Savage
Art

*Jim Thompson—in front of his mother's house, La Jolla,
California, 1942 (Courtesy of the Thompson family)*

A
Biography
of
Jim
Thompson

Savage Art

Robert Polito

Alfred A. Knopf   New York   1995

This Is a Borzoi Book
Published by Alfred A. Knopf, Inc.

Library of Congress Cataloging-in-Publication Data
Polito, Robert.
Savage art: a biography of Jim Thompson /
Robert Polito. — 1st ed.
p.   cm.
Includes bibliographical references and index.
ISBN 0-394-58407-4
1. Thompson, Jim, 1906–1977.
2. Novelists, American—20th century—Biography.
3. Crime in literature. I. Title.
PS3539.H6733Z83   1995
813' .54—dc20
[B]   94-48455 CIP

Manufactured in the United States of America
First Edition

For Kristine . . .

Acknowledgments

Muhammad Ali danced into a Manhattan office as I was recording an interview with an old friend of Jim Thompson's. Drug dealers chased me to the car when I attempted to photograph a former Thompson home. If biographies are quests, their road maps are always out-of-date or imprinted with disappearing ink. *Savage Art*, fortunately, found many friends along the way.

Patricia Thompson Miller fostered my project from conception. Sharon Thompson Reed ministered to my every request, resurrecting details from her splendid memory and documents from her closets, bureaus, and garage. Jim Reed copied photographs with skill and dispatch. The late Alberta Thompson graciously permitted me to consult (and quote from) all her husband's published and unpublished writings. Although this is not an "authorized" biography, I could not have sustained the work without them.

A full list of collaborators can be found among the concluding Notes and Sources, but these claim special citation here: Michael Thompson, J. Anthony Kouba, Edna Myers Borden, Art Kozelka, Sis Cunningham, Gordon Friesen, Arnold Hano, Harlan Ellison, James B. Harris, Lois McDowell, Mel Shestack, Robert Goldfarb, Sam Fuller, Gary Graver, and Jim Thompson's late sisters, Maxine Thompson Kouba and Freddie Thompson Townsend.

Frank Parman was a masterly research assistant, who became a good friend.

My appreciation to those who have written honorably and stylishly about

Jim Thompson, particularly Geoffrey O'Brien, Luc Sante, David Thomson, Barry Gifford, Max Allan Collins, and Ed Gorman.

I want to thank my agents, Glen Hartley and Lynn Chu, and my editors, Edward Kastenmeier, Martin Asher, and Sonny Mehta, for their confidence, engagement, and care. My gratitude to Chip Kidd for his arresting cover, to Iris Weinstein for her elegant design, and to Dori Carlson and Bruce Carr for their scrupulous attention to the text.

This book is dedicated to my wife, Kristine Harris, as its first and best reader, but I would want to gather up into that dedication also all the friends who lifted *Savage Art*—and me—through the many dark passages, especially Marc Gerald, Lloyd Schwartz, David Lehman, Frank Bidart, the late James Merrill, Lawrence Joseph, Peter Carey, Ai, Mark Goodman, John Radziewitz, Samuel Blumenfeld, Sophie Cabot Black, Frances Gouda, Jason Shinder, Jay Pearsall, Andrew Glatzer, Ingrid and Robert Harris, Lucie Brock-Broido, Elizabeth Dickey, Sondra Farganis, Elissa Tenny, Laura Kaminsky, Linda Rodrigues, Judd Eustice, and Linda Dunne.

Contents

Part 3: Ministers of Evil

If you ask an older Ilongot man of
northern Luzon, Philippines, why he
cuts off human heads, his answer is
brief, and one which no anthropologist can readily elaborate: He says that
rage, born of grief, impels him to kill
his fellow human beings. He claims
that he needs a place "to carry his
anger." The act of severing and tossing away the victim's head enables him,
he says, to vent and, he hopes, throw
away the anger of his bereavement. . . .
—Renato Rosaldo, *Culture & Truth*

" There are thirty-two ways to write a
story, and I've used every one, but
there is only one plot—things are not
as they seem."
—Jim Thompson

Savage
Art

His voice became a purring
calm, the intense calm
above a raging subter-
ranean storm.

—*The Getaway*

Prologue:
Art Savage and
His Savage Art

Two Jim Thompson stories:

Shortly before his death on Holy Thursday, April 7, 1977, Jim Thompson instructed his wife, Alberta, to safeguard his novels, manuscripts, papers, and copyrights. "Just you wait," he promised her, "I'll become famous after I'm dead about ten years."

Half pathetic boast, half paranoid prophecy, Thompson's prediction hung like a whiff of purgatory over the desolation of his final days and years. His last important novel, *Pop. 1280,* appeared in 1964. His last notable screen credit, for Stanley Kubrick's *Paths of Glory,* was in 1957. Three of his concluding six publications were commissioned "novelizations" of

3

Hollywood movies and a television show. None of his books remained in print in the United States.

Racked by strokes, Thompson retreated to his tiny apartment on Hillcrest Road in Los Angeles—a few blocks up the hill from his beloved Musso & Frank Grill—to die. "He knew that he would never be able to write again," Alberta Thompson recalls, "so he made up his mind that he wasn't going to eat anymore, and he wouldn't. He literally starved himself to death."

No more than twenty-five mourners—his family and some old friends—attended Thompson's memorial service at the Westwood Village Mortuary on Easter Monday.

"I was feeling bad that there were so few people in the room," remembers Arnold Hano, his editor at Lion Books during the early 1950s. "Then it hit me that this was just another Jim Thompson story. . . ."

Thompson's deathbed long shot finally paid off in 1990 with the release of *The Grifters,* the Stephen Frears film starring Anjelica Huston, John Cusack, and Annette Benning, which garnered four Academy Award nominations. That year saw the adaptation of two additional Thompson novels, *After Dark, My Sweet* by James Foley and *The Kill-Off* by Maggie Greenwald. *The Frightening Frammis,* directed by Tom Cruise from a Thompson short story for Showtime, would follow in 1993, and a remake of *The Getaway,* with Alec Baldwin and Kim Basinger, in 1994.

The reprinting of nearly all of Thompson's major fiction from the 1950s and 1960s capped a quiet, steady resurgence, as alternative weekly newspapers, Sunday arts supplements, national news magazines, and small-circulation literary journals rushed to disclose his rediscovery.

Thompson appeared to have surfaced from nowhere into the cultural mainstream suddenly to be acclaimed as an enduring and significant American writer.

The Thompson revival also smacked of a Jim Thompson story. "This whole revival is pretty amazing," remarks Donald E. Westlake, screenwriter for *The Grifters.* "I think you'd have to say that it somehow matches Jim's view of life, that he gets his fifteen minutes of fame thirteen years after his death."

• • •

Jim Thompson offers a rare instance of a popular art that is also personal and deeply subversive. His fiction is fueled by a lurid intelligence that bulldozes distinctions between sensational and serious culture. Like Weegee's photographs of spectacles and murders, or Andy Warhol's *Death and Disaster* canvases of car wrecks, race riots, and electric chairs, Thompson's novels revel in their own shaky, contradictory status. As Luc Sante suggested in *The New York Review of Books,* "Thompson fills a significant gap in the continuity of postwar American fiction, a link between popular literature and the avant-garde."

Reading a Thompson novel is like being trapped in a bomb shelter with a chatty maniac who also happens to be the air-raid warden. Buried under the shabbiest conventions of pulp fiction—all but three of the twenty-six novels he published between 1942 and 1973 were paperback originals— and picking at the banality with offhand brilliance, his books pursue the most debased imaginative materials.

Thompson turned to crime fiction relatively late in his life, at the age of forty-three, with the publication of *Nothing More Than Murder* (1949). His first novel, *Now and on Earth* (1942), was a thinly veiled proletarian memoir in the style of the 1930s. A second novel, *Heed the Thunder* (1946), recast incidents from his Nebraska childhood along the lines of the regionalist realism of Willa Cather. Thompson subsequently ransacked a variety of popular genres: westerns, historical fiction, true crime, melodramatic thrillers, tall-tale autobiography, and rural soap opera. His most characteristic performances mark him as the blackest beast of what is coming to be known as *série noire.* His notorious novels—preeminently *The Killer Inside Me* (1952), *Savage Night* (1953), *A Hell of a Woman* (1954), *The Nothing Man* (1954), *After Dark, My Sweet* (1955), and *Pop. 1280* (1964)—spotlight edgy, disturbed, insidiously engrossing criminals who often unravel into psychopathic killers. It became Thompson's dismaying gift to re-create his monsters from the inside out, as it were, to roost deep within their snaky psyches, and to embody through imaginative art their terrifying yet beguiling voices on the page.

Listen to Central City Deputy Sheriff Lou Ford run down the death of his fiancée, Amy Stanton, in *The Killer Inside Me:*

> She smiled and came toward me with her arms held out. "I won't, darling. I won't ever say anything like that again. But I do want to tell you how much—"
>
> "Sure," I said. "You want to pour your heart out to me."
>
> And I hit her in the guts as hard as I could.
>
> My fist went back against her spine, and the flesh closed around it to the wrist. I jerked back on it, I had to jerk, and she flopped forward from the waist, like she was hinged.
>
> Her hat fell off, and her head went clear down and touched the floor. And then she toppled over, completely over, like a kid turning a somersault. She lay on her back, eyes bulging, rolling her head from side to side.
>
> She was wearing a white blouse and a white cream-colored suit; a new one, I reckon, because I didn't remember seeing it be-

fore. I got my hand in the front of the blouse, and ripped it down to the waist. I jerked the skirt up over her head, and she jerked and shook all over; and there was a funny sound like she was trying to laugh.

And then I saw the puddle spreading out under her.

I sat down and tried to read the paper. I tried to keep my eyes on it. But the light wasn't very good, not good enough to read by, and she kept moving around. It looked like she couldn't lie still.

Once I felt something touch my boot, and I looked down and it was her hand. It was moving back and forth across the toe of my boot. It moved up along the ankle and the leg, and somehow I was afraid to move away. And then her fingers were at the top, clutching down inside; and I almost couldn't move. I stood up and tried to jerk away, and the fingers held on.

I dragged her two–three feet before I could break away.

Her fingers kept on moving, sliding and crawling back and forth, and finally they got ahold of her purse and held on. They dragged it down inside of her skirt, and I couldn't see it or her hands any more.

Well, that was all right. It would look better to have her hanging onto her purse. And I grinned a little, thinking about it. It was so much like her, you know, to latch onto her purse. She'd always been so tight, and . . . and I guess she'd had to be. . . .

A closeted intellectual who relaxes with Krafft-Ebing's *Psychopathia Sexualis,* Ford calls his public life his "act"—a dumb show where he mimics a stereotypical Texas lawman. Cunningly "in character," he needles incessantly, taking secret vengeance with hectoring platitudes and cornball routines. "Polite, intelligent: guys like that were my meat. . . . Striking at people that way is almost as good as the other, the real way." As Ford presses on, his account proliferates with instances of the "real way" in a deadpan spiral of horror. Every killing demands a sequel, each proceeding from the sadism that infects his sexual relations.

For all the casual ferocity here—the beatings, the shotguns fired into open mouths, the bodies that smash like pumpkins, "hard, then giving away all at once"—the central grotesquery of *The Killer Inside Me* remains Lou Ford's voice. With his shrewd mix of good cheer and hard-boiled idioms, alternately swaggering and shrinking but always observant and self-regarding, Ford cakewalks through his story like a crafty, ingratiating con man. As he juggles his double life, putting on himself and his reader, just as earlier he had toyed with his victims and laughed at his pursuers, you never entirely disbelieve him—although it's certain that he is giving himself away, and likely that he is a callous killer posing as a helpless psychopath.

Neither do you ever wholly part company with Thompson's rock-ribbed sympathy for Ford, even after the inevitable occurs—"All I can do is wait until I split"—and, in one of the strangest and ugliest endings in modern fiction, he and his world blow up in our faces.

• • •

A few years after he wrote *The Killer Inside Me,* Jim Thompson taunted the traditional crime novel audience in *The Nothing Man.* "I suppose it'll baffle the hell out of the average whodunit reader," he quipped, "but perhaps he needs to be baffled. Perhaps his thirst for entertainment will impel him to the dread chore of thinking."

Crime fiction, however violent or macabre or sordid, ordinarily—if paradoxically—constitutes a comforting and conservative genre. Whether the prose is soft- or hard-boiled and the author is Agatha Christie or Dashiell Hammett, Dorothy L. Sayers or James M. Cain, most crime novels tend to borrow their trajectory from (for all the obvious differences) classic comedy: a demonic impulse—greed, lust, jealousy, rage—and a calamitous action—murder—hurl a personality and a society to the rim of annihilation before the crime is solved, the impulse contained, the personality reintegrated, and the society allowed to resume its harmonious mission.

Thompson's boldest writing about criminals transgresses, even inverts, the consolations of genre. A novelist who once told his cousin that there is only one basic plot for fiction—"things are not as they seem"—he overturns the formal and thematic resolutions of the crime novel for a more disruptive, devastating ambiguity. In *The Killer Inside Me,* for instance, Deputy Sheriff Lou Ford is both the detective and the murderer, at once part of the solution and the problem. Thompson's slippery, self-reflexive novels begin with the appearance of integration and order, then chart a descent into madness and extinction. The demonic impulses—what Ford styles *"the sickness"*—are unleashed rather than quelled at the conclusions of his books, with the result that both Thompson's hero and Thompson's society achieve not a new life but a terrifying nothingness.

The Thompson novels, of course, are unthinkable without the precedent of the great crime writers who published in *Black Mask,* the premier mystery pulp H. L. Mencken and George Jean Nathan launched in 1920 to bankroll their tony literary monthly, *The Smart Set.* Hammett, Raymond Chandler, Horace McCoy, Carroll John Daly, Erle Stanley Gardner, Raoul Whitfield, Paul Cain, and the other *"Black Mask* boys" revolutionized—and Americanized—crime fiction, as the elegant British sherlock yielded to the tough, wise-cracking dick, and the country house, book-lined study, and drawing room gave way to the Prohibition speakeasy, hobo jungle, and urban back alley.

The voyeuristic sadism that distinguishes the sleuthing of Race Williams in Carroll John Daly's stories and the surreal violence of Paul Cain's *Fast One* certainly anticipate the cruel habits of Thompson's heroes. The laconic, detached cadences and the acrid wit of Hammett and Chandler—not to mention their more squalid settings, Poisonville in *Red Harvest* or the sun-and-hangover-blinded Los Angeles of *The Long Goodbye*—also have obvious analogies in Thompson. Closer in spirit is Horace McCoy's first-person account of a raging gangster, *Kiss Tomorrow Goodbye*. And closer still (though he scorned the *Black Mask* crowd) are the compact masterpieces of James M. Cain, *The Postman Always Rings Twice* and *Double Indemnity,* especially their headlong narration and bitches' brew of doom and compulsion.

Placing Thompson within this lineage can be a risky venture. True, his crime novels only rarely allude to a social world beyond the pulps. Yet Thompson detonates the clichés of the hard-boiled tradition he inherited—not by seeking to transcend them, as an important writer might be expected to do, but rather by sinking into the clichés so deeply that they are flipped on their heads.

Thus the string-of-firecrackers witticisms that in Hammett or Chandler flaunt the detective hero's masterly ease and stoicism become for Thompson's characters evidence of mental imbalance. Not only are his jokes more bitter and twisted; they often possess a lunatic literalness. Lou Ford, in the passage just quoted, cackles, "You want to pour your heart out to me" to Amy Stanton as he slams his fist through her stomach. Or elsewhere Ford titillates the unsuspecting lover of a woman he's left lying in a bloody heap, "I'd bet money that she's all stretched out waiting for you."

Similarly, the "neutral" style that the crime writers learned from Hemingway—which lives on the surface in tight, worked-over language, so that every perception is immediate and concrete and character is reduced to external action—betokens rampant schizophrenia in Thompson. Ford follows Amy Stanton's dogged fingers up his leg as though he were viewing a movie. By and by he confesses to a lawyer "hypothetically" (as serial killer Ted Bundy later was known to do), simultaneously admitting and disowning his crimes.

Where Thompson does not exaggerate the tough-guy timbre of the *noir* writers, stretching their stagey, willed cool until the mask cracks, he nudges it toward numbness, automatism, walking death. Dolly Dillon in *A Hell of a Woman* reports of himself, "I was like a mechanical man with the batteries run down." Nick Corey of *Pop. 1280* suggests more generally, "So ain't we all inanimate, George?" The logic of the endings of *The Killer Inside Me* and *A Hell of a Woman* requires that we believe that their narrators have been speaking to us from beyond the grave. This might be dismissed as an awkwardness of the genre—in McCoy's *Kiss Tomorrow Goodbye,*

Ralph Cotter describes his own fatal shooting—were not Thompson's characters so despairing of their vital signs. "They can't hang me. I'm already dead. I've been dead a long time," Joe Wilmot insists at the finish of *Nothing More Than Murder*. To Nick Corey, the houses of his Pottsville are indistinguishable from coffins: "Just pine-board walls locking in the emptiness."

Even the feral desire and the-spider-and-the-fly sex that, especially in Cain, triggers all the destruction are flattened out by Thompson into smirking caricatures of passion. Never has the convention of the deadly woman seemed less femme and more purely fatale—or more gratuitous. Whereas Walter Huff in *Double Indemnity* and Frank Chambers in *The Postman Always Rings Twice* lay out their obsessions like big cats pacing off the dimensions of their cages, Thompson's unfortunates aren't finally sure what—or who—is dragging them down. As Dolly Dillon evokes his siren: "And it wasn't a pretty picture, by any means; she was about as far from a raving beauty as I was. But something about it kind of got me. I tripped over a crack, and almost went sprawling." From inside their creeping delusions, Thompson's misogynists are always mixing up the women in their lives. "Yeah, it must have been Doris—or was it Ellen?" slurs Dillon. "Three goddam tramps in a row . . . or maybe it was four or five, but it doesn't matter. It was like they were all the same person." Actual sex is infrequent, and approached as one might the removal of a tick: disagreeable, if necessary, and inseparable from an act of extermination.

Beyond the bits of weirdness about the edges, the cracked fantasy and jagged comedy, the shifts in personal identity that are not so much plot devices as neurotic symptoms, the poems, songs, and left-hand parodies (Willa Cather, Gertrude Stein, Norman Mailer, or a suspiciously recurring alcoholic penman named "Tomlinson or Thomas or something of the kind"), the furious artistry of Thompson's strolls through hell dazzlingly mimics his characters and materials. Fragmenting the popular crime novel against other literary traditions, his books share techniques with vanguard modernist and contemporary American fiction.

The Kill-Off (1957) sets a *Peyton Place* story spinning through a *Rashomon*-like structure in which some dozen different dubious narrators state their case. During *A Hell of a Woman*, as psychotic Dolly Dillon cracks so, in turn, does his story. When Dillon rends utterly on the final pages, the novel splits into two conclusions, cast in alternating lines of roman and italic type, each as hideous and rank as the other, but impossible to read in sequence.

In Thompson's novels the realistic fixtures of crime fiction pass through a wheel of knives on their way to a void. *Savage Night* begins as the routine docket of a consumptive Mafia hit man, Charlie "Little" Bigger, but soon makes room for a writer who grows "the more interesting portions of the female anatomy" on his farm in Vermont and—a decade before the infamous "cut-ups" of William Burroughs and Brion Gysin—also shreds the Bible to create his books. Steadily wasting away through the novel, by the end Bigger loses his limbs, his face, his body. What's left is only a voice signaling from his black hole: "The darkness and myself. Everything else was gone. And the little that was left of me was going, faster and faster." If Thompson assaults the boundaries of American literature, books like *Savage Night, A Hell of a Woman,* and *The Killer Inside Me* slash at the margins of storytelling.

Thompson's fiction is as slithery and treacherous as any of his killers. With so much in motion—the reeling shards of *noir* formulas, the self-consuming narratives, the furtive, often insane raconteurs—there's no comfortable place to sit. Thompson never directs his stories toward redemption. His variations on *Black Mask* formulas serve the same function as Lou Ford's homey jests and impersonations; he trots them out to camouflage *"the sickness."* The nods to hard-boiled conventions do not so much toughen Thompson's novels as humanize them—they're all we have to hang on to in the downdraft. Everything else is a wasted, sucking nihilism that's as unsparing as the most lacerating rock 'n' roll—the Velvet Underground's "Sister Ray," say, or the Sex Pistols' "Bodies"—and as final as a snuff film.

• • •

The Killer Inside Me, like so many of Thompson's novels, turns on an opposition between outer and inner realities. An eerie autoeroticism stokes Lou Ford's imaginations of guilt and self-destruction, revenge and murder, as though he were attempting to repair the ravages of his life with verbal fantasy. Deprived of other sources of power, he possesses only violence and language. Hidden from his everyday world, detached from his own emotions and actions, Ford dwells deep down inside himself, agitated and seething, until he explodes.

Jim Thompson's own relationship to his volatile fiction and the killers inside him—the sources, evolution, and political implications of his *noir* vision—is one, though hardly the only, subject of this biography.

Alienation in its infinite guises drives all of Thompson's writings, from the earliest hobo sketches, through the proletarian novels he produced during the 1930s and 1940s, and on to the mature crime fiction he began to publish with Lion Books during the 1950s. Thompson, as we shall see, was a profoundly alienated man. His alienation stamps nearly every page of this book.

Crime writers are lauded for the ingenuity of their plots and the diversity of their characters and settings. Viewed from this narrow angle, Thompson perhaps "failed" as a crime writer—his plots could be slapdash, and he kept reverting to the same situations and the same sorts of people over and over. He possessed no special knack for impersonal invention. But Thompson was another kind of writer, spikier and harder to categorize. Director Stanley Kubrick praised *The Killer Inside Me* as "probably the most chilling and believable first-person account of a criminally warped mind I have ever encountered." Thompson's novels, however, were not simply brilliant case studies; the fictional issues of his books sprang from the circumstantial issues of his life.

Thompson, of course, never was a killer. Apart from a few youthful arrests in the oil fields, and a flirtation with the underworld during Prohibition in Fort Worth, he had no direct criminal involvement. But at one time or another he held down virtually every job of his marginal men—traveling salesman, baker, bill collector, bellboy, pipeliner, movie house operator, aircraft factory worker, newspaperman, gold buyer, and grifter—or, in a prickly wrinkle, his sheriff father, James Sherman "Big Jim" Thompson, did. Beyond his bedrock personal settings—Oklahoma, Nebraska, Texas— Thompson populated his books with recurrent figures from his family, friends, and occupational acquaintances, and he often represented his masked hustlers and killers under variants of his own 1930s Communist Party alias, Robert Dillon. Stranger and spookier, you will hear in the course of this biography Thompson's family, friends, and acquaintances portray *him* in language that echoes the characters in his novels.

Thompson tended to personalize not just his crime fiction but even his most professional or anonymous writing. An unsigned 1950 article for the men's adventure magazine *SAGA,* "An Alcoholic Looks at Himself," accommodated a more authoritative and vivid probing of his emotional life than he would permit in his tall-tale autobiographies, *Bad Boy* (1953) and *Roughneck* (1954). But the most egregious instance of his impoundment of public forms for private ends is a guilt-and-revenge riddle he cast as an oil field oral history, "The Drilling Contractor," in 1939.

Thompson submitted "The Drilling Contractor" to the University of North Carolina Press as a sample interview for his proposed documentary book on the Oklahoma City building trades, *We Talked About Labor.* During the life history the drilling contractor—who asks that his real name be disguised as "Bob Carey"—reflects on his dry holes and hard luck in Texas; but the bulk of his thirty pages concerns his son, "my boy, Bob."

Young Bob, we learn, while still a freshman in high school, went to work as a night bellboy in a rowdy Fort Worth hotel as a consequence of his father's misjudgments and failures in the oil fields. "It sounds funny that a man running almost $75,000 worth of tools couldn't support his family, but every time I made a good deal I made a bad one . . . well, it just seemed like we couldn't get along without Bob's earnings." Seven mornings a week Bob stumbles home stinking of "whores and whiskey." To revive himself before his classes, "he kept a bottle . . . behind the bath-tub. It didn't do any good to throw it away or talk to him about it. He'd just get more, and sit and stare at you silently until you'd wish you hadn't said anything." By the third year of this devilish routine, "he began to go to pieces completely. . . . He looked like a little dried-up old man, and he was just short of eighteen." Bob ultimately suffers a full physical and mental collapse. "I couldn't stay in the room any longer: Bob stretched out there so still and silent, and the family standing around crying. . . . It was like a funeral."

The secret speaker of "The Drilling Contractor" was Big Jim Thompson, the author's father, a hapless oil tycoon following his sheriff days. But the "oral history" would have been prepared at a time when Pop was about to be committed to a rest home for senility, and too ill to speak for himself. Under the cover of this ghostwritten reminiscence Thompson revisited his own wounded adolescence. With bitter, lacerating phrases he ventriloquized his father's culpability, and heard the penitential words Jim Thompson, Sr., undoubtedly never voiced. A harrowing self-portrait concealed within a knockoff life history, "The Drilling Contractor" also discharged a son's ultimate act of vindication and dominance: Thompson got to write his old man's autobiography.

Novel after novel, Thompson returned to characters who seek revenge through violence and murder—and, when they fail, retaliate through language with compensatory fantasies. "Was every move I made designed to extract payment from the world for the hell I dwelt in?" Clinton Brown asks in *The Nothing Man*, after bludgeoning his wife with a whiskey bottle. Brown is the author of an unfinished manuscript, *Puke and Other Poems*. "I'd written them out of bitterness and brooding," he muses, "out of hate and resentment and restlessness." Brown goes on to literalize—in the spirit of Lou Ford's barbed jokes—a stock decadent Romantic metaphor. "The poet was the killer. The point was indisputable—thanks to me."

Some of the people who were closest to Thompson warily circle the malice in his books. When asked why he might have claimed in *Now and on Earth* that his father committed suicide by gorging on the stuffing in his mattress, his sister Freddie responded, "Because it was the worst possible thing he could think of to say." Or Arnold Hano, his editor at Lion Books: "The anger, the quiet murdering, is Jim getting back somehow. . . . Whatever problems Jim had, he worked them out in his writing." Crime fiction offered Thompson a scaffolding to stage his obsessions and inward dramas, and to transform his chills and fevers into vivid literature.

• • •

In *Texas by the Tail* (1965) Thompson focused the vengeance in his writing with a sly joke, almost a pun. For this late panorama of the oil fields, a book that he told actor and director Tony Bill was his most autobiographical, he divided his West Texas memories among many characters, old and young, male and female. Thompson parceled out a doomed wildcatting adventure in Big Spring with his father to a budding roughneck he called Art Savage, along with "a little black book":

> They were a middling old man and his son. . . .
>
> "I suppose," [the father] said timidly, "you've been counting on having a lot of money?"
>
> The kid said, why not? They'd brought in a good well, and they had hundreds of offsetting acres under lease. Conservatively, they were worth several million dollars. "But I'll settle for a hundred and eighty-two thousand. I won't live long enough to spend any more than that."
>
> "A hundred and eighty-two—Why that particular figure, son?"
>
> "I've been keeping a little black book since I was seven years old. There are one hundred and eighty-two names in it, one for every rotten bastard who's given me a hard time. I've shopped around, and I can get them bumped off for an average price of one thousand dollars."
>
> "Son—" The father shook his head, aghast. "What happened to you? How can you even think of such things?"
>
> "Thinking about it is all that's kept me alive," the kid said. "I can die happy knowing I'm taking all those bastards to hell with me. . . ."

We know from his sister Freddie that during the 1920s Thompson also kept a little black book. "It was a notebook of some kind. . . . Jimmie said that this book contained everybody who had ever been mean to him or who had ever crossed him, and that someday he would pay them all back." In *Texas by the Tail*, when Art Savage grows up and quits the oil fields, "he got rid of the book with the one hundred and eighty-two names. . . . And it was the last book he ever compiled of that kind."

Of that kind. The bias of the blade in the qualification is inescapable. "Art Savage" went on to other books, moved on to other kinds of savage art.

• • •

However private their source, Thompson's obsessions finally are as American as a serial killer. The novels inhabit what William Burroughs describes as "a space *between*, in popular songs and Grade B movies, giving away the basic American rottenness." His paperback originals join a small body of other vital homegrown arts—*film noir*, the blues, documentary photography, early rock 'n' roll—also undergoing reevaluation and reclamation. As

Thompson's literary reputation began to soar during the Reagan-Bush 1980s, it hardly seemed accidental that his posthumous acclaim would occur in a social climate that approximated the political, artistic, and psychic repression of the early Eisenhower years, the period of his most corrosive fiction.

The slippery narrators and materials of Thompson's books pose an arresting caveat for his biographer. A writer's autobiographies might claim much compelling authority in the recounting of his life. But *Bad Boy* and *Roughneck*, unless played against other accounts, are at once too fanciful and evasive. They shape Thompson's own spirited personal myth, often skewing what they take up and omitting entirely many of his most significant passages and detours.

Savage Art draws on vast and scattered lodes of archival documents, letters, and unpublished manuscripts, most of them, like "The Drilling Contractor," unearthed here for the first time. Serendipitous finds—the trail that led to an old fraternity buddy who for nearly sixty years saved a kitty of Thompson's "lost" college stories—proved as fruitful as the patient research that went into this book over half a decade.

Except when he directed the Oklahoma Writers' Project during the 1930s, Thompson really wasn't a public figure with a public record. Published biographical data about him have turned out to be romantically misleading or hilariously wrong. Virtually every current reprint of his novels proclaims, for instance, that he sold his first story to *True Detective* at the age of fourteen—some four years before Bernarr Macfadden founded that pioneering fact-detective monthly. One standard encyclopedia of African-American literature misappropriates Thompson as a black author—on the strength, perhaps, of his late novelization of Michael Roemer's film about racial inequality, *Nothing but a Man*. Despite his astonishing revival, Thompson's story has remained hidden.

• • •

Information about Jim Thompson largely belongs to the surviving individuals who knew him—a medley of American voices, by turns vivid and hesitant, hostile and loyal, agreeing and contradictory, that spans a twentieth-century arc from territorial Oklahoma to 1970s Hollywood. Rather than steamroll the rough edges of their memories into a seamless narrative, I have tried wherever possible, both because it seemed right for Thompson's life and as an experiment in life history, to preserve the language of the more than two hundred of his friends, colleagues, editors, and family who collaborated in the creation of his biography. Some sequences in the pages that follow retain traces of the raw knots and burls of an oral history—an occasional loss of narrative expediency judged as preferable to the loss of these original American voices.

While writing *Savage Art*, I became mindful of the mortality of my informants—Thompson's sisters, Maxine and Freddie, among other central figures, died soon after they were interviewed—and that this was personal and American history just before it vanished into silence. I have introduced the voices of the dead here in the past tense, and only the living speak in the present. The exception is Alberta Thompson. She was a vigorous presence throughout the research, writing, and completion of this book; she died before she could read it. Biographies align photographs focused and shot at particular moments in time. With the passage of a few more years it seems a Thompson biography would have been impossible.

Sheriff James Sherman Thompson
before the Caddo County Jail,
Anadarko, Oklahoma, where Jim
Thompson was born in 1906
(Courtesy of J. Anthony Kouba)

The pure products of America
go crazy—
    —William Carlos Williams (1923)

Part 1

Pure Products
of America

**Well, sir, I should have
been sitting pretty, just
about as pretty as a man
could sit. Here I was, the
high sheriff of Potts
County, and I was drawing
almost two thousand dol-
lars a year—not to mention
what I could pick up on the
side. On top of that I had
free living quarters on the
second floor of the courthouse, just as nice a place
as a man could ask for. . . .**
—Sheriff Nick Corey,
Pop. 1280

Hell's
Fringe:
1906

When Jim Thompson was courting Alberta, he would tease her with the line that he had been born in jail. At their first meeting—on a blind date to the Pink Rose formal dinner-dance at the Holdrege Street digs of the Alpha Gamma Rho fraternity of the University of Nebraska, in Lincoln—he dropped the revelation with a shy whisper barely audible above the stylish swing and sway of Herbie Kaye's orchestra. On subsequent outings, as the young couple more confidently exchanged their secrets and pasts, Jimmie (as he called himself) again and again resurrected the line, as if rehearsing a riddle or a joke. But Alberta, maddeningly, could elicit no explanation from her tall, reed-thin, handsome suitor. Bewildered, then amused, she playfully began to jostle back, announcing that henceforth she would refer to him as "my jail baby." One night sitting behind the wheel of Alberta's 1930 Whippet, while they talked and parked in front of her parents' house, Jimmie at long last rendered the punch line. "Well, you see," he laughed, "my father was a sheriff in Anadarko."

Although Thompson wasn't literally born *in* the Caddo County Jail— but *over* the cell block, inside a comfortable apartment the sheriff enjoyed there—the perception was central to Thompson's own imagination of his Oklahoma childhood, and one of his indispensable myths. The novelist who recurrently chronicled the hustlings of shifty small-town sheriffs, who loaded his books with bitter depictions of the American family as a suffocating prison-without-walls, would replay the story for Alberta, for their children, for his friends, and for virtually everyone he met, all his life.

But then, Jim Thompson told lots of stories.

•   •   •

A future writer of crime fiction and westerns could do worse than turn-of-the-century Oklahoma. During the tempestuous two decades between April 22, 1889—when the lands that the U.S. government had promised to the Five Civilized Tribes for "as long as grass shall grow and waters run" were shamelessly usurped and opened to white settlement—and the coming of statehood on November 16, 1907, the region was divided on the west into Oklahoma Territory, and on the east into Indian Territory. "As the wild West came to a close in cowtowns like Dodge City and Reno City," Oklahoma historian John Thompson (no relation) narrates, "eastern Oklahoma became the last refuge of cattle thieves, gunfighters, and train and bank robbers. . . . Oklahoma, being the last frontier, seemed to be destined to remain the most lawless area in the United States."

The austere landscape of sandstone hills, forests, underbrush, steep gullies, natural caves, and prairie molded a sanctuary for bandit gangs. Quirks in the territorial legal system further obliged fugitives with pasts to live down. Renegades from state laws secured immunity in Oklahoma, as extradition was possible only for federal offenses. Indians could not arraign whites in their courts. As Western writer Glen Shirley recounts, deputy U.S. marshals christened the imaginary border between the Twin Territories "Hell's Fringe."

James Sherman Thompson, or "Big Jim," as Jimmie's father was tagged in territorial lawman circles, was one of the adventuresome men charged with regulating this last frontier: first as a deputy U.S. marshal stationed at Fort Sill, and later as the sheriff of Caddo County, which on its eastern rim bled into Hell's Fringe. Sheriff Thompson—"a heavyset young man with the profile of McKinley," as his son evoked him in his last published novel, *King Blood* (1973)—entered Oklahoma early in 1900. Big Jim rode alongside some of the most celebrated Western peace officers, legends such as Oklahoma's "Three Guardsmen," Bill Tilghman, Heck Thomas, and Chris Madsen, and Chief Deputy U.S. Marshal William D. Fossett (Sheriff Thompson was a "sort of protégé" of Fossett's, according to Elmer LeRoy Baker's *Gunman's Territory*). The bandit gangs likewise composed a rowdy *Who's Who* of pulp and movie lore. Among them: Bill Doolin's "Wild Bunch," Al and Frank Jennings, Bert Casey, Matt Kimes, Wilbur Underhill, Ray Terrill, "Dynamite Dick" Clifton and "Little Dick" West, "Cattle Annie" McDoulet and "Little Breeches" Jennie Stevens, and the "Desperate Daltons."

Myth has glamorized the territorial outlaws and the lawmen who hunted them into homegrown demigods—an "ancient race," as Charles Bronson remarks in Sergio Leone's film *Once Upon a Time in the West*—who, living by their wits and a fatalistic code of honor, blazoned what John Thompson mockingly styles a distinctively American brand of democracy: "God made some men big and others small, but Samuel Colt made them equal."

Oklahoma bandits preyed upon isolated homesteaders and dispossessed Indians. Hardly the iconic free spirits of Western romance, they had short, brutish lives that triggered solitary, nasty deaths. The deputy U.S. marshals, in turn, often emerged from the fiercer strains of the territorial population—on occasion, from the very same gangs they would later hunt and kill. Some peace officers resourcefully plied both sides of the bar, shifting allegiances with a shadowy two-step of law and outlaw.

• • •

Sheriff Thompson's arrival at Fort Sill, a military reservation south of Lawton, continued the westward passage of his clan across the American continent. The migration that began in the late seventeenth century would conclude only in the 1940s, when Big Jim's children moved their own families to Southern California.

Jim Thompson's earliest traceable relation on his father's side was Samuel Dark, a glover of mixed English and Irish blood who sailed from London on the *Content* in August 1680. Devout Quakers, Samuel, his wife, Anne, and their son, John, settled in Bucks County, Pennsylvania. Roughly speaking, the Dark women became teachers while the men worked as farmers and ranchers. John's eldest son, Jacob, farmed in North Carolina, where his son, Samuel, served as a Tory captain in the Revolutionary War before migrating to Tennessee. In the winter of 1829 Samuel's son, also called Samuel—the last Samuel Dark in the line, and Jim Thompson's great-grandfather—moved with his wife, Christine, to Illinois. At some point in their westward journey, the Dark family converted to the Baptist faith. Samuel Dark was a Baptist minister of the conservative "Hard Shell," or "Primitive," stamp. Samuel and Christine's youngest daughter, Harriet, was born in Brooklyn, Illinois, on November 25, 1843. After teaching school in nearby Fulton County for nine years, Harriet met a farmer and Civil War hero named Samuel Thompson.

The first Thompson to emigrate was a Scotch divine. John Thompson had just been ordained a Presbyterian minister in Dumbarton, Scotland, when in 1770, at the age of twenty, he decided to transplant his calling to Maryland. There he married the daughter of another cleric, the aptly surnamed May Bible, and the couple reared eight children. One of their sons, Samuel, relocated to the Northwest Territories in the late eighteenth century. Anticipating his great-grandson James Thompson's career in Anadarko, Samuel served as the sheriff of Coshocton County, in southeastern Ohio, for almost two decades. Samuel's eldest son, John, prospered as a farmer and landowner in Astoria, in Fulton County, Illinois, emerging as a formidable personality in the civic and social life of Astoria and of Lewistown, the county seat. Although not yet middle-aged when he returned from the Civil War in 1865, John retired from the active running of the farm to pledge his time to county politics. He signed over the family lands to his young son, Samuel, who had been born in Astoria on November 6, 1843.

Samuel also distinguished himself in the Civil War. A "small, wiry man," according to his granddaughter Esther Cowan Winchester, Corporal Samuel Thompson was assigned to Company H of the Illinois Volunteers, and fought in battles at Murfreesboro, Chickamauga, Missionary Ridge, Lookout Mountain, and Jonesboro. He witnessed the fall of Atlanta, marching in General William Tecumseh Sherman's scorched-earth campaigns through Georgia and South Carolina. Samuel esteemed a brief, accidental encounter with the general on the outskirts of Savannah in November 1864, as the apex of his life—so much so that he chose Sherman as the middle name for his first son, James.

In the boom years immediately following the Civil War, Samuel Thompson's land flourished. He began to mechanize the farm, burdening himself with seemingly trifling mortgages to acquire the latest grain binders, sickle mowers, and threshers from the nearby International Harvester factory and to broaden the family holdings. Soon the business burgeoned into a thriving combine of Thompson-run granges and leased homesteads. Samuel built a grand house in Ipava, Illinois, the utmost in Midwestern splendor and ease. There, after marrying Harriet Dark on June 21, 1866— and submitting to baptism in her Baptist persuasion—he settled down to the raising of their large family. Subsequent to the birth of stillborn twins in 1868, a daughter, Mary Alice, was born in 1869, and a son, James Sherman, on September 16, 1870. Seven more children followed: John Walter, Christine Agnes, Amy Inez, Lena Leote, Olive Florence, and the twins, Elmer Orville and Arthur Samuel.

The 1870s rocked America with the longest uninterrupted economic depression in its history. The Panic of 1873 triggered five and a half years of plummeting prices and defaulting businesses. Samuel Thompson initially toughed out the crisis, preserving his farms and machinery only by juggling lease money and family savings. But the catastrophic droughts that visited the Midwest in the late 1870s proved more than even a clever landed patrician could weather. After two successive years of total crop failure—and frantic borrowing against future harvests—the Illinois banks called in Samuel's mortgages. Broke and humiliated, he watched as one by one his properties were catalogued and brought to auction.

When finally his Ipava home was placed on the block, and it seemed possible that his still-substantial liabilities would lead to prison, Samuel undertook a desperate action, one he later said cut against the grain of every abiding principle of his life. In the summer of 1879 he gathered up Harriet and the children into a borrowed farm lorry and, under cover of night, fled Illinois for Nebraska. He told no one, not even his father, that he was leaving or where he was heading.

Samuel Thompson ultimately would return to Macomb, Illinois, in 1902, and square his debts and reputation. For his family, though, so long-deferred reparation held no defense against the distresses of paradise lost and the hardships of an upbringing in mulish poverty. The precipitous fall in fortune was especially devastating to the older children, like James, who was about to celebrate his ninth birthday. Like a fairy tale in reverse, the Ipava mansion was transmogrified into a two-room log and sod cabin in Wahoo, Nebraska. The sumptuous world of cooks and servants, private tutors and music lessons, vaporized into a bitter, bygone dream. James toiled upwards of twelve hours a day, clearing and spading the small lot where his father grew all his food. Harriet started a subscription school in the front room of the cabin. There in the evenings, if time allowed, her own children took their lessons. Straw mats then were unhooked from the walls and, wedged in under the desks and benches, James and his siblings slept.

• • •

In 1881 the Thompson family moved to another sod homestead near the North Loup River in Valley County, Nebraska. Their farm, situated within the Michigan township, bordered a small, close-knit community of Czechoslovakian, or "Bohemian," immigrants. Through the next decade Samuel emerged as a progressive force in Valley County politics, leading the fight for an extension of the railroad and a new highway. Nearly an entire lifetime later James would revisit the "old neighborhood" with a few of his sisters and cousins, recording his impressions in a letter ("No man was ever more popular with the Bohemians than Sam Thompson. . . .") he drafted but apparently never mailed to his father.

Big even as a child, James Thompson reached his full adult height of six feet and two inches by early adolescence. His farm chores reined in a lifelong inclination toward obesity—later, he would struggle to hold his weight under 225, before toppling the scales by the 1930s at an astonishing 300 pounds. After he enrolled in high school, James's size combined with a premature thinning of the hair to produce the impression of a man at least twice his age; his son would write savagely of the sadness of "bald-headed men who combed their side hair across the top." A much-remarked dignity of manner that was, perhaps, a consequence of his untimely burdens at home reinforced James's precocious appearance to the point where often he was mistaken for one of his teachers.

Harvests and plantings staggered his education, but James proved a popular student. A quick study, as well as an enthusiastic sportsman, he was elected a class officer each of the six and a half years he attended high school. Despite the decline in his family's circumstances, James manifested early on touches of the cheerful, imperturbable self-confidence that figures in accounts of his adult life. While yet a schoolboy he already struck those around him as preternaturally secure in his own skills and judgments. As James's sister, Christine, told her daughter Harriet:

> I remember my mother saying that he always knew the answer in school. The rest of the students would wave their arms around and shout out their answers, usually wrong. But Uncle Jim would just put his hand up quietly, and he was always right.

James's low-key confidence modulated into heroism during the legendary Blizzard of '88. A freak snow squall, which one survivor described as a "strange wall of blackness that almost instantaneously settled over the land," struck Nebraska on January 12, 1888, between one and three o'clock in the afternoon, trapping teachers and students within the little sod schoolhouses sprinkled over the prairie. While his teachers panicked and determined to dismiss their pupils without delay, James argued for staying inside until the winds died down. Then, as the storm subsided after nightfall, he directed the students to link arms, and led them out through the drifts. Most of the parents, as it happened, had fixed lanterns in their windows, and James easily guided each of his classmates home by dawn. His astuteness in delaying appeared uncanny when it was discovered that in Plainview, Nebraska, a teacher lost three pupils she was escorting from school to a farmhouse only a few hundred yards away. As many as 150 Nebraskans perished in the blizzard, most of them children.

In high school James undertook the role of family arbiter, an honorary position he would hold for—and hold over—his sisters and brothers throughout their lives. As his niece Harriet Cowan Keller notes, "Uncle Jim was an authority on anything and everything, because he was so well informed. He always did a great deal of reading. So his opinion was the one

James S. Thompson and his family, late 1880s.
From left to right, back row: Christine, James
Sherman, Lena, Amy; front row: Samuel
Thompson (Jim Thompson's grandfather),
Elmer, Olive, Arthur, Harriet Dark Thompson
(Jim Thompson's grandmother)
(Courtesy of Pauline Ohmart)

that was valued." Young James studied with the obsessive abandon of the autodidact, storing up an arsenal of recondite information. Harriet adds that while James was a "kind, generous man," he enjoyed startling those who deemed him "a local yokel" with unexpected blasts of medical terminology or classical history—much like Deputy Sheriff Lou Ford in *The Killer Inside Me* or Sheriff Nick Corey in *Pop. 1280*. Harriet's mother, Christine Thompson Cowan, lived for a short time on a farm near Anadarko when James was sheriff:

> She told me that if some man would patronize Uncle Jim, thinking that because of his big size or his sloppy clothes he was just an ignorant country fool, he'd take it for a while. But then he would suddenly start talking in a learned way about anatomy, or the Roman emperors, something they didn't expect him to know about. And they'd just be standing there, she said, with their mouths open.

The Thompsons moved to Ord in 1889 and James graduated from Ord High School at the age of twenty, with the class of 1890. After working his father's farm for a year, he began teaching high school in nearby Burwell, and for much of the next decade he was associated with the Nebraska school system. He served as principal of a high school in North Loup, and finally as superintendent of schools for the entire valley region. At a Nebraska teachers conference in 1895, he met a striking young elementary school instructor from Burwell. Rather, he was reintroduced to her; a few years earlier, Birdie Myers had been his student at the Burwell High School. James and Birdie promptly tumbled into a headlong romance, and soon the pair announced their intention to be married.

• • •

Nine years younger than her future husband, Birdie Edith Myers had not yet turned seventeen. The daughter of a retired farmer and shopkeeper, William Henry Myers, and his wife, Margaret, she was a tall, slender, handsome woman, with deep grey, almost violet, eyes. Her chiseled face and small mouth flowed beneath cascades of dark, wavy hair, which she generally wore up in a distinctly schoolmarmish bun. Birdie's features imparted hints of exoticism that set her apart in Thompson family photos. Perhaps the source of her novel beauty may be traced to her mother, who was herself the daughter of an English father and a Cherokee mother.

James was an instant hit with the Myers clan. His evening visits on horseback to their home on the western boundary of Burwell remain among the warmest early memories of Birdie's niece, Edna Myers Borden, the eldest daughter of her brother David:

> Jim would come to Burwell in the years before he married Birdie, or Aunt Bird, as she was to us. He was such a nice man, a large guy, and quite good-looking. He could sit down at the piano and play all those old-time songs, and entertain you that way. He was pleasant to be around, and brilliant. Both Bird and he were always reading. He was sweet to her, and very generous to our family. We thought he was wonderful.

Yet what was love at first—or, as here, second—sight devolved into a circuitous cat-and-mouse courtship of almost seven years. On at least two occasions the engagement was broken off. Birdie's family, particularly her pious mother, Margaret, began to broach reservations about James's stability. The precipitating episode for their doubts occurred late in the 1890s, when James abruptly resigned his position as superintendent of schools, and departed Nebraska for as many as three years of mysterious wandering through the American frontier.

James's objectives appeared obscure to his family, but perhaps tact demanded they remain that way. His niece Pauline Ohmart speculates that "being a teacher could not possibly satisfy his lust for adventure. Burwell was small potatoes, and he was very ambitious." Her sister Esther Winchester is more pointed: "Mother used to say that Jim rebelled against the hard life of our grandfather. He saw the times they had nothing, in spite of all his work. She used to say that Uncle Jim was not interested in managing money, but in becoming wealthy."

His movements during the last years of the nineteenth century retain the mystery he cast over them on his sporadic trips home. It is known that James resided in Lamar, Missouri, but not when or for how long. He worked as a fireman and, perhaps, also as a detective on the Santa Fe Railroad. Family legend (supported by a passage in Thompson's novel *Heed the Thunder*) maintains that James experienced a "small nervous breakdown" and turned to manual labor for his health. The short biographical note on him in John H. N. Tindall's *Makers of Oklahoma* (1905) indicates that he entered Oklahoma from Colorado. And on his stopovers in Nebraska, James would visit Birdie in Burwell, to patch things up and to ask her for more time.

• • •

In the spring of 1900, James called upon his Uncle Harry in Guthrie, Oklahoma. Canada Harry Thompson had been serving as chief federal law enforcement officer for Oklahoma Territory since November 5, 1897, when Attorney General Joseph McKenna designated him U.S. marshal.

Marshal Thompson, almost fifty years of age, was a tall, leanly muscular man, with hypnotic black eyes and an incongruously soft, lilting voice. He migrated to Oklahoma in 1893, at the opening of the Cherokee Outlet, when President Cleveland issued a proclamation that the "surplus" lands of the Cherokee, Tonkawa, and Pawnee Indians would be opened to white settlement. During the months that James roomed with him and his wife, Alice, at their East Vilas Avenue home, Harry doted on the son of the prodigal brother he had not seen in over two decades. That summer he swore in his wayward nephew as a deputy U.S. marshal.

In *Bad Boy* Jim Thompson stressed his father's fitness for the job, solemnly concluding that "he did not ask for help after that, nor did he need it." But patronage regulated all such appointments in the Twin Territories. With a Republican administration in the White House for thirteen of the seventeen territorial years, Oklahoma swarmed with officials whose passport was loyalty to the GOP.

Marshal Thompson was a case in point. A moneyed rancher and stalwart Republican whip, he delivered the western counties for Dennis T. Flynn, the territorial delegate to Congress, and he was instrumental in the selection of Cassius M. Barnes as territorial governor. His police experience spanned only a term as sheriff of Marion County, Kansas, and a brief outing as a special agent for the Rock Island Railroad. Despite the inevitable nepotism and corruption that patronage wrought, the system—like so many aspects of political life in Oklahoma during the early decades of this century—carried within it forces that were remarkably progressive. The party of Lincoln and the Emancipation Proclamation installed a surprising number of blacks as deputy marshals.

Working from Fort Sill, and then at Guthrie, Tulsa, and Enid, James Sherman Thompson was one of perhaps seventy deputies in the territory. Around the office he kept his uncle's books. On the range he chased cattle thieves, defended the railroad, and enforced laws proscribing gambling, the distribution of illegal whiskey, and adultery. With few rooted local traditions behind them, marshals led improvised careers, devising regulations from circumstance. A fee system that remunerated them for serving writs or tending prisoners, and rewarded the capturing or killing of fugitives, spurred myths of the Western bounty hunter, "murder for hire" sagas grounded in exploits of gunmen like Tom Horn and Frank M. Canton. Horn once confessed, according to historian Frank Richard Prassell, "Killing men is my specialty. I look upon it as a business proposition, and I think I have a corner on the market."

For *King Blood* Thompson spotlighted many of the colorful territorial characters his father talked about: Uncle Harry Thompson and William D. Fossett; the "Three Guardsmen," Tilghman, Madsen, and Thomas; Al Jennings, a legendary lawman turned outlaw; and Isaac Parker, the "Hanging Judge of Fort Smith," who in a twenty-year run dealt 172 death sentences. As for some of the other frontiersmen *King Blood* illuminated in passing, James litigated cases against both Temple Houston, the "Texas flamboyan," and the still more outrageous Moman Pruiett. Dubbed "the murderer's messiah," Pruiett claimed that in his "defense of 343 persons charged with murder, the record shows 303 acquittals, and the only client to hear the death sentence pronounced was saved by presidential clemency." He boasted that he would "quit whenever the death sentence is passed on one of my clients."

Jim Thompson would himself confront the swaggering Pruiett many years later in Oklahoma City. With his foppish threads and his intoxicating courtroom oratory, Pruiett became the principal model for I. Kossmeyer, the histrionic lawyer Thompson reprised in his crime novels, among them *The Criminal* (1953), *Recoil* (1953), *A Swell-Looking Babe* (1954), and *The Kill-Off* (1957).

The territorial tales his father handed down to him shadowed the background of Thompson's fiction, and they even shaped the bedtime stories he would share with his own children, Patricia, Sharon, and Michael. During his final illness in the 1970s Thompson's conversation rebounded with great urgency to his father and the epoch just before his birth. "Even though he couldn't really speak," Sharon relates, "he still told stories about his dad when he was a marshal. I wish that I had written them down."

•   •   •

When the lands of the Kiowa-Comanche and Wichita-Caddo tribes were re-distributed by lottery on August 6, 1901, James Thompson was promoted and transferred to Anadarko, where he set up an office at 429 C. Avenue with J. U. Osburn, a deputy marshal and insurance salesman.

Anadarko sprouted from a cornfield near the Wichita Indian Agency, by the banks of the Washita River, in southwestern Oklahoma. Anadarko is a corruption of Na-dah-ko, the name of an ancient but nearly extinct Caddoan tribe. Noted now for its Southern Plains Indian Museum and annual American Indian Exposition—and as the onetime home of poet John Berryman—turn-of-the-century Anadarko was notorious for its more than fifty saloons and the terror in its streets. An original settler recalled:

> In the seven years of existence before statehood, Anadarko was in the grip of the lawless, when murders, horsethefts and holdups were as common as coyotes, and on one occasion of the convening of court twenty-five cases were on the docket for murder alone, an equal number for larceny, and more for other breaches of law. Then every man had a gun on his hip, some had two, and a man's quickness on the trigger was his passport to a long life. . . .

Celebrating Anadarko's first anniversary, a special edition of the Anadarko *Daily Democrat* opted for a perkier Chamber of Commerce tone, with breathless prose under the booming headline ISN'T IT THE BIGGEST BABY THAT YOU EVER SAW:

> Anadarko, Queen City of the Washita, is one year old today, and in this short time she has grown from nothing to a beautiful, healthy, lawabiding city of four thousand people, the peer of any community in Oklahoma. Carved from a cornfield. It is the living truth for where today handsome business houses, churches, and mansions rear their proud heads, one short year ago waved the tassels of the corn stalk. In place of the streets were foot paths and on the public square was a small clearing in which stood the auctioneer's stand. East of the city perhaps 500 yards beyond the boundary was rag town, the predecessor of Anadarko. It was two long avenues each 100 feet wide and every inch of available space covered with tents, in which were stores of every description, restaurants, barber shops, law offices and real estate firms.

> Nearly seven thousand people inhabited that unique
> city for three or four weeks and such a sight will never be
> witnessed again in Oklahoma. Truly it was a city set on a
> hill whose light was not hid under a bushel, for the glow of
> myriad lights through the white canvas formed a beacon
> that could be seen for miles. . . .

The original settler perhaps shot closer to the bull's-eye. Within the first year of settlement, outlaw Bert Casey murdered Sheriff Frank Smith and Deputy Sheriff George Beck, tossing their bodies under a wagon cover in front of the town's first two-story building, a saloon. On January 23, 1902, Territorial Governor Thompson B. Ferguson appointed James S. Thompson the new sheriff of Caddo County.

James was a "born politician, a real hail-fellow-well-met type," according to his youngest daughter, Freddie. For more than five years he sculled the hazardous waters of Caddo County with rapt poise. Jim Thompson once wrote that his father's "chief talent . . . was the ability to make friends." Garrulous and outgoing, Sheriff Thompson ingratiated himself with his constituency by means of a time-honored formula wielded by king-pins everywhere—sports and favors.

Big Jim joined the Anadarko baseball squad, emerging as the steadiest home run hitter (belting out three in a single game against Lawton in August 1902) and as team manager. He chaired a commission to build the Anadarko Sportsman Park, an ambitious project that planned gun ranges and tennis courts, as well as baseball and other athlethic fields.

Sheriff Thompson dispensed the perks of office from his perch at the center of the "courthouse combine" that determined all Caddo County business. Also known as the "barrel ring" (since the combine convened at a saloon adjacent to the courthouse, where a barrel of whiskey was kept on tap for them), this controversial clique embodied the territorial patronage machine in its rawest state. From the saloon where "orders emanated," as the Caddo County *Times* slyly phrased it, Sheriff Thompson and the County Central Committee bestowed appointments and benefits, settled disputes, and fashioned policy. The barrel ring occasionally practiced politics on a national scale. When President Roosevelt appeared at a Rough Riders reunion in 1905, Sheriff Thompson joined the small cast of dignitaries who entertained him after a wolf hunt in the Wichita Mountains.

Asked to characterize Sheriff Thompson, his niece Pauline Ohmart points to a passage in *The Getaway* (1959) as containing "the very essence" of the Anadarko lawman. There Doc McCoy recalls his father, the "sheriff of a small down-south county":

> . . . the elder McCoy kept his house filled with company. Lik-
> ing his job—and knowing that he would never get another half as

good—he made sure of keeping it. He had never been known to say no, even to a mob's request for a prisoner. He was ready at all times to fiddle for a wedding or weep at a wake. No poker session, cockfight or stag party was considered complete without his presence; yet he was a steadfast church communicant and the ever-present guest at the most genteel social gatherings. Inevitably, he came to be the best-liked man in the county, the one man whom everybody regarded as a friend. He also was the grossest incompetent and the most costly ornament in the county's body politic.

The hint of negligence in the final phrases sounds an ominous note. And the Anadarko papers rumbled about the barrel ring and the high fees Caddo County paid to the sheriff's office. For all that, Republican Sheriff Thompson quickly transformed himself into the most powerful politician and the strongest vote getter in Democratic Caddo County, handily winning reelection three times, in 1902, 1904, and 1906, by ever wider margins.

• • •

Sheriff Thompson celebrated his 1902 victory with a trip to Nebraska. For some years contact had been limited to letters, but his reports of success at Anadarko massaged the skepticism of the Myers family. If Birdie harbored any scruples about her intended, she swallowed them.

A front-page story in the Burwell *Mascot* narrated the inevitable next stage:

CHRISTMAS WEDDING

One of the neatest social events of the season occurred at the home of W. H. Myers and his wife on Bluff street, this (Christmas) morning. Promptly at nine o'clock as Mrs. D. E. Anderson played the wedding march, James Thompson and Birdie Myers took their place in the arch under the bay window, and Rev. C. A. Powers, in his pleasant way, spoke the words that bound these two popular young people together in Holy Matrimony. After congratulation numbers were passed around and each party requested to find the table of the same number, which mixed the guests up in a very pleasant way, a nice wedding breakfast was served. About sixty guests were present and a large number went to the train to bid them adieu as they parted for their future home at Anadarko, Oklahoma. As they boarded the train a heavy shower of rice descended upon them and the many short blasts of the engineer's whistle announced the happy couple aboard. . . .

There survives a matching pair of photographs: one shows James and Birdie departing Burwell Station on Christmas Day, amid a crush of well-wishers; the other captures their arrival in Anadarko, on December 31, where, still in their wedding coats and hats, they encountered another mob. The Anadarko *Daily Democrat* picked up the account:

> Sheriff James Thompson and wife arrived in town yesterday evening on the 3:40 train. They were met at the depot by the band and a great many friends who gave them a hearty welcome to our city. If ever Jim had a doubt about the high esteem in which he is held here and the number of friends that he has, that doubt was certainly dispelled upon his arrival home with his bride. They were escorted from the depot to the American Hotel by the band, where for several hours a constant stream of their many friends called to extend their hearty congratulations. . . .
>
> District Clerk Ned Sisson returned from the city yesterday from a business trip to Kansas City, Missouri. He was at the depot in that city when Sheriff Thompson and his bride arrived there from Nebraska. Ned says that Mrs. Thompson carried two large valises and that Jim only carried a very small paper box, in true Indian style. This story Jim stoutly denies and says he is satisfied that when he met Ned he was in a condition to see double.

Sheriff Thompson surprised Birdie with the wedding gift of a new house. Jim Thompson's sister Maxine was born in this spectacular home on C. Avenue, on October 24, 1903. Edna Myers Borden, who visited her aunt Birdie in Anadarko with Grandmother Myers shortly after the birth of Maxine, recalls that the Thompsons "had a large house, almost a mansion. There were many bedrooms and a big, modern kitchen. Aunt Birdie had a black woman to do her work. Uncle Jim would take me to the old courthouse and the old stone jail, where they had police dogs. I was nine years old, so my grandmother bought me some books and I went to school in Anadarko. I used to walk down the street and the black people would be out on their porches singing hymns."

Two years later Grandmother Myers returned alone to Anadarko for Jimmie's birth. Sheriff Thompson had moved his family into more modest—but gratis—quarters over the new Caddo County Jail. Adjoining the west entrance of the brick county courthouse and entered by a circular staircase from the downstairs jail, the second-floor apartment contained five large rooms. It was on an impromptu delivery table set up in the sheriff's kitchen that the "jail baby," or to give his full name, James Myers Thompson, was born on Thursday, September 27, 1906.

Birdie complained that carrying Jimmie made for a difficult pregnancy—and not just because of the steamy Oklahoma summer or his large

Birdie Myers Thompson and James S. Thompson departing Burwell Station on December 25, 1902, the day after their wedding (Courtesy of Pauline Ohmart)

Sheriff Thompson and his new wife, welcomed to Anadarko, December 31, 1902 (Courtesy of Edna Myers Borden)

size. Sheriff Thompson had subscribed to a correspondence course and was studying hard to become a lawyer. "Mother said that listening to him read Blackstone aloud every night practically drove her crazy," reported Maxine. Nevertheless, Big Jim passed the Oklahoma bar in November 1906.

• • •

The office of sheriff of Caddo County was not all barrel ring logrolling. To keep his frontier boom town booming, Sheriff Thompson regularly staked his life. So anxious was his sister Leote for his safety that she sold her claim to a lot near Apache, Oklahoma, and retreated to Lamar, Missouri, begging him to follow her.

Sheriff Thompson was especially successful in pinching horse thieves. A headline in the Anadarko *Daily Democrat* blazoned, THOMPSON BECOMING TERROR TO THIEVES. The article broadened the claim: "He is rapidly becoming a terror to law breakers and would-be bad men in general." His effective actions during brawls and gun fights at the Anadarko Station also found their way into news stories. Sheriff Thompson undertook the dangerous task of escorting outlaws to prison inside the frontier version of a paddywagon, a crude wooden cart outfitted with chains and leg-irons.

In June 1904, he foiled a wild jail break that rivaled the twists of western pulp fiction. An outlaw gang intended to deliver a bottle of nitric acid to an Anadarko prisoner, "one of the most desperate men ever confined here," inside a bucket of corn syrup. After intercepting a letter that broadly outlined the strategy, Sheriff Thompson cleverly let the escape plan unfold. When the syrup with its secret weapon reached the jail, he surprised the rescue party and arrested them.

Probably his most sensational performance occurred during his first year in office, and involved Bert Casey, a vicious outlaw said to posess many characteristics of Billy the Kid. Jim Thompson would write about Casey at least twice, each time oddly concealing his father's role, first in "Casey the Killer," a 1937 true crime story, and then in "Bert Casey: Wild Gun of the Panhandle," a "book bonus" published in the magazine *Man's World* during the mid-1950s.

Sheriff Thompson was obsessed with Casey. Not only had the outlaw murdered his predecessor, Frank Smith, but he also kept returning to Anadarko for more outrageous and humiliating crimes. Finally, Casey stole two of the sheriff's own ponies from a shed behind the jail, and pinned a death threat brazenly on the door:

> we will get a man next time from your esteemed
> friend Burt [*sic*]

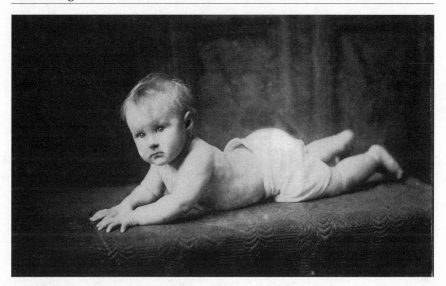

The "jail baby"—
Jim Thompson, 1906
(Courtesy of J.
Anthony Kouba)

Sheriff Thompson set off in pursuit to the Keechi Hills. Conferring with Deputy Jim Bourland, a former member of Casey's gang, he arranged for a captured robber to be released as a "spotter" in the outlaw camp. Although Casey discovered the informer and hanged him as a traitor, a variation on Sheriff Thompson's trick ultimately carried the day. Chief Deputy U.S. Marshal Bill Fossett placed two more spotters in Casey's gang, Fred Hudson and Ed Lockett. On a November morning in 1902, Hudson killed Bert Casey as he was eating breakfast at his camp on the banks of the Eagle Chief River near Cleo, Oklahoma.

Jim Bourland and Fred Hudson later met in a desperate gun battle in Lawton. Drawing their six-shooters and firing at the same instant, both men fell to the sidewalk, Bourland dead and Hudson dying. This was exactly the kind of bizarre "double slaying" that so many of the killers in Jim Thompson's crime novels will try to stage-manage for themselves, arranging their victims' bodies so that each appears to have killed the other.

Sheriff Thompson's cunning in the Bert Casey affair earned the admiration of bounty hunter Frank M. Canton. In his memoir, *Frontier Trails,* Canton hailed "Jim Thompson, the brave and efficient Sheriff of Caddo County."

Behind the old Caddo County Jail, Anadarko,
Oklahoma, 1905. From left to right: Jim
Bourland, J. W. Schrader, C. W. Cooper, D. D.
Hoag, and Sheriff James S. Thompson
(Courtesy of the Thompson family)

• • •

Because of Sheriff Thompson's stature in the Caddo County community, his family acquired all the prestige due regional celebrities. Newspapers attuned more to gossip than to national or even town news dutifully chronicled their goings-on, however slender.

> Sheriff J. S. Thompson left today for a trip in Indian Territory.
>
> Anadarko *Evening Tribune,* February 16, 1902

> Mrs. James S. Thompson, and her father, W. H. Myers, of Burwell, Nebraska, who has been visiting her for some time, went to Lawton the first of the week for a short visit.
>
> Anadarko *Evening Tribune,* May 19, 1903

> Sheriff J. S. Thompson, wife and little daughter, re-
> turned last evening from a week's pleasure trip in Col-
> orado. Mrs. Thompson has been absent from Anadarko
> during the past four months, having spent the greatest
> time at her old home in Nebraska.
>
> Caddo County *Democrat,* September 11, 1905

> Little Maxine Thompson is sick with the measles.
>
> Anadarko *Daily Democrat,* March 5, 1907

> Mrs. J. S. Thompson bought a hat at one of the stores
> yesterday, and last night she read in the *Democrat* of the
> comet which was approaching the earth. She seemed very
> melancholy, and the sheriff asked her what was wrong. To
> which she replied that she wished she had waited until
> after next Friday, and she would have got the hat for a re-
> duced price at a fire sale.
>
> Caddo County *Democrat,* March 22, 1907

The Oklahoma papers also called upon Sheriff Thompson to arbitrate controversies. On one occasion he wrote a mock-heroic essay in scrupulous legalese for the Anadarko *Daily Democrat,* "Chick vs. Stepmother," which addressed the burning questions "What relation is the hen to the chicken she hatched but does not lay, and then what relation is there between the chicken thus hatched and the hen who laid the egg?"

• • •

At the height of his popularity, in 1906, Sheriff Thompson was asked to stand as a Republican candidate for Congress.

Oklahoma rapidly was moving toward statehood. Bird S. McGuire, top dog of the Republican inner circle, insisted that the party nominate its slate before the constitutional convention, scheduled for November. Former Governor Thompson B. Ferguson announced his candidacy in the Second Congressional District. McGuire long had despised Ferguson—with so much mordant ferocity that in 1905 he led an Oklahoma delegation to President Roosevelt and obtained his dismissal as territorial governor. For Sheriff Thompson, a run for Congress against Ferguson would mean double-crossing his old friend, the man who had appointed him sheriff. Nonetheless, when the GOP convened he joined the McGuire-directed crusade to stop Ferguson.

For *Bad Boy,* Jim Thompson reported the episode in the strutting cadences he often slips into when rehearsing his father's ambitions—cadences Maxine suggested echo Sheriff Thompson's own cocky voice:

The ultimate objective of those plans was the Presidency of the United States—for the man believed, and did until the day he died, that any man could be president. As a long step toward that goal, he won the Republican nomination for Congress from his district. . . .

Pop's honesty was something painful to behold. In the relatively minor office of sheriff, he had seen no occasion to discuss his early history and antecedents, nor to promulgate any but the most general of platforms. As a congressman, however, he felt that his constituents had a right to know all about him and what to expect of him as a legislator. Though it damn near killed him—and I mean that literally—he told them.

The great body of voters—men who had moved into Oklahoma from the deep south, men who told each other fondly that "Ol' Jim ain't like the rest of them No'thuhnuhs"—heard him in shocked silence, then with purple-faced fury. They learned that the S in his middle name stood for Sherman, after General Sherman with whom his father had marched to the sea. They learned that the South, whether it liked it or not, was part of the United States, and the quicker it accepted the fact the better. They were told that, as a Republican, he stood for the absolute equality of all races, and that he would fight to obtain and maintain that equality.

Needless to say, Pop's honesty cost him the most smashing political defeat in Oklahoma history.

An autobiographical footnote Jim Thompson printed in *King Blood* added details to this sketch—though Thomas P. Gore, in actuality, was the Democratic candidate for the U.S. Senate:

After three terms as Sheriff . . . James Sherman Thompson ran for Congress against Mr. Gore. Thompson's three-car campaign train carried a banner on each car, the three spelling out his full name. The brass band accompanying the train played *Marching Through Georgia* at each stop. Inevitably, Thompson suffered a smashing defeat. . . .

So remote are these accounts (and a similar recounting, as well, in *Now and on Earth*) from the events of 1906 that it's tempting to dismiss them as a son's wishful fiction—or as the cruelest sarcasm. Yet both Maxine and Freddie also heard the story from their father exactly as their brother wrote it, right down to "Marching Through Georgia" and the Lincolnesque sermon on civil rights. They believed that Jimmie would have been as surprised as they to learn of the sad proceedings that hang in the balance of this chapter.

In the first place, Sheriff Thompson's race for Congress involved only a week-long sprint from the county caucuses on August 21 to the Republican convention in Geary on August 28. The sheriff was a candidate with a peculiar and precise mission: McGuire hoped to deadlock the balloting by springing as many as eight favorite-son candidates. Sheriff Thompson operated as the stalking horse for the McGuire forces in Caddo County.

Secondly, Big Jim Thompson was not nominated by the Republicans for Congress in the Second District. In defiance of the McGuire razzle-dazzle, the more traditional wing of the party—a wing composed largely of progressive Midwesterners—lionized Ferguson. Admirers of the former governor in the Oklahoma County delegation stymied a written agreement between Sheriff Thompson and the other decoys to stick together through the convention. Although he needed thirty ballots, as the McGuire forces craftily reassigned their support from one favorite son to another, Ferguson triumphed. Sheriff Thompson garnered the strongest support of all the McGuire stand-ins. But he never came closer than thirty-eight votes to Ferguson's seventy-four; and even that was not many more than the twenty-eight yeas already pledged to him by Caddo County.

What's finally most misleading about the *Bad Boy* version of the 1906 congressional campaign is the identification of Sheriff Thompson with the progressive spirit within the Republican Party. Not to put too fine a point on it, Bird McGuire epitomized all the sleazy, rabble-rousing impulses in territorial politics. As leader of the GOP in a period of transition, he was both the primary inheritor of the corrupt patronage machine and the principal architect of a remodeled Republican Party that increasingly took its cues from the reactionary Democratic platform. While Sheriff Thompson barnstormed under his umbrella at the Geary convention, McGuire led the party to reverse its anti–Jim Crow tradition for a lily-white posture; as the Guthrie *Daily Leader* euphemistically noted, "The colored brother is getting none of the honors." Closer to home, the Caddo County Republican delegate to the constitutional convention was instructed by the County Central Committee—which Sheriff Thompson chaired—to stand with the Jim Crow clause.

The progressive temper of the party resided in Sheriff Thompson's opponent. Thompson B. Ferguson aroused McGuire's enduring ire by discontinuing the patronage phase of territorial politics during his term as governor. Furthermore, Ferguson remained the only powerful spokesman in the Republican Party for farmers, labor, and blacks. According to the Blackwell *News,* "Governor Ferguson's ideas in relation to social equality for negroes, his opposition to separate schools for white and colored children, and his efforts to abolish the law providing for separate schools would make him obnoxious to every Democrat in Oklahoma and a majority of Republicans." At the Geary convention McGuire exploited racial hatred and directed the enmity of unrewarded office seekers toward Governor Ferguson. Sheriff Thompson not only betrayed a friend; he also was selling out his own Midwestern Republican scruples.

• • •

Despite the defeat, Sheriff Thompson departed Geary on a blustery note. If the coming "con-con," or constitutional convention, should decree a state primary, he would continue the good fight against Ferguson. Before this donnybrook could transpire, the sheriff's bravado mutated to ugly farce and tragedy. Statehood, a boon for Oklahoma politicians, proved a disaster for Big Jim Thompson.

A routine audit of the sheriff's department disclosed $4,920.86 in missing funds. During his reelection campaigns the opposition had fumed about the staggering cost of prairie justice. In 1904 the Anadarko *Democrat* published a cannonade of castigating exposés and editorials, derisively labeling Sheriff Thompson "the taxpayers' friend." As the paper concluded, "We have at different times suggested that the sheriff's office of this county has cost the taxpayer more than it was ever intended that it should cost, by the most reckless legislator . . . his extravagance has raised the tax of this county to the enormous rate of seven per cent. . . . If [opponent] Frank Healy is elected, he will not draw from the treasury $10,383.45 as criminal fees." Other habits riled the Caddo County *Times:*

> The county people are not only against the third term proposition but express a determination as well to vote against any officer who does not enforce ALL LAWS and who violates some of the laws himself by MAINTAINING SUNDAY BALL GAMES AND GAMBLING ON THE RESULTS THEREOF.

Oblique jabs at Sheriff Thompson's gambling agitated newspaper coverage of the 1904 and 1906 elections. The expenses reported in summaries of the Board of County Commissioners meetings do appear top-heavy and swollen. A partial listing of the fees paid over the first quarter of 1902 ran, incredibly:

> James S. Thompson, guarding jai 184.00
> James S. Thompson, boarding prisoners 255.00
> James S. Thompson, fee bill 1257.80
> James S. Thompson, summoning jurors 582.50
> James S. Thompson, attending Dist. Court 37.50
> James S. Thompson, attending Probate Court . . . 96.00

The Anadarko *Democrat* estimated that the sheriff derived as much as $31,150.35 in an eighteen-month stretch ending in July 1904. His official salary for the same period would have been just under $1,500.

The county commissioners suspended Sheriff Thompson in January 1907. He fought the charges, blaming the incompetent bookkeeping of his deputy, D. D. Hoag, and within a month he was provisionally reinstated. But after an investigation divulged the magnitude and character of the crime, the district judge ordered Sheriff Thompson removed from office.

The headlines screamed EMBEZZLEMENT and THE THOMPSON STEAL, and the accusing fingers pointed to the sheriff's gambling. The Anadarko *Democrat* seethed: "Mr. Hoag, the under sheriff, who kept all the books of the sheriff's office, knew all the time that Thompson was playing the bucket shops, and must have more than suspected that it was with money not belonging to him."

Big Jim's friends at the Republican Anadarko *Tribune* pitched an editorial of a more elegiac cast:

> It was with deep regret that the people of Caddo County, without regard to politics, learned of Sheriff Thompson's serious plight. It has developed that he is short to the county about $5,000 taxes collected on delinquent warrants and the commissioners have seen fit to appoint another in his stead. Sheriff Thompson, or 'Jim' Thompson, as he was known to all, was regarded more as a people's official than as a partisan incumbent of office. In two campaigns he led his ticket, receiving the highest vote of any candidate on either ticket. He was a good fellow and made friends of all he met. His principal fault was that he was too good a spender and the people regard his fall more in sorrow than in anger.

A warrant was issued for Sheriff Thompson's arrest, but his deputies refused to serve it.

• • •

For his writing about his father's life in territorial Oklahoma, Thompson ennobled the sheriff whenever he invoked him by name—and then ridiculed him under other names, like Lou Ford and Nick Corey. The books that purport to chronicle his father, *Bad Boy* and *King Blood,* advance a portrait that is respectful to the point of idolatry. Yet their chest-thumping strain of aggrieved naiveté ("Pop's honesty was something painful to behold") hardly sounds persuasive, even if it were not so readily undermined by Oklahoma history.

The Killer Inside Me and *Pop. 1280,* in turn, roil with Oedipal anger: popular, smooth-tongued sheriffs unmasked as psychopathic killers. In *The*

Killer Inside Me, Lou Ford's ingratiating, aw-shucks posture becomes an ingenious torture device. The cavalcade of slayings aside, *Pop. 1280* is probably Thompson's fullest account of "Pop"—from the prickly pun embedded in the title to the snickering conclusion, it is certainly his nastiest. Thompson mugs at Sheriff Corey's loutish overeating and obesity, his aggressive vitality, his lopsided learning, his corny maxims, hypocrisy, and dissembling, and his politician's gusto for any self-serving deal.

How much Thompson knew about his father's troubles in Anadarko remains uncertain. Yet *The Killer Inside Me* and *Pop. 1280* revel in the suspicion that Sheriff Thompson was not what he appeared to be. This novelist son of a lawman would spend *his* life devising crimes and transgressions, rebellions against the law.

• • •

In July 1907, Sheriff Thompson, like his father before him, fled with his young family in the middle of the night, under threat of imprisonment. He put Birdie and the children on a northbound train, and then escaped on horseback to Mexico, a fugitive from justice. No one heard from him for almost two years. Birdie took Maxine and Jimmie, who was not yet one year old, to her parents' home in Burwell. Sheriff Thompson's flight initiated what would be for his children more than a decade of abrupt departures and lonely peregrinations. Though Birdie could hardly have foreseen the circumstances, she reaped the unsettled life her mother had warned against. As for the sheriff, while the criminal charges faded once the insurance company that guaranteed his bond reluctantly covered the shortage, he became something of a local pariah. As Paula McBride, the present associate editor of the Anadarko *Daily News,* comments, "People were ashamed of Jim Thompson's father. So he was left out of all the guides and history books."

> "What's the matter with
> Mama's little sweet-
> heart?"
> "W-where's Papa?"
> "How do I . . . maybe he
> had to see a man. He'll be
> along afterawhile, and if
> you're not good I'll tell
> him about it. . . ."
> ". . . You said Papa would
> be there! You know you
> did! You said—"
> —Edith and Robert Dillon,
> *Heed the Thunder*

White Mother, Black Son: 1907–1919

Heed the Thunder, Jim Thompson's angry novel about his Nebraska childhood, tags Burwell as "clannish," "inter-married," "unfriendly," and "mean," and its settlers—chiefly his own Myers kin—as addled by alcohol, syphilis, and poverty, their lumpish lives a blur of thievery and incest. *Bad Boy* cashiers Burwell with a derisive wave of the hand. "I could say a great deal about the unpleasant features of living with relatives, of living in a gossipy small town where everyone knows your circumstances and has little else to talk about. But I have brooded overlong about these matters in other books (and out of them); so let us dismiss them with the statement that they did exist."

Yet for *South of Heaven* (1967), perhaps the warmest and most nostalgic of his fictions, Thompson rooted his alias, Tommy Burwell, in the family seat his mother fled home to during the summer of 1907—the town where he started school, and the place where more than any other he was raised.

Young Jimmie Thompson displayed the same two-way pull about most aspects of Burwell. First of all, he hated his grandmother almost as much as he idolized his grandfather.

• • •

Grandfather and Grandmother Myers reached Nebraska with their four children, Mel, David, Addie, and Birdie, by covered wagon from Iowa in 1889. William Henry Myers signed a claim on a tract of public land a few miles west of Burwell and erected a sod house. By the measures of the Homestead Act, if he cultivated the farm for five years the spread was his; the soil proving too sandy, the family moved into town. Grandfather Myers purchased the Bluff Street house where Birdie and James would be married, and opened a restaurant by the public octagon at the center of Burwell. Over the restaurant he kept rooms for rent. Burwell was the last stop on the Burlington & Missouri line, and the boardinghouse catered to the railroad crew, who slept over and ate breakfast before heading back on the morning train. Grandfather Myers cooked, while his wife, along with Addie and Birdie, waited tables.

Burwell reposes in a bend of the North Loup River, not far from the mouth of the Calamus. The town belongs to the Great Plains that stretch from the Mississippi River, imperceptibly rising until they run into the Rocky Mountains. Burwell is "seat of Garfield County, the county where the range meets the farm," as the *Nebraska Farmer*—an agricultural periodical Jim Thompson wrote for in the 1930s—enthused for an article about the annual rodeo, apparently not discovering any more colorful circumstances to accent. By Burwell the wheat and corn fields of eastern Nebraska yield to the sandhills: a vast, undulating, nearly lifeless sea of sand, scrubby bushes, and blowing tumbleweeds. Twenty thousand square miles of emptiness and desolation, the sandhills were memorialized in a crude rhyme the Nebraska author Mari Sandoz found carved on an abandoned shack and recorded in *Old Jules:*

> 30 miles to water
> 20 miles to wood
> 10 miles to hell
> And I gone there for good.

Thompson's beloved Willa Cather, who immigrated to nearby Red Cloud the same decade as the Myerses, detected within the Nebraska landscape—which she pronounced "as bare as a piece of sheet iron" and "as naked as the back of your hand"—an awesome, self-annihilating bleakness: "I shall never forget my introduction to it. . . . The land was open range and there was almost no fencing. As we drove furthur and furthur into the country, I felt a good deal as if we had come to the end of everything—it was a kind of erasure of personality."

Settled in the early 1880s, Burwell soon attained a population of just over 2,000 (460 in town, 1,667 rural), chiefly farmers and the merchants who served them. The cruel terrain was aggravated by a capricious climate that might during winter herd the Myers clan into the kitchen to shiver around the stove, as the temperature dipped to 50 below, or during summer thrust them into the cool cellar, as it soared to 120; and the town was no springboard to growth. "Burwell is someplace to escape from," Thompson's younger sister, Freddie, quipped, "a sleepy spot, the size of a stamp."

• • •

The Myers family, like many of Burwell's first citizens, claimed German descent. Originally, the Myerses belonged to the Mennonite Church, the branch of Protestantism that rose out of the Anabaptist movement of the sixteenth-century Reformation. Mennonites observed a strict separation between religion and the world; identifying Christ as the sole Lord of the church, they refused to recognize ecclesiastical or civil authority. Early in the eighteenth century, under threat of religious persecution, the Myerses—or Meyerses, as the name then was spelled, William Henry mysteriously dropping the initial e after he returned from the Civil War—fled Germany for the Mennonite community in Holland. By 1800 the family migrated to America, where Jacob Meyers, his wife, and two children lodged in York County, Pennsylvania, before gravitating west to Illinois. The Myerses spoke of themselves as "Pennsylvania Dutch."

David Newton Meyers, William Henry's father, was born in Whiteside County, Illinois, in 1824. "The Myers men are farmers all down the line," notes Jim Thompson's cousin—and the Myers family historian—Edna Myers Borden. "They always lived in counties, never in towns." With the advent of the Civil War, David drifted from the antimilitarist observances of his Mennonite heritage sufficiently to join the Twentieth Infantry Regiment of the Illinois Volunteers. Alongside his brother Jess, David fought in South Carolina and Virginia and, like Samuel Thompson, participated in Sherman's March to the Sea.

During the siege of Savannah David was captured and dispatched to Andersonville Prison, perhaps the most notorious of the Confederate detention camps. Thirty-five thousand Union soldiers packed an enclosure of fewer than twenty-six acres, corralled without shelter against storms and rain, or the tropical sun. Edna Myers Borden recalls her great-grandfather remarking that he had been confined in an open cattle pen for some seven months and fed only potato peelings and other castoffs from the livestock kept for the Confederate soldiers.

David became one of the plucky few to break out of Andersonville. One night when the guards were distracted by the discovery of a half-completed tunnel, he jumped the wooden balustrade and escaped to the adjoining swampland. A sympathetic Yankee conductor who routinely braked his train near the prison scooped him up and deposited him, not far from home, in Marshalltown, Iowa.

William Henry Myers was the youngest enlistee in the Union army—at least according to Myers family legend he was. Born on his father's farm in Whiteside County on March 1, 1846, young Myers crossed the border into Iowa shortly after his fifteenth birthday and, lying about his age, joined the cavalry. His 1861 enlistment papers claim him as eighteen and record his occupation as farmer. The bugle boy for the Ninth Iowa Regiment, William Henry ranged through Nebraska, Kansas, and Arkansas, but he did not see any action.

Retiring as a sergeant in 1866, William Henry purchased land in Eldora, Iowa, with his army savings and enlistment bounty. On April 20 of that year, he married Marguerite Ellen Cox during a civil ceremony performed in Independence, Iowa.

Jim Thompson understood that Grandfather Myers had been orphaned in early childhood. But the orphan among his grandparents actually was Marguerite. Within a year of her birth on July 12, 1846, her parents died under circumstances that today appear irrecoverable. All that's remembered is that Marguerite's father was an Ohio-born farmer named Cox, and her mother was a Cherokee Indian of the Iroquois Confederation that, emanating from western New York, was scattered through the South and Midwest. The occasion of their meeting and marriage, the fine points of their time together, remains lost.

William Henry and Margaret (as she came to be called) may even have been distantly related. After the death of her parents, Margaret resided with her father's sister, Harriet, and her husband, William Meyers, a Mennonite farmer formerly of Highland County, Ohio, but now in Eldora. At any rate, born during the same year, the future couple crossed paths often when young.

Margaret apparently knew about at least one sibling who did not grow up with her, a brother who subsequently became a doctor serving the Cherokees of Oklahoma. On the 1904 trip that took them to Anadarko, Margaret and her grandaughter Edna Myers Borden visited his home near Guthrie.

All through his life Jim Thompson voiced pleasure in the awareness that he was one-eighth Cherokee. Yet unlike Oklahoma humorist Will Rogers or playwright Lynn Riggs, his Native American heritage never com-

posed a conspicuous plank in his personal identity. "That he was part Indian only supported Jimmie's sense of himself as an outsider, as somebody
a little bit different," suggested Freddie. "He was proud, without making too
much of it." To more than one friend, Thompson also imparted a fear that
his Indian blood figured in his alcoholism. As he aged, his face took on the
high cheekbones and flat countenance of the Cherokee. Elaine St. Johns,
who worked with Thompson at the Los Angeles *Mirror* in 1948, pictures him
in memory as "that big Indian fellow." And his eldest daughter, Patricia, recalls that inside his coffin, "with his flowing mane of white hair and his
broad features, Daddy looked like some grand old Indian chief."

• • •

Grandfather Myers traveled widely during the early years of his marriage,
rarely in the company of Margaret. Between bouts of managing the Eldora
farm he toiled as an itinerant stone mason in Iowa and Ohio. He sold farm
equipment, first on the road and then from hardware stores in St. Louis and
Eldora; later he would own a hardware store in Burwell. He ran a saloon
and hotel in Kansas City. Along the way, Grandfather Myers evolved into a
fierce whiskey drinker and a fearless, high-stakes gambler. He told Jimmie
and Maxine that his pot for a one-year period during the 1870s totaled
$10,000.

After Margaret gave birth to a first son, William Melvin, in 1867, a child
seems to have issued in the wake of each of Grandfather Myers's irregular
sojourns home. David Newton followed in 1871, Adelaide in 1874. The Myerses then suffered the loss of two children who died in infancy. Their
youngest daughter, and Jim Thompson's mother, Birdie Edith Myers, was
born on April 12, 1879.

Like many of the marriages in this book, William Henry and Margaret
sustained a tense union of opposites. That she was "ultra-pious" and he
"the most profane, acid-tongued, harsh, kind, delightful man I ever knew,"
as Thompson summed them up for *Bad Boy,* triggered a spasm of contradictions. Even after the pair relaxed into a routine of cohabitation in Burwell, conflicts persisted. Always restless, William Henry prowled the town,
drinking, talking, and smoking cigars with his cronies at The Forks, his
choice among the taverns, dropping in on his Masonic lodge or playing
cards at his friend Andy Snyder's office. Grandmother Myers never left the
house except to attend Sunday services at the First Christian Church and
to witness at evening prayer meetings. She wouldn't market or shop, and
she banked her money inside a sack at the bottom of her closet. He was fascinated by any new mechanical contrivance, whereas she resisted the
washing machine he purchased for her, still pounding her laundry on a
board.

Even after Birdie returned years later with Maxine and Jimmie, Grandfather Myers prepared the family meals, concocting huge fish and potato breakfasts, aromatic breads, and elaborate stews. On the rare occasions when Margaret did cook, the results proved eccentric. Not eating vegetables herself, she refused to serve them. Roasts and fried rice were her specialties, together with overcooked and overspiced pumpkin pies that her husband branded "leather and lard." Her victuals stuck also in the craw of her young grandson. Maxine reported that six decades later, "Jimmie was still making fun of our grandmother's pies. He always had a thing about those pies."

Retiring on his Civil War pension around the turn of the century, Grandfather Myers luxuriated in the role of patriarch. Mel had died tragically at the age of twenty-nine—a newspaper printer by trade, he contracted a harrowing illness from chemicals in the ink. To hold what remained of the family close by, Grandfather Myers purchased a large farm for David and his wife, Edith, on the western fringes of Burwell. He built a house for Addie, just married to a young Englishman named Robert Wicks, and helped them start a small store. He welcomed Birdie home without condescension or cavil. Margaret, meanwhile, groused about expenditures and toward Birdie assumed a waspish, "Didn't I tell you so" posture. Later, she was not above taking a switch to Jimmie—unless Birdie or Grandfather Myers imposed themselves in her path.

For *Bad Boy* and *Heed the Thunder,* Grandmother Myers looms over Jimmie's boyhood like some Wicked Witch of the West, crabby, closefisted, and unappeasable, a squat fury draped in black. The prayer meetings she forced him to attend may help explain his horror, more than her pies or an occasional whipping, as they tainted his earliest associations with her. From *Bad Boy:*

> I recall an evening when my ultra-pious grandmother had dragged me to a country revival meeting, and I lay shivering in my dark bedroom afterwards. I was too terrified to sleep. I was certain that my six odd years of life—all spent in sinning from the preacher's standpoint—had earned me one of the hotter spots in hell, and I would certainly be snatched there before morning.

Jimmie's memories of the revival meetings, and the sense of unalterable doom that he absorbed there, never deserted him. Grandmother Myers's beliefs embraced a dour tangle of Mennonite dogma and prairie fundamentalism. Life for her, he wrote, "was merely a long trail of hardship which led to a better hereafter." During Jimmie's childhood she lectured him about the imminent end of the world and resurrection of Jesus Christ. "My Grandmother read her Bible every day, and quoted it often to us children," Edna Myers Borden recalls. "She told us that the Bible says that you're not sent to hell, but punished right here. While she spoke of an afterlife, she really believed in hell on earth."

Grandfather Myers served as Jimmie's protector, in the absence of his father, a buddy, and his worldly guide. As the boy grew, there would be outings to the sandhills, card games, hunting trips, and surreptitious sips of "cider." Grandfather Myers was a gifted mimic, a fountainhead of jokes, tall tales, and yarns. "As a child," Thompson wrote in *Roughneck,* "my maternal grandfather had used to tell me all sorts of wild stories, allegories thinly disguised as personal experiences." If the author's note appended to *Heed the Thunder* may be trusted, Grandfather Myers's caustic, irreverent voice ripened into Jim Thompson's literary conscience:

> I was about to pronounce this book the first of a trilogy when the ghost of a hawk-faced old man prodded me with an ethereal cane. "How the hell you know it will be?" he jeered. "Goddam if you ain't a good one!"
>
> And upon that taunt, there came another, in choked explosive tones, "Maybe I had ought to cut his ears off, seein' he don't plan to use 'em."
>
> So I will say this:
>
> This may be the first volume of a trilogy. . . .

• • •

After the furtive trek from Anadarko to Burwell, Birdie settled with Jimmie and Maxine into the tiny back bedroom of the Myerses' Bluff Street home, in suspense about the duration of their stay. While she awaited word from James with every afternoon's mail, there was no certainty she would see her husband again. But guided by the optimism and poise that animate almost every characterization of her, Birdie focused on his return. Because she could not foresee passing the full academic year in town, she reluctantly declined a request, in the fall of 1907, to resume her old post at the Burwell Grammar School; for the same reason, she again resisted offers in 1908 and 1909. She also would tolerate no sniping at James, whatever the source or however long his silence. When not looking after Jimmie and Maxine, for some two and a half years Birdie retreated—Edna Myers Borden remembers—to her room and read.

Not yet thirty, still slim and pretty, Jimmie's mother, for all her burdens, impressed those who knew her with a dignity and humor. The words that recur in family evocations of Birdie are "sweet," "strong," and "patient." Her niece Neddie Pinnell found her "a wonderful person, very kind and sweet and forgiving, and we all loved her dearly." As her nephew Ted Cowan evokes her, Birdie was "tall and beautiful, a very strong woman who didn't brood about her troubles. She was a very patient person, and made the best of it."

Whatever apprehensions Birdie may have sheltered, she kept her reserve before the children. "Mama never complained, though I think she worried a lot," Maxine noted. "She was good and kind to us, never strict, a real softy." Freddie believed that "Mama's dry wit carried her through troubled times." For others, though, like Jimmie's childhood chum Rex Wagner, Birdie's playfulness signaled a "sharp tongue. She could be very sarcastic. Everyone in that family was gifted that way. They would express their opinions very plainly, and were quite outspoken."

While Birdie doted on all her children, Jimmie remained her favorite. "Jimmie was just crazy about Mama," Maxine recalled, "and Mama was crazy about Jimmie. That's all there was to it, really. Jimmie could do no wrong as far as Mama was concerned." By all accounts, Birdie heartily encouraged and stuck by Jimmie, even when she did not entirely grasp what he was up to. Although she would endure long separations from her husband, she was never far from her only son's side. Not only did Birdie always reside with or near him, even after his marriage to Alberta; she also followed Jimmie to some unexpected places—the Texas oil fields in the late 1920s and the University of Nebraska in the early 1930s. Later she researched and co-authored some of his trade journal and true crime articles. Glancing at the intense maternal feelings—by turns nurturing, smothering, and incestuous—that emanate from Thompson's novels, Tony Kouba, Maxine's son, bluntly describes Jimmie as "overmothered."

• • •

***Bad Boy* opens** with what purports to be Jim Thompson's first memory: "an awkward, large-headed tot, much prone to stuttering and tripping over my own feet," having his bottom pinched by Maxine, whom he tactfully designates his "junior." On other occasions, when late-night drinking set him reminiscing, Thompson told Maxine that his earliest recollection was of playing catch with her in the living room of the Myers home, a rolled up pair of socks serving as a ball. Writing *Now and on Earth* almost thirty-five years later, he placed this souvenir of his childhood in a wild, stream-of-consciousness monologue that, spoken to the hallucinated shade of his by then dead father, surges with vestigal traumas and fears before breaking into rushes of giddy laughter:

> Those two years:
> I was wearing dresses, and I laughed when I saw the sun, or the trees making shadows on the grass, or a sparrow hopping through the dust. I laughed because it was good to laugh. There was no bad, only error. (Like the Christian Scientists, Pop.) And I slept

long hours, and I was still fat with mother-fat. Then snow lay on the ground, and in the cold room where Mom watched by the window a little girl and I tossed a ball back and forth by the hour—a ball made out of an old stocking; and there was nothing so funny as when it rolled under the bed or fell behind the door, and I wondered how the little girl could bear to stop. And then the snow was green, and we were like the others now—not the big others but the others that were bigger than we were, and we did not need sleds and warm boots and mackinaws. Barefoot, we walked down to the grove and we laid sticks upon the ground and I sat on the ground with them, holding back the laughter with my hand, and the little girl frowned and she was the teacher. And I laughed when the clods fell around us, and the little girl ran this way and that and tried to climb the trees; ran in circles, crying and screaming until her eyes rolled white in her head; ran because there was nothing to do but run; ran because Mom was at the house and she was not at the house. And I laughed because everything was laughter. There was the smell of fresh earth and yellow dust, and a great pile that was a mountain of gold (like Pop is going to find); and the gold spouted downward from a pipe in the sky, falling around my head, mounting above my feet like golden sand, above my waist and shoulders. And I was looking into the man's eyes, far above, and he was looking down into mine, and I knew that we were playing a game, that he was going to hide me beneath the gold; and I could not understand why Mom came racing across the field nor why the man's teeth bared like a frightened dog's. But I knew everything was good, and I laughed. . . .

His laughter shades to menace. Edna Myers Borden remembers that Birdie used to act out a private little game with Jimmie. From the time that he was old enough to frolic alone in the Myers yard, whenever Jimmie returned to the house covered with dirt Birdie would sweep him up in her arms and scurry to the mirror. Holding his face right by hers, she would stare into the glass and ask him, "Will you take a look at Mama's little black child. Where did your white mother get such a black son?"

"How Jimmie used to laugh at that!" Edna remarks. "Even when he got older, when Bird would do that he'd laugh like it was the funniest thing in the world, and he had never heard it before."

White Mother, Black Son would turn up later as the working title for Thompson's novel about the wrathful progeny of an interracial coupling, eventually published as *Child of Rage* (1972).

• • •

Shortly into the new year of 1910, Jimmie's father finally wrote his family from Mexico. With Bill Tilghman acting as his go-between, the criminal charges against him were suspended. He was free to return to Oklahoma. During his two and a half years on the lam, James experienced his first taste of the life of a minerals speculator, overseeing a copper mine in central Mexico. He earned a degree in accounting through another correspondence course.

By April the Thompsons reunited in a small Oklahoma City apartment, at 432 West 4th Street. Jimmie's father ventured into business as an insurance agent, in partnership with his old friend Logan Billingsley. Born in Tennessee, Billingsley had migrated to Anadarko as a boy. During territorial days, Sheriff Thompson (the story went) saved Billingsley from a lynch mob. Billingsley and Thompson operated out of an office downtown in the Security Building.

Billingsley also owned the Night and Day Drug Store—despite its name essentially a grocery and confectionery market—on West Main Street, and James bought into that as well. The management of the shop rebounded to the Billingsley and Thompson wives. Birdie toted the children to work with her each morning, and the Billingsleys' eldest son, Glenn, became Jimmie's first friend.

• • •

After Burwell, the streets Jimmie explored with Glenn Billingsley around the Night and Day Drug Store augured a dizzying metropolis. The capital of Oklahoma moved in 1910 from Guthrie to Oklahoma City. Opened to white settlement just twenty years earlier, in 1890, Oklahoma City stayed a shaggy town. Its more than 64,000 citizens occupied a strained twilight zone of the old and new. Sleek hotels like the Huckins welcomed patrons who were first befuddled, then angered, by indoor plumbing. Broad, paved streets gave way to a bewildering snarl of narrow footpaths and alleys. As Albert McRill recounts in his wry book about Oklahoma City, *And Satan Came Also,* many backstreets held concealed passageways to illegal saloons, gaming joints, and bawdy houses, or escape routes for those who couldn't afford to be pinched during a raid. Oklahoma had been "dry" since statehood, but this underground economy intersected the public life of the city like a poorly kept secret. While cowboy preacher the Reverend John W. Pruitt railed that "since my visit to Oklahoma City I am confirmed in my belief that hell was made too little from the start," Mayor Henry M. Scales brazenly pantomimed drinking a mint julep at campaign rallies, and not so silently gutted the Prohibition ordinance. When the attorney general seized an occasional stash of liquor, huge throngs jeered as barrels of their "oil of joy" poured down the sewers.

After automobiles began to dodge horses on Main and Grand streets, the question of where else these vehicles might go still hung fire. Roads around Oklahoma City hatched their own small adventures. A classic passage in *The Green Corn Rebellion,* a novel by William Cunningham, Thompson's friend and predecessor as director of the Federal Writers' Project in Oklahoma, examines the mess that attended the presence of more than one car on the same path:

> Once they were plowing along through deep sand when they met another car, and neither car could get out of the ruts. [He] watched the car ahead coming slowly toward them, its wheels cramped, and tightened up all his muscles trying to help. [The driver] stopped and backed a ways, and the other car stopped and the men got out. They started pulling weeds and placing them in the ruts. [The men from the first car] got out and helped them, then the driver of the other car started it, and everybody else pushed. This way they got both cars out of the ruts, and with a good deal of pushing got them past each other.

Jimmie's recollections of Glenn Billingsley in Oklahoma City impart a similar comedy, reminiscent of the silent films of Chaplin, Keaton, and Lloyd that he later admired; and like those films, his recital of his friend's tall-tale shenanigans uphold an air of amused awe before the odd patches of city life:

> Glenn led a charmed life. One Saturday afternoon when he was leaning out the office window, he fell out. But he survived the four-story fall with no more than a scratch. He landed on the awning of the street-level drug store, went through it, and dropped into a baby carriage. The vehicle was empty of its occupant, fortunately, for he made a wreck of it. But, as I say, he wasn't hurt a bit.

Another episode veers from Keaton to the Bowery Boys:

> One morning a bunch of older boys dropped him down a man-hole and sealed the lid back on. Most lads in such a situation would have perished of fright, but not Glenn. He wandered around through the various arteries of the sewer, picking up a sizable quantity of small change from the silt along his way. After a few profitable hours of this, he made his way out through another man-hole. He then phoned the police, quoting that a friend of his had been thrown into the sewer by a certain group of boys—he gave their names. Then, without giving his own name, he hung up and went to town.

The cops collared the youths at school and readily wrung a confession from them. The victim was identified as Glenn. A search of the sewer was begun for his body and the young criminals were taken to the police station, facing a long stretch in the reformatory.

Late in the afternoon, Glenn put in his appearance and was hailed by the admiring and relieved police as a hero. They brought him home where he was tucked into bed, apparently too shocked by his experience to eat. Actually, there was nothing wrong with him but a stomach-ache and, perhaps, eye strain. He had visited four picture shows and eaten several dollars' worth of candy, ice cream, and other delicacies.

After that experience the worst toughs at school shied away from Glenn. He was pure poison.

I always admired him.

As the only childhood companion—and one of the few friends invoked from any period—Glenn holds pride of place in *Bad Boy.* Jimmie actually knew him just a few months. By Christmas, Logan Billingsley departed Oklahoma City to join the Indian Land Service. He subsequently became a real estate developer in New York City, where his brother Sherman managed the Stork Club, and he founded the American Indian Hall of Fame at Anadarko. Later in the decade, Logan would invite the Thompsons to New York for the World Series, but James made the trip alone.

Jimmie also memorialized his young friend in *After Dark, My Sweet.* William "Kid" Collins, the former boxer and escaped mental patient who narrates the novel, keeps repeating to anyone who will listen that he's waiting for "that darned crazy Jack Billingsley. . . . I guess you know the Billingsleys, big real estate family?"

● ● ●

Jimmie's mother made a stab at operating the Night and Day Drug Store by herself, yet without the Billingsleys' experienced hand the business soon foundered. Perhaps for the same reason his father abandoned the insurance agency. Deciding to become a sort of itinerant lawyer, James rented an office near Ardmore and circulated through central Oklahoma. Birdie once more gathered up Maxine and Jimmie, boarding the bus back to her parents. They arrived in Burwell almost exactly a year after they had left it.

The melancholy yo-yoing of 1910 between father and grandparents set a pattern for Jimmie's youth that persisted until he left home for the West Texas oil fields. Brief, concentrated spells of life with father fell between long stretches of exile to Burwell. James would write for Birdie and the children, and for a short time the family would live together in Oklahoma or Texas. But always something happened to separate them again.

Even when the Thompsons ostensibly all resided inside the same house, Jimmie's father slipped away on marathon business trips. "It was almost like having company when Papa returned," Maxine recalled. "Someone would come to the door, and it was Papa." She added that, regarding money, the family reeled through a similar roller-coaster ride. "Our life was very unstable financially. Sometimes there would be just pots of money. Papa would come home with expensive presents for all of us. Then we'd be broke again. There'd be all sorts of men knocking at the door. That's when Mama had to run back to Burwell, and her father would have to take care of everything."

Edna Myers Borden believes that not only work prompted these periodic excursions. She speculates that Jimmie's father might have been manifesting early signs of the mental illness, perhaps a form of manic depression, that devastated him in the 1930s. "I think that he disappeared without any real explanation. I don't think he was a drinker, but something seemed wrong from the way everyone acted. Uncle Jim'd just be gone, and they'd take the bus to Burwell and stay for a couple of years. It's funny looking back on it, but no one ever talked about their father." Elva McWharter, another of Jimmie's Burwell friends, found the silence surrounding his father so strange that she assumed the Thompsons were divorced.

Whatever the cause, Jimmie grew up largely without his father. Absent fathers haunt Thompson's fiction, but the most pathetic imagination of this aspect of his boyhood for the novels—and the saddest, because it probably hews so closely to his own experience and fantasies—agitates *Heed the Thunder*. Through the chronicle of his life among his mother's relatives in a small Nebraska town from 1907 to 1914, recurrent wails of "Where's Papa?" sear the text like a banshee cry. Only in the final pages is the bitter puzzle solved. Papa has not *consciously* abandoned his wife and young son these past seven years, after all—he's merely been the victim of cruel amnesia! And once his memory is restored, after he is cracked on the head with a bottle during a Mexican barroom brawl, he rushes to rejoin his family.

"I think Jimmie resented Papa's being away more than I did," judged Maxine. "I know he resented Burwell more." For *Bad Boy* Jimmie vividly lodged his lifelong difficulties with close friendships directly at his father's door:

> In my earlier years, my father travelled considerably about Oklahoma, seldom staying in any town more than a month—not long enough for me to become accustomed to a strange school, yet too long for me to lay out. Just about the time I began to get acquainted, we would pull up stakes.
>
> So I hungered for friendliness, and no matter how many times I

was duped I never ceased to bite on the bait that was put in front of me. There was a game called "push-over" in those days. A boy would come up to you, put his arm around your shoulder and engage you in kindly conversation. Then just when you were beginning to warm up to him, another boy would kneel behind you, the first would give you a push, and you would fall backwards on your head.

I don't know how many times I fell for this game, and similar ones before I began to get the idea that what appeared to be friendship might be something else entirely. I never liked the idea, and I fought against it. In later life, more or less as a duty, I would draw back from a proffered kindliness and coldly demand the reason for it.

• • •

Back in Burwell, Birdie, Maxine, and Jimmie moved into the house the Myerses had just raised on the western edge of town, not far from the present site of the Cram Field Airport. A photograph taken in June 1911, to commemorate the visit of Grandfather Myers's sisters, Rebecca and Sara, poses the entire Burwell contingent of the Myers-Wicks-Thompson clan along the front porch of the new home. Not quite five years old, Jimmie huddles in the far right corner, almost as tall as his sister Maxine, whose hand he shyly holds; like her, he wears a white dress. And like his cousin Grace Myers, at the opposite end of the photograph, Jimmie has his blond hair cropped short because of a recent outbreak of lice.

Even as the roomier dwelling afforded him more neutral territory in his permanent war with Grandmother Myers, Jimmie thrilled at the discovery that his young cousins lived directly across the road. From a congenial farmhouse on the lip of a vast spread of fields, ranges, barns, silos, and windmills, his Uncle David Myers and his Aunt Edith presided over their brood of seven children: Edna, Frances, Marguerite, William Lyle, Neddie May, Grace, and Donald. Nearest to Jimmie in age, William Lyle Myers was the close companion of his boyhood.

At every opportunity Jimmie forsook the "unfriendly" residence of his grandmother for the place he called "the finest, the best, the friendliest house in the world." All through his years in Burwell Jimmie swapped rooms with his cousin Edna. While she assisted Grandmother Myers, he played or handled light farm chores, such as milking the cows or cleaning the barn, with William Lyle. Edna remembers Jimmie and William Lyle as "nice, quiet boys, given to the usual mischief." At this green stage of their lives, mischief apparently encompassed nothing more than sledding off the farmhouse roof, teasing their sisters with insects, smoking Grandfather Myers's pipe, or trying to pass off some pallid slop intended for the pigs as

*Burwell, Nebraska—June, 1911; from left to right: David Newton Myers, Edna Myers, Frances
Myers (front), Marguerite Gail Myers, William Lyle Myers (front), Nettie May Myers, Grace
Myers (in carriage), Donald Newton Myers, Margaret Ellen Cox Myers (Jim Thompson's
grandmother), William Henry Myers (Jim Thompson's grandfather), Rebecca Schneider, Sara
Dinnell, Byrdie Wicks, Robert Wicks, Mabel Wicks (front), Addie Myers Wicks, Robert Wicks, Jr.,
Olive Wicks (front), Maxine Thompson, Birdie Edith Myers Thompson, and Jim Thompson
(front) (Courtesy of Edna Myers Borden)*

fresh milk—although the boys once "flew" off the barn brandishing flour
sacks for parachutes. Fortunately the harvest was gathered, and the
ground below was piled high with hay.

Jimmie entered the first grade of the Burwell Public School in September 1912. The old wooden structure downtown where Birdie taught had
burned in a spectacular fire. Jimmie attended classes at a modern two-
story, eight-room brick building erected on a field halfway between town
and the Myers farm. The more than three-mile walk to and from school
each day was an infliction Jimmie never forgot. "There was no road to
speak of, just a trail by the edge of the sandhills," recalls his classmate Elva
McWharter. "If it snowed in October you can bet your life it would be there
the next May." Jimmie preserved his "resentment" about his hard trek—
really, of course, about feeling trapped in Burwell—in "A Road and a Memory," a poem he published in the *Prairie Schooner* in 1930:

> I can still see that homely, grass-grown trail
>> That clung so closely to the shambling fence:

Sand-swept, ruts filled with every gale;
    A helpless prey to all the elements.
A shower would make those soft black tracks a mire
    That sucked at wagon wheels and made the horses sweat;
The sun would turn them into flinty fire
    That burnt and tore each unshod foot they met.
In winter, with the grass and sand-burs dead
    I walked the bellying center of the trail
And filled the gopher holes that might have led
    To broken legs when moon and stars should fail.

Each morning found me plodding down that road to school.
    The evening sun was low on my return.
And every roadward thing construed itself into a tool
    To make my hot resentment deeper burn.
Those tortuous ruts were like two treacherous bars
    So spaced to show an eye-deceiving gape
So while one ever struggled for the stars
    They hugged too close for actual escape.

Escape: tell me the meaning of the word:
    Produce the man who's touched a star, for me.
Escape is something for a bird;
    A star is good to hang upon a tree.
Not long, however, lags the flesh behind the mind.
    I left the road, the ruts, the holes, the dust.
And sought a symbol of another kind
    To mark reward for labor, right and just.
. . . and twenty years have trickled through my hand.
    The hand is soft; it's white, preserved and clean.
As unlined, vacant as the wind-brushed sand;
    As meaningless, as—mean.
The road? Why yes, the road is there.
    And it seems the road will always be;
Not white, not soft, not fair,
    But hard and straight as strange eternity.

Written when Thompson was in his mid-twenties but glancing back "twenty years" to his first days at school, "A Road and a Memory" is one of his earliest works that might be dubbed characteristic. While an eerie calm suffuses the surface of the poem, his recollected anger emerges as concentrated, chronic, and pervasive. The harsh Burwell terrain furiously and meticulously observed through the four seasons furnishes the "tools" and "symbols" of an inward landscape charged with "hot" but unnamed "resent-ments" (his missing father? his nomadic childhood? Grandmother Myers? his whole life in Burwell?). As outer and inner adversity intertwine through the personalizing second stanza, and the "tortuous ruts" of the trail mutate into "treacherous bars," "A Road and a Memory" coolly brands this setting of Jimmie's childhood a jail. The menacing, "eye-deceiving" Burwell scene provocatively tempts him with dreams of "escape" that are at once futile and pitiful.

Thompson reprised "A Road and a Memory" in *South of Heaven,* a late novel about the West Texas oil fields. There his roughneck alter ego Tommy Burwell recites some lines as an example of his own youthful poetry. After listening to Burwell on Burwell, his friend Four Trey Whitey responds that while he "liked the poem very much, it always gave him a touch of the blues."

Jimmie is remembered by his Burwell school friends as a promising student. "Jim Thompson was a very smart little boy," Rex Wagner notes. "He had quite a good sense of humor too. Naturally mischievous, I'd have to say, but he never got into trouble with the teachers. He had a real gift for English class, particularly. But like many of us, Jim lost a lot of time at the beginning and close of the school year, having to help out at home with the planting and harvest."

Perhaps to fortify Jimmie against the formidable hike to school, Grand-father Myers inducted him into a perilous routine. First on chilly winter mornings, and then nearly every day, he presented his willowy young grandson with a small therapeutic toddy along with his breakfast of fish and eggs. An "alcoholic" himself who "always was under the influence," according to Elva McWharter, Grandfather Myers may only have been justify-ing his own morning drink. "In days to come," Jimmie wrote in *Bad Boy,* "I was to regret this early acquired taste for alcohol. But, at the time, I did not believe we could have survived without it." Maxine echoed her brother's reproach, tracing his battle with the bottle back to "all those drinks with our grandfather."

• • •

Sometime during the spring of 1913 Jimmie's father summoned the family back to Oklahoma City, where he had set up shop as an accountant in the Baltimore Building. His mother pulled Jimmie from the Burwell Grammar School, and the Thompsons reassembled at a small house at 606 West 9th. James was flush again.

For the next year—the term of their second residency in Oklahoma City—family fortunes seesawed between devil-may-care prodigality and lickpenny poverty. Spectacular homecoming presents still sweetened Pop's absences: a fur coat for Birdie, a violin for Maxine, a smart bag of golf clubs for Jimmie. And, as in Anadarko, he provided a servant to rescue his wife from housework and cooking. "Papa spent his money as fast as it came in," Maxine lamented. "He was incapable of saving anything from the good times for the days when business was slow and we had nothing. For him there was always going to be a lot of money. He just didn't seem to be aware, somehow. He was always hopeful, always thought everything was great." So Birdie reluctantly released her housekeeper after a few months, and once more found herself juggling accounts and dodging creditors. Maxine remembered her mother at meals surreptitiously shifting her own food onto the plates of her children.

Although Jimmie had not completed his first grade in Burwell, the fall of 1913 found him entering the second-year class of the Willard School in Oklahoma City. Never before had he lived under the watchful eye of both parents—and James did not conceal his dismay at what he saw. Tension sparked by mutual incomprehension began to poison any rapport between father and son. "It was a case of their not understanding each other at all," recounted Maxine. "They were two different personalities totally. Papa was all for sports, outgoing, hail-fellow-well-met. My father was the kind of man who would break his neck if he had the money to take the train to New York for the World Series. Jimmie was the introvert. He was not interested in any of the things Papa was. I don't think he ever watched a ball game. Papa never understood Jimmie—at least Jimmie felt that he didn't. Papa could not understand where this boy came from, who blinked his eyes a lot and was shy and withdrawn."

Sprouting up precociously tall—though not rugged and stocky—like his father, Jimmie inherited none of the old man's social sparkle and confidence. Determined to remold his son, James enlisted him in a peculiar apprenticeship that mimicked his own autodidact's training. Arbitrary and perverse, his father's sudden ministrations marked Jimmie with a destructive legacy of deficiency, of "shame." As Thompson wrote in *Bad Boy*, with a deceptive jocularity that sheathes the gut revelation in a shattering parenthesis:

> As an eight-year-old, I can remember his asking Mom about my tastes in literature. He expressed his dissatisfaction with her reply by going out and buying a twelve-volume set of American history and another set of the letters of the presidents. And he pooh-pooed her angry opinion that the stuff was too old for me.
>
> "You're bringing these children up in ignorance," he declared. "Now, when I was four years old, I could name all the presidents. . . ."
>
> There followed a long list of accomplishments, of which I was no more capable than I was of flying. (I suppose the comparison

shamed me all my life.) But for months afterward, I was required to read the books aloud to him every night. I read them at home, while at school I read the adventures of Bow-wow and Mew-wew, and Tom and Jane at Grandmother's farm.

In the same fashion, I was drilled in higher accountancy before I had mastered long division; I was coached in political science before I ever saw a civics class; I learned the dimensions of Betelgeuse before I knew my own hat size. I was always a puzzle and plague to my teachers. I often knew things that they didn't but seldom anything that I should.

I don't mean to give the impression that Pop was harsh. He was anything but. He seldom raised his voice. Never once did he so much as paddle one of us kids. It was simply that he couldn't be content to manage his own sphere and let Mom manage hers.

Jimmie never shed his hangdog sense of inferiority in the face of his father's demands. Maxine underscored the lingering fallout from this early rivalry between James and Jimmie. During the 1960s and 1970s, when Jimmie would retreat to her house on a jag of booze and talk, his conversation reverted to his father. "Much later in life, if Jimmie was drinking, I could sense that he felt he was at odds with his father, that he didn't fit in. Jimmie felt Papa was disappointed in him. I think that he did blame a lot of his problems on that in later years. In his cups late at night, Jimmie would bring that up like he had dwelled on it for a long time. Papa, I'm sure, was completely unaware of his effect."

While Maxine upheld her brother's denial that their father ever inflicted physical punishment on his children, other family members stress the gloomy probability that Jimmie was more than a neglected or discontented child. Thompson's daughter Sharon pointedly remarks, "I think that in his childhood there was what anyone would call child abuse. As my dad told it, without saying too much about it, he was never athletic and not into a lot of boy things like his father. He wanted his father to be proud of him, but there were misunderstandings." His wife, Alberta, who at various junctures in the marriage lived with both of Jimmie's parents, endorses Sharon's appraisal. "I don't think he had a happy childhood. It was unstable financially and emotionally. He had a very lovely mother who was good to him, but his father, well, there probably was some abuse. There was a lot of anger in Jimmie about his father."

Outside the family, Thompson's wellspring of resentment about his father provoked similar suspicions among his friends. Arnold Hano, his editor at Lion Books and perhaps his closest confidant for more than twenty-five years, comments that "I always assumed that Jim was abused to some degree physically, and certainly psychologically, mentally. My wife,

Bonnie, who is a family therapist, says that child abuse is the first thing she would want to ask about. When he'd be drunk, he would get maudlin or bitter about his father, and maybe even cry a little bit. Regarding all the violence [in Thompson's novels], I suspect that it is his relationship with his father that is much more of a causal factor than anything else. The anger, the quiet murdering, is Jim getting back somehow."

Hano emphasizes the recurrent child abuse in Thompson's fiction: "I believe there's an awful lot of the relationship between Jim and his father that you see in the novels."

The crazy, capricious, cruel, and lost childhoods among the Thompson corpus partake of the totalitarian family cast that poet Randall Jarrell termed "one of God's concentration camps." Recollections of vicious beatings, abandonment, deprivation, ritual humiliation, and incest routinely rankle the childhood flashbacks in his novels. As do the subtler forms of what analyst Leonard Shengold calls "soul murder": Critch King in *King Blood* is one of many Thompson scions tormented by his failure to meet his stern father's "standards."

Thompson's novels engage the nuclear family principally in the act of detonation. An astonishing number of his characters are orphans— young Tommy Burwell in *South of Heaven,* as if to italicize the point, is forsaken twice: not only have his mother and father passed away, but even his grandparents, his only remaining kin, die in a freak dynamite accident! A preponderance of the nonorphaned Thompson heroes grow up in single-parent households, overseen by ineffective or brutish guardians.

Sons who can't respect their fathers *(The Criminal),* sons who wish their fathers dead *(A Swell-Looking Babe),* and self-proclaimed prodigies who strive to subvert their fathers' place in their mothers' lives and beds *(A Swell-Looking Babe, Child of Rage)* also stagger through Thompson's books, by turns nursing and picking at their wounds. Others, like Little Charlie Bigger in *Savage Night* or William "Kid" Collins in *After Dark, My Sweet,* are denied all of the succor of childhood and, emerging as doleful boy-men, remain stalled in a state of arrested development.

The Getaway ponders such glitches inside the family machinery with an urgency that resonates through the assaults on conventional values and privileged institutions in Thompson's fiction. During a meditative passage on family and personality that his cousin Pauline Ohmart terms "Jimmie thinking about his father and his own life," Thompson writes of an "insecurity whose seeds are invariably planted earlier in under- or overprotectiveness, in a distrust of parental authority which becomes all authority."

• • •

As Jimmie neared completion of his second grade at the Willard School, his father took the accounting business on the road. Through the good ol' boy network of Chris Madsen and Heck Thomas, the defrocked sheriff whose fiscal hocus-pocus had all but consigned him to a prison cell secured an appointment as chief bookkeeper of the Oklahoma Peace Officers' Association. So well oiled were the wheels of provincial justice that James was able to establish residence once again in Anadarko. The old town became home base for a job that indulged his yen for new scenery and fresh faces.

The summer of 1914 evolved into a spirited family vacation. As Jimmie later told the Oklahoma *News,* "My father became auditor of the Peace Officers' Association and we travelled all over Oklahoma." By fall the Thompsons' gypsy routine proved more unruly. Birdie soon wearied of enrolling Jimmie and Maxine in a new country school system on a monthly, sometimes weekly, basis.

So, when she journeyed north to her folks for the Christmas holidays, Birdie simply stayed there—for almost two years. Jimmie joined the third-grade class at the Burwell Public School. Although nominally an inmate of Grandfather and Grandmother Myers's farmhouse, a permanent bunk was established for him across the road in the bedroom of his cousin William Lyle.

Some seven years Jimmie's senior, and like him shooting up lanky and towheaded, William Lyle goaded his protégé into a frisky round of practical jokes and dares. One winter morning Jimmie and his cousin "shocked" Grandmother Myers by wiring the seat of the wooden privy to a small electric battery. Another time the boys, apparently forgetting their near tragic episode with a homemade parachute, fashioned a glider from scraps of lumber. A dozen years after the Wright Brothers astonished the world at Kitty Hawk, Jimmie and William Lyle stunned their families by attempting to fly out the second-floor window of Donald Newton Myers's barn. Edna Myers Borden witnessed the perilous experiment:

> The boys certainly were clever, but a little reckless. My brother and Jimmie had been busy building an airplane in one of the big barns on my father's land. They put it together by crossing some boards, mainly two-by-fours, but it had a little cabin and two seats. They were going to fly off the roof of my mother's chicken house. She said, "Don't do that, you're going to fall and hurt yourself."
>
> But they did! Or rather they carried the airplane way up into the loft of the barn and flew right out of the big window. The whole family was out there in the yard by now, screaming and yelling at them to come down. We all were terrified. William Lyle was in the front seat, and Jimmie behind him. They didn't go very far, and

crashed right into a load of hay. I can't remember if they were punished or not. I think everyone was happy that the boys weren't
killed.

Edna's sister Neddie Pinnell, also at the scene, adds that "the hayrack they
landed in was only there by accident. Workers loading the barn had just left
off for a while. The boys were lucky—otherwise, they would have really
been hurt!"

Apart from bouts of mischief, Jimmie is generally idealized by his Burwell cousins as quiet, respectful, and thoughtful all through his boyhood
and adolescence. But around the age of nine or ten he began to betray
small premonitions of smoldering anger and emotional distress. Edna remembers that now and again Jimmie would erupt in a weird "jig"; trembling
all over, he'd pogo up and down on his little feet while yelping like a
wounded animal: "Sometimes he did this when he didn't get his way, but
usually there wasn't any reason I could see. You could tell it really upset
Aunt Bird. Jimmie just seemed in a fury about something, and there was
nothing anyone could do to stop him. He jumped and screamed for minutes
at a time until someone grabbed him or, I have to say, slapped him."

In *Heed the Thunder* Thompson ascribed an exaggeratedly antic,
though probably more innocuous, version of this caper to his young stand-
in, Robert Dillon, after he tastes some teasing from his grandfather, here
named Lincoln Fargo:

> The ultimate result of the teasing upon the boy was what Lin-
> coln called a "dance," a term that insulted the art of Terpsichore
> even back to its rudest beginnings.
>
> The tortured youth clasped himself about the middle, in the
> manner of one having overeaten of green apples. Bent double, he
> rocked his head from side to side, hopping first on one foot, then
> on the other—like a rooster on a hot stove. And all the time he
> emitted cries so filled with agony and rage as to turn every coyote
> in the distant sand hills gray-headed. . . .
>
> It was his mother's habit when he was thus seized, to shake
> him until his teeth rattled. And his grandmother had always
> socked him with a dishrag or a handful of scourings from the
> churn, or something equally unpleasant.

More ominous, Jimmie once simulated his own death by hanging. According to Edna, Birdie and Grandmother Myers walked in one evening on
the sight of the boy swinging from the broad beams of the Myerses' front
parlor, his face a purple blur from which protruded a grotesque, swollen
tongue. "He smeared something on his face, and had gotten hold of an ani-

*Jim Thompson—Burwell, Nebraska, probably
1915 (Courtesy of the Thompson family)*

mal tongue—a beef tongue would have been too big, so it probably came from a lamb or a calf. And somehow he fixed the rope that the noose didn't choke him."

If this sounds like an episode, and Jimmie a character from one of Thompson's books, in both spirit and fact they are. Not only did he replay the stunt to haunting effect for *Heed the Thunder,* but, more broadly, the potent mix of perversity, artistry, comedy, sensationalism, and personal pain would also shape many of the violent deaths in his crime novels. Concludes his cousin Neddie: "Jimmie really shocked everybody, which might have been what he wanted to do. He was always very imaginative. Sometimes he told the younger children stories just to scare them. Looking back, I don't think anyone thought that such a quiet, polite boy might have been lonely or unhappy."

Fortunately, Jimmie soon was taken up by another substitute father, his Uncle Bob. Robert Wicks lived with Birdie's sister, Addie, and their six children near the commercial center of town. As a sixteen-year-old stowaway Uncle Bob had absconded from England, apparently to avoid military conscription. Promptly upon debarking at New York he democratized his given surname, Vanwyck, for the social climate of his adopted land. Around 1890 he migrated west to Burwell. After marrying Aunt Addie he ran a tobacco shop, the Racket Store, which also dispensed groceries and yard goods. The enterprise proved so successful that he eventually owned some five hundred acres of rental farm land and built "an elegant home which has cost him at least $4,000," according to H. W. Fought, who profiled Wicks for his 1906 history, *Trail of the Loup*. Uncle Bob became a principal stockholder and sometime officer in the Burwell National Bank.

Whereas Grandfather Myers had diverted Jimmie with jokes, stories, card tricks, and hunting, Uncle Bob endowed him with books and oversaw his fledgling literary education. By contrast to the Draconian study regimen dictated by his father, Robert Wicks's gifts and suggested readings afforded Jimmie profound pleasure, along with instruction—and, moreover, launched his career as a writer.

Uncle Bob initiated his neophyte nephew with McGuffey's *Common Reader*, Palgrave's *Golden Treasury*, the *Encyclopaedia Britannica* in a handsomely engraved edition, and a blissful parade of boy's fiction, mystery, and adventure novels that ranged from Horatio Alger, the Rover Boys series, and *Frank Merriwell's Dilemma* to Lewis Carroll, Wilkie Collins, and Arthur Conan Doyle. Jimmie would retain a lifelong fondness for books of fantasy and adventure. *Savage Night*, for instance, derives an epigraph from H. G. Wells's satiric phantasmagoria, *Mr. Blettsworthy on Rampole Island*. And in a 1941 letter Thompson spoke of his intention to ship out with a San Diego tuna fleet in search of "some good story material." He had "a boy's adventure book in mind."

Uncle Bob introduced Jimmie at a precocious age to American and European classics: Cervantes, Shakespeare, the King James Bible, Rabelais, Dickens, Swift, Poe, Twain, Kipling, Cooper, Chesterton, London, Stevenson, and the Greek tragedies. Thus it was during lively evenings within the Wickses' library that Thompson first kicked around the texts he always cited as his principal literary influences: *Don Quixote, Gulliver's Travels,* and *Oedipus Rex*. His other boyhood reading also stayed with him to animate and nourish his fiction—particularly Poe's tales of terror "The Pit and the Pendulum," "The Cask of Amontillado," and "The Tell-Tale Heart," the pioneering detective stories "The Murders in the Rue Morgue" and "The Purloined Letter," and the atmospheric treatment of the double, "William Wilson"; London's alcoholic memoir *John Barleycorn* and his hobo sketches, *The Road;* and Stevenson's feverish probing of a split personality, *The Strange Case of Dr. Jekyll and Mr. Hyde.*

Jimmie undertook his initial literary experiments at his uncle's appreciative prodding, imitations of his favorite authors, now, regrettably, long lost. A droll sequence in *Bad Boy* on the elusive Scoopchisel suggests the sporting intellectual fellowship between the budding writer and his mentor:

> "Who," he said, "was Scoopchisel?"
>
> "S-scoop . . . ? I don't know," I said.
>
> "You—don't—know? You don't know!" His face colored in a spasm of rage and bewilderment, and, for a moment, I thought surely that this was to be my end. But somehow, though the effort was obviously a drain on his innermost resources, Bob managed to bring himself under control. He addressed me at length and with patience, a fond glow coming into his fine gray eyes. And always thereafter, I discovered, I could move him into this benign mood by raising the subject of Scoopchisel. Scoopchisel, the greatest writer of all time, a man robbed of his proper due by his sneaky brother-in-law, Byron.
>
> It was Scoopchisel who had written the immortal lines:
>
> > *So get the golden sheckles while you're young*
> > *And getting's good.*
> > *And when you're old and feeble*
> > *You won't be chopping wood.*
>
> But he was at his best when annotating the work of other poets. To Fitzgerald's inquiry, "I often wonder what the vintner buys, one half so precious as the stuff he sells," Scoopchisel had retorted, "Protection!" Anent Pope's statement, "Hope springs eternal in the human breast," Scoopchisel had said, "Until you're married, then it moves its nest."

Thompson repaid Uncle Bob's ministrations in typically contradictory fashion. The character modeled after Robert Wicks in *Heed the Thunder,* banker Alfred Courtland, steals from his boss, refuses his own relatives' desperate requests for loans, and brutally disfigures a small boy, as he lurches through the final stages of terminal syphilis. But in a sunnier literary testimonial to his uncle, "Bob Wicks" became one of the pseudonyms Thompson adopted for his magazine work during the 1950s.

The winter of 1915–16 proved momentous for other reasons. For the only time during their many past and future retreats to Burwell, James Thompson visited his wife and children. His considerable charm and self-possession once more galvanized Edna Myers Borden and the entire Myers clan. "Uncle Jim just walked in one day while I was having a music lesson. He sat down at the piano and banged out whatever it was I was trying to play. He really surprised us." If the cause of his arrival remains obscure, one effect soon became evident. For it was during this visit that Jimmie's sister Winifred was conceived.

• • •

Birdie, Maxine, and Jimmie departed Burwell for Oklahoma City shortly before the birth of "Freddie" on October 22, 1916. The period marked the nadir of the Thompsons' helter-skelter finances. Jimmie's father retired his auditor's green visor for the more flamboyant raiment of an oil man. Even as he crisscrossed the state for the Peace Officers' Association he had started to speculate in oil—"Oil Field Operators Since 1914," as the letterhead on his Thompson & Company stationery subsequently averred. Oklahomans had profitably mined black gold since territorial days. But the discovery of the rich Cushing field in 1912, and the Healdton field near Ardmore in 1913, proved an irresistible lure for the man who, as his son once noted, hovered always on "the perilous periphery of the big time." Wheeler-dealers like Roy Johnson and Jake Hamon were pulling upward of ninety thousand barrels a day out of the earth. Precious little of it, unfortunately, gushed into the Thompson coffers at 1314 West Main Street.

Jimmie transmitted those days for *Bad Boy,* with a slight descending twist of the dial toward melodrama:

> My sister Freddie was born during a severe economic depression. It was a hard winter for the nation in general and the Thompsons in particular. Pop had begun to dabble in the oil business, and not very profitably. Mom was in the hospital much of the time.
>
> Our house had twelve rooms (Pop had felt that we needed something larger with the advent of Freddie), and the fires of hell couldn't have kept it warm. The plumbing was constantly freezing and bursting. I froze and burst out with cold sores which my schoolmates promptly diagnosed as cancer. Looking back, I find my cold sores to have been the one cheerful facet of that winter. I had but to wave my festered hands and the toughest bully in school fled before me shrieking.
>
> There were repercussions with my recovery, but even these worked out to my advantage. I got a great deal of splendid exercise in racing up alleys and shinnying over back fences. My reflexes became trigger quick. Without losing the look and feel of it, much of my awkwardness disappeared.

For *Now and on Earth* Thompson remodeled that twelve-room igloo into a "shack deep down on Oklahoma City's West Main Street." His cousin, Harriet Cowan Keller, came to help out after Freddie was born and lingered on through the winter. She reports the Thompsons actually resided in a "run-down two-bedroom house in a rough section of town. The baby slept with her parents. Maxine and I slept together. And there was a little cot in the parents room where Jimmie slept."

The stresses of the Thompsons' poverty rattled Harriet—as did the family's lopsided management of their scant jack. "He was already in the oil business, but there wasn't a lot of money at the time. Still, Uncle Jim wanted to appear like he had money. He didn't have any, they were very poor. Aunt Bird was unhappy because she didn't think he got what he should have out of it."

Between expeditions to the oil fields Jimmie's father brooded at home, concocting madcap commercial schemes. "I could not name all the ventures he was active in during that period," Thompson wrote in *Bad Boy,* "but they included the operation of a saw mill, the proprietorship of a hotel, truck farming, running a bush-league ball club, the garbage-hauling contract for a certain Oklahoma metropolis and turkey ranching."

Poor as Job's turkey and hiding from the landlord at her door, Birdie made stabs at countering her husband's excesses. When James returned from Chicago with more extravagant presents—and no cash—she berated him: "What do I need a new hat for when my children don't have anything to eat!" As Maxine noted, "Mama was trying to be careful and penny-pinching. She was more practical and pragmatic, and Papa was a dreamer in lots of ways." But Harriet recalls that Birdie's gestures seemed halfhearted and, anyway, met with no real success:

> Uncle Jim would bring home a twenty-dollar bill and give it to her to buy groceries and take the house expenses out of that. Then, maybe a day or two later, he'd come and want some of the money back because he was going to take someone out to dinner. She'd say, "You don't have the money to take him out to dinner. Why are you doing that?" But she'd give it back to him. She was not at all aggressive. Another woman would have spent that money and got things she needed for the home.

Around the house Jimmie's mother perpetuated many of Grandmother Myers's domestic quirks. All the Thompson cousins concur that "Aunt Bird wasn't a real homemaker." She inherited an aversion to the kitchen, and for family meals raided the prepared-food counter of her local market. "She tried to keep everyone going on the 1916 version of junk food," Harriet says. Since she often sent the children to the store themselves, "everything we ate was full of sugar. Jimmie was skinny and sickly from malnutrition." Birdie's naive household economy occasionally hatched accidents, one bordering on catastrophe. Through a misreading of the directions for a bottle of cough syrup, she nearly overdosed Maxine and Jimmie on codeine.

Birdie was ill much of the winter of 1916–17. Freddie's hard birth left her with varicose veins, and the swelling would hobble her on and off for the rest of her life. Her doctor also diagnosed a weak heart. With Pop frequently away in the Oklahoma oil fields, the children turned to one another for comfort and care. Maxine watched over Jimmie, and together they looked after the baby.

The chronic disarray of their upbringing hammered a fierce, impenetrable bond among the Thompson children. "The three of them against the world—that was the sense that came from them always," relates Tony Kouba, Maxine's son. Whether at Oklahoma City and Fort Worth in the 1930s, San Diego in the 1940s, New York in the 1950s, or Los Angeles in the 1960s and 1970s, Jimmie and his sisters banded like refugees, sometimes within the same house, but always close by; and whenever one would move, the others followed. "The relationship that existed between Freddie and Jimmie and between Maxine and Jimmie was much closer than the relationships that any of them had with their spouses," Tony Kouba marvels. "I don't know if it was their desperate circumstances or the old man, but whatever happened back there rendered them literally inseparable."

That winter on West Main Jimmie fell in love with—and at—the movies. With no money to burn on heating oil, Birdie conceived the notion that it would be more economical if her family dreamed away the chilly hours after school inside Oklahoma City's nascent movie palaces. Harriet remembers that the Thompsons attended the pictures four or five times a week. "The parents let us kids pick the movies, but we saw just about everything that passed through town, Chaplin, Mary Pickford, Douglas Fairbanks, Fatty Arbuckle, D. W. Griffith, you name it." Not that they were indiscriminate or dispassionate viewers—each of the children pledged devotion to a favorite actor. Jimmie's jewel was the sinister siren Theda Bara. On the wall by his bed he tacked a handbill previewing *The Tiger Woman* that featured a witchy photo of the actress surrounded by snakes, crystal balls, rose petals, and skulls.

Bara, whose publicity gushed that her name formed an anagram for "Arab Death," made an apt seductress for the future author of *A Hell of a Woman* and *A Swell-Looking Babe*. In the iconography of silent film she embodied "the eternal vamp," as beautiful as she was heartless. Her melodramas of male degradation flaunted such vampirish titles as *The Devil's Daughter, Purgatory's Ivory Angel, The Eternal Sappho, The Serpent, Her Double Life, The Rose of Blood, The Vixen,* and *The She-Devil.* Bara's brooding sensual face, kohl-ringed eyes, and slinky chiaroscuro of pale arms and dark silks forged an imago of opulent evil at the crossroads of sex and destruction, eros and thanatos. The tawdrier femmes fatales of Thompson's fiction customarily have been appraised as imitations—or parodies—of James M. Cain's. But it's just as likely that his shabby "vixens" and "she-devils" originated during all those wintry afternoons Jimmie spent in the dark mooning over Theda Bara.

The spare change for these family outings, as for most daily purchases, came from Jimmie's paper routes, the *Oklahoman* in the morning and the *News* in the evening. For larger household expenses Birdie called on Grandfather Myers. "What a shame people have to live this way," Edna Myers Borden recalls him sighing, as he wrote out yet another check.

Then one evening during the spring of 1917 Jimmie's father returned home with a bulging leather satchel. Gathering his wife and children into the master bedroom, he proceeded to overturn the case: a Brobdingnagian bedspread of cash that (depending on who relates the story) totaled $45,000 or $65,000! James had signed on with Jake Hamon.

• • •

Whenever Jim Thompson rhapsodized about his family's lost wealth, he was principally remarking the period when his father worked as bookkeeper, lawyer, and advisor for Hamon. His nostalgic requiem for Oklahoma City at the beginning of *Roughneck*—"and here, across the walk to the right, was the office building from which Pop had directed a multi-million dollar oil business"—essentially recast his father as Hamon, the self-styled John D. Rockefeller of the Southwest. But this would have been a natural enough confusion. A rakish dynamo with a Midas touch, the backroom maker of presidents, Jacob L. Hamon was all that James S. Thompson aspired to be.

The pair first met at the 1906 Oklahoma GOP convention that hatched the backroom campaign for Congress, when Hamon served as chairman of the Republican Territorial Central Committee. Thompson has his father recount his collaboration with the flamboyant railroad, real estate, and oil baron in "The Drilling Contractor," the oral history he submitted to University of North Carolina Press in 1939. James appears as Bob Carey, Hamon as Morris Markham, and Thompson accords his father odd flourishes from his own 1930s Marxist inflections:

> At first I started auditing his books for him, and handling his legal affairs. From that it was an easy step to making leases, and buying supplies and equipment. The oil business fascinated me. It seemed to be one business where you could get ahead without exploiting the labor of others or without injuring anyone; where you didn't rob anyone but old Mother Nature who had plenty more.
>
> I wasn't a full-fledged partner, understand. I didn't want to be. I never had any particular desire to be rich. I just asked for what my services were worth, plus a reasonable amount for taking a chance, and put it back in the business.
>
> We didn't have any big wells or deep wells. Most of our stuff

was shallow—down here in the Healdton field, about a hundred
miles south of Oklahoma City. You could drive along there at night
and see a dozen of our little rigs running, the white signs on the
walking-beams winking under the lights as they bobbed up and
down. . . . Markham and Carey, Maggie Jones Number One. (Maggie Jones would be the name of the lease-owner.) Or Markham and
Carey, Pete Smith Number Three. It was quite an experience: the
boilers hissing and breathing, sending up broad veils of steam; the
pounding of tools that made the whole earth shake; men shouting.
Markham and Carey . . . .

When Thompson has his father claim, "No finer man ever lived than
Morris Markham," some might incline to hear a son's withering irony. A
Kansas-born and -educated lawyer who settled into the old Indian town of
Lawton in 1901, Hamon exhaled corruption like a second language. Swin-
dling oil properties from gullible Indian owners provided the bedrock of his
fortune. As business agent for the Mexican & Pacific railroad, Hamon
placed depots only in those towns that kicked back substantial "bonuses."
As an attorney, he narrowly escaped conviction in 1916 on charges of de-
frauding the federal government for advising clients how to escape to Mexico. During the 1919 Chicago Republican convention Hamon boasted to
friends that he had "signed the check which enabled Warren Harding to run
for president." He was a classic larger-than-life Southwestern tycoon out of
Frank Norris or *Dallas,* greasing his reputation as a drunkard, gambler,
lecher, and bribe giver with lavish donations to the Boy Scouts and Oklahoma churches. Francis Russell, an historian of the scandal-plagued Harding administration, christened Hamon "the last of the Oklahoma bad men."
    At the time of his partnership with Jimmie's father, Hamon commanded
an empire estimated at around $20,000,000 from a suite of rooms at the Ho-
tel Randol, in Ardmore, that he shared with his confidential secretary and
mistress, Clara Barton Smith. When his wife refused to grant him a divorce,
Hamon arranged for Smith to take his name by staging a marriage of conve-
nience for her with one of his nephews. In a sordid scenario worthy of Jim
Thompson's fiction, politics soon made murderous bedfellows. Convinced
that President Harding would appoint him secretary of the interior, Hamon
succumbed to the pressures of domestic rectitude. Spurning the paramour
whom he had transformed from a teenage dry-goods store clerk into the
silent manager of his business affairs, he returned to his wife. On the night
of November 21, 1920, Smith retaliated by fatally shooting Hamon with a revolver he had provided her as protection for a $10,000 "wedding ring."
    Jimmie's father rushed to Hamon's deathbed, according to "The
Drilling Contractor." A coy veil of euphemisms and elisions protects the
guilty:

I caught the first train to Oklahoma City. He was in the hospital and he was dying. . . . Don't ask me that. If I told you you'd know his right name. Maybe you will, anyhow, but I can't tell you and I hope you won't mention it. Morris was my friend.

But he was dying, and he didn't know it. So all I did was sit there at his bedside and talk over old times, and plan things we'd do when he got well. I suppose I was the only living person he really liked and trusted. He was separated from his wife, and his grown son never came around him.

Smith's defense was taken up by Moman Pruiett—the recurring Kossmeyer of Thompson's novels. True to his reputation, the swashbuckling attorney persuaded another jury to return a "not guilty" verdict. Clara Barton Smith Hamon went on to play herself in *Fate,* a Hollywood movie based upon the murder case.

· · ·

As Thompson wrote in *Bad Boy,* "So Pop went to work for Jake, and for the first time in his life he held on to a large share of the money he had made. . . . On at least one occasion Pop's brief case contained a million dollars of Jake's money."

The sudden influx of Hamon cabbage altered the Thompson family in many obvious—and some subtle—ways. Jimmie's father traded in their overcrowded rental and purchased a huge house on Grand Avenue. He leased a suite of offices at the Colcord Building. He bought a fleet of stylish cars. His generosity to his cronies, his presents for his family, knew no bounds. Why not get that $400 violin for Maxine? Why not back that down-on-his-heels friend with trucks, rigging equipment, and some stock options? "The times Papa had money everyone was his 'old pal,' his 'good friend,' " recalled Maxine. "And he closed all his deals with just a hand-shake. He would regret that later."

To Jimmie, his father's meteoric rise mainly bequeathed the bitter-sweet memory of having been, fleetingly, a rich man's son. As he glanced back from the vantage of the next decade's vagaries of fortune:

Here we sat, nominal beggars in a broken-down Ford, at the site of our one-time glory. I closed my eyes against the brilliant sunlight, and I could almost see Pop bustling out of this building—young, smartly dressed, hurrying towards his low-slung Apperson-Jack or the big Cole Aero-Eight. I could see us all riding home together, out to the big-ceilinged house with its book-lined walls. I could see the friendly face of the cook as she dished up the dinner. I could taste—

Jim Thompson—Burwell, Nebraska, probably
1918 (Courtesy of the Thompson family)

For the immediate future, prosperity shifted other aspects of life almost not at all. With her husband busy in Healdton with Hamon, Birdie still lugged her three children to Burwell. Now, however, she returned not to the Myers farm, but to a small clapboard house James rented for them closer to town. "Uncle Jim sent money that year," Neddie Pinnell notes, "unlike other times, when they had to stay with our grandparents."

The fall of 1918, Jimmie rejoined his old classmates in the sixth grade of the Burwell Public School. While he no longer bunked nightly with William Lyle, every morning his cousins picked him up along their walk to school. "We'd pass by their little house and if Maxine and Jimmie weren't out there already waiting for us, then we'd throw pebbles at the door," Neddie remembers. "Aunt Bird hated that. She was a stately, dignified woman. She would try to scold us, but usually she'd wind up laughing."

But for the novelty of his own home, Jimmie plunged into the familiar rituals of Burwell. Afternoons he went back to joining William Lyle at the family farm. Since Uncle David had lost part of his leg in an accident with a mule-drawn tractor, the toil of feeding the hogs and cattle and tending the corn and wheat fields fell to the younger Myerses. After supper Jimmie preferred to do his homework at the Wickses', where Uncle Bob always renewed his stash of books. On weekends Robert Wicks let Jimmie work alongside him in the Racket Store, his tobacco shop.

The Myerses doted on little Freddie. They applauded Maxine's music, her solo concerts on the violin and her duets with her cousin Edna. They fretted over Jimmie, who for all his height appeared gaunt and undernourished; "Skinny Jimmie," the Myerses tagged him, and his grandfather elevated his doses of medicinal "cider." Yet Edna Myers Borden also recalls that her family was chagrined by Birdie's silence about repaying Grandfather Myers. "I can't say if it ever came to words with her, but behind Bird's back they all talked, particularly my grandmother. No one could understand why, when Uncle Jim had prospered, he wouldn't take care of his debts. The Thompsons were always funny about money."

Jimmie remained in Burwell through the completion of the seventh grade. Then, in the summer of 1919, his father dissolved his partnership with Jake Hamon. *Bad Boy* lays the rupture to a colorful, if dubious, quarrel that ignited in a sweltering Oklahoma boomtown hotel when Pop asked his boss how long it had been since he changed his underwear. For "The Drilling Contractor" Thompson has his father more plausibly relate, "Morris and I broke up our partnership in 1919. He'd been expanding very rapidly on his own hook, getting richer every year; and I felt that I was standing in his way."

Or "Morris" stood in his way. Anticipating a cabinet post in the next Republican administration—and, perhaps, a run for office himself—Hamon downshifted his attention from business to politics.

By 1919, with the recent rise in oil prices, the prospects for real money lay in the vast virgin fields of West Texas. On scouting trips with Hamon, James had witnessed a spectacular boom in Ranger when, after the discovery of oil, the sleepy cattle depot thronged with fifty thousand speculators frantic to share the lucre. Many wealthy Oklahomans, moreover, were crossing the border into the Lone Star State to avoid personal income taxes.

Jimmie's father cashed in for a quarter of a million dollars "in round numbers," according to "The Drilling Contractor." He planned a family "trip around the world," and then he would "settle down in some nice section of the country and do the things I'd never got the chance to do." But first he had to help out a "friend" who was experiencing a "lot of hard luck" in Ranger.

He wired Birdie, Maxine, and Jimmie to meet him at Fort Worth.

• • •

Jimmie now was nearly thirteen years old. His literary productions to date were limited to the schoolboy English themes that still are remembered by his Burwell classmates, and to the apprentice exercises instigated by his Uncle Bob. Yet he continued to manifest skill in using his art to terrify and control his family. That summer of 1919 Jimmie kept his younger Wicks and Myers cousins "cowering with stories about the bogeyman," recalls Neddie Pinnell. "When they were playing games Jimmie would scare them with just awful stories about what would happen if they didn't do so and so. Of course they would always do whatever he wanted."

One creation proved more ambitious. In late July or early August Jimmie collected Maxine and his cousins Neddie, Grace, and Donald. Stopping out front of the Myers granary, he directed them to shut their eyes. Neddie continues:

> In the summertime we children used to play at our grandfather's—in the granary on his farm, because it was empty of grain at that time. There were rods across the granary and we used to do acrobatics and all sorts of games.
>
> When Jimmie took us inside and we opened our eyes, there was a great big picture of a man's head—you know, a huge ugly black face on the wooden wall of the granary. It covered the whole wall, and that great black face looked like it was burning up!

Apparently Jimmie had positioned his painting and timed the display such that as the rays from the setting sun shimmered on the granary wall his fierce totem seemed to glower from within the fires of hell. Neddie:

> *Meet the devil!* Jimmie then shouted at us in a dreadful voice which echoed through the granary. . . .
> We ran screaming out of there just as fast as we could!

My Little Black Book: 1919–1929

Oklahoma, Nebraska, and now Texas—the formidable terrain of Thompson's formative years crystallized into the indispensable settings of his novels. From those early Western landscapes he derived his stock of essential images, his prose rhythms, a language.

"Cross the Oklahoma panhandle on a winter's dusk," challenges Texas novelist Larry McMurtry, "and see if you can avoid a sinking of the spirit. . . . Cross the Staked Plains, cross the central Mojave, cross the Donner Pass in a blizzard, cross the Badlands, cross the Canyonlands, cross the Dismal River Country of Northern Nebraska—cross almost anyplace in the West when it is too cold, too hot, too empty, when the sand is blowing in your face or the hailstones are threatening your windshield.

Cross almost any part of it in a lowering light and you may wish heartily that you were back in some civilized place like the Piazza Navonna, eating gelato and feeling cozy."

As a young man Jim Thompson fed on the desolation of West Texas. He thrived on the barrenness, the forsaken isolation and monkish solitude, the outstretched void that if you lived with it long enough surrendered its lean sympathies and spare consolations in a subtle economy of scarcity. "In the beginning, I thought it one of the most desolate areas in the world," he reflected in *Bad Boy.* "As time went on, however, I came to love the vast stretches of prairie, rolling emptily toward the horizon. There was peace in the loneliness, calm and reassurance. In the virgin vastness, virtually unchanged by the assaults of a hundred million years, troubles seemed to shrink and hope loomed large." Most of all, he thrived on the towering West Texas sky—"the bleak, unpromising sky," home to "a Deity whose head seemed forever turned."

Jimmie's fondness for Texas hardly spilled over to its people. The laconic hymns to the "desolate wasteland" that pepper his late novels, especially *The Transgressors* (1961), *Texas by the Tail, South of Heaven,* and *King Blood,* conspicuously shun the "distasteful" Texan:

> Texans made a boast of their insularism; they bragged about such things as never having been outside the state or the fact that the only book in their house was the Bible. . . . I studied their mannerisms and mores, and in my twisted outlook they became Mongoloid monsters. . . . Anything that a Texan might be sensitive about or hold sacred, I jeered at.

Of course if it weren't for Texans, Thompson could have written few of his books. His adopted state coughed up the colorful, sometimes depraved and horrifying individuals he named Four Trey Whitey, Bud Lassen, the Longs, the Kings, Strawlegs Martin, Pancake Butts, Winfield Lord, and the coolly brutal Big Spring deputy sheriff who provided one of the virulent strains that blended into his most celebrated creation, Lou Ford.

While Thompson would go on to set stories in subsequent places of residence—San Diego, New York City, Hollywood—these locales were not vital touchstones for his fiction, only incidental backdrops. No matter where he might live, his novels clung to his three original vistas: Oklahoma, Nebraska, and Texas.

Thompson once summed up his youthful contradictions: "As is apparent, I was a very perverse young man."

• • •

Early in September 1919, the Thompsons reunited at the Westbrook Hotel, where Jimmie's father rented a furnished apartment and an impromptu office. Fort Worth was the concentration point for the West Texas oil operators, and the Westbrook on Fourth Street, between Houston and Main, functioned as their official center. So frenetic were the daily transactions in the lobby that the management removed all the furniture to clear space for an oil mart. Still, crowds overflowed through the big double doors and into the street where a board posted news of the latest trading advances. Inside the Westbrook lobby a pedestaled statue, jocularly dubbed the "Golden Goddess," presided over many "blessed" oil deals.

Before the oil discoveries, Fort Worth served as the strategic marketplace for a great southwestern empire of cattle and cattlemen. Swift & Company, Armour & Company, and Libby, McNeil & Libby erected monstrous stockyards and packinghouses in the Niles City section of "Cowtown."

The oil boom of the teens and 1920s kicked off a stampede of people, money, and development. Cowtown was transmogrified into the "Gateway to the West Texas Oil Fields," as corporations seeking a permanent supply base lodged headquarters there. Oil companies, promotion companies, wildcatters, refineries, automobile manufacturers, rail and pipe lines flourished; and to keep pace, the city annexed surburban properties. The population jumped from 73,312 in 1910 to 106,482 in 1920, and then to 163,447 by the 1930 census. Oil earnings thrust shiny skyscrapers into the downtown horizon, such as the Life of America and the Sinclair buildings, or the W. T. Waggoner Building, where one day James Thompson would keep an office.

For all the cash and glitz, Fort Worth retained an elemental funk. *A Penny in the Dust,* Thompson's abandoned novel about his Texas adolescence, tracks the predominant "Fort Value" odors in a mock-Whitmanesque catalogue of horrors as it spits barbs at the citizenry:

> . . . my olfactory senses were sharpened to their ultimate keen. And the ordinarily accepted and unnoted smells were stenches, bordering on the intolerable.
>
> They were not commingled, arising, as they did, from sources of varied chemical composition. They came to me in crazyquilt, patchwork blobs and gobs like an idiot-concocted *poussé,* each element of which had its own distinct identity.
>
> There was the rotten egg smell (sulphur) from the oil refineries, and the popcornish smell from the 'gins and the cottonseed-oil presses. There was the scalded, spoiled-meat smell from the packing-houses; the smell of coal-smoke from the train yards; of

burning garbage from thousands of backyard incinerators; of
horse- and cow-, pig-, goat- and chicken-shit; for horses still played
a prominent role in transporting people and goods, and even well-
to-do households—many of them—maintained livestock on their
premises. It saved money. Money was good and moneylessness
was bad. Home was good, and all of its suffixes: home-grown,
home-made, home-cooked. "Boughten" was inferior, and cost too
much (whatever that meant).

Strongest of the smells was that of human waste. For Fort
Value poured its untreated sewage into the Trinity River whose
studded mass of offal crawled oozily eastward to Dallas, where it
became that city's problem. (Said the public-toilet graffiti: *Pull the
chain. Dallas needs the water.*)

• • •

Apparently not sharing his grandson's devaluation of Fort Worth, William
Henry Myers accompanied Birdie and the children for the train ride south
from Burwell. When James whisked the family away to West Texas for a
sightseeing trip through the oil fields, Jimmie remained at the Westbrook
under the unsteady eye of his grandfather. Away from the repressive curbs
of his wife, Pa (as Jimmie called him) raised hell. The "medicinal" morning
whiskey-and-hot-water toddies escalated into all-day sipping sessions. Fueled by corn liquor and hotel sandwiches, Grandfather Myers led Jimmie
on his own Cook's tour of the Fort Worth underbelly.

Decked out in the urban cowboy finery that, under Pa's influence, Jimmie would favor for his ten years in Texas, the pair romped among the
honky-tonks on nearby Main and Houston streets. Penny arcades and burlesque houses with names like Phillips Egypt, Electric In-Door Baseball,
Herman Park, the Hippodrome, and the Blue Mouse Theatre pumped them
through a riot of amusement:

> After breakfast we went to a pool hall where Pa beat me five
> games of slop pool and I beat him two. We returned to the hotel,
> then, for a few before-lunch drinks, and following lunch we went to
> a penny arcade.
>
> Pa had brought the bottle with him, and he became quite ram-
> bunctious when "A Night With A Paris Cutie" did not come up to
> his expectations. He caned the machine. I think he would have
> caned the arcade proprietor, but that shrewd gentleman wisely
> gave him no back talk. Instead, he returned Pa's coins and led him
> out to the sidewalk. He pointed to a burlesque house across and
> down the street.

"Why look at pictures," he enquired, "when you can see the real thing?"

"Well, now," said Pa, greatly mollified. "Maybe you have something there, friend."

It was a wonderfully satisfying day. Pa had given a bottle to the ushers and sent a couple of others backstage, and in that place he or I could do no wrong. We hooked the girls' garments until they were reduced to near nudity. Pa climbed upon the ramp and chased them backstage. Yet they responded with laughter and joyous shrieks, and occasionally one would stoop swiftly and plant a kiss on Pa's head.

Each of the succeeding three days, at the end of which the family returned, was a reasonable facsimile of that first day. Hot toddies in the morning, then a pool game, then a burlesque house, with drinks and meals being imbibed at strategic intervals. Also much talk from Pa, much advice delivered in his casual backhanded fashion.

Thompson's alcoholic bonhomie and gallant fondness for Pa in *Bad Boy* aside, his sister Freddie, for one, reproved: "It's all water under the bridge, but I like to think that if our grandfather could have known where the drinking and the fun would lead, he never would have taken Jimmie down that path."

• • •

Whatever the other Thompsons concluded, Grandfather Myers soon was packed up and sent home. The family moved from the Westbrook Hotel into a leased house at 1264 Rosedale Avenue, in south-central Fort Worth, and situated on the so-called mansion end of the street. The command post of the newly incorporated Planters Petroleum Company—James S. Thompson, president; L. E. Lyon, vice president—shifted to a suite at the Texas State Bank Building.

Jimmie enrolled in the freshman class of the Fort Worth High School on Jennings Avenue on September 15, a few weeks shy of his thirteenth birthday. If his parents fled the Westbrook as a caution against big-city temptations, their decision to have him skip a grade was not so much a reward as it was a caustic disciplinary action.

"Papa thought Jimmie needed to be challenged more," recalled Maxine, "and that if he pushed Jimmie he could make more of himself. As he saw it, Jimmie was too introverted, too bookish, and intellectual in a way, although Papa read all the time himself. So he pushed Jimmie into sports, which he hated of course. Papa wanted Jimmie to succeed in the courses which he thought were important, mathematics, science, subjects like that, which Jimmie always did poorly in. I think he felt that the sooner Jimmie finished school he could then help him out in the oil business."

The psychic stretch from the seventh grade of the one-building Burwell school system to an aggressive urban high school might have proved traumatic for any student. But Jimmie had sidestepped almost as much education as he received, between the shuttling back and forth from Oklahoma to Nebraska and the classes lost to planting and harvesting the Myers farm. The happy evenings in Uncle Bob's library and his father's Spartan drills afforded him a precocious erudition without actually establishing the foundation for high school. As Jimmie rued in *Bad Boy,* "I had read voraciously and far in advance of my years. But I was sadly unprepared for the inelastic high school curriculum. I knew nothing of cube and square root and many other things upon which high school subjects were predicated."

The Fort Worth High School marked another skirmish in the war between father and son. For the second time in his life Jimmie dwelled under the same roof as the indomitable man whose sudden wealth only intensified his self-confidence and presumption. What Maxine termed their "basic personality differences" deepened with proximity and age. While she remembered few "blowouts" or "harsh words," she noted that "Papa could bully Jimmie with sarcasm and sharpness, and he usually got what he wanted." Apparently James Thompson, like a few of his son's most memorable fictional characters, was a master needler who wrested his ends through taunts and gibes. In *Bad Boy* Jimmie broadly remarked upon his emotional struggles with his father. Since he shuns recriminating details, and never directly confronts parental authority, his complaints can sound the whiny ring of rain on tin:

> . . . I was a rich man's son, he pointed out, and some day I would inherit great wealth. I must be made into a proper custodian for it—sane, sober, considerate. I should not be allowed to become one of those ill-mannered, irresponsible wastrels, who behaved as though they had been put on earth solely to enjoy themselves.
>
> No error in my deportment was too tiny for Pop to spot and criticize. No flaw in my appearance was too small. From the time I arose until the time I retired, I was subjected to a steady stream of criticism about the way I dressed, walked, talked, stood, ate, sat, and so on into infinity—all with that most maddening of assurances that it was for my "own good."
>
> Always in the past, Mom had served as a bulwark against Pop's extremes of family management, but she proved remiss in this emergency, a fact decidedly less puzzling in retrospect than it

was at the time. Pop had behaved intelligently—instead of with his sporadic brilliance—throughout his partnership with Jake Hamon, and she naturally was inclined to regard his intense interest in me as a continuation of that intelligent behavior. Moreover, say what you will, it is difficult to dispute the judgement of a man who has made a million dollars.

Despite Thompson's equivocation and his hazy self-pity, the enduring ichor from these early wounds blisters the gloss of retrospective tact.

Much as with his father's other best-laid plans in Fort Worth, the scheme to rush Jimmie through high school and into some private fantasy of "Thompson & Son, Oil Operators" unraveled in the event. The spring semester of 1926—some seven years later—would still find Jimmie chasing his diploma. Initially one of the youngest students in his class, he would wind up the oldest. In a curious echo of his father's high school career, "Strangers to the school often mistook me for a member of the faculty." But as we shall see, factors beyond his premature enrollment, and issuing from both sides of the filial fence, conspired to sabotage his schooling.

• • •

All the Thompsons agree that in the unstable realm of family politics Maxine stayed her father's favorite child. Maxine's son, Tony, and Freddie's daughters, Jeremy and Randi, all echo Alberta Thompson's assertion that "their father always made it very clear that she was the special one." While Maxine benefited from a private music tutor, Jimmie was directed to fill his afternoons after school with penny-ante jobs—soda jerk, paper boy, grocery bagger. Even when the Thompsons sojourned to a spa in Waukesha, Wisconsin, after Maxine was diagnosed with a diseased kidney during the summer of 1920, his father apprenticed Jimmie as a plumber's helper. The few surviving letters from James to Birdie during the 1920s brim with inquiries after Maxine. Jimmie will be mentioned near the end, an afterthought, if at all.

Jimmie poured some of his envy of Maxine into his novel *Now and on Earth* (where he renames her Marge):

> Mind, I'm not jealous of Marge, although she always got the best of everything when it was available. Long after Pop had more money than he knew what to do with, I carried a paper route, and worked for Western Union, and caddied, because Pop thought that a job—any kind of lousy goddamned job—"gave character to a boy." And while I was doing that, Marge was taking lessons on the violin at rates up to thirty-five dollars an hour. And she hated the violin, and I loved it. . . .

I used to get her instrument out of its case, and run scales, and saw things out like "Home Sweet Home" and "Turkey in the Straw"; and I guess it was pretty awful. And Pop would fidget, and after a while he'd ask me if I didn't have some work to do. Or he'd dismiss me with: "That's good. Now let's hear you play, Marge."

I wanted to be a violinist. At least, I wanted to get away from jobs where people snubbed and swore at you.

Perhaps because the ten-year difference in age forbade competition, Jimmie remained closer to his baby sister, Freddie, during his Fort Worth years. He enjoyed sitting for her, Freddie disclosed, or exploring the outskirts of town in tandem:

> At the beginning, when there was a little tension between Jimmie and Maxine, I remember going on hikes together. He used to call me 'little fat dale'—I called myself a dale, I couldn't yet say girl.
>
> Once he took me on a hike to the Trinity River, north of town. A lot of sewage used to be dumped into it then, but that didn't mean anything to me. We tried to cross at a lock and I fell in. He made me walk ten feet behind him because of the stench!
>
> Sometimes he took me to the Tandy estate, down the road from us. There was a little creek there and Jimmie would have me dangle my little toes in the water as bait for crawdads.
>
> Jimmie was a real big older brother who took care of me, and teased me, and was very gentle and kind to me. He always was, that never changed.

More than sixty years later, Freddie could still recite a short poem Jimmie wrote for her birthday ("He *said* he wrote it, though I suppose he might have got it from a magazine"):

> Your ears are small
> As the doors in the hall;
> Your face is always pink.
> And, if I'm not mistaken,
> You've often been taken
> For Darwin's missing link.

• • •

Shortly after New Year's Day 1920, the Thompsons relocated to temporary quarters on Handley Drive to supervise the building of a new house near

Tandy Lake. By spring they moved to this baronial home at 3619 Dallas Pike, in an unincorporated suburb of Fort Worth. Their acre of land permitted two garages, a barn, and a small dairy. Jimmie transferred to the Polytechnic High School on Conner Street. He worked as a caddie at the Glen Garden Country Club—the golf course where Robert Talbert carries bags in *The Criminal.*

How Fast Money Goes in Texas would be the working title of Thompson's late novel *Texas by the Tail,* and the phrase might have hung as a caveat over the doors of Planters Petroleum. *Bad Boy* notes that "Pop's luck went sour almost from the day he set foot in Texas. The fortune I was to inherit shrank at the rate of almost four hundred thousand dollars a year." His 1930s oral history, "The Drilling Contractor," provides a fuller account of the actually more precipitate decline. There Thompson has his father recall:

> . . . A friend who was running several strings of tools at Ranger came to me. He'd had a lot of hard luck, and if he couldn't find some one to help him out he was going to lose everything he had. He was in debt as much as his tools were worth, and maybe a little more. But he had interests in the stuff he was drilling, and it looked good. I knew he was honest, and I was afraid that if I didn't help him he'd go off the deep end. . . .
>
> Well, the first well we drilled was ruined by the shooting company. Sixty quarts of nitro went off in the pipe instead of the bottom of the hole. We sued the outfit, but they didn't have anything. We lost the tools in the next well, and before we could get them out or drill any more the price of oil took a dive. Oil isn't like anything else, wheat for instance. It doesn't rise and fall a few cents at a time. Even in these days it takes ten-cent rises and drops. Back then, it fell twenty-five cents, fifty, and a dollar at a crack.
>
> You can see what that meant to me. Suppose you start to build a house that's going to sell for three thousand dollars. It'll probably cost you twenty-seven hundred to build, letting you out with a three hundred dollar profit. But suppose, when you've built the house, it won't bring three thousand—it's only worth a thousand. Or, maybe, you haven't quite got it finished before the drop comes. Then, where are you? . . . Right where I was: broke.

Back where he started before his fat settlement with Jake Hamon, Jimmie's father had no choice but to petition his old confederate. In October he traveled up to Ardmore, hoping to secure a loan that would keep Planters Petroleum solvent.

As James Thompson arrived at the Hotel Randol, Hamon was playing a peremptory role in the Warren Harding campaign that went beyond his post as chairman of the Oklahoma Republican Party. At the June Chicago convention he spent $120,000 to forge a coalition of oil interests and influential GOP senators; that fall he disbursed an additional $400,000 to lock up the Southwest for Harding. When Hamon proposed a last-minute barnstorming of Oklahoma, the candidate came running. "Harding was friendly with everyone" (Thompson has his father remark in "The Drilling Contractor"), "but he was especially friendly when anyone had done him a favor."

Jimmie's father received his loan—and more. Hamon invited him to Kansas, where the Harding whistle-stop would depart from Wichita the following morning. James rode with Mr. and Mrs. Harding in the private campaign car, the *Superb,* for a speaking tour that culminated in a rowdy welcome at the Santa Fe station in Oklahoma City.

Jimmie's father sat next to Hamon on the dais for a banquet at the Huckins Hotel. He walked near the head of a parade of some eight thousand torches that guided the Hardings to an outdoor rally on the fairgrounds. There the GOP standard bearer assuaged the Southwesterners on race. "I believe in race equality before the law. . . . But I want you to know I do not mean that white people and black people shall be forced to associate together." But in Hamon country, Harding mainly talked oil: "I do not favor meddling too much in the affairs of American businessmen." (Presumably the CEO of Planters Petroleum cheered when he linked "the star of empire" to "the star of petroleum.")

Back on the *Superb,* Jimmie's father relaxed into a high-stakes craps game with Harding, Hamon, Jake Babler (an old friend from Anadarko, then under investigation for bribery and campaign fund fraud), and Gaston Means (soon to go to prison during Teapot Dome). He lost $200 before he quit, according to "The Drilling Contractor," while Means dropped $800, Harding $3,000, and Babler a queasy $30,000! Jake Hamon was the big winner.

"It's worth all it cost," Hamon gushed to the *Daily Oklahoman* about the Harding visit.

Jimmie's father left the party at Wichita Falls, Texas, and returned to Fort Worth. With Hamon's check in his pocket and the promise of "as much more as I needed until I could get on my feet," Planters Petroleum was back in business:

> I swung into action. I traded my standard rigs in on a couple of new Stars, got two water well contracts—artesian wells, you know—and had them both drilled inside of a month. I did pretty well on these jobs. I paid off what I owed on the Stars; and bought another one on credit on the strength of them. . . . I felt a lot bet-

Jake Hamon—"last of the Oklahoma bad men"
(Courtesy of the Oklahoma Historical Society)

ter, and my family felt a lot better. They'd been pretty much down in the dumps before.

So what if the next three wells he drilled were dry, or that he broke the mast of his rig and lost his tools in a pipe-pulling job? All West Texas lay before him.

• • •

In Fort Worth Jimmie made the transition from a private writer who shared his work only with his family to a public author ambitious for publication and a large audience. One of the persistent nuggets of misinformation about Jim Thompson—the claim appears in virtually every modern reissue of his fiction—has him selling his first story to *True Detective* when he was fourteen, presumably in 1920 or 1921. *True Detective* did not hit the stands until 1924, and Thompson's debut in this most prestigious of the fact-detective weeklies would not occur until 1935.

There survives no published evidence beyond a single two-installment police serial printed in the *Nebraska Farmer*, in 1931, that young Thompson harbored any "crime" or "mystery" aspirations. In fact, there is no compelling evidence that he viewed himself as a "crime writer" before the late 1940s. Even the myriad true crime articles he produced in the 1930s and 1940s constituted only a lucrative sideline—"just pap" (as he once termed it) dashed off by moonlight to support his family and his other writing.

Jimmie was publishing by the age of fourteen, but his goals were mainstream and, if anything, upwardly mobile. On an author questionnaire submitted to the New American Library publicity department in 1961, Thompson listed his original publications and rooted his writing in the traumas of early poverty:

> Due to family setbacks, spent number of childhood years with relatives. Began to write creatively—or trying to—virtually as soon as I learned the alphabet; an environmental impetus, doubtless, since the most indigent can usually come by a pencil stub and a scrap of paper. Couldn't pass high school English though I was selling jokes and short sketches to humor magazines like *Judge* and *Life,* and also worked as a cub reporter.

The first piece that reliably may be ascribed to Thompson is a joke that appeared in the June 1921 issue of *Judge,* a cheeky Manhattan humor magazine with a national audience:

THE MISSING CHICKEN

> A popular Oklahoma City salesman recently married, and was accompanied by his wife as he entered the dining room of a Texas hotel famed for its excellent cuisine. His order was served promptly, but the fried chicken he had been telling his wife so much about was not in evidence.
>
> "Where is my chicken?" he asked somewhat irritably.
>
> The dusky waiter, leaning over and bringing his mouth in close proximity to the salesman's ear, replied:
>
> "Ef youse mean de li'l gal with blue eyes an' fluffy hair, she doan wo'k heah no mo'."

According to his sister Freddie, Jimmie contributed "dozens" of anonymous squibs to the "Stories to Tell" page of *Judge,* along with some longer

Glen Garden Country Club sketches for the "Told at the 19th Hole" column and a few poems in the mocking style of his birthday greeting. He also lampooned for *Life,* the "Wisdom and Wit Weekly" and a more sophisticated cousin to *Judge* around the 1920s New York humor scene. Since only editors and eminent wits such as Dorothy Parker, Robert Benchley, Alexander Woollcott, and George Kaufman earned bylines, family recognition provides the sole route to Jimmie's publications. Freddie credited another joke—printed in a 1926 issue of *Life*—which cleverly incorporated his name:

AT THE COUNTRY STORE

Mr. Thompson: I would like to buy a dozen balloons.
Clerk: Will you take them with you or shall I send them up?

When *Life* sponsored a campaign to "Save the Poe Cottage" in Fordham Heights, the Bronx, J. M. Thompson of Fort Worth appeared among the contributors, having donated $1 to safeguard a memorial for one of his favorite authors.

At Polytechnic, Jimmie was taken up by a sympathetic English teacher whom he called (shades of Poe!) Edgar Allan Linker for *A Penny in the Dust.* Freddie remarked that it was her brother's ascendancy in composition class that "carried him through high school, even though he had no taste for mathematics and the like. Everyone could see he was just so good in that field that somehow he got by." With his teacher's prodding he joined the Press Club, the prime literary or journalism clique in the absence of a student newspaper. And "Linker" drew on his contacts inside Fort Worth publishing to place Jimmie on plum internships and jobs.

Shortly after the Fort Worth *Press* printed its premiere issue in October 1921, Jimmie went to work for editor Leon Siler as a would-be journalist and general gofer. "In those early days the *Press* was a small, friendly place," recalls Edith Deen, whose "From a Woman's Corner" graced the daily for many decades. "There was a lot of humor in the group. We had more talent than the other papers—high standards but low salaries. So it served as a kind of training school for younger writers."

The *Press* was a flagship in the Southwestern Scripps-Howard chain. A lively journal with a circulation approaching twenty thousand readers, the paper sustained a flair for feisty investigative reporting, breaking open, for instance, the mail fraud scandals that rocked the Texas oil industry in 1923. Every day but Sunday, Jimmie joined the tiny editorial staff of four in the *Press* newsroom at 1007 Commerce Street, close by the Majestic theatre:

I reported on the job at four in the afternoon (at eight a.m. on Saturdays), and remained for as long as I was needed. For my prin-

cipal duties as copy boy, phone-answerer, coffee-procurer and occasional typist, I was paid four dollars a week. For the unimportant
stories I was allowed to cover, I was paid three dollars a column—
to the extent that they were used in the paper.

Due to their very nature, my stories were usually left out of the
paper or appeared in such boiled-down form that the cash rewards
were infinitesimal. About all I could count on was my four dollars
salary—which just about paid my expenses.

This circumstance, coupled with the fact I was away from
home to all hours, soon resulted in a series of conferences between Pop and me.

No writing emerged under Thompson's byline in the Fort Worth *Press.*
For his first incarnation as a newspaperman, Jimmie is mainly remembered
by Mrs. Deen as an after-school office boy, and a stringer who supplied student and faculty gossip for an occasional column spotlighting life around
"Poly Hi" and the other Fort Worth high schools.

After quitting the Press, apparently at the mandate of his father, Jimmie
was briefly affiliated with *Western World,* an oil and mineral promotion
weekly based in Fort Worth but aimed at the entire industry. As at the *Press*
he apprenticed to the top man, publisher Chester R. Bunker, but his role remained accessory and ad hoc. Although it was at the *Western World* offices,
inside the World Building on Sixth and Commerce, that he first met his influential future advocate at *Texas Monthly,* Peter Molyneaux, this crucial introduction—plus a raise to "a magnificent three dollars a day"—hardly
compensated his vexations, both on the job and at home.

As he noted in *Bad Boy:*

I did a little of everything, from addressing envelopes for the
subscription department to reading copy to running errands to
rewriting brief items. Occasionally, when there was space to fill, I
also wrote poems—very bad ones, I fear—of the Robert Service
type.

I never knew when I would be called into work, having to hold
myself in readiness at all times. And the times that I was called
seemed constantly to conflict with my family's plans and sched-
ules. Also, or so I imagined, my adult colleagues were not treating
me with proper respect but consistently took advantage of their
age and my youth to heap me with indignities.

Perhaps Jimmie did infiltrate the hard news and humorless columns of
Western World with his "Robert Service type" verse. Bunker's prosaic

motto, emblazoned at the top of every second page, pitched the trade weekly to "the Reader Who Demands Accuracy." The spotty collections of *Western World* that have survived from the 1920s show no examples of poetry at all—in the breakneck mode of Service's "Rhymes of a Red Cross Man" or any other popular mode.

Maxine suggested that Jimmie primarily assisted Bunker as a freelance copywriter. Alongside the latest oil discoveries and drilling permits, *Western World* featured long and breathless, relentlessly uppercased promotion "letters" from oil promoters hustling leases and stocks: "PUT YOURSELF WHERE FORTUNE CAN HIT YOU! DO IT NOW! THIS IS HOW THINGS HAPPEN IN RICH, LUCKY, MAGICAL WEST TEXAS!" These epistolary advertisements sometimes peddled fictitious stock for nonexistent wells.

By the time Thompson came to memorialize his youth in *Bad Boy,* in 1953, he would have regarded poetry as a more romantic calling than advertising. But in the freewheeling circus of early 1920s Texas oil promotion, the copywriter's craft may have called for greater visionary imagination. "The writing of these letters is a skilled and highly-paid profession, or, more properly an art," Bryce Finley Ryan argued in his pioneering account of the Texas oil promoter. "The letter must be flamboyant enough to bring in money yet innocent enough to be within the law. Few promoters write their own copy because it is a very fine art in its own right."

Jimmie's chief task at *Western World* was to transform the statistics, promises, and lies of oilmen like his father into enticing prose—forgettable hackwork. Yet this is the same coin he would flip over for his oil field novels, *Texas by the Tail, South of Heaven,* and *The Transgressors,* which cauterize the glamour and ostentation of the Texas oil millionaires with bare-knuckled, savage art. Thompson would return to trade journal writing during the Depression, even for a short time running his own oil mail-fraud scam.

• • •

In *Bad Boy* Thompson announced that he departed *Western World* in a bitter huff:

> They were all my bosses. All had the privilege of sending "Kid Shakespeare" and "young Pulitzer" after coffee or carbon paper, and they invariably chose to do so at the worst possible moments. As surely as there were visitors in the office, as surely as I was in the throes of epic composition, frowning importantly as I addressed my typewriter, there would be a cry of, "Hey, kid," followed by the suggestion that I wake up or get the lead out and busy myself with some quasi-humiliating errand or task.
>
> This was probably all for my own good. A writer who cannot

take it may as well forget about writing. But I had taken and was taking so much elsewhere, actually or in my imagination, that I could take little more. And finally, after a wild scene in which, to my horror, I very nearly bawled, I stormed out of the office and returned no more.

Whether his unhappy tenure at *Western World* expired with such high drama—neither Maxine nor Freddie, ordinarily so canny in distinguishing their brother's fact from fiction, could recall the circumstances—the Jim Thompson of the early 1920s was a very irate young man. The slights and affronts around the office excrutiatingly reinforced, as his euphemistic reference to "taking so much elsewhere" suggests, humiliations at home.

Jimmie had reached an awkward age. During his fifteenth year he shot up to his full adult height of six feet, four inches: rail-thin and gangly, yet quietly handsome with thick sandy hair, cobalt eyes and, when he wished, a tender smile. (Maxine: "When he laughed, he looked like a young Gary Cooper.") He seemed, to all appearances, conspicuously mature and grown-up. Jimmie was becoming something of a literary star at Poly Hi, having already laid down the groundwork for a career in writing. Yet around the house his father still infantilized him with carping and criticism—and approached him more in the spirit of one of his oil field reclamation projects than as a son:

> Addressing me as "sirrah," he let it be known that I was pretty poor comfort for a man no longer young whose life's gleanings were slipping through his fingers, never to be grasped again. He said that when he was my age he had done such and such and so and so, and all I could do was get into trouble and sass my betters. He said that I was completely irresponsible and out-of-hand, and that the remedy lay in work and more work. He had been too easy-going with me, he said, but now the old free and easy days were over.

Maxine identified the particular bone of contention that father and son gnawed on: "Papa didn't want Jimmie to become a writer." Despite Jimmie's accolades from "Mr. Linker" and his other high school English instructors, and his precocious credits at *Judge, Life,* the *Press,* and *Western World,* "Papa just couldn't see the point of Jimmie being a writer. He was a man of action himself. I think Papa was very proud of Jimmie later, as far as his brains went, and his writing, but he really didn't think it was any way to support a family."

Even deep into the 1930s his father remained unconvinced about Jim-

Jim Thompson—Fort Worth, Texas, probably
1920 (Courtesy of the Thompson family)

mie's walk of life. "He *never* thought Jimmie should write," maintains Thompson's wife, Alberta. "When he lived with us in Oklahoma City, starting in 1934 or 1935, he'd just come right out and say, 'Go out and get a job.' A job for him meant manual labor. His father was rather indifferent to his writing, though his mother was not. His father had a lot of these old-fashioned ideas, that when a man marries he gives up what he really wants to do. Although he didn't practice what he preached!"

Jimmie preserved a rigid silence about this aspect of his conflict with his father for his autobiographies, allowing himself only the blanket—yet chillingly final—revelation late in *Roughneck:* "I was obviously not the son he had hoped for." But a devastating passage from the long, nightmarish monologue he speaks to the departed spirit of his father in his novel *Now and on Earth* revisits the scene, broken phrases shaping a howl of pain:

What make 'ums so mad! God! You with your fat dignity; and
me with my toes permanently overlapped, and my body outgrown
my organs so that I could never eat what I needed; and what you
might call my soul—ha, ha, my soul!—turned inward because I
knew how unbeautiful it was. Inarticulate, and awkward, and angry.
Angry; raging; suspicious. Not pleasant to have under your eye.
Something that could carry golf clubs, and telegrams, and be kept
out of the way as much as possible, and—

Jimmie acted out his anger spasmodically and sporadically. In 1922 he
ran away from home, riding the rails as far as Houston before he turned
back. His sister Freddie confirmed a seemingly preposterous episode from
Bad Boy when, as a member of the Poly Hi track team, Jimmie figuratively
flipped the bird at his sports-loving father. "While I represented our school
in the intramural two-mile race, I did not run it," Thompson wrote. "I trot-
ted up in front of the grandstand, sat down in the middle of the track and
lighted a cigarette."

Such incidents were rare. Mainly he directed his rage inward and back
into his writing—a pattern that would persist all his life. For it was around
this time that Freddie believes that Jimmie, like his character Art Savage in
Texas by the Tail, began to keep his little black book of revenge. Recalled
Freddie: "I can't tell you now if it was even black, but that's what he called
it, 'my little black book.' It was a notebook of some kind. I don't know if it
was a diary or a book of his writings or if he just put names in it. But Jimmie
said that this book contained everybody who had ever been mean to him
or who had ever crossed him, and that someday he would pay them all
back. We never made too much of it when he talked like that."

• • •

Probably the most resonant guide to Jimmie's mood in the early 1920s is the
novel fragment *A Penny in the Dust.* In a September 23, 1975, letter to his
agent that accompanied the manuscript, Thompson disclosed that "*Penny*
is, in many respects, a true story, and a portrait of the author as a young
man."

A Penny in the Dust contains perhaps Thompson's most introspective
writing. Certainly it offers a profounder, more emotionally plausible probing into his family matrix than either of his putative autobiographies. Set at
"Fort Value," Texas, the fall of 1923, Thompson recasts himself as Robert
Hightower, the only son of a floundering businessman. On the surface the
Hightowers maintain a genial, unimpeachable existence, but subtle tensions agitate the calm exterior. For one thing, everyone is playing a carefully circumscribed "role." Robert narrates:

I gritted my teeth, fought down an almost irresistible urge to say something biting. Pop had little enough as it was. I could not deny him this tiny role he was playing in the final act of his life: the part of the strict but kindly father. Nor could I deny Mom her similar role. But I was finding it increasingly difficult to perform credibly as the Typical Teenage Son. A youth who would come to no-telling-what terrible end, save for the strictest supervision.

The role Robert actually performs is the Prodigal Son—or, as Thompson would put it for the title of his first autobiography, the "Bad Boy." His high school principal shouts at him, "You *are* a behavior problem, Robert. You've given offense to practically every teacher in this school." If his father's secret weapon is belittling sarcasm, Robert's is platitudinous praise. Thus he amiably glad-hands the principal:

"Yes, Sir . . ." I evaded the question, turning on a big smile. "I'm surely glad I ran into you Dr. Parton. I've heard that you were a direct descendant of one of the South's great heroes of the War Between The States, and I thought it would make a fine story for the Sunday newspaper feature section. I've published quite a few things, you know, Dr. Parton, and. . . ."

As Robert portrays his parents, all the labored Hightower role playing emerges as emotional camouflage and protective coloring, the only means of survival in the thwarted and repressive family atmosphere. It's not that the Hightowers lack strong feelings of love and anger for one another; they simply forbid themselves to express those feelings. At one point Robert reaches out to comfort his father but reflexively stops:

He choked up, turning his head away. I wanted to give him a pat on the back or, well, to give him an arm-around-the-shoulders hug or something of the kind—something to let him know that everything was all right. But you don't do things like that in our family. You might possibly brush your lips against a woman's cheeks, or, when shaking hands with a man, add a little firmness to your hand-clasp. But only at weddings and funerals, and similar events: times of great joy and sorrow. The Hightowers frowned upon displays of emotion. They looked askance at anyone who wore his heart on his sleeve.

As *A Penny in the Dust* progresses, Thompson represents Robert as having so thoroughly absorbed the Hightower chill that he passes beyond numbness into a remote psychic terrain where his inner life disconnects from his outward actions. Although more penetrating and far-sighted than his parents, Robert virtually stumbles on his own alienation as he ponders his family and classmates and grapples with his affection for his teacher, Edgar Allan Linker:

> You see, you see, he was all I had. My only friend. The only person in the world I had to talk to. As I liked to talk, and be talked to. A way that apparently seemed natural and unaffected only to the two of us. As much as I loved and respected them, I could not talk to my parents. Mom was too absorbed in the increasing problems of our survival; the shadow of impending doom which the fiercest struggle would not dispel. Pop found sanctuary in dreams of the glorious past, or wandered gloomily, broodingly through a hell without exit; the hopeless, helpless, hideous hell of a man who has never worked for others. . . .
>
> I could not talk to one of my peers (and it had been a very long time since I had tried) without being accused of swallowing a dictionary or showing off. As for conversing with an adult, well, that too could be done only with the utmost wariness. And even then, according to the adult's station in society, I was apt to be dismissed with a patronizing word or the suggestion that I stop flogging my dummy.
>
> I could only talk by being what I was not.

With Robert's final line, Thompson hauntingly links his young surrogate to *The Killer Inside Me,* or *A Hell of a Woman,* or *Savage Night,* or *The Nothing Man,* or *After Dark, My Sweet,* or *Pop. 1280;* the self-estranged refrain, along with the Hightower role playing and the cornball routine with Dr. Parton, will echo through the deepest recesses of at least a dozen crime novels. Clinton Brown of *The Nothing Man* observes in himself "that peculiar two-way pull. . . . I don't wear my emotions on my sleeve. My actions don't necessarily suit my feelings." Lou Ford defines his uncomfortable position, "All I can do is wait until I split. Right down the middle." And Charlie Bigger of *Savage Night* coldly encapsulates, "You can do that, split yourself up into two parts. It's easier than you think. Where it gets tough is when you try to put the parts back together again."

Maxine plaintively underscored Jimmie's own introverted withdrawal from his family in the early 1920s: "Jimmie could be two people. He could be very ordinary, common, and laugh a lot, cook and bake. And then he could be very intellectual. We never knew what he was thinking about because he never talked."

I could only talk by being what I was not. But if Jimmie's talk and

From the Parrot, *Jim Thompson's high school yearbook, 1924 (Courtesy of Fort Worth Public Library)*

actions could not reflect his emotions, his appearance increasingly did. For *Bad Boy* he called up a photo from the 1920s, perhaps the photo that appeared in the junior-class section of the 1924 *Poly Parrot,* his high school yearbook:

> A photograph of this period reveals me as a thin, neat, solemn-faced young man, surprisingly innocuous-looking at first glance. It is only when you look more closely that you see the watchfully narrowed eyes, the stiffness of the lips, the expression that wavers between smile and frown. I looked like I hoped for the best, but expected the worst.

Flip-flopping from a "smile" to a "frown," from the "best" to the "worst"—as he glanced back Thompson appropriately discovered a double image. *That peculiar two-way pull.*

• • •

Behind the scenes of Jimmie's cheerless family drama, his father was starring in "How Fast Money Goes in Texas—The Sequel." On August 31, 1922, James wrote a letter to Birdie, who once more had fled with the children back to Nebraska:

> Dear Birdie & Children:
> Got your letter last night that you were going to Kearney. I sent you a check of $25.00 to Burwell. I suppose it will be forwarded to you. I have chocked this up on my books the sum as cashed so you can cash it. . . .
> I threw up the New York deal I was afraid to risk it with so little capital. . . .
> I am trying to sell our production at Breckenridge.
> I could tell that Maxine had made a great sudden improvement on the violin. I hope I can send her to a conservatory next year. You ought to send Freddie to school what time you are up there. A year now will count when she gets older.
> Write and let me know how much money you will need for the coming month. You must all have some clothes for the cold weather. I was glad you traded the car. What year model is it from?
> Write soon. Jim
> Will write Maxine next letter.

Pop was broke again. For the last two years, in fact, he had been scrambling for cash at the brink of bankruptcy. Records at the Texas secretary of state's office indicate that Planters Petroleum dissolved in April 1921, but the freeze set in even before then. The same Jake Hamon loan that had kept him afloat formed the basis of his new troubles.

When Hamon was murdered by his mistress in November 1921, his fortune reverted to his legal widow, Georgea. Estranged from her husband for more than a decade, and knowing nothing about his elephantine empire, Georgea Hamon hired an accounting firm to organize the estate. Thompson has his father explain in "The Drilling Contractor" about his disastrous encounter with "Mrs. Morris Markham":

> Just when I needed money the worst, I received notice from the executor of Morris' estate that all accounts receivable were being called in and to make arrangements to pay the $5,000 draft. I wrote back that the money had been intended almost as a gift; that, if the truth were known, I probably had it and a great deal more coming to me. I guess he handed it on to Morris' wife, because I got a letter from her about three weeks later. She accused me of almost every mean thing she could think of—of coming between Morris and his family, and trying to steal from him after he was dead. A lot of things like that. She wound up by threatening to sue me.
>
> If I'd wanted to fight she couldn't have collected, but I didn't want to. I borrowed against my drilling contracts, sold a little piece of acreage I'd picked up for some work, and paid back the $5,000. It left me so strapped that I hardly had enough to pay our household expenses, and I had to borrow on our car and some personal jewelry to get money to work on. My family took it pretty hard, and I can't say that I blamed them.

Other factors precipitated the demise of Planters Petroleum. A difficult and unusually deep drill, some 5,800 feet, at Big Spring cost more than it yielded. The oil industry around Breckenridge, which James mentioned during his letter to Birdie, suffered a catastrophic crash in 1921, when prices dropped to one dollar a barrel and the banks folded, spelling ruin for hundreds of operators. Both Maxine and Freddie painted their father as an oddly naive and self-sabotaging tycoon. "Papa was too trusting," suggested Freddie. "He would make deals and just shake hands on them. And they weren't all with savory people. You needed it in writing, with three or four lawyers looking over your shoulder, and Papa didn't always do that."

Jimmie's father kicked against the pricks of his fate, wildcatting through West Texas, with pitiful success. He speculated in the stock market. "Papa thought he had the cotton or wheat or some commodity cornered, and everyone was going to be rich," Freddie recollected, "but of course the bottom fell out." He worked as a traveling salesman (à la William Simpson in *Heed the Thunder*) for International Harvester. But the tragic denouement of his partnership with Jake Hamon cracked his spirit, and it never mended. In all Thompson's portrayals of his father after the mid-1920s, he emerges as a chronically depressed, shattered man. Jimmie henceforth rendered him essentially as Robert Hightower chronicled *his* father: trapped between mournful nostalgia and wretched pipe dreams, wandering "gloomily, broodingly through a hell without exit."

"Papa always seemed cheerful and pleasant," Maxine calculated, "but I think now, looking back, though I didn't realize it then, inwardly he was a kind of broken man. Inwardly, but not outwardly. From then on things started going downhill."

As Pop crumbled before them, the family reeled. For Freddie, too young to have enjoyed the years of plenty, the period before the flight to Nebraska bequeathed a raggle-taggle quilt of absurd, poignant, and stinging impressions:

> There wasn't any money when I was around. All my life, as far back as I can remember was a depression. It didn't bother me because I didn't know any better. It later kept me out of college, which upset Jimmie very much.
>
> I can remember when I was ten or eleven years old playing with the check writer and the stationery from Planters Petroleum, which by then was defunct.
>
> We had a big, brand-new house out on the Dallas Pike. One day I remember Mama telling me to be quiet. She didn't want to go to the door. She knew it was somebody coming to collect on something.
>
> But I think that the fortune kept changing. There'd be another day when Papa would be driving up in a new car, and we'd all dress well. Then things would be at a low ebb again.
>
> Papa lived like there was always going to be plenty of money, but that just about finished him off. Mama was being careful and penny-pinching. But most of the time she just pretended that nothing was happening. Maxine would also be off on a cloud somewhere.
>
> My brother Jimmie was so shy and withdrawn that it was hard to tell what was going on with him. But I really think that he was the only one who seemed to be taking everything in. He tried to talk to Mama about it, but she didn't want to listen. She never liked to hear about problems. Papa became kind of pathetic, it was sad to watch. So Jimmie had to take over, though he was just a big kid himself.

Jimmie was very angry at Papa for losing all of his money, the money he just gave away or threw into some stupid deal. Why didn't Papa save more when he was high and everybody was in clover there? But he never did. Jimmie really was resentful about that.

Jimmie masked his bitterness. He hunted down whatever employment was open to a fifteen-year-old boy, still technically a high school sophomore. "Worked so many time-consuming and exhausting jobs outside of school hours," he rued in his author questionnaire for New American Library. Perhaps taking a cue from his inaugural Fort Worth adventure with Grandfather Myers, Jimmie grubbed at the Gayety Theatre, a burlesque house on Main Street, first as a ticket taker and then as "a candy butcher" and eventually as a Slim Pickens–style comedian chasing $5 door prizes on amateur night. When a film production company—probably the Sunset Motion Picture Corporation of Galveston—shot a two-reel silent comedy at the Gayety, he earned a spot as an extra. (Freddie: "Somewhere we used to have a still photograph of him in a cowboy outfit leaning on a bar rail.")

But the Gayety couldn't appease the Thompsons' penury. In the summer of 1922 Birdie and the children once more bolted north to Nebraska, languishing there for the next fifteen months. This trip fired a scintilla of novelty into the familiar exile. The family rotated residency in Burwell with expeditions to Kearney, the college town where Jimmie's cousin Jocelyn Wicks lived with her new husband. Birdie found part-time work at the Kearney State Teachers College as a grader and tutor.

• • •

Jimmie's father wrote again to "Dear Birdie & Children" from a West Texas tent in the fall of 1922, a subdued, lonesome letter to a family drifting out of his orbit:

> Received your letter yesterday. Will write you a few lines. It has been cool here for several days. Had a slight shower the first of the week.
>
> I suppose it is getting cool up there. I wired you $25.00 yesterday sent you $15.00 more today.
>
> I wish I could run up and pay you a short visit but I have my hands full here.
>
> There is one bright shot in the clouds oil went up 25-cents yesterday in Oklahoma. I hope it will follow here.
>
> I got a letter from [my brother] Elmer in Idaho he was nominated for Lieutenant Governor out there, on the Democratic ticket.

There was a Ku Klux Klan raid at stop six. Some woman took an old lady out and whipped her 100 lashes. There is great indignation over the affair.

School is going on now they are digging a sewer from the new school building to the pasture south.

Maxine how are you feeling I want you to go to the Doctor if you are not well. Have you played in the church yet. Mr. Bigham told me last night Jack was still worrying about Freddie. Jimmie write and tell me how you are getting along and how you like the school.

With love from Papa

It is raining hard just as I was closing this letter.

Jimmie enrolled in the Burwell High School but failed to complete any of his courses. He lost a full year of instruction. When he returned to Fort Worth and Poly in the fall of 1923 it was as a junior. Already Jimmie had fallen two grades behind his entering class.

His father meanwhile struggled on as a mail-order oil promoter. His business consisted of drafting "sucker letters," along the lines of Jimmie's own oily prose for the advertising pages of *Western World,* to solicit cash from the gullible. Instead of drilling oil, James now essentially sold literature.

Ordinarily one of the most lucrative oil-related activities, promotion was a severely threatened species by the fall of 1923. Sensational trials had led to the conviction of thirteen powerful mail-order operators, most notably the Arctic explorer Frederick A. Cook. *Bad Boy* took pains to distance square-shooting, clairvoyant "Pop" from Cook:

> Dr. Frederick A. Cook, the Polar explorer, was our dinner guest one night. . . . He had brought a batch of advertising literature out for Pop to look at. Pop did.
>
> "Don't send this out, Doc," he advised. "It will put you in the pen."

But like his operatic pledges of "Pop's honesty" during the 1906 congressional campaign, Thompson overprotests his father's righteousness into incredulity. Maxine's son, lawyer Tony Kouba, remembers seeing among James Thompson's papers promotion letters of the stamp that sent Dr. Cook to the Kansas Hotel, as the Fort Worth oil crowd tagged Leavenworth Penitentiary, "exactly the kind of thing," Kouba notes, "that the FCC would eventually be there to protect against." Jimmie's father could not have swung into oil promotion at a less propitious moment. Checked by the aggressive federal investigation, his business shuddered to a halt. The coarse fog of his depression darkened.

Jimmie had no choice but to go to work. As his father receded into dullness and paralysis, Jimmie took upon himself the burdens of the family breadwinner—also accepting, in turn, the knottier vexations of family head. Thompson indicated in *Now and on Earth* that initially he strove to carry home the bacon as a writer, but soon reconsidered:

> Oddly enough, I sold the first thing I wrote, a sketch about a golf game; but it was a very long time between that first story and the second. And, although, I never gave up writing, I kept at it largely from habit. Pop went broke and his was the irremediable brokeness of a man past fifty who has never worked for other people. I had to distinguish myself and support the family at the same time. And even at fifteen [*sic*], a high school freshman, I knew I wasn't going to do it by writing.

Jimmie surrendered the hazards of a freelancer for the highest-paying steady job he could find: bellboy at the Hotel Texas. Although actually seventeen (all Thompson's autobiographical writing ad-libs dates "for the sake of a good story," to quote Freddie), he still remained intent on graduating from high school. For the next two years he juggled a standard course load at Poly with full-time employment on the night shift at the Hotel Texas.

At a single stroke, father and son exchanged places. Thompson devastatingly replayed the moment from his father's perspective for "The Drilling Contractor," where he rechristens himself Bob:

> My boy, Bob, was right in the middle of his freshman year in high school. He was a kind of sickly, nervous kid; read a lot and never had much to say. One night about ten o'clock he came out of his bedroom and started for the door with his school books.
>
> "Pretty late to be calling on your friends, isn't it?" I asked.
>
> "I'm going to work," he said.
>
> It was news to me. I kind of laughed. "What kind of work? What are you taking your books for?"
>
> "Nice work," he said. "Hopping bells. Eleven at night until seven in the morning, seven days a week. I take my books so that I can study—whenever the whores stop hollering for men and whiskey."
>
> That's what he said, this fifteen year old kid. Then, he slammed out the door. My wife started crying. Bob had been working for

about a week and he'd made fifty dollars. She didn't want him to work, but she didn't know how we'd get by without the money. It was hard for him to sleep in the daytime, and there wasn't much time anyway, what with going to school five days a week.

Well, I told her we'd put a stop to the business right quick. We might be hard up, but I didn't have to let a kid like that make a living for me. I meant it too, but—well, it just seemed like we couldn't get along without Bob's earnings.

Birdie's tears, like the melodramatic tinkering with chronology, may only have been retrospective. Jimmie's employment at the Hotel Texas would threaten his health as well as his education. Eventually it would also spur a trilogy of hotel novels, *A Swell-Looking Babe, Wild Town* (1957), and *Texas by the Tail*. For the present, though, his job pinned him inside an excruciating double bind. Amid the disintegrating Thompson family drama Jimmie now stretched between two irreconcilable roles: the "disappointing" son of the autocratic father, and the necessary caretaker to the defeated, impotent "dreamer" who no longer could manage his affairs or feed his wife and children. As he bluntly asks—and answers—in *Bad Boy*, "Was a man who had made such a thorough screw-up of his life a suitable mentor for me? (I did not think so.)"

• • •

The fifteen-story red brick Hotel Texas sliced the Fort Worth skyline from its handy downtown site on Eighth Street, between Commerce and Main. Repeated arched windows demonstrated Chicago and Georgian architectural influences while terra-cotta steer heads at street level and at the crest added local color. The six-hundred-room showplace accommodated what Thompson described in *Wild Town* as a hidden metropolis: "Bakery, laundry, grocery. Printers', painters', electricians', plumbers', and carpenters' shops. Ice plant and ice-cream plant. Rug reweaving, upholstering, linen repair. Boiler-room, engine-room, waterworks. . . . The hotel was a city, and it contained everything necessary for the operation of a city." Jack Dempsey signed for the Dempsey-Tunney fight at the Hotel Texas; Lawrence Welk led an orchestra there. President John F. Kennedy spent the night of November 21, 1963, in Suite 850. Gutted and renovated in the early 1980s, the Hotel Texas now stands as the Fort Worth Hyatt Regency.

What the Bellboy Saw served as Thompson's provisional title for his Hotel Texas novel, *A Swell-Looking Babe*. But what this bellboy saw—and committed—could have furnished the lurid details for an entire lifetime's crime fiction. Then, as now, the bellboy in a big-city hotel serviced more of his client's needs than merely transporting heavy bags. "When I found out the other things," he winced in *Now and on Earth,* "it made me a little sick. But I didn't know what to do then; I didn't see any way out. We needed the money, and this, apparently, was the only way of getting it." Through long, wild nights at the Hotel Texas, Jimmie moonlighted as a bootlegger, a drug peddler, a grifter, a pimp, and a male escort.

"I guess a lot of things went on in that hotel," his sister Maxine warily looked back. "He used to tell us some of them when he came home, and it was horrifying. The Hotel Texas was a nice hotel, but things were rough in those days. He was so quiet around home that we never really knew all the horrible things that happened, getting women, booze, cocaine, and whatever for people. But we knew it was rough. We were all kind of scared to death."

This was the Roaring Twenties. In oil-soaked Fort Worth the gaudy revelers not only roared; they bleated and bellowed. Conjuring up "the luxury hotel life," *Bad Boy* evoked "a world whose urbane countenance revealed nothing of the seething and sinister turmoil of its innards, a world whose one rule was that you did nothing you could not get away with." Jimmie stepped into this world for a rowdy eight hours every night.

No desire was off-limits, no vice too vicious, for the guest disposed to compensate the bellhop for his discretion. If someone requested a bottle, Jimmie could nullify the Eighteenth Amendment with either bootleg or drugstore booze. "He would have half-pint bottles of liquor in his socks," noted Freddie, "which he would sell to customers of the hotel to help augment his income." If a guest preferred the headier spice of dope to alcohol, Jimmie would dip down to the Mexican quarter along North Main Street for grass, coke, or heroin. His 1931 short story, "The Car in the Mexican Quarter," finds a bellboy from the "Hotel Lansing" murdered after a drug transaction: "The Lansing is one of the biggest hotels in town, but I knew it stood for a lot of dirty work from its employees."

Call girls ranked high among the privileges of the luxury hotel. One Texas hotel chain fronted a female basketball team to entertain special guests. Sexual commerce at the Hotel Texas was less stylized. Freddie: "Jimmie once told me that when a customer wanted a woman, the bellboy gave a special signal and one was sent up to the room. I was just horrified to hear he was involved in that!" Apparently the bellhop earned a tip from both sides of the transaction. Female guests also were accommodated. As Thompson hinted in *Bad Boy,* "Nominally, there were strictly enforced rules against such things as . . . intimacy with female guests. As long as you did them in such a way as not to give rise to complaints or disturb the routine of the hotel, nothing would be done."

The Texas expected their bellboys to chaperone the rough-and-tumble gambling parties that blew into Fort Worth for the large stock and rodeo conventions. Twenty-four-hour-a-day dice and card games devoured entire floors, and the staff mingled with the hustlers. Sitting in was discouraged, but the bellhops cut into the haul by "feeding them mooches": bringing fresh blood to the tables. Predictably these gaffs often erupted in violence. On at least one occasion Jimmie paid for his attendance with his safety. Recalled Maxine: "A party of gamblers was upset with Jimmie about something or other, and the situation got out of hand. Two or three of the biggest men picked him up and held him upside down over an elevator shaft. I don't know how he got out of it, but he really was frightened over that for a long time."

Thompson confessed in *Bad Boy* that while hopping bells at the Hotel Texas he acquired the "grift"—the tricks of the short con, which he later handed down to Roy Dillon in *The Grifters* (1963)—from a friend he calls Allie Ivers. "Thanks to a confidential talk with Allie Ivers, I did not do too badly in these games. . . . By the process of 'rat-holing'—surreptitiously palming an occasional ten or twenty—I often got away with hundreds." Thompson claimed, in fact, that it was Allie Ivers who first introduced him to the night manager of the Texas.

The wily Ivers occupied a curious niche in Jimmie's unfolding private mythology. Most of the shenanigans and malefactions he laid at Ivers's feet in *Bad Boy* and *Roughneck* truly were committed by a con man and mobster of his acquaintance, Red Brown. As Thompson wrote to editor Marc Jaffe of the New American Library, in a 1958 letter about his novel *The Getaway*,

> I have been on a first-name basis with a number of criminals. Following his release from prison, I was the room-mate one summer of the notorious bank-robber, "Airplane Red" Brown, and I served as best man at his wedding. You'll realize that I'm not bragging about this; as the son of a well-known peace officer, I am no admirer of criminals. But this background does allow me to write with authority.

Brown is the hoodlum behind the wisecracking, bamboozling Ivers, and the Ivers-like Turkelson in *Texas by the Tail;* he also floats behind Carter "Doc" McCoy, the unflappable bandit of *The Getaway,* and "Airplane Red" Cosgrove, the young bank robber of *Recoil.* But the name Allie Ivers commanded greater personal significance for Jimmie than as a "real life" source for his novels. Freddie remembered "Allie" as an imaginary *Doppelgänger* her brother maintained throughout adolescence. "Allie Ivers," in Freddie's account, hovers between Jimmie's spectral evil twin and a cartoon devil spitting advice over his left shoulder:

That was a little joke Jimmie had when he was younger. He didn't pronounce it the way it's spelled in his books—more like "Ollie Avers." I can't tell you where it came from. I want to say Laurel and Hardy, which Jimmie always loved. . . . Anyway, when Jimmie wanted to tell us something silly or very outrageous he'd say, "as Ollie Avers," like it wasn't really him saying it. And sometimes if Mama caught Jimmie doing something he shouldn't, or something happened at the hotel, he'd tell her, "Ollie Avers did it," or "Ollie Avers made me do it." It was just a funny little excuse he'd make up. Jimmie could be very funny when he wanted to.

Thompson employed "Allie Ivers" to precisely this effect in *Bad Boy* and *Roughneck:* he's an enchanting imp of the perverse who lures Jimmie down the forbidden path into grifting or bootlegging or petty larceny. Thompson virtually gave away his dry joke when he reported that the Fort Worth police believed that Ivers was a "fictitious fall guy," or when he bestowed on his shifty "friend" a physical description that intriguingly matched his own. "He was thin, blond and pale, with the most innocent blue eyes I have ever seen. Our paths crossed and recrossed during those years, and he often referred to me as his best friend (a reference which I often found debatable). I knew him far better than anyone else. Yet throughout our association, I never knew where he lived, I never learned anything about his background or antecedents, and I was never sure of how he would behave from one day to the next."

• • •

Jimmie officially earned $15 a month at the Hotel Texas—but gratuities sent him home with as much as $300 each week. Pocketing more than enough cash to support his family, he splurged on a new car, a stylish Dort coupe. Jimmie began to affect modish, expensive clothes: flashy suits, Borsalino hats, imported shoes. He became so much the Texas dandy that the hotel staff nicknamed him "Dolly."

For all his adventures, perks, and pleasures, Jimmie's schedule carried within it the seeds of physical and mental ruin. Released from work at 7 in the morning, he barely had time to shower and change in the bellhops' locker room before he was due at school. Classes at Poly lasted until 3:30 in the afternoon. Sleep occupied the early evening—yet not too much of it, as Jimmie needed to rise by 9:30 in order to eat and be back at the Hotel Texas for his shift at 11. Homework might be accomplished between calls in the slow dawn hours; but his leisure to study on the job can be judged by the fact that after two years at the hotel he had yet to complete his junior courses. *A Penny in the Dust* features this gruesome exchange between Robert Hightower and his principal, Dr. Parton:

"You look very tired, Robert. Run around a lot at night, do you?"

"Yes, sir," I said. "I'm afraid I do."

"Well, you'd better start getting to bed earlier. Try getting nine or ten hours sleep a night. I'll bet it will do wonders for you, all the way around."

Yessir, yessir, kiss my ass, sir. I'll work nine hours a night, and I'll sleep nine hours a night, and study nine hours a night, and—

"Now, I can understand how a young man from the North might have trouble adapting to the South. Texas and Texans must have seemed rather strange to you. . . ."

Oh, no, sir! It took my Pop just three years to go bust here. A million bucks down the bucket. My Mom and I are just crazy about Texas.

"But you're really a very lucky young man, Robert. How many other boys have the fine home, the fine clothes, that you have? How many other boys have. . . ."

Piles that you can stack washers on, falling arches, veins that are going varicose. A wageless bellboy job, a job that paid only in tips, nine hours a night, seven days a week. . . .

"Well, you better run along now, Robert. You've got to spend three hours in detention hall, remember, and you're looking awfully tired."

"Yes, sir," I said.

Jimmie turned to whiskey as a surrogate for rest and to keep his body traveling through his inverted routine. He sipped all night at the hotel for refreshment and "to forget my shame and fear of exposure and arrest"; afternoons he drank in the bath to steer his jittery brain toward sleep. Jimmie took to stashing bootleg all over the house: in his room, the cellar, the garage, even "behind the bath-tub," as Thompson has his father relate in "The Drilling Contractor." And when liquor couldn't jump-start his weary system, Jimmie—Maxine recalled—would sniff cocaine.

Although Thompson never evolved into a Jekyll and Hyde drinker prone to blackout rages and violence, the bottle subtly alchemized his personality. Under the influence, his stammering self-consciousness, introversion, and timidity melted away and—as Freddie fascinatingly characterized his alcoholic sea change—"Jimmie became more like Papa."

Both sisters seem to have welcomed the transformation at this early stage of his drinking. "When Jimmie had a few drinks his personality would change," Freddie explained. "But then we all thought it was great fun. Before that he'd get so nervous, stutter and blink his eyes a lot. Drinking he'd become like his father, outgoing, funny, more of an extrovert, flamboyant.

From a shy, withdrawn person he would become a hilarious bon vivant. He used to say, 'It gives me courage to be more outgoing.' "

Drunkenness lifted the ponderousness of Jimmie's reserve in another crucial aspect. If alcohol released his secret social graces, it also authorized him to probe the dark corners of his life with a searching candor he would otherwise unleash only under the smoke screen of his fiction. "You see, Jimmie never really went into his own personal feelings very much *except* when he was drinking," his elder sister, Maxine, cautioned. "Then I could see how sensitive he was, and how the hotel or some of the things Papa did damaged Jimmie. These horrible stories just poured out of him. They scared and upset me. It was how I felt reading his books, like I really didn't know him. I don't think I ever had a close conversation with Jimmie when he hadn't been drinking."

Freddie perhaps inclined to the silver lining in the gathering thunderhead of Jimmie's dissipation, because he so tenderly doted on her at home. With the Thompson family foundering around them, Jimmie emerged as her foster parent as much as her teasing older brother:

> You could say that Jimmie brought me up, and I don't mean just because he was paying the bills. Although I'm sure he had torments from lack of money and worrying about his miserable jobs, he was so patient and gentle with me.
>
> Jimmie helped me set up a little cold drink stand on the highway. He built me a little shack right by the Dallas–Fort Worth Pike—of course, it was more rural then—and got the Coca-Cola people to bring me a little refrigerator and a hat. He was helping me make money. But he couldn't make me understand that when someone gave me 50¢ I didn't get to keep the whole thing, that I had to give back 45¢ in change!
>
> I remember when he got me my first bicycle, and I didn't know how to ride well. Jimmie had his car by then, and we both chose to ride that day on a road up the hill from our house. He was sort of watching over me. I was riding along, trying to manage the bicycle, wobbling a little, and I headed for the front of his car. He was petrified and couldn't seem to get out of my way, so I was hurt a bit. The steering wheel of my bicycle had poked me in the throat, and I thought I was dying! Jimmie bundled me up and drove me home. He was so anxious and upset about me.
>
> In his books, which are sort of autobiographical, Jimmie makes himself into quite an exaggerated person—harder than he was, maybe as he wished he could have been, but really wasn't, at least with me. I thought of him as very funny, very witty, not above any

Jim with his mother, Birdie—Fort Worth,
Texas, probably 1925 (Courtesy of the
Thompson family)

kind of joke. Jimmie was always tender with me, very sweet and
very caring.

•   •   •

Amazingly, Jimmie endured his vicious regimen for almost two years. From
the fall of 1923 into the summer of 1925 he lurched between Polytechnic
High School and the Hotel Texas, squaring the nurture of his family against
the temptations of the Fort Worth underworld. His education sideslipped.
After twelve semesters he now was about to begin his senior classes, a rite
of passage that would coincide with his nineteenth birthday. The overwork
and fatigue, all the stress and alcohol, mounted a hellish assault on Jimmie's health. As Freddie characterized him mid-decade, he was "eighteen
going on fifty."

Apparently the first symptoms were a chronic cough and a constant
clearing of his throat—Jimmie had commenced his lifelong sixty-plus-
cigarettes-a-day habit while bellhopping at the hotel. Then in the spring of
1924 he suddenly started to lose weight. Already gaunt and pinched, he
shrank to an alarming one hundred pounds. His mother could barely rouse
him from his sodden evening sleep. When shaking him wasn't enough, she

took to playing the phonograph loudly by his bed, and Jimmie started turning up late for work. Finally one summer evening he couldn't get up at all. Jimmie slept for an agonizing twenty-seven hours while his family kept vigil over him, until his father telephoned the hotel physician. When an ambulance rushed him to the hospital, the diagnosis was nervous exhaustion, tuberculosis, and alcoholism.

Thompson positioned a lurid recapitulation of his collapse as the centerpiece of "The Drilling Contractor," discharging a vengeful, unappeasable docket of his illness from his father's self-condemning perspective. Bitter, deadpan phrases dig into every revolting physical detail:

> The third summer he worked he began to go to pieces completely. He had the piles so bad from being on his feet and not resting that it looked like about half of his insides were hanging out. I peeked into his bedroom one day while he was sleeping, and I was shocked and sick for days afterward. I knew that he was in a bad way but I hadn't realized how bad.
>
> He had the pillows piled under his stomach so that he was crouching on his knees, and he had the electric fan turned on his rump. It was sickening; it looked like a rope of raw meat: all stuck up with powder and vaseline where he'd tried to relieve the pain. You could count the bones in his body through his skin. You could even see his heart beat with his back turned to you. He looked like a little dried-up old man, and he was just short of eighteen.
>
> He never seemed to eat anything. When he got up at night he'd go into the bathroom and take a drink of liquor, and start vomiting. Then, as soon as he'd stopped he'd take another drink, and vomit some more. He'd keep that up until you'd think he would shake himself to pieces; and, finally, he'd make a drink stay down, add a few more to it, and get ready to go to work. I don't know how much money he was actually making, but he always gave at least thirty-five dollars a week to his mother, and he was always buying something for the girls or giving them money to buy things with. The truth of the matter was I borrowed quite a bit from him myself, ten or twenty dollars at a time. I asked him not to mention it to his mother, and he never did.
>
> Well, late in the summer he got to where he couldn't rest at all. He'd talk in his sleep for an hour at a time—mumbling, you know— and then he'd let out a yell and jump clear of the bed. He'd do that a dozen times a day until he'd get so nervous and shaky that he'd sit down on the edge of the bed with his head in his hands, and

start crying. Sometimes he cried when he was trying to eat, or when he was dressing or shaving. He'd just start in, whatever he was doing, and there wasn't anything you could do to make him stop. He'd cry until he couldn't cry any longer, and then he'd start laughing, and all you could do was sit and watch.

The cure proved as sordid as the disease. On his fourth day at the hospital delirium tremens set in. Jimmie experienced delusions and violent screaming fits accompanied by a spastic twitching of his face and limbs. As two orderlies held him down, his doctor poured whiskey into his jerking body, tapering the dose until by the end of the second week Jimmie was resting quietly on less than a pint a day. Thompson termed his disorder "a nervous breakdown" in the New American Library questionnaire. For many years afterward, he noted, his lungs remained "badly spotted."

Coaxed back from near death by the alcohol that had nearly killed him, Jimmie was released for a slow recuperation at home. While his Hotel Texas insurance covered his medical expenses, he planned to support his family with his savings, a neat $1,100 in a period when bread sold for 7¢ a loaf. Except that, after Jimmie left the hospital, he discovered that his bank account was empty.

His father had hit on another sure thing: drilling an artesian well in South Texas. "Borrowing" liberally from Jimmie for the past three years, James Thompson doubted that his son could object to a deal that would net a quick $3,000. Inevitably, complications ensued, culminating in a freak cyclone that devastated the site. Just as Jimmie arrived home with a stern warning from his doctor not to work for at least four months, his father staggered back to Fort Worth owing a small fortune.

When Birdie made the inexorable return trip to Burwell in the fall of 1925, her family couldn't conceal their shock. "Jimmie was so sick, pale, and thin," recalls Edna Myers Borden. "It was really sad to see him that way. Everyone was very upset and worried over him. He had fevers and terrible abdominal problems that whole year he spent with us. Of course, we all blamed his father." James Thompson's own Nebraska relations lodged a similar grudge against him. As his niece Harriet Cowan Keller remarked, "The fact that Uncle Jim couldn't hold on to his money caused him to let his son work as a bellhop. That was an awful thing for the young boy to do. Not only his illness but many of Jimmie's later troubles I always laid to his environment in the hotel."

• • •

Jimmie's sickness carried its privileges. While Birdie and the girls slept on davenports in the living room of the small house Grandfather and

Grandmother Myers now occupied a few blocks south of the center of town, his ailments earned him a prized rear bedroom with a private entrance. Although he still railed against his grandmother's cooking and, apparently, found his visiting aunt Addie a gossipy, nagging affliction, he regained enough vitality by winter to resume classes at the Burwell High School.

Jimmie's closest Burwell friends, his Myers cousins William Lyle and Donald, and Carl Grunkemeyer, of course had long since graduated. He took up with a younger crowd that included Carl's brother Ralph, Vance White, Terrence Downey, Rex Wagner, and Carl's future wife, Elva McWharter. If back in Fort Worth Jimmie had impressed his sisters as incurably self-conscious and clumsy, these new chums celebrated his urban polish and savoir faire. Although accustomed to twenty-year-old high school seniors, rustic Burwell never saw the likes of the post–Hotel Texas Jim Thompson.

"He brought a lot of the cosmopolitan to Burwell, to us, our class," enthuses Elva McWharter. "We thought he was very sophisticated. He knew all of the nicetudes to impress a girl. He was very attentive to his friends. And he was always well dressed, nice sweaters and other sharp clothes."

Jimmie's mind, as much as his jazzy asphalt jungle threads, dazzled his classmates: "He gave the sense of knowing a lot. My strongest memory is from English class, because there he impressed me the most. Jim was a brilliant writer. Even then he wrote highly poetic, metaphorical prose. I can still remember a phrase from one of his essays: 'the highway stretched like a ribbon.' " Like McWharter, Rex Wagner "wasn't at all surprised that Jim became a writer. He had a real good sense of expressing himself. That year we had Mr. Smatt for English—not a good teacher. But Jim wrote some very outstanding English papers for him about places in Texas and Oklahoma where he had lived or visited."

A "splendid dancer" in McWharter's admiring judgment, Jimmie attended "all of our school parties," where he "enthusiastically" partook of such homespun parlor games as rook and musical chairs. On the sly, though, his intemperate proclivities rebounded. Despite the cautions of his doctors he raided Grandfather Myers's stock of "cider," and purchased moonshine brewed in stills concealed throughout the sandhills. "There were times when he clearly was drinking," notes McWharter. "We just didn't have much experience with that."

Burwell High School lacked a formal athletic program that year, as the coach himself had been fired for drunkenness. Jimmie exercised by running laps every morning and evening. As his father wrote, belatedly, from Fort Worth:

Mama just told me about your running on the track, I want
to caution you against straining your lungs in this and if you feel
them hurting you don't do it. I had a friend once who caught
consumption from heavy track work at least the doctors said
that this caused it.

When Birdie attempted to restore the old Livingston Hotel, Jimmie
pitched in with all his Fort Worth know-how. Burwell's first hotel, now de-
cayed into a seedy boardinghouse, the Livingston became the model for
the Verdon Hotel, which Edie Dillon and her son Robert reopen with spectacular success in *Heed the Thunder.* The Livingston was not so blessed.
The Thompsons slaved over the hotel through the fierce winter months.
"But they couldn't make a go of it," reports Edna Myers Borden. "Birdie just
wasn't a homemaker. So, frankly, nobody would stay in it."

Jimmie abruptly departed Burwell early in the spring of 1926 and returned to Fort Worth. His mother and sisters stayed on while Jimmie entered into uneasy residence with his father inside the gloomy house on the
Dallas Pike. Though the Thompsons still retained ownership, the cars and
much of the furniture had been sold for necessities. "We were like polite
strangers to one another," he later reflected, "rather than father and son."
Jimmie purchased back his old job hopping bells and dutifully reported to
class, recommencing his murderous rotation of nights at the Hotel Texas
and days at Polytechnic High School.

Thompson asserted in *Bad Boy* that he finished high school only by
doctoring his grades with the aid of a pliant Poly secretary. In the absence
of his Fort Worth and Burwell academic records it's impossible to dismiss
this as merely another fanciful episode of his personal mythology, a further
stage in the devolution of a "Bad Boy," though that's probably the best way
to understand his story. Fascinatingly, the only paper evidence—his 1929
University of Nebraska identification card—finds Jimmie attempting to
pass himself off as a high school graduate and failing to get away with it.
After shrinking his high school years from seven to a more conventional
"five," he wrote on the standard form required of all entering students that
yes, he graduated from "Poly Hi School" in " '25." Someone at the college
apparently checked further or requested a transcript, for another hand
subsequently crossed out Jimmie's own statements and carefully penciled
in the words "did not graduate."

Jimmie tarried in Fort Worth barely long enough to have his senior
class picture snapped for the 1926 *Parrot.* In both the casual and formal
yearbook portraits he appears distracted, tired, and sad. More haunting
still is the descriptive italic legend printed below his name: *"His mind was
keen, intense."*

Come June, Jimmie would already be in the oil fields courting another

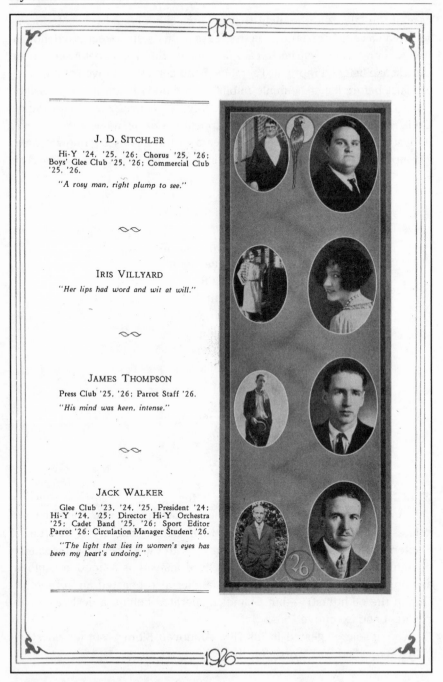

J. D. SITCHLER

Hi-Y '24, '25, '26; Chorus '25, '26;
Boys' Glee Club '25, '26; Commercial Club
'25, '26.

"A rosy man, right plump to see."

IRIS VILLYARD

"Her lips had word and wit at will."

JAMES THOMPSON

Press Club '25, '26; Parrot Staff '26.

"His mind was keen, intense."

JACK WALKER

Glee Club '23, '24, '25, President '24;
Hi-Y '24, '25; Director Hi-Y Orchestra
'25; Cadet Band '25, '26; Sport Editor
Parrot '26; Circulation Manager Student '26.

*"The light that lies in women's eyes has
been my heart's undoing."*

The Parrot, *1926. "On the night that my high school
graduated I was seated on a generator, far out on the
Texas plains. . . ," Thompson wrote in* Now and on
Earth. *(Courtesy of Fort Worth Public Library)*

case of the DTs. "On the night that my high school class graduated I was seated on a generator, far out on the Texas plains"—he wisecracked, not entirely accurately, in *Now and on Earth*—"and on the ground below me a huge rattlesnake listened raptly as I screamed and cursed and raved at him."

Just before leaving Jimmie published a moody poem in the May-June issue of *The Will-o'-the-Wisp,* a bimonthly verse magazine. "The Darker Drink" is the earliest known work to appear under his name and, however derivative and brittle, whispers portents of the novels to follow. "James Thompson"—if not yet Jim Thompson—officially kicked off his life as a writer:

THE DARKER DRINK

Whether it be with dawn,
Or when the blue moon
Broods on the hill,
Or in the twilight
When the day is gone,
Or in the midnight
Lone and dark and chill. . . .
Some where, some time
Each mouth must know
Death's kiss. . . . .
O waiting heart if Love
Were sure as this!

• • •

When Jimmie hitchhiked to West Texas in the spring of 1926, he was escaping, of course, to the arena of his father's most spectacular triumphs and failures; his first stop, Big Spring, had figured prominently in the ruin of Planters Petroleum. But he did not run away to the oil fields as a would-be operator, contractor, or promoter. He lived instead as a hobo, a gambler, and an itinerant laborer. Raymond Chandler also boasted an apprenticeship in the oil industry—but Chandler operated behind a desk, as an accountant and executive.

Thompson suggested in his New American Library author questionnaire that he fled Fort Worth for his health:

I wandered through West Texas and Far West Texas during several years of my youth; bumming and working at a variety of jobs while recovering from a nervous breakdown and purifying my badly-spotted lungs with the high dry air. 'Jungled-Up' along the Pecos River, I did my first serious writing at that time.

Even more than the Hotel Texas and its ready entrée into the Fort Worth underground, the oil fields constituted the formative work experience of his youth. He discovered his politics through conversations with the Wobblies he met at the drilling camps and hobo jungles. Moreover, oil field narratives galvanize four of his novels, *South of Heaven, Wild Town, The Transgressors,* and *Texas by the Tail,* and circulate incidentally through many others. As for Thompson's "first serious writing," seven of the surviving eleven prose sketches and stories he produced during the late 1920s and early 1930s have the West Texas oil fields as their setting: "Oil Field Vignettes" and "Thieves of the Field" (published in *Texas Monthly*); "Character at Iraan" and "Gentlemen of the Jungle" (the *Prairie Schooner*); "Bo'ger" and "Incident in God's Country" (the *Cornhusker Countryman*); and "The Picture" (unpublished).

Thompson bitingly encapsulated the late 1920s for *Roughneck:* "I had grown up in a world, in jobs, where the roughest justice prevailed, where discipline was maintained, more often than not, with physical violence." So decisive for his maturation as a man and writer, his roustabout life in the oil fields can be overromanticized—a temptation Thompson himself did not always resist. His standard chronology inflated the duration of his wanderings. *Bad Boy* claims three years, while an author's note for "Bo'ger" in the *Cornhusker Countryman* asserts that "five years of actual life in the oil fields of Texas are behind this story." The tally offered by his first published novel, *Now and on Earth,* "something more than two years," cleaves more closely to the actual twenty-eight months Jimmie freelanced along the razor's edge in West Texas. Similarly, his self-styled "roughneck" persona (the word simultaneously designates a "rowdy" and a "member of a crew that builds and repairs oil wells") tended to exaggerate his isolation from his family. The oil fields section of *Bad Boy* portrays twenty-one-year-old Jimmie as such a solitary animal that James, Birdie, and his sisters might as well be dead, for all the communication Thompson admits with them.

This roughneck, however, rarely lost touch with his parents during his stretch in the muddy boomtowns and oil patches. Not only did Birdie regularly hear from him in the form of letters and money (when working he would send as much as $150 a month to Nebraska); she also eventually joined him. A token of their unusual closeness, Jimmie may have been the only oil tramp in West Texas toiling alongside his mother. For much of the winter of 1927–28 they ran a restaurant from a shotgun shack near Four Sand. "Mama went out there just to be with Jimmie for a while," remembered Maxine. "Somehow they got a sort of diner going for the men."

In *Texas by the Tail,* the novel he told Tony Bill was his most autobiographical, Thompson accorded this restaurant to Houston oil magnate Jake Zearsdale:

> We ran the cookshack for the drilling crews. My mother and I did. . . . A drilling rig runs twenty-four hours a day, of course, which meant that we had to serve meals around the clock. I don't think my mother and I ever got to sleep more than two hours in a row.
>
> We did all the cooking on a four-burner oil-stove, and we lived and slept in the same room we cooked in.

He even drew his father back to the fray. Late in 1926 Jimmie collected his earnings from a salvage contract job and, summoning the old man, leased a drilling rig. Thompson & Son finally wildcatted together outside of Big Spring. *Texas by the Tail* dealt this memory card to Art Savage, also the recipient of Jimmie's little black book, for a withering double portrait:

> They were a middling-old man and his son. The father wore the unmistakable stamp of defeat, a man who had drilled one dry hole too many. The kid looked mean and snotty and very sick, and he was all three and then some.
>
> Into the rig and the job it had to do, the old man had sunk his home, his furniture, his insurance policies; every nickel he could beg and borrow. That still left a hell of a hump to get over, for an outfit and a job like this, so the kid had kicked in for it. The kid was a loner, he'd been one almost since the time he was old enough to walk. Some things had begun to happen to him about then that shouldn't happen to kids, and maybe they could have been avoided and maybe they couldn't have. But it was all the same to him. He didn't ask for excuses, he didn't give any. As far as he was concerned, the world was a shitpot with a barbed-wire handle and the further he could kick it the better he liked it. As far as he was concerned, he had plenty owing to him. And he was hell on wheels at collecting.
>
> He was now nineteen years old. He was suffering from tuberculosis, bleeding ulcers, and chronic alcoholism. . . .
>
> Wildcats are always Jonahs. You're in unexplored territory, and you never know what you're going to get into until you've already got into it and it's too damned late. This particular wildcatter had enough hard luck for a hundred wells.
>
> The boiler blew up. The rig caught on fire. The mast snapped.

The tools were lost in the hole a dozen times. The drill cable bucked and whipped, cleanly slicing off a tooldresser's head.

The kid announced that he had gone his limit; he had nothing left but his ass and his pants and they both had holes in them. . . .

Mainly Jimmie traveled solo, a transient and drifter. He became a habitué of the hobo jungles at the edges of the teeming ragtowns and company camps that attended the sudden discovery of petroleum. For his prefatory note to "Gentlemen of the Jungle," his 1931 sketch of three oil tramps, Thompson defined the jungle as "largely a state of mind; to the bum it is a home, temporarily—a home because he has become accustomed to the surroundings, which for him fill the need of rest and nourishment." His necessities attended to, the hobo exudes a skeptical, leathery lovelessness: "He does not find love there, it is true, because the jungle is strictly masculine; but in spite of the Guest sagas and the epigrams to the contrary it has never been proved, conclusively, that love made the home; no one, to my knowledge, has ever banished the javelin-pitching elf to see whether or not his absence made any serious alteration in the atmosphere." And released from conventional desires, the hobo reposes and dreams: "The jungle from which the characters of this group were drawn is Texan. The ground swoops down to the river, there, just outside of town; and the wind, blowing constantly, lays the grass low against the sun. Here, one may lie and reach out to grab some weatherstained piece of paper that blows past him, and read and think, then let the paper blow on again; nothing to worry about—no next book-of-the-month to fret over."

Hobohemia was a complex and highly politicized social institution with its own unwritten system of laws, etiquette, mores, and division of labor. Although "tramp" and "bum" were sanctioned synonyms, "hobo" specifically designated a wandering laborer (the word probably derives from "hoe boy," a seasonal farm worker). A catalyst for hobo culture and traditions, the jungles operated as nomadic democracies, welcoming all arrivals regardless of race, nationality, or personal past. As migrant workers, the Texas hoboes affiliated with the revolutionary Industrial Workers of the World. IWW publicity touted the itinerant bindle stiffs as "the guerrillas of the revolution" and remarked that the "nomadic worker of the West embodies the very spirit of the IWW. His cheerful cynicism, his frank and outspoken contempt for most of the conventions of bourgeois society, including the more stringent conventions which masquerade under the name of morality, make him an admirable exemplar of the iconoclastic doctrine of revolutionary unionism." The more stable jungles sometimes excluded any oil tramp not carrying a red IWW membership card.

Jimmie signed on with the Wobblies shortly after his arrival in West

Texas. The celebrated "shock troops of labor," the IWW concluded their brief *Preamble* with a blunt call for militant action: "It is the historic mission of the working class to do away with capitalism. The army of production must be organized, not only for the every-day struggle with the capitalists, but also to carry on production when capitalism shall have been overthrown. By organizing industrially we are forming the structure of the new society within the shell of the old."

Thompson's late screenplay about the oil fields of the 1920s, *Bo,* featured a heroic Wobbly montage. While Earl Robinson's ballad "I Dreamt I Saw Joe Hill Last Night" played in the background, the camera would dissolve to:

> About a dozen STILL bust shots of hoboes and their leaders, Joe Hill, Bill Haywood, etc. Men in caps, felt hats, perhaps an occasional stocking cap or derby. One by one, we bring them out of a seeming void, and HOLD CLOSE in front of the camera. The 'boes— all with the level-eyed, firm-jawed stamp of their breed. (Shots should be timed to end coincidentally with below.)
>
> VOICE (over)
> (with above)
> In those days, there were giants in the land . . . Unassuming, unrecognized, unhonored . . . Fighting in dubious battle for a world they would never see. . . .

Ostensibly in West Texas to repair his health, "Slim"—as Jimmie was tagged by his hobo brothers—seems to have mounted a total assault on his physical and mental well-being. Starting with a brief incarceration in the resort town of Mineral Wells, he was pinched frequently for drunkenness and vagrancy, and at least once for assault. Run-ins with the capricious and often brutish Texas law were hardly accidental as Jimmie hankered after the fierce "white lightning" and "ginger jake" favored by the fieldworkers. When hard-pressed, he even strained canned heat.

Home-brewed white lightning, the infamous corn whiskey distillate, stunned, stupefied, and occasionally blinded its serious consumers. The more lethal and addictive jake, a peppery Jamaica ginger concoction sold as medicine in drugstores, ravaged the nervous system, inducing a crippling disorder known as jake leg. As a Texas roughneck recalled, "I've seen a lot of 'em that had jake leg. You can't walk straight, and you have to have crutches and walking canes, and then whenever you step, why, your leg goes to trembling. Your feet goes to trembling. And they're mighty near jerked out from under you." Jake leg was immortalized in "Jake Walk Blues," a 1930 song by the Allen Brothers.

Thompson stocked his oil field novels with grisly testimonials to his intoxication and the violent hallucinations that twisted the Texas prairie into a lower circle of hell. "I did not know when it was safe," he wrote, "to walk through the things in front of me and when it was not. Sometimes, most times, my feet would melt through their bodies." Yet his 1930 short story "Character at Iraan" spiked perhaps his most fearsome drinking phantasmagoria.

Arriving in the tiny far West Texas town of Iraan, Slim and two pipeline 'boes he calls Strawlegs Martin and Ted McKelvie purchase a quart of jake and rent a room. A few gulps of the "choking greenish liquid" pleasantly enhance the vista: "I looked at the road and it did not bother me as it had before. It looked hazy and unreal." A few more, and Slim can barely manage the short walk to a diner for breakfast:

> My legs moved as separate units on the way back to the Greek's. I stepped on Martin's feet a couple of times before he caught my elbow. I laughed then. This was something like life. Where else was there anything like the oil towns. I asked Martin, and he told me.
>
> The blood boiled in my cheeks and my head kept forcing itself higher and higher. I told Martin about all that I was going to eat, and asked him what he was going to have. He didn't answer me but asked how old I was.
>
> "Twenty-one in five more days," I said.

Back in their room, Slim's premature bout with jake leg gives way to wretched vomiting ("my head drooped forward and I was the sickest human in West Texas"). While his companions watch in horror, Slim slips into an alcoholic coma. Comatose yet eerily aware, he hears Martin pronounce him gone:

> McKelvie and Strawlegs got me back on the bed after a while. There was the feeling that a belt was being tightened on my chest. Ted kept bathing my head in cold water and that seemed to make my chest worse.
>
> Martin asked me if I couldn't eat some soup or something. Then Ted asked me. I didn't answer either although I heard them perfectly. I just lay there and looked at them. Ted leaned over me and looked into my eyes. I looked back into his at the little pictures in the pupils. Then Ted passed his hand back and forth in front of my face. It came very close, so close that I could see a faint little cross in his hand joining the life- and the heart-line.

I wished I could have seen how Martin was taking all this hocus-pocus, but he had stepped out of my view, and the desire was not strong enough to move the eye-nerve. And while I wondered I heard Martin scream.

"He's dead! Oh, Christ—he's dead!"

When Slim revives in an impromptu pipeline hospital "two weeks from the day" later, he finds a note from Martin urging home to "go on home."

• • •

Strawlegs Martin—or his real-life model, Harry Kirby "Haywire" McClintock—would repeat his avuncular advice a few more times before Jimmie finally listened and returned to Fort Worth. Despite the pounding to body and soul, for two-plus years he scoured the oil fields for any available work, however lowly or hazardous. On the first leg of his odyssey Jimmie joined a team of salvage contractors near Big Spring. Soon to be a popular Depression sideline, salvage involved the purchase of bankrupt or abandoned oil derricks and dismantling them for lumber and tools. Tearing down a hundred-foot-high tower involved considerable ingenuity and peril. Since razing the derrick necessarily meant disassembling the crossbeams that held it erect, for the salvage gang the situation was rather like the old adage about sawing off the limb you are standing on. Mishaps proliferated, especially for inexperienced hands like Jimmie. "My survival," he noted, "can only be credited to a miracle."

While in Big Spring, Thompson linked up with some Oklahoma-based wildcatters and found a position as "shooter" in a drilling crew. Probably the most reckless of all his oil field exploits, the shooter sank a small torpedo loaded with nitroglycerin into the hole of an oil well and detonated it. Jimmie also took charge of a "soup wagon," the horse-drawn cart that conveyed nitroglycerin to a drilling site over the rough, makeshift "roads."

Big Spring contained other explosive materials. It was there, Thompson recounted in *Bad Boy,* that he ran up against the sinister deputy sheriff whom he later "recreated" as Lou Ford, "the sardonic, likable murderer of my fourth novel, *The Killer Inside Me.*" Coming to collect Jimmie's fine for disturbing the peace, the grinning deputy discharged his own torpedoes of laconic menace:

> He was a good-looking guy. His hair was coal-black beneath his pushed-back Stetson, and his black intelligent eyes were set wide apart in a tanned, fine-featured face. He grinned at me as I dropped down in front of him on the derrick floor.
>
> "Now, that wasn't very smart," he said. "And that's—"

"And that's a fact," I snapped. "All right, let's get going."

He went on grinning at me. In fact, his grin broadened a little. But it was fixed, humorless, and a veil seemed to drop over his eyes.

"What makes you so sure," he said, softly, "you're going anywhere?"

"Well, I—" I gulped. "I—I—"

"Awful lonesome out here, ain't it? Ain't another soul for miles around but you and me."

"L-look," I said. "I'm—I wasn't trying to—"

"Lived here all my life," he went on, softly. "Everyone knows me. No one knows you. And we're all alone. What do you make o' that, a smart fella like you? You've been around. You're full of piss and high-spirits. What do you think an ol' stupid country boy might do in a case like this?"

He stared at me, steadily, the grin baring his teeth. I stood paralyzed and wordless, a great cold lump forming in my stomach. The wind whined and moaned through the derrick. He spoke again, as though in answer to a point I had raised.

"Don't need one," he said. "Ain't nothin' you can do with a gun that you can't do a better way. Don't see nothin' around here I'd need a gun for."

He shifted his feet slightly. The muscles in his shoulders bunched. He took a pair of black kid gloves from his pocket, and drew them on, slowly. He smacked his fist into the palm of his other hand.

"I'll tell you something," he said. "Tell you a couple of things. There ain't no way of telling what a man is by looking at him. There ain't no way of knowing what he'll do if he has the chance. You think maybe you can remember that?"

I couldn't speak, but I managed a nod. His grin and his eyes went back to normal.

"Look kind of peaked," he said. "Why'n't you have somethin' to eat an' drink before we leave?"

Although Thompson only encountered him on two brief occasions, this anonymous Big Spring deputy sheriff emerged as the most vividly rendered presence in *Bad Boy* and *Roughneck*. His personality, carriage, and especially his voice leap from the prose with a conspicuous clarity that the author was unable to accord his own mother and father, his wife and children, his Burwell relations and his Fort Worth cronies—and perhaps suspiciously so. Thompson of course wrote the passage *after* he already had nailed Lou Ford to the page for *The Killer Inside Me*. The singular intensity and precision of the exchange may involve another form of retrospective literary camouflage: Thompson's wish to disguise how much of his sheriff father—and, as the self-portrait in *A Penny in the Dust* suggests, also of himself—he poured into Ford.

Surely the spooky Big Spring lawman, whoever he was, contributed a key element to the volatile compound that ultimately stabilized as Lou Ford. Even after *The Killer Inside Me,* Thompson would return to him again and again—for *Wild Town, The Transgressors,* and *South of Heaven.* As Thompson concluded his *Bad Boy* vignette, "I never saw that deputy again, but I couldn't get him out of my mind."

• • •

In 1927 Jimmie began to work the pipeline.

That year saw massive pipeline construction all through the American Southwest. By December, four new major trunk lines in West Texas alone transported the ever-increasing yield of oil and gas to refineries and shipping points on the Gulf Coast. Jimmie appears to have participated in the building of at least three pipeline projects: the Humble Pipe Line Company line from Reagan County to Ingleside; the Gulf Pipe Line Company line from the Church and Fields area through Midland to Ranger; and the Texas Company line to Port Arthur.

Pipeline cats owned the rep of being less educated than other oil field laborers. Poorly paid (Jimmie said that he earned "four-fifty a day less a dollar for 'slop and flop' ") and with no opportunities for advancement, anyone with a bendable back and a tolerance for physical pain could be a pipeliner. In *South of Heaven* Thompson catalogued his pipeline brothers with pungent humor: "jailbirds, mission stiffs, hoboes—and hardly a man-jack among 'em with more than an empty gut and the raggedy-ass clothes he wore."

For some of his pipeline year Jimmie served as a night watchman near Iraan. This permitted him to carry a gun and operate as a kind of unofficial deputy sheriff, guarding costly truckloads of pipe from the pirates and con men he chronicled for his short story "Thieves of the Field." But the chief task of the night watchman was to service the generators and other machinery with oil, gas, and water.

The daily grind out on the line proved more grueling. Pipeliners in the 1920s cleared the right of way through the motley West Texas terrain, dug the ditches, wrapped the pipe, screwed it together, and refilled the ditch, all by hand. Jimmie toiled for a time with the "dope gang," the men who encased the pipe inside a protective cotton coating and then sealed it with hot, smelly gobs of liquid asphalt. A doper, it was said, could be identified by his wracking cough and the strips of burned skin that sometimes hung from his face and neck.

Jimmie also worked as a "powder monkey." Running ahead of the assembly crew he helped cut a pathway to the gulf with a rock drill and dynamite. This hairy business, "blasting a trail through a world where no man had gone before," would be the burden of *South of Heaven:* "Dyna was a touchy girl, but she was absolutely predictable. You knew how she had to be treated, and as long as you treated her exactly that way you got along fine. But never slight her, or it'd be the last time you did. Never let your mind wander when she demanded your attention."

A meditative set piece late in *South of Heaven* pondered the awesome scale of the pipeline, invoking the pandemonium and cruel human toll:

> Sometimes when the fire was in the hole, and I was taking distance from the blast, I'd look back down the line behind me. And it seemed as long as I looked I could never look enough. There was so much to see, so much that would never be seen again. *Paso por aqui*—passed by here. And then no more.
>
> Men and machines, stretching endlessly into the distance. Men and machines, only a thin almost invisible rivulet, at first, a tiny thing lost in the horizon. It seemed to come up out of the ground like a puny spring, back there at the start; a near-nothingness amidst nothing. And then slowly it grew larger, the men and machines grew larger, and the sound of them grew greater; the rivulet became a river, and its thunderous surging shook the earth.
>
> The long thin line of burnt-black men, their shovels glinting as they caught the sun. . . .
>
> The yellow-painted generators, peering down into the ditch, periodically breaking into fits of chugging and coughing as though startled by their surroundings. . . .
>
> The mammoth ditchers rocking to and fro, grunting and quavering like fat old ladies. . . .
>
> The jackhammers jouncing and jigging as they pounded the hard rock. . . .
>
> The razzle-dazzle of sparks raining upward where the welder's torches pencilled fire against the pipe. . . .
>
> > *Throw out the lifeline,*
> > *Here comes the pipeline.*
> > *Somebody's going to drag up!*
>
> A lot of 'em would drag up, I reckoned. Paid off with money or the ditch for a grave. *Paso por aqui*—and then no more.
>
> But it was something to see, something to remember. The men and the machines—dying, smashing up, wearing out—but always

moving forward. Creeping through a wild and lonely world toward Port Arthur on the Gulf.

Throw out the lifeline, indeed. The powder monkey, on one occasion, found himself entombed by a freakish cave-in—more than three hours, Jimmie wrote his family, under the exploded dirt, rock, and rubble before rescuers could dig him out. Thompson subsequently told friends that the oil fields left him with a deep-seated hatred of insects, and a lifelong fear of being buried alive.

• • •

While jungling up along the pipeline in the late 1920s Jimmie made two important friendships.

Between oil field jobs he apprenticed to Whitey Ford, an itinerant entertainer and gambler. Ford was one of a pair of musicians who float behind the composite character in *South of Heaven* he called Four Trey Whitey—whose name, like many of Thompson's characters, is a close approximation of Ford's actual name. ("Four Trey" is crapshooter slang for a four-three roll of the dice.)

Under his comic stage handle the "Duke of Paducah," Ford eventually evolved into a featured performer at the Grand Ole Opry. A gifted musician and songwriter who toured with Otto Gray's Oklahoma Cowboys as well as with his own Dixie Land outfit, he earned his greatest renown as a hillbilly vaudevillian. Attired in a too-tight bright green suit with large brass buttons, red bow tie, high-button shoes, and tiny bowler hat, the ruddy-faced, husky comedian would spray his audience with rapid-fire country-bumpkin patter. "I'm going back to the wagon, boys, these shoes are killin' me" became Ford's famous signature exit line.

All through the 1920s Whitey Ford traveled the oil boomtown circuit from Arkansas to California, making sideline forays through the camps and jungles between his official stints with the Dixie Land Jazz Band or Otto Gray. Thompson and Ford apparently first met at a makeshift gambling house near Big Spring. Jimmie was marking time there as a "sweater," a lowly, usually dipsomaniac hanger-on who fetched drinks and sandwiches for the gamblers in exchange for chips and the right to sleep on the dice tables. Soon they began to range the pipeline together in Ford's tumbledown Model T, operating payday games of bones, blackjack, klondike, and the random short con in the camps and jungles of West Texas. Ford bankrolled the floating casino, while Jimmie took a small cut of the profit for his troubles. For the first time since his debut at the Fort Worth Gayety Theatre Jimmie ascended the stage, functioning as straight man for his older partner's humorous sketches and musical burlesques.

In an interview with John W. Rumble for the Country Music Foundation

Harry Kirby McClintock ("Haywire")
and his wife, Bessie, 1929 (Courtesy
of Henry Young)

Oral History Project, Ford reminisced about the oil fields and the violent
Texas boomtowns he and Jimmie rambled and gambled through, highlight-
ing the uproarious and almost self-consciously mythic milieu:

> A lot of guys there in Smackover had played over in Border,
> and they said, "If you think *this* is rough, you oughta go over there."
> They told a story, just a story, about Border, Texas. They said that
> they'd had a big riot and fights in the street and everything.
> So they sent for the Texas Rangers. A guy in a truck with a horse in
> the truck showed up, went up to what was called the deputy sheriff
> or whatever he was. He unloaded his horse and saddled him up.
> He went in and reported and he said, "You the deputy sheriff?"
> "Yeah." (This is the story, now.) "Well, I'm the Texas Ranger that
> was sent here to handle this riot." "Where are your men?" "Just one
> Texas Ranger's all you need. One riot, one Texas Ranger." We al-

ways laughed at that story, but that wasn't true. They had all kinds
of trouble over there.

Although Thompson assigned Whitey Ford's surname (and some of his
cornball routines) to his most infamous literary character, Deputy Sheriff
Lou Ford, another musician he befriended in West Texas—and the other
half of Four Trey Whitey—wielded significantly greater impact on his life.
Harry McClintock (whose nickname, "Haywire," Thompson punningly
transformed into "Strawlegs" for *Bad Boy* and "Character at Iraan") was the
union organizer who inducted Jimmie into the Wobblies and tagged him
with his hobo moniker, "Slim." Probably the supreme influence on Thompson's political thinking, McClintock also proved a catalyst in his decision to
quit the oil fields and become a writer of prose. Jimmie and Haywire Mac
would remain close through the late 1940s.

At the time of their meeting, McClintock worked as a San Francisco–
based tramp entertainer, or "busker." An intimate of the legendary Joe Hill
(he was present when Hill brought "The Preacher and the Slave" into the
IWW hall at Portland, Oregon), Mac played an E-flat baritone horn for the
first Wobbly street band. He co-edited *The Little Red Songbook,* which became the official union primer. The preeminent figure in the American folk
song of protest between Hill and Woody Guthrie, McClintock claimed authorship of at least two classics: "The Big Rock Candy Mountain," a children's "nonsense" favorite that actually encodes a homosexual tramp
serenade, and "Hallelujah, I'm a Bum," a spoof of an old gospel hymn that
served as the unofficial IWW anthem.

On his periodic sweeps through the West Texas Wobbly strongholds
the charismatic busker adopted Jimmie as one of his young protégés. They
tramped, organized, and odd-jobbed through Big Spring, Midland, Four
Sand, Chalk, and Borger. Musically, Mac instilled in him a fondness for folk
and country ballads that never departed him. Politically, he arranged for
Jimmie's first red union card, and introduced him to the writings of Eugene
Debs, Big Bill Haywood, and, above all, Karl Marx.

Thompson later told his Oklahoma City friend Gordon Friesen that
reading Marx in the oil fields was "the turning point in his life," his "first
real education," and that "Marx had given him the words to understand his
life." Friesen believes that during this conversation, which took place in
1938, "Jim was talking about the autobiographical novels he was trying to
write, not just his politics at that time." Another friend, French *cinéaste*
Pierre Rissient, notes that as late as the 1960s Thompson still correlated
his fiction to his early study of Marx:

> When one would ask him what were the things that, in his
> opinion, he broached in his novels, he would say that all writers

have but one theme, in all literature there is but one theme which is, moreover, the theme of *Don Quixote,* and which is that things are not what they seem. He would always come back to this phrase. He could not formulate anything else but this; he would return to it unceasingly. What followed, generally, was that he would say that he had begun to understand the world when he read Karl Marx. His interpretation of *Don Quixote* and of all literature came to him, then, from his reading of Marx.

If Thompson discovered in Marx "the words to understand" his own anger and alienation, his becoming a Marxist also thrust a fist into the face of his capitalist father's life and career. Thompson would not fully develop the literary implications of his Marxism until almost ten years after McClintock led him to *The Manifesto of the Communist Party* and *Capital.* But "Incident in God's Country," a 1931 pipeline story, soon displayed his Wobbly sympathies.

The most overtly political of all his oil field writing, "Incident" bristles with the casual brutalities of hobo subsistence. As a sick, hungry Slim awakens in a jungle by the Pecos River, he coldly observes his battered companions: Tin-Pan, whose eye has been "rotted by canned-heat," and Big Torpy, who "had been an agitator during the war, at Devils River. At the hands of the patriots there he had received cause for permanent exemption from military duty—a great hot R on either foot."

Slim saunters into town to panhandle some change:

I went down to the pool hall and bummed along the line of sweaters, but most of them were as broke as I and the hour was early so I got nothing. Too, some bum had been there ahead of me.

There was nothing to the town besides the pool hall, two cot houses, and two cafes. The few men working were drillers and tool-dressers with an occasional roustabout. There were no great bands of workers to pander upon as there were in other fields, altho it was the largest producing field in the world. A few shallow wells drilled here occasionally with a minimum amount of labor kept up the so-called overproduction indefinitely.

Yet I was not greatly interested in the trusts that morning, nor would I have been greatly disturbed by some independent operator committing hari kari upon the doorstep of the nearest Standard Oil official. The thought that I wish to convey is, any panhandling that was done had to be done either early in the morning or at night, for during the day the town was empty.

When news comes of hirings on the pipeline, Slim joins the "forty odd" oil tramps for the long trip to camp. There armed thugs—"three men I recognized as professional gunmen and strikebreakers. . . . Each of these was levelling at us a sawed-off shotgun"—reinforce the strident anti-union posturing of the field boss:

> "I want to be square with you men," he said, "but I'll do it in my own way. I won't have a bunch of wobblies and bums telling me how. You've been used to high wages in this country. I won't pay high wages. This job will pay thirty cents an hour, with one dollar and a half out for board."
> "That only leaves us a dollar and twenty cents clear!"
> "No. This is a ten hour job. You can clear a dollar and a half per day on it!"
> "Straight time?"
> "No. No money when you can't work."
> "You can't get white men to work for that."
> "All right then; I'll get Mexicans."
> We cursed him. "Yah! you greaser-loving scoundrel!"
> He only smiled as a man can afford to smile who has the whip hand and knows it. . . .

In the near riot that follows, Tin-Pan is struck in the face with a rifle butt. As Slim comments, "From the socket where his rotted eye had been something leaped forth and fell sickeningly in the mud. His face, as he turned, looked surprised thru an avalanche of blood. Then, like a man fresh in hell, he began to scream. . . ."

Thompson punctuated this grim business with quotations from "Hallelujah, I'm a Bum," advancing the chorus as an at once inspirational and mocking gloss:

> *Hallelujah! (I roared)*
> *I'm a bum!*
> *Hallelujah!*
> *Bum again!*
> *Hallelujah! Give us a handout*
> *To revive us again.*

• • •

The homage to McClintock in "Incident in God's Country" marked a debt honorably repaid. For it was Haywire Mac who directed Thompson back to his real work. The Wobbly busker provided his greatest service to Jimmie when he finally persuaded him to leave the oil fields and get on with his life and education. Thompson told Mel Shestack, a University of Southern California student whom he introduced to the singer in the late 1940s, that "if it weren't for Mac I might still be a bum today."

South of Heaven framed the situation of Tommy Burwell in much the same terms. During this bittersweet coming-of-age novel, Burwell is haunted by the fear that he will always be a vagrant and a drunkard: "I took a long look at myself, trudging along in the dust, with my hat brim turned up back and front and my belly burning with before-breakfast booze. And the picture wasn't a nice one at all. There was nothing romantic or dashing about it. I was a drifter, a day laborer, a tinhorn gambler—a man wasting his life in a wasteland. That's what I was now. That's what I'd be in another twenty-one years if I lived that long, unless I started changing my ways fast."

But for all Burwell's self-knowledge, only the kindly nagging of Four Trey Whitey puts him back on track. After hearing him recite from his poetry—including "A Road and a Memory," Thompson's *Prairie Schooner* poem about his Burwell schooldays—Four Trey scowls: "What kind of life is this for a kid as bright as you are? Why do you go on wasting your time, year after year? Do you think you're going to stay young forever? If you do, take a look at me."

Thompson's "first serious writing," as he termed it for the New American Library author questionnaire, emerged through McClintock's example and guidance. Shortly before Jimmie departed West Texas in 1928, he drafted "Oil Field Vignettes" and mailed it off to Peter Molyneaux, a journalist he knew from his internship at *Western World.* Now editor of *Texas Monthly,* Molyneaux accepted the piece and published it early the next year. As Thompson remarked in *Now and on Earth:*

> One evening while I was killing time in the library, I picked up a copy of the *Texas Monthly.* And there on the title page was a line *"Oil Field Vignettes . . .* By James Dillon." I had written that story almost a year before, one bitter night down on the Pecos—written it by lantern-light with the sleet beating down against the nickel tablet and my hands swathed in mittens. And I had sent it to town with the provision truck and promptly forgotten about it.

The jungle setting here is significant. "Oil Field Vignettes," like much of the prose Thompson produced in the late 1920s and early 1930s, belongs to the hobo literature genre. Harry McClintock not only directed him to Marx; he also placed before him the burgeoning tradition of tramp ballads, folklore, stories, and autobiographies, some of which, such as Jack London's *The Road,* Jimmie already had read with his uncle Bob Wicks. Although conventionally associated with the Depression because so many 1930s writers first etched their mark with fictionalized accounts of their days riding the rails—Edward Anderson, Nelson Algren, even Louis L'Amour—the hobo was an established literary fixture by the time "Oil Field Vignettes" appeared in *Texas Monthly.* Tramp autobiographies formed a persistent subgenre: W. H. Davies's *Autobiography of a Super-Tramp* (1908), Vachel Lindsay's *A Handy Guide for Beggars* (1916), and Jim Tully's *Beggars of Life* (1924). George Milburn edited *The Hobo's Hornbook,* an encyclopedic miscellany of tramp writing and lore, in 1930. Nels Anderson published his pioneering study, *The Hobo,* as far back as 1923. Rootless, disdainful of authority, and alienated from the paradigms of success and failure, the vagabond adventurer established a code of American toughness that predates Hemingway and Hammett. The sardonically self-sufficient hobo lies behind the more aggressive outcasts of subsequent proletarian, tough-guy, and crime fiction.

For "Oil Field Vignettes" Thompson strung together a trio of oil tramp yarns. Subtitled "Thumbnail Biographies of Three Picturesque Characters of the Drilling Fraternity," the discrete episodes focused some incisive close-ups: Jake Fanner, who "simply could not bear to say an unnecessary word"; Big Hole Ben, who "drew the handle by refusing to drill anything smaller than a ten-inch hole"; and Baldy Sealbridge, whose wife "had also married a baker's dozen of other servicemen and had drawn thirty dollars a month from each during the war." Darkly humorous, "Vignettes" suffered from an irritatingly antique tone as Thompson stretched to sound more seasoned—and simply *older*—than he really was. "I met Baldy Sealbridge right after the war; a little runt, he was. . . ."

The cultural terrain that "Oil Field Vignettes" staked out involved folklore more than memoir or fiction. The stylized portraits might have run in *Folk-Say,* the annual anthology of folk songs, old-timers' reminiscences, and local color sketches and poems that Ben Botkin was then assembling for the University of Oklahoma Press. Thompson, who would collect folklore for Botkin during the late 1930s, did not so much memorialize his own oil field adventures in "Vignettes" as he did spin variations on contemporary Texas legends. "Big Hole Ben," for example, belonged to the popular "Big Hole Bill" family of tall tales. As Mody C. Boatright summarized for his book, *Folklore of the Oil Industry,* "Big Hole Bill was a cable-tool driller who boasted that he was a big-hole man. The bigger the better, and he refused to work on any less than ten inches in diameter. When it came time to reduce the hole below this size, he would quit. He would leave little holes to little men. This was his boast, but he did not fool his peers. Every driller knows that the big part, that is the beginning of a well, is easier drilling than the deep part."

•   •   •

Thompson, as suggested earlier, often romanticized his oil field experiences for his books. But even more than his flirtation with the underworld at the Hotel Texas, the danger, deprivation, and strain of his hobo years beg the question of why Jimmie so consistently sought out such threatening circumstances.

As a "key to his behavior" his sister Maxine underscored what she described as "Jimmie's tendency to throw himself into jobs and situations that were against his nature. That was something he always did, back then and later." Although Thompson's "nature" perhaps embraced more than his family was disposed to admit, Maxine advanced a flexible interpretation that stipulated courage, self-destruction, and a writer's search for material in complementary doses:

> Money really doesn't explain the depressing and frightening jobs he took on. There were so many times he did things he didn't have to do. Jimmie was a deeply gentle man, more sensitive than anyone I have ever known, but also determined to do things a lot of people would hold back from, saying, "I want to be comfortable." He was always plunging into circumstances that emotionally he wasn't equipped for, jobs that required someone who was more of an easygoing, extrovert type, and jobs that put a terrible strain on him physically, though he was a big man. I don't think that many men would have tried to endure those hardships, and it often seemed unnecessary to us. He did those things looking for stories as well as for a living.
>
> When he became a hobo I was horrified. But Jimmie wanted to do it just to see what it was like. He constantly wanted to take up something new, wanted to learn what was going on, even when it went against his basic nature.

In this Thompson resembled Jean Genet, who once said that everything he wrote was *"contre moi-même."*

•   •   •

Jimmie reappeared in Fort Worth late in the fall of 1928—on Thanksgiving Day, he announced in *Now and on Earth* with his melodramatic eye for dates. Much in the Thompson household had changed during his absence.

Or, rather, households. Jimmie's parents, who for many years had been leading separate lives, now maintained separate residences. After lodging with the Myerses in Burwell, and then cooking alongside Jimmie at Four Sand, Birdie settled herself and Freddie into an apartment in Oklahoma City. His father meanwhile moved to a tiny rental at 329 Blevins Avenue, closer to downtown Fort Worth. Claiming "oil leases" as his occupation, he essentially lived off the proceeds from the sale of the Dallas Pike house. As further evidence of Birdie's increasing partiality to her son, she rejoined her husband only upon Jimmie's return. And pronto. By Christmas, Birdie and Freddie gravitated to Blevins Avenue.

Maxine too had attempted a fresh start as the bride of Russell Boomer. The Thompsons and the Boomers were old familiars from turn-of-the-century Nebraska education circles. Russell was the son of George Boomer, then a professor at the University of Nebraska but, many years earlier, a rural high school principal and superintendent of schools. When, in 1927, Maxine wished to continue her violin studies in Lincoln, the Thompsons wrote the Boomers asking if she might board with them. Within a year she and Russell married and struck out on their own in Fort Worth, where he managed a grocery store in the Piggly Wiggly chain.

Fired up by Harry McClintock's confidence in his prose and with the imprimatur of *Texas Monthly,* Jimmie departed West Texas carrying what Freddie recalled as "all these fat notebooks of his work," determined to become a writer. However, his own desires once more vied with the need to support his family. Jimmie tarried as a clerk in Russell Boomer's Piggly Wiggly. Then, after Maxine and her husband drifted back to Lincoln, he reconnected with the Hotel Texas. "Soon Jimmie was up to all his old stunts," chastised Freddie, "bootlegging, call girls, you name it."

But Freddie was thrilled to have her brother on the scene. Although she worried over his morals, and laughed at the mustache he flaunted like a hobo souvenir, "Jimmie could do no wrong as far as I was concerned then." She turned to him for help with her schoolwork, and he read aloud from his oil field stories, and passed on his new enthusiasm for music.

One evening on a family outing to a local fair Jimmie even talked Freddie into entering the talent show. Backed by a string band the Young Thompsons belted out a few of the songs Haywire Mac taught him, including "Frankie and Johnny," the classic American folk tune (originally "Frankie and Albert") of adultery and murder:

> Frankie and Johnny were lovers,
> O lordy how could they love,
> Swore to be true to each other,
> True as the stars above;
> He was her man, but he done her wrong, so wrong.

> Johnny saw Frankie a comin',
> Down the backstairs he did scoot;
> Frankie had the little gun out,
> Let him have it rooty-de-toot;
> For he was her man, but she shot him down.

"Jimmie was a little high," remembered Freddie, "otherwise I'm sure we wouldn't have done that, since neither of us could really sing. We hadn't told Mama. . . . She was pretty shocked when she heard our voices, and that wild song coming from the stage. Mama came running over to get us off." Jimmie maintained a lifelong fascination with the dark edges of folk and country-and-western, from Hank Williams, Woody Guthrie, and Leadbelly to Webb Pierce and the Louvin Brothers.

• • •

Thompson concluded *Bad Boy* with the story of how he left Fort Worth in 1929 and went to college. Persuaded by "Allie Ivers" to expand his bootlegging from his customary pint-at-a-time transactions to a full-tilt racket, Jimmie started to order upward of ten cases of whiskey a week from "Al's boys," Capone's local mob. Soon he hit upon a madcap scheme to pay for college by selling twenty cases during a convention and skipping town with the "four or five thousand" dollar haul. Only, of course, federal Prohibition agents seized his stash at the Hotel Texas, forcing Jimmie to flee Fort Worth with his mother and sister—"Al's boys" and the government in hot pursuit.

A hair-raising ending, a bracing parable, and, as like as not, the only fitting denouement for the "Bad Boy" turned writer manqué Thompson was carving into his personal mythology. . . . But the episode never took place, evidently by Thompson's own admission. "When I read that story in *Bad Boy* about the federal agents taking his whiskey and the family being run out of Texas," Freddie noted, "I said to him, 'You know that didn't happen, Jimmie, I was there.' He answered, 'You know, and I know,' and just sort of chuckled."

Jimmie reached college by a less sensational, though probably more interesting route. Shortly after the February publication of "Oil Field Vignettes," he descended upon *Texas Monthly*'s offices in the Texas National Bank Building with more oil field sketches. After reading and accepting "Thieves of the Field," editor Peter Molyneaux apparently urged him to continue his education. When Jimmie replied that he hadn't been able to finish high school, Molyneaux told him about a program at the University of Nebraska that accepted promising students who lacked the standard credentials for college. Molyneaux, who carried a reputation for assisting young writers, offered to provide Jimmie with a letter of introduction to his old friend Robert Crawford, a professor of agricultural journalism.

Other sirens summoned him to Lincoln. Maxine, for one, lived there with Russell. And at Maxine's instigation he had lately been corresponding and exchanging poems with Russell's sister, Lucille, a musician in her all-girl traveling orchestra, the Joybelles. On the strength of these poems Professor Boomer tagged him, not entirely without irony, the "next Walt Whitman," and promised to do what he could to help.

In September Jimmie loaded his books and clothes into his car and, after reluctantly depositing Birdie and Freddie at Burwell, set about registering in the University of Nebraska.

•　•　•

The writing Thompson published in 1929 shows him experimenting with his name: for each of the three times he appeared in print he choose a different byline. '

The March-April issue of *The Will-o'-the-Wisp* featured a new poem, "Winter Trees." More skillfully rhymed than "The Darker Drink," this displayed the author's touch principally in the slyly lethal final line:

WINTER TREES

The crystal scissors of the frost
Have cut the leaves, in wood and field,
From summer trees. Beauty long lost
To admiring eyes is now revealed.

By noon or starlight brightly glow
Enamelled leaves in quaint design
Against pale banks of drifted snow,—
Laurel and holly, yopin, pine.

No longer can the eye ignore
Such lusty, patient dignity,
When birch, ash, poplar, sycamore
Seem smitten with a leprosy.

This poem was signed, with conventional formality, "James Thompson."

"Thieves of the Field," published in June, employed the same structure as "Oil Field Vignettes"—three discontinuous "Anecdotes of the Gentry Who 'Borrow' Pipe in the Oil Fields of Texas"—and a similarly corny style: "Down in East Texas there was a farmer who got the oil bug." Although in no sense a crime story, this was Thompson's earliest attempt to write about criminals. While his oil field backdrops crackled with authenticity, the outrageous thieves and their extravagant scams emerged as all down-home cock-and-bull. Here too the young author seemed to be striving not so much for realism as folklore.

This sketch was signed, in a bizarre conjunction of the unassuming and the affected, the maternal and the paternal, "Jim Myers Thompson."

Only "Oil Field Vignettes," the earliest printed piece, bore the name that he would henceforth use for all his serious writing: Jim Thompson.

Jim standing by Alberta's 1930 Whippet, 1931
(Courtesy of the Thompson family)

I been a-havin' some hard travelin',
I thought you knowed,
I been a-havin' some hard travelin',
Way down the road,
I been a-havin' some hard travelin',
Hard ramblin', hard gamblin',
I been havin' some hard travelin', Lord.
—Woody Guthrie (1941)

Part 2

Hard Travelin'

> If you're like I am you've
> probably spotted a thou-
> sand couples during your
> lifetime that made you
> wonder why and how the
> hell they ever got together.
> And if you're like I used to
> be you probably lay it to
> liquor and shotguns.
>
> —Joe Wilmot, *Nothing
> More Than Murder*

An American Tragedy: 1929–1935

Whether proudly or reluctantly damned, the wounded, haunted spirits of Jim Thompson's fiction slip into a void many of them label "hell." For Clinton Brown, castrated by an antipersonnel mine in the Second World War, the wound if not the hell is literal. "Was every move I made," he wonders in *The Nothing Man* after crowning his wife with a whiskey bottle, "designed to extract payment from the world for the hell I dwelt in?" For Edie Dillon, the abandoned wife cast among nettlesome relatives in *Heed the Thunder,* the damage is internal but her nightmare pervasive. When asked by her dying father whether she believes in hell, she responds with a home-spun paraphrase of Mephistopheles's famous declaration in *Dr. Faustus* that where we are is hell: "I know doggoned well there is. And you don't have to dig for it."

The Getaway marks Thompson's boldest invocation of the hell within. Through fifty feverishly claustrophobic pages he casts bank robber Doc McCoy's cross-country escape as a descent into crime fiction Hades, the dominion of El Rey. "You tell yourself it is a bad dream. You tell yourself you have died—you, not the others—and have waked up in hell. But you know better. . . . There is an end to dreams and there is no end to this."

Often in Thompson's novels, though, hell entails a more specific nether realm: sex. In *Now and on Earth* James Dillon depicts making love with his wife, Roberta, as being "in heaven and in hell at the same time. . . . A cloud surrounds me, a black mist, and I am smothered." Charlie Bigger of *Savage Night* plumbs similar depths with his landlady, Fay: "I struggled and strained, aching clear down to my toenails; and I kept my eyes closed, afraid to let her see what she might see in them . . . *and I was in that drab desert where the sun shed neither heat nor light, and. . . ."* Roy Dillon in *The Grifters,* after what Thompson describes as his "hell of a time" in the arms of Moira Langtry, worries that blustery cliché until it becomes a demonic epithet for postcoital torment:

> But afterward, after she had gone back to her own room, de-
> pression came to him and what had seemed like such a hell of a
> time became distasteful, even a little disgusting. It was the depres-
> sion of surfeit, the tail of self-indulgence's kite. You flew high, wide,
> and handsome, imposing on the breeze that might have wafted you
> along indefinitely; and then it was gone, and down, down, down
> you went.

And so on. . . . Thompson conceived about as many different kinds of hell as novels. Outside of his books he also brooded over the abyss, telling one of his literary agents, Robert Goldfarb, that his "idea of hell was killing what you loved most in order to survive."

Yet Thompson's most insistent and crotchety consignment of hellfire, undoubtedly, implicated his alma mater. "Hell, in case you're interested," he asserted in *Now and on Earth,* "is actually the College of Agriculture of the University of Nebraska. You can take my word for it."

• • •

Jim enrolled in the College of Agriculture of the University of Nebraska, at Lincoln, on September 20, 1929, one week shy of his twenty-third birthday, and barely a month before the "American Earthquake," as Edmund Wilson dubbed the Wall Street crash that announced the Great Depression. The Thompsons had been riding out their own family depression for nearly a decade, so perhaps Jim scarcely felt the tremor, at first. But Nebraska too had experienced hard times in the midst of prosperity, straight through the 1920s. During the unrelenting postwar agricultural recession farmers defaulted on loans to the extent that four hundred banks closed their doors in 1928 alone. The Lincoln that Thompson moved to already was burdened with foreclosed mortgages, vacant buildings, and unemployment lines.

The Depression and the drought of the early 1930s devastated Lincoln. As the WPA authors of *Nebraska: A Guide to the Cornhusker State* relate:

> The condition of the farmers affected Nebraska merchants, lumber dealers, realtors, school teachers, laborers, and artisans. Housewives stocked their pantry shelves with the simplest essentials; construction lagged; school administrators curtailed their programs as tax receipts went down; day laborers, formerly sure of a place on Nebraska farms and in Nebraska industries, began the long trek of the unemployed.

Drought summers in the city packed an infernal wallop. Many citizens, Jim occasionally among them, forsook their beds for the cooler grass of the state capital lawn.

People who lived in Lincoln during the late 1920s and early 1930s proclaim it "very New England." They mean, on the positive slant, to designate the city as a haven for "culture." Anchored by the university, an energetic Nebraska Art Association, and a respected symphony orchestra, Lincoln offered a more vital and various cultural life than any burg from there to Chicago. They also mean, on the negative slant, to paint the city as classconscious, puritanical, snobbish, and smug. The wide paved streets, beautiful parks, fine restaurants, cosmopolitan hotels, theaters, concert halls, and bookish "discussion groups" sheltered a wasp's nest of strictly observed social hierarchies. Houses in Lincoln were known by the names of their original owners, irrespective of how distantly they might have occupied them. The leading department stores, law firms, and insurance companies all were "family" enterprises. No shows or other entertainments opened their doors on Sundays. A sanctimonious tone of Prohibition mulled the air—and one of Thompson's college mentors, Professor Lowry C. Wimberly, found himself publicly chastened for sharing a beer with an undergraduate.

"Lincoln was mudflats on the outside and Boston on the inside," went an inspired local phrase. Jim would spend his Lincoln years mostly on the outside looking in. On his one romantic foray inside the social loop he would be rejected, humiliated, crushed.

● ● ●

But why the Ag College? For his account in *Roughneck* Thompson appeared
embarrassed and angry as he struggled to explain how the would-be novelist conked out in a College of Agriculture. If *Bad Boy* personalized the parable of the Prodigal Son, so the animating inner myth behind *Roughneck* was
the Victim. Like many alcoholics Thompson tended to characterize himself
as the unwitting, helpless chump of "circumstances," "fate," or "others." As
he self-pityingly catalogued a later misstep:

> All my life, it seemed, things had been turning out this way. I
> would work myself into exhaustion, maintain the most correct of
> attitudes. Then, flukish Fate would take a hand and something pre-
> posterous and wholly unrelated would edge into the picture. And
> all my work and rightness would be as not.

The *Roughneck* rendition of his entrance into college faults "flukish
Fate" under the guise of two magazine editors Thompson did not name but
who were, in fact, Glenn Buck and Francis Flood of the *Nebraska Farmer*.
Dressed in his Hotel Texas finery, Jim approached them for part-time work:

> It was at a farm magazine. The two young editors looked me
> over fondly, ascertaining that I was entering the university, and,
> after a significant glance at one another, took me into firmly courte-
> ous custody. . . . So I was from Texas, eh? (Here an awed look
> into the lining of my forty dollar Borsalino.) And I wanted a job, eh?
> (A glance at label of imported tweed topcoat.) Well, they could un-
> derstand that. It gave a man a certain independence, helped his
> standing on the campus. Now, of course—*naturally*—I had enrolled
> in the College of Agriculture?
>
> "My God, no!" I said, and then seeing the pained looks on their
> faces, "Why should I want to do that? I'm in Fine Arts."
>
> They shook their heads. I had made a terrible mistake, they
> said. No one enrolled in Fine Arts, absolutely no one. The degree
> was worthless, you know; one might as well have a diploma from a
> barber college. The thing to do—and they would take immediate
> steps to arrange it—was to switch to the College of Agriculture. I
> could take journalism there, also as much English as I liked; and
> with a B.Sc.A., I would be fixed for life. It was practically as good as
> an M.D.
>
> Now, I was to become very cross with these young men in en-
> suing months. . . .

Buck, the first student at the University of Nebraska to major in agricultural journalism and, later, publisher of the *Nebraska Farmer,* became one

of Thompson's closest faculty friends. Buck "rushed" him into the Alpha Gamma Rho fraternity. He hired Jim as a technical writer for the *Farmer* and published his only surviving detective serial in its pages. Buck chaperoned the frat house dance on Jim and Alberta's first date.

Thompson found other inducements, besides Buck and Flood, for choosing "the farm," as the east-campus Ag College then was known, over the "city campus" of the College of Arts and Sciences, three miles downtown. Depression economics was one. A concentration in farm journalism smoothed the path to a career as a professional writer. In 1929 Alpha Gamma Rho included several aspiring authors, among them Jim's pals Art Kozelka and Boyd Von Seggern, who opted for the security of agricultural journalism over the vagaries of liberal arts. Perhaps more to the point, Thompson's only Lincoln contacts, Robert Crawford and George Boomer, both taught at the College of Agriculture. As he acknowledged on the New American Library author questionnaire, "Not much talent or taste for agriculture, but it was the one school that offered help."

He entered the university as an "adult special" student, a category that (as the catalogue states) specified "Persons of at least 21 years of age who *cannot* fulfill the regular admission requirements for freshman standing, but who present an equivalent academic training, or who have otherwise acquired adequate preparation for collegiate courses." Thompson noted in the NAL questionnaire that his *Texas Monthly* pieces "didn't pay much, but led to the opportunity to go to college." So it's likely that "Oil Field Vignettes" and "Thieves of the Field," along with Peter Molyneaux's letter to Crawford, substituted for a high school diploma.

On his student identification card Thompson scrawled "Mrs. Birdie E. Thompson" after the entry, "Father, nearest relative, or guardian"; likewise, he claimed her religion, Baptist. But the most interesting wrinkle on his application forms—aside from the clumsy whack at impersonating a high school graduate—is a statement that Thompson has been "Reprieved from Military Science." The University of Nebraska required four semesters of military instruction from all male undergraduates. According to the catalogue, "Excuses from this requirement are granted only on the grounds of conscientious scruples, physical disability, or other reasons equally valid." Since Jim had regained his health by 1929 and, moreover, passed a vigorous course in gymnastics and athletics his first semester, the only credible explanation is that he was asserting his Wobbly pacifism.

For his freshman year Thompson rented room 1111E in the Volga Apartments, before moving to an apartment over a drugstore with Maxine and Russell at 1504 North 27th Street, after his sister returned from a summer tour with the Joybelles. He embarked on the standard first-year course load, which included classes in agricultural journalism, English composition, physical education, botany, agronomy, and rural economics.

• • •

But in order to pass into "Hell" Jim first had to eat the humble pie of "Hell Week."

Hell Week designated the period of fraternity initiation or hazing. Boyd Von Seggern reflects that "in 1929 our Hell Week was tame compared to previous years, since not long before there had been a scandal where a few boys got hurt and the dean of the college cracked down." Most of the high-jinks predictably involved ritual humiliation. Pledges were assigned "funny names" and entered the Holdrege Street fraternity house through a hole in the basement; they were run up and down the stairs on their hands and knees; they bobbed for apples in epsom-salted water. At dinner, Joe McGuiness reports, "We had to turn our chair around with our fork tied to one finger and eat the food through slats in the chair. That was a messy deal. Then, we had to stand at the door when people came in and expound a little bit. They had me shout at everybody, 'I'm an old she wolf from Honey Creek and this is my night to howl.' I've forgotten what Jim had to say."

Some of the pranks turned kinky. Eugene Dowell remembers, "We had to go downtown wearing an overcoat with nothing on underneath it, and walk around Lincoln all night." Other rites, even in "tame" 1929, incorporated some violence. "There was a lot of paddling with barrel staves," recalls William Ralston. "The actives all had barrel staves with handles cut in them. They'd make you get up on your chair and give long, silly speeches. And if you didn't get it right, you'd have to bend over and they'd give you four or five swats. That kind of brought your senses back." But McGuiness memorializes the culminating and most grotesque rite of Hell Week:

> They lined us up and told us to undress while they stood around us with their paddles. They said, "Stick one thumb up the guy's butt in front of you." We did that. Then, "Stick the other thumb in your mouth." We did that. Then, after a few minutes, they said, "Change thumbs." So we did, and those that didn't got swat on the caboose!

As Ralston wryly concludes, "Hell Week was rough, but we survived. It helped build character. Going through Hell Week helped me get through Marine basic training later."

Jim and his fellow pledges amply degraded, Alpha Gamma Rho settled into a calmer routine of Monday-night meetings, a weekly open house, and monthly dances. One of the newest fraternities at the university, AGR lacked the prestige of Phi Sigma, the Betas, and the other established Greek clubs that figured so prominently in Lincoln social life; most of the members were poor, ambitious farmboys. Their distance from the fashionable whirl can be judged by a comment of Emory Fahrney, the 1931 AGR president. "I found out one thing," he quipped, "a tux makes an awful good wiping rag when you get back on the farm." Yet the tiny band that overlapped with Thompson—never more than thirty, and shrinking through the Depression—produced a newspaper publisher and novelist (Von Seggern), a horticultural editor of the Chicago *Times* (Kozelka), and a *Life* magazine reporter and playwright (William McCleery).

Although Jim did not room at the AGR house at 3605 Holdrege, across from the main entrance to the Ag College, he is remembered by his brothers as a diligent, enthusiastic member. "He took a lively interest in house activities," Von Seggern recounts, "until the jobs he worked to earn his way through school kept him too busy. But he still attended the social hours and the dances and paid his fees." Full house dues totaled $70, but those who, like Jim, found cheaper lodging elsewhere paid only $6. His first campus work came through AGR. Like several of the boys, Thompson was on "night call" at Castle Roper & Matthews Mortuary his freshman year; weekends he toiled as a "batch man" at the Butter-Nut Bread Company, a job he later gave to Charlie Bigger in *Savage Night.*

His college friends echo the warm if abstract descriptions of his Burwell High School classmates. They remember Jim as "quiet," "a nice fellow," "very considerate of other members," "liked by everybody," and yet as "someone who didn't have many close friends," "a loner." Because of his "exceptional writing," they term him "a very interesting guy" and "brainy."

• • •

Thompson's AGR brothers also brand him as "well dressed" and "handsome." Von Seggern: "He was a tall, lanky fellow, hawk-faced . . . he looked like Gregory Peck." Yet it appears to have been the lean, muscular vigor of his prose, as much as of his person, that appealed to Lucille Boomer. Pen pals through the summer and early fall, they finally met when the Joybelles came home from barnstorming the Midwest Chautauqua circuit with the Summer Shows of 1929:

> I corresponded with him before we met, through knowing his sister Maxine. He wrote to me from Fort Worth, Texas, lovely, lovely letters, and I wrote to him. He was a very sensitive young man. And I felt as if I knew him before we met.
>
> Jim wrote a great deal of wonderful poetry and sent me some of it, lots of poems. I was brought up in a family that enjoyed literature and poetry, and I was very impressed by his ability. "A Road and a Memory," published by the *Prairie Schooner,* that was the kind of poetry I remember reading and being impressed by.

Jim Thompson with Lucille Boomer, Lincoln,
Nebraska, 1929 (Courtesy of Maxine
Thompson Kouba)

His letters were like that too, on a poetic plane. I met him
through his sister, but more that way, through his writing.

For Jim Thompson, meeting Lucille in the fall of 1929 was the supreme
event of his freshman year. She was "the first real girlfriend" his sisters remembered, though Freddie remarked on "several vague high school flings";
and, of course, Thompson knew women at the Hotel Texas and in the oil
fields. His first known love, by all accounts he fell hard. Jim's relationship
with Lucille eventually formed one of the still centers around which his
subsequent emotional life revolved. "She was the great love of Jimmie's
life," Maxine judged. "He was just crazy about her."

One year younger than Jim, Lucille was the only daughter of George and Grace Boomer. Professor Boomer taught classes in rural economics at the university, but chiefly he traveled the state giving lectures to farmers and businessmen as a state extension agent in marketing. Mrs. Boomer ran an educational employment bureau in Lincoln, Boomers Teachers Agency. She cut a wide swath in Lincoln society. Maxine found her a "little pretentious," but appraised her "a very strong-willed businesswoman."

Lucille entered the College of Arts and Sciences in 1927, with a major in music and fine arts. She took a leave of absence after her sophomore year to travel with the Joybelles—onstage, she played the flute and presented dramatic readings. She returned to class in 1930, earning A's in all her courses.

Although Lucille appears robust and high-spirited in photographs, a tragic car crash of a few years earlier left her rather fragile: "When I was sixteen I was in an accident that kept me out of high school for two years. At the University of Nebraska I had to drive from class to class on that big campus, and was kind of impaired in what I could do."

Jim and Lucille began dating right away. "I fell in love with him immediately," remembers Lucille. She invited him to teas and social hours at her sorority, and he escorted her to all the Alpha Gamma Rho parties and dances. Some squibs from the Lincoln *Sunday Star*—the first composed by its 1930 "Campus Life" correspondent, Jim Thompson—render the tone of these affairs:

GIVE "SWEETHEART DINNER"

The Alpha Gamma Rho spring party at the Lincoln hotel Friday evening was attended by three hundred couples. Professor and Mrs. H. J. Gramlich, Professor and Mrs. E. Mussehl, and Professor and Mrs. F. D. Keim chaperoned the dance.

The Alpha Gamma Rhos will entertain thirty guests today at their annual "sweetheart dinner" at the chapter house. A color scheme of gold and green will be used in table appointments. Dinner will be at 1 o'clock. Mr. and Mrs. R. M. Cole and Mrs. and Mrs. Glenn Buck will chaperone.

LIGHTS DECORATE LAWN

Vari-colored lights on the lawn of the Alpha Gamma Rho house told passers-by Friday evening that the fraternity was entertaining at a house dance and lawn party. After an evening of dancing, chaperoned by C. W. Nibler and Mr. and Mrs. Dick Cole, refreshments were served in the yard.

Jim and Lucille mainly kept to themselves, taking long drives, attending movies, and, above all, talking. "Jimmie was a very quiet person, not an extrovert at all," says Lucille. He read a lot, and we talked and talked about books, about ourselves. It was a close, warm relationship, very serious." Or Jim would join the Boomers in their book-filled living room at 1745 D Street for evening concerts around the grand piano. "Much of the time we stayed at our home with my parents and Maxine." Lucille recalls her father's praise and encouragement of her new boyfriend's writing. If the Boomers granted Thompson his first experience of a blue-blooded household, they also, after the madness of his own childhood, provided his first glimpse into a cheerful, supportive, functioning American family. Apparently he fell deeply in love with everything he saw.

Maxine believed that "Jimmie and Lucille were made for each other; they were just so right together. She was someone he could talk to on his own level. Jimmie wanted to marry her right away."

• • •

Thompson's other important early Lincoln friendships were with his favorite teachers, Professor Crawford, who lectured on agricultural journalism, and Professor Prescott, who taught English. He took two classes from Crawford, agricultural journalism and advanced agricultural editing, and three classes in composition and literature from Prescott. These added up to the only courses in which Thompson can be said to have done well. Both men returned his respect and fondness with striking generosity. Professor Prescott employed him as a teaching assistant and grader, and steered him around to the offices of the *Prairie Schooner*. Professor Crawford not only greased Jim's entrance into college; he also loaned him money, in 1931, to cover his books and tuition.

Russell True Prescott was a young instructor in English, a writer of short stories, and associate editor of the *Schooner*. He carried a bad rap among Thompson's AGR brothers as a "stern teacher," a "tough grader," and an "uninspired grind" who drilled students in spelling and vocabulary. Says AGR president Emory Fahrney:

> Prescott blackballed me from the honor society because I told the head of the department that he was the worst teacher I had in a hundred and some odd college hours. He didn't know how to motivate his classes. He sat on his desk, took his watch fob out, and swung it back and forth. It was the most hypnotic device you ever saw. That and the fact it was a one o'clock class really put you to sleep!

But Fahrney harbored no writerly ambitions. Jim Thompson idolized the teacher who permitted him to submit short stories and poems in place of the assigned themes and exercises. Prescott, a self-proclaimed "Midwestern regionalist," introduced him to the work of Willa Cather, the Nebraska novelist who influenced Thompson's 1946 novel *Heed the Thunder,* and whose fiction Jim later recommended to his own writing students at USC. The professor endorsed his application to Sigma Upsilon, the honorary literary fraternity. Jim would maintain an energetic correspondence with Prescott for many years after he departed Lincoln.

It was for Professor Prescott's two-semester freshman English composition course that Thompson drafted "Oswald the Duck" and "The Picture," his earliest extant college prose. Apparently never published, the pieces (along with a 1931 effort, "Sympathy") have survived through the admiring preservation of AGR buddy Art Kozelka. "I kept the stories in my files because I thought his style at the time was terrific. Jim's stuff captured my fancy. I've reread these many times."

"Oswald the Duck" (fall 1929) is the wild card among Thompson's student writings, partaking of neither oil field folklore nor gritty naturalism. Subtitled "A Little Story for Big Children," the fable perhaps derived from the Oswald the Lucky Rabbit cartoon by Disney, though the precise satiric objective remains obscure. With giddy wordplay Thompson charted the escapades of a wiseacre drake that "had been a rathskeller and rakehelly from birth, and early acquired the name of a quack." His slapstick resisted few opportunities for other howling puns—"lame ducks," "bad eggs," or "talking turkey."

"The Picture" (spring 1930) staked out more promising turf. Although steeped in Hemingway, Thompson's first full-blooded short story forcefully laid out some of his abiding preoccupations: sexual malaise, improvident couplings, guilt, paranoia, fatalism, and deadly self-delusion. A portrait of two roughnecks, "The Picture" pivots on an irresistible premise. The life of a young tool dresser hangs—literally—on a thin rope held by a friend he has betrayed by sleeping with his wife. The incriminating evidence, a passionately inscribed photograph of the woman, rests in the inside pocket of the cloth jumper that the tool dresser, known only as Cunningham, removed before descending into the oil well. Like many of Thompson's classic protaganists, Cunningham senses his doom right from the antsy opening:

> Cunningham knew that he was going to be killed as surely as he knew that three tons of drilling tools hung above him. They would come down on him presently, those tools. They would hurl him, crush, bury him, in the red mud two hundred feet below. They

would come down on him in one big rush of steel against iron. He couldn't get out of their way wedged in twenty inches of pipe. He couldn't stop them; three tons of steel with a fifty foot drop are not easily stopped. They wouldn't stop, or even hesitate. They would go on and he would go on.

Thompson loaded the tool dresser's reverie with laconic axioms loosely translated from *Men without Women* and *A Farewell to Arms:* "Ordinary death wasn't so bad; Cunningham had the oil man's expectation and nonchalance for that"; or "with the reflection which comes before death—when reflection makes the least difference"; and "[he] had a code and a temper. If you were his friend you were likewise a follower of his code." But he trenchantly mined the tension as Cunningham hears his partner, also designated tersely by his last name, Gaunce, announce his intention to search the jumper for a match:

> There was no doubt as to what he would do. Gaunce's first instinct would be to kill. And circumstances had made killing irresistably easy. The tools over the hole, and Cunningham in the hole . . . An accident.
> Not once did Cunningham doubt that Gaunce would find the picture. He had to. He pictured Gaunce feeling through the outer pockets, then reaching inside. He would hesitate a moment, curious, considering ethics; then shrug his shoulders and smile at the thought of some jibe he would give his tool-dresser later. Then he would look at the picture.

Thompson locked the story securely within Cunningham's guilty, self-torturing head. When the tool dresser hears Gaunce shout—menacingly, he believes—"Cunningham, you won't wear that jumper any more," he surrenders to his panic and fixes his own mordant death:

> To Cunningham the problem of life in those last few moments was a problem of death. He knew he had to die; he never considered anything else. But to wait for the bit to rush down on him, grinding him into the mud while he was still alive—that was too horrible. The bit could come down, but on a dead man.
> Somehow, he wormed one arm down to his side and got his knife. He brought it back over his head and sawed at the rope that held him. Overhead, he thought he heard the clanking of the tools, and he hurried at the task. He laughed a little with relief when the last strands parted.
> For a moment he held himself with his feet and hands. Then he

straightened, drew in his chest. He shot downward, past all stopping, all hope of life.

And as he went, Gaunce's voice followed him. Loudly, at first,
then tapering off until the last word seemed to be allowed him only
by grace of an irony-loving Fate.

"Hey, Cunningham! Your jumper blew out in the slush-pit an'
sunk!"

The fluent narration and inward texture of "The Picture" signaled a literary breakthrough after the piecemeal folklore portraits of the previous
year. On the strength of Thompson's freshman stories, Professor Prescott
presented him to Lowry C. Wimberly, the famed founding editor of the
Prairie Schooner. Jim became "one of Wimberly's boys," as the university
grapevine tagged the select young men—and women—who gathered at the
editor's R Street home on alternate Sunday nights to read aloud their poetry and fiction in an early incarnation of a creative writing workshop. Wimberly had instituted his circle of artists and scholars by the mid-1920s,
when novelist Mari Sandoz was a student. By the time of Thompson's entrance, the group was "long-haired, avant-garde, and for Lincoln quite un-
conventional," as fellow member Kenneth Keller recalls it. Ben Botkin, then
an English Ph.D. candidate; Loren Eiseley, a poet and, eventually, the author of such classic texts as *The Immense Journey* and *Darwin's Century;*
and actor William Thompson enlivened the discussions. Poet Weldon Kees
would join a few years later.

Kenneth Keller remarks upon Jim's "unique" standing among this
Who's Who of budding Lincoln intellectuals:

> The group was composed mainly of the best English under-
> graduates and a few graduate students. Jim was unique, I think,
> coming from the College of Agriculture—just as he must have been
> the only Ag student ever to have his work published in the *Prairie
> Schooner.* That was quite an honor, even for the students in the
> writing group. I should know—I kept submitting my stuff to Wim-
> berly, but he never published any of it!
>
> Professor Wimberly took an interest in just about every stu-
> dent who was interested in writing. There were about a dozen of us
> that would meet every other Sunday night, usually at his house,
> but sometimes in his office in the College of Law building. This was
> the Depression, and I've often thought that Wimberly must have
> been making hardly enough to live on. But still he'd have us guys
> out there, give us donuts and coffee and popcorn.
>
> We would take turns reading what we'd written. Wimberly had
> a droll way of speaking out the side of his mouth. We sort of knelt

before Doc, as we called him, and what he said was both inspirational and the law for us. He liked to have us spread our wings, use
our imaginations, and break away from the stodgy standards of the
twenties. He also had us read a lot—Middle-western writers
mostly, Willa Cather, Glenway Wescott, someone named Dorothy
Canfield Fisher, who was big then. Doc was the first person I knew
to speak of William Faulkner, but he also read the crime magazines,
like *True Detective,* with relish. We talked over problems of technique and style. And Wimberly let us air our grudges about the
University or Lincoln.

Wimberly's writing workshop provided a refuge for talented bohemians, rebels, and misfits in a rigid, preachy society. The intense conversations about art and artists often spilled over into all-night gab sessions at
the coffee shop of the Lincoln bus depot where, Keller reports, Jim would
try out his West Texas anecdotes before running them through his typewriter. Besides affording him a supportive and discriminating audience, the
group had a peculiar dynamic that mirrored Thompson's deepening ambitions. While folklorist Botkin encouraged his investigations of oil field traditions, Wimberly persuaded him to "spread his wings" into sustained
narratives.

Thompson would subsequently publish folklore in the *Prairie Schooner*
his sophomore year. But he produced his strongest poem, and his sharpest
college fiction, as an immediate consequence of Wimberly's workshop. The
winter 1930 issue of the *Schooner* carried "A Road and a Memory," Thompson's tightly wound stanzas about walking to school in Burwell. "A Road"
became his first work to be reprinted in a national anthology, appearing in
Cap and Gown (1931), a compendium of the best undergraduate verse. And
the spring 1930 edition of the *Schooner* featured "Character at Iraan." Although also invoked earlier, Thompson's boldest and most prescient early
story merits additional brief mention. Building upon his performance in
"The Picture," the author confidently rendered the anxieties and tediums of
the oil field hobo from the inside out. The prickly first-person narration of
"Iraan" juggled multiple characters, whimsical dialogue, and a graphic appreciation of the violent West Texas setting:

> Strawlegs and I went down to the ladies' ready-to-wear-and-
> grocery store and hocked our jackets at fifty cents per. We spent
> the rest of the morning playing pool. We still had a dime or two at
> noon; so we went back to the Greek's. Ted McKelvie was there
> playing "I Love My Gamblin' Man" on the phonograph, and drink-
> ing coffee.

He took us over to a table in the corner and handed us twenty-one dollars apiece.

"I thought I could beat that nigger," he said, tapping sharp nails, carelessly. "Never saw a nigger yet I couldn't beat some way."

Martin winked at me. "Ted," he said, "I'm afraid I'll have to tell that nigger you didn't win this money on the square or my conscience will hurt me."

Ted told us not to lose any sleep over it. "He already knows I cheated him, anyway," he said. "He felt all right about it when I left."

The strangest moment in "Iraan"—narrator Slim's descent into a jake-induced coma until he hears himself declared dead—proved the most characteristic. From *The Killer Inside Me* to *A Hell of a Woman* and *Savage Night*, many of Thompson's first-person crime novels will conclude with the narrator dying on the final page.

Thompson's *Prairie Schooner* writing exposed a starker pessimism than can be detected in any other contemporary contributions to the quarterly, whether by established or student authors. Founded in 1927, and instantly achieving a literary stature that belied its regional bent and tiny circulation, the Schooner actually ignited controversy because of what some Lincoln critics condemned as a preoccupation with "doom, gloom and tragic stuff." Yet, next to young Jim Thompson, the prairie naturalists and realists all now appear housebroken. "Character at Iraan," in fact, was printed only a few pages away from a protest against "psycho-pathological fiction" by one Ada Jean Mecham—a protest that could have served as an inverse blueprint for Thompson's mature novels:

It is time to question the popularity of a novel which has for its basic idea the underlying cause of crimes of violence or murder or mental depression that results in madness. . . . For there are normal, happy people in the world; there is love that is unselfish; and there is courage that is capable of sacrifice.

This duly noted, mainstream literature and film of the 1920s and early 1930s, it should be remembered, cultivated a blunt edge. F. Scott Fitzgerald's *The Great Gatsby* (1925), Ernest Hemingway's "The Killers" (1927), and William Faulkner's *Sanctuary* (1931)—to spotlight only the most conspicuous literary appropriations of violence—crisscrossed the popular gangster novel. A cool, casual savagery rippled through such box office smashes as *Doorway to Hell* (1930), *Little Caesar* (1930), *The Public Enemy* (1931), and *Scarface* (1932). On the newsstand, *Black Mask* led the monthly and weekly detective fiction pulps, publishing Dashiell Hammett, Carroll John Daly,

Paul Cain, Raoul Whitfield, and Raymond Chandler. Bernarr Macfadden's success with *True Detective*—within whose lurid pages Jim already, accord- ing to Lucille Boomer, was printing anonymous tidbits—set off a spree of fact-detective knockoffs, along with oddball "true story" sensations like *Strange Suicides* or *Medical Horrors* ("76 Babies Murdered," "Chloroformed," "Confessions of a Nurse," "Million Dollar Baby Farm"). Beyond the internal pressures bearing down on his writing, the culture that surrounded Thompson hankered after the hard-boiled.

● ● ●

Thompson's other beloved professor, Robert Crawford, shouldered the rep- utation of a campus eccentric. A plump, owlish man with an M.A. from Columbia University and a background in news reporting, Crawford insinu- ated himself into the faculty by the mid-1920s after he was hired to draft a history of the College of Agriculture, *These Fifty Years*. Soon he was serving in a dual capacity as an assistant to the chancellor in public relations and as chairman—and sole instructor—of a department in the relatively new discipline of agricultural journalism. Crawford later became famous for a self-help theory, "Creative Thinking," which he advanced in two other books, *Think for Yourself* and *The Technique of Creative Thinking: How to Use Your Ideas to Achieve Success*. During class Professor Crawford main- tained an odd habit of laughing at unexpected moments. According to Thompson's friend Kenneth Keller, "He would be lecturing and just stop and laugh. None of us ever understood why." A bachelor, he left a pile of money to the city of Lincoln for a park to be created in his name one hun- dred years after his death.

Although Crawford billed his course "agricultural journalism," the in- troductory class Thompson attended his freshman year covered (in Keller's words) "just about every type of journalism there was at that time." The teacher's focus "was never theoretical but practical. He'd always have the student write an article that might have some chance of publication."

Professor Crawford presently printed his lectures as a small book, *The Magazine Article* (1931). Thus it's possible to reconstruct what Thompson studied in the field that would provide his basic living for the next two decades. As he calculated in a 1948 letter, "I've written several million words for newspapers and magazines."

The Magazine Article confirms Keller's recollection that "agricultural journalism" comprised an encyclopedic survey, and offers a few intriguing biases and premonitions. Ranging from "The Business Article" to "The Hu- morous Article," with week-long stopovers in "The Agricultural Article," "The Outdoor Article," "The Woman's Article," "The Interview," "The Liter- ary Article," and "The Romantic Historical Article," Crawford's course not only encompassed more than a dozen different species of popular journalism, it also beguilingly found room for "Fiction Writing" as well. Common-sense recommendations about researching the magazine market, catching an editor's attention, or gathering illustrations mixed with cranky schematic diagrams that, for instance, compared the structure of an article to a ladder. (The rungs lifted the writer from "Words" and "Phrases" up through "Sentences," "Paragraphs," and "Themes," and on to the pinnacle, "The Idea." Crawford's giddy caption cautions, "Watch that final step!")

Still, Thompson absorbed much that sooner or later he put to use. His professor's crisp review of the agricultural feature would enable him, by the mid-1930s, to parlay his scant farm experience into hundreds of articles. And with grander consequences for his income—as well as for his future fiction—Thompson would heed Crawford's directives for "The Confession Article":

> There has been a great interest in recent years in the confession type of magazine. Ostensibly posing as facts, many of the stories have undoubtedly been fiction. But here we are not going to deal with sex stories, half fact and half fiction, but rather with those articles that tell worthwhile personal experiences in certain fields.
>
> To a large extent, you see, confession articles are really personality stories telling actual experiences in the first person. Perhaps a very large proportion of the articles ostensibly written by noted people are not written by these people at all. This is nothing more or less than "ghostwriting," as it is sometimes called. Some magazines give the real writer credit as joint author of the article; sometimes there is a statement that it is written in collaboration with or in an interview with "So-and-so."
>
> Usually the real writer receives the money for the article and of course a much larger check than if the article had been signed with his own name. . . . Since you will not likely have had the experiences that you propose to write about in this type of article most of such writing you will do will be ghostwriting. To a large extent you must put yourself in the position of the person who has had the experience.

Thompson subsequently slipped into the first-person ghost wherever possible. Contrary to the omniscient overview favored by *True Detective* and other fact-detective weeklies, nearly all his true crime stories find him ventriloquizing the voice of the criminal investigator and securing for himself only a collateral "as-told-to" credit. He eventually became so comfortable doing the policeman in different voices that he retained the ghost-written model even when, as in the case of his *Master Detective* feature "The

Dark Stair" (1946), the crime was his own invention. Thompson, significantly, also would "put himself in the position of the person who has had
the experience" for the terrifying impersonations of psychopathic criminals that spur his brashest novels.

Crawford's course ventilated a strident lowbrow posture conspicuously at odds with the Midwestern aestheticism Thompson was gleaning
from Wimberly and Prescott. "One may study 'English' for years, submit
manuscripts to every publisher," the journalism professor huffed, "and yet
fail to have a single one accepted." The fiction Crawford promoted in class
aimed to ascend another ladder, the best-seller list, before dropping off into
high-yield oblivion. Even this antiliterary bias cut its way into Thompson's
consciousness. Reading Crawford on "Fiction Writing," it's hard not to recall that his student would achieve notoriety through mass market paperback originals emblazoned with sensational, alliterative titles:

> If there is one outstanding word of advice to the fiction writer,
> it would seem to be this: Quick success is usually achieved by
> novel or unusual treatment. There are plenty of people who can
> write ordinary stories of a more or less routine type, and write
> them well. Something new, to break this routine, is more apt to be
> accepted by a publication. . . . On the other hand, some writers
> in their efforts to achieve novelty in stories or novels have become
> so grotesque as to be almost absurd, or in a few cases so sex-con-
> scious as to be repugnant to good taste. . . . Most good fiction
> titles today introduce some imaginative qualities—mystery,
> curiosity, suspense—or they may make use of some structural de-
> vices such as interrogation or alliteration.

Whether the subject was true confessions or novels, agricultural journalism accented "the business of writing," and promoted the writer as businessman. What Thompson ultimately derived from Crawford was a
conception of himself as a *professional* writer. "Crawford taught us not to
take ourselves too seriously," notes Kenneth Keller, "but to pay attention to
the professional bottom line." Throughout his career Thompson never, for
letters and interviews, on his income tax returns and author question-
naires, advanced himself as an artist or, even, a novelist. He was a "professional writer" or, simply, a "writer."

Thompson earned a grade of 90 in agricultural journalism, and the
same score from Prescott in English composition. His freshman report card
otherwise was a mess: 77 in rural economics, 75 in physical education, 65
in agronomy; he failed botany. Some years later when he applied for a writing grant from the Rosenwald Foundation, Thompson felt compelled to ap-
pend an explanatory note about his transcript:

I feel that I should make some comment on my university
record, which, with the exception of the grades in English and
Journalism, is anything but good. I enrolled in the college of
agriculture, although I knew nothing about farming, because of
the better opportunities to work. During the time I was in
school, I had no more than four hours a day to study and attend
class; my outside working hours ranged from eight to sixteen
hours a day.

For a full-time student Jim indeed tracked a stupefying concatenation of
part-time jobs. Along with his night watchman stints at Castle Roper &
Matthews Mortuary and his weekends at the Butter-Nut Bread Company,
he ushered at the Lincoln Auditorium; he peddled radios on commission
from a small shop, Radio Sales and Service, down the road from the apartment he shared with Maxine and Russell; he temped as a stenographer in
the collection department of the Liberty Stores, a Midwestern installment-
sales outfit; he graded papers for Professor Prescott, and enjoyed a brief
term (January to April 1930) as campus correspondent of the Lincoln
Sunday Star. When summer rolled around he juiced up the pace, signing
on with the Harris-Goar Store to pen advertising in a Crawford-directed
independent study project that advanced him credits in agricultural
editing.

Any one of his college jobs should have covered his rent and modest
tuition ($40). But Jim now was supporting two additional households. Duti-
fully each week he sent a check to his mother and Freddie in Burwell and
another check to his father, still struggling in Fort Worth.

During his years in Lincoln, Thompson essentially reproduced the
schedule that had nearly killed him in high school. A college update of an
old snapshot, from *Roughneck:*

. . . there was little time for rest and relaxation in the months
that followed. I seldom got to bed before midnight, and I had
to be up at dawn to make my seven o'clock classes at the university. . . . My last class let out at 11:50 in the morning, and I had to
be at the store at noon. I had no lunch period, then, as the other
employees had. . . .

Jim resisted other ruinous habits. Aside from an AGR buddy's surmise
that he was the undergraduate nabbed with Wimberly at the infamous beer
bust, drinking figures in no account of Thompson's college life. As Maxine
recalled, "Jimmie was trying so hard to get back on track, burning the midnight oil, as they say, to keep it all together with studying and all his jobs
and not drinking, staying healthy. Every night he'd come home dead tired,

but he would park himself at the kitchen table and begin to write. Jimmie was just determined to succeed as a writer. Plus, he was in love."

· · ·

Lucille Boomer "felt very proud when Jim's writing was accepted by the *Prairie Schooner.* That was our high literary magazine, and coming from Lincoln my family knew what an honor that was." Professor Boomer especially marveled at Jim's promise, and became his champion within the household. He encouraged the romance, defending the young couple against the nagging doubts of his wife. By all accounts he welcomed Jim as his future son-in-law. But Lucille notes that her father "was already ill when Jimmie entered our lives." George Boomer died in March 1930.

Jim stood by Lucille at her father's funeral. While their relationship drifted along through the summer, that probably marked the last occasion when the pair would be so close. Grace Boomer set about dislodging Jim and finding her only daughter a more genteel mate. As Maxine remembered,

> Though Jimmie loved Lucille—and I know she liked him, liked him better, I think, than the fellow she did marry—her mother did everything she could to break them up. She wanted her daughter to have someone with a lot of money. Mrs. Boomer never felt that Jimmie would amount to anything. She thought he would never be able to support Lucille in the style she was going to have to be accustomed to because of her terrible automobile accident. Professor Boomer would have approved but, of course, he was no longer running the show.

Maxine added, "Jimmie always said that Mrs. Boomer drove a wedge between them. He really blamed her, and Lucille blamed her also."

Lucille agrees that "mother was troubled by how deeply we felt about each other." Yet, for her, the decision not to marry Jim Thompson involved more than crass maternal bullying. She wrestled with her own qualms and fears:

> Ours was a close, warm relationship, not in the way they are these days, but there was a period of time when it was very serious. But it wouldn't have worked out. I liked him, and I admired many qualities of his, but others not so much.
>
> He wasn't crude, not at all, that was never the problem. The Thompsons were a very fine family, educated and refined. But Jim seemed too much a vague introvert, unsettled, not really knowing where he was headed. "Loner" describes him very well. I don't be-

lieve he had much time just to be social or make friends or have what we might consider a normal life in college.

Jim had writing ability, and he was working odd jobs to keep body and soul together. But he did not appear to have any kind of stable profession ahead of him. Naturally any family wants their daughter to be settled that way.

He was very important to me for a short period of time . . . a short time in the scheme of things.

Lucille finally broke off with Jim early in the fall. On Valentine's Day, 1931, she married Walter Larson, a student at the dental college. Within a year she left Lincoln for Hartford, Connecticut, where Dr. Larson established his practice. According to Lucille, she never saw Jim after her marriage.

Jim was devastated. "I don't think I ever saw him so broke up about anything," Maxine recalled. "He moped all that winter, hardly eating or studying, not writing much of anything. I considered Lucille the love of his life. He just thought it so unfair."

His rejection on grounds of class, money, and work—the rallying cries of the Marxist social theory Thompson had imbibed from Haywire Mac in Texas, now replayed as bedroom farce—rankled and haunted for many years. In 1941 he took his revenge, injecting a barbed account of an— apparently imaginary—adulterous tryst with Lucille into his novel *Now and on Earth:*

> One day, after she was married and I was married, we met on the street in Lincoln. And I undressed her with my eyes and she met me with hers. And nothing mattered but that we should be together again. We drove to Marysville, Kansas, and registered at a hotel. We even wrote letters—unmailed, fortunately—explaining why we had to do what we had done. Then the physical reunion, and after that, talk, lying there together in the dusk. She had it all planned. She had a sorority sister whose husband owned a big advertising agency in Des Moines, and he was a perfectly gorgeous person. If I would just be nice to him—
>
> "What do you mean, nice? I've never spit in anyone's face yet."
>
> "Well, that's what I mean, dear. You say so many things that are misunderstood. They give people the wrong impression of you. They think that—"
>
> "—that I've been in some pretty nasty places. Well, I have been. And anyone who doesn't like it can lump it."
>
> "Please, dear. I think it's marvellous the way you've worked to make something of yourself—"

"—with so little success, is that what you mean? Well, what do you want me to do? Never mind—I'll tell you . . . 'Ooh, my deah Mrs. Bunghole, what a delightful blend of pee—excuse me tea! And what are your beagles doing this season, Mrs. Bunghole? Beagling? Why how gorgeously odd! Do tell me—' "

"Now you're becoming impossible!"

"Perhaps I always was."

"Perhaps."

We went back to Lincoln that same night. . . .

In a comforting coincidence Birdie and Freddie joined Jim during his breakup with Lucille. Burwell family politics had steadily soured after the death of Grandfather Myers in 1928 ("No one knows better than I do," Thompson wrote in a letter to his mother, "just what a poor place Burwell is for Freddie"). Rather than return to her husband in Texas, Birdie shifted to Lincoln. For academic year 1930–31 the three Thompsons rented a house at 2985 Holdrege, not far from AGR headquarters. To help pay for the spread Birdie took in boarders and baked pies, which she peddled along fraternity row. She enrolled as an extension student in the university. Following in her son's footsteps, she elected an evening English class with Professor Prescott.

Although their boxy home functioned as a second AGR command post, Jim remained (in Freddie's words) "sad and depressed. He stayed in bed a lot, basically getting up to go to work. He wouldn't join in all the fun Mama arranged for his friends." Jim likewise resisted the repeated attempts of his brother-in-law, Russell, who apparently felt guilty over the Lucille affair, to stage-manage blind dates for him. Unable to write—Thompson published nothing during the fall of 1930—his grades continued to plummet. This time he achieved a disappointing pair of 85s from Crawford and Prescott (in advanced agricultural editing and advanced composition, respectively). His farm grades were worse: 65 in poultry; and 65 also in agricultural engineering. He passed animal pathology with a minimal 60 only after the AGR council interceded with his teacher.

• • •

After Christmas Jim began to crawl out from under his malaise. Tapped for Sigma Upsilon, the coveted literary fraternity, he returned to Wimberly's workshop. Once more he broached his chary presence at AGR meetings and socials. Finally, late in February 1931, needing a date for the celebrated Pink Rose formal, he acceded to Russell's sedulous matchmaking. All winter Russell had touted the charms of a certain young Lincoln telephone operator. Thus Jim, only days after Lucille Boomer's dreaded wedding, rang the doorbell of Alberta Hesse's North 25th Street home. Natty in his borrowed tux, he carried, appropriately enough, a corsage of miniature pink roses.

Alberta fleshes out the story:

> It was a blind date. I had known Russell for years. When he called and said, "Alberta, would you like to go out on a date with my brother-in-law to a fraternity dance," first I said no. But he pleaded, "Oh, come on, he really needs a date. He's just broken up with a girl." That did it.
>
> So I asked my mother if it would be all right if I went dancing. You see, I had given up dancing for Lent. Mother said, yes, go ahead. She was a good sport.
>
> Well, the next thing I knew Jimmie showed up at the front door, all by himself. We stood and looked at each other. . . . Then I introduced him to my father—my mother, I think, wasn't there at that particular moment.
>
> We went off to the fraternity dance and had the best time in the world, which surprised me. At the end of the evening he said, "I'll call you." But two weeks went by after that dance, and no call. . . .
>
> So I said, to heck with him! I was really disappointed. I thought to myself, here I've been acting so horsey. . . .

Jim, of course, ultimately did phone. "Sometime in early March. . . . From that point on you couldn't tear us apart."

Jim Thompson's "Rock of Gibraltar" (as one of his literary agents, Robert Mills, hailed her), Alberta Helen Charlotte Elizabeth Hesse was born in Fort Madison, Iowa, on August 12, 1908. The Hesses moved to Lincoln when Alberta and her sister, Pauline, were babies. Her father, John, opened a restaurant downtown and, after this failed in the 1920s Nebraska recession, sought his luck as a traveling salesman. Her mother, Elena, kept the house. Just twenty-two when she met Jim, Alberta was a slim, tall, shapely woman with light brown hair and an eye for fashion. After graduating from high school she applied to the Lincoln Telephone & Telegraph Company, where she quickly worked her way up from operator to supervisor.

In *Now and on Earth* Thompson contrasted his visits to the Hesse and Boomer homes. Scarcely disguising the names—Roberta for Alberta, Lois for Lucille—he called down a plague on both their houses:

> The first time I called at Roberta's house she and her mother were in the kitchen. Roberta let me in and whispered I'll be right with you honey; and then she went back into the kitchen and I could hear her and her mother talking in low voices. I wanted to

Jim and Alberta—Lincoln, Nebraska, 1931
(Courtesy of the Thompson family)

smoke, but I couldn't find an ashtray; I looked around for something to read and there wasn't anything. Not a newspaper, not a
book or magazine of any kind. I began to get nervous. I wondered
what in the name of God they were talking about, whether the old
lady was trying to talk her out of going out with me. Lois' mother
hadn't been exactly fond of me either. . . . But it hadn't been like
this. . . .

There:

"My dear boy! Aren't you just frozen? Lois will be right down.
She's had such a cold today; barely able to drag herself around. I
don't suppose I could persuade you two to spend the evening
here? The doctor and I are going out—goodness gracious! You're
sneezing! Aren't you afraid that Lois will catch—?"

"It's nothing serious," I'd say. "Just t.b."

"Oh . . . now, you're teasing me, aren't you? By the way, I've a book you must take with you when you go. Dear, dear Willa! I do know you'll enjoy her. What sacrifices she must have made! What a lonely life she must have led!"

"Willa? Which Willa do you mean?"

"Why, Miss Cather!"

"Oh. I thought you were talking about the other one."

"Which—what other—is there another—?"

Then the doctor chuckling: "Martha, Martha! . . . By the way Jim. I've just received my copy of the *Prairie Schooner*. Your story is very well done. Too bad there isn't some money in that sort of thing. Too bad."

That's the way it had been at Lois' house. They didn't hide you in the kitchen there. They seated you in a room with a baby grand and more books than a branch library, and then they pelted you with words until your hide became so sore that you began to shout and snarl even before you were touched, until you made such a fool and a boor of yourself that you could never go back.

But at Roberta's:

I got up and began to pace the floor, and finally, call it eaves-dropping if you will, I stopped where I could hear:

"Why Mother! You don't mean it!"

"Yessir, that's just what she did! She took a little cornmeal and beat it up with some canned milk and water, and she dipped the bread in that. And it made the finest French toast you ever saw!"

I thought, well for the love of—But it went on and on. . . .

"You can't guess how much I paid for eggs today."

"Well, now—how much was that last dozen?"

. . . When we were outside in the car, I said, "Do you always keep your dates waiting while you discuss the price of eggs?"

For all that, Jim was smitten. His free evenings, they went dancing at the Avalon or Rosewilde ballrooms, frequented the movie palaces along O Street, or cruised Lincoln in her new car. Alberta worried over his punishing schedule: "He'd leave one job and have to run clear across town for a class. The job ended at noon, which is when his class started. He was always tardy, because you can't be in two places at the same time!" And much as later she would edit and proofread his novels, she began to accompany Jim on the nightly rounds of his current venture: selling door-to-door for the Kay-Bee Clothing Company. His routine also involved collecting on overdue accounts: "Jimmie really hated the work, bugging the poor people who couldn't pay their bills. He felt sorry for them—remember, this was the height of the Depression. But occasionally the people got angry and threatened Jimmie. Those times he'd come back to the car white, just shaking." Thompson eventually assigned this cheerless living to Dolly Dillon in *A Hell of a Woman,* sardonically rechristening Kay-Bee the Pay-E-Zee Stores.

Alberta's physical relish in her future husband still radiates after sixty years:

> Jimmie was a handsome brute. . . . He was tall, six feet four inches, lean, almost thin, really, and a smooth-looking person. He had thick brown hair, greyish-blue eyes, and a very pretty smile . . . Jimmie also was a stylish dresser; he had very good taste. He always wore a Steinblock or another name-brand suit. And back then he always wore a hat—sometimes a Stetson, but other kinds as well. All in all, he looked very elegant. . . . When I first saw him, I knew I was going to marry him!

Jim palpably returned her passion. As he would soon write her from the road, shortly after the birth of their first child, Patricia:

> Yes, I surely do remember those happy days and nights together of last year, this time, with you going to sleep in my arms at night, and waking me up in the morning with a kiss. . . . I'm afraid Patricia is in for a little neglect when we get together again. I'm going to need her mama's undivided love and attention for a while. Will I get it—lots of love, I mean?
>
> . . . God, it's been so long, hasn't it? I'm glad it's only a matter of days, now, and not weeks and months. I don't think I could see much point in living if I didn't know you were going to be with me soon.

Jim and Alberta Thompson were married on September 16, 1931. On the Wednesday morning he was scheduled to register for his fall classes Jim stole over to Alberta's house and together they drove across the state border to Marysville, Kansas—the site of his fictional rendezvous with Lucille in *Now and on Earth.* They stopped at the first justice of the peace, Probate Judge W. W. Potter. As the couple approached the bench, the office staff whistled "Here Comes the Bride." When the time came to pay for the license the bride reached into her purse and loaned her husband twenty dollars. As Alberta concludes the oddly unceremonious day that would chart their lives for nearly the next fifty years:

We went out and had an ice cream sundae. Then we drove back to Lincoln, where they were having a fall fashion show. Later that night we saw a film of *An American Tragedy* by Theodore Dreiser. Then I went to my home, and he went to his home. . . .

The Thompsons kept their marriage a secret because the Lincoln Telephone & Telegraph Company, where Alberta wished to continue to work, maintained a strict no-married-women policy. But they eloped because both Jim and Alberta feared the opposition of their families. A neighborhood flibbertigibbet soon rendered all precautions moot. "When Maxine and her husband would go out, we'd go over there. Some old woman phoned my mother and said, 'Do you know where your daughter is?' Well, that just let the cat out of the bag." With a flick of the gossip's tongue Alberta was fired, and the families were in an uproar.

Elena Hesse bruited many of the same misgivings that had deep-sixed Jim with Grace Boomer one year earlier. Reports Alberta:

My parents always felt I never should have married Jimmie. My mother thought that he wasn't good enough for me—she was a very German woman, very set in her ways. I was engaged several times to lawyers and doctors, and I don't think she ever thought that Jimmie was going to make anything.

My mother always believed I had made quite a mistake. Of course I didn't think so, but it was hard for me to convince her. She reconciled to it, more or less, but she was never happy about it. Jimmie was aware they didn't care for him. He visited back there after our son was born [in 1938], and he was welcome—they never would have put him out. But they had their feelings, and didn't hide them.

The Thompson sisters betrayed even more hostility to the marriage. Rarely ones to mince words . . . as Freddie recounted:

We were all, Mama included, very disappointed when he married Alberta. I remember Maxine said to him, "How could you have done such a damn fool thing as marry her!" She knew about the Hesse family, and she also was very close to Lucille Boomer. . . . Alberta was a cute young woman, pampered by her parents, and at twenty-three Jimmie apparently didn't need the intellectual stimulation. That was the one thing that was missing there—an understanding of his thinking process, his brain, and being able to sit and really discuss things the way he might have wanted to.

That marriage was just something that two people should not

have gotten into, one of those deals. But it lasted all those years, and wasn't all that bad. And it's hard to look back and tell how people should have been.

Personally, I think the marriage was almost a rebound thing for Jimmie, from Lucille. . . .

Thicker than spouses, the three Thompson siblings, Maxine, Jim, and Freddie, always remained very proprietary about one another. And Maxine especially, through her marriage to Russell, carried a torch for the Boomers, which she never dropped, even after her divorce in the early 1940s. Outside of the family, though, some friends—like producer David Foster—actually found Alberta "more sophisticated" than her husband.

But as Freddie intimated, the Thompsons' aversion to Alberta proved deeper than the passing territoriality of a battered family. Aggravated by proximity—the various wings of the family would share cities and, often, cramped residences for the duration of their lives—tensions festered. With Alberta evidently returning the volleys, the carping of in-laws vaporized into the noxious background noise against which Jim Thompson struggled to write and raise his children. As he rued in *Now and on Earth:*

> . . . I thought about Roberta, about Mom. About the kids growing up around me. Growing up amidst this turmoil, these hatreds, this—well, why quibble—insanity. I thought and my stomach tightened into a little ball; my guts crawled up around my lungs and my vision went black.
>
> I took a drink and chased it with wine. . . .
>
> I wish, I thought, that Mom could understand what Roberta means to me—why I am like I am with her. I wish Roberta could understand what Mom means to me. Maybe they do understand. Maybe that's why things are like they are.

When Jim and Alberta renewed their vows before Father Quinn of the Sacred Heart Catholic Church on April 6, 1932, the couple was already expecting their first child. Alberta's parents, sister, and assorted kin witnessed the informal ceremony. Jim's side of the rectory stayed empty but for a scattering of AGR buddies. By then Birdie, Freddie, and Maxine were in Fort Worth, attending James Thompson, who had shattered his leg in a fall. No one from his family managed to return to Lincoln for his wedding.

•   •   •

If Jim married "on the rebound from Lucille," as his sister believed, his suddenly recharged creativity indicated otherwise. Immediately upon meeting Alberta he embarked on the strongest run of literary work in his

college career, indeed for the entire 1930s. During the interval between February and September 1931, Thompson produced at least seven new
pieces—one for each month of his courtship.

The *Cornhusker Countryman,* an Ag College monthly "devoted to the advancement of scientific agriculture," served as the unlikely vehicle for
much of this writing. Edited by AGR brothers Boyd Von Seggern and Art
Kozelka, the *Countryman* featured the latest bulletins from the campus
Experimental Farm alongside reports from livestock shows, faculty vignettes, and alumni chat. Much as Jim Thompson emerged as the only Ag
student to crack the *Prairie Schooner,* his contributions to the *Cornhusker
Countryman* marked that journal's sole foray into fiction. Von Seggern
trumpeted the *Countryman's* new wrinkle when his editorial note introduced Thompson's debut, in February: "Never before has this magazine
had the privilege of presenting an honest-to-goodness story of fiction." A
flattering author's profile (complete with photograph) in the May issue
marked the first appearance of a distinction that would be repeated by
nearly everyone who subsequently knew Thompson: the jarring, even
shocking contrast between his gentle social manner and the "hardness" of
his writing.

> Jim Thompson, in his story, "Incident in God's Country," pre-
> sents the last of his four short story series. The "Incident" is a
> longer story than his others, and it is that much more interesting,
> too.
>
> Jim gives a background of a region in which he has spent many
> months—the Texas jungles; the oil fields. It was a life that would
> harden most any man. Jim's own words, perhaps, reflect hardness,
> but you will know different if you know Jim.
>
> For as busy as Thompson is in trying to earn his way thru
> college, we are more than greatly pleased that he found time to
> dash off these stories. Journalists and writers in the know have
> typified him as a "promising comer." Jim is a sophomore on the
> campus.

Open to a broader range of topics, and crossed by a quirkier tangle of
literary influences, Thompson's four *Cornhusker Countryman* stories were
loose and experimental, compared to his *Prairie Schooner* efforts. "Chink"
(February) mixed Sherwood Anderson with O. Henry as Thompson pursued the effects of gossip on a small town (probably Burwell) to a surprise,
about-face conclusion. When Cal Peters sees Chink Halleck, confectioner
and suspected ladies' man, climb through Madge Hornbeck's window one
night, first comes the feverish speculation, and then the sweet—for
Thompson, anyway—O. Henry twist:

THIS ISSUE

Here's the last for the present fiscal school year. Eight issues of the Countryman have been published and we hope you have enjoyed them all. Next fall a new editor will take charge of the magazine, according to the practice of changing every semester.

●

This semester there has been a diligent effort to present something new in college of agriculture magazines. Several features were created, some of them entirely different from anything in parallel publications in the country. Most prominent among these additions has been the use of pure fiction written by college talent.

Jim Thompson

Jim Thompson, in his story, "Incident in God's Country," presents the last of his four short story series. The "incident" is a longer story than his others, and it is that much more interesting, too.

Jim gives a background of a region in which he himself spent many months—the Texas jungles; the oil fields. It was a life that would harden most any man. Jim's own words, perhaps, reflect hardness, but you will know different if you know Jim.

For as busy as Thompson is in trying to earn his way thru college, we are more than greatly pleased that he found time to dash off these stories. Journalists and writers in the know have typified him as a "promising comer." Jim is a sophomore on the campus.

●

Profile of Jim Thompson, from the
Cornhusker Countryman, *May 1931*

"Just think of it," [Mrs. Halleck] said to Cal and me. "Every night that I've been sick and needing all the fuel to make fire for my room, he's slipped over to Madge Hornbeck's and made his candy to sell the next day. One night she forgot and locked the door and he had to crawl in the window."

. . . I looked at Cal who was pretty red in the face and remarked that that was one couple that didn't need a thing from anyone else.

"Maybe not," said Cal. "But from now on Chink can have anything he'll take."

And when the story got around we all felt the same about Chink that Cal did.

The ironically titled "Close Shave" (March) exploited the curveball ending to droller, meaner effect. A nervous, Walter Mittyish rooming house bachelor loses the girl of his daydreams with a catty note addressed to the person who's been cadging his razor—not his jocular rival, as he believes, but his comely beloved, Myra:

There was nothing but silence from the other side of the door. It was some minutes before he noticed that a piece of paper had been shoved inside. It was his own note with some lines added.

"I don't use it much," they said.

"I'm sorry I used it at all. But
I'm glad I found out how small
you really were."

The signature was Myra Mallory's.

Thompson also reanimated his familiar subjects. The oil fields continued to provide his major backdrop, both inside and out of the *Cornhusker Countryman*. Besides "Incident in God's Country" (May), his audacious tribute to Haywire Mac and the Texas Wobblies, he published "Bo'ger" (April), a boomtown tall tale about Toots McKie, a powder mucker and "snow bird" (cocaine addict) who "accidentally" blew up Borger, Texas. And Thompson returned to the *Prairie Schooner* in the fall 1931 issue with "Gentlemen of the Jungle," his canniest bit of oil field folklore prior to the Federal Writers' Project. Following his customary layout he aligned three hobo snapshots: Pancake Butts, a Wobbly hash slinger who "treats his deepest thoughts as if they were so axiomatic as to be humorous"; the illiterate "Poor Boy," who ran away from home at the age of twenty-five—"Just as soon as I got big enough"; and Tin-Pan Artie, so called since he lost his face in a pipeline dynamite "experiment." Prepared under folklorist Ben Botkin's practiced eye, "Gentlemen" advanced a leaner, less self-consciously folksy idiom than

Thompson's previous excursions into West Texas oral history. As he now trusted his hobo voices to make his points for him, the portraits acquired more bite. Here he pokes fun at Tin-Pan Artie's naiveté simply by quoting him:

> Still, he insists that it was no accident, but premeditated. "For years," he says, "I'd been wondering just what would happen if I slowed up a little, and I just wondered until I had to find out. Oh, maybe I didn't plan on it turning out as bad as it did; I was more like the little boy that tried to see how far he could lean out the window than anything else. It sounds funny as hell, but I guess I just wanted to see how close I could come to getting killed."

"Gentlemen of the Jungle" earned Thompson an honorable mention in Edward J. O'Brien's prestigious annual anthology, *The Best Short Stories* (1932).

One of his hardest stories that year failed to reach print. For "Sympathy" (preserved in Art Kozelka's files) Thompson embroidered his ordeals in the collections department of the Kay-Bee Clothing Company. Agents of the "Planet Credit Stores" attempt to elicit payment from an unemployed laborer, one Oscar Bordes, by crafting an ingenious "sympathy" letter after his children die in a tragic fire caused by an inflammable nightgown he purchased on credit. Their grotesquery culminates in a newspaper article about Bordes's "reply" to their letter, his suicide: "In a note attached to his pillow, he requested that his body be shipped to the medical college of the state University, and that payment for same should be sent to the local office of the Planet Credit Stores." If "Sympathy" proved too nasty for the *Countryman* or the *Schooner,* Thompson would resurrect similar materials for his 1954 crime novel, *A Hell of a Woman.*

The young writer's persistence paid off when, in the summer of 1931, Thompson achieved his splashiest publication—and biggest check—to date. His old friend Glenn Buck agreed to serialize "The Car in the Mexican Quarter" in the August 22 and 29 issues of the *Nebraska Farmer.* Not only is this Thompson's longest and most ambitious college story; it's also his only known piece of detective fiction.

> It was about three in the morning at Mexican Joe's. A dingy lantern hanging from the unused electric chandelier cast an eerie light against the cobwebbed walls. Everything was quiet except for the gentle snores of Joe who lay beneath the counter. I was eating hot tamales while I waited for my relief on the Mexican quarter beat.
>
> There was little sound on the brick street outside. Occasion-

ally a giant beetle whirling around the street light would crash to the pavement. At least it sounded like a crash. Then you could hear, furtively, the smothered wail of an infant or the half-muttered speech of someone turning in his sleep. That was about all.

Thompson lifted the spare, hard-boiled rhythms and the flippant phrasing of "The Car in the Mexican Quarter" from the pages of *Black Mask* or *Red Harvest.* But he pulled the squalid Fort Worth setting, the hotel heroin ring, and the murdered bellboy directly from his own experiences with the Lonestar underworld at the Hotel Texas.

Police Detective Marshall, while munching on his tamale in the Mexican quarter, sees a car run over Charles "Skippy" Kahn. A "sneak thief," a "capper for crooked games," a stool pigeon and dope peddler, Kahn recently signed on as night bellboy at the Hotel Lansing. Marshall's investigation of the killing leads him through the drug underground to a familiar Fort Worth gangster—"Airplane Red" Brown, here represented under a curious mongrel of his real name and the alias Thompson would assign him in *Bad Boy:*

> Dago Red Ivers was inside at his desk. I have known Dago Red for several years, but he did not offer to get up or to shake hands. He merely stared at me out of his brown eyes.
>
> "Well," he said, finally, "what do you want?"
>
> "The man who killed Skippy Kahn," I replied, without hesitation.
>
> He sniffed. "So do the police."
>
> I grabbed him by the shoulder and whirled him around facing me.
>
> "None of your wisecracks," I snarled. . . .

Since Dago Red's alibi involves his having been in jail at the time of the killing, Marshall is humiliated, his case in tatters. Following a few more comic turns, the detective concludes where he should have begun, with Kahn's wife:

> "Skippy kept a supply of the stuff here in the house . . . I was surprised last night when he called me and told me to bring it down. . . .
>
> "I have never driven a car a great deal so that I was deathly afraid as I went along the dark streets of Mexican town. . . . You saw the result . . . I had my elbow against the gear lever and my foot was over the accelerator. As I slid down in the seat my toe naturally came down on the gas. The jerk threw my arm against the

gear lever and clashed the gears. Thoroughly frightened now, I jerked at the gear desperately bringing my foot down on the gas harder than ever. Then, I shut my eyes. I don't know how I got around the corner nor how I got home. But here I am, wanted for the murder of Skippy Kahn."

Whether Marshall believes her story or not, he proves more romantic than the Continental Op or Sam Spade:

> I started toward the door.
> Frightened, she stopped me.
> "Where are you going?"
> I grinned. "To look for the party who killed Skippy Kahn."
> "But I just told you—"
> "You didn't tell me anything," I interrupted. "Not a thing. That's the only thing you'll have to remember. Can you do it?"
> For the first time she really smiled. "You're square," she said.
> I went out the door.

Not until nearly eighteen years later, in 1949, would Thompson publish his next bona fide work of crime fiction, *Nothing More Than Murder.* By then, of course, he had shifted his narrative focus from the detective to the criminal.

Alberta's gifts as a muse, unfortunately, did not carry over from Thompson's fiction to his grades. His new writing garnered a solid 90 from Professsor Prescott, but his report card, mainly failures and incompletes, put his name on the college probation list. Thompson, however, managed one other psuedoacademic success that semester. In May he wrote and performed in the costume pageant that capped the annual Lincoln Farmers Fair. Art Kozelka previewed the spectacle for the *Cornhusker Countryman:*

> The pageant this year is the work of the girls in the pageantry class and according to Ruthalee Hollaway the presentation will surpass any of the previous ones. It is the first time that male characters were asked to take part in a pageant and it is surprising to note the eagerness that is displayed by some of the boys.
>
> Depicting the history of costume, the pageant will bear the title of "Now and Then." Jim Thompson, a sophomore, has penned the prologue.

• • •

During the days following his September wedding to Alberta, Thompson attempted to register for his junior year classes by borrowing tuition money

Arnold's Revenge

By Jim Thompson

A short-short-short-short novel by the author of "Concessions of a Husband"

Part One

Trouble Brewing

FIRST, the door-bell rang, Marcia looked at Arnold. He gestured with his revolver.

"Come in," she called.

The outer door opened, and feet walked and scraped uncertainly in the hallway. Arnold gestured again.

"In here," said Marcia.

There was a moment of silence then, like the silence a thunderbolt undergoes when deciding between a prize bull and a rotten tree. Marcia felt tense, but strong. That had always been the way with Marcia; she had great tensile strength. The door opened.

"Come right on in and make yourself at home," said Arnold cordially. "Before I blow hell out of you." *(To be continued.) Who has Arnold threatened to blow hell out of? Yes, yes, the man at the door, of course! But who is the man? Is it someone Marcia knows? If not, what is he doing there? If so, ditto. Be sure to read the next episode on page 182 of this swiftly moving novel of today.*

from Professor Crawford. But his plans to complete college ran smack into the wall of the Great Depression. The Kay-Bee Clothing Company went belly-up and, as he wrote home to his parents, many of his other opportunities also slipped away:

> Of the thirty dollars Crawford loaned me I was only able to get back $13.00. Of course, about five went for books, but the rest was lost in the maze of University red-tape. . . .
>
> Max Johnson has sold the Auditorium to a chain so I suspect that I am knocked out there. Prescott's enrollment was so low this year that he is reading his own papers. He does have some bulletins for me to work on but there is no hurry about that as I could not get a check for it before the 10th of November. Took a story over to the *Nebraska Farmer* this morning. I don't know if they will take it or not. . . .

Forget about States Securities. That's what I'm going to do.
The payments are six dollars per week and I couldn't begin to
keep them up without a good steady job.

I know that you must all be practically mad from living in
that morass of boredom and just as quickly as I can I want you
to get out of there. How is Pop's leg?

Thus Thompson dropped out of the University of Nebraska on October 1, 1931, bringing his formal education to a close.

Jim intended to remain in Lincoln through the birth of his child. As Alberta still resided with her parents, he struggled to pay his own rent with a
pair of publishing schemes, one ingenious, the other illegal. With partner
Russell Boomer, Thompson persuaded Lincoln merchants to advertise in a
discount coupon book. "Jimmie and Russell originated the idea of the
coupon book," recalls Alberta. "They printed up the books and sold them
for a few cents—you got something free or a little off. Everybody was so
hard up."

On his own Thompson hazarded a riskier venture. Drawing upon his internship at *Western World,* he drafted a series of oil promotion "sucker letters" and had them typset on showy "Thompson & Company" stationery
("Oil Field Operators Since 1914"). Listing offices in Fort Worth, Dallas, Lul-
ing, Lincoln, Oklahoma City, and Witchita Falls, Thompson & Company
seemed a bizarre fulfillment of James Thompson's dream of going into business with his son. The promotion letters themselves have disappeared, but
Jim worried over them in a nervous note to his father:

I was already in the mails on this letter so I couldn't back
down. I do not believe that there is anything incriminating in it,
anyway. I realize that the postal laws are strict, but I have a
hand-picked mailing list and I am only sending mail out, due to
necessity, in small batches. I could not write about silver mines
because I know nothing about them. I believe that this deal will
go through, in spite of rather shabby printing and everything
else. I had only seven dollars to get started on and I have bought
my stamps out of that, but I believe it is going to go. Only time
will tell, of course. Let me know right away what you think about
the letter. Study it carefully, also the letterhead. It is full of innuendo but that is about all.

Whatever the fate of Thompson's seven-dollar oil company, the Depression drove him from Lincoln soon after his church wedding, in April.
He drifted to Big Springs, Nebraska, a wispy town of five hundred people
near the Colorado border, leaving his pregnant wife behind. Summoning his

father from Texas, Thompson took over the Big Springs Theater. Through the spring and summer they operated a small movie house. Jim ordered the films and worked the projector, while Pop sold tickets and popcorn. James catalogued their ill-fated plunge into show business with a letter to Birdie—now in Burwell, where, unwittingly, she had just passed one of his bad checks:

> . . . all of us have got you in a bad fix and we should not have done it.
>
> But we have had a terrible week. The last five days have been blizzards and cold. Two nights we could not open and two others we took in an average of three dollars. So much of our trade comes from the country.
>
> We have Wheeler and Woolsey in Peach O'Reno tonight. It has snowed last night but it looks like the weather might improve.
>
> I am sending a check for six dollars. I would rather have it turned down there as my check than to have yours turned down here.
>
> We have lost fifty dollars by losing the last two shows. I am busy working on our program for tonight. . . .

Jim returned to Lincoln for the debut of his daughter, Patricia, on September 9, 1932. Alberta notes that "he was very excited about it. He stayed with my sister for a time, just a block from where I lived. Jimmie used to walk to the hospital, at least twenty-five blocks, to save his money so he could buy me a dozen roses when Pat was born."

Once Alberta and the baby were safely lodged in her parents' house, Jim took off again. "My family wasn't happy about it," she recalled, "but I thought it was necessary. He tried very hard to get a job in Lincoln—we would have been happy to settle down there." Leaving atop a boxcar, he became a hobo for the second time in his life.

"During the next two years," Thompson related in a 1937 interview with the Oklahoma News, "I worked in harvests, oil fields and did anything else I could find to do. Much of the time it was simply a hobo existence, drifting throughout Oklahoma, Texas, Nebraska and Kansas in search of work."

For the first phase of his travels Jim rode the rails from Lincoln to Omaha to Kansas City. Following the magpie aristocracy of the boxcar he preferred the "old-time hoboes" over the "Depression-born bums." But the 1930s vagrant, peerage notwithstanding, hard-traveled a dreary, dangerous track. Instead of a job, hunger, illness, and a night in jail usually waited at the end of the line. Thompson played cynical games of hide-and-seek with the legendary railroad bulls and notched his share of arrests for vagrancy. He learned, he later said, how to strain canned heat through his handkerchief and rubbing alcohol through stale bread. Often sheltered from the snow and cold by only the tall weeds of the freight yard jungles, he was sick much of the winter of 1932. He credited some "hobo benefactors" near Kansas City for nursing him through a devastating bout of pneumonia.

Thompson chronicled his lonely, frustrating passage in a Swiftean memoir he wrote a few years later as a member of an Oklahoma Popular Front organization, the Social Forum School. "A Night with Sally" was one of his most malignant bits of invective as well as one of the most revealing of his "lost" works. Fired by a "pen, hotter than the Martyr-fires of Rome, keener than the blade of Damocles," he spat back his humiliations with a vengeful screed:

> At morning of the day before, after a jungle breakfast of coffee seconds, I had definitely promised my stomach something substantial in the way of lunch. At noon, concealing my economic deficiencies under a sudden interest in zoology (the park squirrels) I had deferred the gastric engagement until dinner time. And dinner time found me striding firmly toward the freight yards with nothing more nourishing than a piece of advice from a plainclothesman, i.e., "Don't hang around here, buddy." I would have been stubborn and let him run me in, but I had heard pretty authoritatively that the city fathers of Omaha did not feed their indigent guests. Thoughtfully, they provided large quantities of cold water; and if a transient was still reluctant to leave at daybreak he was given a rather crude but invigorating chiropractic treatment. But there was no food. Not even one of those elastic, puncture-proof doughnuts which, considering their lonesome importance on the menus of most charitable institutions, must run the gamut of vitamins.
>
> At that time, the winter of 1932, one could hardly pass a corner in Omaha without seeing a sign which warned the public of the dangers of encouraging beggary. The signs advocated two methods of ridding the town of such unconscionable rascals as had the abysmally bad taste to become hungry: Ignore them entirely, and let them starve to death. Or send them to the City Mission where they would surely die of indigestion. These sentiments were not as concisely expressed as I have set them down here, of course; and in adopting either method I feel sure that the good townsmen had no idea of the inevitable objective. Only a few weeks before, the family of a man who had been imprisoned for chicken theft had died of dysentery colitis after a feast of cantaloupe rinds salvaged from a garbage can. The Community Chest and other benevolent

agencies had stoutly refused to bury the paupers—six in all—so the expense had fallen on the city. Beyond a doubt, no right-thinking citizen of Omaha wanted any more deaths of this kind—within the city limits. In the matter of the City Mission I am doubtless guilty of overstatement, also. The fare there was five slices of bread and a cup of coffee per day per man. I use the words bread and coffee advisedly. No one could eat the bread until it had been soaked in the coffee; and no one could eat it afterward. Naturally, then, there was no danger of death from indigestion.

My impressions of the second day of my fast are a trifle vague. As I have said before [sic], I sat in the library for the greater part of the day watching the snow fall on the street outside. But along about six in the evening, just after I had picked up the organ of the United States Chamber of Commerce, my mind seems to have gone blank; and when I recovered I was standing on a corner talking to a Salvation Army Santa Claus. And after leaving him, and walking block after block to the north side of town, I arrived at the Salvation Army Hotel.

The Hotel was an imposing structure of red brick and had been used as a school house until its condemnation by the Health and Fire Departments. It provided a haven for most variety of animal pests which foolishly lingered in the walls and halls in the hope of finding someone worth biting. Except for the shower room which was equipped with circulating ice water, the interior was one of Spartan simplicity. The bedding consisted of newspapers (provided by the guests), and the beds were on the floor. Toilet facilities were available in the basement; but since the basement floors were occupied by sleepers, the windows and certain corners were used by tacit consent.

I had arrived too late for dinner, I was told. Meals were served at seven in the morning, and seven in the evening. After a few nourishing drinks of water and an invigorating shower, I settled down in the upper hall spreading newspapers beneath me, and pulling my coat over my chest, box-car fashion. After a while the lights were turned out, but this did not stop the influx of bums, most of whom managed to step on me. One crippled man, stumbling along the hall, put the end of his crutch in my mouth, and when I got up to look for a less travelled route I fell down the stairway. The clerk looked up from the bible which he was reading beneath a dim desk lamp and stared at me severely.

"What are you doing down there?"

"I—"

"Where's your coat?"

"I—"

"Traded it for whiskey, I'll bet. . . . Oh, how do you expect the Lord to do right by you when you won't do right by him?"

"I'm hungry."

"You're drunk. Now, listen. I'm going to take you downstairs and see that you get located. And you'd better stay there when I do."

He marched me down to the lavatory. Mostly Negroes and Mexicans were sleeping there. A quarter-candle power bulb burned in the ceiling; and I could only make out the shadow of the snoring bums, the filth-encrusted toilets, and the gray sinks; but their odor was nothing so ethereal. It was a firm, solid thing that you had to push out of your eyes with your hands or kick out of the way with your foot.

The floor was wet, so I sat down on a toilet, turned sideways so that I could pillow my head on the reservoir. I would not care to go on record as saying that I went to sleep; but I did become unconscious. Miraculously, morning arrived.

The dining room was divided in two parts: The dining room proper, the part in which we stood, consisted of row after row of chairs with table arms. The kitchen, on the other side, contained a huge coffee urn, a coal range, piles of tin cups and plates, and forks and spoons; there were no knives.

Two men stood at the counter. One snatched hot cakes from a table near the stove, slapped them onto the tin plates, and shoved them out to the bums. The other drew the coffee, and slashed syrup over the cakes which the bums held out to him. Butter, cream, and sugar were not served.

I took my plate and cup and sat down in one of the chairs. I took a huge gulp of the coffee, and almost strangled. That was not coffee as I had known it. It was colored water; it smelled like the henna water I had seen my sister use years before. It had always made me sick, that odor. It made me sick now. Dying of thirst or hunger, I could not have consumed it. I forked off a bite of the cakes, mopped them around in the syrup, and raised them to my mouth. They were green. I loosed them from my fork and experimented with another bite. As I traced around the plate, I noticed that the metal became brighter and the cake became greener. I got up and started for the door.

"What's the matter with you fellow? Food not good enough for you?" It was one of the countermen.

"No," I said, decidedly. "It isn't."

"Reckon you could eat it if you was hungry."

I should have told him to go to hell; but I was always a little different about giving directions to strangers. I mounted the basement stairs and went out into the snow, started toward town. In the library the day before I had read Wolfe; or was it Hecht? At any rate, trudging along the crusted walk, I found myself sulfurously alliterative:

"Ah, you hymnalistic harlots" (I muttered) "you ballading bastards, you poverty-prowling prostitutes, you religion-ranting rabble. May your drums burst from a hot wind of hell fire. May nothing but the offal of the birds decorate your tambourines. May you smother in a sea of your own filth. Some day, you mushmouthed mongers of the War Cry, when I am less hungry and less cold—and I will not starve or freeze, you Sabbatical sons-of-bitches, you apologetic anus-openings—I will lay your organization open with a pen, hotter than the Martyr-fires of Rome, keener than the blade of Damocles. You will wish, then, as I carve your cancerous flesh. . . ."

His own flesh battered and weary, Thompson swapped the boxcar for a makeshift bunk with his father in Oklahoma City. Old family friends, Billy and Effie Stoors, had taken pity on the ailing ex–oil man and slipped him a room on the sly in an apartment house they managed on Northwest 5th Street.

Jim joined them there in January 1933. Oklahoma City held few consolations. Farmers who had lost their land swelled the restless army of the unemployed; hungry crowds raided grocery stores or broke into vacant apartments, burning doors and woodwork for fuel, resisting eviction with clubs. A sprawling Hooverville overran the banks of the North Canadian River. Thompson subsisted by "ditch digging, circular distributing, dish washing," as he tersely recorded on his New American Library questionnaire. Hired as a relief laborer he cut sewer ditches through the half-frozen mud for a fixed twelve days each month—his only reliable employment in a state that counted 301,310 out of work. Taking his first significant political action since leaving the oil fields, Thompson participated in a May "food riot" at the Oklahoma City Civic Center. After a peaceful march to the Federal Commissary, several thousand demonstrators were greeted with tear gas and fire hoses. Eleven activists from the Communist-led Unemployed Councils subsequently were convicted of seditious conspiracy.

Jim's letters home rippled with kindly remarks about his father's projected "acreage deals" and "oil wells." Yet even with the Stoorses' help James Thompson was rapidly declining into an unmanageable burden. When he felt up to it, he enlisted in relief work or scrubbed toilets at the Oklahoma Publishing Company. During less lucid moments he wandered

Arnold's Revenge

Part Two

Harve Bannister and Marcia Are Caught
in a Web of Circumstances

HARVE BANNISTER, in the doorway, felt a warm Niagara of perspiration cascading down the back of his neck. At least it seemed to him that it must be cascading.

"Before I blow hell out of you," repeated Arnold, transposing, "come right on in and make yourself at home."

He nodded approvingly as Bannister wobbled into a chair.

"You've come to see my wife, I suppose?"

"W-why—"

"I'll blow hell out of you if you lie to me!"

"W-why—yes. I came to see her."

"You've been here before when I was gone?"

"W-why—"

"I'll blow—"

"Yes!" *(To be continued.) Who is this—oh, all right, all right! But what's going to happen next, if you're so smart? Save yourself a headache and read the next exciting episode on page 186.*

Oklahoma City streets in a blue funk; frequently lost, he also neglected his appearance and "forgot" to eat. His broken-record patter rambled the remote past—West Texas, Anadarko, Nebraska.

Freddie and Maxine believed that their father "was a victim of Alzheimer's disease, though we didn't know to call it that back then." But Jim, like his cousin Edna Myers Borden, concluded that the sixty-three-year-old man's confusion and carelessness stemmed from chronic depression. "My brother thought that a lot of it was Pop's inabilty to cope with the stress and disappointments of the last fifteen years," Freddie recalled. "Losing the respect of men his age, being too much down on his luck—Jimmie said that Pop just couldn't handle it anymore."

James Thompson's "acreage deals" were imaginary; the "oil wells" he drilled were in his head. During one sad letter to Birdie, dated January 12, 1933, and apparently dictated to and typed deadpan by his son, he reported that he "went down to see Jake Hamon at Ardmore about helping out on the deal, but he was out of town." Hamon, of course, had been dead for nearly twelve years.

• • •

That bleak winter in Oklahoma City Thompson struggled to launch his career as a freelance writer of trade articles. Yearning for his wife in Lincoln,
and fearing for his family in Burwell, he formulated his plans with a desperate, secret dispatch to Birdie:

> . . . Alberta is quite anxious to get away from up there;
> said she would be glad to come down when you came, but did
> not want to count on it and be disappointed. I think that you
> and I could make a living for us (please don't quote me now or
> hereafter) especially since this trade-journal business has
> cropped up. But it will take "feeder" income to carry on the
> trade-journal work. I am doing all I can with it under the present
> circumstances. I thought, somewhat, as soon as we are perma-
> nently located here of putting a typing ad in the writer's maga-
> zine, as I talked of doing before. This and the other, with very
> little help, should comprise a living for all of us. Now, here's
> something else strictly on the q.t.: Would it facilitate your exo-
> dus from Nebraska if I were to send you an urgent telegram or
> letter? Let me know what you think. I believe the time has come
> for drastic action of some sort. I know I will have to do some-
> thing about Alberta within the month. Better burn this letter
> when you are through with it.
> Things are very cheap here. Food took another big drop
> this week. Eggs, eight cents a dozen; sausage or liver five cents a
> pound; milk five cents a quart; and other things proportionately.
> Rents, too, if you can get out far enough from town are cheap. I
> saw a two-room house in Capital Hill with two lots, modern ex-
> cept for gas, advertised for fifty dollars. Terms of $10.00 down
> and $10.00 per month. . . .
> I believe you would feel a whole lot better down here in a
> warmer climate, and I know I would feel better having you here.
> There is a University right in the town Freddie could attend as
> soon as the money was forthcoming. I've got to see Alberta
> pretty soon. It's been almost four months now. If nothing else
> happens I think I'll go back and see her if only for a day.

During the 1930s Thompson dashed off "many hundreds" of short technical pieces for such regional farm and oil trade magazines as the *Nebraska
Farmer,* the *Blue Valley Farmer,* the *Oklahoma Farmer-Stockman,* and the *Oil
and Gas Journal.* Since this work rarely merited bylines, it's impossible to

chart his contributions. The only certain specimen, a five-page handwritten article titled "Drilling for Oil," survives because Jim folded it into a letter to his mother. "The enclosed shows something I have been working on for a long time," he added. "I will have several articles to send them in a few days. I don't know a thing about their rate of pay or whether it is on publication or acceptance; I will let you know when I know." If nothing else, "Drilling for Oil" demonstrated his ability to parrot the generic trade-journal voice:

> Oil is graded according to the per cent of gasoline it contains. The grading is done by finding the gravity of the oil. Oil that shows forty per cent gravity is considered high grade. This grade is found in Texas in the Ranger, Breckenridge and Electra fields. At Big Spring, Pecos and Wink the gravity is thirty degrees. East Texas, Oklahoma City, Seminole and most of Kansas produces a gravity of thirty-eight degrees.

Thompson estimated that in 1933 alone he sold "three hundred thousand words of trade-journal material and collect[ed] on less than a tenth of it." Even fractional remuneration for so much writing constituted a fruitful Depression sideline. After a few sales he tempered his anti-Burwell paranoia with a bullish letter to Maxine:

> Nothing much new, here. Pop got two days [relief] work this week. Or rather, he worked two-thirds of a day and got two days time for it. I guess they don't intend to let me work this time. Yes, I have been working on something for the trade journals; but since I only have three on the string I can only write a limited amount; and I need supplementary funds. I will have everything written that can be written by next week, and then my string will be "loaded" for two months. That is why it is necessary to have a number of these magazines lined up.
>
> I don't know of any author in the U.S. who can command an arbitrary agreement from a magazine to purchase his stuff whether it is good or not; but this group certainly sent me a very strong invitation, outlining their needs and telling me how to go about the collecting and writing of it; and concluding with the statement "trusting that you will be able to get some good stories for us, we are, cordially, etc."
>
> I heard from Mom last Monday. She had been sick again. I guess Ma has been wearing her out. I urged her to get away as quickly as she could. Alberta will come down with her when she

comes. I don't know how we will get by; but I think the group perishing plan has its advantages over the old unit idea. . . .

Well, there really isn't much to write about, and my mind is too empty to ad lib. . . .

P.S. I got this out of Shelley. Kind of encouraging, isn't it?

"O, wind,
If winter comes, can spring be far behind?"

The wild west wind of Shelley's ode bolstering his optimism and industry, Thompson realized his ironic "group perishing plan" early in the spring of 1933. His trade-journal business proved lucrative enough for him to assemble the scattered "units" of his family. Alberta bundled Pat into her Whippet and, after fetching Birdie and Freddie from Burwell, reached Oklahoma City by April. Jim and Alberta dwelt under the same roof for the first time in almost three years of marriage.

That spring counted another milestone. Between caring for his father and marketing his trade features, Thompson somehow managed to complete a draft of a novel—a "thriller," as he then styled it, tentatively titled *The Unholy Grail,* and set in the Big Springs Theater. Much revised over the succeeding sixteen years, *The Unholy Grail* eventually evolved into his first crime novel, *Nothing More Than Murder.*

• • •

On Northwest 5th Street conjugal bliss contended with congested quarters and sparring in-laws. But Jim and Alberta were "thrilled" to be living together, finally, even as five adults and a baby squeezed into the poky one-room-plus-kitchen flat. "Let's just say we all had our moments," admits Alberta. With his mother at his side Jim accelerated his trade-journal production. While Birdie dictated anecdotes and data from her farming background, Jim shaped and polished the articles.

Come summer, Birdie tired of the catfights and decamped with Freddie to Maxine and Russell's home in Fort Worth. Jim quickly followed, but alone. After a short vacation with his mother he returned to the West Texas oil fields, where once again he worked as a salvage contractor. He exited Fort Worth just before Lucille Boomer Larson arrived for a visit with her brother.

Compounding the déjà vu, Jim backtracked to Fort Worth in September, and took a job as night doorman at the Worth Hotel, a plush three-hundred-room establishment on the corner of Seventh and Taylor. His official title was "Starter, Parent Garage"; a passage in his hotel novel *Texas by the Tail* unravels the confusion:

He wore the hotel's livery, but he was actually employed by the garage-taxi company which serviced the hotel. Thus, since the latter company could hardly hire a supervisor for one man, he was pretty much his own boss. Then (and this was more important to him than he had previously realized) he was no longer addressed as "boy." Lifted out of the category of faceless flunkies, he became a person—a man with a name, who was to be consulted with at least a measure of respect on the vital matters of transportation and the maintenance of ultra-expensive cars. . . .

The Depression licensed the Worth to devise fresh degradations and torments. Although the repeal of Prohibition diminished some near occasions of sin, Jim logged a merciless seven-day, eighty-four-hour week without breaks or relief. The grind flattened his feet and permanently insulted his kidneys. Despite prevarications about his elevated starter status, he re-

---

Arnold's Revenge

Part Three

Harve Bannister and Marcia Are Still Caught in a Web of Circumstances

Aʀɴᴏʟᴅ sat down in a corner easy-chair and pulled out the reading lamp. Lifting the shade, he focused the rays on the lounge where Marcia half-reclined, her white face angrily enigmatic under the improvised spotlight.

"Tableau!" His voice was a trifle insane. "Come on, you rat-eared, back-belted mess of slumgullion, make yourself at home!"

"Y-you mean me?" quavered Bannister.

"You're the only rat-eared, back-belted mess of slumgullion here, aren't you?"

"I—I believe so," said Bannister, eyeing the revolver.

"Well?"

"I'm perfectly at home, thank you."

"If," Arnold warned him solemnly, "you lie to me again I'll blow hell out of you . . . I said make yourself at home. Get over there with her. Act as though I wasn't here. Kiss her. Make love to her. But do a good job of it, or I'll bl—" *(To be continued.) Can you guess what Arnold is about to say? Ah-ah—mustn't say it! You cannot afford to miss a single line of the next exciting episode on page 191.*

mained a twenty-seven-year-old man in a quintessentially "boy's" profession. As Thompson added in *Texas by the Tail*, "The hotel boy, you see, is ageless. As long as he is reasonably able-bodied, he is a 'boy' at sixty-five just as he was at sixteen when he began his career as a page, valet or bellboy. Throughout his years his earnings remain about the same; he is making no more at the end than he was at the beginning. . . ." Jim's wages at the Worth, excluding gratuities, never exceeded $14 a week. One happy night Will Rogers tipped him a $50 bill for retrieving his car.

Jim rented the apartment over Maxine and Russell in a duplex at 1630 Mistletoe Boulevard, and sent for Alberta, Pat, and Pop. Cushier accommodations failed to ease Thompson family tensions. "Jimmie often found himself in the middle," Freddie recollected. "Petty annoyances, usually—money, the joint kitchen, the old in-law business—Mother was kind of outspoken. . . . One time in Fort Worth, Alberta and I had a real falling-out. We cried and made up in the end, but those things were so hard on Jimmie. Each time he would try to smooth it over, to balance it out, and keep things peaceful on both sides. He couldn't stand all the stress in the family—all the criticism, one putting down the other, that just drove him crazy."

· · ·

Thompson orchestrated an apt family cottage industry from the contentious duplex: true crime.

Chained to Fort Worth by his hotel schedule, he sent Birdie, Freddie, and Alberta out scouring the state for sensational murders he could write up for the fact-detective monthlies. "Jimmie's mother would keep track of the money on these trips," Alberta remembers. "So much for gas, so much to stay in a motel, so much to eat. Often we'd come home with just a nickel! But he got some pretty big checks for those pieces."

True crime pulps (so dubbed from the wood pulp they sometimes were printed on) paid at substantially higher rates than the oil and farm journals. *True Detective* tendered a rosy $250 for a six-thousand-word article during the 1930s (exactly the same money it offers in the 1990s). Thompson had been hustling unsigned $25 squibs to the fact-detective magazines at least since freshman year in college. He earned his first byline with "The Strange Death of Eugene Kling," an investigation into the slaying of a young Fort Worth drifter for the November 1935 issue of *True Detective*.

Enthusiasts of *The Killer Inside Me* may be startled to discover that the novelist who so deeply indwelt Lou Ford's sadistic psyche that he splattered the murder of Amy Stanton through ten grisly, grinding pages was himself squeamish about violence. Thompson served as a medium for some of the most monstrous impulses in American life, yet he lacked the ordinary citizen's appetite for vicarious carnage—and the ordinary citi-

*Jim Thompson poses as a murdered drifter
for "The Strange Death of Eugene Kling"
(* True Detective, *November 1935).*

zen's self-protecting detachment from it. According to his sister Freddie's portrayal, Thompson killed alongside the murderers in his true crime stories, and died with the victims:

> You wouldn't gather this from anything he's written but he was very sensitive. He couldn't stand to read anything in the paper that was a horror story—the murders and the other things that happen, they just made him cringe. He was also on the shy side, and he hated to go to the scene of a crime, look up the sheriff, and do the interviews. But I loved that part. I don't ever remember Jimmie doing his own research.
>
> It was a family affair. My mother and I would go down to the morgue and go through the newspapers until we found a murder story. We'd follow it through to the end to make sure there was a trial and a conviction. My mother was very good at endlessly going

through all of these clippings taking notes. There were some very colorful murders in those days.

We'd go back and tell Jimmie briefly what it was about. Then, with her notes I would go to the town where it happened and interview the sheriff and all the people involved, get the court record, and take the pictures. The guys were always so happy to talk about themselves and see their names in a magazine. Usually the crimes had been years before—we tried to make sure everyone was in jail—but I remember one of them was more recent. I went to the jailhouse and interviewed the so-called killer. . . . Most of them were crimes of passion, family squabbles, not at all like he wrote in later years.

I used to pose Alberta when she went along. If there was nothing available, I would say the body was found in this position, and she would stretch out on the ground and I would take her picture with my $9 Kodak. I'd sell the photographs for $3 apiece, so I thought I was in the money.

Then I would just come back and tell the story to Jimmie as I'd gathered it from the people I talked to. I would tell it to him with relish and glee, and he would write it up that way. He would write it as though he had been there and done the whole thing himself.

I remember walking in on him one night when I'd just come back from one of these trips. He was sitting in the kitchen engrossed over the typewriter, deep into something. I knocked and went in and he just about jumped out of his shoes! He'd been reading over one of our horror stories, I guess, and he leapt up scared, frightened for a minute. He'd get so nervous and upset hearing those things. Jimmie took it all very personally, like, I don't know, it was something that involved *him.*

But he needed the money. When the check from whatever magazine finally came in, Alberta would put a white handkerchief on the downstairs porch light, so that we would see it walking in. . . .

From catchpenny broadsides hawked in the London streets of Elizabethan England to the current boffo true crime dramatic reenactment television programs, *America's Most Wanted* and *Unsolved Mysteries,* so-called murders for the millions have enjoyed a continuous, if often clandestine, run. Eighteenth-century Grub Street hacks cooked up cheap biographies of celebrated thieves and murderers, while the *The Newgate Calendar* (first issued in 1773 and steadily expanded into the next century) disseminated the latest trials and executions. Richard Altick, perhaps the foremost scholar of nineteenth-century popular culture, focused the subterranean persistence of publications of violent crime for his *Victorian Studies in Scarlet:*

Their popularity in the pre-Victorian decades was a modest but unmistakable indication of the increasing and enduring taste for tales of fatal violence which was about to be so memorably exploited. . . . The passion for real-life murder was most unapologetically manifest among the "millions," as the Victorians called the working class, but it prevailed as well by the firesides of the middle class and sometimes, though rather more covertly, in the stately halls of the aristocracy. . . .

"Real-life murder" penetrated the American mainstream in 1924. Bernarr Macfadden—a physical culturist, sex lecturer, newspaper-and-magazine magnate, occasional presidential candidate—adapted the confessional formulas of his best-selling *True Story* and created *True Detective Mysteries.* Circulation spiraled toward a stunning two million readers. During the peak period—roughly 1935 to 1945, also the peak period for Thompson's involvement—*True Detective* presided as the premier publication in a dense field. As many as seventy-five different fact-detective monthlies heaped the nation's newsstands. Macfadden led the pack with *True Detective* and *Master Detective.* Wilford H. "Captain Billy" Fawcett followed with *Daring Detective, Startling Detective,* and *Front Page Detective;* and Arnold Kruse's Detective Stories Publishing Company of Chicago rounded out a prestigious (and high-paying) triumvirate with *Official Detective, Actual Detective,* and *Intimate Detective.*

"For years I wrote for every magazine in the 'true crime' field," Thompson later told Joan Kahn, his editor at Harper and Brothers Publishers for *Nothing More Than Murder.* Family and friends recall him appearing "constantly" in "dozens" of fact-detective monthlies throughout the 1930s and 1940s. A search of the thin holdings at the Library of Congress and serendipitous finds in private collections expose what is surely the tip of his true crime iceberg: thirteen signed articles between 1935 and 1949, all of them for periodicals controlled by Macfadden, Fawcett, or Kruse (see the concluding Notes and Sources for complete titles and dates).

Thompson produced at least four additional pieces in 1945 under a tantalizing masculinization of his mother's name, Bird E. Thompson, for the Canadian pulp outfit Superior Publishers/Duchess Printing & Publishing. Long after he established himself as a regular writer of fiction, he reverted to true crime whenever his finances dictated—for *Police Gazette* and the New York men's adventure magazines of the 1950s or back to *True Detective* and *Master Detective,* under the avuncular alias Bob Wicks. As late as 1959 Thompson circulated a proposal for "a book-length fact story," *The Slave Girl in the Cellar,* based on the Dora Jones peonage case.

He became what Jack Heise calls a trained seal. (The all-time true crime champion, Heise joined *True Detective* the same issue as Thompson,

Arnold's Revenge

Part Four

Harve Bannister Confesses

TWO FIGURES, male and female, clasped upon the lounge. Merely clasped. Arnold shook his head.

"No life. No feeling. Let's see how you kiss. And keep in mind that I'm not supposed to be here."

Harve Bannister stared deep into the black pools of Marcia's eyes. There were questions in them; questions but no fear. Then their lips met and there was a long, pleasant silence.

"Let's have a little action," growled Arnold, peevishly. "Marcia, don't be so particular about your dress. I'm not supposed to be here, you know. Young man, will you take your coat off or will I have to blow hell out of you?"

Bannister arose with alacrity, and shucked off his coat. A hard oblong object fell out of a pocket. Arnold leaped to his feet, his eyes glowing.

"What's that?"

"One of our brushes," explained Bannister, with pride, for he was a proud man. "My sample case is out in the hall. I've been here several times before, but your wife wouldn't let me in." *(To be continued.)* Now, do you want to read the next and final exciting episode on page 196 or not? Yes, or no. We're not going to tease you.

and still covers the beat today.) "Throw us a fish," Heise quips, "and we'll write anything." The American penmen who sleuthed in the fact-detective pulps for quick cash constitute a motley line-up—Dashiell Hammett, Lionel White, Harry Whittington, Day Keene, Anthony Boucher, Harlan Ellison, Ellery Queen, Bruno Fischer, Laurence Treat, D. L. Champion, Erle Stanley Gardner, S. S. Van Dine, Brett Halliday, even Ralph Ellison and screenwriter Nunnally Johnson.

Yet Jim Thompson was the only major crime novelist, and the only significant writer of any stripe, to hone his craft principally on true crime. Crime novelists tended to surface from the detective fiction pulps and slicks. Thompson's unique—and uniquely long, since fourteen years separate "The Strange Death of Eugene Kling" from *Nothing More Than Murder*— apprenticeship inside the more lurid lowlife of real-life murder inescapably stamped his mature work. The detective fiction and fact-detective monthlies vented different aims, assumptions, and constraints, particularly concerning sensationalism, and appealed to distinct audiences. Against the broad national demographics of the detective fiction magazines, the true crime readership concentrated in Southern and Midwestern towns. The urban following of *Black Mask, Dime Detective,* and *Black Aces* recoiled from the fact-detective pulps, disdaining their shrill headlines ("The Illicit Lovers and the Walking Corpse," "4 Murders in 4 Minutes," "Ditch of Doom—The Crimson Horror of the Keechi Hills," to cite Thompson's raciest), their grainy, morbid snapshots, and their slasher pyrotechnics ("One step, two steps, *slash!* Three steps, four steps, *slash!,* " as he telegraphed in "Ditch of Doom").

Thompson dismissed his true crime writing as "just pap" during a 1940 letter to William Couch at the University of North Carolina Press. And he groaned in *Now and on Earth,* "I'm getting plenty sick of writing with a picture of a cop and a kindergarten tot pasted on my paper carriage." But story by story he absorbed the trademark tone of incredulous horror and, eventually, carried it over to his novels.

That Thompson's fiction evidenced *any* lingering fallout from the pulps perhaps is surprising, because the true crime story adhered to a stricter formal protocol than the Harlequin romance. No writer could resist the intricate prescriptions regarding style and content—many set down in printed "writer's guidelines" that over six decades, Jack Heise reports, have changed only with the libel laws. Thompson observed the house rules:

> All stories must be post-trial, with the perpetrators convicted and sentenced at the conclusion. . . . We also prefer that cases involve not more than three suspects. . . . Do not pinpoint the guilty person too early in the story because it kills suspense. . . . Use *active* writing, avoid passive constructions. Remember that detectives probe, unearth, dig up, ferret out, determine, deduce, seek out, ascertain, discover, hunt, root out, delve, uncover, track, trace, inspect; they canvass, inquire, question, interrogate, quiz, etc. . . .

He also respected the still more baroque silent decrees involving purple leads ("The morning of February 12th, 1935, dawned gray and cold. . . ."), surreal clues (a pair of giant footprints, a woman's slipper with a missing heel, a kicking horse), and twisted riddles that with minimal ratiocination ("Something clicked in my brain. . . .") all but solve themselves.

Even as he replicated the snug routines, Thompson insinuated quirky, personalizing flourishes that stitched his signature into his best true crime stories. "Solving Oklahoma's Twin Slayings" (*Master Detective,* March 1938) subverts the obligatory atmospheric prologue with a rumble of Wobbly politics:

It is a dingy and shabby section of town, the far southwest corner of Oklahoma City, and on that humid afternoon of July 23rd,
1934, with the sun raising a greasy miasma from each oil-coated
slush-pit and creek, the air was most depressing.

Half-starved dogs wandered listlessly through weed-grown
tangles of abandoned drilling equipment. Long ago, color lines had
been forgotten; negroes and whites lived side by side in ragged
tents and shacks of wood and tin, salvaged from near-by junk
heaps: lived and died there along mean, twisting, narrow alley-like
streets.

Nature had banked a billion dollars under the ground; banked
it in the black liquid currency of oil. And in tapping that treasury
man had spent millions on towering derricks, hissing boilers, and
sinuous miles of pipe. But on the people who lived there, on the
outskirts of the world's greatest oil field, both Nature and man had
skimped. Poverty-stricken, wretched, they clung to a miserable existence. On the crest of this wave of wealth they starved. And, as is
always the case where great wealth is contrasted with deplorable
poverty, the evil overshadowed the good. Death loved such places.

So protested Oklahoma County Evidence Officer Claude Tyler, "as told to
Jim Thompson."

Thompson opted for the first-person "ghost," as recommended by Professor Crawford, for all but three of his extant fact-detective stories. "That
so many of his pieces are in the 'as-told-to' manner really amazes me,"
Heise remarks. "This wasn't common practice at all. Most of us found that
style too limited because the peace officer came on the scene long after the
crime had been committed. Plus, it usually meant handing over part of the
check to the sheriff or the prosecutor!"

The freshest and most prophetic passages in Thompson's writing for
the pulps originated with his Crawford-inspired ambition "to put yourself in
the position of the person who has had the experience." Many of his true
crime stories hint at the experimental split narration of *The Killer Inside
Me, A Hell of a Woman,* and *Savage Night.* His detectives will casually oscillate between first- and third-person voices, much like the schizoid raconteurs of his novels, and the individual vantage point of a criminal
investigation will atomize into a cross fire of multiple perspectives.

A Thompson detective in routine pursuit (as Sergeant Friday might
say) of a homicide could slip, by turns, into the role of the killer, the victim,
assorted eyewitnesses, or virtually anyone else who intersected his case.
Midway through "Solving Oklahoma's Twin Slayings" Claude Tyler, for instance, bizarrely recapitulates the murder of Leona Seals from deep inside
her own terrified consciousness:

Slowly, with the sureness of a serpent, a hand stole around the door; a hand bearing a heavy blue-black automatic. Deliberately, the evil black muzzle swept the room like the eyes of a periscope until it pointed directly at her breast. For a moment, perhaps, it remained there, almost motionless. Then an arm followed the hand, then a shoulder.

Instinctively, Mrs. Seals clasped the baby to her breast. In her first surprise and terror she had been unable to cry out; her vocal cords were paralyzed. Only her mind worked. Was it someone she knew playing a joke on her? Was it a prowler intent upon stripping her of the few pennies she possessed? Or was it—with a sickening wave of horror, another contingency flashed through her brain.

"Oh, God, no! He wouldn't do that!"

The head of the intruder appeared in the doorway, and all doubt vanished. A scream tore through her chalk-white lips, shattering the quiet air with the awful fear of the hideous. Higher and higher rose the cry.

Flame flashed from the assassin's gun, and the canvas walls rocked with the reverberations. Once again it flashed. With a little moan, the girl wife sank back on the bed. She saw, in the last moment of consciousness, that a bullet had torn through her baby's arm, and with a pain that was not born of her own great hurt she saw its frenzied sobbing.

Then, the little door of the tent closed, and her eyes shut in the last long rest.

For "Oklahoma's Conspiring Lovers and the Clue of the Kicking Horse" (*True Detective,* August 1939), County Attorney J. A. Shirley also staggers his otherwise stolid first-person inquiry with a ventriloquized re-creation, this time from the slippery perspective of conspirator Ila Hughes:

Ila Hughes sat up in bed, and drew the bedclothes up over her shoulder. It was about 9:00 p.m., November 26th, 1929, and a bitter wind howled through the eaves of the little farmhouse. She listened intently, every nerve strained. Then she heard a series of dull thumps that were almost lost in the noise of the gale. She shook her husband, muttering in exasperation as he burrowed deeper under the covers.

"Wake up, Will!" she exclaimed. The horses are in the corn!"

William Hughes was almost stone deaf and did not waken easily. She shook him again, raising her voice to a shout.

"Will, you've got to wake up!"

He stirred sleepily and opened his eyes. "What's the trouble, Ila?"

"The horses—I hear them out in the corn! You'll have to lock them up again!"

With a groan of dismay, he leaped from the bed. He jerked on his boots, and pulled an overcoat over his flannel nightshirt. Mrs. Hughes also slipped into shoes and coat, and lighted a lantern. Together they went outside.

The barn lay about 150 feet south of the house. In it they kept a cow, two work horses and a supply of corn. Judging from the sounds that were coming from the building, one or both of the horses had gotten free and were gorging themselves on the grain.

Almost fifty feet from the building, Hughes turned to his wife. "You'd better stay here, Ila," he advised. "Those horses are apt to be feeling pretty frisky, and you might get hurt. I can probably handle them better by myself."

Mrs. Hughes nodded. "All right—but be careful!"

She stood at the side of a hayrack and watched as her husband picked up the lantern and walked into the darkness. For a moment, as he entered the barn, his figure was silouetted in the doorway. Then, suddenly, as though an unseen hand had snuffed out the flame, the light went out.

She took a step forward and shouted, but the cry was lost in the sudden bedlam that filled the night. In the terrible uproar, she could hear the startled and angry neighings of the horses, the sound of thudding blows, and her husband's frantic cries for help.

It was minutes after the tumult ceased before Mrs. Hughes could force herself forward. Inside the barn, she struck a match with a trembling hand. The flickering light revealed a ghastly scene. . . .

One Thompson fact-detective story advanced beyond flickering portents of the novelist to come. "Ditch of Doom—The Crimson Horror of the Keechi Hills" (*Master Detective*, April 1936) decisively laid claim to the thematic obsessions and narrative attack of his crime fiction in a compact masterwork. William "Uncle Billy" Royce, a gruff, reclusive octogenarian and self-proclaimed member of the James gang, has spent the last thirty years excavating his farm in Oklahoma's Keechi Hills for the vast store of stolen gold Frank and Jesse told him was buried there: "A good fifth of his hundred and sixty acres were one shovel-scarred battlefield. There were holes in the barn, the chicken-house, the pigpen, along the creek—in every place that a person might look. And still his digging continued. . . ." When a bloody trail in the kitchen leads to a shallow grave beneath the chicken-

Arnold's Revenge

Part Five

After Troubled Seas

Brandishing his gun, Arnold fled the room, a wild cry on his lips.

Marcia's first words to Harve Bannister were pregnant with meaning.

"When," she whispered, "you are through with the toothpaste, do you always replace the cap on the tube?"

"Never," he replied. "I always drop it down the drain."

"Darling!" said Marcia. And threw her arms around him.

She stayed there for a long time, reveling in this new love. Only when the shot rang out upstairs, did displeasure cloud her eyes. "Well," she was on the point of saying, "Arnold has finally succeeded in blowing hell out of something."

But she did not say it. There was something so unspoiled—something that needed sheltering about Bannister. It would be like a slap in the face to confront him with any further crudity.

"Just Arnold," she whispered again. "Just Arnold—clearing his head."

THE END

house and the mutilated body of his latest "wife," the eccentric treasure hunter turns out to be a demented murderer. And what about all those other holes? Suspicions reel through a sickening cavalcade of mysterious disappearances: Uncle Billy's six previous housekeepers, some overnight guests whose abandoned auto rots in his barn. . . . "There were thousands of possible graves on that farm."

Ostensibly reported by Caddo County Deputy Sheriff C. C. Ruff, Thompson's earliest portrait of a serial killer actually derived from a newspaper article, "Uncle Billy and the Mystery of the Stolen Gold," which Bob Kniseley published in the *Daily Oklahoman*, February 3, 1935. Thompson cadged his facts and a great deal of incidental imagery, including that poignant "shovel-scarred battlefield," from Kniseley. Even Uncle Billy's confession, supposedly taken down firsthand by Deputy Sherriff Ruff, appeared in the original interview.

Here Uncle Billy Royce, speaking—it should be noted—from the very same Anadarko jail where Jim Thompson was born, reprises the murder of his wife, Lela Ethel, for the *Daily Oklahoman:*

"She found $5,000 buried on the farm, down in the valley just below the barn, and when I told her I wanted part of it she told me it was hers—that I should have none of it."

The old voice grew a little wild, eyelids flew wider open, face muscles worked and their playing up and down showed under gaunt cheek bones of the slender visage. Then they knotted on jaws that a moment before had appeared hollow and devoid of strength.

"It was mine! It was mine! It all belonged to me! Frank James told me where to look for it, and it was mine!" The more timorous of the men sitting around the walls of the room seemed to shrink from the sound.

Then in a flow of fluttering words a story came out.

"She wouldn't give me my share, and we fought. She chased me with a butcher knife. She wanted all of my land—all of my money. I hit her—hit her with a piece of pipe, and she fell, but she got up, and so I hit her again, and again, and then I drug her into the hole in the hen house and covered her up."

This is Thompson's hasty reworking in *Master Detective:*

And Uncle Billy was insane. Waiting there in the Anadarko jail, he told still another story of the tragedy. But no longer did he talk mildly, with a bold eye. His eyes rolled, and his voice rose to a screech.

"She found money! She found $5,000 buried on the farm, down in the valley below the barn. When I asked her for part of it she told me it was hers—that I should have none of it. She wouldn't give me my share, and we fought. I hit her, and she fell down. Then I dragged her into the hole in the hen house and covered her up."

The most arresting moments of "Ditch of Doom," however, have no parallel in the newspaper source. Whereas Kniseley scarcely mentions the Caddo County sheriff's office, Thompson cunningly positions Deputy Sheriff C. C. Ruff at the center of his story. Ruff's shell-shocked reactions and his slow-dawning insight into Uncle Billy inflame the "crimson horror":

Turning to enter the kitchen, my gaze was arrested by something I saw on the north wall of that room. Startled, I leaned closer. It was a tiny clump of fuzz, glued to the siding by a thin dark streak of what was unmistakably blood. A few feet further along the wall was another of those curious stains; I counted eight in all.

Eight streaks of splattered blood. Eight murderous strokes of an axe or knife. . . . We retraced the spots on the walls; and through them the details of the tragic drama that had been played

in that lonesome shack became almost as clear as if we had witnessed it.

Pulling out all his stops, Thompson would switch perspective a dizzying half-dozen times. As the first- and third-person voices merge and jar, he
downshifts from Deputy Ruff to the anguished final moments of Lela Ethel,
to the skeptical queries of neighbor Tom Taylor and the confrontational
cross-examinations of Royce's stepdaughter and stepson. With his boldest
stroke, the hallucinatory prologue, Thompson transports the reader into
the disordered mind of Uncle Billy:

> Vague whisps of moonlight filtered through the dust-grimed
> windows. Shadows fell upon the bed, the shabby sticks of ancient
> furniture—crept through the dingy rooms in quiet terror and van-
> ished. In the black-jacks, the wind soughed miserably; and from
> the ghostly hills an owl hooted his eternal question. . . .
>
> He shot the rusted bolt of the door, and pulled it open. Again,
> standing on the porch he listened. Again, he heard the owl's echo-
> ing cry.
>
> That, and other sounds.
>
> The soft shuffle of a spade. Digging. The quiet click of a pick,
> striking its way through the rocky shale. And. . . .
>
> The grisly crunching of an axe; the terrified pleading of a
> woman—choking, groaning.
>
> Then—silence!

Writing for the fact-detective monthlies taught Thompson how to relate a complicated story in a few crisp pages. True crime allowed him to ex-
plore character, language, atmosphere, pacing, and rhythm without the
burden of inventing a plot (and plot would always be a burden for Thompson). In 1940, when he applied to the Rosenwald Foundation for a grant to
compose an oral history of "Business, Labor, and the Unions," Thompson
explicitly rooted his legacy from the pulps in the first-person ghost:

> The first-person device, by permitting the reader to identify
> himself with one character from beginning to end, not only serves
> to juxtapose one force with another and gives both meaning, but
> makes for easier reading. In writing for popular magazines I have
> found that the first-person—as-told-to or ghostwritten—story has
> a far wider audience than the third-person narrative; it gives the
> reader a feeling of being part of things rather than an observer.
> That this type of writing is not for the "intellectual" is doubtless
> true, although it should not offend them. . . .

The subjective reenactments and re-created conversations of Thompson's true crime stores offhandedly mingle fact and fiction, a predicament

Jim Thompson poses as the investigator for
"Case of the Giant Footprints" (Startling
Detective, *May 1940).*

that on least two occasions demanded discreet acknowledgment from *Master Detective.* "The Dark Stair" (June 1946) and "Case of the Catalog Clue" (July 1948) each carried a baffling caveat in tiny italic type: *"Real police procedure and detective work form the basis for the following stories, although they are not fact cases. Models posed for the photographs used with these stories and any resemblance of the names used to those of actual persons is coincidental."*

Even a true fact–detective story, of course, could not be printed without illustrations. Here too Thompson improvised liberally. Alberta served as a willing victim, crawling into a ditch for "The Illicit Lovers and the Walking Corpse" (*Daring Detective,* January 1940), or lying facedown in the leaves for "The Riddle of the Bride in Scarlet" (*Daring Detective,* October 1936). Birdie grimly played solitaire in a photograph accompanying "Catch the Keeper of the Calendar" (*Intimate Detective,* May 1940), and Freddie starred as the "Dead Man's Wife" in "The Dark Stair." Jim himself fittingly portrayed multiple parts, posing as the brutally murdered transient for "The Strange Death of Eugene Kling" and as the stalwart investigator for the "Case of the Giant Footprints" (*Startling Detective,* May 1940).

• • •

Thompson owed the next major change in his life to true crime. Late in 1935 he gleaned an assignment to profile an Oklahoma police chief, "a model of public officialdom," and the promise of a cool $2,000 for the long serial. After turning in his uniform to the Worth Hotel, he moved his extended family back to Oklahoma City. Three months and some "forty thousand words of the best damned detective story I had ever written" later, the crime-busting chief of police was locked up in his own jail, charged with heading an interstate auto theft ring. As Thompson moaned in *Roughneck,* "I came to a trash receptacle, tossed the thick, carefully prepared manuscript inside. . . . It was a ludicrously comic situation, but somehow I couldn't laugh a bit."

But for once "flukish Fate" was secretly spinning in his behalf. Returning to Oklahoma City meant more than cashiering a demeaning, dead-end hotel job. For the first time since leaving the University of Nebraska, Thompson would have the support of a community of serious writers. His initial contact, editor Martin Heflin, had already published "Arnold's Revenge," a parody of the radio cliffhanger, in the February 1935 issue of *Bandwagon,* Oklahoma City's lively "Magazine of the Southwest" (the five "episodes" are serialized within this chapter).

Since Thompson's new writing increasingly would be fueled by his radical politics, he also was about to become a public figure. Soon after his arrival he helped organize an Oklahoma City John Reed Club. And in the spring of 1936 he joined the Communist Party.

The Concrete Pasture: 1936– 1940

Jim Thompson once whispered to Ted Cowan that during the 1930s he had clandestinely operated as state secretary for the Oklahoma Communist Party. This conspiratorial boast, the crowning provocation in a taunting progression calculated to affront and panic his earnest, baby-faced cousin, then in the service of the U.S. Navy, exaggerated significantly Thompson's standing among Oklahoma Communists—though not at all, however, his pride in his Party affiliation or the powerful role the Party would play in his future.

Around New York, Chicago, and San Francisco young writers rallied to the Communist Party as the primary source of political alternatives for artists, especially after the advent of the Popular Front in 1935. John Reed

Club magazines and agitprop theaters served as vehicles of revolutionary culture. Party activists and their close collaborators dominated the American Writers' Congress and the League of American Writers, which developed in its wake. But when Jim climbed the stairs to the Progressive Book Shop at 29½ West Grand Avenue, site of the new Oklahoma Communist Party headquarters, state membership comprised only "twenty-eight comrades, mostly isolated in rural sections," according to his friend—and the bona fide Party secretary—Robert Wood. "In Oklahoma City we had a few, disconnected from the masses. . . ."

Through the tireless recruiting of Bob Wood and his wife, Ina—the illustrious "Union Maid" of Woody Guthrie's song—the Oklahoma Party prospered. "During the latter part of the decade," historian Harvey Klehr observed in *The Heyday of American Communism,* "remote outposts like Oklahoma . . . developed thriving Communist parties." As the Depression continued to desolate the state with all the random brutality of a natural disaster, Party registration leapt to 114 by January 1, 1937, and quadrupled again to an impressive 500-plus by 1938. Eli Jaffe, who came to Oklahoma in 1938 and organized for the Workers' Alliance, recalls:

> In those days it was not too difficult to become a radical. If you had any sensitivity at all, you had to feel that things weren't working, and that something had to be done. Oklahoma was in bad economic trouble. The oil industry was badly depleted, and there was an agricultural crisis. Many Oakies flooded into Oklahoma City from the oil fields, along with the farmers who had lost their land to the dust storms. Many unemployed collected along the banks of the river, in Community Camp, Walnut Grove, the "Hoovervilles" where people lived in shacks made of tin cans, license plates, and cardboard cartons. There was a great deal of unrest, and a lot of humane, humanity-minded, and progressive people were affected by the plight of native Oklahomans. Spain also was a watershed issue for many of us, and a number of Oklahomans went under the umbrella of the Abraham Lincoln Brigade.

As the Party base shifted from the outlying farms to Oklahoma City, writers began to haunt the weekly meetings at the Progressive Book Shop. Nearly all of Thompson's closest friends on the Oklahoma Federal Writers' Project also would affirm Party membership: William Cunningham, Ned DeWitt, Fred Maxham, Dan Garrison, Joe Paskavan, and Gordon Friesen. The nostalgic engagé life of "meetings . . . lectures . . . rallies," which Thompson ascribed to Galen White for *The Concrete Pasture,* his unfinished 1954 novel about the Party, dovetailed with his own. The Oklahoma City Communist Party, like its national counterpart, offered writers comrade-

*Robert Wood—Secretary of the Oklahoma
Communist Party, inside the Progressive Book
Shop, 1939 (Photograph by C. J. Kaho,
courtesy of the* Daily Oklahoman*)*

ship and a sense of common purpose, along with political action. Thompson enjoyed the group solidarity, study sessions devoted to readings of Marx, Lenin, and Trotsky; lectures at the Social Forum School; speeches to the Southwest Writers' Congress; fund-raising dances for the Abraham Lincoln Brigade—even if, as always, he stood a little off to the side. "Jim was always writing," remembers Ina Wood, "sometimes during our meetings!"

For sensitive communications the Oklahoma Communists addressed one another under nondescript Party pseudonyms. Secrecy and a low profile were particularly crucial to Thompson as he climbed the rungs of the Writers' Project, though his identification with the Party eventually would burst forth into destructive controversy. "Bill Cunningham or Jim Thompson could not have lasted a day on the project," suggests Jaffe, "if that was common knowledge." Thompson's alias, intriguingly, contained a surname he would repeatedly reassign to his fictional characters, Robert Dillon.

During the late 1930s Thompson's personal history merged with the public history of his generation: the writers who threw body and soul into the revolutionary left, worked the Federal Writers' Project, grew disillusioned, and ultimately broke with the Party.

Many in that generation, both on the national scene and in Oklahoma City, paid dearly for their radicalism with arrests, persecution, and blacklisting. Thompson too would suffer, as we shall see, in one spectacular confrontation with the Oklahoma power structure. Yet the outcome for him otherwise proved considerably more providential. Nearly everything good that happened to Jim Thompson as a writer—starting in 1936, and continuing deep into the next decade—came about as a result of his involvement with the radical left.

• • •

On first arriving in Oklahoma City, Thompson seemed to be staring straight into the maw of ruin. The cruel fiasco of his true crime serial left him scrambling for fresh cases to dramatize. The trade journals had recently cut their rates in half. And Alberta, in premature celebration of their fortune, was pregnant with a second child.

Shoehorning his family into a rooming house on the rim of the business district, Thompson kept writing. In collaboration with Birdie he continued to storm the trades—a thousand words on fruit jars, caning chairs . . . anything for a sure $20. Freddie resumed her runs through the newspaper morgues and county jails. But Thompson sold perhaps as few as three true crime stories in 1936.

Between checks he searched for more secure work. Thompson presented his clips to all the Oklahoma City daily newspapers, garnering kudos but no job. After one frustrating interview, he reported, a friendly editor drew his attention to a new organization that appeared to be hiring unemployed writers. As he sketched the moment in *Roughneck:*

> I started for the door, very dejected as you may guess.
>
> An elderly copy-desk man followed me out into the hall.
>
> "Too bad, son," he said. "If you're not too particular about money, I may be able to put you next to another job."
>
> I said that I would be grateful for anything at all, for the time being. He told me what the prospective job was, and my face fell again.
>
> "Writers' Project? But that's relief work, isn't it? I'm not a relief client."
>
> "They have a few non-relief people—men who really know writing and editing. Sort of supervisors, you know, for the non-professionals. One of the fellows who got laid off here is over there now."

"Well," I said dubiously, "I suppose it won't hurt to look into it."

"Sure it won't." He gave me an encouraging slap on the back. "They've got a big set-up over there, a hundred and twenty-five people, I understand. Maybe you can get to be boss of the whole shebang!"

Thompson signed on with the Oklahoma Federal Writers' Project on April 1, 1936. His cornball shuffle with the rustic "copy-desk man" partook of retrospective leftist camouflage. He already was acquainted with the project through his friendship with the state director, William Cunningham.

A tall, raw-boned, and ruddy-complexioned Oklahoma farmboy, Bill Cunningham was five years older than Thompson and a regional novelist with an increscent national reputation. In 1935 Vanguard Press published *The Green Corn Rebellion,* Cunningham's sympathetic re-creation of the attempt by some two thousand Oklahoma tenant farmers to march on Washington as a protest against the 1917 draft. Jack Conroy of the *New Masses* praised the book as "not only an excellent specimen of sectional realism, but a proletarian novel in the best sense of the word." Cunningham followed this in 1936 with *Pretty Boy,* a mythic celebration of Oklahoma outlaw Charles Arthur "Pretty Boy" Floyd. He had contributed folklore to Ben Botkin's *Folk-Say,* and one of his poems, "The Old Time Fiddler," appeared in an Oklahoma textbook for ninth-grade English students. Like Thompson, he also cranked out stories for the pulps.

Prior to his appointment as state director, Cunningham had spent five years as an instructor in proletarian literature and Marxian economics at Commonwealth College, a self-styled "united front labor college" near Mena, Arkansas. Commonwealth students, mainly workers, farmers, and artists, crafted an experiment in communal living and cooperative education. Students and teachers toiled side by side in the fields, kitchen, and laundry; they jointly established the curriculum, and even constructed their own campus buildings. As an advertisement in the *Windsor Quarterly,* the college's "revolutionary movement" literary magazine, defined the school:

> Believing that the working class must and will develop a new art and culture, and believing that the young American writer can find artistic power and maturity only by identifying himself with this class of the future, Commonwealth College welcomes as students young men and women with literary power who seek clarification on the great social issues of the day.

Thompson admired *The Green Corn Rebellion* and prized his rapport with its author. Soon Jim was a regular visitor at the apartment that Bill, his wife, Sally, and younger sister, Agnes, shared on Northwest 5th Street. "Around Bill," Agnes "Sis" Cunningham notes, "Jim's strange shyness disappeared in long afternoons of drinking and literary talk."

Bill Cunningham "wanted Jim Thompson on the Writers' Project right from the time they first met in the winter, I think, of 1935," according to Sis. "But he couldn't on account of the federal regulations that limited the number of non-relief workers." Dismayed by the paucity of professional writers on the Project, the director hired his friend at the earliest possible opportunity.

Thompson joined the project as a half-time non-relief worker with a salary of $68 a month. His first assignment: the Oklahoma state guide.

•   •   •

The Federal Writers' Project, a program of the New Deal's Works Progress Administration (WPA), opened in 1935 with a mission to create suitable work for America's destitute writers. For nearly nine years the Writers' Project carried between 3,500 and 6,686 employees on its rolls, many of whom were aptly ridiculed as "near writers" and "would-be writers," since almost any person on relief who could sign his name might claim eligibility. "What a collection of oddballs we had!" the executive secretary for the Oklahoma project, Alta Churchill DeWitt, remembers. "A few who had written, more who hadn't written, some who wanted to write, and others who were just there." Yet a galaxy of America's aspiring poets and novelists turned to the Federal Writers' Project for sustenance early in their careers: Conrad Aiken, Nelson Algren, Saul Bellow, Sterling A. Brown, John Cheever, Edward Dahlberg, Ralph Ellison, Kenneth Fearing, Zora Neale Hurston, David Ignatow, Claude McKay, Kenneth Patchen, and Richard Wright.

The collective goal was the production of the American Guide Series. Across the nation Project reporters compiled life histories, preserved folklore, and classified local records in an unprecedented reclamation of homegrown experience. "Certainly few, if any, decades in our history," Warren I. Susman has written of the 1930s, "could claim the production of such a vast literature—to say nothing of a vast body of films, recordings, and paintings —that described and defined every aspect of American life."

Baedekers of cultural diversity, the state guides spotlighted what Whitman called this "nation of many nations." Their texts blended a practical manual for automobile tourism with speculative essays on history, natural settings, labor, economy, racial and ethnic groups, the arts, and recreation. Often to the consternation of legislatures and Chambers of Commerce, the guides shaded their nationalism not with rosy boosterism but with thorny social criticism.

Thompson began at the back of the Oklahoma book, with the automobile tours. Alma Churchill DeWitt recalls that "Jim was part of a close group of Project writers that included Ned [DeWitt], Joe Paskavan, and Louis L'Amour. They were all young and very ambitious about writing. In the mornings they'd go off and visit Indian mounds, bat caves, fields of wild-flowers, driving all over the state to get information for the tours." He quickly worked his way up to drafting early versions of the "General Information" directory and the essay on "Folklore and Folkways." Within months Thompson became so indispensable to the Oklahoma guide that Bill Cunningham tagged him "the most capable writer on the Project," and recommended him to Henry Alsberg, the national director of the Federal Writers' Project, for a promotion:

> One of our own workers has displayed considerable competence. He is Jim Thompson, now on the operating Project as professional, non-relief. He has been writing Tours and now is re-organizing and rewriting the Introductory Essays. He is a professional writer (wood-pulps), about 32 years of age, is quiet and commands a great deal of respect on the Project.
> I should like to put him on the coordinating project at about $125 per month, full time, as Guide Book Editor. He has wide, general interests and a better grasp of things than has anyone else on the Project. . . .
> Another reason I should like to get Thompson in a position like this is that he, of all those I know about, would be best qualified to take over the job of state director in case I should be struck by lightning. The stormy season is approaching. . . .

He ascended to guide book editor in September 1936. Over the next few years Thompson would have many occasions to excoriate the meddling state bureaucracy. "Oklahoma City," Cunningham quoted him in a letter to Alsberg, "is a big town built upon the ideas of still smaller men. . . . A city whose artistic ideals are hung on the long horns of a lean steer and whose cultural life is wrapped in the rusty hide of the same steer, said steer having died long ago." And he came to loathe the long hours spent untangling the clotted "research" his relief reporters deposited in the guide book files—"It's like trying to work with a ball of yarn that the cat has been playing with."

The position proved a mare's nest. Still, Thompson's pride in his tiresome labors surges through an article he later wrote for the *Sooner Magazine* about the Oklahoma state guide:

> . . . It might be well to mention here, that the *Oklahoma Guide* is much more than a "guide." In many respects it resembles an encyclopedia. The book opens with a series of essays on the

state's social and economic life: the educational system, transportation, racial elements, and many other topics. Following these,
and occupying approximately three-fourths of the volume, are
twenty-three tours covering every federal highway and several important state highways. The tours not only take cognizance of
camping sites, important towns and important people—the usual
things—but also discuss the history, the mode of living, the industries and agricultural practices of each locality. Obviously, the one-
man-and-stenographer idea has its drawbacks.

The writer in a work of this kind has a thousand chances
to madden the reader and make himself ridiculous. "Fifty years
ago . . . " he says, and the reader picking up the book a few years
hence will have to guess the date referred to. "On your left," says
the scribe, "is the largest Masonic Temple in Oklahoma." And the
tourist, who has stubbornly entered town from the wrong direction, looks to his left and sees an undertaking parlor. . . .

Our tourist can never be lost because we orient him constantly and the orientation is not dependent on red barns,
haystacks, and whoops and hollers. He can start out on one highway, turn off on a country road, double back, and take another
highway, and he'll always know exactly where he is and the exact
distance to his destination. If he likes oil wells we'll take him right
up to the derrick floor and give him the history of the industry
from spring-pole to rotary; if he's a golf nut we'll show him the best
courses. Whatever he does is all right with us. . . .

Now, after two years, we have some 4,000,000 words in our
files, probably the largest collection of Oklahoma manuscripts in
existence. Our guide-book manuscript of 180,000 words is the concentrated essence of the file material.

As guide book editor Jim took home a substantial salary, at least for
Oklahoma, where average annual earnings still hovered below $800. His
raise allowed him to swap the dismal rooming house for a duplex at 429½
West 6th Street. Like many Depression families, the Thompsons took ad-
vantage of the volatile housing market and kept moving to larger quarters.
The National Archives preserves a comical correspondence between
Thompson and Henry Alsberg, initiated when one of the national director's
letters came back to him "Address Unknown," which plots four new
Thompson residences in a scant seven months. (The incessant motion also
apparently confounded the FBI. A sentence in Thompson's small bureau file
reads, "Will attempt to ascertain the present whereabouts of James M.
Thompson.")

At home, wherever that was, mayhem persisted. Alta Churchill DeWitt, an occasional supper guest, recalls that in the late 1930s "the Thompsons led a kind of harum-scarum life. His father's senility was a big problem. But in general, life was different for them than it was for other people—that whole huge extended family of Jim's. Things just happened to them, both good and bad. The sense I got was that everything was serendipitous, full of accidents and surprises. Nothing was planned out."

But whether planned or not, the year that had dawned so darkly rang down on a joyous note. December 25, 1936, the Thompsons welcomed the birth of a second daughter, Sharon, a Christmas baby.

• • •

The peppery smoke of politics permeated the offices of Oklahoma Federal Writers' Project. Thompson supported Bill Cunningham in a tacit radicalization of the administrative agenda. Their insurgent program—and occasionally graceless maneuvering—split the Project into divisive factions: a left-leaning nucleus of writers and editors led by Cunningham, Thompson, and Ned DeWitt; and a conservative main body of clerical workers whose mouthpiece was assistant state director Zoe Tilghman. The founder of the Oklahoma Poetry Society, a former literary editor of *Harlow's Weekly,* and the widow of Marshal Bill Tilghman, Sheriff Thompson's old territorial sidekick, Zoe Agnes Tilghman intimated that she—and her kind—had been "frozen out by the Communist group."

The Oklahoma Writers' Project sustained a concentration of Marxists in executive positions that, perhaps, only was exceeded by the New York City and San Francisco offices. For obvious reasons Cunningham, Thompson, and DeWitt steadily disavowed Party membership while on the Project. Sis Cunningham reveals the hidden threads fastening the Writers' Project to the Oklahoma City CP:

> The Oklahoma Party had a few hundred members on paper. Bob Wood would go on field trips through the state signing up members who never came to meetings. The Oklahoma City meetings could have as few as seven or eight people, intellectuals, writers, with a few working people.
>
> The Party was stronger than that, of course, and had other wings. To protect themselves in case of a crackdown, many would not usually go. For instance, the Red Dust Players [her agitprop theater group] almost never went. Around Oklahoma City the heaviest concentration came from the Writers' Project—Bill, Jim, Ned, Alta, Gordon [Friesen], Dan Garrison, and a few more.
>
> The meetings sometimes took place in the bookstore, but more often in people's homes. Or we would rent a room at one of the hotels downtown. We'd start off with some singing—"The Inter-

nationale," "Brother, Can You Spare a Dime," "Solidarity Forever," "Casey Jones, the Union Scab," "Commonwealth of Toil," "Pie in the Sky," lots of songs. Then we made reports. In Oklahoma City one of the main focuses of the Communist Party was organizing the un-employed workers into the Workers' Alliance. The Writers' Project members were heavily involved in that, working with what used to be called the Unemployed Councils.

Jim Thompson sometimes came to the meetings with his sis-ters, but mostly he came by himself. I remember staying up with him many nights stuffing envelopes. Bill always was very circum-spect and careful about his involvement—no one was ever able to link him to anything. Jim, Ned, and some of the others were more up-front, but still pretty secretive. . . .

Cunningham and Thompson screened anti-Fascist films and staged benefits for the Spanish Loyalists on Project time. Project reporters under their supervision inventoried the state's cooperative institutions, noting that "the cooperative movement in Oklahoma may well be regarded as a modern method of the struggle for economic liberty dating back to Pharaoh's oppression of the children of Israel." In another Commonwealth College–inspired venture, the Project mounted "A Survey of Community Sales" in Oklahoma. "The community sale brought consumer and producer together, thereby eliminating the economic middlemen," an introduction asserted. Cunningham encouraged his secretary, Alta Churchill DeWitt, to visit the Southern Workers Anti-War Summer School at Commonwealth Col-lege, and promptly increased her salary when she returned.

The Marxist inner circle also quietly orchestrated a movement to es-tablish an Oklahoma Writers' Project union. In the summer of 1936 Cun-ningham hired Fred Maxham, ostensibly as a reporter assigned to a labor survey, and provided him with a mysterious assistant, Thelma Shumake. The pair produced exactly one short paper over five months, a rough draft of an "Industry and Labor" essay for the state guide. Off the public record, Fred Maxham "was a paid Party functionary Bill brought in from Common-wealth College," his then girlfriend, Sis Cunningham, relates, as well as the new state organization secretary for the Oklahoma Communist Party. Max-ham and Shumake went to work promoting the union.

Thirty Project writers met at the Huckins Hotel on August 17, blocked out a tentative program, and selected officers. While Ned DeWitt was elected president, Alta Churchill secretary, and Louis L'Amour delegate to the national Works Progress Administration convention, Jim Thompson served as chairman of the union's organization committee.

During a follow-up assembly early in September, wrangles over a con-stitution threatened to choke the union in its cradle. Zoe Tilghman included a personal report on the gathering among a docket of materials she subsequently leaked to Congressman Martin Dies, chairman of the House Committee on Un-American Activities:

> About two months after Maxham's appearance, he and Mr. Cunningham promoted formation of a Union, which it was expected would include not only the writers but all white-collar workers. . . . However, a radical constitution was submitted, causing a considerable fight, and finally the adoption of another which eliminated the more radical sections. The union was carried on for some time, and Maxham, with Cunningham's open approval (although as director he had officially resigned from the Union on the ground that a "boss" couldn't belong) made strong efforts to join the union to the national Workers' Alliance which, at least in its leadership and policies is strongly communistic. They tried to rush this through on a minority vote but others made parliamentary objections and this also failed. . . .

Undaunted by internal dissension, Thompson and DeWitt endeavored to push the union to bolder actions. When word reached them that six employees on the Missouri Project had been fired, apparently for organizing a union, they quickly called a solidarity meeting. Thirteen Oklahoma writers mailed letters of protest to Henry Alsberg. As cooler heads invoked the WPA regulations sanctioning unions and requested a federal investigation, Thompson went for the throat:

> I wish to protest against the recent outrage in St. Louis which for sheer tyranny and the usurpation of human rights has not been equalled since the Homestead strike.
>
> As I understand it, six union writers there were dismissed from the Writers' Project because of some very reasonable requests they made to the Project director; another cause for their dismissal, I understand, was their attempt to organize their fellow writers and thus improve the working standards.
>
> Who is this martinet who violates the cardinal principles of human liberty? Why does she stop with sic-ing the police on the picketeers? Why doesn't she equip herself with thugs and tear gas and completely annihilate these villains who have the base temerity to "ask for more"? Why doesn't she show herself for what she is—a disciple of Bergdoff, Pinkerton, and William Randolph Hearst?
>
> I cannot believe that when you know of the true state of affairs in St. Louis you will allow it to continue. I feel sure that you

will have these writers reinstated, and at the same time familiar-
ize the director with the rights of employees to organize. To
adopt any other course—to allow the wrong to go unrighted—
would strike a severe blow at the labor movement, and render
"free speech" an empty phrase.

He wasted his breath. Alsberg's inquiry concluded that the Missouri
writers misrepresented their grievances to their Oklahoma brethren. But
the "martinet," Project director Geraldine Parker, was forced to resign on
grounds of incompetence.

The hastily convened session, unfortunately, proved the undoing of the
Oklahoma Writers' Project union. As an anonymous memorandum from the
brief Zoe Tilghman released to the Dies committee discloses:

At that time the Federal Writers' Project of St. Louis were out
on strike, a thing we the loyal group considered a disgrace to our
Government. Wires came from them to the project union here in
Oklahoma City for aid to assist them while on the strike. A few
days later we were asked to contribute to another group going out
on strike. A meeting was called to decide whether or not we would
go in with the Workers' Alliance.

At this meeting many of the workers knew nothing of it, [and]
therefore were not present. Maxham rose and in loud exciting
tones endeavored to railroad the vote over, when a lady arose and
stated that the workers had not been properly informed regarding
the holding of the meeting, that the Roberts Rules of order were
not followed and there was less than two-thirds of a majority vote,
which was necessary in the case. Others came out boldly and
stated they were not in favor of this picketing of the Capitol in
Washington and asked to withdraw from any such union. This put
a quell on the reds for they were aware the scales had fallen from
the eyes of the "Conservatives," as we were called, and as the
press quoted, the union died a quiet death. Nevertheless its power
was still felt in the office. Mrs. Tilghman, the assistant state director, lost everything but her title. . . .

For its final act the Oklahoma Writers' Project union threatened a November strike, after Washington proposed broad cuts in relief personnel. A
mass meeting chaired by Thompson and DeWitt at the Labor Temple, on
West California Avenue, induced local WPA officials to promise that all
ousted white-collar workers would be reassigned to other state projects.
But another rash motion to reconsider linkage with American Workers Alliance shattered the shaky union.

Following the demise of the Writers' Project union, the executive cadre affiliated independently with the American Writers Union. Thompson was elected district representative, and for the rest of the decade served on the executive board of the AWU.

Accusations of Communist domination on the Project reached Oklahoma Congressman R. P. Hill. Citing Cunningham's sponsorship of "an abortive union movement designed to embarrass the Administration," his "favoritism" and "communistic activities," Hill demanded the director's dismissal in January 1937. The Oklahoma Project, by then, had already weathered a visit from the Federal Bureau of Investigation. Cunningham shrugged off the Feds with an unruffled letter to Henry Alsberg:

> As you may know the Writers' Project here has been rather thoroughly investigated by the F.B.I. The matter is unimportant but I thought perhaps you should know about it. . . .
>
> . . . A complaint was made secretly that four persons among those active in the union were not doing any work on the Guide. This complaint went to the State office, then to Washington, and about two weeks ago the G-man appeared. His name is Van Doren. It seems that he is one of the men who was active in establishing the Pretty Boy Floyd's guilt in the Kansas City Massacre. Van Doren seems to be a very capable and intelligent man. He interviewed the four workers accused. One of these is the Tour Editor and another has been one of the hardest workers since the beginning, putting in overtime consistently. The third wrote the articles on Oil and Oklahoma Labor. The fourth has been working on Principal Cities. The first two are still on the Project; the latter two we had to lay off December 15th, because they were non-relief. Our G-man talked to these persons and others on the Project and I gave him a report of what these workers had done. Fortunately the four persons investigated were among the dozen most useful persons on the Project. As I told the G-man at the time, we have had on the Project persons so incompetent or so unstable nervously that they have been of no use whatever, but we kept them on simply because they had no means otherwise to feed themselves. These latter took no part in union activities and so were above suspicion.
>
> Van Doren said after his investigation that the charges were absurd and that he would turn in a very favorable report. . . .
>
> The Project workers enjoyed the sensation of being investigated by G-men, but otherwise all is quiet.

Harder to deflect were the suspicions of partisanship toward Marxist writers on the Project. Zoe Tilghman regarded Alta Churchill DeWitt's pay

raise after her summer vacation at Commonwealth College as a cynical reward for her raised consciousness: "Since then [she] has been foremost in
all Communist work of the group." Thelma Shumake, Tilghman also discovered, "has for a long period been secretly paid a higher wage than her rat-
ing entitled, and more than others doing similar work." When Washington
finally succeeded in pruning the Oklahoma WPA, in July 1937, Cunningham
demoted Tilghman and assigned Thompson and Alta Churchill DeWitt the
only two nonsecurity wage positions. Mrs. Tilghman's conclusion? "The
Communists were definitively and openly favored . . . continued support
of them is a slap in the face to workers who are faithful and loyal citizens."

Similar charges rattled WPA windows across America. From Cunningham and Jim Thompson on down, the dominant figures on the Oklahoma
Writers' Project undeniably harbored Communist sympathies. But Tilghman's McCarthyist vilification of her colleagues' patriotism threw a grimy
veil over her private ambitions and political itinerary. As Oklahoma writer
Frank Parman concludes,

> Tilghman's fight with the Marxists on the Project really was
> personal, though it had roots in Oklahoma history. Her attitude
> was that of many of the '89ers and pioneers in the state—"We're
> proud and we own it." She thought she should be the director, and
> everyone else was an interloper. Apart from herself, her group con-
> sisted of the stenographers and typists, and she played up their re-
> sentment of the writers on the Project.

Without the Communist writers Tilghman denounced before the Dies committee, there could have been no Oklahoma Federal Writers' Project. The
Marxists also, for all their heavy-handed politicking, proved the most sensitive administrators. As J. Ellen Wolgamuth, no friend of the Communists,
evoked Zoe Tilghman for Henry Alsberg, "So cruel and overbearing was she
that whether we liked his politics we were driven to our director for
refuge—and we must all say for him that he was always kind in manner."

Wolgamuth spoke up as an assistant guide book editor and, by her own
admission, one of the two craftiest wordsmiths on the Project. Of herself—
and Thompson—she confided to Alsberg, "As it is I acknowledge only Jim
my superior in the writing game."

• • •

Behind the scenes Thompson catwalked along the fringes of the Oklahoma
City left. On September 17, 1936, Oklahoma *Labor* published "A Night with
Sally," his memoir of the lonely months he rode the rails after his marriage
to Alberta, and his sneering assault on the "hymnalistic harlots" of the

Omaha Salvation Army. "A True Story," as the subtitle read, "A Night with Sally" comprised an early fragment of Thompson's proletarian novel-in-progress, *Always to Be Blest.* The author's credit identified him merely as "Member of the Social Forum School," concealing his professional standing as guide book editor on the Writers' Project. During the bitter imbroglio that subsequently erupted on the editorial and letters pages of Oklahoma *Labor,* he was further characterized as "not only a member of the Social Forum School but he is our first graduate."

For a lifelong atheist like Thompson, the Social Forum School put forward a dubious public face. Equal parts Marx and Jesus, this primary instrument of his political writing and teaching during 1936 and 1937 sprang from a Social Gospel column, "A Layman to His Pastor," which Lawrence Lay contributed to Oklahoma *Labor.* Week after week the Reverend Lay preached a new social order grounded in a fusion of Christian ethics, Marxist class consciousness, Utopian pedagogy, and revolutionary fervor. "You will find Jesus and Marx," he proposed in Oklahoma *Labor,* "digging in the same field, having the same objective, and both recognizing the same problem as the one of first importance—poverty." The early Christian church "was unequivocally communistic, and yet the churches today are being supported by some of the most ruthless capitalists on earth." The Bible "is the poor man's book; its message is the voice of God against tyrants, idlers, and parasites. . . ."

The "Marxian-Christian union" Lay sought for the Social Forum School cut across a vortex of local and national currents. Oklahoma possessed a powerful Social Gospel crusade as far back as 1913, when socialist weeklies like the *Sword of Truth* and the *Sledge Hammer* merged political reform with evangelical spirit. As the Social Gospel movement gathered steam in the course of the Depression, the Reverend Lay, under the influence of Harry F. Ward and Claude C. Williams, joined the radical People's Institute of Applied Religion. Williams and Ward, moreover, maintained close ties with Commonwealth College, whose cooperative program and labor curriculum Lay assimilated into the Social Forum School. And Nicholas Comfort, an outspoken Presbyterian minister and the dean of the Oklahoma School of Religion, established the Norman Forum in 1936 as an agency for introducing controversial speakers into the community. Lay consulted Nick Comfort before he organized his own forum later the same year.

Jim Thompson's ardent fellowship in a spiritual assembly predicated on the realization of the "Perfect Man" probably would have been absurd, even during the heady 1930s, before the arrival of the Popular Front. Under the slogan "Communism Is Twentieth Century Americanism," the American Communist Party in 1935 reversed its insistence on class struggle and a Soviet system of government. The Party started to laud the virtues of American democracy and patriotism, American institutions, history, and rituals, and urged collaboration with the American bourgeoisie. Despite the Reverend Lay's "old-time preacher manner," as Alta Churchill DeWitt recalled, the Social Forum School's place in the Popular Front could not escape the local press. The *Daily Oklahoman* charged that "a school for communists flourishes in Oklahoma City." The sweeping condemnation linked the "school in city training reds" to the Writers' Project. "Subversive influence is at work in the federal writers' project of the WPA here."

Although the Social Forum School claimed at its peak perhaps eighty active students and faculty, the articles of incorporation Lay filed with the Oklahoma secretary of state on September 3, 1936, listed twenty-one directors. At least half of these came from the Writers' Project. Along with Thompson, DeWitt, and nearly all of the other Writers' Project union members who mailed protest letters to Henry Alsberg during the Missouri project strike, the directors included the Reverend Lay, Louis L'Amour, a smattering of Oklahoma City labor leaders, and some names that Sis Cunningham brands "obvious Party aliases."

For the official articles of incorporation Lay defined the purpose of the Social Forum School in noncombative Newspeak. "By assembling data on conditions as they are," and "by assembling expert sociological opinion on the dangers that threaten our civilization and on the relation of crime, immorality, and war to economic injustice and the commercial conflict," through "open discussions" and "mass meetings," he wrote, the school would "promote non-political education on the social issues."

In practice the Social Forum School honed a sharper blade. "This school has as its openly announced objective the peaceful transformation of our present political and economic system into one of co-operation and justice," an advertisement in Oklahoma *Labor* somewhat disingenuously clarified. And with bold caps: WE ARE SOON GOING TO FIND OURSELVES IN THE CHAINS OF FASCISM IF THE MASSES DO NOT UNITE ON A SOUND SYSTEM OF EDUCATIONAL PROPAGANDA.

From the battery of programs chronicled by the Social Forum Arsenal, it appears that operations around the school whirled in two contiguous orbits. The main focus of the Social Forum School inhered in small weekly classes, conducted largely out of view in the Labor Temple, the Veterans of Industry Hall, the Downtown Baptist Church, or the Writers' Project office in the old City Hall at Grand and Broadway. A student, like Jim Thompson, would follow a program patterned after Commonwealth College's, with courses in such subjects as "social security law, conservation of our natural resources, the employment of supported married women in industry, forces that are making for war and for peace, America's chance to preserve democracy, and the function of the churches in the struggle for social justice." The writings of American progressives like Lincoln and Thomas

Paine, some Social Gospel literature, and the Reverend Lay's own tracts supplemented the standard reading in Marx and Lenin.

After graduation the student could conduct his own classes and lectures. Jim Thompson, according to Alta Churchill DeWitt, led evening discussions of proletarian authors, apparently touching on John Dos Passos, James T. Farrell, Nelson Algren, Edward Anderson, and William Cunningham, among others. And he presented an early version of a talk he later delivered under the title "The Economic Plight of the Writer."

Open symposia on topical questions occupied the school's second track. Following the example of Nick Comfort's Norman Forum and, Lay once suggested, the adult education lectures at the New School for Social Research in New York City, the Social Forum School hosted speakers, panels, and debates. Starting on November 16, 1936, when six religious and political leaders, including Bob Wood, interpreted the results of the recent election at the Oklahoma City university auditorium, large forums convened every other Tuesday evening. At least one of these seems to have turned rowdy. A conservative clergyman, the Reverend Rembert Gilman Smith, later charged in the *Daily Oklahoman:*

> About two years ago, the most costly church building in Oklahoma and in the southwest, permitted the use of one of its lecture rooms for the holding of a series of lectures under the auspices of one of the reddest organizations in the United States. These lectures caused a sensation in that city and almost a riot at one of the meetings. Such an incident was possible only because of the ignorance of the church authorities as to the nature of the organization, whose aim includes the destruction of all religion.

"A Night with Sally" marked the first volley from "The Social Forum Arsenal" discharged by a writer other than the Reverend Lay. For all its private fury, Thompson's broadside against the "hymnalistic harlots . . . ballading bastards . . . poverty-prowling prostitutes . . . religion-ranting rabble" of the Salvation Army (see "An American Tragedy" for the full text) chiefly whipped up a Rabelaisian reprise of the Social Gospel axiom that disparaged charity as an insulting stopgap for the poor. Oklahoma *Labor,* just a few months earlier, had editorialized that "charity is a theft." Imagine, then, Jim Thompson's shock at finding himself dead center in a public catfight—not with the reactionary clerics of Oklahoma City, but with the very same leftist newspaper that sponsored his riposte.

One week after publishing "Sally," Oklahoma *Labor* weighed in with a stunning lead editorial. L. N. Shelden—not only Oklahoma *Labor*'s editor but also a founding director of the Social Forum School—denounced his own author's journalistic integrity, intelligence, and literary style:

THE JIM THOMPSONS

In Oklahoma Labor last week there appeared under the heading "A Night with Sally" what was purported to be a true story and the experience of one Jim Thompson, member of the Social Forum School.

The reason it passed by the editor will soon be apparent.

If you read it you will recall that Jim Thompson represented himself to have been one of society's derelicts, hopelessly struggling in the quicksands of an economic system that sucks forever downward the frail bark of the under-privileged and the disinherited.

You will recall that this particular episode was supposed to have occurred in Omaha, in 1932; and that after he had knocked at every door, and tried every agency known for offering shelter and food to the homeless and hungered, he was finally directed to the Salvation Army Home.

Then begins the recital of what is purported to be an actual picture of conditions and treatment at the Salvation Army refuge. Whether true or not is beside the question, and verification can be left without harm to those who have had experience with the work of the Salvation Army.

First of all, there are too many Jim Thompsons who lack the intelligence to distinguish between the cause and the effect; and not having the intelligence they foam, and froth, and rant and curse at the effect instead of trying to seek a solution to the cause of why the Thompsons and the Salvation Army are a product of the same social system.

Without the fool Thompsons there would be no need of the Salvation Army, so far as material needs are concerned; and so long as the Thompsons remain the deluded scavengers of the capitalist system, just so long will the social sewage find its way into whatever clarifying crucible the Salvation Army can provide.

Read "A Night with Sally" and you will be convinced, as we are, of the utter hopelessness of trying to build a new and better social order out of such material as the Thompsons; and if Lawrence Lay, conductor of the Social Forum School, succeeds in getting an intelligent thought into the head of the least of these he will have earned a niche in the hall of fame.

Thompson's friends in the Social Forum School and on the Writers' Project entered swinging in his defense. The following issue of Oklahoma *Labor,* Lay struggled to defuse the squabble. Deflecting the ugly personal strain in Shelden's editorial, the Reverend paid tribute to his first graduate:

I see in your editorial, entitled the The Jim Thompsons, something which Mr. Thompson himself does not seem to see, and I fail to see what he and others seem to see. To me you obviously speak of the Jim Thompsons in a figurative sense, meaning the class of people who submit to what Jim experienced and yet make no discovery of the cause of their misery and feel no revulsion against the system that produces such derelicts and the "Sallys" that show them such mercy as Jim received. You did not mean to infer that the author of "A Night with Sally" was, in reality, one of these Jim Thompsons.

If you meant anything to the contrary of my interpretation, you are altogether wrong . . . I, as director of the School, am ready to recommend to the executive board that Mr. Thompson be granted some formal recognition of superior fitness for service in the Social Forum School's field of endeavor. . . .

Louis L'Amour, in his letter to editor, aimed lower and swung a bit harder:

. . . Naturally, being a short story writer, I found the editorial exceedingly unpleasant as well as unfair. I am not referring now to the terms in which you addressed Mr. Thompson, or the terms you applied to him, but rather of the misapprehension under which you apparently labor. Being a literary critic and book reviewer of some years standing, I believe I am in the position to judge Mr. Thompson's sketch. For your information I might say that it is not the place of the writer of stories to discuss the causes of conditions; it is his place to portray the true state of affairs, to present a picture. . . .

There was no blanket indictment of the Salvation Army contained in the story; it was an indictment of a purely local state of affairs. However, I will take an oath that similar conditions existed in the Salvation Army flophouse in Galveston a few years ago. And I do not feel you had a right to imply that Mr. Thompson's statement was untrue without being familiar with the facts. . . .

The condition Mr. Thompson painted was not pretty, but neither are the pictures painted by Erskine Caldwell, Ernest Hemingway, Thomas Wolfe, Sinclair Lewis, Upton Sinclair, Sherwood Anderson, or Theodore Dreiser. . . .

As for Mr. Thompson, I am slightly acquainted with him, and have found him a university man, a gentleman, and a student with an earnest wish to better the lot of the under-dog. It would be wise to consider before again hurling such obloquy and vilification at a man you do not know because he has exposed a condition of which you are obviously ignorant.

Granted his own space to reply, a manifestly hurt and bewildered Jim Thompson dispensed with the alliterative clamor of "A Night with Sally." Marshaling his anger in clipped, insinuating phrases, he pointed the accusing finger back at Shelden's hypocrisy and corruption:

> I have read your editorial of September 24th in which you describe me as a fool and a deluded scavenger of the capitalist system. Knowing as I do your reasons for writing it, I am only alarmed for your readers who have as an editor a man who tries to run with the hares and hunt with the hounds. As a writer, writing without pay and by request, it was my privilege to write as I pleased. And it was your privilege—your duty, rather—to reject the article or edit it so that nothing in the content or language would be offensive to your readers. It was not your privilege to publish the article, then—to salve a few indignant subscribers—to attack the author. You will forgive this brief outline of editorial prerogatives; your own diagnosis of me was rather illuminating.
>
> In your necessary polemic against me (necessary to save your meal tickets) you take me to task because I write entirely of effect and not at all of cause. If you had any real knowledge of economics, instead of a few pat phrases, you would know that there are a thousand and one real and fancied causes of the depression, while there is only one effect—the depression, itself. We can see the effect, know that it exists; but the cause is pure theory. For instance, we have the case of an editor of a liberal paper calling a writer names. This is the effect—but of what? Pressure on the editor from subscribers or advertisers?
>
> I might say that you were a fool and a deluded scavenger of the capitalist system, too, and probably come fairly close to the truth. But as to how you arrived at such a state would be beyond my deductive ability. At any rate, in the case of self-evident facts, proof is not necessary.

At this point Shelden appears to have become embarrassed by the strident overkill of his editorial. The next week he prefaced a fresh batch of outraged letters—from Project writers Ned DeWitt, Joe Paskavan, and Fred Maxham—with a rambling, circular apology. He echoed the Reverend Lay's Jesuitical distinction between "the Jim Thompsons that make up a large part of our social order" and "Jim Thompson, the author" ("the fine and sincere gentleman his sponsors claim"). Yet the implications of Shelden's parting shot might have alarmed *any* Jim Thompson:

> And since one of our correspondents asks how we propose to build a new social order, we make answer by saying: "Breed more Lawrence Lays and sterilize the Jim Thompsons."

On the Writers' Project—Joe Paskavan, Louis
L'Amour, and Jim Thompson, Oklahoma City,
1936 (Courtesy of the Thompson family)

On that bizarre injunction the feud sputtered to a standstill. Shelden continued to accommodate "The Social Forum Arsenal" within the pages of Oklahoma *Labor.* Thompson remained on the Social Forum School faculty until Lay recast the political platform along stricter religious lines, as the Social Justice Crusade of the Downtown Baptist Church, late in 1937.

Readers may be surprised at the recurrent surfacing of Louis L'Amour, Presidential Medal of Freedom recipient and Ronald Reagan's favorite novelist, from the murky depths of the Oklahoma left. Two years younger than Thompson, L'Amour settled in Oklahoma City sometime during the mid-1930s after a youth spent as a hobo, merchant seaman, and wandering laborer. A published poet and the author of numerous short stories—not of the West, then, but of South Seas adventures, prizefighters, and gangsters—he became a regular book reviewer for the lively Sunday literary page that University of Oklahoma Professor Kenneth Kaufman edited for the *Daily Oklahoman.* Many of L'Amour's Depression essays espoused a distinctly radical stance. Praising Edward Anderson's hobo novel *Hungry Men,* he wrote in 1935:

> . . . It seems highly improbable that a revolution will take place in this country at the present time, or near it, although the subject is interesting, but one wonders what will become of a country where young men such as [Ace] Stecker [Anderson's hero] are forced to wander helplessly, driven by the police, in fear of chain gangs, and out of work through the force of economic changes over which they have no control.

L'Amour was only the second writer, after Jim Thompson, to take over the Reverend Lay's slot in "The Social Forum Arsenal."

L'Amour joined the Writers' Project the same year as Thompson. By December 1, 1936, he advanced to the full-time position of cities editor. The *Handbook of Oklahoma Writers* (1939) listed Thompson, Ned DeWitt, and L'Amour as the three foremost writers on the Project.

By all accounts Thompson and L'Amour developed an intense friendship that shortly faded. Alberta Thompson recalls "a time when Louis was around nearly every day, eating us out of house and home! But Jimmie decided that he was an incompetent writer who didn't know anything above a two-syllable word." Others suggest that Thompson's impatience with L'Amour's flair for sham and pretense occasioned the break. "Jim and Ned used to make fun of all those tall tales of his," notes Alta Churchill DeWitt. "Louis would talk about going to China to work, and the boys figured out that he would have had to have been ten years old! I guess Jim just got tired of hearing them."

Gordon Friesen, another Writers' Project buddy, remembers interrupting Thompson one afternoon as he was speaking on the telephone in his office. "I went up to Jim's desk to turn in some copy. He was on the phone lambasting someone, shouting 'You goddam phony!' After he hung up he turned to me and said, 'That's the biggest fraud in the world. That was Louis L'Amour.' "

Muses Friesen: "I've sometimes thought that Jim wrote what he did in answer to L'Amour's sentimental gook. Jim Thompson's was the real story—*How the West Was Really Won.* . . ."

• • •

Thompson was wrapping up the first installment of that secret history even as L'Amour championed "Sally" against the unsavory slurs of Oklahoma *Labor.* Henry Alsberg solicited contributions of off-time creative work during the fall of 1936 for a national anthology of WPA employees. Envisioned as a literary alternative to "the made work for hopeless hacks" in the state guide books, *American Stuff* was published in August 1937 by Viking Press, with an ample first-edition hardcover press run of five thousand copies. *American Stuff* featured the prose, poetry, and artwork of fifty Project authors and artists, among them Richard Wright, Kenneth Rexroth, Sterling Brown, Hubert Davis, and Robert Hayden. For a collection that accentuated Depression themes and a bracing American vernacular, Thompson's selection, "The End of the Book," proved the most vernacular—and the most depressing.

"The End of the Book" (as his totemic titled implied) was the concluding section of Thompson's hobo novel, *Always to Be Blest*. The startling fragment dramatized the final day of a drifter, Lester Cummings, as he wakes up in an Oklahoma oil field toolshed, breakfasts on a live rat, butchers a family of tenant farmers, and is himself slain by a rifleman. Alsberg shuddered as he relayed the chapter to his editorial board: "I am also sending in a story entitled 'The End of the Book,' by Jim Thompson, Oklahoma City. I think this shows a lot of talent. It is perhaps gruesome, especially in the beginning, almost to the absurd." Reviewers with stronger stomachs found space to commend Thompson alongside the better-known contributors to *American Stuff*: "Faulkneresque" (Brooklyn *Eagle*), and "astonishes the unsuspecting" (Washington *Times*).

The chapter also earned him his first book contract. David Zablowdowsky, an editor at Viking Press and one of Thompson's New York contacts with the American Writers Union, sent a tantalizing letter of inquiry a few months before *American Stuff* reached the bookstores:

> You know of course that your piece "The End of the Story" [*sic*] is appearing in our volume of WPA selections. It is about time, too, that you knew that we consider it among the few very best pieces in the collection.
>
> Does your title literally mean what it says, and are these few pages the end of a longer story of perhaps book length? If so we should very much appreciate the opportunity to consider the larger work with an eye to continuing as your publishers. In any case, even if "The End of the Story" does not form part of a larger whole, we are still interested in reading anything of book length that you may have written or be writing. May we hear from you soon about this?

Thompson signed with Viking Press to write *Always to Be Blest* in the fall of 1937. A special agreement was tailored to his chronic difficulty managing large amounts of cash, in this case no more than $500. Each week Thompson would send Viking a five-thousand-word installment and receive a partial advance on royalties in return. Publication was scheduled for March 1938.

In an October 1937 interview with the Oklahoma *News* ("Depression Launches City WPA Writer on Road to Fame and Fortune"), Thompson admitted that he "wrote the last chapter last fall when the national WPA organization requested that samples of employees' work be submitted for approval." But he revealed that he "conceived the idea more than two years ago when the initial chapters were written." He judged that "about one-fourth of the book has already been sent to the publishers" and "several other chapters [have been] completed, including the final ones."

Thompson indeed completed *Always to Be Blessed* on schedule, but the novel was never published by Viking, Simon and Schuster, Vanguard Press, or any of the other houses he later consulted. He consigned the blame to his installment contract with Viking Press in a rueful 1940 letter:

> . . . It's so simple, and tempting, to turn out a lot of stuff, week by week, that would be impossible to correlate; and no one has better reason to know it than I do. My first and only novel was sold to Viking in installments. . . . Every installment was accepted with enthusiasm, but when they were all in I didn't have a book and it was impossible to make a book of them. In my eagerness to put across every installment I had lost my theme.

Since Thompson later destroyed the manuscript of *Always to Be Blest,* the full scope and texture of the novel evades description. Only two sections survived, "A Night with Sally" and "The End of the Book," along with a thumbnail précis scattered through the Oklahoma *News* interview:

> One of the vast army of unemployed that drifted from place to place during the turbulent depression period, Mr. Thompson is capitalizing on his experiences and observations in the novel.
>
> Entitled "Always to be Blest," the book presents an account of the major highlights of the depression from the standpoint of the jobless man in Oklahoma, Texas, Kansas and Nebraska, said Mr. Thompson. . . .
>
> Oklahoma City's contribution to his novel will include the food riot of 1933 which resulted in several persons being sentenced to federal prison, and will also have a chapter devoted to the kidnapping and subsequent release of a wealthy city oil man, without mentioning any names of actual principals involved.
>
> "Small town stockholders in Nebraska banks trying to give away their stock and in some instances even paying persons to take it off their hands," will be included in the book, said Mr. Thompson. Other chapters will deal with proration battles, the drought, and other depression catas-

> trophes such as the farmers pouring out milk because of
> no market, while people in cities were starving. . . .

As so often with Thompson, the evidence for *Always to Be Blest* crooks in contrary directions. "Sally" and the *Daily Oklahoman* plot summary suggest a conventional, if highly politicized "bottom dog" saga along the lines of the proletarian novels he might have discussed in his class at the Social Forum School: Edward Dahlberg's *Bottom Dogs* (1929), Nelson Algren's *Somebody in Boots* (1935), and Edward Anderson's *Hungry Men* (1935), with their Depression inventory of boxcars, hobo jungles, Hoovervilles, and violent political protests.

But "The End of the Book" indicates that Thompson projected a more innovative and personal, wholly stranger novel. The final pages of *Always to Be Blest* relinquish documentary realism for an hallucinatory experiment. The ambitious chapter blasts off with a blunt encapsulation of Marxist alienation. Circumstances have reduced drifter Lester Cummings to an "animal," just as the rat who shares the metal toolshed with him is an "animal." Yet the perspectives of the paired beasts disorientingly cross and intertwine. When Cummings bludgeons and then devours the still-writhing rat, Thompson plays the hellish moment like one of the murder scenes in his *Master Detective* stories, narrating from the dying victim's—here, the rat's—point of view:

> The paws of the other animal scooped him up and held him
> level with its laughing gray eyes. The mouth laughed, too, and
> saliva dripped from the corners. He came closer to the mouth, saw
> it open wider. His head passed through the opening, and he gazed
> down the concave hall of the throat. An instant only. Suddenly
> there was no light, no sound. Only something hard and sharp clos-
> ing upon his neck. He felt his eyes leap from their sockets, his
> tongue crawl through his teeth. He felt the rush of blood from his
> jugular, jerked with the sudden energy of his heart. He felt. Then he
> felt no more.

After his grisly meal "the other animal," Lester Cummings, walks through the rain, backsliding into delirious fantasy; as Marx predicted, alienated man is also self-alienated man. Cummings's inward conversation increasingly detaches from his outward actions, and Thompson in turn shifts from roman to italic type. When the narrative splits, a disembodied second voice signals the hobo's psychic fragmentation. Cummings murders a passing tenant farmer and his family, seemingly oblivious to his own movements. Speaking from deep inside his derangement, he imagines that one of the blood-splattered women is his lost love, Lois:

"Rain. Even the road is red with it . . . And—wait a minute! This looks like Lois!"

"It . . . it is Lois!"

"I would not be too sure. Remember how you were fooled before. Lift her out of the car. Lay her there on the ground. That dress is rotten; it will tear easily. Now, do you think it is still Lois?"

"Ah, God! It is Lois. Kneel down by her. Kiss her lips, her breasts, take her into your arms. Hold her against your shoulder. This is good, isn't it? Just to hold her and protect her; let her sleep while you stand guard. All these days, these months, these years, and now you are together again. It was a long time but it is past now. Remember the last day of school when you walked home together? Remember the night you drove your new car around to her house? Remember the lane with the tall elms, the elms dripping diamonds of sunshine from their leaves, the robins teetering on the fence wires, the grass singing in the wind? Ah, God! And the little apartment over the drugstore. The smell of hot coffee on a cold morning. Hands ruffling your hair, probing your ribs, tickling you into wakefulness. Remember the days when you lived for the nights, the nights with Lois asleep on the lounge while you sat at the kitchen table poring over your correspondence course in accounting . . . Ah, God! Do not speak! Let me give back what has been taken from you. Her nose is not flat and negroid as you see it; her hair is not a stringy mass of wool, green with dirt at the roots; her breasts are not brown with sun and rust. She is clean, clean and pure as you remember her. . . ."

His ghastly monologue concludes with a rapid-fire inversion of the opening sequence. Cummings now, not the rat, relates his own death *("that fellow in the black hat, settling on one knee, lifting the long barrel of a rifle . . . The noise! That numbing, grinding pain in your skull!")*, convinced that he is returning home with Lois to Nebraska.

For all Thompson's political and literary service to the Party there is no sign here that *Always to Be Blest* succumbed to the innocence, the sentimentality, or the refusal to see complexity in the world that enervated much 1930s writing.

"The End of the Book" anticipated by almost twenty years the split narration at the close of *A Hell of a Woman*. Thompson, like many American writers, probably learned how to use italics from reading William Faulkner, who, according to Thompson's wife, Alberta, was his favorite novelist. Faulkner once remarked that the italic passages in *The Sound and the Fury*, Thompson's likely model here, indicated a break between the "objective picture" and a "subjective . . . thought transference." Thompson would employ italics correspondingly all his future writing life.

Closer to home, the rat-eating episode bore the literary fingerprints of William Cunningham. *The Green Corn Rebellion* also had served up a hideous rodent meal. At the crushing emotional climax of Cunningham's novel, Bill Johnson, a disabled black wagon driver, attempts to collect his pay for deliveries during the wheat harvest. The white mill owner drunkenly taunts him with an offer of a costly wagonload of wheat—"Lissen, nigger. If you'll eat that there mouse, tail and all, I'll give you that load of wheat." Humiliated yet desperate, Johnson complies:

> . . . He picked up the mouse and brushed the grains of sand off it. He crammed it into his mouth. It was too big to swallow at a gulp and he crunched down on it two or three times and swallowed hard. It was down then, and the wheat was his. He felt sick. The men stared at him with expressions of horror. Suddenly he doubled up and retched and the whole mess in his stomach flooded through his mouth and nose.

Written barely one year after *The Green Corn Rebellion,* Thompson's brutal sequel shows him raising the stakes as if in a private contest with his friend and boss to see who could devise the grosser shock.

Always to Be Blest acquired its title from an improbable source for a proletarian novel, Alexander Pope's "An Essay on Man" in heroic couplets:

> Hope springs eternal in the human breast:
> Man never Is, but always To be blest:
> The soul, uneasy and confin'd from home,
> Rests and expatiates in a life to come.

From *Nothing More Than Murder* (1949) to *The Getaway* (1959), the theme of sacrificing the present for the sake of an unknown future animated Thompson's major crime fiction. "I still wasn't hot for the killing," Joe Wilmot typically argues in *Nothing More Than Murder,* "but if that was the only way to lead a happy, decent life, why. . . ."

"The End of the Book" nearly failed to reach Henry Alsberg or Viking Press. Alta Churchill DeWitt, the executive secretary on the Writers' Project charged with typing the manuscript, held on to it right up to deadline. "Because of me," she recalls, "Jim almost didn't get started on writing his book. He wrote a short story and asked me to type it and send it to Mr. Alsberg. It lay on my desk for a month or more. To my Oklahoma ears it just sounded horrible—someone biting the head off a rat and eating it. . . . I was almost too scared to type it. It was so revolting that I didn't think Mr. Alsberg would be interested in it. Anyway, I finally did mail it in, and the story developed into Jim's first novel. . . ."

• • •

American Stuff certified Thompson's promise. As one marker of his elevated status among Oklahoma writers, Ben Botkin invited him to partici-
pate in the formation of a Southwest Writers' Congress. An old friend from
Professor Wimberly's Sunday-evening workshops in Lincoln, Botkin was
himself now an assistant professor of English and folklore at the University
of Oklahoma. For many months he had been promoting the notion of a regional writers' conference in the spirit of the first American Writers' Congress held in New York City in April 1935. By the spring of 1937 he secured
promises of sponsorship from Witter Bynner, Lynn Riggs, Oscar Ameringer,
Kenneth Kaufman, Joseph Brandt, George Milburn, Mabel Dodge Luhan,
and William Cunningham, among other prominent Southwest writers, editors, and academics. Louis L'Amour obliged as secretary to Botkin's provisional committee.

L'Amour's invitational letter of May 10 set down the broad objectives of
the congress. "For some time," he wrote, "Southwest writers have felt the
need of an organization for the discussion and clarification of problems peculiar to Southwest writers in the present national and international scene.
Such an organization would give contemporary meaning and direction to
Southwest culture, viewed in relation to both its past and its future, its social and economic as well as its aesthetic and intellectual factors." Subsequent fine-tuning by the sponsors produced four more specific aims:

1. To defend the democratic liberties of free speech and free
    assembly. . . .

2. To support regional as well as national mediums of commu-
    nication devoted to these ends. . . .

3. To encourage and protect regional writers and writing by
    means of conferences, recognition, exhibits; to consider
    craft and professional problems and to raise the standards
    of regional criticism; to discourage unfair practices in the
    writing trade. . . .

4. To cooperate with other regional and national organizations
    devoted to similar aims. . . .

More than 150 writers from Oklahoma, Texas, and New Mexico attended the first Southwest Writers' Congress in Oklahoma City on May 22.
The all-day conference of papers and discussions convened at the YMCA
on Northwest 2nd Street. Botkin presided over a morning program devoted

to "The Writer and His Region," during which Bill Cunningham spoke on "Social and Economic Factors." According to the Norman *Transcript,* "Cunningham painted a hopeful outlook for regional writers who try to understand their Indians, their oil millionaires, their early-day outlaws, their community camps." The talk, it would seem, all but reproduced the regional Oklahoma texture of *Always to Be Blest.*

Thompson presented his paper "The Economic Plight of the Writer" at the afternoon session on "The Writer and Society," chaired by Mrs. Walter (Lucia Loomis) Ferguson, a columnist for the Scripps-Howard newspapers and the daughter-in-law of Thompson B. Ferguson, the territorial governor who had appointed his father sheriff in 1902. Thickening the incrustation of family ghosts, he also shared the podium with his nemesis, Zoe Tilghman. Professor Winifred Johnston of the University of Oklahoma completed the panel.

Alta Churchill DeWitt, in the audience that afternoon with Ned, remembers that "Jim spoke in a kind of nuts-and-bolts way about his experience on the Writers' Project and with the different kinds of magazines he wrote for back then, like *True Detective* and so forth, how they treated the writers, what they paid—and sometimes didn't pay. What I recall Jim saying is that a writer really was a worker, like other sorts of workers. Everybody was very proud of him." No printed record of Thompson's speech survives.

An evening program on the Spanish Civil War concluded the Saturday conference. A "Continuations Committee" to carry on the work of the Southwest Writers' Congress replaced the largely ceremonial board of sponsors. Professor Johnston was elected chairman, Mrs. Walter Ferguson vice chairman, journalist Hope Holway secretary, and Jim Thompson treasurer. The delegates selected Ben Botkin as their representative to the second American Writers' Congress, meeting in New York City in June.

The Oklahoma City press bandied the inevitable allegation of Communist subversion. "Was Writers' Meeting Red or Wasn't It?" challenged the *Daily Oklahoman* for the following morning. Zoe Tilghman indicated anew that she had been misled and betrayed by her writing brethren (Bill Cunningham would remove her from her position as assistant director shortly after the congress). But the local media, for once, appeared mollified when a group of University of Oklahoma professors denounced the Communist charge as an "amateurish attempt at sensationalism."

Within the Southwest Writers' Congress, however, the red issue continued to rankle. After Botkin reported on the American Writers' Congress at a July 12 executive meeting, the committee debated whether to join forces with the League of American Writers. Dissension over national affiliation splintered the Southwest Writers' Congress at their next regional conference on December 27. The Tulsa *World* reported,

Communism and Fascism went to the mat Monday when more than a score of Oklahoma writers gathered in Tulsa for the Southwest Writers' congress at the All Souls Unitarian church.

Ralph Bates, English novelist, who spoke at afternoon and midnight meetings, introduced the controversial issue early in the morning business meeting.

"Many liberal people fear that anti-Fascist sentiment in writers' organizations is a cloak for communistic activity," said Bates. "This is not true. You will find some radical elements in any group, anywhere, but I assure you that no writers' organization in the world is actively supporting communism.

"The reason why national and international groups of writers oppose the evils of fascism and not of communism is because we see the former as an immediate danger, and consider it necessary to combat a threat to our existence as writers. I am not suggesting that we go as far as certain oil magnates and keep a private army."

Discussion from the floor raged upon whether a writers' group should espouse any political matter or remain strictly a craft group. Many authors present expressed themselves as being thoroughly opposed to any diversion of the congress' energy into channels outside their professional work.

Vigorous discussion was held on the question of affiliation with the National Congress of Writers [sic] but the question was tabled until a future meeting should allow a larger representation of members.

The Congress voted to accept the aims of the organization as set up by the executive committee with the amendment that "improper" censorship should be used to qualify the original statement which implied that the group condemned all censorship. . . .

The Southwest Writers' Congress arrived at the same dead end as the Writers' Project union before it. When the delegates retrenched, Winifred Johnston and Hope Holway resigned from the executive committee. Thompson remained with the watered-down congress, sliding into Holway's position as secretary. This post may have provided the loose factual underpinning for his assertion to his cousin Ted Cowan that he served as secretary to the Oklahoma Communist Party. Another regional congress, planned for Santa Fe or Dallas, apparently never took place.

Thompson, Cunningham, and Botkin, among others, affiliated independently with the League of American Writers.

• • •

As executive secretary of the Southwest Writers' Congress, Jim Thompson intended to travel to New York City for the third American Writers' Congress in June 1939. By then, however, he was thoroughly consumed by his responsibilities as director of the Oklahoma Federal Writers' Project—the "boss of the whole shebang."

Bill Cunningham had complained to Henry Alsberg, as far back as 1936, that administering the project made a hash of his creative life. "My own hours are between 170 and 177 hours a month," he lamented. "Last winter I wrote a book but in order to do so I worked from five until eight a.m. on week days and all day Sunday. Both my health and writing suffered." Cunningham amplified his complaint in a May 1937 letter to the national director: "I find it impossible to do any writing on this job and I am thinking of quitting about September 1." He requested a secret meeting with Alsberg in Washington "to discuss the personalities here. . . . I am not advertising the fact because the matter of a successor is difficult."

Cunningham's problems mounted off and on the job. Under his directorship the Oklahoma Writers' Project failed to carry any of its work to publication. The dearth of capable writers, bureaucratic snarls, and the reluctance of conservative Oklahoma businessmen and Chambers of Commerce to bankroll New Deal crusades contributed to the drag. Office discord, particularly the rift between Cunningham and Zoe Tilghman, undermined the collaborative spirit necessary for any Project success. Manuscripts on "Indian Schools and Missions," "Musicians of Oklahoma," and "Cooperative Associations," guides to Tulsa and Oklahoma City, collections of regional folklore, and interviews with former slaves living in Oklahoma all languished, only partially completed or lacking sponsors to finance printing and distribution. In May 1937, the same month that Cunningham confided his resignation plans to Alsberg, Joseph Brandt, director of the University of Oklahoma Press, rejected a draft of the state guide.

A frustrated and demoralized Cunningham went on half-time in September 1937. Still retaining the reins of power, he arranged for Thompson— rather than former assistant director Tilghman, the local politicians' fair-haired girl—to assume chief responsibility for all editorial work. Thompson gained experience as acting director until the following February, when Cunningham tendered his resignation in another hush-hush letter to Alsberg that promoted his friend and effectively axed Tilghman:

> Mrs. Cunningham has to leave Oklahoma because of an allergic condition. It is impossible to discover the exact cause, but the dirt storms seem to have something to do with it. At any rate it happpens only in Oklahoma and no relief is possible here.
>
> And so I want to leave also. . . .
>
> There is only one person here who can take my place. You remember Jim Thompson as one of the contributors to "American Stuff." Viking is bringing out his first novel, "Always to Be

Blessed" [*sic*], next fall. He has been guide book editor on the project for a long time and is now in charge of the University of Oklahoma Guide. He wrote, or rewrote most of the introductory essays.

Mrs. Tilghman could not make a go of it. She gets along well with the average, fairly docile worker on the Project, but she fights with both the mental cases and the above-average folks. She is by conditioning and inclination a Sturdy Pioneer, and she has devoted her life to the Winning of the West, to Building an Empire in a Vast Wilderness. The English language is too complex for her, and no paragraph is safe with her.

My suggestion is that Jim and I come to Washington March 1, and you can give him the once-over. If he seems O.K. he could take my place March 15. I have not discussed this matter with anyone here and shall not do so until I hear from you. Perhaps you should send your reply to my home address. . . .

Sally Cunningham's illness (her sister-in-law Sis admits) was "a ruse Bill cooked up to get himself out of an impossible political situation in Oklahoma." Cunningham and Thompson traveled to Washington on March 3 for a week of meetings with Alsberg. The national director persuaded Cunningham to accept a position in Washington as his chief administrative assistant. Cunningham remained with Alsberg through 1939, whereupon he moved to New York City to become an editor with TASS, the chief news agency of the Soviet Union.

Thompson returned to Oklahoma City the director of the Project, at an annual wage of $2,300. Among his first official actions he elevated Ned DeWitt, his ally from the Writers' Project union, to state editor, and assigned Lawrence Lay to compile a *History and Present-Day Life of the Negro in Oklahoma.*

Cunningham's gambit predictably riled the Tilghman contingent on the Project. Still smarting from her peremptory demotion, Tilghman later grumbled to the Dies committee that, "No Congressman or Senator was consulted as to Mr. Thompson's appointment, his sole recommendation being the request of Mr. Cunningham. . . . This enabled them to have Ned DeWitt the remaining member of their Communist group on non-security wage. . . . They have continued the policy of openly favoring the Communists."

Thompson attempted to finesse the feud by asking Henry Alsberg to promote Tilghman to a traveling position, "setting up the machinery for, and supervising, place-name work in other states." When Alsberg demurred, Thompson vented his anger in a blunt and personal letter to Washington:

I have no dislike for Mrs. Tilghman, on the contrary, because of the friendship of my father—who was an old-time officer—for her husband, I have nothing but the kindest feelings for her. But the situation here in the office is rapidly becoming intolerable. From all that I understand, it would be far from politic to discharge Mrs. Tilghman, but sometimes I do not see how I can put up with her. She has suffered a great deal from imprisonment, on criminal charges, of her two sons, and is not even when in the best of spirits, a good person to have working around others. She also is more than slightly deaf and naturally she speaks in a very loud voice. It is hard to preserve discipline when—as was recently the case—a person warns you flatly in a tone that carries at least one hundred yards that unless you give her a better position you will be discharged from your own. . . .

If there is a some way in which she could be removed from the Oklahoma Writers' Project I would appreciate it very much. I think that the morale of the project will improve considerably and I know that with her going a considerable source of embarrassment for me will be missing.

"Tilghman tried to take the project away from Jim," Alta Churchill DeWitt insists. "The old lady wanted the job for herself." Formally regaining her title of assistant state director, but stripped of any real power, Zoe Tilghman persevered as a burr in Thompson's hide his entire tenure as director. Thereafter, of course, she informed on him to Congressman Dies.

Thompson for his part stepped up his radical activities and, if anything, lodged a more conspicuous public profile in the Oklahoma City left after he assumed the director's chair. Somewhat recklessly, he continued to attend Party gatherings, occasionally in the wary company of his wife. "I went to one or two meetings, simply to be with Jimmie," Alberta recalls. "I was appalled, you see, because I'm a Catholic. But Jimmie said it was the right thing to do during that troubled time, and he had to do it. So I said okay, and went along with him. All the writers on the Project were scared to death someone would find out about it." Thompson's older sister, Maxine—now separated from Russell Boomer, on account of his drinking and womanizing—appreciated the social side of the Oklahoma City CP: "Those people were really, really smart, very intellectual, and I liked every one of them. They were such fun to be around, and it was so much fun to go to their dances and concerts and things."

From Project headquarters Thompson furthered the political program set by Cunningham. He raised money for the Abraham Lincoln Brigade and

scheduled leftist films and speakers. He instituted a mandatory Monday re-
medial English class for Project reporters and typists that stressed essays
on the Spanish Loyalists and the American labor movement. He upheld
Thelma Shumake's superior wage by promoting her to head reporter. And
he staffed the Project with comrades, such as playwright Dan Garrison
and novelist Gordon Friesen. Garrison, a member of Sis Cunningham's Red
Dust Players, seemed needlessly brazen about his Party identification. He
signed one letter on official Project stationery, "Daniel M. Garrison, fellow
traveller."

Indeed, Thompson approached his role as director in uninhibitedly
Marxist terms. Defending a projected essay on "Racial Elements" for the
state guide, he wrote Washington that "I believe that it is wrong to write of
the Negroes, as Negroes, instead of members of the working-class with
working-class problems. The entire Negro essay is built around the theme
that poor whites and poor Negroes are in the same boat."

Some Oklahoma historians, such as Mary Ann Slater in her pioneering
thesis on the Oklahoma Writers' Project, have argued that Thompson and
Cunningham simply were out of step with the state, and that their "social
concerns . . . did not coincide with the political realities in Oklahoma."
During the 1930s, it's true, many Oklahomans failed to acknowledge the
needy, the unemployed, and the homeless in their streets, just as many Oklahoma politicians frowned on relief programs and blamed the victims for
their distressed circumstances. The decade saw a resurgence in Klan violence, and Oklahoma City embraced its own Father Coughlin in the person
of radio preacher E. F. Webber. Yet Oklahoma also possessed a vigorous socialist tradition. At its peak, just prior to the First World War, the Socialist
Party achieved nearly one-third of the vote and elected six candidates to
the legislature, making Oklahoma the foremost Socialist stronghold, pro-
portionately, in the nation. By the spring of 1917 the more militant Working
Class Union claimed thirty-four thousand followers in eastern Oklahoma
and Arkansas. In the early 1930s the Communist-led Unemployed Councils
organized as many as thirty thousand farmers and laborers, staging massive demonstrations in Oklahoma City, such as the food riot Thompson witnessed in 1933. Oscar Ameringer edited the *American Guardian,* a socialist
weekly with a national readership of forty-five thousand, from Oklahoma.
And the state placed the persuasive New Deal progressive voice of Josh
Lee in the U.S. Senate.

Yet no sooner had Thompson repainted his office when a fresh wave of
red stories rippled through the Oklahoma papers. The *Daily Oklahoman,*
after singing the standard aria (Maxham, Shumake, the Writers' Project
union, the Southwest Writers' Congress), trumpeted fresh scandal on May
27: executive secretary Alta Churchill DeWitt was in New York City with
Bob and Ina Wood, Sis Cunningham, and Fred Maxham for the Communist

Party national convention. Also, the Tulsa *World* publicized a rumor that government agents would be investigating "reported communist activities" among WPA workers.

Ominous signals. His first few months as Project director Jim Thompson nonetheless negotiated more administrative triumphs than Bill Cunningham managed during his nearly two years in Oklahoma City. By May Thompson convinced the Tulsa Federation of Women's Clubs to sponsor *Tulsa: A Guide to the Oil Capital,* and in June the state travel and tourist bureau agreed to publish the *Calendar of Annual Events in Oklahoma.*

Bagatelles, no doubt, to a man who peppered his official correspondence with references to "class consciousness"—but as director, Thompson hit the ground running. At the urging of Ben Botkin, the new national folklore editor, Thompson intensified the Project's gathering of Oklahoma folk tales and songs. The Negro history, when completed by Lay, would comprise an exhaustive manuscript of nearly forty-eight thousand words. An ambitious stereopticon series on Oklahoma history would tour the public schools. The state guide would be revised for resubmission to the University of Oklahoma Press. And most intriguing of all, perhaps, Senator Josh Lee suggested that the Project compose a labor history.

· · ·

For a notoriously shy and introverted man, Thompson seemed unable to resist those aspects of his new job that called for extroversion and personal display. During the fall of 1938 he performed on the radio in a cycle of plays, coauthored by him, Ned DeWitt, and other Project writers.

Starting on November 5 and for the next twenty-six weeks, KOMA radio, Oklahoma City, broadcast *Prairie Playhouse,* half-hour dramas mainly drawn from Oklahoma history, each Saturday night at 7:30. Thompson and his staff honed the scripts from research materials prepared for the state guide. "For music," Thompson wrote Henry Alsberg, "we are largely dependent upon the broadcasting station, although the Federal Music Project, I believe, will help us with the arrangement of very old tunes, Indian songs, etc. Then, too, a Negro choir of twenty-five voices will donate their services for at least one of the plays. Our acting talent will be derived from several sources: professionals on the studio payroll, talent schools, speech classes of the public school system, and the Project." Many of the plays dramatized events that would have been familiar to Thompson from his father's recollections of territorial days. *The Fort Smith Trail,* for instance, treated Isaac Parker, the "Hanging Judge."

Thompson supplied the voice of Sim Durkin for the *Prairie Playhouse* premiere, *The Barrel of Salt.* His press release sketched the comic, cliffhanger plot:

The opening scene of *The Barrel of Salt* is in the Muskogee boarding house of Mrs. Mamie Durkin, in the year of 1874. Mrs. Durkin, a harried but aggressive woman, is cursed with a $1,000 mortgage on her establishment and an easy going, meddling husband, who is even more of a permanent fixture than the mortgage.

Hiram Cosgreave, an inspector from Washington, has been sent to Indian Territory to determine which is the best site for the proposed agency of the Five Civilized Tribes, Muskogee or Eufaula. Naturally, the agency with its great volume of business will "make" the town that is fortunate enough to secure it and Mrs. Durkin is doing all that she can to favorably impress Cosgreave, who has just arrived. In her attempt, she has the undesired and blundering help of her husband, Sim, and his illiterate companion Pede Walters. They make the mistake of offering the dignified Cosgreave a bribe to locate the agency in Muskogee, and even insist upon his accepting it in spite of his angry refusals. Finally, Cosgreave becomes so infuriated that he tells them outright that he has as good as made up his mind to give the agency to Eufaula. Sim is alarmed. If Muskogee does not become the site of the agency they cannot remove the mortgage on the boarding house and he will never be able to face Mamie, who has no great appreciation for his talents. He attempts to appease Cosgreave, but to no avail, and his desperation grows. But just when things seem darkest he evolves a scheme to save the day.

The scripts of the radio plays have been lost. Other titles suggest their range and flavor: *These Are Our Lives, Seminole, Pat Hennesy, First Murder, Snake Doctor, Adobe Walls, Why the River Is Red, Steel Coronado, Early Bird, Step-en-Fetch It, People on Relief, Nobody with Sense,* and *Old Oklahoma.*

First Murder is the wild card on this list. The play in all probability sprang not from territorial Oklahoma annals but, rather, from a colonial episode that captivated Thompson from the moment he first encountered it in William Bradford's *History of Plymouth Plantation,* perhaps as a boy rooting through his Uncle Bob's Burwell library, and haunted him the rest of his life: the story of John Billington, the *Mayflower* voyager who became the first man to be tried and executed for murder in what is now the United States.

Thompson kept circling back in his writing to John Billington. He tore into the subject for true crime articles—"America's First Murder" (in *For Men Only*) and the more provocatively titled "Murder Came on the Mayflower" (in *Mercury Mystery Magazine*). He eventually proposed a true crime book, *The Mayflower Murder,* and even a rickety historical novel, *Billington.* This forgotten founding father also ranked high in Thompson's bedtime entertainments for his children, and for his nephew, Tony Kouba. "My uncle Jimmie was completely obsessed with that murder," Kouba contends, "like it was some sort of primal scene for the country. I can't tell you how many times he told me the story. It fascinated him that the founding of the country and the first murder coincided like that."*

•   •   •

Thompson opened his home to his staff and a round robin of visiting writers and artists. Directing the Project brought some stimulating friendships, along with many hours of enforced fellowship. He particularly enjoyed the company of Joe Jones, a young Missouri painter whose Depression murals adorned Commonwealth College, and of Thomas Hart Benton, frequently in Oklahoma on sketching tours.

By virtue of his new post Thompson suddenly emerged as one of the major attractions on the Oklahoma culture circuit. "One night Jim and Ned DeWitt were invited to dinner in Oklahoma City by a count and countess," Gordon Friesen remembers, "who for some reason were passing through and wanted to meet some writers. Jim went, expecting some high-level conversation. He was pretty surprised when the countess reached under the table and grabbed his prick and tried to masturbate him!"

Alberta Thompson objected to her husband's open-door policy, and frowned on his strange friends with their raffish manners and bohemian tastes. "Jimmie felt that as the director he had to entertain a lot," she notes, "and sometimes we would pawn things for a week to pay for it." Thompson re-created what Alberta terms a "representative" late-1930s domestic squabble, probably about Joe Jones, for his novel *Now and on Earth:*

> ". . . Sunday was the worst day of all. . . . We'd hardly get out of bed before Jimmie's friends—they weren't my friends, I'll tell you!—would start coming in. And they'd be there all day, drinking coffee and scattering ashes all over everything, and—you'd have thought it was their place instead of ours. They'd flop right down on my clean bedspread and sprawl around on the floors, and go to the toilet—and you could hear them going. . . . They'd go in there and leave the door wide open and holler in to the front room when they had anything to say. And if they wanted something to eat, they just went right into the kitchen and helped themselves.

* The convergence of idealism and destruction on the *Mayflower* fascinated another American writer, William Carlos Williams. "The result of that brave setting out of the Pilgrims has been an atavism that thwarts and destroys . . . a panorama of murders, perversions . . . ," Williams wrote in the "Voyage of the *Mayflower*" chapter of *In the American Grain,* a book that Thompson recommended to his writing students at USC during the late 1940s.

There was one fellow that always wore dirty old corduroys, and I know he hadn't had a bath in years, and he was the worst one of all. One Sunday I had half a roast I'd been saving and he got it and brought it into the front room with the salt and pepper shakers. . . ."

"If I remember rightly," I said, "he paid rather handsomely for everything he ever got from us. He was just about the best painter in the Southwest. Before he went to Washington to do some murals, he gave us a portable electric phonograph and a complete set of Carl Sandburg recordings and—"

"Don't mention those records. . . . I never got so sick of listening to anything in my life. I heard them from morning until night. Every time Jimmie couldn't think of anything to do; when he was tired or nervous or cross . . . he'd get those records out. And of all the disgusting filthy—That's where he got that 'Foggy, Foggy Dew' business, and 'Sam Hall'—"

"They're old English folksongs. You can't expect—"

"Old English folksongs, my eye! I guess I know when I hear filth, and I certainly heard those things enough."

"Well, I got rid of them . . ."

Thompson was absent from the house a lot, traveling for the Project. During the period of the labor history he would sweep up Gordon Friesen, Dan Garrison, and Clyde Hamm and vanish for days—interviewing union leaders or, as likely, swimming and fishing at Hamm's mother's farm in western Oklahoma. Friesen recounts another Project outing when Thompson returned to Anadarko, his birthplace, for the annual August All-Indian Fair and Exposition:

Jim and Ned DeWitt drove over to Anadarko in Ned's car, a Ford coupe. They picked up two huge Indian women and spent a day and a half with them eating Cracker Jacks and popcorn, and drinking up on Choc Beer, named after the Choctaw Indians who brewed it for the white man. They all got pretty well stoned.

Driving around, Jim tried to make out with one of the Indian women, who weighed about four hundred pounds. The car fell into a ditch, and Jim and the woman tumbled into the space between the front and back seats of the small car. They got wedged there with her on her back on top of Jim, her asshole pressed against his nose. In this position she unloosed all the gas that had accumulated from the Choc Beer. She had passed out. Ned tried to pry them loose, but failed; and he and Jim then passed out. The next day a passing mule driver pulled them out. I am describing this as

Ned told it to me when we were on the project together, with Jim standing by smiling shyly. . . .

A much sanitized version of this spree would appear in *Roughneck.* Ned DeWitt was Thompson's closest friend on the Project, after the departure of Bill Cunningham. Born in Fayetteville, Arkansas, in 1911, DeWitt entered the University of Oklahoma following a stint in the oil fields. He published poems and satirical sketches in *Poet Magazine,* Oklahoma *Labor,* and the *State Anthology of Oklahoma Poetry.* Signing with the Project in 1936, he married Alta Churchill two years later. Jim, Ned, and Alta formed a faithful trio in the cafés around West Main Street. "We were all so young then," Alta comments. "I remember the night in a place called Joe's, a kind of labor hangout around the corner from the Project office, when Jim and Ned first introduced me to beer. They were so disappointed that I didn't like it, so I compromised with black coffee."

The frantic socializing, his eighty-hour week at the Project, and the tense mood at home exacted their toll. Thompson had many pressures bearing down on him during the late 1930s. Both of his sisters, now, and his mother looked to him for support; his father demanded almost constant observation so that he wouldn't get lost or injure himself. Viking, moreover, rejected *Always to Be Blest* in the fall of 1938. A plan to carve the novel into discrete short stories failed to turn up any interest at the literary magazines he queried.

To counter the strain Thompson developed a routine of checking into Oklahoma City hotels to rest and write. On the job he reverted to his old Hotel Texas habit of popping pills to clear his head for the long days of editing and rewriting. And for the first time since leaving the oil fields Thompson was drinking heavily again.

Drinking had nearly cost him his friendship with Bill and Sally Cunningham. "One thing Sally held against Jim," Sis Cunningham relates, "was that he would visit them drinking whiskey as he came in and then pass out on the floor. At first this amused them, but when it got to be a regular thing, Sally had enough. She was real mad that she had to clean up his vomit." Thompson apparently never drank at the Project, but he began to miss work due to the previous night's imbibing. J. Ellen Wolgamuth delicately hinted to Henry Alsberg in December 1938 that the director "often is not very well."

A binge drinker, Thompson was an alcoholic of a particularly frustrating stripe. His ability to drink socially, taking only a glass of beer with his dinner, or to abstain completely for days or weeks camouflaged his problem. "Jimmie was an alcoholic, I'm sure now," Alberta admits. "Even in those days when they said it was not a disease I always felt he couldn't help it. Yet Jimmie could go for a long time and not take a drink. Then all of a sudden something would set him off, and the whiskey bottle would come out. Things might be going along beautifully, but good or bad really didn't seem to matter. That was the mystery to me." Like many who learned to drink during Prohibition, when virtually all liquor was bootleg, strong and bad, Thompson developed a tremendous tolerance for high-voltage spirits. "Jimmie could drink very heavily at night and then be up bright and early writing the next morning, and you'd never know he had a drink."

Thompson had a progressive disease that, as we shall see, assaulted his health, marred his work, and injured his family. So many of the characters in his novels, of course, would also be heavy drinkers, and he passed on his own understanding of his situation to them. Thompson's boozers often joke about their intake. "I have never been able to understand the high regard that leaders of dangerous missions have for sobriety," newsman Clinton Brown quips in *The Nothing Man.* "Sober, one challenges the fates; unsober, the fates cannot be bothered with you." But more anxious and incisive observations crawl between the cracks. Roughneck Tommy Burwell, for instance, in *South of Heaven:* "When you drink like we did you don't think much about sex." Or hit man Charlie Bigger in *Savage Night:* "I'd had enough. More than enough. Or I never would have. You take just so much from the bottle, and then you stop taking. From then on you're putting."

Hard drinking in Thompson's fiction usually is assigned to fear. "A person that drinks a lot is always frightened," Kid Collins reckons in *After Dark, My Sweet.* "They may act just the opposite—tough and hard, like they don't give a damn for anything. But inside they're scared. They have too much imagination. Everything is magnified in their minds, made a hundred times worse than it really is." *The Alcoholics* (1953), Thompson's novel about a Los Angeles sanatorium, distills Collins's suggestion to fear of failure:

> The alcoholic's depressed mood pulls him two ways. While it insists that great deeds must be done by way of proving himself, it insidiously resists his doing them. It tells him simultaneously that he must—and can't. That he is certain to fail—and must succeed.

And fear of self:

> Alcoholics can't be frightened away from drinking. Their own fear of self, until they can recognize it for the baseless and unreasonable thing it is, is much greater than their fear of anything else. No, you can't frighten them. . . .

Thompson's people tend not to like themselves very much sober. Even Clinton Brown finally can't stand what he sees at the bottom of his empty glass:

Without whiskey, that circle in my mind began to dissolve, I ceased to move around it endlessly, and my vision turned inward. And while I caught only a glimpse of what lay there, that little was so bewildering and maddening—and frightful—that I could look no more. . . .

• • •

The Thompson's third child and only son, Michael, was born in Oklahoma City on May 17, 1938. Jim had long been complaining to friends that Alberta's strict Catholicism would not allow her to consider birth control. So later that summer he submitted to a vasectomy. A friend, Otto Lucy, performed the procedure under local anesthetic in exchange for a bottle of whiskey. A delirious Thompson apparently whacked the so-called doctor in the face, and Lucy was able to finish the snipping and slicing only by hunkering down on his chest.

Another of Thompson's offbeat guides to the criminal underworld, Otto Castro Lucy and his wife, Lillie Belle, operated the Lucy Psychological and Speech Clinic from a succession of Oklahoma City addresses. A former dean of men in the state college at Edmund and a 1936 candidate for the Oklahoma City school board, Lucy served as a consultant in psychiatry for several county judges. With no medical training, he dubbed himself "Doctor" because of his studies toward a master's degree at the Harvard Graduate School in Education. Fired from a Stillwater college, allegedly for molesting boys, Lucy became the model for the bug-eyed psychiatrists and physicians who periodically crop up in Thompson's novels—Fritz Steinhopf of *Texas by the Tail,* Max Vonderscheid of *The Getaway,* and, especially, Roland Luther of *Recoil.*

In *Recoil* Dr. Luther and his blackmailed "wife," Lila, front a corrupt political lobbying campaign from the Luther Psychological Clinic. Seeking a disposable fall guy, Luther sponsors the release of bank robber Pat "Airplane Red" Cosgrove (Thompson's Fort Worth crony "Airplane Red" Brown) from the Sandstone State Reformatory. Otto Lucy, in fact, worked out of the office of Mabel Bassett, the Oklahoma commissioner of charities and corrections, and the woman behind the gallant Myrtle Briscoe in *Recoil.*

"Dr. Lucy claimed that Jimmie was a genius," Alberta recalls. "He was a close friend of the family back then. One day we were sort of kidding around, and Lucy said something about Jimmie being a genius. I laughed and said, 'Oh, of course he is.' But Dr. Lucy replied, 'I'm really not kidding Alberta.' Jimmie by that time was director of the Writers' Project, but he hadn't yet written very much."

Thompson took to accompanying Lucy on his rounds of interviews with Oklahoma parolees. Many afternoons he slipped away from the Proj-

"Doctor" Otto Lucy in his cell, 1940
(Photograph by Bill Johnson, courtesy of the
Daily Oklahoman*)*

ect to pore over the psychology textbooks, patient files, and case studies at
the clinic. Thompson's sister Freddie believed that Lucy's contribution to
his fiction was incalculable:

> I'll tell you where in my opinion a lot of his strange and violent
> material came from. Jimmie met a psychiatrist in Oklahoma City
> named Dr. Lucy, a crazy man with really weird, funny eyes. He
> looked just like Edmund Lowe. He was the first homosexual I had
> ever seen.
>
> Doctor Lucy was a brilliant man, claimed to be a Harvard grad-
> uate. He had this extensive library and Jimmie loved to go over
> there and read and just devour all of those books. I've often since
> wondered when I read something in one of Jimmie's novels which
> case study this might be.

Thompson transferred this autobiographical wrinkle to Lou Ford for *The
Killer Inside Me.* Deputy Sheriff Ford winds down with the bulky old volumes of morbid psychology in his father's study: ". . . Krafft-Ebing, Jung,
Freud, Bleuler, Adolf Meyer, Kretschmer, Kraepelin. . . . All the answers
were here, out in the open where you could look at them. And no one was
terrified or horrified. I came out of the place I was hiding in—that I always
had to hide in—and began to breathe."

Lucy was arrested in 1940 for a $75 abortion he performed on a twenty-five-year-old Oklahoma City department store clerk, Mary Ellen Legge, who subsequently died. While free on bail he was busted again when he terminated the pregnancy of Mrs. Goldie Crow, the wife of a city milk truck driver, who also died. Both women believed that Lucy was a medical doctor. He denied his guilt until investigators turned up surgical tools and a bloody newspaper from his basement. Other problems converged. A taxicab accident, he averred, left him subject to catatonic seizures. And Lillie Belle filed for divorce, on grounds of neglect.

Something of a wag, Lucy tried to banter through his trial like, well, a Jim Thompson character. "There are some soldiers and former soldiers in here," he told the *Daily Oklahoman* from his jail cell, as he waved his ivory cigarette holder, "and we're thinking about organizing a company to do our part for national defense. The sheriff might let us have some wooden guns, and we might be able to do a little drilling."

Convicted on two counts of first-degree manslaughter, Otto Lucy was sentenced to twenty-five years in the Oklahoma State Penitentiary at McAlester. Almost that many years later Thompson would tuck into the pages of *The Getaway* his eulogy for the odd, troubled healer and murderer: "Herr Doktor . . . abortionist, physician to criminals; a man who had never been able to say no to a need, regardless of laws and personal ethics."

• • •

With Ben Botkin as national folklore consultant, the Writers' Project's conservation of America's folk heritage underwent an ideological shift. Botkin thickened the concept of historical folklore to include contemporary industrial, urban, and oral sources with a vertical proletarian twist. "The folk movement must come from below upward, rather than of above downward," he argued. "Otherwise it may be dismissed as a patronizing gesture, a nostalgic wish, an elegiac complaint, a sporadic and abortive revival—on the part of paternalistic aristocrats going slumming. . . ." Jim Thompson rode the transformation more smoothly than most Southwestern and Southern state directors. He had already been there, not only with Botkin at the University of Nebraska but also with Haywire Mac in the Texas oil fields.

Thompson early on established folklore as his specialization at the Writers' Project. He first researched a "Folklore and Folk Customs" chapter for the guide book in 1936. With a lean essay, some thousand words shorter than national specifications, he surveyed Oklahoma square dances and rural pastimes, oil field speech and tall tales, Negro lore, outlaw fables, superstitions, and cures. After Thompson mailed his draft to Washington for approval, associate director George Cronyn wrote him that "this is such an excellent, well-written essay that our few minor suggestions may appear carping." John Lomax, then Henry Alsberg's folklore editor, proclaimed it "a most satisfactory essay" and distributed copies to the other state offices as a model. Reordered and tightened over the next three years, the article would enter the Oklahoma state guide as "Folklore and Folkways," essentially as Thompson phrased it but minus his droll heading "Bad Men and Bad Women" and spiky references to "class differences" and "political and industrial strife."

Following Botkin's emphasis on "living lore," as well as his own West Texas stories from the *Prairie Schooner* and *Cornhusker Countryman,* Thompson in 1938 engaged a team consisting of Gordon Friesen, Dan Garrison, William Caywood, and Welborn Hope to comb the Oklahoma oil fields and refineries for legends, songs, and colloquialisms. This fieldwork yielded "about 100,000 words of folklore material," which Thompson dismissed as "pretty poor stuff," yet also occasioned a few trenchant industrial tales and interviews, particularly Hope's "The Doodlebug," Garrison's "Rigbuilders," and Thompson's wry "Snake Magee's Rotary Boiler."

One offshoot from his folklore essay for the state guide was a fascinating glossary, *A Dictionary of Oklahomaisms,* which Thompson and his staff compiled but never published. Covering perhaps 250 specimens of regional folk-say and concentrating on roughneck, miner, rancher, and cowboy slang, the *Dictionary* accentuated linguistic ingenuity, if not perversity. Thompson's high-spirited preface set the tone:

> Being an Oklahoman is largely a state of mind. Some people who made the run of '89 still are "from the East." Others, who arrived last year, from Kansas or New Jersey, are as much a part of the state as the red beds. It all depends on how much you will admit, or what you care to claim. If you see a gentleman with his hair braided and a blanket for a topcoat it is reasonable to assume that he is a native; providing, of course, that there are no traces of his complexion on his shirt, and he does not try to sell you corn salve. . . .

The Oklahoma Writers' Project exhumed gems: *burr-head,* an unusually stupid person; *crumb-boss,* the man who has charge of tents or bunkhouses, derived from the humorous supposition that he is able to command the crumbs (bugs) that infect the beds; *git-up sooner,* an early riser, sometimes used to designate a rural Shylock; *Jerusalem Slim,* Jesus Christ; *Kinesy Knob,* used in reproving an immodest female, "I kin see Kinesy Knob a'showing!"; *wingie,* a one-armed man. . . . Thompson introduced samples and lectured on *A Dictionary of Oklahomaisms* at the annual meeting of the Oklahoma Folklore Society in February 1939.

Botkin planned to feature Thompson's recent oil field tales in a Project anthology, *American Folk Stuff,* including "The Laziest Man in Oklahoma," his slight roustabout yarn, and "Snake Magee's Rotary Boiler." Snappy and modern, "Snake Magee" spun an Einsteinian fantasy about the oil driller whose exploding boiler sends him hurtling through space with such speed that he arrives back in town slightly before he left it. As Botkin informed Thompson, "Your 'Snake Magee' has attracted much favorable comment in the states where it has been circulated. Charles K. Madsen, the Utah supervisor–state editor, writes, 'This is one of the best tall tales I have ever read.' "

When *American Folk Stuff* fizzled, Thompson published "Snake Magee" in *Direction,* a Connecticut literary monthly. The folk tale, in a ludicrous tangent, then drew the notice of the FBI. "Editorial policy adheres strictly to the Communist Party program," the report in Thompson's file solemnly intoned.

He later attempted to expand his roughneck fable into a 6,500-word narrative, "Snake Magee and Johnnie Too-Late." His own prognosis of the sequel in a 1940 letter to Botkin, "not very good," stands.

• • •

For his most heartbreaking and polished short story of the 1930s Thompson turned to neither folklore nor radical politics. Cooperative Books, a Norman, Oklahoma, press, released *Economy of Scarcity: Some Human Footnotes,* a pamphlet of off-time creative work by four members of the Writers' Project, in June 1939. The title spoofed Stuart Chase's New Deal book, *The Economy of Abundance.* As editor Winifred Johnston announced in her introduction, *"Some Human Footnotes* presents the reverse side of that glamorous world of penthouses, furs, and shining cars which the movies give us. But for a complete reflection of the economy of scarcity this picture also is needed." With their contributions Welborn Hope, Dan Garrison, and Ned DeWitt each worked over Depression icons of poverty and injustice—a cotton picker, tenant farmers, the Salvation Army mission. In "Time Without End" Jim Thompson exposed instead the crumbling interior economy and solitary mental depression of a senile old man.

"Time Without End" accompanied the failing, befuddled Joseph Mazinky through an entire vacant day. Thompson's surprisingly formal delivery grasped a seasoned tenderness far removed from the bitter ironies and violent thunder claps of his prior 1930s fiction:

> Mr. Joseph Mazinky waddled painfully along under the August sun, stepping as gingerly on the hot bricks as if they had been so many red, rectangular eggs. He was neat and slovenly at the same time, having used, apparently, all his strength and discernment in attending to a few details. His shirt was clean, but buttoned

crooked. He had laced one creased trouser leg to the top of his shoe. He was clean-shaven, but there were gray blobs of soap in his ears. Each conventional thesis of attire and toilet had its antithesis: from his head, where his crisp straw sailor rode backwards, to his shoes, only one of which was shined.

Mr. Mazinky struggles to find his way through a private labyrinth of the few city blocks that separate the residence hotel where he lives from the apartment of his son, also named Joe, with whom he takes his nightly meals. Blundering down the strange streets, he loses his abilty to distinguish past from present, "what was real and what was not." As with "The End of the Book," italics designate his slide back to childhood:

> *The shabby facade of the apartment house, a half-block away, drew down to the familiar walls of the soddy. The heat-spotted pavement glistened with the yellow-black of scorching stubble. The hot wind soughed over the prairie, swaying the sheet that hung in the doorway.*
>
> *He was so tired that he wanted to fall forward on the dirt floor and go to sleep; but, no, there was Ma squatted before him, holding out her work-red hands urgingly.*
>
> *"Just one more step, Joey. Just one more."*
>
> *He took it and she moved back.*
>
> *"That's a big boy. Now another one."*
>
> *"Huh-uh."*
>
> *"Aw, Joey . . ."*
>
> *"No," he said. "No, no, no."*
>
> *It began to rain, and he was sure that she would pick him up and carry him to the window. Instead, she disappeared with the soddy and the swaying sheet and the scorching stubble.*

When not lost in the past Mr. Mazinky knows only shame—shame for burdening his family, insulting Joe's wife, Myra, or disappointing his granddaughter, Little Myra; shame for his appearance, his confusion, his fumbles. But "Time Without End" is also his son's story. Caught between his helpless father and his own needy family Joe too contends with a maze of knotted feelings:

> "I gave you the money every Saturday, Pop. What'd you do with it?"
>
> "I—I guess I lost it."
>
> "But, Pop, you couldn't—" Joe stopped himself, taking a deep breath. "Well, don't lose it any more. And don't charge anything to

your hotel bill. Do you understand, Pop? I don't want to be tight; God knows you never were with me. I just can't make it. The kid needs her tonsils out, and Myra ain't got a decent dress to her name. And my insurance ain't paid yet, and . . . But don't do it any more. You won't, will you?"

"Sure not, Joe."

"You're sure, now? You won't forget?"

"Of course. I won't forget," said Mr. Mazinky, a little stiffly. "I reckon I got a few brains left."

"Okay," said Joe. "Just don't let me down." He stood up and dug two one-dollar bills from his watch pocket, extended them silently. . . .

Mr. Mazinky arrives back at his hotel room broke—and broken. Absent-mindedly he crushes, and then consumes the box of candy he purchased for his granddaughter with the food money Joe gave him. His "time without end" closes in, disordered and blurred:

> The fan sang in a tone above tonelessness—*like the little wheel on the cream separator.* And in the alley below the garbage cans rattled as. . . .
>
> *As Pa rinsed out the milk pails.*
>
> Firmly, the tether of the past tightened, drawing Mr. Mazinky away from the frightening crevices of the present.

The situation of Mr. Joseph Mazinky paralleled, of course, the pitiful descent of James Sherman Thompson. By the summer of 1939 the Thompsons were casting about for a private institution in which to settle the enfeebled former sheriff and oil man. "I doubt whether Pop ever saw that story Jimmie did about him," Alberta posits. "He was too far gone by then, I think. But Jimmie was very proud that he had done it." He had reason to be. Ben Botkin wrote him from Washington: "Your story is the best of the lot and the best thing of yours I have seen. The illusion of age and decay is perfectly created and controlled. Congratulations on a swell job."

Nearly everyone who knew Jim Thompson in the late 1930s marveled at his incredible energy. His predecessor, William Cunningham, had protested that editing left him no time for writing. Yet Thompson finished a novel, executed his finest short story, and coauthored as many as twenty-six radio plays during his first year as director of the Project, not counting his monthly quantum of trade and true crime articles.

That was just the work he signed his name to. Beyond the Saturday-night dramas, Thompson supplied KOMA with hours of advertising copy and "continuity" between song chitchat and jokes for the record spinners.

Gordon Friesen remembers that his friend also was contributing anonymously to *True Story,* still the leading confession magazine. "Jim was making up and sending stories into *True Story* every month. He was being paid something like $25 for a short article," Friesen remembers, "and turning them out as fast as possible."

• • •

During the spring of 1939 the Oklahoma Writers' Project moved toward completion of its chief outstanding tasks, the state guide and the labor history. National director Henry Alsberg indicated his pleasure at recent progress on both fronts, and urged Thompson to nail down sponsors for publication. For much of his directorship Thompson was able to ignore the innuendo that shrouded his office in red. His federal mandate meant that he answered only to Washington, and Alsberg, with Bill Cunningham at his side, shielded him from the censure of Oklahoma politicians and newspapers. The Emergency Relief Act of 1939, which would transfer control of most WPA arts projects to the individual states by September 1, changed all that. Thompson found himself on a collision course with Oklahoma authorities, not only for sponsorship of the state guide and the labor history but also for his survival on the Project.

Thompson sniffed trouble with the labor history from the moment the volume was broached in May 1938. "The idea of the history was not mine," he notified Alsberg. "Responding to requests from Senators Lee and Thomas . . . Mr. E. M. Fry, Deputy WPA Administrator, called me to his office and asked me what I thought about writing a Labor History. I told him that while I was deeply in sympathy with the labor movement, I could not help but feel hesitant about undertaking a work which was apt to be, to say the least, so controversial." But once Thompson recognized that the political clout of Oklahoma's two senators made the labor history inevitable, he plunged into the research with characteristic vigor. "I had my people working on the history for more than ten months," he added to Alsberg. "I dictated the final manuscript from more than a million words of source material." Washington applauded the results. "You have produced a good interpretive job," Alsberg wrote back, "which when published should be a real credit to the Project."

Thompson secured a promise of sponsorship from Oklahoma Commissioner of Labor W. A. Pat Murphy, but the state budget office vetoed the request. He then arranged meetings with representatives of Oklahoma labor unions to see if they might underwrite the history with subscriptions. These conferences, which Thompson financed out of his own pocket, were tense affairs, as many of the unions demanded approval of copy before they would commit to advance orders. As Thompson apprised Alsberg of his heated life around the Project:

> . . . Representatives of the brotherhoods, the bricklayers, and several other crafts accepted the manuscript without reading it. Mr. Tom Cheek, president of the Farmers' Union read and approved it and promised to ask for funds at the July convention of his organization. . . .
>
> David Fowler, president of District 21, United Mine Workers of America, and also advisor to the Arkansas-Oklahoma CIO groups did not attend the meeting. . . . I called Mr. Fowler at his Muskogee headquarters and found him extremely antagonistic. He not only refused to subcribe to the publication but emphatically declined to discuss the history . . . I went to Muskogee to see him.
>
> He had been informed, as I understood it, probably by rivals in the labor movement, that the history was unfriendly to the miners and the CIO. I insisted that he read it and point out our errors, if any, and we went through the manuscript together. . . . I am returning the pages—as they were returned from your office—on which we made changes, and the revised copy of each. . . .

With Alsberg's authorization, Thompson sent the manuscript to the printer by late July. He expected to have galleys ready for final formal approval in Washington within a few weeks.

Thompson simultaneously was seeking a sponsor for the guide book, which had been his central activity at the Project since his 1936 appointment as editor. Most state projects looked to local government funding for their guides. But Thompson doubted that Oklahoma Governor Leon Phillips, a blustery opponent of President Roosevelt and the New Deal, would release his regressive hammerlock on the legislative coffers. "It will be almost impossible," he predicted to Alsberg, "to obtain a subsidy from any state agency under the present political set-up."

At the suggestion of Ben Botkin, Thompson entered into correspondence with Savoie Lottinville, the new director of the University of Oklahoma Press, in April 1939. He reported to Alsberg that Lottinville appeared open to discussions but needed to "secure reports from his readers [to] decide whether or not the guide is something they would like to publish." Thompson cautioned that "the future of the press is very much in doubt because of the economy drive of the present legislature." He reminded Alsberg that the University of Oklahoma Press rejected a previous draft of the guide in 1937, mainly for copyright objections. Yet he hoped "these difficulties can be ironed out if the report on the book is favorable."

Thompson anticipated a positive reading. After months of relentless fact checking, line editing, and rewriting, Washington had approved his revised guide in March and scheduled it "for early publication." Alsberg and the national staff corrected errors, recommended fresh topics and approaches, and encouraged a reliance on vitalizing "visual" details. Yet Washington also tossed off a few red herrings. Alsberg, for instance, fixated on *The Grapes of Wrath* when it appeared in 1939, and seemed determined to retool the Oklahoma guide book according to John Steinbeck's novel. "Are the conditions in the country around Sallisaw as they were when Steinbeck collected material for his book?" Alsberg queried. And again: "I can only suggest that you read Steinbeck's *Grapes of Wrath* to discover how descriptions of the ordinary and the commonplace in concrete terms make literature." Thompson shot back an intemperate response from his hobo years in and out of the state:

> . . . Concerning your questions on *Grapes of Wrath:* It is difficult for me to believe, although I am a Steinbeck fan, that the author of the book ever was in Oklahoma. There never were dust storms around Sallisaw. This town is in the Ozark Mountains section. The land of this area, as elsewhere in eastern Oklahoma, suffered greatly from erosion but it was not caused by the wind. . . .
>
> You can gather from this that knowledge of the State is an insurmountable obstacle to writing of Oklahoma as Steinbeck would write of it. The effect of the hegira of Okies upon the trades people in the towns was imperceptible. And to write of the food and the eating houses, the dance halls, the churches and schools—well, again we are handicapped by our knowledge of actual conditions. Every two or three years for the better part of my life I have traveled from Texas up through North Dakota and back again, and for the average person I have found conditions much the same in one State as I have in another. Your 25¢ plate lunch in Texas will be equipped with poke salad; in Oklahoma and Kansas perhaps, greens; in Nebraska, Iowa and points north, garden sass. But it's still spinach, whatever you call it. If we had the room, as Steinbeck had, for characterization, and if we were writing fiction rather than fact, we could bring out the subtle differences in people and places such as Washington would like to see. . . . We must always keep in mind that our manuscript has to be read and approved by local people and that inaccuracies, such as Steinbeck's book was filled with, will not be excused when we are the authors. . . .

Thompson was still excising mistakes from the guide even after Washington certified his copy. "In gathering material for our Labor and Negro

Histories," he advised Alsberg, "we have uncovered facts which contradict a number of statements in our essays. We had adopted a policy in the past of depending on 'authoritative' works, such as Harlow's *History of Oklahoma,* when we were in doubt about certain points. Now in the light of our new research matter, we find that Harlow's contains a number of statements which are hard to characterize as anything but barefaced lies. For instance, this 'history' indicated by omission and statement that the coal mine strike of 1919 was settled in favor of the operators, when as a matter of fact it was one of the greatest union victories in the labor annals of Oklahoma. . . ."

As the September 1 deadline neared, Savoie Lottinville informed Thompson of his interest in signing a contract for the Oklahoma state guide. He calculated that the massive volume would cost the University of Oklahoma Press nearly $6,000. However, the press itself, he judged, could contribute only half that amount. Other sponsors would have to furnish the balance.

Lottinville, a panelist at the Southwest Writers' Congress, may have been bargaining in good faith and offering all the resources at his disposal. Thompson initially wrote Alsberg of Lottinville's "valuable and contagious enthusiasm for the manuscript. . . . I do not believe it will be any problem to secure . . . subsidies." But he soon recognized that in Oklahoma politics, Lottinville's insistence on outside subvention was tantamount to canceling the guide.

On July 20 Thompson submitted a letter of resignation to Henry Alsberg:

> As you probably know, our project becomes State-wide, instead of Federal, on September 1st.
>
> For several reasons, I do not believe I could fit into the State-wide set-up so I am submitting my resignation to become effective the first of September. Since I have accumulated considerable annual leave, I will submit my resignation to the State office on July 24th—this coming Monday—and will take no active part in project affairs after that date. . . .
>
> If you care to write me, you should do so immediately, so that the letter will reach me by or before Monday. . . .

His friend, Ben Botkin, took Thompson at his word:

> Henry showed me your letter announcing your resignation and asked me if I could do anything to keep you on the job until the guidebook is finished. The only thing I can suggest is that if the State Administrator will guarantee you your annual leave (in accrued salary) at the end of August, you should hang on, for

the sake of writing 30 [a conventional journalistic way to mark the end of a story] to the guide. . . . But I doubt (and I suppose you know better than I do) whether you will have the Administrator on your side. So I am really more worried what will become of you than I am about what will happen to the guide, anxious as I am to see that out of the way. Knowing (from your long letter of some time back) how you feel about the project, I can only wonder that you stayed as long as you did. A good many of us here were quite in agreement with what you said about the evils of standardization and believe that the individuality of state writers should never have been sacrificed to a formula. Now that the formula is threatened with breakdown, I regret that you have felt it necessary to quit before you could show what you could do under state sponsorship. (Here my acquaintance with Oklahoma interposes the comment that under state sponsorship you might as well quit, knowing what this means in Oklahoma City.)

Your resignation is only the first of many that will probably take place, and there will be many dismissals for political reasons. The breaking-up is going to be a sorrowful process. . . .

Alsberg immediately dispatched three administrative emissaries to Oklahoma City and wired Thompson to hold off his resignation until they arrived.

His accumulated annual leave, perhaps, preyed upon Thompson that turbulent summer of 1939, as his letter testifies. But his resignation, more likely, constituted a power play intended to tip Lottinville's hand and steer Washington's attention to the imperiled state guide. Thompson's ploy, if that's what it was, appeared to spark the desired effects. When Alsberg's delegation, led by regional supervisor Lyle Saxon and regional director of division of professional and service projects Leo Spofford, reached Oklahoma City at midnight, July 25, they briskly mobilized all the sparring parties. With a series of meetings Saxon patched up Thompson's difficulties with local WPA administrators, Ron Stephens and Eula Fullerton. And when he brought Thompson together with Lottinville and W. B. Bizzell, president of the University of Oklahoma, it seemed that the university would sponsor not only the state guide but also the new state-controlled Writers' Project. After Thompson agreed to remain as director, Saxon returned to his home base of Louisiana convinced that "all previous troubles were ironed out, and I was most hopeful that the Oklahoma Project would continue to function as before."

Saxon left—and spoke—too quickly. During his visit problems emerged that undercut his hasty conclusion. Ron Stephens, for one, wished to examine the labor history, since "if some criticism followed he would be held responsible." As Saxon reported to Alsberg:

> The only thing that worried me was this: Mr. Thompson told me that a labor history of Oklahoma had been taken to the printers that day and that the printing had begun. He had the approval of the national office for this he told me. I am quite sure that Mr. Thompson and Mr. DeWitt and their assistants had worked long and hard on this labor history, and insofar as I know (I haven't seen the manuscript) it is not of a controversial nature. . . .

The University of Oklahoma, moreover, had disclosed during the conference with Thompson the real reason for Lottinville's caution about the state guide. Again, as Saxon reported to Alsberg:

> They seemed entirely willing to cooperate and said that it was highly probable that the university would take on the sponsorship of the Writers' Project, after certain matters were cleared up. He wished to make some sort of an examination into the workings of the Writers' Project, he said. There had been some accusations as to Communism on the Writers' Project in the past, he said, and while he did not believe that there was any truth in these accusations he felt that the university should not sponsor the Writers' Project until he was able to assure himself that no future trouble would ensue . . . the whole tone of the meeting was so cordial and so friendly that I felt Mr. Thompson and Mr. DeWitt would have no further trouble.

Thompson attempted to settle the labor history and agreed to provide Eula Fullerton with a carbon copy for reading by her and Ron Stephens. But his compromise disappeared down a blind alley. He complained to Saxon:

> As you told me to do, I submitted the manuscript to the state office for approval by their labor department. After reading half the manuscript—the whole thing could have been read by anyone in forty-five minutes—I was notified that the rest could not be read for approximately two weeks. I then went to Miss Fullerton and asked her if she would not read it, as, obviously, we were very short on time. It was at this point that she advised me that the Project could not be sponsored on account of the book.

Only a few days after Saxon departed Oklahoma City, the University of Oklahoma withdrew its offer of sponsorship for the Writers' Project, citing the labor history. "The University was not willing to sponsor the Project unless this manuscript was recalled," Leo Spofford briefed Washington, "and unless it was definitely understood that the University was not sponsoring the Project while this book was being printed."

The Communist issue proved still more damaging. Lottinville and President Bizzell were nervous about the Project because the school was itself under siege. "The University of Oklahoma must be very, very careful since it is at the mercy of the State Legislature and the Governor," Eula Fullerton instructed Spofford, "and whether deserved or not, the Writers' Project in Oklahoma is branded as being a Communist group. . . . One of the first acts of Governor Phillips was to launch a bitter attack against the University of Oklahoma as encouraging Communism among the faculty members and on the teaching program." When Phillips repeated his charges during the spring of 1939, Thompson scoffed at them in letter to Botkin:

> The rumpus at the University turned out the same as usual. Everyone was accused of being a communist but the party members and Bizzell emerged the legislative cloaca every bit as pure as his bible collection. Faint rumblings are still coming from the State house, but with the *Daily Oklahoman* decrying the investigation, I look for no more trouble.

That "legislative cloaca" sealed Thompson's doom at the Project.

On August 4, Henry Alsberg telephoned Thompson and asked him to halt production on the labor history in order to save the Oklahoma Writers' Project. Thompson replied by mail the following morning that this would make him personally responsible for paying off the printer—but that principle, more than money, was at risk:

> It is a much more serious matter to me to junk ten months work, simply because it is the convenient thing to do. I am wondering also if, having done it once, we will have to continue to buckle under to expediency. I am wondering if some excuse will not be found to toss out our Negro history, our oil stories, and so on. And I am wondering why if we are not permitted to do any honest or original research, why, if we are never permitted to move out of the safe and beaten path, there is any use in having a Writers' Project.

By then he knew from conversations with Fullerton and Stephens that his politics, not the labor history, was the snag in his negotiations with the University of Oklahoma.

Through late August Thompson urgently wired Alsberg: "Think I could save Project if I could talk with you" and "I refuse to leave job under cloud. Want talk with you and get to bottom of affair." With the national office also about to close, there was no money for travel.

The afternoon of August 31, mere hours before the Federal Writers' Project expired, Governor Leon Phillips put the muscle on. Through an intermediary, Ira Finley, president of the Veterans of Industry of America, the governor notified Ron Stephens of his willingness to sponsor the Project "provided Thompson and DeWitt were fired, and we appointed someone who was not associated with the Oklahoma Communist movement in any way."

Thompson shut down the Oklahoma Federal Writers' Project that same night. The office reopened nine months later with historian Angie Debo as director.

• • •

Labor History of Oklahoma appeared in November 1939. Detached from its scorching political context, the slim volume of 120 pages seems muted, impersonal, almost prosaic—hardly the raw material of sensational resignations, ultimatums, and firings. Gordon Friesen worked closely with Thompson and principal researcher Clyde Hamm, a labor history student at the University of Oklahoma, as they resolved the final text. "Jim went out of his way to make the labor history noncontroversial," he maintains. "Compared to what it should have been, the manuscript that everyone attacked so bitterly was pretty tame. The radical labor history we started with got severely trimmed back."

As Thompson anticipated, any labor history of Oklahoma was fated for contention. He opened the book with a somber recital of hazardous conditions in the McAlester mines, where on January 14, 1892, a coal dust explosion killed one hundred miners and mutiltated two hundred more. Field disasters made up only the natural portion of peril for workers during the inauguration of the Oklahoma labor movement. Strikers against the Choctaw Coal & Railway Company in 1894, for instance, were seized from their homes by the federal infantry, loaded into boxcars, and deported to Arkansas. Succeeding sections examined agrarian movements, such as the Farmers' Union, the Renters' Union, and the Green Corn Rebellion; the anti-labor Coronado case, which forced the dissolution of District 21 of the United Mine Workers of America; the Oklahoma City Packing-House strike of 1921, when a black strike breaker was lynched; and the creation of the Farmer-Labor Reconstruction League, which dominated the 1922 Oklahoma election.

As the *Labor History of Oklahoma* adventured closer to the present, Thompson and his Project staff scanned struggles they had themselves been party to, either as union activists or observers. The chapter on "Depression and Recovery" charted the rise of the Unemployed Councils and the food riots of 1933 and 1934, the formation of the Southern Tenant Farmers Union, the bloody Pure Oil Refinery strike of 1938, and the ongoing Mid-Continent Refinery strike—all, according to Sis Cunningham, missions of the Oklahoma City CP. Yet even for events witnessed firsthand, Thompson emitted mechanical, committee prose; and perhaps because he dictated rather than wrote, the history missed the luster of his folklore essay for the guide book and the sting of his official letters to Alsberg. A steely cynicism occasionally crosscut the run of facts, names, and dates. Here Thompson pokes around the edges of the Oklahoma City food riot seditious conspiracy trial:

> In January preceding this trial, members and sympathizers of the [Unemployed] Councils conducted a vigorous campaign to raise funds for the defense and to indicate broad public protest against the arrests. Thousands of postcards, letters and telegrams, poured into the offices of Judge Vaught and Federal Prosecutor Lewis, demanding the release of the prisoners. Many people contributed to the defense fund. In an attempt to check this movement, more were arrested, charged with "Conspiracy to obstruct justice." Among these were Marshall Lakey, well known Oklahoma sculptor, who had offered to do a bust for the person raising the greatest sum for the defense fund, and Harry Bender, who had just been exposed by the Communist Party as an agent provocateur sent into Oklahoma City to attempt to smash the growing Oil Workers' Union.
>
> Bender pleaded guilty, asking for a suspended sentence, and was sentenced to serve eighteen months in the Federal Penitentiary. Lakey and others entered pleas of nolo contendere and were released for lack of any evidence of conspiracy.

Despite Thompson's efforts to soft-pedal it, the book never wholly concealed its labor bias. More damaging, perhaps, the mercenary Oklahoma government—"the rottenest, politically, in the country," Thompson gauged in *Roughneck*—rather than management, emerged the dominant villain.

The labor history garnered a respectful notice on Professor Kenneth Kaufman's Sunday book page for the *Daily Oklahoman*. But Thompson brooded on another critique to Ben Botkin: "I've only seen one review of the labor history, so far. It was by a liberal (self-named), O. L. Crain, and, as you might expect, he managed to contain his enthusiasm for the volume. He termed it, 'interesting but incomplete, a typical result of a forced-writing project. . . .' Hell, I knew it was incomplete; but I don't know what a forced-writing project is. If anything our organization was a forced-not-to-write project."

Oklahoma: A Guide to the Sooner State was published in December 1941 under the auspices of the University of Oklahoma Press—the last entry in the American Guide Series to reach print. Angie Debo and her assistant, John M. Oskison, signed the editorial preface, and neither Thompson nor Cunningham received acknowledgment for his years of toil.

Prior to directing the Project, Debo had authored two superb Native American histories, *The Rise and Fall of the Choctaw Republic* (1933) and *And Still the Waters Run* (1940). Because of her fearless scholarship Debo subsequently attained the status of an Oklahoma legend, especially among the state's young women historians. But her personal myth has needlessly embellished her role in the state guide. A recent reprint of *Oklahoma: A Guide to the Sooner State* awards her sole editorial responsibility for its contents. Assessing each of the directors' respective contributions to the printed text is a quagmire as, during the 1950s, the Oklahoma Historical Society reports, two hundred boxes of Project papers were apparently shipped to Fort Worth for storage and lost. Debo, it's certain, overhauled the automobile tours; she solicited an expert article from Professor Edward Everett Dale on "The Spirit of Oklahoma." But her handiwork otherwise seems less decisive. Where dated, sequential drafts survive, as in the case of the "Folklore and Folkways" essay and "General Information" section, the manuscripts entered the published guide essentially as they had exited Thompson's typewriter.

• • •

Three months after he left the Project Thompson put on a brave front to Botkin, who had hoped to find him a position with the revamped WPA:

> I've settled down in earnest to free-lancing, and have made one sale and sent out five stories since I wrote you. Naturally, since a fifty per cent selling average is pretty good in this business, I'm not becoming wealthy. But I feel better, being my own boss, and I know that, in the long run, I'll be better off. I wouldn't want another regular job, even if I could get one; security, with all it connotes, is, I think, a bad thing for me. . . .
>
> Incidentally, I want to thank you for your efforts on my behalf in Washington. I was pretty sure that I would never be re-employed in any branch of the WPA, so I wasn't at all disappointed. No, I haven't seen Newsom [Alsberg's successor at the WPA] or heard anything of him. And, frankly, I don't give a particular damn if I never do.

Yet Jim was reeling—angry, troubled, and slightly out of control. The devastation of his dismissal settled over his mood like a corrosive fume. His letter boasted "rumors that a tri-state labor newspaper is about to be launched, and that I'm in line for the job of editor." But Thompson lost out on that prize, he later admitted, because of his excessive drinking. In fact, his 1950 confessional essay for *SAGA*, "An Alcoholic Looks at Himself," charged nearly all of his erratic movements for the next year and a half to the haze of alcoholic shame:

> . . . an alcoholic is driven by an urge which no one but another alcoholic can understand: He must justify himself (or stop drinking). He must justify a career, which, to the normal man or woman amounts to outright shamelessness. Pulling an ordinary rabbit out of a hat is not sufficient justification. He was to come up with a Chinchilla.
>
> In 1939, drink cost me an excellent editorial job. The position was a highly specialized one, and for many people the setback might have been permanent. But not for me, an alcoholic.
>
> Disgraced, broke and faced with an increasingly frigid home atmosphere, I blotted everything out and plunged into free-lancing for the pulp-paper magazines. I had been out of that field for years, but within months I was making more than I had been on the job I had lost.
>
> Having therefore justified myself with a Chinchilla, so to speak, I, of course slackened up on my work and stepped up my drinking. It wasn't long before another rabbit was demanded. I had one; I had begun a subconscious search for one months previously. One out of a hundred letters I wrote to friends, associates, and friends of both, asking for help, finally bore fruit. I received a research fellowship from a philanthropic foundation.
>
> The money involved was not much, but it practically amounted to a year's pension. My time was my own and during the year I did almost nothing but drink . . .

Thompson actually earned his fellowship from the Rockefeller Foundation with minimal melodrama. During the spring of 1939 the Oklahoma Project was approached by William Terry Couch, regional director for the Southern states and director of the University of North Carolina Press, with an idea for a book on oil field workers. Couch had recently edited *These Are Our Lives,* a collection of life histories gathered by Project writers in North Carolina, Tennessee, and Georgia. "Mr. Couch was here two or three days last week and we had some swell discussions," Thompson enthused in a May 15 letter to Botkin. "We have arranged tentatively to do a book on the

same order as *These Are Our Lives,* but dealing entirely with the oil industry. What do you think of the idea? The boys here are very much pepped up
about it."

During his twenty years in Chapel Hill, William Couch established the
University of North Carolina Press as "the single most influential institution
in launching Modernist thought in the South," historian Daniel Singal
wrote. More than most university publishers, Couch put his stamp on
every book he printed. He furnished his oral historians with comprehen-
sive "Instructions to Writers." And, as he challenged in his preface for
These Are Our Lives:

> The idea is to get life histories which are readable and faithful
> representations of living persons, and which, taken together, will
> give a fair picture of the structure and working of society. So far as
> I know, this method of portraying the quality of life of a people, of
> revealing the real workings of institutions, customs, habits, has
> never been used for the people of any region or country. . . .
> With all our talk about democracy it seems not inappropriate to let
> the people speak for themselves.

The "documentary book" became a leading new genre of the late Depression. From Margaret Bourke-White and Erskine Caldwell's popular
essay in photojournalism, *You Have Seen Their Faces,* to Walker Evans and
James Agee's magisterial *Let Us Now Praise Famous Men,* American modernist artists worked to represent the texture of everyday reality with the
pliant tools of life history.

Couch admired Thompson. "I feel that the discovery of Mr. Thompson
and the few others I have located," he declared early in 1940, "far more
than compensates for the time I wasted with the imbecilities of the WPA."
When the Project terminated, he still wanted Thompson and Ned DeWitt
for his Chapel Hill occupational "lives" program. DeWitt, all agreed, could
continue with the oil field volume, now titled *People in Oil,* provided he
could obtain the necessary funding. Thompson, with Couch's assistance,
would apply for a fellowship to support his research on another book.

Thompson's life history project absorbed some false starts before he
cut his way to a viable subject. Initially, he explored a book on "hunting and
trapping in Louisiana." But early in January 1940 Thompson applied to the
Rosenwald Foundation for a grant to write about the Oklahoma coal-mining
industry:

> There is nothing unique about my plan of work; it was used
> successfully in compiling the volume *These Are Our Lives,* and
> other books. It consists, simply, of obtaining first-person stories

from people engaged in the various branches of the industry, from actual mining to merchandising. The workers tell their stories in their own language—as much of their personal histories as is pertinent and significant, and the details of the jobs that they do. By means of a keen regard to dialectical peculiarities, careful selection of the subjects for interview, and thoughtful editing and arrangement of the material, it should be possible to formulate a factual yet highly entertaining document on the industry. . . .

Oklahoma's coal-mining area is among the oldest industrial regions in the Southwest. A part of the domain of the Five Civilized Tribes, at the time the mines were opened, it was settled by workers of a dozen nationalities. The story of these people and their descendants is more than one of an industry; in a sense, it is the story of America.

Long on process, short on scintillating particulars, Thompson's prospectus failed to impress the Rosenwald board. But before he received its decision, he had already moved on to a topic whose history and curiosities he didn't have to fake. On January 19 Thompson petitioned the Rockefeller Foundation with a vigorous and highly personal proposal about "Business, Labor, and the Unions":

Scope: The book should treat the CIO, the AF of L, one or two of the Railway Brotherhoods, the Farmers' Union and the Southern Tenant Farmers Union, and one of the unions for the unskilled or unemployed such as the Workers' Alliance or the Veterans of Industry. . . .

Objectives: It is difficult to set down the purposes of such a book except in very general terms, nor is it possible to do more than hope that those purposes will be achieved. Discussion will be directed, of course, towards the various breaches between the organized and unorganized, employer and employee, the CIO and AF of L, yes, and the actual if unofficial hostilities between the industrial and the agrarian worker. What are the real issues behind these quarrels? Why do they recur, continue, in the face of the obvious disadvantages to the participants? I believe—or I hope—that the answers to those questions can be found; that the trouble arises not from any differences in aims, but by unnecessary divergence from the same aim. And I think this can be shown through depicting the men in labor and industry as they are—not as they might like to be, think they are, or should be. Last year, in preparing a

Labor history of Oklahoma for the Federal Writers' Project, it was necessary to call a meeting of the representatives of the CIO, the AF of L, the Farmers' Union, the Railway Brotherhoods, and several other organizations. Their backgrounds were, in many respects, identical; in general, they all wanted the same thing. Yet they were hardly free of suspicion of one another. I wondered just how much of their antipathy and distrust was due to their being inarticulate, to self-deception, inhibition, and habit. I could not help but think of the fable of the mother duck who scolded her ducklings for waddling. I think that capital and labor need to be divested of their habiliments, cartoonist provided, of silk hat and square cap.

I believe, in short, that they need a mirror.

Method of Work: I have a good many friends and acquaintances in the labor movement, from the state commissioner of labor to the secretary of the local hod-carriers union. Most of them trust me to be honest and conscientious, and would give me such help as they were able. This help might consist of technical advice on trade terms and lingo, invitations into the homes of workers, and rides from one point to another. Having been a worker in a great many occupations, I make a sympathetic and understanding listener around workers, and have no trouble in feeling "at home." At the same time, I can adjust myself to, and converse sensibly with, the employer groups. I have been an employer; I was, until recently, a member of the Oklahoma City Chamber of Commerce.

Briefly, I think that I might serve as the above-mentioned mirror.

Thompson received a one-year fellowship of $1,800 from the Rockefeller Foundation General Education Board, to begin February 1. By then he had further refined the scope of his book to the Southwestern building trades. His working title: *We Talked About Labor.*

That winter and spring Thompson roamed all over Oklahoma, Texas, and Arkansas, assembling labor news and interviews. Soon he was bombarding Couch with 2,500-word life histories—at the rate of four or five a week: "Commissioner's Office," "We Need Education," and "Common Laborer" (February 13); "I'll Get Ahead," "All the Lads Were Good," and "The Sum of Our Moments" (February 17); "Labor Editor," and "Electrician's Hall" (February 26).

The interviews, Thompson reported, demanded diplomacy: "There is a feud for almost every square foot in the labor temple. To be seen talking with the b.a. [business agent] of one craft is to invite a snub or suspicion from another." His travels called for patience. "For the past week I have been trying to get an interview with the business agent of the electricians union. . . . He is always scooting off madly, before the admiring members of the local, for some unknown destination, at the approximate time I appear. He is just finishing a domino game and must leave as soon as it is over."

Couch praised Thompson's first stories for their "genuineness," but he worried that the life historian was imposing his own personality on the voices of his subjects. "In my opinion," he advanced, "the best stories are those in which you have the least to say." By May, Mary Bobbit Littlejohn, Couch's assistant, injected a more devastating criticism:

> After reading this material, the main question that comes to my mind is how a book can be made from it to cover the whole building industry. . . . It seems to me that very soon Mr. Thompson, from the material already gathered, should form an outline of how he wants to do the book, then work on gathering material to fill in the outline. . . . I do think that much more of the kind of random gathering already done will involve a good deal wasted time.

Thompson finally ceased accumulating life histories in June and sat down to devise a structure for *We Talked About Labor.* "I know I'm working myself right out of the only job I ever enjoyed," he anxiously wrote Couch, "but there it is, anyway."

• • •

We Talked About Labor thrust Thompson back into the thick of the Oklahoma workers' struggle. In the spring and summer of 1940 he was spending more time than ever on Grand Avenue at the Progressive Book Shop. In May, Bob and Ina Wood invited him to a concert some visiting musicians were throwing at the Hooverville by the banks of the North Canadian River.

Woody Guthrie and Pete Seeger came to Oklahoma City on a cross-country drive that carried them from Washington, D.C., to Pampa, Texas, an oil boomtown where Guthrie's wife, Mary, was raising their children. As Guthrie recounted his stay:

> We bought us a Plymouth and drove down through the South and then crossed over into Oklahoma to sing for the Hooverville Camptowners "Community Camp" on the rim of Oklahoma's worst garbage dump. I made up my song "Union Maid" on the typewriter of Bob and Ina Wood, the organizers of the Communist Party in Oklahoma. They gave me as good a feeling as I ever got from being around anybody in my life. They made me see why I had to keep

going around and around with my guitar making up songs and singing. . . .

Thompson joined the outdoor sing-along near the wretched shantytown where thousands of Oklahoma's unemployed huddled in hammered tin shacks, coffin crates, or the huge pipes left over from the city sewer project. He attended another benefit performance with the Red Dust Players, a few days later, for the Workers' Alliance and striking oil workers.

"Woody and Jim took to each other right away like a pair of old hobos," Gordon Friesen marvels. "You could see that they had a lot in common." Thompson apparently pleased the singer with his knowledge of Haywire Mac and the Texas Wobblies. But neither Friesen nor Pete Seeger can recall anything that these pure products of America—both sons of Oklahoma, perennial vagabonds, and homegrown radicals inclined to disguise their subversive tidings behind a cloud of hayseed—said to each other. Thompson didn't accompany Sis Cunningham and Bob Wood when Guthrie offered them a ride to New York City for the Communist Party convention in the huge black Plymouth he then donated to the Oklahoma City CP. Guthrie's pivotal role in Thompson's literary life would have to wait.

Jim's political energy that summer wore also the garb of family. His sister Freddie, now married to Charles Johnston, a young grocer, announced her candidacy for the Oklahoma state senate in the Fourteenth District. Thompson threw in with the campaign, essentially a lark, as a speechwriter and advance man. Dubbed the "oomph candidate" by the local press, Freddie finished a distant third in a field of three, but no matter. The barnstorming excused a lot of soggy evenings. "Jimmie was with me every step of the way, enjoying it like mad," Freddie remembered. "His speeches were spellbinding. I memorized them carefully, but I had no idea what I was talking about. . . . One night in a little town on the outskirts of Oklahoma City Jimmie decided that they were country people and he should introduce me in a way that they would be comfortable with. So he got up there with his few drinks and talked about how I had slopped hogs, and all these other dreadful things. . . . Jimmie had probably one of the most fun summers. . . ."

But in August disaster struck the Oklahoma City left. For months the Reverend E. F. Webber had been inflaming anti-Communist hysteria with his weekly sermons over KOMA. One May night the Progressive Book Shop was broken into and ransacked. Although the Reverend Webber denied any knowledge of the burglary, he soon announced to his radio audience that some Communist propaganda "has come into my possession" and that as "a special treat" there would be a civic book burning. In June he sponsored a huge bonfire in the stadium adjacent to his tabernacle. Thirty-one copies of the Constitution of the United States, stolen from the Progressive Book

Shop, swelled the pyre of Marxist tracts and periodicals. Oklahoma City became the sole American metropolis to sustain a public book burning prior to the Second World War.

Then on Saturday, August 17, a police raid descended on the Progressive Book Shop, seizing more than ten thousand books, papers, and pamphlets and arresting everyone on the premises. Simultaneously across Oklahoma City, officers led by Assistant County Attorney John Eberle invaded five homes. Personal libraries and files were looted and, as at the bookstore, anyone in the vicinity, resident or visitor, was hauled off to jail. Eberle held the prisoners incommunicado for nearly a week, concealed from their families and friends under aliases assigned them by the police. Slowly, names drifted out to the press and the crowd rallying on the steps of the courthouse. The eighteen eventually were arraigned on charges of "membership in the Communist Party" or of distributing literature "advocating . . . crime, criminal syndicalism, sabotage, and doing acts of physical violence and the destruction of and damage to property" included Bob and Ina Wood, Fred Maxham, Eli Jaffe, and Herb Brausch (a hod carrier who contributed the "Common Laborer" life history to *We Talked About Labor*).

During the chaotic news blackout of the shakedown, Sis Cunningham and other party leaders fled to the "Western Badlands," hiding out in family farms or with sympathizers unknown to the police. Thompson stood his ground in Oklahoma City and, with Gordon Friesen, organized the Oklahoma committee to Defend Political Prisoners. Believing that a celebrity attorney might best confront Eberle, the committee approached Moman Pruiett—Sheriff Thompson's flowery foe from territorial days, and the colorful Kossmeyer of his son's crime novels. "Since Pruiett immediately obtained a writ of habeas corpus for us that forced Eberle to release the names of nine of the prisoners, that probably was a smart tactic," Friesen discloses. "But we never should have sent Eli Jaffe's girlfriend to talk to him. Nena Beth was just a teenager then, pretty innocent, and Moman Pruiett tried to get her to lie down and urinate on his stomach!" Oblique planes from Thompson's past intersected at the Oklahoma County Jail that August: Jaffe and Brausch wound up as cellmates with Otto Lucy.

Thompson himself avoided arrest—no doubt, Friesen calculates, because his stature as former director of the Writers' Project "made him too big a fish for a little assistant county prosecutor to haul in." Unlike the Woods, Sis Cunningham, or Friesen, he would never endure the silent scourge of the blacklist. During the weeks following the raids Thompson presented his situation to William Couch more like a journalist than a potential victim. "The labor scene, here, has become so interesting," he hedged. "Herb Brausch, of *Common Laborer,* is in jail in lieu of $50,000 bond on a charge of criminal syndicalism." Yet by all accounts he was deeply frightened, then and later. Thompson placed a fictional interview with the

Criminal lawyer Moman Pruiett—the re-
current "Kossmeyer" of Jim Thompson's fiction
(Courtesy of the Oklahoma Historical Society)

FBI over communism at the center of his novel *Now and on Earth,* but his own case proved luckier. "Nothing ever came of it, no problems, no real harm," his sister Freddie recalled. "But after that he was always afraid."

• • •

As the first criminal syndicalism trials proceeded to speedy convictions in the fall of 1940, Thompson made plans to leave Oklahoma City. For some time Alberta had been talking of moving the family to California, where she thought Jim might find a job writing for the movies. With so many of his closest friends facing stiff prison sentences,* Thompson's only significant

---

* After separate trials, Robert Wood, Ina Wood, and Eli Jaffe were each sentenced to the maximum penalty of ten years' imprisonment and a $5,000 fine. In 1943 an Oklahoma appeals court reversed the convictions. "By then the Soviet Union was America's ally in the war with Germany," Gordon Friesen notes, "and Communist books couldn't justify the witch hunt anymore."

tie to his native state was his Rockefeller Foundation grant and the building trades book.

Over the summer he had managed to map out a synopsis for *We Talked About Labor*. Apologizing for his "agonizing slowness," Thompson mailed a draft of the opening sections, "Foundation" and "Framework," to the University of North Carolina Press in early August. A revised outline, together with a draft of the third section, "Finishing," followed a few weeks later. Near the end of September he sent 119 more pages and still another synopsis, listing some twenty-nine life histories out of a projected thirty-five. With each fresh submission Couch and his readers grew more baffled and testy.

Thompson had appended a brief artistic statement to his original proposal for the Rockefeller Foundation:

> In writing the book, I would follow the case-history scheme insofar as it shows the developments of character, the personal history of the interviewed, the way he lives and has lived. However, I intend to connect one story with another by means of first-person narrative: sidelights on the countryside, the towns, a square-dance, a farmer's balky mule, the reception clerk in a business office. Not much of this, but enough to hold the bricks of the book together—as they must be held together to have their full significance. The connection, the common ground between one character and another, is, in a way, the principal theme of the book.

This design must have seemed straightforward enough for Couch and the Rockefeller board to approve his project. Yet no "documentary book" before *Let Us Now Praise Famous Men* aimed for such an autobiographical and multifaceted text.

As *We Talked About Labor* neared completion, Thompson's first-person experiment antagonized the University of North Carolina Press. Couch indicated that the interstitial "sidelights" threatened to overwhelm the life histories, and although "I understood what you are trying to do when I read it," he bristled at "the upside down approach." An anonymous outside reader railed against the "whimsical quirks" and "stylistic tricks," before throwing up his hands:

> Is he writing for his own amusement, without caring whether he is understood or not? . . . Sentence after sentence in the first ten or so pages, does not make sense to me. The approach gives no indication that the author is (as I am told on good authority) being ironical. . . . The personal idiosyncratic twists and the sprightly tone seem out of place unless the author is joining the company of Charles Lamb and is in the realm of the personal essay.

. . . It does not seem to me that the people who want information
on this subject would be able to get it from the MS as it is.

Evidently Thompson was forging his book with the techniques of his 1930s
fiction, including the mocking satire of "A Night with Sally" and, perhaps,
even the double-edged split-narration of "The End of the Book." And the
University of North Carolina Press would have none of it.

After receiving Couch's report, Thompson disgustedly tore up his draft
of *We Talked About Labor,* three-quarters of his way to the end, and planned
to start over. His only surviving life history, "The Drilling Contractor," his
memoir of his father, oddly bears out at least one of his readers' objections.
Composed in 1939 when James Sherman Thompson was too sick to speak
for himself, the ghostwritten "oral history" offered a chilling Oedipal parable of abuse, revenge, and redemption, but next to no information about
the oil industry. When Thompson allowed "The Drilling Contractor" to wander from the claustrophobic father-and-son drama, the history was all
charged tangents—Jake Hamon, Frederick Cook, Harding's train, bad business deals. And far from removing himself from the writing, as Couch insisted, Thompson insinuated *his* personal life history into nearly every line.
As noted earlier, he made his father wallow in the muck of the Hotel Texas,
his own alcoholism, and his high school nervous breakdown, the old man
gamely confessing mea culpa every step of the way.

The haunting self-portrait of "The Drilling Contractor" marked Thompson's frankest expression to date of his desire for vengeance against his father, and of his wish to be forgiven by him. He concluded the life history on
a prickly note, at once redemptive and sour. His father, as always, is speaking of his son "Bob":

> . . . Bob? Well, he's about as husky a specimen as you'll run
> up against. He finished high school and took a couple years at the
> university; and then he dropped out and knocked around the coun-
> try for six months. When he came back he'd made up his mind to
> be a writer, and lately he's been making almost enough to keep
> himself going. I asked him one day if he didn't need a little more ed-
> ucation to be a writer. He didn't say anything. He sat there looking
> at me for a minute, and then he ripped up the story he was working
> on, and tore out of the house like he'd been shot. That was the
> last time he was drunk. He won't even drink a bottle of beer any
> more. . . .

By the winter of 1940 this too was fantasy. His drinking, ironically enough,
reactivated his Hotel Texas tuberculosis. Thompson complained to Couch
that his lungs were hemorrhaging and he was coughing up blood: "The con-

dition has been aggravated by strep and the substitution of stimulants for rest." His health and his book in tatters, he looked to a new life in California.

On December 8, Bob Wood offered Thompson the official Party car if he would drive it to San Francisco for use by the International Labor Defense lawyer who was handling his appeal. He gathered up the family, closed down the apartment, and left the following afternoon.

Sheriff Thompson didn't make the trip. Just prior to departure, Thompson installed his father in the Lamoine Nursing Home, a small house on Northwest 3rd Street, where Karl and Hazel Tempus took in elderly patients. *Now and on Earth* re-created the painful deceit:

> Remember how easy it was? Come on, Pop, we'll have a bottle of beer and go for a little ride. Pop didn't suspect. He'd never think his family would do a thing like that to him. . . .

• • •

Thompson drove the Party automobile, Woody Guthrie's old black Plymouth, to San Diego, where he deposited his wife, their children, his mother, and his newly divorced sister, Freddie, with his cousin Neddie Pinnell, before making his way alone to San Francisco. On the drive up the Pacific Coast Highway, he later wrote, a hitchhiker tried to rob him at knifepoint after hearing him drunkenly boast about his success as a writer.

Coming back, Thompson stopped off in Hollywood. He tried to see Donald Ogden Stewart, screenwriter, that year, of *The Philadelphia Story,* and president of the League of American Writers, but he was turned away. In a Hollywood Boulevard bar he met Sam Fuller, then a reporter for the San Diego *Sun.* Fuller dragged Thompson to a Christmas party in National City, and introduced him to novelist Nathanael West (West would die in an automobile accident ten days later). Thompson also made the rounds of the studios and talent agencies with *Always to Be Blest,* but no one was interested. Fawcett Publications dangled the possibility of an assignment with their movie magazines—his only prospect.

On the bus to San Diego, Thompson pulled the brittle typescript of *Always to Be Blest* from his knapsack and pitched it out the window.

"Well I'm thirty-five. Thirty-five, can you understand that? . . . Skip through fifteen million words for the Writers' Project. Skip through half a million for the foundation. Skip through the back numbers of five strings of magazines. Skip through forty, fifty, yes seventy-five thousand words a week, week after week, for the trade journals. . . . What did it get me? Shall I tell you? You're damned right I shall. It got me a ragged ass and beans three times a week. It got me haircuts in barber colleges.

It got me piles you could stack washers on. It got me a lung that isn't even bad enough to kill me. It got me in a dump with six strangers. It got me in jail for forty-eight hours a week and a lunatic asylum on Sunday. It got me whiskey, yes, and a woman to sleep with, yes. It got me twenty-five thousand reminders ten million times a day that nothing I'd done meant anything. . . ."

—James Dillon, *Now and on Earth*

If Tears Were Bombs: 1941– 1951

Jim Thompson entered California convinced of his failure as a writer and a man. After five years of promise, the books he counted on to ransom his future, *Always to Be Blest* and *We Talked About Labor,* miscarried in the execution, flowers in the dustbin. Thompson merely transplanted his problems to a sunnier climate. "Befuddled with booze," he conceded, "I even insisted on moving to California, away from people who might be willing to help me. . . . The fellowship was not renewed. My family and I were stranded in a place where I knew no one and had absolutely no credit. My creative talents were at least temporarily burned up by alcohol."

Failure would become Thompson's great subject. The bleakest of his novels radiate his empathy for those misfits and rejects ground up by the

American machinery of individualism, progress, and success. Proletarian and hobo literature or the raw, heartbreaking oral histories of Studs Terkel's *Hard Times* have engraved a profile of the Depression "marginal man" who underlies the essential Thompson character. The crushing legacies of 1930s marginality—rootlessness, alienation, fear, anger, despair, impotence, shame, drunkenness, and violence—would coalesce into the themes of his mature fiction. Thompson's crime novels of the 1950s and 1960s, with their shadowy Depression settings and anachronistic antiheroes (grifters, roughnecks, traveling salesmen), reanimate this 1930s marginal man, but without the typical 1930s suggestion that his terrible circumstances are remediable. Stripped of any mitigating social or economic context, the evils Thompson went on to limn, the ooze and slime that Lou Ford calls *"the sickness,"* seem as basic to the creation of the world as hydrogen. At the conclusion of *The Killer Inside Me,* Ford spews a prayer for "all of us that started the game with a crooked cue, that wanted so much and got so little, that meant so good and did so bad. . . . All of us."

But a novelist of failure is not the same as a failed novelist—and that was the specter Thompson faced in his shaving mirror every morning as early in 1941, closing in on thirty-five, he took a job scraping plaster off a San Diego airplane factory floor.

Later that year he sneaked a peek at his father's record of misfortune, defeat, and loss as he contemplated his own downward spiral. "I said to myself . . . , Were you ever happy? Did you ever have any peace? And I had to answer, Why no, for Christ's sake; you've always been in hell. You've just slipped deeper. And you're going to keep on because you're your father. Your father without his endurance. . . ."

• • •

Thompson's frustrating Hollywood sojourn persuaded him to linger in San Diego. The family packed Neddie and Richard Pinnell's Goldfinch Street home for a 1940 clan Christmas reminiscent of his Burwell childhood. As he puzzled out his next step, the rotation of the new year and the new decade inflamed his old devils. "Cousin Jimmie drank himself right into the gutter," Neddie Pinnell declares. "More than once we found him unconscious in the street."

He beat the drum for *We Talked About Labor* during his transcontinental letters to William Couch: "I've been up as far north as Frisco, and back again, and I've got some good material. The change in background will, I think, add to the interest of the book." But he was firmly reminded that his Rockefeller grant expired in January. Moreover, Couch warned him, "the war has taken all interest from internal problems, and I'm afraid there is going to be no chance of any real attention to our internal problems until after that thing is settled." The war in Europe snuffed Thompson's other

Jim and Alberta—San Diego, 1940 (Courtesy
of the Thompson family)

contingencies. "I had thought about shipping out with the tuna fleet," he wrote Couch from the Pinnells in mid-January. "The boats go down below the equator, and are out as long as three months at a time. I could make a little something at it in wages, and, more important, get some good story material. I had a boys' adventure book in mind. But, even since I have been here, the government has bought so many of the boats for mine-sweepers that hundreds of experienced fishermen have been beached and it's practically an impossibility to get a berth." True crime, his port during previous financial squalls, also suffered the squeeze. "The pulp situation, generally, is pretty bad due to the increase in the cost of paper. The magazines are either cutting in size or rates, or both." But even without the war, these prospects all were will-o'-the-wisps. Thompson found himself in the midst of an agonizing, nearly year-long writer's block.

On February 1 he rented half of a house at 2130 Second Avenue with his final foundation check. The pretty Spanish-style duplex, with white stucco and a terra-cotta tile roof, perched at the top of a steep hill over-looking San Diego Bay. "How they managed to pour concrete on those hills is beyond me," Thompson subsequently wondered. "You can tie your shoelaces going up them without stooping."

San Diego, those uncertain months prior to the Japanese attack on Pearl Harbor, was a genial retirement town clandestinely clearing the decks for battle. Over the next five years the oldest Spanish settlement in Califor-nia would be transformed into a dense grid of aircraft plants, navy yards, and boot camps. As the prewar population of 147,995 doubled in the after-shock of December 7, San Diego pulsed to the rhythms of the war industry. Contemporary accounts report, "Aircraft factories rang with the sound of work around the clock, and along Broadway, some cafes never closed. Long troop trains rolled in and out of the Santa Fe Depot. Darkened warships slipped out of the harbor and armed men patrolled the city's beaches. . . . Barrage balloons dangled over the city to snatch Japanese airplanes from the air. Cavalry patrols rode around reservoirs, watching for saboteurs." Even San Diego Gas & Electric enlisted in the war effort, equipping its "Reddy Kilowatt" symbol with a helmet and rifle.

Thompson complained to William Couch that the cost of "living [here] is too high," but he appreciated the physical amenities of Southern Califor-nia: strolls in Balboa Park, weekend outings with Alberta to the Del Mar Race Track or to the ballroom on Crystal Pier, and Sunday-morning family breakfasts at Mission Beach, where he scalded the coffee, hobo-style, over a wood fire. A lifelong insomniac, Thompson enjoyed the night-life south of Broadway, or he rambled the Spanish Old Town, unchanged since the 1850s. Although the three-bedroom Second Avenue duplex forged a pres-sure cooker for his acid-tongued kin, from his front steps he could smoke cigarettes and watch tramp steamers glide out of the harbor. A covert door by the driveway furnished a hasty exit when domestic stresses over-whelmed or when the landlady rang the bell for her late rent. Yet on the few occasions Thompson attempted to write, he was forced into the bathroom, his typewriter plopped down on the toilet seat as he straddled the rim of the tub.

That February Thompson applied to the U.S. Employment Service. His Rockefeller money long spent, he accepted the first job offered, in the stock room of Ryan Aeronautical, a sheer mile down the cliff on Harbor Drive. He represented the daily grind to Couch as a lateral extension of his research on *We Talked About Labor*. "I went to work shortly after leaving your em-ployment for the Ryan Aeronautical Co. here, as a stockroom clerk," Thompson apprised Chapel Hill in May, "and am now production and stock bookkeeper for the firm. The company manufactures trainers for the Army and Navy. I plan on making a connection in the near future with Lockheed or some other manufacturer of bombers; and then I want some experience on fighting planes. I believe that, within a year or less, I will be able to write competently on airplane manufacturing, and there should be a large field for such writing in the future." But the labor writer was now a laborer.

Thompson started off as an unskilled workman, cleaning after the plasterers and painters who were expanding the Ryan plant. But on the strength of a bibulous brainstorm, he quickly progressed. He reviewed his curious rise in "An Alcoholic Looks at Himself":

> . . . I had thrown away one magnificent opportunity after another; and there I was reduced to cleaning floors at a wage that would not properly feed and house my family, and at home all I had to do was look at a drink to get a reminder that my children needed milk . . . I felt every edged word and reproachful glance.
>
> The only advantage of my job was that it allowed me to roam the plant from one end to another . . . I got a broad and original conception of the workings of the great factory. That led me to produce one of the prize rabbits of my career.
>
> One day I got up from the floor, dusted my hands against my shirt and accosted the plant superintendent. "You seem to be having a lot of trouble with your parts records," I said boldly. "I'd like a chance to straighten them out."
>
> The boss gave me a quick glance, grinned out of the corner of his mouth and started to turn away.
>
> "I believe I can do it," I insisted. "I've held some pretty important jobs. I got down on my luck through drinking, but I'm all right now."
>
> He hesitated. "Know anything about accounting?"
>
> "Well . . ."
>
> "I see. Can you read blueprints?"
>
> "Well, not exactly, but—"
>
> "Better get back to your work," he said.
>
> As soon as I finished dinner that night, I hurried down to the public library. I drew out every book I could get on blueprint-reading and accounting and took them home. I was still reading the next morning when my wife set toast and coffee in front of me.
>
> Red-eyed and weary, I accosted the plant superintendent again.
>
> "I know something about accounting now," I said. "And I can read blueprints. I sat up all night studying."
>
> Before he could turn away or tell me to get back to my work, I reeled off the titles of the books I'd read. Some of them apparently struck a familiar chord, for he gave me an appraising look.
>
> "All right," he said. "What do you think our trouble is?"

"Everything. Whoever installed your system of records didn't know what they were doing."

"No? It was installed by a firm of industrial engineers. A very good firm."

"The system's very good in theory," I said. "But it doesn't work out in practice. It overlooks the human element; it would take a corps of high-paid experts to keep it going. Now . . ."

While he fidgeted, wavering between interest and irritation, I went on talking, working on him with all the terrible intensity that seems to be one of the peculiar characteristics of alcoholics. In the end, I got my chance. I was put in the "Parts-control" department for a week, at my regular salary. During that week I was to study the system and recommend changes which I felt would rectify the trouble.

I did not need a week. I already knew what the trouble was and how to eliminate it. Before the week was out I made a number of recommendations. Added up they amounted to scrapping the expensive but unworkable system and installing the one I drew up. It was a large order, and coming from an inexperienced man, a seemingly presumptuous one. Nevertheless, I was right and could prove it. Eventually, every one of my recommendations was carried out. I was rewarded with four pay raises and three promotions within seven months. . . .

With similar self-satisfaction his accountant father had straightened out Jake Hamon's books and salvaged his own financial life. Like the 1920s adolescent venture into the West Texas oil fields, Jim Thompson once more was competing with Pop on the old man's turf—but absurdly, and somewhat pathetically, for a menial job he had no stake in and essentially despised.

By August he had enough of Ryan Aeronautical and quit. Despite raises and a new title, the weekly rent and grocery bill for his pinched household outran his salary. His sister Maxine—fresh from divorcing Russell Boomer, whom she now, in tears, denounced as a drunk and a skirt chaser—joined the testy swarm that doleful summer, broadening the burden and thickening the tension. The six-day workweek, the arduous walk home up the almost vertical pitch of Second Avenue, and binges on cheap, fortified wine had plagued his sensitive lungs. Vomiting blood, scarcely able to eat, he feared that he was headed for another breakdown.

Thompson sent his wife and children, in a further echo of his father, to Nebraska. Bill Cunningham had wired him about a high-paying writing job in New York City. As Alberta moved back to her parents in Lincoln, Jim boarded an eastbound bus.

He departed San Diego the first week of September. A few days out, he stopped at Oklahoma City to check on his father. Thompson was dismayed, by all accounts, at what awaited him in the Lamoine Nursing Home. "My mother, Christine, and her sisters, Leota and Olive, went up there to visit Uncle Jim a few times earlier, and said that he looked so bad," cousin Harriet Cowan Keller recalls. "The man taking care of him made a remark that he would see to it that Uncle Jim wouldn't weigh three hundred pounds. They figured he must have starved him, because when they next saw him he had lost a lot of weight. He knew them, and could talk with them, but the place kept him strapped to the bed because he would wander off. He wasn't capable of knowing when to eat or go to the bathroom."

Shaken, Thompson caught the morning bus after a one-night layover. The ride, he wrote, was emotional and uncomfortable. Nursing a stomach ailment, incapable of sleep, he sipped whiskey all the way to 42nd Street.

• • •

Thompson subsequently recast his New York trip into one of his elemental personal myths. He honed the saga during late-night talks with friends, such as Arnold Hano and Jim Bryans, his editors at Lion Books, and he crafted versions for "An Alcoholic Looks at Himself" and *Roughneck*. The legend, as he polished it, ran like this.

Fired by the notion of writing his first novel, Jim set out for where the publishers were, New York City, late in the fall of 1941. After pausing at Oklahoma City, he pledged to return with his advance in exactly one month, spring his sick father from the sanitarium, and bring him home to San Diego. Arriving in New York by early November (on "election night," November 4), he quickly made the rounds of the publishers. He told them that he could complete the novel within two weeks, if they would loan him a typewriter and stake him cash for a room in which to write it. The first five editors he saw sent him out the door with varying degrees of politeness. But an amused editor at the sixth house, calculating how little the company had to lose, agreed to the terms. Following ten days of continuous drinking and writing, he submitted the manuscript. He was then rushed to Bellevue Hospital, a victim of nervous exhaustion and alcoholic poisoning. Upon his release a week later, he returned to the publisher to learn that the novel had been accepted. But just as he heard the good news, Jim was handed a telegram, sent by his mother, notifying him of the death of his father, two days earlier.

In conversation Thompson usually added that Pop killed himself by ripping the wadding out of his mattress and stuffing it down his throat. He would be in tears, inconsolable. As Arnold Hano remarks, "When Jim would drink he would sometimes cry and say, 'Why couldn't he have waited another day? He knew I was going to show up. Why did he have to kill himself?' " Hano, a trusted confidant, was so moved by the suicide story that he reproduced the macabre particulars for his Los Angeles *Times* obituary of Thompson.

Like the sly claim that he had been born in jail, or the evil-twin conceit of "Allie Ivers," or the brassy assertion that he graduated from high school by forging his academic record, Thompson's sensational New York misadventure possessed enough solid pegs for him to hang his fantastic garments—and his soiled linen—on; and his urgent manner ("the terrible intensity that seems to be one of the peculiar characteristics of alcoholics") precluded awkward interrogation. But from the convenient oversight of Bill Cunningham's job offer and his postdated departure to Sheriff Thompson's grisly, wretched death, his tale bristles with omissions, self-censorship, reversals in chronology, and wild idiosyncratic invention.

• • •

A more literal narrative provided by his New York City friends, while not so tragic, is hardly less dramatic.

Thompson, as far as can be determined, reached New York City late on September 14, the evening of the state primary election. He made his way downtown to Bill and Sally Cunningham's apartment at 328 West 21st Street in the Chelsea section of Manhattan, expecting to room with them until he could afford his own place and send for his family. Thompson blew in drunk, and sick to his stomach with a virus he had picked up en route. Alarmed, Sally insisted that he check into a hotel. Bill escorted him around the corner to Allerton House, at the intersection of Eighth Avenue and 22nd Street.

By the time Thompson reached New York, the writing position Cunningham proposed to him was filled already. In his only near contemporary recollection, a 1942 interview with the San Diego *Tribune-Sun,* he described the work as "a $21-a-day publicity job with a government bureau engaged in writing radio dramas for broadcast to occupied countries." Cunningham was an assistant editor at TASS, and it's likely that the assignment involved the Soviet news agency—circumstances Thompson would have justifiably elided when he came to write about the trip in the McCarthyist 1950s.

Thompson's own renditions of his stay present himself, true crime writer fashion, as a lone wolf sleeping on rainy park benches, single-handedly assaulting the cruel city and the fickle publishing world. "He told us he lived outdoors in Union Square half the time, and other awful things," his sister Maxine shuddered. "It was hard for us to picture." But New York in the fall of 1941 remained the vital epicenter of the American Communist Party, and while Thompson was in the process of rethinking his Party affiliation, he had some old friends there. In addition to Bill and Sally, Gordon

Friesen and Sis Cunningham (married earlier that year), and painter Joe Jones now resided in the city.

Sis Cunningham played accordion, wrote, and sang with the Almanac Singers, the influential urban folk group that included Woody Guthrie, Pete Seeger, Bess Lomax, Arthur Stern, and Millard Lampell. The musicians lived communally in a town house by 10th Street and Greenwich Avenue. The Friesens invited Thompson down to Almanac House for the Sunday-afternoon hootenannies and rent parties, where he renewed his acquaintance with Guthrie. During these informal concerts they introduced him to Nicholas Ray, then a network radio director, actor Will Geer, novelist and *Daily Worker* columnist Mike Gold, and Alan Lomax. Jim chased the Almanac Singers on their round of bookings at union halls, War Relief benefits, and old age homes. As Guthrie biographer Joe Klein notes, the Almanacs "tended to mythologize themselves and each other shamelessly" with mysterious pseudonyms and proletarian backgrounds. Thompson may have absorbed his *lumpen* New York posturing from them. For his entire Manhattan transfer, after the lonely self-exile of San Diego, Jim mingled with writers, artists, and activists.

His Oklahoma friends expressed concern at his condition. Nimble and matinee-idol handsome when they last saw him, Thompson appeared bloated and jowly, his body drifting toward a middle-aged drinker's paunch. "Jim changed a lot physically during the 1940s," Gordon Friesen remembers. "He suddenly put on weight, and he looked gray and sick a lot of the time." Friesen also remarked the recurrence of a "unique neurosis" he had first witnessed in Oklahoma City, and "which manifested itself later when Jim visited us in New York. He had to be within walking distance of a bar with a toilet. I remember he and I zigzagging across town to a meeting of the Writers Guild. Jim knew of a route which would take us from bar to bar—without necessarily stopping in any of them. He needed to be assured that he had immediate access to a toilet. As soon as we got two or three blocks from a bar he would start to get jittery; but when we got close he would be calm. Jim had this whole route mapped out beforehand, and we arrived at the meeting from behind." Many alcoholics develop stomach and abdominal problems. For the rest of his life, Thompson's daughter Sharon intimates, "Daddy was always very peculiar about having a bathroom nearby."

Thompson told Friesen and Bill Cunningham about his Hollywood washout, and how he had pitched *Always to Be Blessed* from the bus. Bill, in particular, encouraged him to return to fiction, and volunteered to show anything he produced to his editor at Vanguard Press. Borrowing a typewriter from Bill and Sally, Thompson broke his writer's block in his room at Allerton House. Over four intense days (he informed the San Diego *Tribune-*

Sun) he pounded out the opening of a novel, some fifteen thousand words, as a "sample" to entice publishers. In a white-heat he spat back the arid past year of his life—family quarrels, his humiliations at Ryan, his aimless tippling, the strains on his marriage—scarcely pausing to change the names (Alberta to Roberta, Freddie to Frankie, Maxine to Marge, Sharon to Shannon, Mike to Mack, Pat to Jo, and so on).

His father died in Oklahoma City on October 2, just sixteen days after Thompson arrived in New York. No other family member has ever suggested that he committed suicide. The death certificate, supported by recollections of the widow of his physician, Dr. Ralph A. Smith, listed pneumonia, cardiovascular disease, and senility. He was seventy-one years old. Birdie raced back for the quick burial in Memorial Park on October 3, alone. She logged New York City as the residence for her son in all the obituaries.

After receiving the telegram at Bill and Sally's, Jim confided to Gordon Friesen his disappointment that he could not attend the funeral for the sake of his mother; otherwise he held his feelings to himself. Friesen can't retrace whether Thompson had completed, or even started, the sample chapters of his novel. A later section incorporated the death, backdating it to his residency in San Diego.

Over the following weeks his friends noticed other changes in their old Oklahoma City comrade. Thompson rebuffed Bill Cunningham's overtures to help him place his work-in-progress. Vanguard had rejected *Always to Be Blest* back in 1938, and apparently he was still smarting. Moreover, he began to voice reservations about the New York City leftist literary avant-garde.

"No more of that esoteric shit! I want to write books about the way people really live," Jim erupted one night to Friesen, during a rare recorded declaration of his ambitions. "From now on I'm going to write about life as it is. I'll show those motherfuckers!"

He used words like "earthy," "sexy," and "violent" to characterize the novels he envisioned. But, as Friesen expounds, Thompson's objectives were fiercely double-edged: he aspired to be at once more popular and more subversive. "Jim was fed up with not making a living. He spoke of writing for money by talking about what people wanted to read, sex and violence. But he also said he wanted to be truer to his own life, and to life as he had seen it. The heroic Party line became something of a straitjacket for Jim, as far as his writing was concerned."

Thompson probably resisted Bill Cunningham and Vanguard Press because his new novel, despite his apparent flirtation with TASS, would record his break with the Communist Party. His title, *Now and on Earth*, in fact derived from a poignant scene where he directly challenged Karl Marx.

As San Diego "hack-writer and aircraft flunkey" James Dillon comforts his young daughter Shannon, Thompson performed an autopsy upon the American Dream, assailing in the same breath both God and the God that failed:

> . . . oh, Christ, as she lies here in my arms, exhausted but afraid to sleep, living on hatred, even the thought that we did not want to want her makes me feel like a criminal. And I am not. And Roberta is not. We wanted Jo, and we wanted Shannon, and we wanted Mack. Six in all, we had dreamed of; and a big white house with a deep lawn and many bedrooms and a pantry that was always full. We wanted them, but we wanted that, too. Not for ourselves, but for them. We wanted it because we knew what it would mean if we didn't have it. I knew how I was, and Roberta knew how she was. And we knew how it would be: As it had been with us.
>
> We did want her. Goddammit, I say we did! We want her now. I was crazy to say that we didn't or hadn't. But we are getting tired, and we are so cramped, and there are so many things to be done.
>
> Why? I ask, why is it like this? Not for Roberta, not for myself; but for all of us.
>
> Why, Karl? And what will you do about it? Not twenty years from now when Shannon and all the Shannons have bred, and a plague spreads across the land, and brother slays brother.
>
> Not then, when it is too late, but now!
>
> And you, God? What have you to offer? Sweet music? Pie in the sky? Yes. But, on earth . . . ?
>
> Now and on Earth?

Thompson called himself a Socialist for at least another decade. The bloodline of his 1930s Marxism circulates through all his subsequent fiction. His crime novels routinely appropriate the lingua franca of alienation. "In a sense they were an autonomous body," he comments of some migrant farm workers in *The Getaway,* "functioning within a society which was organized to grind them down." For *Texas by the Tail* he laments "the cruel shearing away of all but the utterly practical, as pastoral man was caught up in an industrial society." Where Marx rued the powerlessness of "mechanized" man, Dolly Dillon of *A Hell of a Woman* says, "I was like a mechanical man with the batteries run down." And, as suggested earlier, the Marxist concept of self-alienation infused the chilling split narration of *A Hell of a Woman, The Killer Inside Me,* and *Savage Night,* among other crime novels. Thompson continued to write political fiction all his life. Animated by his rock-ribbed sympathy for those the system doesn't work for, his books root through the dark patches of American experience, undermining privileged institutions and values. *Pop. 1280* and *Child of Rage* ridicule the grinding heritage of racism. *A Swell-Looking Babe* sketches a red scare at a Texas high school. *South of Heaven* chronicles oil field Wobblies. *Recoil,* as Geoffrey O'Brien suggests, "provides a prescient critique of a right-wing pressure group which more than slightly resembles the Moral Majority." The recurrent surname "Dillon," his Party alias, itself lodged a silent homage to his Communist past. But the utopian uplift of the dialectic and a purely economic interpretation of society no longer satisfied him.

"Jim's point of view was that of an Anarchist and not as a Communist," observed John Hammond, the Columbia Records executive who later became a close friend, with perhaps the shrewdest appraisal of Thompson's ideological sea change in the early 1940s: "Jim's political instincts were formed by the IWW in Oklahoma, and he was somewhat influenced by the great Wobbly writer Oscar Ameringer, whose wonderful magazine the *American Guardian* was published in Oklahoma . . . and although he was very briefly a member of the Party in the forties, being an Anarchist meant that he couldn't possibly subject himself to the disciplines of communism."

Gordon Friesen stresses that Thompson's dissatisfaction with the Party in the fall of 1941 stayed personal and literary, and did not mark a response to public events, such as the Moscow Trials, the Nazi-Soviet Pact, or other expired hopes of a low, dishonest decade. "I believe that he was only thinking about the writing he wanted to do, and the problem of finding the right publisher for his book," Friesen recounts. "As I remember, Jim took it around to four places, all established publishers, and all of them turned him down. But still he wouldn't take Bill up on Vanguard."

His publishing problem bumped into an unexpected solution one Sunday night at Almanac House. Woody Guthrie recently had become friendly with Richard S. Childs, the founder of Modern Age Books, and a young editor there everyone called "Doc" McDowell. After listening as Thompson talked through his plans for *Now and on Earth* during the lively suppers that followed the hootenannies, Guthrie asked to read his sample chapters. A few days later Woody accompanied Jim uptown to 432 Fourth Avenue, and presented him to Modern Age.

Richard Childs established Modern Age Books in 1937 as an experiment in mass-market publishing. The house, as initially announced, aimed to furnish quality paperbound originals at cheap prices for sale in drugstores, on newsstands, or through a mail-order subscription service. But their unusual format (5$\frac{1}{2}$ by 7$\frac{1}{2}$ inches), a harbinger of the trade paperback, restricted distribution and display. By the time Thompson encountered Modern Age, the firm released only clothbound editions through bookstores.

An economist and a leader of the New America Party, Childs emphasized topical titles on social trends and current events. But he also printed novels, travelogues, detective stories, books for children, and an innovative photojournalism monthly, *Photo-History,* a kind of radical *Life,* that ran four thematic issues (on "Spain," "Labor's Challenge," "War Is Here," and "China Reborn"). His small editorial staff included Samuel Craig, the founder of the Literary Guild, Louis Birk, a former Macmillan college textbook traveler, writer Arthur Pound, and Elliott "Doc" McDowell.

"Without exactly being Communist," McDowell's widow, Lois, discloses, "Modern Age was the headquarters for all the radicals in the literary field. It was financed by a wealthy liberal, Dick Childs. There was a whole movement of people in the mainstream part of publishing who were close to a left-wing trade union called the Book and Magazine Guild. Woody Guthrie was up there a lot—he was the reason, of course, Thompson found Modern Age. Will Geer, Burl Ives, and Nick Ray hung around all the time, too."

Unbeknownst to Thompson, he already possessed an admirer at Modern Age. David Zablowdowsky, the Viking editor who signed *Always to Be Blest,* joined as a managing editor in 1940. But it was McDowell whom Guthrie first approached with *Now and on Earth.* Dubbed "Doc" on account of his physician father, McDowell taught English at the University of Illinois before Childs brought him aboard. On the strength of Woody Guthrie's recommendation, he offered Thompson a contract for his novel. "Woody virtually agented Jim's first book," Lois McDowell explains. "He was keen on Doc to publish it."

More than his editor, Doc McDowell became one of Thompson's closest New York friends. Soon the writer was making his way across town to the McDowells' chic Art Deco apartment on East 22nd Street, in a building decorated with glistening bands of glazed terra-cotta, for convivial home-cooked dinners. As Lois McDowell recalls:

> Jim was on the rebound from the Party, and we were what you'd call disillusioned fellow travelers. Doc took a great shine to him, and he used to be in our home a lot. He had many meals with us. Jim was a large, bulky, ruddy man then, very friendly. We knew he had a drinking problem, and I always had the feeling that there was something odd about him. He seemed like someone who had some kind of flaw. Probably this was the drinking, but it was more in the mysterious way that he lived. He never mentioned his wife or his family, and we never knew where he was going when he left us.
>
> He was one of the strange people my husband brought home, but that didn't make me like him any less. Jim was one of perhaps thirty wonderful people we knew in our lives.

Thompson received a standard advance of about $400 for *Now and on Earth*—half on signing, the remainder on acceptance of the novel. With the money he paid up his bill at Allerton House and rented a small room over a Chinese restaurant on Eighth Avenue, by 23rd Street. When Friesen visited, he found "Jim hunched over his portable typewriter, the toilet by his shoulder—just so he knew it was there—and a bottle of good whiskey beside the desk." Thompson completed his book in about five weeks—hardly the ten-day marathon of his own legend, but a steeplechase nonetheless.

On submission of *Now and on Earth* he indeed entered Bellevue Hospital for a few nights' rest. For *Roughneck* he dramatized his rescue from alcoholic delerium by "Bill" of Alcoholics Anonymous. Bill—or, more properly, Bill W.—is a stock A.A. euphemism. But if this part of his story was true, Thompson may not have been speaking figuratively. In 1941 Bill Wilson worked out of the A.A. 24th Street clubhouse, a former stable just around the corner.

· · ·

Modern Age accepted *Now and on Earth* with minimal changes and announced the book for its spring list. Doc McDowell signed Thompson to a contract for two additional novels—a revision of his 1932 "thriller," *The Unholy Grail,* and a fictionalization of his family's history during the Civil War. "Most of the Civil War books I've seen have dealt with the southern viewpoint," Thompson briefed the San Diego *Tribune-Sun.* "I'd like to write one with a northern locale." The newspaper added, "As an authentic source of material, he has letters and other documents left by his paternal and maternal grandfathers, both of whom marched with Sherman to the sea."

Thompson wired Alberta to join him in New York. Waiting on her arrival from Lincoln with the children, he toured the city in a style befitting a rising author. He attended *My Sister Eileen,* Ruth McKenney's play about Nathanael West's wife, whom he had met in Hollywood with Sam Fuller almost exactly one year earlier. And he participated in an art auction to benefit the Oklahoma Committee to Fight Syndicalism Cases at the Puma Galleries, where he sold a painting by his friend Joe Jones.

The reunited Thompsons moved into a residence hotel on 14th Street near Union Square in early December. For Alberta, Jim was already rehearsing his quixotic Manhattan fable: "He told us that he slept in the park until Modern Age gave him a typewriter and the money for a room." Thompson tended to compartmentalize his life, maintaining an adamant division between home and work, his family and his friends. Gordon Friesen and Sis Cunningham, for instance, never knew that Alberta came to New York; and Alberta never saw any of his new companions, such as the McDowells or Woody Guthrie. Only once did Thompson relent, gathering up his brood for a publishing Christmas party. "It was a really lavish affair," his daughter

'Who's Who' Crashed by Timekeeper

Jim Thompson, Solar Aircraft Co. timekeeper, is author of a novel that has just landed him in "Who's Who."

Shortly after the publication of Now and on Earth, *San Diego* Tribune-Sun, *June 6, 1942*

Sharon, then five years old, avers. "I kept asking for beer, and finally someone gave me a little bit. . . . Back at the apartment house my brother,
Mike, ran through a plate glass window while we were playing! We were
pretty wild."

Thompson intended to "relocate in New York," Alberta remembers.
"But the city was just too much for us." Shortly after Christmas he retreated to San Diego. For "An Alcoholic Looks at Himself," he chalked up
the decision to abandon his Eastern friends and contacts as more pie-eyed
self-aggrandizement: "Look around for a job in New York? Nonsense. I was a
novelist now. My book was being rushed toward early spring publication.
The Hollywood studios would be beating on my door as soon as they saw
the galley proofs. . . . Before returning to California, of course, I had to
celebrate my triumph. . . ."

On January 17 Thompson took a job with the Solar Aircraft Company.

• • •

Wrapped in a modish dust jacket of cubist design and bearing acclamatory
blurbs by novelists Richard Wright, Louis Bromfield, and Millen Brand, *Now
and on Earth* appeared in March 1942. Charting a hellish summer in the life
of James Dillon and his family with an offhand, conversational style that
perhaps reflected the velocity of composition, Thompson's first published
book juggled three complementary narratives. Equal parts a classic blue-
collar novel, a plaintive confession, and a searing portrait of an incipient
psychopath, *Now and on Earth* refocused his social protest efforts of the
1930s even as it looked forward to the Lion crime fiction of the 1950s.

Now and on Earth, despite Thompson's midnight rant to Friesen against
"esoteric shit," shaped a radical cultural document no less than *Always to
Be Blest,* and an aggressive labor study no less than *We Talked About Labor.*
Thompson zeroed in on the inner workings of an unnamed San Diego aircraft plant. He surveyed the defense industry from the perspective of a former writer turned factory drone, devoting many engrossing pages to Jim
Dillon's promotion from the broom-and-scraper brigade to stockroom
bookkeeper via an ambitious inventory overhaul—and some numbing
paragraphs to airplane arcana. Through the treadmill of plant operations,
the insipid factory politics, particularly Dillon's rivalry with Gross, his
double-dealing predecessor as bookkeeper, the beggarly milestones such
as a 4¢ an hour raise after a thirty-day probationary period, and the more
sinister shadow of a Communist inquest, Thompson remained as absorbed
by the sheer accumulation of fact and data as any proletarian firebrand.

But Ryan Aeronautical was not the only private stock he grafted onto
Dillon's pedigree. *Now and on Earth* in crucial ways pushed closer to
Thompson's new goal of a more personal and subversive fiction. The famil-

iar contours of the naturalistic assembly-line plot masked a sour, sullen autobiography. By proxy of Jim Dillon, Thompson probed his past with grittier emotion and candor than he would display in his well-armored memoirs, *Bad Boy* and *Roughneck.* With bird's-eye flashbacks and razor-edged crosscuts, he reconstructed his entire history prior to his arrival in San Diego: his abandoned Rockefeller Foundation research, the Oklahoma Federal Writers' Project, *Always to Be Blest,* his marriage to Alberta and his thwarted affair with Lucille Boomer, the University of Nebraska, the *Nebraska Farmer* and the *Prairie Schooner,* the West Texas oil fields, the Hotel Texas, and back through the obscure recesses of his Oklahoma City and Burwell, Nebraska, childhood. The dirty engine of family, however, rather than economics or work, drove the novel, as it would nearly all his subsequent fiction. "If anyone wants to know my father they have to read *Now and on Earth,"* Thompson's elder daughter, Patricia, affirms. "I think so many questions about him could be answered if people would really read that book. I see gross exaggerations in some things, but that was the way he saw it. *Now and on Earth* was not fabricated in any way."

Now and on Earth mounted a merciless dissection of the American family as Thompson carved up his nearest and dearest with an icy scalpel. Pop is rotting away in a sanitarium, "a broke and friendless old man . . . still drilling oil wells—very real oil wells, to him at least." Mom, a distant matriarch hobbled by varicose veins, maintains her poise by elective deafness. " 'That's nice,' " she responds to Dillon after he recounts his first day at work on his hands and knees chipping up plaster, "and I knew she hadn't really heard a word." Dillon's younger sister, Frankie, becomes pregnant by his boss at the aircraft factory, while his older sister, Marge, breezes in, high-flown and foolish:

> There'll be Turkish cigarettes everywhere you turn. The bathroom sink will be filled with henna, always. There'll be fudge in the ashtrays, and lipstick on the drinking glasses, and moving-picture magazines from hell to breakfast. I'll never be able to write or read. The house will be filled constantly with the "handsomest fellow" and the "most refined man," and the phone will ring unmercifully and the doorbell likewise. And always, always in that timid-half-hesitant drawl of hers Marge will give us her views, her advice, on everything from intercourse to the international situation.

Roberta, Dillon's martinet wife, is a writer's nightmare. "Why, in the name of God," he shouts at her during an argument, "won't you just once read a *book?*" Discontented and hot-tempered, contemptuous of her in-laws, she alternately infantalizes her husband:

Roberta got red, and her nostrils trembled. "Now James Dillon! Don't you dare swear at me!"

"I'm not swearing. I'm praying for forbearance."

"And don't get smart, either."

"Dammit," I said, "how many times have I asked you not to talk about me getting smart? I'm not six years old."

—and controls him by playing her trump card, sex:

> . . . Roberta had taken off her dress and hung it up, and was lying on the bed, hands over her face. I looked down at her and began to tingle. I knew how it was going to be, and I hated myself for it. But I couldn't help it. Roberta didn't need to do anything to win an argument with me but let me look at her. I knew it from the moment I saw her. She knew it after a few years.

The Dillons occupy a domestic prison as desolate, stifling, and soul-destroying as any that Thompson will create for the toxic families in his crime novels. The chronic angers of their house, their sniping sarcasm and grinding quarrels, their disappointments, grievances, and poverty mold a demonic "heritage of lunacy" for the Dillon children, Jo, Shannon, and Mack: "Growing up amidst this turmoil, these hatreds, this—well, why quibble—insanity." During one after-dinner wrangle, Shannon sinks her teeth into Roberta's leg and won't let go. During another, Jo performs a grotesque pantomime of her mother experiencing an orgasm.

A self-confessed "outsider" in his own family, Jim Dillon seems more like the vacant eye at the center of this family cyclone. Sick, alcoholic, a blocked writer, marginalized at home and at work, he emerges as preternaturally observant yet chillingly detached from the chaos tumbling down around him. In this thinly veiled autobiographical novel, Thompson endowed Dillon with many of the same disturbed qualities he would later consign to Lou Ford in *The Killer Inside Me,* Dolly Dillon in *A Hell of a Woman,* Charlie Bigger in *Savage Night,* and his other murderous psychopaths and sociopaths: self-pity, paranoia, sexual malaise, self-estrangement, an abiding sense of failure, and an inclination to violence. Nightly Jim Dillon numbs his senses with drink and withdraws into silence. Sex is "an insane unaccountable hunger . . . ugly despicable"; it leaves him "tortured, haunted, feeble, inarticulate." He admits to a cleanliness fetish: "[Roberta] had no girdle on (I think they make a woman look cramped), only the frilly white panties which she buys—or used to buy—by the dozens because she knows I am disturbed by the potential uncleanliness of colors; and she used no perfume because I object to that for much the same reason." He whines about his bad breaks, his bad luck, his fate, and begins to suspect that there is a "plot" working against him:

> I know I mustn't start thinking that way. But it's hard not to at times. . . . All I've ever asked is to be left alone. And no one will leave me alone. Someone is always doing what's best for me; making me do what I should do from their standpoint.
>
> But I mustn't begin thinking it was deliberate. That, baldly, there is a plot against me. It is becoming harder not to, but I know I must not.
>
> *I must not!*

Lest anyone think he is sliding into mere delusion, Dillon paraphrases a short story by the science fiction writer Robert Heinlein, "They," which Thompson would have read the previous spring in the April issue of *Unknown,* a fantasy pulp. Dillon personalizes Heinlein's stark metaphysical parable of the solitary genius into a tall tale about "an inmate in a private nut house," his "employer" and his "wife." The "lunatic" complains to his psychiatrist that "the whole world is in a conspiracy to make him do things he doesn't want to do." In college he couldn't study what he wanted; now he has to work a job he can't stand:

> The psychiatrist shakes his head sadly and gets up and walks out.
>
> Then comes the final scene:
>
> The man's wife, his employer, his college teachers, and a host of other demons—yes, demons—are in conclave. There *is* a plot.
>
> He's getting on to us, says the wife. I think he's going to run away again. What'll we do this time?
>
> Let him go, says the psychiatrist. We'll get him back. We always get 'em back . . .

Although Dillon is anything but a criminal (like Thompson, he "cannot stand anyone who is unkind to children—children, dogs, or old people"), he often hovers on the brink of violence. He relates a childhood dream in which his mother beats his unborn first daughter to death with her bare fists. An empty ice cube tray sets him raving. And near the end of the novel he pummels a co-worker with a broom.

"Lou Ford, by all means," Thompson's daughter Patricia elaborates. "The pain in *Now and on Earth* really gets to me. It's scary and devastating. I know, I lived through a lot of it. So many people so unhappy, really confused, and not knowing it with the exception of my father. It's like he's there and not there, part of him just standing back observing and analyzing like they're characters on the stage. And with such clarity—he didn't miss a trick."

Thompson has Dillon report his father's suicide in a slashing obituary:

> William Sherman Dillon, well-known inmate of the H— Sanitarium, and former millionaire, oil-man, politician, and attorney, died at his residence early Sunday morning after gorging himself on the excelsior from his mattress. At his bedside was his wife, who had to be, his daughter Margaret, who didn't know any better, and several imbeciles who wanted to taste the excelsior themselves. While the will has not yet been probated, it is understood that the entire estate, consisting of unpaid bills and a heritage of lunacy, is to go to Mr. Dillon's son, James Grant Dillon, prominent hack-writer and aircraft flunkey of San Diego, California. . . .

The hallucinatory interview that supplants this necrology splits open the linear narrative of *Now and on Earth,* as in alternating blocks of roman and italic type Dillon cross-examines the spirit of his departed father. The relentless postmortem ("Pop, did—did you hate us very much?" *"I did. . . ."*) voids the facile reconciliation between the oil man and his wayward boy that concluded "The Drilling Contractor," Thompson's ghostwritten oral history of just a few years earlier. Rasping their mutual resentment into the black hole of eternity, both father and son remain unaccommodated and unpurged.

"The distortion of a text," Freud once observed, "is not unlike a murder." The disembodied italicized voice that interrupts and disorders *Now and on Earth* after the suicide of James Sherman Dillon will reappear in *A Hell of a Woman* when Dolly Dillon commits his first killing. The myth Thompson reconstructed out of his New York trip connected his solitary completion of *Now and on Earth* to the death of his father, forging a sad, guilt-ridden story of bad luck, bad timing, and a son's inability to save his father—"Why couldn't he have waited another day? He knew I was going to show up." His account continued the *Roughneck* theme of Thompson as Victim—a friendless animal undone by "flukish Fate." But the available facts, and Thompson's handling of his father's death in his novel, move beyond his guilt to another old myth: a son's vengeful—if here, literary—slaying of the father. "Why would Jimmie say that his father killed himself?" Thompson's sister Freddie asked. "Because it was the worst possible thing he could think of to write."

The famous writers who lent blurbs to *Now and on Earth* underscored the documentary aspect of the novel. Richard Wright: "Here is a document as true as a birth or death certificate." And Louis Bromfield: "It is a remarkable transcription of a world which seldom finds its way into fiction." Yet early reviewers recognized the creepier strains at the margins—even if they sometimes recoiled from what they saw. Max Miller, author of *I Cover the Waterfront,* dismissed the book as "a psychopathic novel" and "downright morbid" in the local San Diego *Union.* But the Springfield *Union-Republican* praised it as a "continuation . . . of the hard-boiled school of literature." And Milton Hindus, for the New York *Herald Tribune,* noted—presciently—that "Jim Thompson has a trick of thrusting a scene close up to you so that your interest is involved whether you like it or not. . . . It has a passionate immediacy of utterance which makes the reader jump as if he'd accidently touched a live wire." *Now and on Earth* also drew respectful notices from the *New Republic* and the *New Yorker,* which compared Thompson to James T. Farrell.

• • •

Despite a sheaf of friendly reviews, *Now and on Earth* met with indifferent sales. Discouraged ("My book, when it was published, aroused no enthusiasm whatsoever in Hollywood and not a great deal elsewhere"), Thompson wrestled with his revision of *The Unholy Grail* between shifts at Solar Aircraft. A registered letter from Modern Age rendered his struggle moot. With the staff about to enter the armed forces, Richard Childs intended to dissolve the publishing firm in October. Since Thompson once again had arranged for a weekly remittance in return for a set number of new chapters, he lost out on much of his advance.

He entered the Solar Aircraft Company, then located on 12th Street between Taft and McKinley, as a timekeeper. On July 10, after six months watching the clock, he moved up to payroll clerk—but abruptly resigned in August, citing "insufficient income." The War Manpower Commission had frozen many San Diego industries, and by mid-September Thompson entreated Solar and was rehired as a production planner.

The Thompsons abandoned pricey downtown San Diego for suburban Linda Vista, and leased half of an ugly saltbox of a house at 2601 Nye Street—"temporary" accommodations they would endure for the rest of the decade. Domestic unrest eased somewhat when Maxine, Freddie, and Birdie found their own apartment. But Thompson still was distracted by his sisters' problems. Freddie, also at Solar as a switchboard operator, gave birth to a daughter, Randi, out of wedlock in April. "She tried to have an abortion with me in Mexico," Randi discloses, "but it didn't work. My real father was a Marine, married, who had his own family, and she didn't even tell him I was coming along. He has no knowledge I was ever born. . . . I found out about all this just a few years ago. That's the secret part of the family—the three of them [Freddie, Maxine, and Jimmie] had lies and secrets all their lives. None of us children could ever figure out what the big

Alberta (standing) and Freddie (seated front)
at Solar Aircraft Company, San Diego, mid-
1940s (Courtesy of the Thompson family)

A family spree in Tijuana, Mexico: Michael,
Sharon, Jim, and Patricia, 1943 (Courtesy of
the Thompson family)

dark secret might be that made them all want to band together and protect each other."

Solar Aircraft soon evolved into a Thompson family shop. Maxine slipped into Jim's old timekeeper slot, and, come October, Alberta joined Freddie on the switchboard, a post she held through the war, until 1950. In order to care for the children during the day (Patricia now was ten, Sharon six, and Mike four), Thompson rotated onto the four-to-midnight swing shift, and obliged as a house husband. "He came to a lot of school functions that my mother couldn't attend because she was working," Sharon recalls. "Usually he'd be the only father there among all these women! And every Saturday he took us downtown to the public library. My dad cleaned the house, ironed our clothes, and told us stories about the old-time outlaws and sheriffs his father knew. He did all the cooking—barbecued ribs, Spanish omelets, onion soup, delicious pies, he could cook anything."

His benders eventually scotched hopes for a long, tranquil run of *Life with Father*. Depressed by the cancellation of his publishing contracts, and stuck in another senseless job, Thompson—by his own stupefying tally— "was moving toward a consumption of six pints per day. . . . I knew I was drinking ostensibly lethal quantities of whiskey. And yet, not only could I not stop, but I had to have ever larger and larger amounts." From the missed meals to his disruptive disappearances, he increasingly left his children alone to scramble for themselves. Much as in the rudderless household of his childhood, the young Thompsons learned to care for, and raise, one another. Patricia casts a chary eye back to the 1940s on Nye Street:

> I know what they say about the children of alcoholics. . . . The person who took over was me—and then, as we got older, Sharon. I assumed a tremendous amount of responsibility very young. It was like, well, my mother had to work, and my father was busy, and this was what I had to do. It was a three-way partnership in my mind from a very early age. Later I went to football games and dances, but those things were always done after my responsibilities at home.
>
> I came home from school to clean the house, and depending on what Sharon and Mike were doing I'd pursue them or do homework. I was in charge of Sharon and Mike, and they gave me a horrible time. They were always difficult to control. There were a great many chaotic moments, but at the time I didn't feel that it was anything out of the norm. It was just the way my family was.
>
> I didn't see the family as unusual until high school, when I became more aware of the drinking, and the impact it had on my mother. We never knew what set it off. Everything would be fine,

but then it would start. My father wasn't the same person—it was a different personality completely. He wasn't the same quiet person. He talked a great deal more, on things I really didn't understand. My mother would be upset and fearful, things would get to a very strained level, and sometimes this would go on for days.

I always wanted to help and protect my mother from it, if I could. Not physically, there was never anything like that, but emotionally, as he could get very sarcastic with her. . . . Staying up late at night, not being able to sleep, wondering if things would be okay, hoping he would get over it and be like my father again. . . . That he might fall and hurt himself, would get sick from it, always was a concern. He'd get sick, very sick to his stomach. It was scary. . . . When he stopped, he'd be very apologetic, on an even keel, very low-key.

That period wasn't a particularly glorious time for me. I don't care if I ever go back to San Diego—I wouldn't care if I never heard the name San Diego again. . . .

By the summer of 1943 Thompson drank himself into another nervous breakdown. He resigned from Solar on Independence Day, July 4, because of "illness," and earned medical disability benefits for the balance of the year. "He was very irritable," Alberta remembers, "and I was always careful that the children didn't make noise or do anything else to make him nervous." During his convalescence Thompson affiliated with A.A. and abstained from all alcohol. But like his encounter with "Bill W." in New York, the twelve-step program carried no lasting effect. Shortly after he received his first-year anniversary cake he fell off the wagon, claiming he had "nothing in common" with the members of his A.A. group.

At Alberta's urging, Thompson returned to *The Unholy Grail* and sat down for another whack at the movie house mystery that had vexed him since 1932. "That novel was always one of my favorites," she notes. "He had put it up on the shelf, and said he might as well forget about it. I said, Don't forget about it, because it's a good book. When he started to get better I took his typewriter out. I encouraged him to write. I used to tease him a lot, call him some endearing name, or tickle him under the chin and say, Come on, Jimmie, we have children and you have to raise them, so you better get busy and go to work. He'd start to laugh, and he eventually got going on it."

The innermost core of any relationship, especially a marriage that could withstand the abrasions of nearly fifty years, pulses behind a veil no outsider can presume to lift. Yet Alberta's playful ministrations to her husband during his recovery suggest that the Thompsons were hardly as mismatched as the storming Dillons of *Now and on Earth*. Proximate witnesses,

like the Thompson children, although by no means disinterested specta-
tors, are keen to protest that the scathing Punch-and-Judy disunion of that
novel "is pretty unfair to our mother." Sharon proposes that "even in the
darkest of times [the early 1940s] theirs was a good marriage, but a hard
marriage. I think my father would have died a lot earlier if it hadn't been for
my mother, because she really did take care of him." As Patricia amplifies:

> My parents balanced each other. Each one provided the other
> with what they themselves didn't have. My mother gave my father
> the steadiness that he greatly needed, her undying love and devo-
> tion, a commitment, and a willingness to go the long difficult road
> no matter what. He challenged her mind and gave her intellectual
> stimulation. And he gave her all of his love. As demanding as he
> was, there still was a tremendous give-and-take in that marriage. I
> could not imagine one without the other.
>
> There was peace and tranquillity there even in the midst of all
> the chaos, a true meeting of the minds, and, except when the drink-
> ing was going on, a sense of them basically standing together. I
> think that whatever demons were within my father they had noth-
> ing to do with my mother.

Thompson polished *The Unholy Grail* and mailed it off to his new agent,
Franz Horch, in New York. There were no takers. He would rewrite the
blighted book a total of eight times—"in the alcoholic determination to
prove myself right and the nation's publishers wrong"—before it finally appeared as *Nothing More Than Murder*.

The spring of 1944, he thought he saw another way out. He would find
his luck—and his fortune—as a foreign correspondent for one of the armed
services newspapers. Thompson had registered for the draft in Oklahoma
City back in 1940; now, as a thirty-seven-year-old father of three, with his
long history of physical and emotional illness, he doubtless could have escaped induction. But much to the astonishment of Alberta and his sisters,
he enlisted in the U.S. Marine Corps on April 13, and commenced basic
training in San Diego. Thompson never made it overseas. A few weeks shy
of his graduation from the grueling boot camp, he collapsed and was
rushed by ambulance to the Navy Defense Hospital at Camp Pendleton.
The diagnosis was rheumatic fever.

Honorably discharged as a private on June 9, Thompson returned to
Nye Street downcast and exasperated. "When he came home from the hospital he was completely dissatisfied with his life," Alberta recalls. "Everything would have changed for him if he could have survived basic training
and become a foreign correspondent." He buried himself in a battery of
mediocre jobs—building inspector for the city of San Diego or door-to-door

gold buyer for Joseph Fleishman's pawnshop on 5th Avenue. Thompson later mined his brief stint persuading suburban housewives to surrender their high-karat watches, necklaces, wedding rings, heirlooms, and dental fillings for a novel, *The Golden Gizmo;* a pair of con man novellas, "The Cellini Chalice" and "The Frightening Frammis," published in *Alfred Hitchcock's Mystery Magazine;* and a short story, "Blood from a Turnip," printed in *Collier's.*

Weekday mornings he began to drop by the Navy Housing Unit on Blakely Drive, where his mother and Freddie lived with Maxine and her new husband, Joseph Kouba, a career soldier in the USMC. No longer able to manage the stairs, Birdie slept on a bed in the kitchen next to Randi, Freddie's daughter. After breakfast Thompson helped his mother clear the dishes from the table, set up a typewriter, and together they settled down to write true crime. Responsible for the first draft, Birdie apparently stumbled upon a homespun version of the "cut-up technique" that William Burroughs and Brion Gysin would pioneer in the early 1960s. She surrounded herself with dozens of issues of *True Detective, Daring Detective,* and other pulps, according to Freddie; randomly working through them, "she cut and pasted passages until she developed a crime and a set of characters." Thompson then smoothed out the story, carefully converting the names and locales, and mailed it out under the pseudonym Bird E. Thompson. Probably to throw off the scent, the Bird only flew in Canada, appearing (often anonymously) in true crime anthologies issued by the Superior Publishers/Duchess Printing & Publishing Company of Toronto. A Bird E. Thompson letter to editor L. C. Steele at Duchess indicates their handiwork:

> Thanks for the check for the two stories, "The Corpse in the Clearing," and "Murder in the City of God." You didn't mention the art in these cases. I can furnish a few if wanted, there is no profit to me in these.
>
> In "The Corpse in the Clearing" the following are available, Emit Giles, murderer; George Rose, victim; Sheriff Orren Wester and Under Sheriff Henry Hardy.
>
> In the "Murder in the City of God," Robert Cargo, murderer; Oklahoma County Court House, and Evidence Officer Claude Tyler.
>
> Please write if you want them.
>
> I did not receive a check for the art in the "Mountain Massacre" case. I believe you used five pictures, I sent six.

"The Corpse in the Clearing" was collected for two Superior/Duchess digests, *Marijuana Murder* ("Authentic Police Cases Every Story True") and

The Weeping Widow ("Sure-Fire Detective Book"), a few years later. Another Bird E. Thompson story, "The Innocent Double," features the slaying of Pearl Pearson, a former "stage actress and contortionist," and an accused murderer who is set free after a five-hour speech by none other than Moman Pruiett. Thompson and his mother also collaborated on a lumbering western set in territorial Oklahoma, "The Fort Smith Trail," and based, most likely, on his 1938 Writers' Project radio play of the same name.

Thompson played host that summer to his cousin, Ted Cowan, a sailor coasting through San Diego on his way overseas. He enjoyed rattling Cowan, whose devout Methodist father condemned *Now and on Earth* as "pure filth." He coolly informed the young patriot that he was the former secretary of the Oklahoma Communist Party, that the only way he could relax was with alcohol, and that he had written more than two thousand books and stories. "Jimmie joked quite a bit, but he also lectured me about writing. He said, 'There are thirty-two ways to write a story, and I've used them all, but there is only one plot—things are not as they seem.'"

The "one plot" routine became one of Thompson's favorites, and he reprised it for Arnold Hano, cineaste Pierre Rissient, and the students in his USC writing class. Ultimately he handed the line over to a lewd, bitter drunk—"His name was Tomlinson or Thomas or something of the kind, and I gather from certain things he said that he was a writer"—for his late unfinished novel *The Horse in the Baby's Bathtub:*

> . . . I seemed to hear another voice, to see a bloated red-eyed face, and to smell the sour sachet of whiskey.
> *"Plot? There ain't but one plot in the world, m'boy. Give 'em somethin' else they'd clobber you with it."*
> *"Polti says there are thirty-two plots."*
> *"They all got the same daddy, one basic plot. Things're not as they seem, that's the papa of the whole thirty-two. Things're not as they seem."*
> *"Nothing? Nothing is ever as it seems?"*
> *"Only—hic!—only if it stinks. If it stinks then that's the way it is. Livin' proof of it. . . ."*

• • •

*. . . **Things are not as they seem.*** Early in the spring of 1945 he decided to return to New York, the scene of his greatest success. But broke, Thompson first rode the bus to Chicago, where he burst in on William Couch, now the director of the University of Chicago Press, and begged for a loan. Couch was still piqued over *We Talked About Labor*—he complained to the Rockefeller Foundation that "Mr. Thompson's work was disappointing,"

and pronounced *Now and on Earth* "totally worthless." Even so, he welcomed the prodigal novelist into his home for the night, and then purchased him a seat on the Pacemaker train to New York City. "I remember
very little about that journey," Thompson wrote. "The one recollection that
stands out clearly is of my being hidden by drinking companions beneath
the table of a crowded dining car while railroad detectives held up the train
for ten minutes in an attempt to find me and unload me. What I had done to
deserve their attention is, mercifully, unknown to me."

Thompson journeyed east to confront his agent over his latest revision
of *The Unholy Grail.* Franz Horch appears an improbable representative for
a Midwestern movie house thriller. Born in Vienna at the turn of the century, he assisted Max Reinhardt on a number of theater and film productions in Berlin during the late 1920s and early 1930s. Horch came to New
York in 1938 as a political refugee from the Nazi regime in Austria and
opened a literary agency that specialized in the American rights for émigré
authors and in the European rights for American writers. His august client
roster included Thomas and Klaus Mann, Erich Maria Remarque, Alma
Mahler, Franz Werfel, Ferenc Molnar, John Dos Passos, E. B. White, James
Thurber, Upton Sinclair, James Hilton, Jim Bishop, Edna Ferber, and Anaïs
Nin. An obese, balding man with a thick mustache, Horch discovered
Thompson through Modern Age.

"An Alcoholic Looks at Himself" documented his face-off with the old-
worldly Horch at the agent's West 73rd Street office:

> My literary agent was not exactly happy to see me when I con-
> fronted him, half-drunk and wholly broke. He believed the manu-
> script I had sent him was unsaleable. He would not approach
> publishers for an advance on anything else I might write, at least
> until I had put that "anything" into concrete form.
>
> He was definitely "unable" to lend me money.
>
> I thanked him brusquely (for nothing, my attitude said), with-
> drew my manuscript and stalked out. I was determined to sell it
> myself. . . .

This was only the first scuffle of a running donnybrook. Thompson shortly
staged a public shouting match with Horch at the Eclair, the Viennese pas-
try and schnitzel restaurant favored by Jewish expatriates, on West 72nd
Street.

Borrowing money from Bill Cunningham, he checked into a waterfront
hotel by the West Village and looked up his other New York pals. He frequently ate his meals with Sis Cunningham and Gordon Friesen at their new
place on East 84th Street, where he "always arrived hoisting a big whiskey
bottle." Thompson took to stopping by Lois McDowell's office at the J. Ster-

ling Getchell advertising agency in the Chrysler Building. "Doc and Jim kept in touch after the failure of Modern Age," she remarks. "I remember Jim coming up to visit me where I worked, and I'd usually bring him home to supper." Doc recently had joined Greenberg: Publisher, a small mainstream firm that "had nothing to do with the radical experience," Lois McDowell adds, and emphasized popular psychology, education, cooking, and how-to books.

But just as they had in 1941, Thompson's radical New York friends came through for him. With the assistance of Doc McDowell, he outmaneuvered the recalcitrant Horch and negotiated the sale of his next book—not the bedeviled movie mystery, which Greenberg: Publisher also passed on, but an "historical novel." He hammed up his triumph for "An Alcoholic Looks at Himself":

> Sitting in a bar, I conceived the germ of a historical novel and I began presenting that. Fortunately, or otherwise, I had that first novel to my credit, book manuscripts were in heavy demand at the time and an alcoholic can be a very convincing and likable person when he feels he must. So. . . .
>
> Six weeks to the day after I left my agent's office, I walked back in again. I laid a hundred-dollar bill on his desk and placed a fifty beside it.
>
> "That's your commission on a hundred-twenty-five-thousand-word novel I just sold," I said. "Plus your commission on an advance for an unwritten novel."
>
> His astonishment was gratifying, as it should have been. Much of my maniacal, brain-and-body-sapping effort during the past few weeks had been so much stage-setting for this brief moment. . . .

Greenberg: Publisher paid Thompson $500 for the novel, tentatively titled *A Portion of the Land.* Although his contract, signed on May 22, allowed him until September 1 to deliver the manuscript, by working sixteen to eighteen hours a day at his dockside hotel he finished the book in five weeks. Come early July, he was back in San Diego.

Prior to departure, though, Franz Horch suggested that he schedule an appointment with an émigré physician who had a reputation for "curing" alcoholics. Many of Horch's authors consulted Dr. Max Jacobson for a variety of physical and psychological complaints. One, Anaïs Nin, was instrumental in luring the German refugee to New York:

> When I was ill with bronchitis I was happy to rediscover Dr. Max Jacobson, the German *emigre* doctor, whom I had helped indirectly to reach America. He rushed over with his miracle bag and cured me instantly. . . . He is becoming known for the amazing

doctor he is. Intuitive, alert, observant. He has almost no need of a laboratory. I have never seen a human eye so like an X-ray when he scans a human being for signs of illness.

"Dr. Feelgood" or "Miracle Max," as Jacobson came to be known in the 1960s, dispensed high-octane injections of multivitamins, steroids, hormones, placenta, animal organ cells, and amphetamines from his crowded office on East 72nd Street. Like Horch, he numbered among his clients the eminent and mighty: President John F. Kennedy and Jackie, Judy Garland, Truman Capote, Marlene Dietrich, Cecil B. DeMille, Henry Miller, Billy Wilder, Van Cliburn, Edward G. Robinson, and Tennessee Williams. Dr. Jacobson's medical license would be revoked by the New York State Board of Regents in 1975.

For the next decade Thompson visited "Miracle Max" whenever he was in New York and needed to sober up in a hurry. Back in California, he received vials of his formula and disposable needles through the mail. Jacobson's widow, Ruth, relates:

> In those years Dr. Jacobson was preparing injectable materials for his patients' own use. Thompson would have seen Dr. Jacobson and a multivitamin formula would have been determined for him. There would be these 30-cc vials of injectable materials. Thompson would have reported by mail or phone on how he was progressing, and on how he felt, and a vial would be sent to him with a recommended dosage—1 or 2 ccs per day, week, or whatever. Dr. Jacobson was treating a number of alcoholics, including Tennessee Williams.

Thompson learned to administer his shots, but the "cure" never held. As he wrapped up his final showdown with Horch: "Having wrung the last drop of pleasure from my act, I boarded a train and crossed the country again—drunk, of course."

•   •   •

Heed the Thunder (as he redesignated *A Portion of the Land*) was published in February 1946, with a dedication to Lois and Elliott McDowell. For his populist epic rooted in the verdant farms and desolate sandhills of his Burwell childhood, Thompson reverted to the "Midwestern regionalism" of his college mentors, Russell Prescott and Lowry C. Wimberly—a fifteen-year step back from the subversive, personal fiction he espoused to Gordon Friesen. Yet *Heed the Thunder,* like *Now and on Earth* before it, harbored several books within the same jacket: a panoramic country life chronicle after the model of Nebraska novelists Mari Sandoz and Willa Cather; a scurrilous family history; and a brutish descent into degradation, sadism, incest, homicide, and dementia.

Edith Dillon and her son, Robert, retreat to her ancestral Fargo family farm in Verdon, a valley town along the crest of the sandhills, after the mystifying disappearance of her husband, an Oklahoma City lawyer and former peace officer. The novel covers the years 1907 to 1914. Thompson dramatically enhanced Robert Dillon's age ("slightly less than seven") and isolated him as a forlorn only child. But he infused *Heed the Thunder* with the spirit of his Nebraska youth: the fishing trips and cider-drinking sessions with Pa, the tiffs with Ma, Uncle Bob's books, the pranks with his cousins, the abortive airplane flight from the barn, Birdie's hotel, and his mock suicide with a makeshift noose and animal tongue.

The only Thompson character to bear his full Party alias, Robert Dillon, like young Jimmie, is a "thin, gawky boy, pale, and with a big head and sandy hair." By the time he reaches thirteen, he seems "a mass of contradictions, infinitely more worrisome to himself than he was to others":

> Generally, he did not swear much. He did not object to others cursing—he even enjoyed it. But for himself he preferred using, searching for, words and phrases which expressed the same vehemence and decadence, but yet were acceptable in any company.
>
> His companions were of all ages and sizes. . . . He had that mixed curse and blessing to make people laugh without trying to, even when trying not to. . . . He could not diagram a sentence and such terms as "past participle" and "present imperfect" filled him with amused annoyance. But he could write better themes than the examples in the text. . . . He had read every history, ancient and modern, in the public library, but he passed the subject in school by the skin of his teeth. . . . Extremely credulous, he was also suspicious of almost everyone.

Robert remains nominally polite and cheerful amid the betrayals and lies of his elders. He inherits a rucksack of instinctive snakes—suspicions, angers, insecurities, fears, aggressions—which the novel deposits at the doorstep of his absent father. "W-where's Papa?" Robert bawls. *Heed the Thunder* subsequently would be reprinted in Canada as *Sins of the Fathers*.

Thompson ripped through his Burwell relatives with travesty and vitriol. Grant Fargo (patterned after his uncle William Melvin Myers) is a besotted dandy who sleeps with his cousin Bella and, most likely, murders her by crashing their car. Sherman Fargo (after his uncle David Newton Myers) is an obnoxious, swaggering hayseed. He scoffs at indoor plumbing —"It ain't healthy"; disdains to oil his new thresher—"the damned thing could get along without oil, seeing how much it had cost"; torments his siblings, and finally loses his mismanaged farm. Sherman's wife, Josephine (after his aunt Edith), swaddles her unhappiness in fat: "a quaking, bread-pudding of a woman. . . . She had the ferociousness of a rat and the timidity of a mouse."

Transplanted Englishman Alfred Courtland (after Bob Wicks) swindles $25,000 and the ownership of the Verdon bank. Half-mad from syphilis, Alf flogs a sandhills schoolboy with his riding crop:

> Courtland struck him in the face with the doubled quirt. . . .
> Blood burst from his face in a dozen places, and a great red welt
> coiled snake-like across his cheeks. He staggered to his feet half-
> blinded, and his great fists doubled and undoubled harmlessly. If
> Courtland had struck him with his hand he would have fought, but
> the whip . . . the whip had done something to him. It had broken
> worse than his skin—something that would always lie festering,
> unhealed. . . . And as Courtland swung the quirt again and again,
> the only sound that came from him was a low sobbing, an almost
> animal whining.

Pearl Fargo (after Ma Myers) reaped the harshest scorn. She is physically repellent: "She wore her hair on top of her head in a slightly pyramided coil which, according to her husband, resembled a cow chip." And this scolding, stony-hearted taskmaster can't conceal her irritation with Edie and Robert: "He supposed that all grandmas disliked little boys." Pearl stays housebound except for her tent-meeting revivals. Under the spell of the Reverend-Parson Silas Whitcomb, she deeds the Fargo farm to God, in expectation of His imminent return "should He decide to remake the earth instead of destroying it."

Only Lincoln Fargo, the character based on Pa Myers, escaped Thompson's shooting gallery of small-town grotesquery. Gruff "Link" Fargo is a retired stonemason, saloon keeper, and homesteader, a veteran of Sherman's march to the sea and a "first-rate storyteller, gambler, and judge of good whiskey and food." Robert's champion and stand-by father, Fargo molds a moral center for *Heed the Thunder* with a pair of fatalistic set pieces.

"That was all there was to life," he calculates in the first, "a gift that was slowly taken away from you. An Indian gift. You started with a handful of something and ended up with a handful of nothing. The best things were taken away from you last when you needed them the most. When you were at the bottom of the pot, when there was no longer reason for life, then you died. It was probably a good thing."

On his deathbed, Fargo then gauges his personal losses against the imponderables of his life—any life—and his tragic sense that, just out of comprehension, everything matters more than he can say:

"I guess we don't never learn, Edie. We don't never learn. There ain't none of us can tell whether it'll rain the next day or not. We don't know if our kids are goin' to be boys or girls. Or why the world turns one way instead of another. Or—the what or why or when of anything. Hindsight's the only gift we got, except on one thing. On that we're all prophets.

"We know what's in the other fellow's mind. It don't make no difference that we've never seen him before, or whatever. We know he's out to do us if he gets the chance."

"Pa!"

"You got plenty of time to talk, Edie. I ain't. . . . We came to a house one day—not far from Atlanta it was—and I was bringin' up the rear an' all I got was a book . . . I don't remember the words no more, but I got the idea. . . . There ain't no death, no deed, no o-mission or co-mission that don't leave its mark. . . .

"We plow up the prairie because it's ours to plow, and we dam up the cricks because they're ours to dam. We grab everything we can while the grabbin's good, because it's ours an' because some other fellow will do it if we don't. . . . And, hell, there ain't nothin' that's really ours, and we don't know what's in the other fellow's mind. . . ."

"How say the unsayable?" Thompson will ask twenty years later, at the conclusion of *The Grifters.* Lincoln Fargo's vision of diminution and waste, guilt and unknowability, resonates through all Thompson's crime fiction.

Heed the Thunder placates the household gods of the historical novel with rustic slapstick, the flutters of first love, some operatic nature ("Spring slipped like a virgin into the bed of the valley"), and a loose net of anecdote tightening—barely—to a plot. After seven years, Robert Dillon is rescued from Verdon through a deus ex machina more convenient than convincing, as his father suddenly surfaces from Mexico, no longer a victim of amnesia.

The novel culminates in a mushy page-long hymn to the land: "The good land, the bad land, the fair-to-middling land. . . ." Yet the pervading politics of *Heed the Thunder* is anything but sentimental. Through the Fargos, Thompson shadowed the closing of the Great Frontier and the industrialization of the West, the ravishing of natural resources for short-term profit, and the conflicts between the farmers and the railroads, the homesteaders and the banks.

Heed the Thunder intoned an elegy over a ruined family and a vanished way of life, binding the clan and the land, the familial and the political, in a fatal equation. Resurrecting the title of his 1939 pamphlet, *Economy of Scarcity,* Thompson lamented, "It was a condition bred of the vast loneliness of the prairies and nurtured by the same force—a sort of economy, or civilization, of scarcity. As the years passed and the population increased and there was room for more than one bank, one barber shop, one hotel to the community, the clan would break up or submerge. It was cracking even now, but the fissures were imperceptible."

But, as with *Now and on Earth,* it is *"the sickness"* crackling along the novel's lunatic fringe that more accurately anticipated Thompson's future direction as a writer. Stray bolts of madness shoot through the prairie pieties and hard-won wisdom. As Grant Fargo drunkenly whips his horse, the face of his incestuous lover, Bella, pops into his head: "He lashed out at the mare, noting with enjoyment the pained flicker of her flanks. . . . He'd show her what was what, who was boss. . . . He'd show them all. Yes, Bella, too. . . . He'd have her following him around like a whipped puppy." Mike Czerny, the sandhills schoolboy mauled by Alf Courtland, metastasizes into a "monster":

> *By morning he was raving, by that evening his head was puffed to twice its normal size; he was a festering, bleeding, sightless mess. . . . When his insanity became uncontrollable, they chained him in the cellar, and there he remained for three months. By fall, he seemed completely normal again—except for his looks. His face looked as though it had been branded with a running iron; his mouth had been chewed and clawed until it was almost twice its original size, and there were only a few stumps of teeth in his rotted gums. He was almost wholly blind, but he could see enough to know what they saw, and he could hear. . . . So the days, the weeks, the months passed for the boy, the monster who was Mike Czerny. . . . And sometimes he would slip away from his drudgery and lie concealed near the road, peering at the infrequent passers-by out of his almost blind eyes. Waiting. . . .*

Thompson's first full-tilt psychopath, Czerny slices Grant Fargo with a husking mitt and then scourges him with a strand of barbed wire in the belief that he is Alfred Courtland.

Heed the Thunder attracted some positive but mainly baffled reviews. The *Saturday Review* ticketed the novel a "Sears-Roebuck epic. . . . There are a number of good stories in this book but the whole effect is moderately confusing." The New York *Herald Tribune* polished it off with a wisecrack: "The prose is vigorous, and domestic dialogue has a barroom bluntness. If sufficient readers are 'interested or amused,' says the author, he will do a trilogy. No comment."

The strongest reaction came from Burwell. "Jimmie's novel upset everyone here," Edna Myers Borden remembers. "The family was very hurt by that book. We all saw ourselves in it. The language disturbed us, but we were more upset because a lot of it just wasn't true. No one could understand why he wrote it that way—what he said about our grandmother or Robert Wicks—or even believe that he wrote it at all. Jimmie was a sweet boy, and we didn't see him like that."

Pained letters flowed back to Birdie in San Diego, and stinging accusations. Addie Wicks charged that it was James Sherman Thompson who died from syphilis of the brain. Maxine hastened to heal the schism with some fanciful footwork—and a few outright lies. "As for Jimmie's book causing such a furor in Burwell, I can't understand this," she wrote back to her Nebraska cousins. "It was purely fiction. Why should he be spiteful? It is not one of our family traits. . . . If everyone would read *Grapes of Wrath, Tobacco Road, Hell's Half Acre,* or any number of well-known books by prominent writers, they wouldn't be shocked by Jimmie's *Heed the Thunder.* He is mild in comparison. . . . I'm sure the Burwell Library is *full* of books dirtier than Jimmie's, and if the people want to pick out themselves in those books they could probably do so. . . . Perhaps it was unfortunate that the setting should be Nebraska and the characters familiar to you. . . . The people's names had a similarity to those in Burwell. He used some of the characteristics of the people he knew there and pictures Pa to some extent. The rest was what could be written of any place. It's all purely imaginary. . . ."

The Myerses never forgave Thompson. And the Burwell Library "kept *Heed the Thunder* on the shelf for a while," Edna reports, "so anyone who wanted could read it. But then they sent it on to Omaha—they didn't like it either!"

• • •

For much of the 1940s Thompson was living two lives. Manic sprees in New York City, where he dispatched his novels and caroused with old literary and Party friends, alternated with long, stagnant lulls in San Diego, where he lapsed into deadly jobs and reclusive intoxication. He seemed incapable of building on his laurels once he returned to his daily routines, as though he could only do his work far away from home, under the threat of his self-created crises. Although his legend glows with the heat of his relentless productivity, Thompson wrote as he drank—a novel within five weeks, a half-dozen true crime features over a single month—in binges.

The publication of *Heed the Thunder* triggered a precipitous deterioration. "Back home again," he confided in "An Alcoholic Looks at Himself," "my drinking entered a new and terrifying phase. Heretofore its tendency had been to make me amiable and gregarious. Now I became dopey, antisocial and abusive. . . . In the earlier stages of my alcoholism I was content with inflicting mental anguish on those near to me. But in recent years I have become violent. . . . The publishing date of my written novel and the deadline for the undelivered one virtually coincided. Thus, when the former flopped resoundingly, I used that fact as justification for refusing to meet my obligations to write the other."

No contract for an additional novel survives in the Greenberg: Publisher archives. Thompson projected *Heed the Thunder* as the cornerstone volume of an old-fashioned trilogy that would retrace his bloodline through the Civil War to colonial America. But his determination fizzled— a victim of Burwell family friction, or the incapacitating "shame" he imputed to childhood "comparison[s]" with his father, or the whiskey. Over the next year Thompson confined his writing to true crime. Besides all the Bird E. Thompson trumpery, he also condensed *The Unholy Grail* into an 8,500-word feature, "The Dark Stair," for *Master Detective* (June 1946). This fictional case history preserved his trusty "as-told-to" format: By County Evidence Officer Chester L. Stacey with Jim Thompson.

Alberta's wages at Solar provided the capital source of family income. When he was drinking, Thompson burned up the telephone wires—and her scant treasury—with expensive long-distance calls to his pals and publishing contacts in New York; and he affrighted the children with impulsive flights from the house. "He used to disappear for days at a time," according to his son, Michael. "I remember one night my mother left him out on the porch, and when she came back he was gone. Another time he ended up in a bar in Tijuana; or another night, we went to pick him up in downtown San Diego. . . . He left us up in the air quite a bit."

The assignment of tracking Thompson down often fell on his sister Freddie:

> Jimmie wouldn't come home, and everybody would say, Oh dear, where is he, we got to find him. Usually I was the one who went off to search the bars. I'd have to hunt for him all over town, bar to bar. He would leave amiably, but sometimes there had been some incident, some little hassle, like he had poured a pitcher of beer over his companion's head as a joke, something that if he were sober Jimmie would be totally horrified at. Once or twice—I never would tell this to Alberta—I found him with a prostitute. He would come willingly, laughing, but he was always afraid he was going to get it when he got home, and I think he did.

Jim began to frequent the drying-out clinics of San Diego, the Hygeia Sanatorium on Ivy Street, or the Paradise Valley Sanitarium and Hospital on National Avenue. "In three years I was hospitalized twenty-seven times for

Jim Thompson (left center) reporting for the San
Diego Journal *(Courtesy of the Thompson family)*

alcoholism," he half-boasted, half-rued. "I got nothing but temporary sobriety and enormous bills."

• • •

His talent for fiction "all-but-exhausted," Thompson reluctantly sought out his first professional writing job since leaving Oklahoma. The San Diego *Journal* hired him to fill a temporary reporter's slot in June 1947, for $67.50 a week. "When I interviewed him, Jim said that he had a drinking problem but had been on the wagon for a while," *Journal* city editor Fred Kinne recalls. "I had someone out on illness, so I said, Why don't you sit down and sub for him and we'll see what happens. I just kept Jim on when the other guy came back, because I was so impressed with him. Jim was a helluva good reporter, and one of the finest writers I ever worked with."

The San Diego *Journal* (published in multiple afternoon and evening editions) hit the streets on Saint Patrick's Day, 1944, as the liberal Democratic alternative to the Republican establishment, Copley family papers, the *Tribune* and the *Union*. Edited and printed from an old Masonic temple at the corner of 5th and Ash, the *Journal* accented local news, mixing aggressive investigative exposés and consumer caveats with light features. Thompson occupied the second desk in the airy newsroom, close by the city editor's command post. "I kept him there because Jim could handle any kind of story—politics, the police, the courthouse," Kinne remarks. "I could assign him to anything. But Jim had a particular touch for human pathos, for sob stories. Anytime there was a child involved in a story I made sure Jim went out on it. Once I asked him, How can you do that so well? He said, 'Well, I set my mind as though it were my child.' He wrote without strain or effect, and he could make you cry."

Kinne was able to recite the conclusion to a tiny, ten-sentence eulogy, "Goodnight, Son, You've Had a Busy Day," which Thompson delivered on November 12, retrieving favorite phrases from the vacuum of nearly fifty years:

> Little Billy Nolting is dead.
>
> Bill suffered from nephrosis, a rare kidney ailment.
>
> Only exposure to measles could alleviate or cure it, and no sufficiently severe case of the disease could be found in San Diego.
>
> It was just a week before his fourth birthday when the child, son of Mr. and Mrs. George Nolting, La Mesa, gave up the painful struggle for life.
>
> But perhaps "gave up" is misleading.
>
> Billy had been sick for a very long time, but he probably never was conscious of the fact that the deep sleep he was passing into would be his last.
>
> There was his birthday only a week off. Little more than a month away was Christmas, the first he had ever really known. . . . Children don't give up such things easily, and probably Billy didn't.
>
> He was just tired, and he went to sleep for a while.
>
> And when he awakens the birthday cake and the Christmas presents will be there waiting . . . in a land where there are no diseases to torture children.

Little Billy Nolting vaulted Thompson's byline onto the front page. Aficionados of *The Killer Inside Me* may be even more dismayed to learn that it was a cute "interview" with a cat that placed his photograph there on August 26. As the hard-bitten Scoop posed with his notebook and pencil, a cigarette pasted to his lip, next to the fluffy calico, the *Journal* headline blared: AL E. KATT, SPITTING MAD, DEMANDS HIS RIGHTS; HAS BACK IN AIR OVER "DOG TERROR" IN SAN DIEGO. His full text ran:

> "Thousands of dogs are being smuggled across the Mexican border every month. . . . Dogs have approached me on the street and called me vile names."
>
> These were the grim revelations made this morning by

Al E. Katt, during a surprise visit to The Journal editorial rooms.

Documenting his statements that San Diego is in the grip of a "dog terror," Katt cited recent negative action on a canine-control ordinance and a pending increase in the price of milk.

He also declared that a proposed hike in bus fares was dog-inspired.

"If bus fares go up," he meowed, twisting his whiskers, "people will start staying home. And if they stay at home, how can us cats snitch stuff—I mean, exercise our rights as free-born felines.

"Dogs ain't got no rights. We cats have a majority and the majority ought to rule."

A graduate of Yeowl University, Katt came here from Persia six or seven lives ago. He claims an hour's sleep at night is enough for anyone, attributes his good health to milk, mice and frequent sponge baths.

His favorite song, which he sang as he swaggered out the door, is "Get Along, Little Doggies. . . ."

The wily Mr. Katt turned out to be a Ms. and deposited a litter of kittens in the newsroom. When one of them crawled up the leg of his trousers, Thompson named him Deadline, swept him into his jacket pocket, and carried him home to his kids.

Thompson squeezed out puff pieces on his ailing Old Town bartender and on a mock edict in La Mesa that required all bearded residents to shave one side of their face. In keeping with contemporary newspaper practice, he tended to earn bylines for his comfy chitchat ("Artistic Bent Found Vent in Baking of Great Cakes," "Shipping Fresh Flowers by Mail May Become $1 Million Dollar Business") or his hometown highlights ("County School System Called One of the Best," "Animal Hiring Agency Just One Role of S.D. Zoo"), while the six or seven hard news items he wrote up every morning for Kinne entered the paper uncredited. A prominent exception was his series in July on the trial of Albert and Elizabeth Ingalls, former Boston socialites charged with confining their black maid, Dora Jones, in involuntary servitude. Covering this sensational "slave" trial with *Journal* reporter Logan Jenkins, Thompson produced a daily court transcript—no mean feat for someone lacking shorthand—and a daily news summary, along with the occasional sidebar profile ("Mrs. Ingalls Worries About Photos, Obeys Husbands 'Shh's' in Interview," "Dora Taunted Own Marriage Failure, Says Mrs. Ingalls"). The case manifestly impressed Thompson, and he pursued it long after the commotion faded with the conviction of Mrs. Ingalls. As late as 1959, he developed a proposal for a kind of nonfiction novel about Dora Jones, *The Slave Girl in the Cellar*.

A generation older than most of his colleagues, Thompson largely kept to himself, eating his lunch alone at the Peacock Cafe and politely refusing invitations for after-work drinks and poker. To a young rewrite woman like Esther Gwynne, then twenty-two, he "seemed a wreck of a man at that point, red-faced, ragged, with an untidy look about him, but a terrific writer." His only real friend on the staff was Lionel Van Deerlin, subsequently city editor of the *Journal* and a Congressman from south San Diego (1963–81). "Jim was such wonderful company," Van Deerlin describes his companion inside and out of the newsroom. "He was interested in so much more than the surface events which claimed the attention of reporters. And so creative—that piece he wrote on a dying child actually had me in tears. Of course Jim was a dreadful problem. But, my God, once you dried him out, what a talent!"

Since Van Deerlin also lived in Linda Vista, he found himself fetching Thompson from the Hygeia Sanatorium:

> I would get a call from his wife saying that he was ready to go back to work. Mrs. Thompson was extremely devoted to him. She knew that if I picked him up he would get there all right. This was Godawful early in the morning—we started around 6:30, and our first deadline for the afternoon edition was 9:30. So I would go in the dawn hours down to this place, and he'd be ready to leave, and I'd take him in. He was such an intelligent man that he wouldn't offer a lot of silly excuses that you often get from alcoholics. Jim didn't drink in the city room. He just wouldn't come in some morning, and I knew that it had started again.

The saddest of all Thompson's articles for the *Journal* was his conventionally cast obituary for Birdie, after her death from a cerebral embolism on November 29.

THOMPSON FUNERAL RITES SET TUESDAY

> Funeral services for Mrs. Birdie E. Thompson, 68, who died Saturday at her home, 3207 Blakely, will be held Tuesday at 3 p.m. from Johnson-Saum Mortuary. Interment will be in Mt. Hope Cemetery.
>
> A native of Eldora, Iowa, Mrs. Thompson attended the University of Nebraska, after which she taught school in Burwell, Neb., Oklahoma City, and Ft. Worth. She came to San Diego in 1940.
>
> Her husband, James Sherman Thompson, died in 1941. He was [a] widely known pioneer peace officer in Oklahoma and Texas.
>
> Surviving are her son, James Thompson; two daughters, Mrs. Joseph Kouba and Mrs. Winifred Johnston, and five grandchildren, all of San Diego.

The passing of his beloved mother, his compeer and collaborator, stunned Thompson, even though Birdie had been infirm with heart trouble for years. "My dad was literally devastated when Mom died," Sharon remembers. "He cried and cried, and just had a real bad time handling it." But in his grief he stayed scrupulously attentive to the feelings of his children and, for a committed nonbeliever, their trust in the Catholic Church. "I hopped a bus the minute I heard she was really bad and lit some candles in our church," Sharon adds. "I knew that if I lit the candles she was going to live. But my grandmother didn't live. My dad was extremely worried, and he told my mother that he didn't want my faith to be shattered because my grandmother died."

Thompson lasted some nine months at the San Diego *Journal,* exiting in a blaze of rage and glory that instantly notched a Southern California newspaper legend. City editor Kinne narrates:

> This is the way I lost Jim. He had written a hard-hitting story about a San Diego assemblyman. The assemblyman phoned the publisher, John A. Kennedy, a well-connected, self-important man with a rich wife, who insisted that everyone call him "Captain" because of an honorary commission he got during the war. Kennedy came storming out to the city room, ran right by my desk, and chastized Jim for writing an inaccurate story—which, of course, it wasn't. I followed Kennedy right back into the publisher's office, and said, "Kennedy, don't you ever come into my city room again. You just cost me a great reporter." Kennedy shot back, "You call me Captain Kennedy." So I said, "Good, then you call me Colonel Kinne"—that was my rank in the Second World War.
>
> I knew Jim well enough to know how he would react. He went out and got drunk and never came back. I looked for him at the Peacock Cafe and a few other places, but couldn't find him. The next I heard he was up in Los Angeles.

Thompson put the vindictive bite on Captain Kennedy a decade later with a pair of satirical newspaper novels, *The Criminal* and *The Nothing Man.* "The Captain," as he christened the publisher of the *Star* in *The Criminal,* is a "monster, bastard, inhuman son-of-a-bitch" who strong-arms his reporters with spies and threats to their health insurance, destroys innocent citizens through vicious circulation-boosting slander mongering, and casually confuses himself with God. Kennedy also backdrops Austin Lovelace, the dimwitted yet imperious owner of the Pacific City *Courier* in *The Nothing Man.* Publisher Lovelace "frowned on what he termed the 'negative type' of story. He was fond of asserting that Pacific City was the 'cleanest community in America,' and he was very apt to suspect the credibility of reporters who produced evidence to the contrary. . . . He couldn't be kidded. However good you said he was, it wasn't ever quite so good as he *thought* he was."

The *Journal* contributed other details to *The Nothing Man.* "Colonel" Fred Kinne floats behind "Colonel" Dave Randall, the long-suffering city editor of the *Courier.* Poet-journalist Clinton Brown's happy-news column, "Around the Town With Clinton Brown," parodies Forest Warren's "People I Know," a sunny *Journal* digest of gossip, gassy verse, and bromides ("The grand essentials of happiness are something to do . . . something to love . . . and something to hope for. . . ."). Even the first "Sneering Slayer" murder, the death of Brown's wife, Ellen, in a fire, and the clue of an incriminating poem may rebound from a front-page story in the *Journal,* "Young Love Main Motif of Beulah, Bud at Boat Explosion Trial," that crisscrossed doomed passion, fiery homicide, and a love sonnet.

Thompson published his final signed article in the San Diego *Journal* on Friday, February 13, 1948, a cheerful summary of all the "lucky" events that transpired on that "unlucky" day. "Let's have no more nonsense about Friday the Thirteenth," he decreed shortly before John A. Kennedy blindsided him in the city room. "F. the T. is as shot with good luck as a goat in a junkyard. . . ."

•   •   •

Come September, Thompson was in Los Angeles interviewing for a position with the soon-to-be-launched Los Angeles *Mirror,* an afternoon tabloid publisher Norman Chandler envisioned as a breezier, working-class companion to his Los Angeles *Times.* The trip up seemed auspicious—riding on the train, Thompson told Alberta, he sat and conversed with novelist Raymond Chandler, who had recently moved to La Jolla—and he got the job. By October 1 he began commuting every workweek to Los Angeles. He rented a room in the Case Hotel on South Broadway, home to the Los Angeles Press Club, and then a suite in a boardinghouse a silent screen star named Mary MacLaren managed from her crumbling mansion in the Wilshire district. Thompson would be spectacularly fired after only 130 days on the *Mirror.* Yet however brief, his first installment in the City of the Angels proved one of the woolliest episodes of his life.

Managing editor J. E. "Ed" Murray engaged Thompson not as a general correspondent but as a rewrite man. Unlike the movie cliché "Get me rewrite!," where a glamorous roving reporter dictates his story verbatim to an idle lackey, the rewrite battery crafted publishable stories from often bewildering field notes and police bulletins amid a remorseless pressure cooker. As Thompson characterized rewrite for *The Nothing Man,* "There'll be a deadline every hour, and all hell will pop if you miss one. There's no time to work your stuff over. You have to hit it on the nose the first shot. And you can't let everything else slide while you're doing it. You'll have to keep answering your phones, two of them, taking down notes on other stories. You'll have a half-dozen stories going at the same time. . . ."

Thompson held down the last desk along rewrite row near the entrance to the stylish *Mirror* newsroom (colors coordinated by Mrs. Norman Chandler's own decorator), and earned $85 a week. By most accounts he proved incapable of managing the stress. "Whenever there was any pressure, Jim couldn't take it and got drunk," comments George Getze, a rewrite man who shared the San Diego commute. "Around the office he was pretty unreliable. If the paper called a big meeting at 5 a.m., that would be the morning Jim wouldn't show up. He couldn't stand this feeling of responsibility. He would vanish every time there was something special like that."

Thompson appeared not so much irresponsible as bored and unhappy, to Hollywood reporter Kendis Moss:

> Jim was a very good rewrite man, but he hated every minute of it. This was a new paper with a jazzy young press corps, but he wasn't romantic at all about the newspaper business. He had contempt for the whole thing. Jim was at a stage in his life when newspaper work was pretty miserable for him. Sometimes he'd be at his desk seemingly busy—madly typing away, but we knew he was working on his own books. He never wanted to take a story from the desk because he was always working on his own stuff. I don't remember ever seeing him excited about a story. Then he'd be drunk in the city room and they wouldn't dare give him a story. He'd just sit there with his headphones on, sort of sad and seedy in an out-of-fashion suit that had been worn too many times, looking very depressed. We never knew where Jim hid the bottle. But we knew it was there.

He erected even more of a wall about himself than he had at the *Journal.* When the staff broke for breakfast after the first deadline at 6 a.m., he remained at his desk. He drank his solitary lunch at the Liberty Bar. He fled the party the Chandlers threw after the paper held a dry run on October 1. Moss found Thompson "remote and hard to get to, very much a loner. Jim had as much talent as any of us, but he never joined in. He was never rude, but he could remove himself. His body was sitting there, but he wasn't. There was little two-way communication with Jim. He deliberately tuned out, but I thought he was observing everything very clearly. His books show this—he didn't miss anything."

Still, Thompson enjoyed playing the roué for his younger male colleagues. He shocked Getze one night when he injected himself with the elixir he still received in the mail from Dr. Max Jacobson. "Jim always acted so furtive. We were going out drinking with Steve Healy, whom he shared a room with for a while at the Case Hotel, and they left me out in the hall while they disappeared into their room. They came out completely changed. When I asked, what's up?, Jim said, 'Just some vitamin B shots,' and they both sort of snickered." And he startled Getze another afternoon, by the *Mirror* elevator:

I was getting into the elevator just as he was getting off. Jim was with this woman—a frowsy-looking thing, older, kind of battered and beat-up. She looked like an old whore, I'm afraid to say. He said, "I'd like you to meet my roommate." I must have stood there with my mouth open, because he winked at her and said, "Don't pay any attention to George. He's too young to understand."

Mary MacLaren, presumably the "frowsy-looking thing" in question, *was* Thompson's roommate—or, at least, she owned the tumble-down rooming house at 127 North Manhattan Place, where he resided, along with her brood of transients, dogs, cats, and pigeons, after he vacated the Case Hotel. A fashion model by the age of thirteen, and a Broadway chorus girl at fourteen, the ash-blond beauty came to Hollywood in 1916, starring in more than a dozen films for Universal Studios and the Famous Players–Lasky Corporation. She played the queen of France in Douglas Fairbanks's 1921 production of *The Three Musketeers,* and features with Wallace Reid and Lionel Barrymore soon followed. "My dressing room at Universal Studios was next door to Valentino's," MacLaren told an interviewer. "He used to come in and take me in his arms and hug me and kiss me. I really think that if it hadn't been for my mother I would have been the first Mrs. Valentino." She abandoned her movie career in 1924 to marry a Scottish-born colonel in the Indian army who took her to Bombay. But divorcing him less than a year later—because, she said, she could not tolerate his love of sport hunting—MacLaren opened her Los Angeles mansion to a string of increasingly disreputable boarders. One roomer was convicted of lewd vagrancy after the former actress testified that he had insisted on spanking her, to "see if I could become one of the family." Another, a self-proclaimed Roman Catholic bishop, used the house as a church and rescue mission after he "hypnotized" her into deeding it over to him. MacLaren eventually wed lodger Robert S. Coleman, a blind amputee veteran of World War I, in a tabloid-celebrated "marriage of mercy."

While Jim Thompson boarded with her, MacLaren was finishing a novel, *The Twisted Heart,* which she published in 1952. The wife of an army colonel who served in India rents out rooms after her husband dies. She finds herself drawn to a tenant, Dee Richards, who turns out to be homosexual. "My mind was centered on Dee as I went about my work that day," MacLaren wrote. "I realized how trying it might be to have as a lover a man who so attracted me, yet was unable to give me the normal satisfactions of love." She marries him anyway, musing on her wedding night: "Intoxicated as I was with the wonder and beauty of the universe, I was still painfully conscious of my problem with Dee."

Thompson helped Mary MacLaren edit *The Twisted Heart*—but probably little else. "At that time Jim was the kind of drunk who is not interested in women," *Mirror* writer Elaine St. Johns judges. "He was only interested in drinking."

St. Johns, the daughter of popular California novelist and Hearst journalist Adela Rodgers St. Johns, was as close to Thompson as anyone at the *Mirror.* "I was pretty green then, and Jim kind of was my mentor. He used to give me tips about how to handle a story." Although "Jim was shy with women," he lowered his guard after St. Johns rescued him from the Liberty Bar:

> Jim and I got to be buddies. He had a drinking problem, and I was a recovering alcoholic. Jim got loaded at the Liberty Bar, where my mother used to go to get my grandfather, Earl Rodgers, out of there. There was some sort of trouble, and the bartender called Sid Hughes, our assistant city editor. I was sent over to get Jim to come back to the paper. Sid then told me and Skip Joyce, another rewrite man, to take Jim down to the Case Hotel and put him to bed.
>
> We couldn't get Jim to go to sleep. He kept wanting another drink, thrashing around, getting pretty belligerent. I had broken my neck, so I was carrying some Nembutal capsules. Skip and I decided that we would let Jim have another drink if he would take a pill. Steve Healy came in to see how we were doing—and he was drunk too. Steve said that if we stuck a pin in the capsule the Nembutal would work faster. Well, Jim went out like a light, scaring the hell out of me. I went down to the Press Club to drink coffee. I kept sending someone up to the room to see if Jim was still breathing. For six hours I was sure I had killed him.
>
> Eventually I went home. But I called the Press Club every half-hour to check if Jim was alive. By this time I was beside myself—I couldn't sleep—the idea of me murdering Jim Thompson! So I

phoned his wife in San Diego, told her who I was, and what I had done. But she said, that's just fine, the pill ought to keep him quiet for a few hours. She seemed pretty used to the whole thing.

When I went to work the next morning, Jim still hadn't shown up. Skip and I conferred, and he said that he would take the blame for the murder.

Finally Jim showed up, around eleven. I walked right over to him and let go. I hit him as hard as I possibly could. Of course the whole city room was in hysterics. Fortunately, Jim thought it was very funny, and we became fast friends.

When a bartender would shut Jim off there could be a lot of trouble. But after that, whenever Sid sent me out to get him, he'd come like a lamb.

Thompson, by his own inventory, arrived sodden on the *Mirror's* opening day; he was "drunk on election day . . . drunk on every occasion when it was most important to be sober and at work." For a paper generous with bylines, he garnered only one—"Luers Link Up Million Weiners Daily, No Joke!" (January 11, 1949). After repeated warnings, managing editor Ed Murray sacked him in February, indicating sternly on Thompson's employee card: "Discharged for drinking on the job. Would not reemploy, unreliable."

Rumors about his dismissal circulated through the city room. "The story we all got," George Getze recounts, "was that the paper sent Jim down to the San Diego Zoo to interview their mynah bird. While he was on the train they telephoned his wife and told her Jim was fired, and not to come back."

• • •

Thompson's firing from the Los Angeles *Mirror* (February 11, 1949) synchronized with the official publication date of his next novel (February 16)—his justification, perhaps, for his conspicuous disgust around the rewrite desk. After seventeen years and eight radical revisions he clinched his quest for *The Unholy Grail* with a new agent, Ingrid Hallen, an eminent new publisher, Harper and Brothers, and a catchy new title, *Nothing More Than Murder.* Although the small-town movie theater plot was set by the time Thompson sent "The Dark Stair" to *Master Detective* in 1946, he overhauled his "thriller" during the vacant months between the *Journal* and the *Mirror* with a sweet boost from "Miracle Max." The crime novel—Thompson's first, at forty-two, the brink of middle age—bore the dedication, "To Max Jacobson, M.D., New York."

On the surface *Nothing More Than Murder* is a classic doomed love triangle/insurance scam shocker from the tradition of James M. Cain: in the

Jim Thompson with his cat, Deadline, on the
jacket of Nothing More Than Murder

Midwestern town of Stoneville (population 7,500) a mismatched husband
and wife and their hired hand play out a game of fatal attraction, the perfect murder, and a double indemnity policy. But Thompson transposed
more than he borrowed from *The Postman Always Rings Twice* and *Double
Indemnity,* turning Cain inside out with a run of dazzling sexual inversions.

In *Nothing More Than Murder* it's the husband, Barclay Movie House operator Joe Wilmot, who tumbles into a destructive coupling with the household employee, business college student Carol Farmer. The inconvenient
spouse, blue-blooded Elizabeth Barclay Wilmot, not only knows about the
illicit duo between her sheets; she's also been subtly encouraging them.
She emerges as both the principal architect of an ingenious insurance
dodge—when another woman's body is substituted for her's, Elizabeth will
appear to have died in a fire ignited from a faulty movie projector cord and
sixteen reels of explosive film—and the principal beneficiary, as Joe and
Carol agree to pay all of the $25,000 to her. Next to such carnal avatars
as Frank Chambers (*Postman*) and Walter Huff (*Double Indemnity*), Joe
amounts to a tin icon, an emasculated, bungling con man whose wife
"treats [him] like a dog," and who mistakes his self-pity for lust. And his

femme fatale? Carol seems anything but, as Thompson skews Cain's erotic
tragedy into farce:

> . . . She looked like hell. She looked like a sack of bran that
> couldn't decide which way it was going to fall.
> And then the curtain rose or however you want to put it, and
> everything was changed.
> And what I began to think about wasn't laughing or crying.
> That tiny bit of cockeyedness gave her a cute look, and the
> way she she toed in sort of spread her buttocks and made a little
> valley under her skirt, and—it don't—doesn't—make sense but
> there was something about it that made me think of the Twenty-
> Third Psalm.
> I thought she looked awkward and top-heavy, and, hell, I could
> see now that she didn't at all. Her breasts weren't too big. Jesus,
> her breasts!
> She looked cute-mad and funny-sweet. She looked like she'd
> started somewhere and had been mussed up along the way.
> She was a honey. She was sugar and spice. She was a bitch.
> I said, "Come here Carol," and she came there.
> And then I was kissing her like I'd been waiting all my life to do
> just that, and she was the same way with me.
> I don't know how long it was before I looked up and saw Eliza-
> beth in the doorway.

A murderous hero concealed behind a torrent of glib prattle and his
preposterous Lorelei, Joe Wilmot and Carol Farmer established the para-
digm for Thompson's novels to follow. Carol is a projection of Joe's own
fears and self-doubts. "I knew how she felt," he posits, "because I felt the
same way. I knew what it meant to be nothing and to want to be something." Joe's history as an orphan shunted from foster homes to reform
school to prison has left him insecure about his intelligence, his social
standing, even his grammar. The genial, back-slapping mask he wears on
his rounds among the movie distributors of Wheat City camouflages his
petrified soul. "All of a sudden it came over me why I'd had so many blue
spells lately," he whimpers. "It was because I felt like I didn't amount to
much anymore. It was because I didn't feel I was as good as other people—
that I shouldn't put myself with people who wouldn't do what I was doing."
Joe lists like a zombie in the wake of the deadly fire, eerily detaching
his feelings from his words and actions: "I nodded. Something seemed to
nod my head. And when I spoke it was as though someone were whispering
the words to me." Numbed by guilt and suspicion ("we weren't the same

people any more"), his never-solid identity splinters into psychosis. *"They can't hang me,"* he blurts at the end. *"I'm already dead. I've been dead a long time."*

Joe and Elizabeth do not so much have a marriage as a business merger. He signed on with her because she needed help with her family movie house. Joe ruthlessly built the Barclay into "the most modern, most completely equipped small-city house in the state, and there's just one guy responsible. Me." Yet the knowledge that the enterprise is not really his gnaws like a wolf under his coat:

> I was about to tell him off in a nice way when the manager came out. . . .
>
> "Getting along all right?" he said. "Everything going to suit you Mr. Barclay?"
>
> I could feel myself turning red. "My name's not Barclay," I said.
>
> "Oh," he said stepping back a little, "I thought you were from Barclay Operating Company at—"
>
> "I'm Joe Wilmot," I said. "I've operated Barclay for the past ten years. The property's in my wife's name. Okay?"

"Property," or the Barclay, is their only bond, a sly parody of what Marx called commodity fetishism. But Thompson allows the reader to discern what Joe's self-denying chatter cannot—that it is his own depression and negativity that compel him to thwart Elizabeth's efforts to draw them closer. He resists her appeals for sex. He seems to gloat over the memory of her miscarriage. He sabotages her adoption of a child. The murder of an unsuspecting old woman in a booby-trapped inferno, ironically, embodies Joe's yearnings for domestic bliss. "I still wasn't hot for the killing," he puns, "but if that was the only way to lead a happy, decent, life, why. . . ."

As the insurance scam unravels, *Nothing More Than Murder* juggles a plot as intricate and suspenseful as any that might be found in an Agatha Christie mystery. But "plot" here—as for all Thompson's subsequent first-person-narrator crime novels—remains inseparable from character and voice. The scheme is doomed from the start not because of any inherent flaw, but because of Joe's self-fulfilling bad attitude. Unable to imagine that he might succeed, he fails. The glitches, snags, and leakage in the conspiracy match the hesitations, the false notes, and the accidental admissions in his prose. "I'd stepped into one again," Joe splutters, signaling another slip-up in the plan—and in his story. Doubting himself, he cannot believe that Carol really loves him until after she kills herself. The blackmailers who close in on him, like film distributor Hap Chance, or real estate agent Andy Taylor, or union boss Mike Blair, crawl out from under the rock of Joe's own

revengeful disposition as a businessman. The insurance investigator Appel-
ton, like Wilmot, only wishes to save his company money. The setting is
even insistently filtered through his character. After Elizabeth's funeral, the
realistic landscape of the crime novel folds into a pasteboard hell out of
Doré or Grosz, allegorical and surreal:

> I guess almost the entire county was at the cemetery . . . It
> gave you an awfully funny feeling. It made you feel almost like it
> was Judgement Day; like they'd all been pulled up out of every-
> where for the trumpet's blast before they could move. It was kind
> of scary.
>
> I remember one woman in particular. She was standing up in a
> wagon box with a big fat squawling baby in each arm. They looked
> damned near as big as she was; and she'd started to feed them, I
> guess, because she had her blouse open and what babies go for
> was hanging out on each side. It wasn't hanging right, though, and
> the kids were as mad as all hell, twisting and screaming and grab-
> bing at it, and trying to raise their heads up. But she stood there
> with her head bowed down like everyone else.

Thompson constructed a tightly wound, self-reflexive fiction that spun
out spoofs of Gertrude Stein and a familiar "big gawky guy named Thomas
or Thompson" at the Stoneville Literary Club. *Nothing More Than Murder*
contains a detective figure in the form of investigator Appleton, but the
novel is neither a whodunit? in the style of Christie nor a will-they-get-
away-with-it? in the style of Cain. The stranger riddle that hounds Joe
Wilmot might best be formulated as, Who done what? Ignorant of his own
nature, he knows little about the motivations of others; but even as the
quintessential bumbling criminal, he is more unwitting than he and his
reader realize. In another kind of crime novel reversal, only on the last page
of *Nothing More Than Murder* will Joe discover—like the audience of a
British mystery—the truth about his crime. Carol never substituted another victim for Elizabeth. His wife has been brutally murdered. And he is
still in love with her. "Jesus Christ!" he laughs to Appleton, "I gave you all
the cards myself."

"Nothing" is the key that turns the lock of the title. Joe and Carol are
nothing. Their murder accomplishes nothing. *"Wouldn't that be hell?"* he
asks himself. *"Wouldn't it be just sweet hell to mix yourself in a murder and
then find out it hadn't got you anything?"*

With *Nothing More Than Murder* Thompson finally realized his ambition
of a popular, personal, and subversive fiction. The character of Joe Wilmot

allowed him to dramatize the essential cruxes of his life—a dramatization safely distanced by the slippery formulas of the crime novel. The shame, the self-pity, and the resignation in the face of "flukish Fate" and failure that seems a soft spot in his autobiographies *Bad Boy* and *Roughneck* crystallized into the whine of a sniveling murderer. The veil that, as his sisters, wife, and friends have remarked, Thompson cast over his most private feelings, the split between the hardness of his work and gentleness of his manner that his Alpha Gamma Rho buddies at the University of Nebraska were the first to question, the avenging anger that he pitched at his family in *Now and on Earth* and *Heed the Thunder,* the remorse, the guilt, the intensifying "tendency toward violence" that he exposed in "An Alcoholic Looks at Himself," and the melancholy remoteness and self-estrangement that scared Kendis Moss at the Los Angeles *Mirror,* all hardened into the mask of a disintegrating psychopath. Even the need to pull a "Chinchilla" out of his hat that he once identified as symptomatic of his alcoholic aggrandizement narrowed into the perfect murder. Refracting his personality and personal experiences, such as his management of the Big Springs Theater back in 1932, through the rituals of crime fiction, Thompson turned weaknesses to strengths, his chills and fevers to savage art. It was a practice that, after a few more false moves, he would follow for all his best novels.

"Jim was someone who worked through his problems in his writing," advises Arnold Hano, his editor at Lion Books. "The fact is that so many of the same things tend to recur in his novels, sometimes in the same words, certainly in some of the same images. And the women seem to be very much the same—all those women in the books who are to some degree like Alberta, and who are abused or killed. Whatever his problems were, Jim worked them out in his novels."

Thompson's correspondence with Joan Kahn, legendary editor of the Harper Novels of Crime and Suspense, provides some additional background to *Nothing More Than Murder.* When Kahn queried the blaze that consumes Elizabeth Wilmot, he responded with a grisly anecdote from his criminal research in Oklahoma:

> . . . I'm not an expert on bodies and fires, either, but I probably do have a little more than average knowledge on the subject. For years I wrote for every major magazine in the "true crime" field; I worked closely with peace officers and police departments in three states, and had the inside track with the Oklahoma State Bureau of Corrections. I wrote up one case, which I could never sell because it was "too gruesome," in which a Southeastern Oklahoma family of five was nailed inside a log cabin and burned alive. There was nothing left of them but

teeth, ashes and a few remnants of bone—the crime bureau op-
eratives were able to get it all in a few quart pails—but it was
possible to establish identification. Exactly how I don't know, of
course. Only a trained criminologist would.

And after Kahn wondered whether his treatment of the movie industry
might subject Harper to libel action, Thompson fired back a volley of facts
and a litany of corruption:

> . . . The people, places and plot of Nothing More Than
> Murder are entirely my own creations and have never existed
> outside of my imagination. The background of the book, of
> course, is a straight from the record portrayal of the motion pic-
> ture industry. I don't know how many times the film companies
> have been found guilty of acting in restraint through block-
> booking, preference-booking, chain-exhibitor tie-ups and similar
> practices and devices. Only a few weeks ago Interstate The-
> aters, the big southwestern chain, was found guilty of monopo-
> listic practices; and I don't think there's been a single year in the
> last twenty that the chains haven't found themselves on the los-
> ing end of a lawsuit—the exchanges with them. (For example:
> Paramount Pictures was forced to sever connections with Pub-
> lix Theatres, Fox with Fox West Coast Theatres, etc.)
> The only place I may have strayed from the record was in
> dealing with the projectionists' union. That—since I believe that
> any union is better than none at all—I put in a much more favor-
> able light than it is entitled to. As you doubtless know, this is the
> Bioff-Browne outfit; one could safely impute to it every crime on
> the calendar. I've merely implied that the lads may be a little too
> high-spirited and high-handed. . . .
> One final word of reassurance: I've written several million
> words for newspapers and magazines in which an overstate-
> ment or error would bring immediate and expensive retalia-
> tion—and I've yet to be involved in a libel suit.

The novel drew no lawsuits, only his most illustrious notices to date.
The *Saturday Review* stuttered, "Grim—but very good!" And the *New Republic:* "For those sure they can take it, I recommend the grimmest tale in
several seasons." Reprinted in paperback, *Nothing More Than Murder* would
sell 750,000 copies over the next decade.

• • •

Thompson insisted "I was glad I was fired," and that he "esteemed" his pink slip from the *Mirror* more than a letter from his agent announcing the sale of the French and Australian rights to *Nothing More Than Murder.* "Sooner or later an alcoholic is faced with the question of *not* whether to go on or give up drinking but whether to live or die," he avowed in "An Alcoholic Looks at Himself." "I have decided to live. The letter of dismissal has helped me to make this decision."

Back in San Diego, Thompson for once wasted no time. He immediately embarked on a new crime novel, *Recoil,* which intertwined "Airplane Red" Brown, his Fort Worth bank-robber roommate from the late 1920s, with "Doctor" Otto Lucy, the "inside track to the Oklahoma State Board of Corrections" featured in his letter to Joan Kahn. But come October, he was once again boarding the Los Angeles train—to teach creative writing at the University of Southern California. Adela Rodgers St. Johns, on the strength of *Nothing More Than Murder* and a recommendation from her daughter Elaine, asked him to take over her fiction seminar when she was hospitalized with a heart ailment. For three months Professor Thompson joined an elite USC writing faculty that included Christopher Isherwood and Aldous Huxley.

"He was the kind of teacher that you called Jim," quips Mel Shestack, a USC student who would go on to edit *True* magazine and an encyclopedia of country music. "This was a formal age, remember—Jim always wore a tie to class, one of those short ties from the 1930s, and a gangster suit—but he was very casual and low-key. He was nice in a gruff sort of way, and I just loved him. At the same time I was taking a course from Isherwood, and later I studied with Huxley, but Jim was the best for me. Maybe I found him so marvelous because I was interested in *Black Mask,* the pulps, all the things he knew so much about."

Thompson conducted his classes much as Lowry C. Wimberly led the Sunday-evening workshops at the University of Nebraska. "St. Johns talked about herself and the background to her stories, but Jim read our stories aloud," Shestack reviews. "He read them paragraph by paragraph in his courtly, slight Southern accent. He was big on getting a lot of stuff into a paragraph. He was Hemingwayesque in the sense of everything being cold, hard, and clean—tight writing. And he emphasized art through dialogue. But he wanted us to pack as much into our paragraphs as possible, without going into unnecessary description. 'You don't have to describe the furniture,' he'd say. Jim was against 'over-furnished rooms'—a phrase he picked up from Willa Cather."

He assigned an eclectic reading list. Some of his choices were predictable, a roster of the influences on his 1940s novels. "Jim had us study *A Farewell to Arms* and *Double Indemnity,*" as Shestack says, running down the syllabus, "along with Cather's story 'Coming, Aphrodite,' about a lonely

Jim Thompson–type character who lives in Greenwich Village, and her essay, 'The Novel Demeuble.' "* His other selections were more adventurous—Robinson Jeffers's poetry; William Carlos Williams's poems, short stories, and *In the American Grain*—and, in one instance, astounding:

> All semester Jim was carrying around this heavily marked-up copy of a novel, *Stranger in Town,* by Howard Hunt, which he made us read at the end. It's a pretty good book about a major who returns to New York after the war. Jim talked a lot about the different kinds of speech in the novel—how you could change the way a character is perceived by changing the way he talked.

E. Howard Hunt was not yet the CIA spook or Watergate burglar, but a Guggenheim Fellow and a novelist both mainstream (*East of Farewell, Limit of Darkness*) and crime (*Maelstrom*). Apart from Hunt's fondness for italics, *Stranger in Town* (1947) produced no specific impact on Thompson's novels.

But of Thompson's insistence on poetry in a fiction writing class, Shestack comments, "Jim kept saying that a writer of prose has to read poetry to keep his ear tuned. He talked a lot about writing in the vernacular as opposed to the highfalutin and literary. One of his assignments was for each of us to take a passage from an established author and rewrite it in the vernacular, the language of real people. Pulp was poetry for Jim. William Carlos Williams—whom I'd never heard of then—expressed the vernacular for him, but also was kind of experimental, kind of avant-garde. Jim said that we shouldn't be afraid to experiment with our stories."

When late in the semester Shestack turned in a "little piece about hoboes on a train, something I knew nothing about," Thompson asked if he had heard of Haywire Mac. Soon Professor "Slim" and his pupil were driving down to San Pedro for a meeting with Harry McClintock:

> Jim said that Mac was a guy I'd like to know. I had a 1938 Chevy and we went down in that. He told me that Haywire Mac had been writing and recording hobo songs long before Jimmie Rodgers. He sang "Hallelujah I'm a Bum" and "The Big Rock Candy Mountain" for me. Many years later I would interview Haywire Mac and Hank Williams and write about country music, but back then I didn't

---

* "The Novel Demeuble" (1922) was Cather's polemic against a realism that "asserts itself in the cataloguing of a great number of material objects." Believing that "the novel, for a long time has been over-furnished," she touted "the inexplicable presence of the thing not named. . . . Whatever is felt on the page without being specifically named there— that, one might say is created." Cather urged writers "to present their scene by suggestion rather than enumeration." Shrewd counsel to a crime novelist like Thompson.

know any of this. Jim told me about the oil fields and the Wobblies, and how Mac had been a tramp, a bum, and a private detective. He said Mac had saved his life in Texas.

At one point he had me stop and pick up Bill Miller, who was one-half of a San Diego mystery-writing team by the name of "Wade Miller." We barbecued back of Mac's house, and everyone but me did a lot of drinking that day. There was a great deal of affection between Mac and Jim. I used to have a photograph taken of Jim, Bill Miller, Haywire Mac, and myself, with our arms around each other, all of us decked out in Hawaiian shirts.

Bob Wade, the other half of "Wade Miller," had recently interviewed Thompson for his local KGB radio program, *San Diego Scrapbook*. "Bill and I were younger than Jim, less sophisticated, and a lot less cynical," Wade explains. "We were admirers of *Nothing More Than Murder*. I asked him on the air if he would have any advice for young writers. 'Take up plumbing' was all he'd say."

On his free nights in Los Angeles, Thompson hung out at Ciro's, the Hollywood nightclub on Sunset Boulevard where Mel Shestack parked cars—not for the music or the movie stars, but for the bouncers. "He liked the tough old birds who watched the door and checked people's signatures at Ciro's. Jim had a real *film noir* attitude."

Working weekends out of his small front bedroom on Nye Street, Thompson completed *Recoil* early in 1950. For his second crime novel he essentially rewrote his first but swapped the horror, loathing, and greasy genre play of *Nothing More Than Murder* for the resolutions of a conventional thriller.

The cast resurrected some familiar spirits from Thompson's 1920s and 1930s. "Doctor" Roland Luther sponsors the parole of a bank robber, Pat "Airplane Red" Cosgrove, who has written him from the Sandstone State Reformatory. A psychologist turned political lobbyist, Luther presides over a shadowy Capital City junta that includes state senators and lawyers, the Highway Commission, and the National Phalanx, a right-wing pressure group.

Endowed with his model Otto Lucy's shifty bug eyes, Luther lodges an elusive, two-faced presence. "It settled down to who he really was," Cosgrove wonders, "the threatening, cold-eyed man who had bullied [Senator] Burkman, or the man who had been angry over the pollution of a river and ashamed of being part of the general pattern of pollution."

Orbiting the dubious doctor is a pair of mysterious women. The seductive Lila Luther slides "in . . . [and] out of character." Madeline Flournoy—though idealized by Pat Cosgrove—also appears to possess the same Janus face as Luther:

. . . The bedroom door was still open, as I had left it, and I could see her almost as plainly as though I had been in the room with her. And what I saw sent a cold chill of shock along my spine. . . .

Always before, even when she was serious, she'd appeared gay, good-humored, light-hearted. I'd never seen her any other way. *She'd never let me see her any other way.* And now not a vestige of that gaiety and good humor remained. I could hardly believe it was the same girl, the same woman—this woman whose face was a hideous and sinister mask of hatred.

Lila and Madeline both make plays for Pat.

Cosgrove initially seems a younger Joe Wilmot—and an embryonic psychopath. Like Joe, he is an orphan with a cloudy criminal past. He hides behind a similarly bland false front, "this bleached mask that does duty as a face." Pat too has a taste for pain and violence:

. . . I slid out of my coat and shirt and undershirt. . . .

"You were looking at these welts, sir?" I said. "Why they were nothing, relatively speaking. A little annoying, perhaps, when you get them full of gnats and salt sweat and rock dust; but nothing compared to those ribs. You should have seen them popping out through the flesh like splinters bursting through tree bark. You should have seen this arm the day a friend tried to chop it off me. That's right, sir. A friend. He got three days in the hole and I got three weeks in the hospital."

. . . I chopped him down and in, with the edge of my hands, getting both kidneys at once. His arms came down and I cuffed him, spinning him around. I jerked his tie, as tight as I could get it, took a turn around his neck with each end, and knotted it in the back.

I let him drop to the floor and watched him thrash about, scratching and clawing at his throat.

Cosgrove shares Wilmot's bewilderment at his own motives and behavior. The jug heist that originally committed him to Sandstone sneaked up on him like the ambush of some alien force—"all I'd intended when I entered the bank was to draw a dollar out of my savings account." And Pat is a bungler. His struggle to ditch a corpse he's stumbled upon tumbles into slapstick, *Grand Guignol* style:

I lifted Eggleston's body. I clawed the [elevator] door open with one hand, and staggered outside. Only seconds, now. Only a few seconds to get the body into the car and get away. The steps on the stairs were rushing downward. They'd passed the second floor. Any moment the door would fly open, and—

I ran toward the entrance. Only a few feet to go. Out of the lobby and across the walk and into the car. Only a few feet and— and I couldn't make them. I couldn't go back and I couldn't go forward. Someone had stepped into the entrance.

A blue-uniformed cop. . . .

He had been looking at something down the street as he stepped into the entrance, and his head was still turned now. I stopped dead in my tracks, paralyzed for the moment with shock and fear. Then, as his head started to turn toward me, I acted. I did the only thing there was to do.

I ran forward and hurled the body at him.

It struck him high in the chest, obstructing his vision—I hoped—and bowling him over backwards. He yelled and grappled with it blindly, and I darted around to one side and sprang for the car.

For *Recoil* Thompson once again framed an interior riddle whose solution is beyond the ken of his narrating hero: What is Pat Cosgrove's role in Dr. Luther's secret plot? As Pat confronts the irreconcilable evidence and checkered characters of his story, he is forced to become a kind of private investigator into his own life. "I was in a trap," he agonizes, "and I couldn't go out by the door. That led back to Sandstone. I had to stay in until I found my own exit." Suspicious of everyone—even the stalwart Commissioner of Corrections Myrtle Briscoe—Cosgrove appears destined for the same psychic hell that swallowed Joe Wilmot:

> I didn't know anything. All I had was guesses. Guesses which, when you probed them and tried to follow them, became ridiculous. . . . I had the impression of being drawn into a game while a flood tide rose around my neck.

In the end Thompson wrenched *Recoil* back from the trapdoor void of *Nothing More Than Murder*. Pat Cosgrove is smarter than Joe Wilmot— Thompson, not very convincingly, outfits him with a photographic memory and a prison library that all but reproduces his own childhood in Uncle Bob's Burwell study ("Shakespeare, Dickens, Swift, Twain . . ."). Pat cleaves to a core of innocence that, despite his quirks and chinks, shields him from the "general pattern of pollution" in Capital City. He stands apart from the corruption that imbues Wilmot's every atom, from his dreams to his language.

Thompson steered the volatile contradictions of *Recoil* to a Hollywood finish, as though hoping for a movie deal. Through the agency of Myrtle Briscoe and the ultimately true-blue Madeline Flournoy, the external dark forces—Dr. Luther, Senator Burkman, the National Phalanx—are routed in the suspenseful exposure of another double-indemnity insurance scam. Pat marries Madeline and takes a job with the Department of Corrections.

Recoil found no buyers among the hardcover publishers that Ingrid Hallen, Thompson's agent, circulated with the manuscript. The novel would appear only after he established himself with Lion Books, in 1953.

The failure of *Recoil* left Thompson with the superstition that the books he wrote at home were "jinxed." So in the spring of 1950 he made plans for a trip to New York. But before departing San Diego, he penned the words to his only known song, "When I Go Home and You're Not There," a collaboration with Old Town drinking buddy Maurice Devin. Over Devin's meditative torch-and-twang, Thompson cast his strange, passive-aggressive lyric:

> When I go home and you're not there
> Oh! Gosh how much I care
> What shouldn't happen to a collie
> Happens to me oh golly
> Are you lost or strayed
> In mischief or mislaid
> It feels like when you tumble on a big bumble bee
>
> If tears were bombs
> I'd have enough to blow this whole old world afar
> I'm sorry for those names I call
> Though that's just what you are
> Most of the time why I'm no saint
> But never think I ain't when I'm alone
> When I go home and you are not there

• • •

Thompson didn't travel to New York City in the spring of 1950 for a show-down with his agent over *Recoil;* nor did he land with the seeds of a new novel he would cultivate in a squalid downtown hotel. He followed the irresistible magnetic lure of his sisters, who had migrated cross-country to Queens after Maxine's husband, USMC Warrant Officer Joseph Kouba, was transferred to the Brooklyn Navy Yard. And he came in hot pursuit of an editorial position with *SAGA,* "The Magazine of True Adventure" Macfadden Publications announced as a replacement for *Master Detective.* By late June, Thompson joined Freddie and Maxine at the Elizabeth and Gregory apartment complex in Astoria, a few blocks from the East River. Alberta and the children remained back in San Diego, awaiting his word.

"Although my dad was always there for us," his daughter Sharon cautions, "it seemed like whenever there was a big tragedy he wasn't there. My brother was badly burned—one of the neighbor kids picked a rag out of a bonfire and twirled it around on a stick; it flew off and stuck around Mike's neck. And he was in New York for that. Or we had a dog named Sandy that Daddy dearly loved, and he bit somebody, and the neighbors got up a petition to kill him. That was also while my Dad was in New York. Every time something really bad happened he was gone."

SAGA emerged from the back pages of *Master Detective* during the summer of 1950. Macfadden Publications ventured to supplement the standard crime fare with "thrill stories" it termed "sagas" in the expectation of thoroughly transforming the magazine by fall:

> Beginning next September issue, *SAGA* will be the new title of this magazine. Quite a step—there being not even a semblance of resemblance between the old and the new.
>
> As the old Scandinavian sagas of long ago told of the heroic deeds of brave men, so in this entirely new magazine which *Master Detective* will be, we are going to give you their modern counterparts—the thrilling adventures men have today, in all fields of human activity, and in wide variety—all types of stories men find exciting. . . .
>
> Our present plan is to present two or three of these new type stories in June, three in July, four in August and then in the September issue have an all-out 100 percent *SAGA* magazine.

After the conservative true crime readership protested, Macfadden decided to continue *Master Detective* and pitched *SAGA* to an independent market. As a "men's adventure magazine" *SAGA* would be distinguished from the more familiar "men's magazines," such as *Playboy,* which flourished later in the 1950s. Shunning nude pictorials and titillating sexual fantasy, *SAGA* operated in a strictly womanless universe. Paeans to athletes, soldiers, cops, fire fighters, hunters, Hollywood stunt men, self-made millionaires, Old West legends, celebrity mobsters, and other super-males proclaimed a strident cult of masculinity: "We think you will like personal sagas of real people, engaged in man's adventure with life."

SAGA debuted on schedule under the editorship of David Dressler. A past executive director of the New York State Division of Parole, an academic sociologist, and the author of *Parole Chief* and *Probation and Parole,* Dressler hired Thompson shortly after Labor Day as an assistant editor earning $85 a week. "Jim came in with Dave," Margaret Joyce, another assistant editor, recalls. "Everybody was surprised that these two established writers would have anything to do with *SAGA.*" Soon Thompson's letters home to Alberta bore warm allusions to Dressler and intimations of fellowship both inside and out of the Macfadden offices on East 42nd Street:

> . . . Things go satisfactorily on the job. Like Dave Dressler very much, and he seems to like me and appreciate my work more every day. We went to lunch together yesterday and kicked around the idea for a motion-picture story treatment—he sold his last one for $35,000. When Sam Goldwyn comes to town, the three of us are due to get together to talk story. . . .

Dressler promoted Thompson to associate editor in May 1951, and then to managing editor in July. "Jim was a solid managing editor," as Joyce portrays him. "He was very pleasant to work with, and extremely good at what he was doing. He had a sharp sense of humor—very witty. He had high standards for his own writing, and for all of us. He worked hard, and he expected those around him, the assistant editors and the copy editors, to work hard. But Jim was fair. All the employees liked him."

Thompson discovered that he could augment his *SAGA* salary with articles at upward of $75 or $100 a shot, depending on length. Beginning with the November 1950 issue he published six signed Jim Thompson features, two stories under the pen name "Dillon Roberts," a transposition of his Party alias, and at least three substantial anonymous items, including "An Alcoholic Looks at Himself" (see concluding Notes and Sources for titles and dates). But this scarcely hints at his total contribution—or his hack work—over the next eleven months. Thompson subsequently indicated that he ghosted nearly all of the "filler" departments in the magazine, from "*SAGA*'s Bargain Counter" to the "You Said It!" letters-to-the-editor column.

His output at *SAGA* ranged from professional to deadly. Some pieces, such as "He Supplies Santa Claus," his profile of toy magnate A. C. Gilbert, merely punch the clock. But it's painful to watch a die-hard sports debunker like Thompson toot a lumbering hurray for Jim Thorpe and the Indian Industrial Institute of Carlisle, Pennsylvania, football team ("Those Amazing Gridiron Indians"); and it's grievous to find the onetime Communist parroting the rankest saws of cold war jingoism ("A G.I. Returns from Korea" and "Who Is This Man Eisenhower?").

His stronger features predictably chewed on the same meat as his books. "Prowlers in the Pear Trees" and "Death Missed a Bet," in fact, would reappear as chapters of, respectively, *Bad Boy* and *Roughneck*. "Two Lives of John Stink," about an Osage Indian who was mistakenly buried alive, would return in *Cropper's Cabin* (1952). "Oil Sleuths" provides a knowing commentary on the oil fields. And "This Could Be Gold, Lady," a first-person chronicle of a gold-buying con man, Thompson would quickly put to use for a short story, "Blood from a Turnip," published by *Collier's* in 1952, and for his next novel, *The Golden Gizmo*.

"An Alcoholic Looks at Himself" marked his boldest gesture at *SAGA*— at once idiosyncratic and insurgent. With this printed rendering of an A.A. qualification, Thompson not only confronts his alcoholism, he also manages to undermine the virile code of the magazine in which his essay appeared with a harrowing study of human frailty, suffering, and defeat. Although chest thumping and bathos occasionally enervate his confession, Thompson dispatches a more accurate probing of his professional and family life than he would brook in his autobiographies.

He concluded his alcoholic self-portrait with an affirmation of hard-won sobriety. But this, alas, was a vain—or short-lived—dream. As his sister Maxine recalled, Thompson needed to be sobered up for his article on the returning Korean War veteran that graced the very same issue of *SAGA:*

> I remember so well when Jimmie had a drinking spell and he had an appointment with a young soldier in Washington. We didn't think it was a good time to take him, but he said, "Just get me to Dr. Max, and I'll be okay." Well, Dr. Jacobson gave him a shot—and it must have really been something, because Jimmie's face was just florid, fiery red and flushed. But he was sober. We drove him down to Washington, he kept his appointment, and he wrote what he had to write.

Thompson reclaimed his traditional politics during his final months at *SAGA*. Over the summer of 1951 the Macfadden employees attempted to organize a union. "Dave Dressler, while not openly in support of these activities, was known to be in favor of the union," reports Margaret Joyce. "As a result, he got on the bad side of management." When Dressler was fired in August, Thompson immediately tendered his resignation. "Jim was a strong backer of union activities," Joyce continues. "He had strong convictions about Dave being fired, the union, and the way management was treating everybody."

As one of his last editorial edicts, Thompson spurned a submission from his old Social Forum School comrade Louis L'Amour. "Did you really think you could put this stuff past *me*?"—Gordon Friesen quotes him as scribbling on the rejection slip. The story, "How Tough Can You Get?," ran anyway in the October issue, a month after Thompson's name disappeared from the masthead.

• • •

Thompson had sent for Alberta and the children the previous October. He leased another apartment in the Elizabeth and Gregory complex, at 20-61 18th Street, around the corner from Maxine and Freddie. The tidy, three-floor postwar brick building bordered Astoria Park, the site of an expansive WPA-era pool and picnic ground, in the shadow of the Triborough Bridge. The view from the bedroom window looked out over the churning waters of Hell Gate.

During the weeks following his departure from *SAGA* he ground out *The Golden Gizmo*. Thompson's dark comedy about the mishaps of a gold buyer, Toddmore "Toddy" Kent, actually sprang from two articles in the true adventure magazine: his own "This Could Be Gold, Lady" and a droll entry by David Dressler about a singing Airedale, "See What Nature Hath Wrought!" For *The Golden Gizmo* Thompson cut a classic opening sentence around a more gifted and menacing Doberman—"It was almost quitting time when Toddy met the man with no chin and the talking dog." But the novel continued his retreat into the consolations of genre.

Toddy Kent is a seasoned grifter with the intrinsic Thompson pedigree. A runaway from a broken home, he "half-killed his step-father with a two-by-four." Former bellboy, hobo, and Reno gambling house hustler, Kent "moved into the con games as naturally as a blonde moving into a mink coat. . . . Since he shunned working with others, he was confined to playing the 'small con'—the hype and the smack and the tat." On the run from the Chicago police, he remains married to the "vicious, selfish, totally irresponsible, physically unattractive" Elaine, for reasons "that cannot be put into words." Driven by his luck, his "gizmo," Kent treads suburban Los Angeles shaking down housewives.

The conceit of the "golden gizmo" elegantly literalized all Thompson's invocations of "flukish Fate":

> Todd Kent (the *more* was phony) had been born with a gizmo. That—the GI term for the unidentifiable—was the way he had come to think of something that changed in value from day to day, that was too whimsical in its influence to be bracketed as a gift, talent, aptitude or trait.
>
> For most of the thirty years of his life, the gizmo had pushed him into the smelly caverns where the easy money lay. All his life—and always without warning—it had hustled him out through soul-skinning, nerve-searing exits.

The gizmo shifts into overdrive the afternoon Kent "accidently" pockets a solid-gold watch from the house of the chinless man. Suddenly ensnarled in a Gordian knot of schemes and counterschemes—involving Nazi collaborators, local racketeers, a crooked bail bondsman, the Treasury Department, his wife, and his pawnbroker—he must penetrate this maze of his own unlucky trespass to save his life.

Thompson encircled Kent with his proven props and stratagems: an outwardly sympathetic, glad-handing confederate who is exposed as a snaky villain (Milt Vonderheim, curator of the Los Angeles Jewel & Watch Company and Kent's boss), a duo of contrasting women (Kent's "clowning" psychotic wife and the enigmatic yet faithful Dolores), a faked murder (for much of the novel Kent believes he may have killed Elaine), and a prole profession from his past. Always fascinated by work, Thompson dug as deeply into the gold trade here as he had into the film industry for *Nothing More Than Murder*.

As Kent chases his "stubborn" gizmo through the insidiously overlapping cabals, *The Golden Gizmo* flaunts a farrago of absurdist flourishes. Perrito, the talking Doberman, croaks a chorus of "Nearer My God to Thee" at a fatuous Salvation Army prayer service out of Thompson's 1936 jeremiad "A Night with Sally." Fleeing Perrito, Kent wanders onto the stage of a burlesque house, where he hot-dogs with the house comic. And when the resourceful bail bondsman, nicknamed "Airedale" (after the dog in Dressler's *SAGA* story), arranges for a paid ringer to impersonate Elaine for a short jail sentence, she turns out to be a junkie in need of daily deliveries of heroin.

But for *The Golden Gizmo* Thompson opted not to stage his purblind hero from within, his first experiment with omniscient narration since he turned to crime fiction. While he would shortly learn how to cast prickly, obsessive novels in the third person, here the manic action checks any intimate psychological engagement with Kent. For a story-driven machine the intrigue often appears forced and confusing; the reader, no less than Kent, falters amid the breakneck convolutions and revelations. *The Golden Gizmo* shadows Toddy Kent's plunge into nightmare from a sheltered perch, and then abruptly rescues him. A tacked-on happy ending, the ultimate genre nod, only belies his conflicts and his pain.

• • •

Thompson must have suspected his own gizmo when his literary agent, Ingrid Hallen, returned the manuscript of *The Golden Gizmo* to him, no sale. Desperate for cash—his apartment in Astoria rented at more than three times the price of the San Diego house—he allowed himself to be recruited by the *Police Gazette* as a managing editor in the fall of 1951. Thompson negotiated a mid-morning arrival, as the rush-hour New York subway induced claustrophobia and panic attacks, and he retired early to the Irish bar on the ground floor of the *PG* offices at 1819 Broadway, a few blocks south of Columbus Circle.

The *Police Gazette* "was a colorful, chaotic place to work," recounts

Betty Widmayer, then a young graphic artist in charge of layout and design, "and Jim came in with a big buildup. We were told that he had won a Pulitzer Prize for journalism out West before drinking led him into hard times." Owned by Harold Roswell, the sensational monthly tabloid mixed show-biz gossip with yellow factoids, such as "Hitler Is Alive!," their biggest story in 1951, according to Widmayer. The small staff comprised a crusty gang of flacks and hatchet men out of Damon Runyon. Editor Nat Perlow knocked around with Senator Estes Kefauver. Sports editor Ed Van Every managed the career of boxer Ezzard Charles. Oscar Fraley, also on sports, ghosted *The Untouchables* for Eliot Ness. And Kermit Jaediker, a novelist who would publish *Tall, Dark and Dead* and *Hero's Lust* with Lion Books, covered the crime beat. But however "colorful," the *Police Gazette* for Jim Thompson was like pouring water on a drowning man. Betty Widmayer elaborates:

> The job was beneath his ability—needless to say, the stories weren't the greatest—and he disliked the idea of what he had to do there. But he did it for the money. Jim was very nice, very considerate, and very sensitive—but sensitive was not a good thing to be in that office. He was a nervous man, anxious and worried, and he needed a lot of help talking with people. On summer weekends we all used to go out to a house Harold Roswell kept in Southampton and go over the different manuscripts and the layout of the magazine. It was not a happy experience for Jim—he really disliked it, and felt frustrated with Roswell. Ros was not the type of person who cared about a person's feelings or weaknesses, he just wanted to get the job done. Jim needed a little more soothing and sensitivity. He was very aware of other people's feelings—too much so for his own good.

Thompson published only one signed article for the *Police Gazette,* a puff profile of entertainer Ted Mack (November 1951). Much as at the Los Angeles *Mirror,* he refused to disguise his disappointment and disgust. "Jim obviously didn't enjoy being there," Widmayer adds. "One Friday afternoon the editor, Nat Perlow, was getting ready to go on vacation. Jim was upset about something, so he went down to the bar. He had a number of drinks. When we filed out and saw him, it was clear that we had to do something. Nat had a plane to catch, but we took Jim home to Astoria in a taxi. His wife met us at the door."

Around the Elizabeth and Gregory complex Thompson's drinking also was beginning to frighten his young nephew and nieces. As Freddie's daughter Randi, then nine years old, remarks:

My earliest recollections of my Uncle Jimmie are of him being over at our apartment because he was drunk and had been kicked out of his home. There would be some kind of upheaval, Alberta would throw him out, and Maxine would take him in. My mother and Maxine would sit up with him all night long while he drank and talked and talked. They would sit with him until he got through whatever it was that was causing him to binge. Then he would go back home. Sometimes it seemed he was there for a long time, a week or more, and other times it was a few days.

When drinking he was always extremely depressed—always just sitting in a chair with the whiskey bottle beside him, head down. And there were always tears, everyone would be crying and upset, and I would usually be sent out of the room. He was a little bit scary to me at that point because he was so huge, and I only saw him when he was drinking.

Thompson subsequently told the California magazine *Westways* that his editorial stint at the *Police Gazette* was "about as low down as you can get." But after some eight months in the depths, Ingrid Hallen telephoned him about a public appeal for "paperback originals" that Arnold Hano, editor of Lion Books, recently had issued in *Publishers Weekly.* Hallen arranged a meeting at Lion's headquarters in the Empire State Building. "Jim was a big sheepdog of a guy following docilely behind his agent, a tall, Valkyrie-like woman," Hano recalls. Two weeks later, Thompson reappeared with the opening chapters of *The Killer Inside Me.*

SAGA *editor—Jim with sister Maxine and*
his niece Randi, Queens, New York, 1950
(Courtesy of the Thompson family)

"The trouble is, however, that men
in general do not create in light and
warmth alone. They create in darkness and coldness. They create when
they are hopeless, in the midst of an-
tagonisms, when they are wrong,
when their powers are no longer
subject to their control. They create
as the ministers of evil. . . ."

—Wallace Stevens (1951)

Part 3

Ministers
of
Evil

How
Now,
Brown
Cow:
1952–
1956

> I began to feel those
> twinges of mental nausea
> that always herald the
> arrival of my muse.
> —Clinton Brown,
> *The Nothing Man*

If Jim Thompson had died before the fall of 1952—pickled in Jack Daniels, cured again in Pall Malls, and burnt out by forty-six—his only memorial would have been a fistful of tantalizing footnotes. His directorship of the Oklahoma Federal Writers' Project should have grazed histories of the New Deal and the WPA. *Now and on Earth* and *Heed the Thunder* might have crashed academic inventories of the proletarian and agrarian novel. *Nothing More Than Murder* may have penetrated pricey catalogues of vintage hard-boiled crime fiction, perhaps even snared a coterie of wistful fans chasing the phantom question of what-if.

Thompson blazed his reputation deep in middle age. Discharging an entire misspent lifetime's industry and artistry into a decisive nineteen months, he stacked up twelve new books between September 1952 and March 1954, nearly all of them for Lion Books. His staggering output of the early 1950s distorts the smooth contours of his chronology like a large animal passing through the belly of a python, and comprises his most ambitious and devastating work: *The Killer Inside Me; Savage Night; The Criminal; A Hell of a Woman; The Nothing Man; After Dark, My Sweet;* and *The Kill-Off.* His publishers would not catch up with his production until 1957. Although Thompson would go on to devise other audacious, unflinching fictions, if he had died in the spring of 1954 his literary legacy would have remained essentially what it is today.

Thompson's novels look back to the marginal men of the 1930s, but they belong to the 1950s. "These have been the years of conformity and depression," Norman Mailer rumbled in "The White Negro," the essay that popularized the hipster as psychopath. "The Second World War presented a mirror to the human condition which blinded anyone who looked into it . . . if society was so murderous, then who could ignore the most hideous of questions about his own nature?" Against the Eisenhower grin and the confident smiles of corporate advertisements, Thompson pronounced a negation, a refusal, picking out—and picking away at—a culture of loss, alienation, hopelessness, and failure. Against the suburban utopia of *Father Knows Best*—the long-running television series introduced the same season as *The Nothing Man*—he lanced a boil on the American Dream, flaunting a nightmare family of feeble, abusive fathers, suffocating mothers, martinet wives, impotent husbands, and incestuous siblings. The 1950s forged a complex, multifaceted decade, resistant to tidy encapsulation. Soon after the turn of the half-century, "psycho" serial killers—a boy-next-door spree gunsman like Charley Starkweather, or a wisecracking cannibal like Ed Gein—made news and myth, their crimes spurring a media folklore of movies, books, and songs. Thompson's novels join, even anticipate, such quintessential violations of "Silent Generation" decorum as William Burroughs's *Junky,* Allen Ginsberg's *Howl,* Mailer's *Advertisements for Myself,* Robert Frank's *The Americans,* Laslo Benedek's *The Wild One,* Nicholas Ray's *Rebel Without a Cause,* and the rock 'n' roll of Little Richard, Chuck Berry, and Elvis Presley.

One misconception of the Thompson revival is the belief that he published as he perished, a lost and neglected writer. His novels of the 1950s sold out their printings of 200,000 to 250,000 copies. During an era when the label "a $10,000 man" designated a handsome yearly wage, Thompson pocketed $2,500 advances for the books that dented his typewriter in bimonthly spasms. His publishers respected his gifts and his unique stature in the 25¢ brigade, even as they occasionally vied to tame his vision. Lion Books attempted to nominate *The Killer Inside Me* for the 1952 National Book Award as "the most authentically original novel of the year." An editorial memo at New American Library boasted, "Jim Thompson is a special writer and yet, though it appears to be a paradox, is a writer for hundreds of thousands of readers. His short prose serves to illuminate events in which the passions of men and women are revealed in their naked, primeval fury." Thompson's books found honor at unexpected heights. Anthony Boucher, the dean of American crime and fantasy fiction, celebrated nearly all Thompson's paperback originals in *The New York Times Book Review*—and in terms that anticipate the current critical reclamation of his work. Reviewing *Savage Night,* Boucher marveled: "Written with vigor and bite, but sheering off from realism into a peculiar surrealist ending of sheer Guignol horror. Odd that a mass-consumption paperback should contain the most experimental writing I've seen in a suspense novel of late."

Thompson's blackest books of the early 1950s ushered in his golden age, and the only period of his life that provoked any visible nostalgia. Novelist Harlan Ellison met Thompson at Lion Books in 1956 when the older writer asked if he had an extra stick of Dentyne gum and, more than a decade down the line, renewed the friendship in Hollywood. "I would go over, and we would reminisce like people who were a lot closer than we actually were," Ellison remembers of long afternoons with Thompson at All-American Burgers or the Musso & Frank Grill during the late 1960s. "Jim was kind of played out at that point, and nobody was paying a lot of attention. We would sit and talk for hours and hours—about writing, learning to write—but mostly about what New York was like in the 1950s. Jim seemed to lament the passing of that time."

• • •

When Thompson trailed Ingrid Hallen into Arnold Hano's suite at Lion Books he arrived, almost inadvertently, at his life project. But his was not the predicament of David Goodis or Cornell Woolrich, who, after the commercial and critical rejection of early "serious" work, shifted to suspense fiction, gnawing the marrow of defeat into the grave. Thompson more closely resembled Chester Himes, whose first published novels, *If He Hollers Let Him Go* (1945) and *Lonely Crusade* (1947), emerged, like *Now and on Earth,* from the California defense industry. Amid the obscurity of his self-exile in France during the mid-1950s Himes was commissioned by Marcel Duhamel, the influential originator of *série noire* at Gallimard, to write a *roman policier.* The result was *A Rage in Harlem,* and then the extended Coffin Ed Johnson and Grave Digger Jones cycle, his most incisive and radical fiction.

Thompson's inaugural Lion books, as well as some later efforts for New American Library, also sprang from commissions and publisher synopses—fatal grounding ordinarily for a novelist. But as Hano recalls, "Without really knowing what we were doing, we were developing at Lion the whole *série noire* kind of novel to a greater degree than anyone else had, or was."

Lion Books started in 1949 as a sideline of the Magazine Management Company, owned by Depression pulp pooh-bah Martin Goodman. The heart of Magazine Management resided in Marvel Comics—Stan Lee was Goodman's nephew—and an empire of interchangeable men's adventure rags led by *Male* and *Stag,* with circulations exceeding eight hundred thousand monthly copies. "Goodman had a sixth sense for publishing," suggests Noah Sarlot, director of a men's adventure division at Magazine Management that encompassed *Man's World, Men, For Men Only, Action for Men, True Action, Sportsman, Fishing Adventure, Hunting Adventure,* and *Sports Life.* "Almost every week he'd come in with another title. He used to say that if you don't create your own competition someone else will." Goodman launched profitable raids on other markets, in the true confessions, screen, cheesecake, and women's magazine racks. Moreover, he maintained his own distribution operation, Atlas Magazines. As Sarlot traces the humble genesis of Lion Books: "With Atlas Magazines at his disposal, it just made sense for Goodman to have a line of paperbacks to distribute."

Goodman packaged a run of bawdy paperbacks under the imprint of Red Circle Books for sale in the cigar stores, newsstands, and train stations that featured his comics and magazines. Then late in 1949, with the publication of the eighth title, a reprint of Edward Anderson's hobo classic *Hungry Men,* the name was changed to Lion Books. The focus expanded from mild sexploitation to embrace a diversity of popular genres: westerns, crime, sports, and movie tie-ins. Goodman enlisted a staff of bright, young editors—Jim Bryans, William Goldberg, and Walter Fultz—with Arnold Hano, formerly at Bantam, as editor in chief. Lion soon borrowed a trick from Fawcett Gold Medal Books and began to slip an occasional original onto the monthly list—not for the sake of literature, but to dodge the costly bidding wars for best-selling hardcovers.

Paperback originals in the early 1950s contrived a bridge between the pulps and mainstream publishing. "These were the last years of the pulp magazines," Harlan Ellison explains. "Writers drifted into the men's magazines, and fiction writers into paperback originals. If you weren't a name writer there was no place else to go. Lion, Pyramid, and a few others were creating incredible stables of writers." Mavericks like Hano, or Ralph Daigh and Jim Bishop at Fawcett Gold Medal, approached paperback originals in the spirit of a magazine editor soliciting articles. They decided on a type of book, sketched a premise and a springboard plot, and then located an author to write it. As Hano reviews his editorial program:

> We started a line of paperback originals. That way we could
> get young writers and new writers to do things for us. Jim Bryans

suggested that we write synopses of books that we thought would have the substance we were looking for, and all we had to do was find a writer who could do that kind of book.

Bryans was very good at this. He would take classics, he would take *Oedipus Rex,* he would take *Hamlet,* he would take *Macbeth,* and he would turn them into modern suspense novels, in synopsis form. These weren't lengthy synopses, probably two-thirds of a page.*

Lion continued to function mainly as a reprint outfit. But the writers discovered, the careers nurtured, and the gritty, offbeat books cooked up by this absurd fiction mill—upward of 120 original titles—lodged a vital episode in American *noir.* "These were pretty rough and tumble days," Ellison comments, "and these were real editors, who knew how to do a book."

Hano & Co. solicited three of David Goodis's most baroque novels, *The Burglar, Black Friday,* and *The Blonde on the Street Corner.* They contracted horror maven Richard Matheson's first novel, and important early work from Robert Bloch and Richard Prather. Day Keene found a niche at Lion for three books, including *Sleep with the Devil,* his racy study of a loan shark enforcer and a country preacher's daughter. Bruno Fischer crafted *The Lustful Ape* under the pseudonym Russell Gray. Cyril Kornbluth, the science fiction innovator and activist, likewise retained pen names for his astute fictions on sexually daring themes—Simon Eiesner for *The Naked Storm,* which featured a lesbian novelist, and Jordan Park for *Half,* a rare odyssey into hermaphroditism. Lion, in fact, became quietly notorious for stylish lesbiana with a crime twist. The intriguing Fletcher Flora, an education advisor to the Department of the Army in Leavenworth, Kansas, made his debut with the subtle *Strange Sisters,* and then followed it up with *Desperate Asylum,* before moving into an orthodox mash of adultery and murder.

Lion originals trafficked in iconoclastic politics. David Karp exposed a secret college society with insidious tentacles through the U.S. government—Yale's Skull and Bones, apparently—in *The Brotherhood of Velvet.* The firm introduced an imaginative regional anthology series, spotlighting *Strange Barriers* (on interracial relationships), *Great Tales of the Deep South,* and *Great Tales of City Dwellers.* Hano invested in young African-American writers, particularly Curtis Lucas and the tragic Jay Thomas Caldwell, killed during a robbery after the appearance of his boxing novel, *Me an' You.* Lion Books advanced a distinctive look—menacing yet elegant—at the

---

*Few Lion books flaunt their purported mythic origins so plainly. George Milburn's *Julie,* rooted in Chaucer's "The Miller's Tale," appears an exception. Neither Hano nor Bryans, for instance, can recall what classic stories—if any—underlie *The Killer Inside Me* or *Cropper's Cabin.*

newsstand, with such artists as Robert Maguire, Rudolph Belarski, Harry Schaare, Lou Marchetti, Mort Kunstler, and Rafael DeSoto illustrating the covers.

Thompson chafed under the sensationalism at Lion, and the distortion of his fiction into a disposable commodity. "I'm sure you understand that the lurid titling and blurbing of my books is strictly the work of the publisher," he complained to Anthony Boucher in 1954, during a letter that also lamented "the practice of chopping a manuscript to fit an arbitrary length." But he recognized that with Hano and Lion he had stumbled upon a home, a safe house for his boldest and most challenging work, and a last shot at reinventing himself. "They took me as I was," Thompson continued to Boucher, "allowed me to write in the only way I know how. Other publishers, excepting those in the hardcover field, have never been willing to do that."

• • •

Rumors of his talent and troubles preceded Thompson to Lion. Editor Jim Bryans was already familiar with his novels of the 1940s. "I had read *Nothing More Than Murder,* and at least one of the other hardcover books, and enjoyed them. When Ingrid Hallen mentioned him as someone with a lot of ability who was down on his luck, a heavy boozer who was back on the wagon, I asked her to drop by. So she brought him up to see us. Hallen was a very stately lady of a certain age who looked exactly like Helga in those paintings by Andrew Wyeth—not at all the kind of agent you would associate with a Jim Thompson."

Hano and Bryans immediately introduced him to the manila folder of Lion plots. "We handed him about five synopses or so," Hano recounts. "Bryans had this one about a New York City cop who got involved with a prostitute and ends up killing her. It was kind of a cheapo suspense novel. Jim looked it over and said, 'I'll take this one.' That's how *The Killer Inside Me* became *The Killer Inside Me*—though we didn't call it that then, as I don't remember any of the synopses having titles. Also on the list was a kind of pastiche of the Erskine Caldwell novels, another Bryans synopsis, which became *Cropper's Cabin.*"

Thompson impressed Hano at that first meeting in the Empire State Building with "his huge size and gentleness. He was big—over six feet four, and 250 pounds—but he had this low, soft voice and his handshake was soft as a child's. Courtly, deferential, the Southern gentleman type, but his face was kind of stony, guarded, not much change of expression. He smoked a lot, letting the cigarette burn down to the absolute nub. His skin was very pale, almost sallow, no sign of the sun there at all. I liked him right away."

The novelist startled his future editors when he casually volunteered that he had spent the previous decade inside alcoholic institutions. "He was trying to explain the gap, where his writing career had been, and it hadn't been anyplace for so many years," Hano reflects. "I know now he was exaggerating. But I understood him to say that there was a nine-year period when he was totally out of it. He told us he was dry then, he wasn't drinking at all, and as far as I know, that turned out to be true."

Bryans too found Thompson "courtly and pleasant." Yet, he counters, "there was a load of bitterness somewhere in there, and that was clear to me right from the start. He was not unaware he had something special—modest, not a braggart, but he had a sense of his own gifts. You could see he was struggling, that he probably was broke, and that he was kind of bitter about his lack of success."

Thompson arranged with Hano that he would draft the opening forty or fifty pages of the policeman-prostitute potboiler, and an outline for the rest. "We would either give him a go-ahead or not on the basis of that. We discussed a contract—since it was his first book for us, probably a $2,000 total advance, $1,000 if the sample worked out, another $1,000 on completion."

When Thompson returned to Lion Books "not more than two weeks later," Hano was stunned. Not only did the writer arrive with half of *The Killer Inside Me* in tow—twelve of the eventual twenty-six chapters—he also had thoroughly transformed the synopsis, twisting it around the coils of his own history and temperament. The sadistic New York City flatfoot of Bryans's précis evolved into West Texas Deputy Sheriff Lou Ford, whose Central City approximated the oil boomtown of Big Spring. Furthermore, he murdered with his mouth as much as with his hands. Hano subsequently wrote:

> [T]he glory of Jim's writing is what he did with those synopses. He took our banal plot outline and our trite characterizations and he turned them into—well, he turned them into *The Killer Inside Me* and *Cropper's Cabin*.
>
> I read that portion of *The Killer* that night. Immediately I knew it was good, and when he reached the scene of Lou Ford coming to the dark jail cell of young Johnnie Pappas, the Greek kid who'd been arrested with one of the bills that connected him to the first murder, I started to feel the hair on my skin rise. And when Lou Ford reached his hand to the youngster's throat, my brain exploded gently and the top of my head seemed to blow off. . . .

"Jim introduced the genius," Bryans adds, "like having Lou Ford find an outlet for his sadism by boring people to death. Anybody can write a storyline. But nobody but Jim Thompson would have thought of doing that."

After *The Killer Inside Me* and *Cropper's Cabin,* Lion Books never again bound Thompson to a synopsis. "Very early on I realized that what Jim needed was encouragement more than anything else," Hano remarks. "As far as I was concerned, he was inventing a new genre for us. You unleash a guy like that, you simply don't try to direct him."

• • •

Thompson retreated to Virginia to complete *The Killer Inside Me*. Still anxious about the books he hatched at home, despite his recent lucky stroke with Lion, he called on Maxine and Sergeant Kouba at the Quantico Marine Corps Base, a forty-five-minute drive south of Washington in Prince William County. Toiling in the upstairs maid's quarters he fell into the disciplined groove of a writer attending an artist's colony.

"After his breakfast Jimmie would just sit up there in that tiny room and write until I'd call him for supper," Maxine recounted of her brother's visit during the stifling Southern summer of 1952. "Because the housing units had just been built, all day long great big trucks would go by, and steamrollers leveling the mud and making a lot of noise. I'd go up there and look in on him, and you'd never know anything was happening around him, he was so deep into that book. He'd write ten pages every day. Each night I'd read the ten pages, and I was horrified all the way through, but I never said so. I did ask him finally, where in the world did you get all this? He said that he had acquired a lot of it from reading, from research and looking things up." Given some three months to turn in the manuscript, he wrapped *The Killer Inside Me* with another mind-boggling two-week surge.

Thompson banished the fulsome genre exercises of *Recoil* and *The Golden Gizmo* and intensified the more personal and subversive experiment he initiated with *Nothing More Than Murder. The Killer Inside Me* (Lion Books, September 1952) is regarded by many readers as his masterpiece. Described by Stanley Kubrick, who would direct *Lolita* after the Thompson-scripted films *The Killing* and *Paths of Glory,* as "probably the most chilling and believable first-person story of a criminally warped mind I have ever encountered," the novel sustains comparisons with Vladimir Nabokov's representations of lunatics, pedophiles, and assassins. With *The Killer Inside Me* Thompson dramatically deepened his skill at staging his contradictions in the public theater of the crime novel. Along the way to his amiable monster Lou Ford, he honed a cunning allegory on the situation of the pulp novel and its creator.

The posthumous memoirs and confessions of a justified sinner, *The Killer Inside Me*—as Thompson's title predicts—is probably his most interior fiction. Yet narrator Ford—as the title also signals—could not be more alarmingly self-estranged. Pausing before a mirror in his dead father's labo-

ratory early in the novel, the smooth deputy sheriff is not so much reporting his appearance as critiquing a character:

> I was still wearing my Stetson, shoved a little to the back of my
> head. I had on a kind of pinkish shirt and a black bow tie, and the
> pants of my blue serge suit were hitched up so as to catch on the
> tops of my Justin boots. Lean and wiry; a mouth that looked all set
> to drawl. A typical Western-country peace officer, that was me.
> Maybe friendlier looking than the average. Maybe a little cleaner
> cut. But on the whole typical.
>
> That's what I was, and I couldn't change. Even if it was safe, I
> doubted if I could change. I'd pretended so long that I no longer
> had to.

Through a lifetime of "standing outside of myself," Ford has replaced
the spontaneous impulses and movements of his personality with an "act."
This chatty hayseed routine, "just old dumb Lou from Kalamazoo," he dons
as defensive camouflage for what he repeatedly italicizes as *"the sickness,"*
and suggests the protective coloring certain animals adopt to deceive
predators by blending into the natural landscape:

> I've loafed around the streets sometimes, leaned against a
> store front with my hat pushed back and one boot hooked back
> around the other—hell, you've probably seen me if you've ever
> been out this way—I've stood like that, looking nice and friendly
> and stupid, like I wouldn't piss if my pants were on fire. And all the
> time I'm laughing myself sick inside. Just watching the people.

"It was in character," he drawls, "and my talk was a big part of me—part of
the guy that had thrown 'em all off the trail." When not "in character," Ford
lounges at home skimming German and Italian periodicals, solving calculus
problems "for the hell of it," and studying "bulky volumes" of morbid
psychology.

"The sickness," he informs us, began with the sexual abuse inflicted on
him by the family housekeeper, Helene. A discarded mistress of his father's
(Lou's mother died when he was a baby, perhaps during childbirth), Helene
spitefully transferred their sadistic games to Dr. Ford's only child. "With
Dad finding out about us . . . I'd been made to feel," he explains, "that I'd
done something that couldn't ever be forgiven—that would always lie between him and me, the only kin I had . . . I had a burden of fear and
shame put on me that I could never get shed of." Along with his inheritance
of "fear and shame," a hunger for ultraviolent mating has passed down the
chain of flesh from father to son. Lou wallops his girlfriend, Amy Stanton,

"until she had to take it kind of easy when she sat down." And his ferocious coupling with prostitute Joyce Lakeland stirs from her near death:

> I jerked the jersey up over her face and tied the end in a knot. I threw her down on the bed, yanked off her sleeping shorts and tied her feet together with them.
>
> I took off my belt and raised it over my head. . . .
>
> I don't know how long it was before I stopped, before I came to my senses. All I know is that my arm ached like hell and her rear end was one big bruise, and I was scared crazy—as scared as a man can get and go on living.
>
> I freed her feet and hands, and pulled the jersey off her head. I soaked a towel in cold water and bathed her with it. I poured coffee between her lips. And all the time I was talking, begging her to forgive me, telling her how sorry I was.
>
> I got down on my knees by the bed, and begged and apologized. At last her eyelids fluttered and opened.
>
> "D-don't," she whispered.
>
> "I won't," I said. "Honest to God, ma'am, I won't ever—"
>
> "Don't talk." She brushed her lips against mine. "Don't say you're sorry."
>
> She kissed me again. She began fumbling at my tie, my shirt; starting to undress me after I'd almost skinned her alive.
>
> I went back the next day and the day after that. I kept going back. And it was like a wind had been turned on a dying fire. . . .

The Killer Inside Me opens as Ford's encounter with Joyce inflames the smoldering guilt and revenge he has masked since he molested a little girl fifteen years earlier. That adolescent episode also kicked off his double life, as Dr. Ford insisted that Mike Dean, Lou's newly adopted brother, take the blame. The deputy sheriff has devised two allied outlets "to ease the terrific pressure that was building up inside of me." The more innocuous safety valve he terms "dead-pan kidding," or "the needle." Ford hooks the well-mannered citizenry of Central City and tortures them with platitudes:

> "Well, it's like this," I said. "Now, I've always felt we were one big happy family here. Us people that work for the county. . . ."
>
> "Uh-huh. One big happy family, eh?" His eyes strayed again. "Go on, Lou."
>
> "We're kind of brothers under the skin. . . ."
>
> "Y-yes."
>
> "We're all in the same boat, and we've got to put our shoulders to the wheel and pull together."

His throat seemed to swell all of a sudden, and he yanked a handkerchief from his pocket. Then he whirled around in his chair, his back to me, coughing and strangling and sputtering. I heard his secretary get up, and hurry out. Her high heels went tap-tapping down the corridor, moving faster and faster toward the woman's john until she was almost running.

I hope she pissed in her drawers.

Ford's clichés often sheathe a squirrelly, macabre literalness. "I think we've broken the case," he taunts his fellow officers after he snaps the neck of young Johnnie Pappas in his jail cell. "Something to warm you up, eh?" Ford queries a bum begging money for food, just before he grinds a lit cigar into the drifter's outstretched palm.

His other outlet, of course, is murder. The verbal needle, Ford confides, is merely "a substitute for something else," and *The Killer Inside Me* eventually releases that "something else" in a caravan of beatings, strangulations, smashed bodies, shotguns fired into gaping mouths, and a giddy, final explosion. Consistent with his own recounting of *"the sickness,"* Ford's victims mainly are women—almost any woman, Amy, Joyce, or that nameless girl child, standing in for the original, Helene:

> She was gone, and I couldn't strike back at her, yes, kill her, for what I'd been made to feel she'd done to me. But that was all right. She was the first woman I'd ever known; she *was* woman to me; and all womankind bore her face. So I could strike back at any of them, any female, and it would be the same as striking at her. And I did that, I started striking out . . . and Mike Dean took the blame. . . .
>
> If I could have gotten away somewhere, where I wouldn't have been constantly reminded of what had happened and I'd had something I wanted to do—something to occupy my mind—it might have been different. But I couldn't get away, and there wasn't anything here I wanted to do. So nothing had changed; I was still looking for *her*. And any woman who'd done what she had would be *her*. . . .
>
> Anyone. Amy. Joyce. Any woman who, even for a moment, became *her*.
>
> I'd kill them.
>
> I'd keep trying until I did kill them.

Ford's killings, like his "act" and his sex, command a volatile mix of compulsion and theater. Joyce's death should look like a double murder involving her sometime lover Elmer Conway. He meticulously stages Amy's demise as the handiwork of a passing derelict.

Late in the novel Ford diagnoses himself as a paranoid schizophrenic or—with the magpie pedantry he's absorbed from his father's library—as a victim of "dementia praecox. Schizophrenia, paranoid type. Acute, recurrent, advanced." More colloquially, he tells doomed Johnnie Pappas, "I guess I kind of got a foot on both fences. . . . I planted 'em there early and now they've taken root, and I can't move either way and I can't jump. All I can do is wait until I split. Right down the middle."

The vision Lou Ford sees in his mirror is clear, if double and loathsome. But what anyone else in Central City—Amy, Joyce, Sheriff Bob Maples, county attorney Howard Hendricks, oil man Chester Conway, or Joe Rothman, president of the local Building Trades Council—knows about this "typical Western-country peace officer" is a trickier question, as every word of *The Killer Inside Me* trickles through Ford. For most of his spree he reiterates his conviction that no one can, as he claims of Amy, "get around the image she had of gentle, friendly, easy-going Lou Ford." Yet between the lines of his hypnotic patter his disguise seems riddled with rifts and holes. Twice Rothman cautions him against overplaying the cornball—"It's a good act but easy to overdo." And Sheriff Maples all but reveals he's on to Ford as he drunkenly inverts one of the deputy's banalities:

> "Wash—watch y'self," he mumbled. "Stop man with grin, smile worthwhile—s-stop all a' stuff spilt milk n' so on. Wha' you do tha for, anyway."
> "Aw," I said. "I was only kidding, Bob."
> "T-tell you somethin'," he said. "T-tell you somethin' I bet you never thought of."
> "Yeah?"
> "It's—it's always lightest j-just before the dark."
> Tired as I was, I laughed. "You got it wrong, Bob," I said. "You mean—"
> "Huh-uh," he said. "You got it wrong."

Only after the whole world seems to be bearing down does Ford recognize he has been giving himself away from the start, dropping clues and missing cues. But these are time bombs Thompson planted for a second or third reading. On the first run through *The Killer Inside Me* such pointers slide by virtually unnoticed, so reasonable is Ford's demented monologue. Once drawn in, we follow his snake-charming twang, fascinated and repulsed, to the brutal finish, even as the deputy sheriff begins to torment his readers with the same linguistic games he worked on his victims. For Ford gradually turns his clichés against us. With no one but the reader to

squirm, he sustains his aggressive prattle: "It had always made me feel better to come here, back from the time I was kneehigh to a grasshopper. It
was like coming out of the darkness into the sunlight, out of a storm into
calm. Like being lost and found again." He cruelly stops and starts his narrative of Amy Stanton's murder through ten maddening pages, like a sadist
dallying the climax of his partner.

During his dance around Stanton's death, Ford styles himself a
novelist:

> In a lot of books I read, the writer seems to go haywire every
> time he reaches a high point. He'll start leaving out punctuation
> and running his words together and babble about stars flashing
> and sinking into a deep dreamless sea. And you can't figure out
> whether the hero's laying his girl or a cornerstone. I guess that
> kind of crap is supposed to be pretty deep stuff—a lot of the book
> reviewers eat it up, I notice. But the way I see it is, the writer is just
> too goddam lazy to do his job. And I'm not lazy, whatever else I am.
> I'll tell you everything.

Ford—like any naturalist novelist—plays God, controlling the flow of
information, and meting out punishment. But can he tell us "everything"?
For all the insane violence, *The Killer Inside Me* poses an elegant Chinese
puzzle of a book. Is Ford, as he purports, a helpless psychopath driven by
"the sickness"? Or is this just another, more sophisticated wrinkle in his ingratiating con? That the deputy sheriff himself first frames the problem en-
hances the mystery. "We might have the disease, the condition," he blandly
summarizes, "or we might just be cold-blooded and smart as hell; or we
might be innocent of what we're supposed to have done. We might be any
of those three things, because the symptoms we show would fit any of the
three."

In the end, Ford really can't say anything about his motives, his nature,
what's inside or outside of him. He marshals a set of alibis, explanations,
and rationalizations for Central City, and then marshals a second set for
himself and us. His *"sickness"* seems another false front, a slick code for the
rampant nihilism Ford can only approach obliquely, as in the tabloid
tragedy he recites while driving home:

> Years ago there was a jeweler here in Central City who had a
> hell of a good business, and a beautiful wife and two fine kids. And
> one day on a business trip over to one of the teachers' college
> towns he met up with a girl, a real honey, and before long he was
> sleeping with her. She knew he was married, and she was willing to
> leave it that way. So everything was perfect. He had her and he had

his family and a swell business. But one morning they found him and the girl dead in a motel—he'd shot her and killed himself. And when one of our deputies went to tell his wife about it, he found her and the kids dead, too. This fellow had shot 'em all.

He'd had everything, and somehow nothing was better.

Roger Caillois, a French anthropologist who, with Georges Bataille and Michel Leiris, founded the College of Sociology in Paris during the late 1930s, once proposed that animals, such as the praying mantis or box crab, that camouflage themselves by mimicking their environments are motivated not only by "the instinct of self-preservation which, in some way orients the creature toward life," but also by "a sort of instinct of renunciation that orients it toward a mode of reduced existence, which in the end would no longer know either consciousness or feeling." Ford's country-bumpkin act, "just old dumb Lou," charts the same forked path, until his self-preservation and life shatter into renunciation and death. On the final pages of *The Killer Inside Me* he consummates the terrifying logic of his split and, like a crackpot Sampson in the temple of the Philistines, destroys his house, his enemies, and himself along with it. "And it was like I'd signaled, the way the smoke suddenly poured up through the floor. And the room exploded with shots and yells, and I seemed to explode with it, yelling and laughing. . . ."

Along with Ford's divided house, *The Killer Inside Me* detonates some myths of small-town America—the benevolent cop, the kindly physician, the free and open country. The public guardians of morality, justice, and power all are whitened sepulchers, privately depraved or criminal. Ford's family, Central City—each is a stinking prison.

Like Robert Hightower, the young bellboy in *A Penny in the Dust,* Thompson's shelved "portrait of the author as a young man," Lou Ford can only talk by being what he is not. The mutant lawman may have sprung full-grown from a Big Spring deputy sheriff, as alleged in *Bad Boy.* But, as suggested earlier, Thompson diverted a lot of his own character—and of his sheriff father—into *The Killer Inside Me.* More commandingly than in *Nothing More Than Murder,* he exposed ambivalent and dangerous feelings by assuming an identity that is at once the insidious voice of madness and the naked voice of grief and pain. And Ford came laden with many smaller souvenirs from his creator's past. When the deputy visits Fort Worth, he stays at a hotel on West Seventh Street—the site of the Worth Hotel, where the writer worked in 1933. Ford reads the psychological case studies Thompson pored over in Otto Lucy's library, shoots himself up with B-complex vitamins, and even drops the name of "Max Jacobsohn" *(sic).*

But perhaps Ford's slyest role is as a stand-in for the medium in which he first appeared. Many of Thompson's recent admirers have wondered what it must have been like to grab *The Killer Inside Me* from a subway newsstand in 1952, seduced by the tawdry cover and blurb ("You see—I *had* to destroy them") into the anticipation of escapist kicks, only to board an express train to hell. Ford's brilliant dumb show, the killer inside the clown, grinds a mordant analogy for this original, revolting novel disguised as just another two-bit thrill. For his Lion debut Thompson, if not Lou Ford, aspired to "tell you everything."

• • •

The Killer Inside Me laid down the map for his writing life during the Lion years. Although Thompson executed at least some of his novels in New York City, either at his Queens apartment or assorted Manhattan hotels, he preferred Maxine's. Every few months he would board the train for Quantico, and then, later in the decade, for the Homestead Air Force Base in Dade County, Florida. It's odd to think of Thompson releasing his horrors from Southern military installations—the Stars and Stripes rippling in the warm breeze, the spruce troops parading, as he set another terminally alienated American spinning toward another ugly dead end. And odder still that the original audience for his misogynist heroes consisted exclusively of women—his sister Maxine, on the road; at home his wife, Alberta, who proofread and edited all his Lion books.

While he plotted his new novels, which revolved, more often than not, around an obsessive contrast between outer and inner lives, Thompson appeared to flourish as a modest burgher: enveloped in work and family, pulling down a steady, even liberal income, a creature of moderate habits. Arnold Hano claims that he never once saw the writer take a drink during the early 1950s. Hano and his wife, Bonnie, evolved into the Thompsons' closest New York friends. "He and Alberta and Bonnie and I spent many evenings together," Hano recalls. "Supper and talk. People ask us today what did we talk about. We talked banalities. We talked about kids and work and how to make a dollar last longer. We talked about politics and other writers. We talked about ourselves."

Others around Thompson were not so blessed. His daughter Sharon concealed her embarrassment when a teenage chum observed him wandering the streets of Astoria intoxicated. "I was shaken that this man I loved, that I looked up to for everything, would get like that. I tried to convince my girlfriend that it couldn't have been my father she had seen."

Thompson reserved his binges mainly for new acquaintances like George and Mary Milburn, whose Greenwich Village flat by the corner of Eighth and Macdougal constituted a handy refuge. Born in Indian Territory the same year as Thompson, George Milburn was a talented Oklahoma short story writer, novelist, and essayist, a contributor to *Folk-Say*, the editor of *The Hobo's Hornbook*, and the author of *Oklahoma Town, No More*

Trumpets, Catalogue, and *Flannigan's Folly.* During the 1930s Thompson and Milburn kept almost meeting at the University of Oklahoma, where mutual friend Ben Botkin touted one native son to the other. Milburn fled to New York City in 1948 after a calamitous stint in Hollywood, nursing a vicious writer's block with alcohol while he held down a job as a receptionist in the emergency room of St. Vincent's Hospital. His early stories for the *American Mercury,* thumbnail renderings of tragic or ludicrous Oklahoma lives in a deadpan style *The New York Times* once praised as "heartless," were a key influence on Thompson's fiction. Thompson squared the debt when he insisted that Arnold Hano reprint *Oklahoma Town* and *No More Trumpets*— the paperbacks retitled, with typical Lion sensitivity, *Sin People* and *Hoboes and Harlots.* Thompson also brokered Milburn's final novel, *Julie,* with Lion. "Jim was the only one who never gave up on George," Mary Milburn acknowledged. "Jim helped and encouraged him, and stuck after him to write and work. But George didn't work, though."*

Sometimes accompanied by Alberta, Thompson rode the subway over from Queens on the promise of a Milburn-cooked meal that would evaporate in a fog of whiskey and Chianti when George or Mary woozily forgot to ignite the stove. Weekends the couples might more soberly convene at Penn Station for a visit to Botkin, now residing upstate in Croton-on-Hudson. But usually Thompson arrived solo after dinner for a marathon of conversation about the Sooner State and books. "Jim and George were both great talkers," remarked Mary Milburn. "They would settle down in the living room for hours and hours, and I would just leave them and go to bed. Jim had a very strong personality, full of recommendations and advice, and he would show his writing to George as he was working on it. George loved Jim's novels, but I found them too violent, which seemed to surprise him. Jim had a tendency to get angry at people—he could be accusative and testy, saying that so-and-so had promised to do something and hadn't. But around us he was very friendly, and made you feel comfortable. I never saw two men who could drink as much as George and Jim when they got together. Then Alberta would have to come in on the subway and take him home."

Despite the random blowout, Thompson managed to temper his drinking for the longest interlude since he joined A.A. back in San Diego. The result was not only a groaning shelf of murderous fiction, but also, perhaps, his nearest approach to a secure, ordinary American existence.

---

*George Milburn wrote Thompson in 1959, "I don't mind telling you that we were kind of worried abt you when we first heard abt yr illness, & it put me in a prayerful attitude, skeptic though I am, when I began remembering all the good turns you have done me. . . . Jim, sometimes at night I try adding up all the good people I have ever known, instead of counting sheep, & you & Alberta always pop into my mind first. Is this a dubious compliment?"

For almost two years Thompson appears to have done little else except write, revise, and publish. In accounts of family and friends he virtually disappears from his own life—and disappears into his work.

• • •

Thompson followed *The Killer Inside Me* with *Cropper's Cabin* in November 1952, a scant two months later. The dating and even the order of composition of his other novels during the Lion years can only be approximated. The official roster of his publications is deceptive. *Recoil* and *The Golden Gizmo,* although not released until 1953 and 1954, of course were completed long before Thompson heard of Lion Books. *The Nothing Man,* issued by Dell in 1954, was actually edited by Arnold Hano, the manuscript changing publishers because of an excess of Thompson product at Lion. *After Dark, My Sweet,* printed by Popular Library in 1955, similarly seems to have been developed at Lion before Hano left the firm in the fall of 1954. Corporate difficulties at Magazine Management delayed *The Kill-Off* until 1957, yet the book was a near contemporary of *The Criminal,* distributed four years previous. Since their precise chronology remains irrecoverable, Thompson's novels of the early 1950s might most advantageously be retraced by reference to genre and strategy.

First-Person Psychopathic Novels

The quartet of first-person narrator, psychopathic killer novels that Thompson refined from the fires of *The Killer Inside Me* intensified his reputation as a *noir* stylist and unsavory "minister of evil." In *The Mask of Sanity,* Dr. Hervey Cleckley identifies some characteristic points in the profile of psychopathic disorder, including "superficial charm and good intelligence," "untruthfulness and insincerity," "lack of remorse and shame," "inadequately motivated antisocial behavior," "pathological egocentricity and incapacity for love," "general poverty in major affective reactions," "fantastic and uninviting behavior with drink," "sex life impersonal, trivial, and poorly integrated," and "failure to follow any life plan." During examinations of the psychopath, Cleckley continues,

> the observer is confronted with a convincing mask of sanity. . . . There is nothing at all odd or queer about him, and in every respect he tends to embody the concept of a well-adjusted happy person. . . . Only very slowly and by a complex estimation or judgement based on multitudinous small impressions does the conviction come upon us that, despite these intact rational processes, these normal emotional affirmations, and their consistent application in all directions, we are dealing here not with a

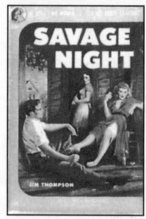

Courtesy Jay Pearsall;
Now and on Earth *and*
Nothing More Than
Murder *courtesy Fales*
Library, New York
University

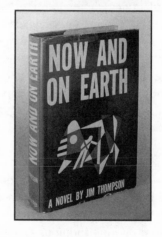
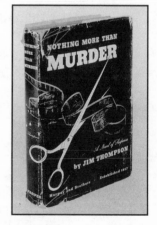

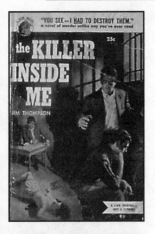

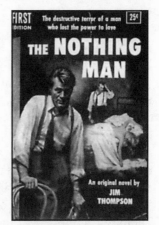

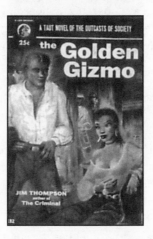
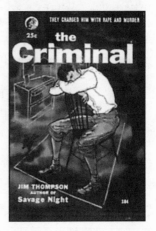

complete man at all but with something that suggests a subtly constructed reflex machine that can mimic the human personality perfectly.

Savage Night; A Hell of a Woman; The Nothing Man; and *After Dark, My Sweet,* like *The Killer Inside Me,* fall among the few clinically accurate re- creations of the mask of sanity in crime fiction. Still, the radical storytelling in these novels is anything but conventionally realistic. Writing at the height of his ambitions and skills, Thompson devised a thorny pop- modernism—"a link," as Luc Sante proposed, "between popular literature and the avant-garde"—available for 25¢ at any newsstand.

Savage Night (Lion Books, October 1953) originated as a private wager. Thompson informed Arnold Hano, "I want to do a Syndicate-type novel, and I want to use just 500 words, 500 basic words, because I think that will reduce it to what I want to reduce it to." He ultimately abandoned his 500- word straitjacket. But restriction, diminishment, and loss continued to stagger this spare story of Charlie "Little" Bigger, a tiny, consumptive con- tract murderer blackmailed out of retirement by "The Man" to kill Jake Win- roy, key witness against the Mob in a racketeering case.

A "Syndicate-type novel" rouses expectations of *Little Caesar, Red Har- vest, The Big Heat, Kiss Me Deadly,* or, for a contemporary audience, *The Godfather.* With *Savage Night,* however, Thompson travestied the American gangster cult. Sickness, passivity, anxiety, decay—along with a sheer reck- lessness of style—designate a literary genre running out of bounds.

Traveling under the alias of "Carl Bigelow," Charlie Bigger is agitated by his size from the moment he arrives in Peardale, the New York college town where Jake Winroy's wife, Fay, operates a boardinghouse. With his lift shoes, dyed hair, contact lenses, and dentures, Bigger is all spare parts passing as callow charm. He reluctantly takes stock of his looks—and fal- tering identity—alone in his bedroom at the Winroys:

> I lay still, forcing myself to lie still when I felt the urge to get up and look in the mirror. . . . I closed my eyes, looking at myself in my mind's eye.
>
> It gave me a start. It was like looking at someone else.
>
> I'd seen myself that way ten thousand times and each time it was a new experience. I'd see what other people seemed to see, and I'd catch myself thinking, "Gosh, what a nice little guy. You don't need anyone to tell you *he's* all right—"
>
> I thought that, now, and somehow it sent a shiver through me. I started thinking about the teeth and the other changes, and I knew it didn't really matter. But I made myself think about them.

I felt safer, some way, believing it was those things instead of—instead of?

. . . The teeth and the contact lenses. The tanned, healthy-looking face. The extra weight. The added height . . . and only part of it due to the elevator shoes I'd worn since 1943. I'd straightened up when I shook the bug, and—but had I shaken it? Suppose I took sick now, so sick I couldn't go through with this? The Man would be sore, and—the name? *Charles Bigger*—Carl Bigelow? Well, it was as good as any. It wouldn't have been any better to call myself Chester Bellows or Chauncey Billingsley; and it would have to be something like that. A man can't get too far away from his own name, you know. He may try to but he's asking for trouble. There's laundry markings. There's answering when you're spoke to. So. . . .

Bigger/Bigelow's obsessive profile scores a mischievous Thompson jab at Lion sensationalism. Publisher Martin Goodman—according to Hano— "wanted every writer to show in the opening pages of a novel a woman getting undressed or taking a bath, so that she could describe her beautiful form in the mirror." Yet more than a joke, Bigger's self-appraisals remain reflected, distanced, or secondhand. He quotes a frightening account of his appearance from a true crime magazine. And "standing outside myself," he watches and listens for what others observe and hear. "And it was like seeing a movie you've seen a thousand times before. And . . . and I guess there wasn't anything strange about that."

The "bug" Bigger almost names is tuberculosis. From the "faint trace of blood in his spit" on the opening page, he is slowly wasting away through *Savage Night.* Every cough, each fresh jag of "blood and phlegm" seems to erode his physical and social stature. "What there was of me was all right," he quips, "but there wasn't much of me any more." Establishing his cover, Bigger enrolls in the local teacher's college. But when his teeth slip in class, and "everything I said sounded sort of like baby talk," he shrinks still further: "I'd thought that school couldn't be any worse than it'd been that Friday, but it was. Maybe it just seemed worse because there was so much more of it and so much less of me." Tortured that his illness and ravaged frame mark him a figure of fun, Bigger follows his shame into self-hatred and delusion. Is Fay Winroy, whom he deftly if cynically beds, also working for The Man? Is old Mr. Kendall, the kindly boarder who hires him at the bakery? "The only person I could trust was Charlie Bigger, Little Bigger," he cackles. "And that sawed-off-son-of-a-bitch, I was beginning to have my doubts about him."

Thompson awarded Bigger his special student status from the University of Nebraska, his batch-boy job at the Butter-Nut Bread Company, and his Hotel Texas TB. Half-child, half-monster, the elfin hit man packs a lethal combination of fastidiousness and violence. Capable of elbowing a woman in a crowded New York City train station "so hard she almost dropped the baby she was carrying," Bigger enjoys drying the dishes after dinner, laments the quarreling of husbands and wives, and takes quiet Sunday drives with the elderly Peardale sheriff and his wife. Both strains converge in his brutally elegant slaying of a minor mobster named Fruit Jar:

> I gave it to him in the neck. I damned near carved his Adam's apple out. I took the big silk handkerchief out of his breast pocket, wiped my hands and the knife, and put the knife in his pocket. (That should give them something to think about.) Then I shoved him down on the floor in the car, and caught the train to town.

Boasting that he's "pretty good at putting myself in the other fellow's place," Bigger enters into a paralyzing identification with his intended victim, Jake Winroy. "The poor bastard was kind of like me. He hadn't been anything, but he'd done his damnedest to be something. . . ." Later, amid sad puns on his name, "Little" Bigger and Winroy virtually swap places: "He seemed to be getting bigger, and I was getting littler." Bigger recognizes himself also in Ruthie Dorne, the crippled college student who cooks and cleans for the Winroys. "I knew how she felt," he confides. "Why wouldn't I know how it felt to be a kind of joke, to have people tell you off kind of like it was what you were made for?" Ruthie, even more than Carol in *Nothing More Than Murder,* embodies Thompson's sourest parody of the femme fatale:

> . . . one good look was all I did get. But what I saw interested me. Maybe it wouldn't interest you, but it did me.
> She had on an old mucklededung-colored coat—the way it was screaming Sears-Roebuck they should have paid her to wear it—and a kind of rough wool skirt. Her glasses were the kind your grandpa maybe wore, little tiny lenses, steel rims, pinchy across the nose. They made her eyes look like walnuts in a plate of cream fudge. Her hair was black and thick and shiny, but the way it was fixed—murder!
> She had only one leg, the right one. The fingers of her left hand, gripping the crosspiece of her crutch, looked a little splayed. . . .

After Bigger rapes Ruthie, the couple sinks into a hideous cartoon of hothouse passion:

. . . She stopped begging.

There was nothing left to beg for.

I looked down, my head against hers so that she couldn't see that I was looking. I looked, and closed my eyes quickly. But I couldn't keep them closed.

It was a baby's foot. A tiny little foot and ankle. It started just above the knee joint—where the knee would have been if she had one—a tiny little ankle, not much bigger around than a thumb; a baby ankle and a baby foot.

The toes were curling and uncurling, moving with the rhythm of her body. . . .

"C-Carl . . . Oh, C-Carl!" she gasped.

After a long time, what seemed like a long time, I heard her saying, "Don't. Please don't Carl. It's a-all right, so—so, please, Carl. . . . Please don't cry anymore—"

If sex, as so often in Thompson, seems monstrous, there are few intact bodies—and people—in *Savage Night*. Ruthie limps along with a mechanical *thud-tap,* as inwardly traumatized as outwardly deformed. Mr. Kendall, we learn, is not only a thwarted academic but also dying. Jake is "some wild sick animal," "a beaten dog," and "dead, the same as." Fay is only an "actress," pliant, desperate and lost. Carl is stunted by his height, of course, but even more by memories of his drunken father and Depression past, and his need for disguise and double dealing. "You can do that, split yourself up into two parts," he admits. "It's easier than you'd think. Where it gets tough is when you try to get the parts back together again."

At every turn, *Savage Night* proclaims a hatred of the human body. The astonishing emblem for this disgust is—there's no comely phrase for it—a cunt farm Bigger evokes one night after sleeping with Fay. The farm permeates an obscene flashback (or fantasy, it's impossible to say) the hit man provides of a drunken novelist whose tale bitterly reproduced Thompson's visits to New York City during the 1940s:

He was a writer, only he didn't call himself that. He called himself a hockey peddler. "You notice that smell?" he said, "I just got through dumping a load of crap in New York, and I ain't had time to get it fumigated." All I could smell was the whiz he'd been drinking. He went on talking, not at all grammatical like you might expect a writer to, and he was funny as hell.

He said he had a farm up in Vermont, and all he grew on it were the more interesting portions of the female anatomy. And he never laughed or cracked a smile, and the way he told about it almost made you believe it. "I fertilize them with wild goat manure," he said. "The goats are tame to begin with, but they soon go wild. The stench, you know. I feed them on the finest grade grain alcohol, and they have their own private cesspool to bathe in. But nothing does any good. You should see them at night when they stand on their heads, howling."

I grinned, wondering why I didn't give it to him. "I didn't know goats howled," I said.

"They do if they're wild enough," I said.

"Is that all you grow?" I said. "You don't have bodies on any of—of those things?"

"Jesus Christ!" He turned on me like I'd called him a dirty name. "Ain't I got things tough enough as it is? Even butts and breasts are becoming a drug on the market. About all there's any demand for is you know what." He passed me the bottle, and had a drink himself, and he calmed down a little. "Oh, I used to grow other things," he said. "Bodies. Faces. Eyes. Expressions. Brains. I grew them in a three-dollar-a-week room down on Fourteenth Street and I ate aspirin when I couldn't raise the dough for a hamburger. And every now and then some lordly publisher would come down and reap my crop and package it at two-fifty a copy. . . ."

After the author's debauched walk-on, Bigger botches his mission in typical Thompson fashion, slipping into the same mistakes as Lou Ford and Joe Wilmot before him. He can't read The Man, misjudges Fay and Mr. Kendall, and only after Ruthie carves out Winroy's throat with a razor—curiously offstage, for a crime novel—does he recognize her as The Man's ruthless plant.

Savage Night begins in a solid world of train stations, rooming houses, highways, bakeries, and schools but gradually angles into a void. Early in the novel Mr. Kendall touted "the satirists" to Charlie Bigger. But when Bigger and Ruthie Dorne escape via car or delirium to that writer's Vermont farm, the concluding chapters shape a psychic hell that seems a collaboration among Swift, Edgar Allan Poe, and William Burroughs. Hiding among the howling and shrieking goats, and the jungle of wiggling, squirming vaginas, Bigger and Ruthie, like the Yahoos in *Gulliver's Travels,* lapse into bestial silence, "just grunting and gesturing and pointing at things." Bigger pores over the novelist's writings, all Burroughsean cut-up words and phrases from the Bible, rearranged as babble. And chased by Ruthie's ax, he scurries, like the condemned man in "The Pit and the Pendulum," down into the cellar, to die.

Ruthie completes with her blade the erosion that Bigger's anxiety and sickness previously broached only as paranoid metaphor. As she slices his limbs and organs and dismantles his senses, he numbly recounts his reactions, and Thompson's chapters shorten and shrink until the last is a single sentence. What's left at the end is a disembodied voice narrating through his death, and Bigger—it must be assumed now—was dead even from the beginning of the novel.

Savage Night, as Anthony Boucher declared in *The New York Times,* hazarded "the most experimental writing" of any crime fiction published in 1953. The following year Thompson escalated the experimentation—and the psychic shocks—with *A Hell of a Woman* (Lion Books, July 1954). The novel superficially replays its immediate antecedents. *A Hell of a Woman* features another psychopathic narrator of debatable intelligence who dies on the final page. As in *The Killer Inside Me,* the central crime is a double-murder staged so that it appears the victims killed each other. Like *Savage Night,* the storyline slides from a vividly nuanced physical setting into fantasy and nothingness. But as he recycled his wardrobe, Thompson ransacked so many other literary closets, both high and low, that *A Hell of a Woman* ranks as his wildest book.

Frank "Dolly" Dillon—the name blends Thompson's Party alias, Dillon, with Dolly, his handle at the Hotel Texas—is a door-to-door salesman for the Pay-E-Zee Stores in what appears to be Lincoln, Nebraska, during the early 1950s. At thirty, he has devolved into his job—similar to the one at the Kay-Bee Clothing Company Thompson despised as a student in 1931—after a lifetime of humiliations and scams. Expelled from high school for hitting on his English teacher ("I thought she wanted it. . . . But . . . it was a trap"), Dillon drifted to the Southwest, buying gold, selling coupons, or chasing a magazine circulation crew.

With a depression in full swing, Dillon doctors his sales cards to pay the bills and come by his drinks. During the day he tails deadbeat accounts, like the hapless Swedish immigrant Pete Hendrickson ("Chunk you sell me. Suit no good—like paper it vears! In chail you should be. . . ."), and suffers the sarcasm of his boss, Staples. Nights, at home in his "four-room dump," Dillon knocks around his wife, Joyce, "a lazy, selfish, dirty slob," he fumes, "Kid Sloppybutt, Princess Lead-in-the-Tail, Queen of the Cigarette Girls and a free pinch with every pack." If Lou Ford was an intellectual disguised as a backwater oaf, Dillon is that oaf straining to remain sane as he keeps missing the American Dream—or, as he puts it, a "crack . . . at the big dough." So, when he stumbles on Ma Farrell, and she offers him sex with her niece in exchange for a chest of Pay-E-Zee silverware, Dillon believes he has glimpsed the promised land.

Mona plays the siren role in *A Hell of a Woman.* Thompson shades their meeting with Gothic lightning effects and a comic pratfall:

> I'd gotten out of my car and was running for the porch when I
> saw her. She was peering through the curtains of the door, and a

flash of lightning lit up the dark glass for an instant, framing her
face like a picture. And it wasn't a pretty picture, by any means;
she was about as far from a raving beauty as I was. But something
about it kind of got to me. I tripped over a crack, and almost went
sprawling. When I looked up again she was gone, and the curtains
were motionless.

Dillon's attraction to Mona, like Charlie Bigger's with Ruthie, is not so much
rooted in lust as in identification and pathos: "She was too beat-down, completely lacking in confidence. If there was someone to take her away from
here, keep her going until she built up a little. . . . I hadn't had many people believe in me like that. Many? Hell, any." He protectively resists Ma Farrell's pimping, and only pretends to sleep with Mona. Yet, from Dillon's
suspicious angle, Mona continues to serve as a charged commodity. She
posts Dillon's bail after his rummy bookkeeping sends him to jail. And the
revelation that her aunt is hoarding a $100,000 cache in the basement ig-
nites the plot to kill Ma and pin it on Hendrickson.

Dillon lacks Bigger's background in murder, or Ford's glacial poise. The
pressure of juggling Joyce and Mona, Hendrickson and Staples, starts to tilt
his scales. As Dillon unravels, so also does his narrative. He talks to himself
in long, whimpering rages. " 'You're doing swell Dolly,' I told myself. . . ."
He casts episodes in the second person:

> . . . All you can do is go on like those other guys go on. The
> guy giving haircuts to dogs, and the guy sweeping up horse ma-
> nure. Hating it. Hating yourself.
>   And hoping.

The text erupts with electric italics and slashing capitals:

> *"Why, you're crazy, man!" I thought.* "YOU'RE *going to kill some-
> one?* YOU'RE *going to kill a couple of people? Not you, fella. It just
> ain't in you.*"

He raves to himself aloud in the third person:

> "Nothing wrong," I said—and I said it out loud—"Dolly Dillon
> says there's nothing wrong with it—the rotten son-of-a-bitch!"

Finally, after the murder of Ma Farrell and Hendrickson, Dillon—and *A
Hell of a Woman*—splinters. The novel cracks open as Dillon confronts us
with whole chapters in an alternative pulp mode, part Horatio Alger, part
frothing nonsense, which breezily whitewashes his guilt. Under the title

"THROUGH THICK AND THIN: THE TRUE STORY OF A MAN'S FIGHT AGAINST HIGH ODDS AND LOW WOMEN," he begins his story over with a new name, Knarf Nollid: "I was born in New York City one score and ten years ago, of poor but honest parents, and from my earliest recollections I was out working and trying to make something of myself and be somebody."

This rival pulp novel within the novel reappears after Dillon murders Joyce, and again after Mona falls in front of a truck. For his first direct treatment of the Depression marginal man since the 1930s, Thompson reanimated the split narration of "The End of the Book" sequence in *Always to Be Blest*. The alternate story releases Dillon's septic inner life, as he revisits scenes he has already narrated. Here is his initial, hard-boiled account of an ugly round with Joyce:

> "I'm warning you, Joyce. I'm giving you one last chance."
> "All hail the king." She made a noise with her lips. "Here's a kiss for you, king."
> "And here's one for you," I said.
> I brought it up from the belt, the sweetest left hook you ever saw in your life. She spun around on her heels and flopped backwards, right into the tub full of dirty bath water. And, Jesus, did it make a mess out of her.
> I leaned against the door, laughing . . .

This is the sensitive Knarf Nollid version:

> . . . the babe I'm married to then, she's out of this world, what I mean. The queen of the tramps, and a plenty tough bitch to boot.
> To get ahead of myself a little, she starts giving me a hard time one night, talking dirty to me and using bad language. So like I always do, I try to be reasonable and show her the error of her ways. I say it is not the best time to talk when a man comes home from work, and perhaps we will both be in a better mood after we have a bite to eat. I say, will she please fix us a bite, and I will cheerfully help her. Well, for answer she gives me some more of the dirty talk. And when I try to pet her and soothe her down, gently but firmly, she somehow slips and falls into the bathtub.
> I helped her out and apologized, although I hadn't done a goddamned thing. . . .

Along with some obvious satire, the pulp trappings of the rival novel hone a shrewd social point. As Dillon lurches through his self-serving revision, abruptly shifting tone, style, and diction, it is as though an inmate has escaped from the collective popular unconscious.

Dillon's black hole is sex. "I think I'm getting this thing all fouled up," he sputters. "I believe it was Doris who acted that way, the gal I was married to before Joyce. Yeah, it must have been Doris—or was it Ellen? Well, it doesn't make much difference; they were all alike." Like Frank Chambers in *The Postman Always Rings Twice* or Walter Huff in *Double Indemnity,* Dillon portrays himself as a victim of female wiles. "Three goddamned tramps in a row . . . or maybe it was four or five, but it doesn't matter. It was like they all were the same person."

Dolly Dillon forces the question of Thompson's misogyny. The glib answer is that Thompson was beastly to everyone regardless of gender, and that the women baiting belongs to a pervasive misanthropy. Yet that won't entirely hold up. The men in his books tend to be murdered outright, while the women are beaten or tortured and then killed.

A Hell of a Woman can, however, help focus the issue. Thompson's own relations with the women of his life—Alberta, Lucille Boomer, his mother and sisters—frequently were, as we have seen, frustrating, angry, and tangled. Yet when he refracted his private struggles into crime fiction he secured a dramatic distance on the problems of his nights and days. In the novels Thompson stylized his characters' repellent misogyny and avenging fantasies. When Dillon mixes up the women he abuses, for instance, the author makes it clear that the mushrooming hatred signals another downturn in his disintegration.

The original title of *A Hell of a Woman,* Thompson wrote Anthony Boucher, was *How Now, Brown Cow.* That nonsense phrase, borrowed from a children's elocution exercise, underscored Dillon's regression, unlike the catchier Lion title, which echoes his psychotic fears of the femme fatale. Dillon lacks a language for all the urgent stories of his life, *How Now, Brown Cow* seemed to say, Joyce, Mona, Ellen, or Doris among them.* Although Dillon sees "tramps" and female "traps" as the source of all his troubles, Thompson steadily italicized—often literally—his character's self-delusion and blindness. For all Dillon's rants, Mona and Joyce aren't tramps. Each could love him, if he would let them. He is responsible for his ruin. And, with his slyly feminine nickname, this Dolly is no tough guy at all. Dillon may mine the misogynist vein in American crime fiction. But once again Thompson inverted more than he borrowed from James M. Cain.

The conclusion of *A Hell of a Woman* all but crosses over the bound-

---

* When French director Alain Corneau adapted *A Hell of a Woman* with novelist Georges Perec for his film *Série Noire,* "he wanted the spoken language to be made up of clichés and stereotypes, in order to communicate directly the absence of an inner core" (according to David Bellos's biography *Georges Perec: A Life in Words*).

aries of storytelling. Hopelessly fragmented now, Dillon and the novel fall through a trapdoor and, as he notes, "there was nothing familiar to hang onto." Claiming he is on the lam in Oklahoma City and buying gold door to door under the name of Fred Jones—or Derf Senoj, as his backwards alias runs—Dillon tries to relate his happy new life with Helene, "my princess charming . . . beautiful and classy and all that a man desires in a woman." But as Fred Jones talks, Derf Sonej's counterpoint shoots through his text with bitter italicized phrases like static on his internal radio. When Fred says "beautiful and classy," Derf breaks in, *a bag in a fleabag, for Christ's sake. . . .* " Or while Fred and Helene mix fancy "drinks," his double toots, *"wow! the wine and the hay! yeeoweeeee."*

The battle within Dillon between Derf and Fred churns until, on the final pages, *A Hell of a Woman* rips apart into two simultaneous narratives. Thompson planned a cinematic finish for the novel, a kind of split screen. His manuscript concluded with two parallel columns of type. On one side, Fred plays out Dillon's terror of the emasculating she-demon. After Helene fixes him a cocktail, she takes her hair shears, lowers his trousers, and un-sexes him. On the other side, Derf consummates Dillon's self-destruction. After binging on wine, marijuana, cocaine, and heroin, he breaks a window with his foot, straddles the shattered pane, saws off his penis, and throws himself to the street. Either way, a night to dismember.

Lion editor Arnold Hano found the split screen confusing. "I didn't know whether the reader would read first the right-hand column, then the left-hand column, or jump back and forth." That anarchy, presumably, was Thompson's goal. But with the author's approval, the printed novel inter-weaves the endings into alternating lines of roman and italic type, in-evitably granting one voice—Derf's—the last word. *"I threw myself out the window."*

Perhaps nervous about the risks of even the muted finale for the paper-back audience, Lion published *A Hell of a Woman* with a preface by Thomp-son's friend George Milburn. "There will be those who will see in *A Hell of a Woman* traces of James Joyce's *Ulysses* and of William Faulkner's *Sanctu-ary,"* Milburn expounded. "And, as is to be expected, there will be those who will declare author Jim Thompson to be shameful or obscene—as readers have on occasion charged Joyce and Faulkner . . . Jim Thompson is the finest crime novelist going, Simenon and Graham Greene notwith-standing." *A Hell of a Woman* made a peculiar package: a standard Lion lurid cover, the highbrow preface, and a mindless blurb—"She lured him into the world's oldest trap."

For *The Nothing Man* (Dell, December 1954) Thompson amplified the closing strains of *A Hell of a Woman* into a total novel of castration and sui-cide. Narrator Clinton Brown, poet and rewrite man for the Pacific *City Courier,* lost his penis to an antipersonnel mine in the Second World War.

Ashamed, lonely, and relentlessly articulate, Brown emerges as probably Thompson's most sympathetic psychopath. "Was every move I made," he asks, "designed to extract payment from the world for the hell I dwelt in? Had I tried to destroy slowly and, failing that, killed wantonly?" *The Nothing Man* will be Brown's death song as, sitting late at his typewriter in the empty *Courier* newsroom, he prepares to take his life.

Clinton Brown is Hemingway's Jake Barnes transported to the seedy, apocalyptic Southern California of Nathanael West. He rolls a sallow eye over the newspaper trade and Pacific City politics. Prim, boosterish *Courier* publisher Austin Lovelace "wants the *Courier* all sweetness and light. No scandals, no exposes, nothing that would reflect on the fair name of Pacific City." The *Courier,* Brown rhapsodizes, is a non-union shop. "We take no dictation from labor bosses. . . . Thus, desk men may do reporting; re-porters may work the desk; and rewrite men such as myself may give fullest play to the talents which, on so many newspapers, are restricted and stunted by the harsh mandates of the Newspaper Guild." He taunts po-lice detective Lem Stukey, "chief pimp, gambler, all-around and overall racketeer of Pacific City. . . . I will say this for Stukey: he is absolutely fearless and relentless where vagrants are concerned." A blackout drunk with "cirrhosis of the soul," Brown revels in his alcoholism, ridicules his in-sipid column, "Around the Town with Clinton Brown," and experiences vi-sions of the Golden State as "nothing but desert, parched and withered and lifeless, where a dead man walked through eternity."

Brown can sound like Lou Ford in overdrive—not so much the verbal needle as the verbal buzz saw. His edgiest barbs are aimed at "Colonel" Dave Randall, *Courier* editor and, moreover, the army officer who ordered him into that minefield:

> "Uh, working pretty late, aren't you, Brownie?"
>
> "Late, Colonel?" I said. . . . "Well, yes and no. Yes, for a papa bird with a nest. No, for a nestless, non-papa bird. My work is my bride and I am consummating our wedding."
>
> "Uh . . . I notice your picture is badly smudged. I'll order a new one cut for the column."
>
> "I'd rather you didn't, Colonel," I said. "I think of the lady birds, drawn irresistibly by my chiseled, unsmudged profile, their tail feathers spread in delicious anticipation. I think of their disappoint-ment in the end . . . you should excuse the pun, Colonel. As a mat-ter of fact, I believe we should dispense with my picture entirely, replace it with something more appropriate, a coat of arms, say—"
>
> "Brownie—" He was wincing. I had barely raised the harpoon, yet already he was wincing. And there was no longer any satisfac-tion in it for me—if there had ever been any—but I went on.

"Something symbolic," I said. "A jackass, say, rampant against two thirds of a pawnbroker's sign, a smug, all-wise-looking jackass. As for the device, the slogan—how is your Latin, Colonel? Can you give me a translation of the phrase, 'I regret that I had only one penis to give to my country'?"

He bit his lip, his thin face sick and worried. I took the bottle from my desk and drank long and thirstily.

"Brownie, for God's sake! Won't you ever give it up?"

Grinding his quips and hallucinations, the castrato reporter ironically is something of a ladies' man. His ex-wife still carries the torch for him. Now a prostitute, Ellen remains unaware of his injury; rather than tell her, Brown divorced her when he returned from the service. "She wasn't bad, you see. She was weak, spiteful, stubborn; she'd made her own life a hell as a means of making mine one. But, except for what had happened to me, she wouldn't have done what she had." And Lovelace introduces him to Deborah Chasen. Initially, she seems more misogynist folderol. "Added up feature by feature," Brown rudely calculates, "she was anything but pretty. Corn-colored, almost-coarse hair, pulled back from her head in a horse's tail; green eyes that were just a shade off center; mouth a little too big . . . but when you put them all together you had a knockout." Yet once the widow Chasen penetrates his hard-bitten armor ("You're sad. . . . Funny and sad"), she evolves into Thompson's tenderest female portrait. The writer even has her repeat some love lines that Jim Dillon's wife, Roberta, pronounced in his autobiographical novel *Now and on Earth:*

"I knew it had to be you or no one; that if it weren't you then there simply wouldn't be anyone. . . . You'll see, darling." Her voice sank to a throaty, caressing whisper and her eyes burned like green fires. "It'll be all right for both of us. It'll be like nothing there ever was before. . . ."

Living in constant fear of exposure, Brown undertakes to silence his wife, and then Deborah Chasen. He clubs Ellen with a whiskey bottle, and sets her cabin on fire. "Remember, Ellen?" he jeers. "You always said to burn you up. . . ." Brown strangles Chasen, and tosses her into the dog pound. When both bodies turn up clutching bits of randy doggerel, he inflames the story into the sensational "Sneering Slayer" murders for the *Courier.* He also chokes Constance Wakefield, a dowdy publisher who holds the only copy of his incriminating poetry manuscript, stuffing a handful of coins down her throat.

As the author of a proto-beatnik work-in-progress, *Puke and Other Poems,* Brown justifies the "Sneering Slayer" murders—or "rhymes," as he rechristens them—with a pair of decadent literary equations. "The poet was the killer," he prates like some dazed acolyte of Rimbaud. "The point was indisputable—thanks to me." The poet-killer, he continues, is the scourge of God: "Something very bad has happened; that bad has to be off-set." Brown will not be the last Thompson murderer to recast his crimes as the actions of a righteous deity. As on Judgment Day, everyone must be punished according to her kind. "Ellen had wanted to be burned up and Deborah had wanted—wanted something else—and Constance Wakefield had wanted money. So I'd given it to her, and in such a way as to give her the utmost pleasure from it."

The Nothing Man features some of Thompson's nerviest writing and most demonic conceits. But the novel is not so formally innovative as *Savage Night* or *A Hell of a Woman*. The split narration appears here only as a psychotic "two-way pull." Early on Brown confesses, "I was experiencing that peculiar two-way pull that had manifested itself with increasing frequency and intensity in recent months. . . . Simultaneously I wanted to lash out at everything and do nothing about anything." And later:

> The old two-way pull began to assert itself. I headed for town, sitting very straight and circumspectly in the car seat but moving sideways, mentally. Moving off to one side, off into a world known only to me, where I could see *them* without being seen.

But the contradictions that radiate from the "two-way pull" crackle the spine of the traditional crime novel. If Brown, for instance, talks like Dr. Jekyll and Mr. Hyde, he behaves like Sherlock Holmes to his own Professor Moriarty. The Sneering Slayer murders are ingenious and, probably, unsolvable. The only clues come from Brown himself, in the form of his *Courier* columns or his conversations with Chief of Detectives Lem Stukey. He keeps the investigation running long after he would have been off scot-free. The crimes display the same doubleness. Playing out Brown's revenge and his guilt in equal measure, they seem, as Stukey observes, the work of two hands: "I was just going to say that it looks almost like two guys. One of 'em, this joker, he half asses the job up and the second makes it stick."

Similarly, Brown only *believes* he is the murderer. Operating in an alcoholic blackout, "I couldn't be sure that I had actually killed. . . ." Each of his victims, as it turns out, was already dead from causes different from what he can remember. Too impotent even to consummate his crimes, Brown technically is guilty of, as the title puts it, nothing:

> All I had wanted was to keep everyone under my thumb, to gouge and nibble away at them while I watched them squirm. . . .
> Then, when I wearied of the game, when I could no longer continue

it, I would kill myself. Or, no—No! I would make *Them* kill *me*. I would do something so blatantly criminal—so botched—that They would know I was guilty, and They would have to. . . .

They *would* have to, wouldn't they?

They couldn't leave me to go on . . . into nothingness.

"I suppose it will baffle hell out of the average whodunit reader," Brown chortles, "but perhaps he needs to be baffled. Perhaps his thirst for entertainment will impel him to the dread chore of thinking."

Dell Publishing Company obviously thought differently. As Thompson complained to Anthony Boucher, "I spent more time arguing about *The Nothing Man* than I did writing it; and then, in order to make a sale, I had to botch up the ending." Dell insisted that he tack a happy resolution onto the novel, as the chastened reporter promises to clean himself up and fly straight. But it's easy to see where Thompson intended *The Nothing Man* to conclude—a few pages earlier, with Brown twisting in the wind, incapable of either murder or suicide. "You've been slidin' down the rope and havin' a hell of a time for yourself," Lem Stukey tells him. "And now you're at the bottom, and all you can do is hang there. You can't let go and you can't get anyone to give you a shove. It wouldn't make 'em nothing. They can't do your job for you. It—it ain't much fun, is it, keed?"

For all its flagrant perversity, *The Nothing Man* is one of Jim Thompson's most personal fictions. Clinton Brown vented his creator's fury over the affronts and follies of the San Diego *Journal* and the Los Angeles *Mirror* during the 1940s. The novel, for as intimate an observer as his eldest daughter, Patricia, spilled over from Thompson's inner world. "The theme of that book," she believes, "came out of his life. It's a feeling that's so difficult to verbalize, but you have such a strong sense of certain things. I can see how he would have written that book."*

After Dark, My Sweet (Popular Library, December 1955) reshuffles the cards of Thompson's psychopathic deck into a suspenseful blind poker of sex, kidnapping, and salvation. William "Kid" Collins initially seems fated for the same psychic shredder as Brown, Dillon, Bigger, or Ford. A former boxer and recently escaped mental patient, he announces his split with only the second paragraph of his story:

---

*His friend Pierre Rissient traced *The Nothing Man* (resonantly titled *M. Zero* in French) to Thompson's 1938 vasectomy: "One day he confessed to me that his wife was such a Catholic that, when they did not wish to have any more children, she forced him to submit to a surgical operation in which he was sterilized, because she wanted nothing to do with contraceptives, and for her the slighter, lesser sin was for him to be sterilized. This is very important regarding *The Nothing Man,* for example, since in *The Nothing Man* the character is completely castrated.

Around four in the afternoon, after I'd walked about ten miles, I came to this roadhouse. I went on past it a little ways, walking slower and slower, arguing with myself. I lost the argument—the part of me that was on-the-beam lost it—and I went back.

Some lines from his psychiatric dossier flesh out the Thompson type: "Collins is amiable, polite, patient, but may be very dangerous if aroused." He wears a genial mask of sanity ("I played it dumb—kind of good-natured dumb"), but violence is never far from his surface. Inside the roadhouse, he punches a bartender "so hard it made my wrist ache."

Collins is haunted by the life-changing moment in the ring when, goaded by the referee's indifference to his opponent's low blows, he murdered the "Burlington Bearcat." The memory overtakes his present mind like an LSD flashback. "The veins in my throat were swelling," he notes. "Everything began to look red and blurred and hazy." Collins slips into a trance:

> It came back with neonlike clarity. The lights were scorching my eyes. The resin dust, the beerish smell of ammonia, were strangling me. And above the roar of the crowd, I could hear that one wildly shrieking voice. "Stop him! Stop him! He's kicking his brains out! It's murder, MURDER!"

As his boxing nickname implies, the "Kid" retains many childlike qualities despite the brutality and suffering of his past. Stalled in a state of arrested development, he emerges as both innocent and deadly.

After Collins is swept up by a mysterious, displaced couple and enlisted in their kidnapping plot, "Uncle Bud" Stoker, Fay Anderson, and the "Kid" forge a stunted triangle, a postnuclear family of damaged outsiders. A disgraced ex-policeman turned con artist, Stoker is one of Thompson's minor gems. He alternately flatters and browbeats Collins. "You meet guys like Uncle Bud once—just over a drink or a cup of coffee—and you feel like you've known them all your life. . . . Sooner or later, of course, they want something; and when they do it's awfully hard to say no to them. . . . Even when it's like something *this* Uncle Bud wanted."

The enigmatic, alcoholic Fay is harder for Collins to scan. "She was on and off like that all the time, I found out—nice to you one minute, needling you the next." Fay and Collins circumscribe a frustrating cat-and-mouse courtship of suspicion and desire. When she first meets him in Bert's Bar, she regards him only as a pickup and convenient stooge in the Vanderventer snatch. After she learns that he has escaped from a sanatorium, she fears for her safety and flees. But however warily, Fay grows protective of

Collins—"Listen closely to Old Mother Anderson," she entreats. If he is in a sense her son, he also becomes her pet. She calls him "Collie," sometimes fondly, other times contemptuously: "Down, boy. That's a good Collie."

Collie and Fay are plangent mirror images. His longing for her, his need to shelter her, is blocked by his own insecurity, confusion, and mistrust. He taps into a conundrum similar to the one that whirled around Pat Cosgrove in *Recoil.* What does Fay want with him? Will she, like Uncle Bud, double-cross him? Recognizing that his "judgement is anything but good," Collins sideslips and skids:

> Maybe it had all been a build-up, a way of pointing me in one direction so she could move in another. Why not? Fay couldn't get me to clear out, and leave her and Uncle Bud or someone else with my share of the loot. So she'd picked up with another plan, another way of cutting me out of the deal. She'd know just how to go about it. Right from the beginning, she'd been able to get me so rattled and mixed up I didn't know what I was doing.

In the opaque atmosphere of *After Dark, My Sweet,* it's only while "Mother Anderson" and the "Kid" make love that the fog lifts. During their finally unrestrained intercourse, perhaps Thompson's only unsmirking sexual episode, Collins observes, "There wasn't a second of pretense in that long hour we were together. . . . There are some things you can't fake, you can't pretend about, and that's one of them." But this still center cannot hold against the absurdist calamity of the kidnapping. And he rises from their bed with his doubts intact.

Collins identifies with little Charlie, the sickly, neglected scion of a wealthy Southwestern family. "The more I thought about it, the more it seemed to me that Bill Collins and Charles Vanderventer III were in the same boat . . . no one was interested in either of us until the kidnapping." As Fay and Uncle Bud collapse amid the news reports, ransom notes, and the diabetic Charlie, Collins eerily gathers confidence and focus from the troubled boy. He steals insulin and administers the shots. He punishes Fay when she wants to leave Charlie in a culvert to die. And he turns the tables on Uncle Bud, prodding a confrontation with the police that leaves the con man in a railway station riddled with bullets. But even as he asserts his new strength, Collins is disintegrating, sliding into his old "red haze," and "Rushing toward the end. . . . This was what I wanted, you see, the end."

For *After Dark, My Sweet* Thompson devised his most subtly modulated double ending. As Collins takes to the road with Fay and Charlie, the question for him is still whether to trust and believe her. He wearily concludes that in spite of all her previous feints and hesitations he does—and more:

When a man stops caring what happens, all the strain is lifted from him. Suspicion and worry and fear—all the things that twist his thinking out of focus—are brushed aside. And he can see people as they really are—as I saw Fay then.

Weak and frightened. Self-pitying, maybe. But good, too. Basically as good as a woman could be, and hating herself for not being better. She'd planned to call the cops, telling them the boy was in the culvert, after we'd made our escape. I *knew* that now. I knew that if it came to a showdown, she'd protect him with her life. I *knew* it, and suddenly I wanted Fay to live.

Suddenly, it made sense for Fay to live; it was the only way my having lived would make any sense. It was why I had lived, it seemed like. It was why I had been made like I was. To show her something, to prove something—to do something for her that she could not do for herself. . . .

Collins transforms himself into Jesus Christ, much as Clinton Brown in *The Nothing Man* merged with the wrathful God of the Old Testament. This "psychotic-of-good-will," as Boucher wittily tagged him in *The New York Times,* proceeds to sacrifice his life to save Fay's, provoking her to shoot him as he appears to go for the boy.

Director James Foley in his 1990 adaptation of *After Dark, My Sweet* played this moment as pure nobility. But Thompson allows the reader to view Collins's sacrificial gesture as at once heroic and the culmination of all his childish, infantile impulses. The novel concludes with Fay and Charlie alive and safe, as the dying Collie rolls over and barks like a dog.

After Dark, My Sweet exchanges the verbal or structural pyrotechnics of its predecessors for bold, filmic imagery. Thompson, in fact, projected *After Dark, My Sweet* as a movie right from conception. Alongside his first-person manuscript he prepared a third-person treatment, called *The Concrete Pasture.* This haunting title, a recurrent Thompson favorite, could be engraved over the portal to all his 1950s fiction. "The concrete pasture," he brooded. "You keep going and going, and it's always the same everywhere. Wherever you've been, wherever you go, everywhere you look. Just grayness and hardness, as far as you can see."

•   •   •

A coruscating whirl of pop and high culture, of private obsessions and American pathology, the first-person narrator, psychopathic killer novels became Jim Thompson's signature and passport, both in the 1950s and later. Early on they secured his name as an influential "writer's writer." While Anthony Boucher publicized his "sharp and markedly individual studies in crime and punishment" in the Sunday *New York Times,* novelist

R. V. Cassill argued that Thompson "is exactly what the French enthusiasts for existential American violence were looking for in the work of Dashiell Hammett, Horace McCoy, and Raymond Chandler. None of those men ever wrote a book within miles of Thompson's." French literary critics eventually would salute him as *"le plus noir, le plus amer, le plus pessimiste de tous les auteurs des romans policiers américains"* and *"un des grands écrivains américains du XX° siècle et le plus grand auteur de la Série Noire."* When contemporary journalists tout a new book, film, or CD as "in the style of Jim Thompson" they also are paying homage to his psychopathic ventriloquism. But during the Lion years Thompson conjured up other kinds of books, which he wrestled to the page with varying gusto and skill.

Multiple Narrator Novels

With *The Criminal* (Lion Books, December 1953) and *The Kill-Off* (Lion Library, January 1957) Thompson moved from split narrations and dual personalities to a multiple first-person technique. Nine different questionable narrators drive an evolving story in *The Criminal,* while *The Kill-Off* circulates an even dozen. Hattie, the African-American housekeeper and mistress of a white doctor in *The Kill-Off,* dubs the shifting points of view "keyhole thinking":

> Reckon you know what I mean. . . . May be a mighty big room, but you sure ain't going to see much of it. And you keep looking through the keyhole long enough, nothing ain't never going to look big to you.
>
> Get to where that eye of yours just won't spread out.

An individual's perspective—or keyhole—is limited, homespun Hattie adds, by his or her language: "The mind can't go no farther than a person's 'cabulary. You got to have the words or you can't talk, and you got to have them or you can't think. No words, no thinking. Just kind of feeling."

Thompson would have encountered multiple first-person narration in William Faulkner's *As I Lay Dying* while a student at the University of Nebraska. Martin Goldsmith adapted the mode for crime fiction in 1939 with *Detour,* later stunningly filmed by Edgar Ulmer. At least two other crime novels known to Thompson, Kenneth Fearing's *The Big Clock* (1946) and Bruno Fischer's *More Deaths Than One* (1947) enhanced suspense with multiple narrators. Fischer was a Lion author, and "Jim told me that he admired Kenneth Fearing," reports Arnold Hano. Yet the device in Thompson's hands remained truer to Faulkner. The multiple voices in *The Criminal* and *The Kill-Off* do not so much stagger mounting excitement as assemble a social theater for the display of collective evil and guilt.

The Criminal commences with a tabloid atrocity of the rape and murder of a promiscuous schoolgirl, and brilliantly proceeds to forget about it. The death of Josie Eddleman in the Kenton Hills district of a city that resembles the suburban Fort Worth of Thompson's adolescence is never solved. The novel swerves from the resolution of a crime into the cultural network of greed, deceit, and betrayal that surrounds the arrest of the last person to see Josie alive, young Bob Talbert. Everybody admits that the tongue-tied, hot-blooded teenager did not kill the girl. But if he isn't "the criminal" of the title, who is? Could it be the publisher and self-styled "God" of the *Star,* known only as the Captain, who sensationalizes the scandal to sell papers? "We'll run them off the stands," the Captain hoots at his journalistic rivals. "Just what do we *know* about this boy, anyway. . . ." Or could it be *Star* reporter William Willis, who stokes the smear campaign against Bob in his "grudge play against the paper"? Or District Attorney Hargreave Clinton, who badgers his confession? *"Is that what you mean, Bob,"* Clinton hisses. *"You want me to help you, put it in the right words. . . ."* All the major players of *The Criminal* are soiled. The police vie to trade information for cash with I. Kossmeyer, Bob's flamboyant lawyer. Bob's parents indict his character as they act out their dismal marriage before Willis. Even Kossmeyer pays for the testimony that secures Bob's release.

Thompson focuses the accidents that shape a life with weary tenderness. Writing in his own middle age, he summons a shuddering, washed-out sense of disappointment and decline. "You just rock along, doing the things that you have to," Allen Talbert, Bob's father, shrugs, "and you get kind of startled sometimes when you stand off and look at yourself. You think, my God, that isn't me. How did I ever get like that? But you go right ahead, startled or not, hating it or not, because you don't actually have much to say about it. You're not moving so much as you are being moved." Still more plaintively, Arlene Clinton, the D.A.'s neglected wife, wonders, "Isn't it terrible? You're just like you always were, the very same person, and suddenly that isn't good enough anymore." With the insoluble murder lodging a vacuum at the core of the novel, *The Criminal* is all anxious resonance.

For this slender tour de force Thompson dictated distinctive intonations for his gallery of speakers, spreading out from hysterical chatter of Martha Talbert, Bob's mother, to Willis's cynical gamesmanship and the Captain's omniscient leer.

One voice he adapted from the ethnological "Ex-Slaves" narratives he compiled as director of the Oklahoma Writers' Project. Here is Kossmeyer's conversation with Pearlie May Jones, as recounted by her son President Abraham Lincoln Jones:

Lil man say, Well, mam, I couln pay you tuh say you see iss boy. You unnerstan at, mam.

> Mammy say, I unnerstans, mistah. I unnerstans, awright.
>
> Lil man squirm. He say, I like be vey cleah on dis point. I could not n would not be pahty tuh procurin false witness. I wan nuffin fum you but de troof. Dey is no connection between whut you say n any sistance I give you.
>
> Mammy grin. Sho dey ain, she say. We just do it fo favuh.

This is the less stagy model from the "Ex-Slaves" oral histories:

> He's might old, is Uncle George King, and he'll tell you that he was born on two-hundred acres of Hell, but the whitefolks call it Samuel Noll's plantation.
>
> Kinder small for plantation, but plenty room for that devil overseer to lay on the lash, and plenty room for the old she-devil Mistress to whip his mammy til' she was just a piece of living raw meat!

I. Kossmeyer himself was based on Moman Pruiett, the theatrical Oklahoma lawyer who shadowed the Thompsons from territorial days to the Writers' Project. "Jim hated Pruiett since the time of the Oklahoma Committee to Defend Political Prisoners," Gordon Friesen recalls. "He was outraged when Pruiett tried to get little Nena Beth to piss on him. Jim really had it in for him after that." The mocking metamorphosis of Pruiett into Kossmeyer suggests that the revenge instincts behind Thompson's fiction rarely imposed a simple mechanical bludgeon. "Jim could be pretty funny sometimes," Friesen comments. "Pruiett was a virulent anti-Semite and reactionary in his politics, although he always talked about the common man. So Jim made him into a liberal and a Jew—probably the most terrible fate he could imagine for him!"

Kossmeyer retains Pruiett's dramatic flair, his eloquence and gift for mimicry, along with his success in the courtroom. "My clients are seldom convicted," he brags. Yet only Kossmeyer is willing to acknowledge the wreckage of Bob Talbert's future. And Thompson slips the lawyer a compassionate set piece about the Jones family that homes in on the many bruised souls of *The Criminal:*

> . . . Two Negro boys, perhaps thirteen and fifteen respectively, were shucking peas into a kettle while a third boy—ten or thereabouts—looked on. I said, hello, and they leaped to their feet. The older boy placed himself in front of the other two. "Mammy," he called over his shoulder, not taking his eyes off me, "some white man heah."
>
> There was trouble in the way he said white man. There was

trouble in the woman who squeezed through the door and silently confronted me, hands on hips. I could see what Bob meant when he said she was plenty mean-looking.

This was going to be tough, as tough as it could be made on me. But I was thinking not so much of the fact as the causes that lay behind it. What had been done to them, said and done to them, to make them like this?

Kossmeyer was Thompson's first serial character, apart from an extraneous Fruit Jar or Billingsley, and he returned to introduce *The Kill-Off.* The *Peyton Place* plot radiates around the murder of a town gossip in a dying Long Island, New York, resort. Luane Devore in her prime "had resembled Theda Bara," the silent-screen vamp of Thompson's damp afternoons at the movies in Oklahoma City. Now a flabby, talcum-caked hypochondriac, Luane terrorizes the town of Manduwoc from the telephone in her sickroom. "There was nothing at all wrong with her," Kossmeyer relates. "Nothing but self-pity and selfishness, viciousness and fear: the urge to lash out at others from the sanctuary of the invalid's bed." The lawyer warns Luane: "You'd better stop telling those rotten lies about people before one of them stops you. Permanently, you know what I mean?"

The flibbertigibbet's charges of adultery, incest, impotence, miscegenation, or bankruptcy may be "rotten," but are they "lies"? The multiple narration of *The Kill-Off* matched the mudslinging theme and the furtive, inbred village. Thompson commanded his difficult technique, interlocking the twelve guileful voices of his main story as he made room for lively side dramas. Each of the narrators is guilty of what one, local drunk Marmaduke "Goofy" Gannder, labels "the original sin, the one we all suffer for: the failure to attribute to others the motives we claim for ourselves." Everyone in Manduwoc, it seems, harbors a secret and thus a powerful inducement for silencing Luane. (The peculiar title of the novel probably alludes to that 1950s phenomenon, the bake-off. *The Kill-Off* is a contest to see who can get Luane first.)

Thompson took greater risks with his characters for *The Kill-Off* than he allowed himself in *The Criminal.* He enjoyed revisiting events *Rashomon*-style, deflecting the epiphanies against discordant perspectives. Rags McGuire, for instance, an old-time jazz bandleader, bitterly asserts that his absent wife, Janie, is "at home looking after the boys, whoring and guzzling." Some hundred pages later we hear that his two sons died in a car crash that left Janie without "a nose and only part of a tongue, and no teeth . . . and hardly any place to put teeth." Thompson more elaborately diffracts the mutation of Pete Pavlov from a straight-shooting if gruff family man into a psychopath through his contradictory narrators. Pavlov eventually confesses to—but then disclaims—the murder of Luane Devore, all the while pledging his high principles. "I have to live a certain way or I'd rather be dead," he says, "which I'm just about to be."

The Kill-Off struts a cracked surrealism. "Goofy" Gannder renames the local cemetery "The City of Wonderful People" because of the testimonials on the tombstones. "They're DUTIFUL AND LOVING PARENTS, they're GOD-FEARING AND LOYAL, they're HONEST and KINDLY and STEADFAST and GENEROUS and MERCIFUL and TOLERANT and WISE. . . ." Stopping at his grandmother's grave, Gannder unloads another Swiftean parable:

> Once upon a time, there were two billion and a half bastards who lived in a jungle, which weighed approximately six sextillion, four hundred and fifty quintillion short tons. Though they were all brothers, these bastards, their sole occupation was fratricide. Though the jungle abounded in wondrous fruits, their sole food was dirt. Though their potential for knowledge was unlimited, they knew but one thing. And what they knew was only what they did not know. And what they did not know was what was enough.

Bobbie Ashton is the most perverse citizen of Manduwoc. The illegitimate scion of the black maid Hattie and her physician employer, Bobbie quotes the Bible and proclaims himself "a loving god" as he channels his racial self-hatred into intricate feats of revenge. He taunts his mother with libidinous innuendo. He steals drugs from his father's office and addicts Pete Pavlov's daughter Myra. Bobbie Ashton provides the prototype for the teenage evil geniuses in Thompson's late novels *Child of Rage* and *The Horse in the Baby's Bathtub,* the recurrent "white-mother-black-son" prodigies that his French admirer Pierre Rissient would label his "most savage . . . most violent . . . and most provocative" creations.

Writing in the Third Person

The smooth timing and indirection of *The Kill-Off* mark it a high point of Thompson's first-person novels. *A Swell-Looking Babe* (Lion, July 1954), however, is evidence that the writer did not require a ventriloquized "I" to create lethal fiction. This book scavenged so deeply beneath Thompson family trauma that the bloody trench probably could be surveyed only by a distant third-person narration.

A Swell-Looking Babe twists the struggles of Thompson's Fort Worth adolescence into a pulp *Oedipus Rex.* Bill "Dusty" Rhodes is an intelligent, handsome night bellboy (like Jim, nicknamed "Dolly") at the Manton Hotel who walks the razor edge of the Texas underworld. Once intent on medical school, he was forced to work after his foster father (like James Sherman Thompson, a former teacher and principal) lost his post in a red scare when his name turned up on a Free Speech petition. "Learn[ing] simply to accept . . . and hate," the bellhop conceals a homicidal ire for William Bryant Rhodes, Sr., and a simmering erotic obsession with his deceased foster mother, "the woman, the only one." When Dusty meets "her counterpart," the mystifying Marcia Hillis, at the Manton, and lines up with mobster Tug Trowbridge to rob the hotel, the caper surges with reveries of incest and patricide.

If Dusty seems a terrifying projection of Jim Thompson at the Hotel Texas during the mid-1920s, Professor Rhodes is a fair facsimile of Pop circa 1932. The aloof, sullen son has long been a "disappointment" to his father, his "conduct . . . below standard," as Thompson encapsulates in a snug parallel to his autobiography *Bad Boy*. Now parent and child have swapped places as a result of the old man's sudden enfeeblement. "Only a little past sixty, and . . . practically senile," the absent-minded professor wanders the streets unable to control his money, his time—or his face: "His father's mouth had drooped open in that loose, imbecilic way. His eyes were vacantly bewildered. Swiftly, as he always did when the perplexing or troublesome loomed, he had retreated behind the barrier of helplessness."

More than in any other of his Lion novels, Thompson thrust his early domestic crises—and private myths—to the forefront of *A Swell-Looking Babe*. Dusty fancies himself a paragon of filial concern, indulging his father's whims, enduring a crummy job, and contending with the family lawyer—"Caustic" Kossmeyer. Yet inwardly he sizzles, blaming Professor Rhodes for the destruction of his career, and for coming between him and his foster mother. Dusty is a master of subliminal aggression. It was he, we eventually discover, who signed the petition that led to his father's dismissal from Central High School. When the professor kills himself, Dusty saunters off to the Manton, misconstruing—or ignoring—the death rattle behind the bedroom door:

> It sounded like he was praying. Or singing. Kind of like he was praying and singing together. And occasionally there was something like a sob . . . choked, strangling, rattling.
>
> Dusty went on to the hotel.

The scene echoes the choking suicide Thompson imagined for *his* father in the Oklahoma sanitarium of *Now and on Earth*—"gorging himself on the excelsior from his mattress"—and repeated, as though it were public record, to friends such as Arnold Hano for the rest of his days. "He knew I was going to show up. Why did he have to kill himself?" Thompson sobbed to Hano. "I demand to know, Rhodes," Kossmeyer confronts Dusty, "why you did not intervene to save his life? Why, instead, you walked callously out of the house and left this helpless old man to die!"

Dusty's yearnings for his foster mother are harder to accommodate, or abide. Thompson's nephew Tony Kouba believes that "Jimmie was over-mothered as a child. From my own mother [Maxine] I know that his mother would have killed herself to get him anything he wanted. He moved out from this heavily mothered environment into a really tough, wild place. There were some strange circumstances at that hotel, and Jimmie wasn't cut from that cloth."

Still, nothing in Thompson's anecdotal history prepares a reader for Dusty's peekaboo assaults on Mrs. Rhodes's bed:

> . . . he had been about eleven when it happened. It was on a Sunday morning, and she had been awakened by a rainstorm, and so she had awakened him (not intentionally) with drowsy kisses and hugs. He burrowed close to her. He moved his head, sleepily, feeling an unusual softness and warmth. And suddenly he felt it withdrawn, or, rather, since he did not release his hold, an attempt at withdrawal.
>
> "Bill! Let go, darling!"
>
> "Huh?" He opened his eyes unwillingly. "What's the matter?"
>
> "Well, you can see, can't you?"—her voice was almost sharp. "I mean, Mother has to fix her nightgown."
>
> She fixed it hastily, blushing. She sat back down, rather stiffly, and then, seeing the innocence of his expression, she drew him close again. . . .
>
> He was silent, but it was a different kind of silence. Warm, expectant, deliciously shivery. They lay very still for a moment, and then she sat up, and there was the sound of soft silk against silken flesh.
>
> She lay back down. She whispered, "B-baby. Turn around, baby. . . ." And he turned around.
>
> Then, right on the doorstep of ultimate heaven, the gates clanged shut.
>
> She lay perfectly still, breathing evenly. She did not need to push him away, not physically. Her eyes did that. Delicately flushed a moment before, the lovely planes of her face were now an icy white. . . .
>
> *"You had it all figured out, didn't you? Your—poor old Dad, sick and worn out so much of the time. And me, still young and foolish and giddy, and loving you so much that I'd do anything to save you hurt."*
>
> *"I—you mad at me about somethin', Mother?"*
>
> *"Stop it! Stop pretending! Don't deceive yourself, Bill. At least be honest with yourself."*

"M-Mother. I'm sorry if I —"

*"Not nearly as sorry as I am Bill. Nor as shocked, or fright-
ened. . . ."*

Dusty's midnight encounter with Marcia Hillis at the Manton Hotel triggers both his incestuous memories and the doomed robbery. "All women—
the personification, the refined best of them all," Marcia is the flip side of
Dolly Dillon's "Three goddamned tramps in row. . . . It was like they were
the same person." When Marcia cautiously resists him, Dusty recalls his
foster mother and beats her. Too late, in typical Thompson fashion, does
he shed his past to recognize her honesty and kindness, or the cynical ma-
nipulations of Tug Trowbridge. A Capone-style racketeer, Tug emerges as a
sort of surrogate father to Dusty, plying the self-confidence he misses at
home. The gangster, in fact, dies in a police shoot-out at precisely the same
moment that Professor Rhodes chokes in his room.

A Swell-Looking Babe is Thompson's ugliest dramatization of the guilt
and revenge that haunts his 1950s fiction—and the most self-chastising.
The novel closes with lawyer Kossmeyer jauntily mimicking Dusty's hanging for the murder of William Bryant Rhodes, Sr. "Freudians will have a field
day here," Anthony Boucher raved in *The New York Times*. "But Thompson
never overtly diagrams his psychoanalytic patterns. On the surface he's
content to tell a rattling good story. . . . Beneath that surface there's a
subtle study of the interplay of conscious and subconscious motivations, a
full-length picture of a Rex-size Oedipus complex, and an almost Aris-
totelian sense of tragic form. It's a good value, on whichever level you
choose to read it."

Cul-de-Sacs

Not all of Thompson's Lion novels proved so formidable. Despite daunting
runs of sevens and elevens he rolled an occasional snake-eyes. If *The Killer
Inside Me* suggested, in Geoffrey O'Brien's inspired phrase, a "Dimestore
Dostoevsky," then *Cropper's Cabin* (Lion, November 1952), its fumbling sequel, is Cut-Rate Caldwell and Fire-Sale Faulkner. For this latter-day *God's
Little Acre* or *Sanctuary*, Thompson exhumed the stereotypes of the rustic
soap opera.

Tom Carver is a young cotton farmer in love with Donna, the beautiful
daughter of a prosperous Indian landowner, Matthew Ontime. His father is
so mean that he let Tom's mother die during childbirth while he spent a
week in the arms of a whore. That whore, Mary, lives with the Carvers in
their shack on a tiny field at the center of Ontime's five-thousand-acre
spread, and shares both of their beds. Tom's father wants to lease the oil
rights to their land. Ontime blocks the deal, drawing Tom into a family feud

that pits him against Donna. When Ontime perishes in a hog pen, stabbed with Tom's knife, not even Kossmeyer—here tracking even closer to the vicious Moman Pruiett, as he destroys Donna's reputation on the witness stand—can keep the country boy out of Sandstone State Reformatory.

Thompson steeped his sharecropper's melodrama in territorial Oklahoma and Native American history. The opening chapters review the migration of the Five Civilized Tribes along the "Trail of Tears" to southeastern Oklahoma and the opening of Indian Territory to white settlement with an angry emphasis, as in *Heed the Thunder,* on the destruction of the land. But *Cropper's Cabin* comes alive only in patches. The fatal miscue is Thompson's hazy trajectory of narrator Tom Carver. Although a talented student beloved by his teachers, Tom swells with rancors and tantrums. He enjoys hurting people: "Maybe you don't know how it is when you're so sick inside, sick and hopeless-feeling, that you want someone to cross you a little; just enough so's you'll have an excuse to make them feel bad too." And Tom enjoys being hurt, laughing as his father whips him:

> He brought the strap up fast. It whistled and popped as he swung it up above his head. And I grinned at him, feeling the bad feeling that was now good to feel. It was like a coon must feel when a trap gets him, and he has to chew off a leg to get out.

Only his hatred for Pa—"the picture I had in my mind of facing Pa with the axe"—keeps Tom sane in Sandstone. To a young prison doctor he coughs up a clipped parable that allies him with the other walking dead of the Lion novels:

> "It's—well, it's kind of like this, doc. Like a story I read one time about a man. He got to where he couldn't see, not really see, you know. He had eyes, but somehow they didn't tell his mind anything. And his ears were the same way. And his mouth. Somehow he couldn't find any words to come out of it; and he couldn't taste anything. Not really taste it. And all over his body, doc, he was kind of numb. He couldn't feel anything. And he knew there was something wrong—he knew *what* was wrong. But there wasn't a thing he could do about it, him or anyone else. Not a thing, and it was a waste of time to try. Because he was dead."

Tom Carver takes shape as a trademark Thompson psycho—who is promptly healed at the end. After a Creek Indian janitor named Abe Toolate admits to the theft of Tom's knife and the murder of Matthew Ontime, Tom is released from Sandstone to a joyous "new life" with Donna. The burden of this implausible resolution probably belongs more to a rare editorial lapse by Arnold Hano than to any conversion to the redemptive powers of love and bourgeois marriage on Thompson's part. "I think when we did *Cropper's Cabin,* we asked Jim whether he could come up with a more up-beat ending," Hano reports. "He said, oh, like . . . , and mentioned another novel—I forget which one it was. I said, yes, like that, and he said, sure." The upshot of their *folie à deux* is that *Cropper's Cabin* turned out the limpest of all Thompson's Lion novels.

Abe Toolate's confession involves an oddity from the annals of the Osage Nation that Thompson had chronicled in "Two Lives of John Stink" for the March 1951 issue of *SAGA.* Tom invokes the strange fate of John Stink as he observes the ceremonial "execution" of Toolate by a Creek medicine man:

> . . . I wasn't any Indian, of course, but I knew that what had happened to [Toolate]—though he hadn't been harmed physically—was about the worst thing that could happen to a man.
>
> A few years ago, during a smallpox epidemic, an Indian died up in the old Osage Nation. The doctors pronounced him dead, and all his kinfolks and friends came to his house and began mourning. And he wasn't really dead—just in a state of coma—and all the racket snapped him out of it. He sat up in bed and asked them what the heck was going on. And no one heard him—no one would admit hearing. They just got up and walked out.
>
> From that day on, as far as the Osages were concerned, he didn't exist. He'd "died" and the dead don't come back to life. No one would speak to him. He'd try to stop them on the street, and they'd just look right through him and keep on going.

Thompson was remembering an article by Lorren Williams, "The Saga of John Stink: Oklahoma's Rugged Indian Individualist," which appeared in the Oklahoma *News* on March 14, 1937, opposite a story by his Writers' Project friend Ned DeWitt on the Cherokee "outlaw" Ned Christie. John Stink—or Ho-Ta-Moi, "Rolling Thunder," his Osage name—lived some sixty years after his ritual ostracism. The beneficiary of more than $200,000 in headrights to the oil revenues from the Osage Reservation, he forsook his modern log cabin to sleep with his dogs in the woods near the Pawhuska Country Club. John Ha-Ta-Moi could be observed, Williams wrote, mimicking golfers as he puffed on a fat cigar, or sitting behind the steering wheel of a motor car he never removed from the garage. His obituary in the *News* would read, "Rites for John Stink Are Final, This Time."

Thompson drew on the more recent past in *The Alcoholics* (Lion Books, March 1953). His periodic visits to the Hygeia and Paradise Valley drying-out clinics in San Diego during the 1940s afforded a stark backdrop for this slight social comedy, his only Lion novel not focused on a crime. Thompson planned *The Alcoholics* as a breakaway best seller, according to Arnold Hano: "His marketing theory was that there are forty million alcoholics, so I should sell forty million books."

The novel, Thompson also told Hano, "would be a twenty-four-hour kind of book," set on a single day in the life of El Healtho, a run-down Southern California spa specializing in "Modern Treatment for Alcoholics." Any ambitions toward plot melt away into a rolling tableau of crackpots and dipsos. El Healtho director Peter S. Murphy is a failed suicide with a split personality. Head nurse Lucretia Baker masturbates against the bound body of a lobotomized patient and distributes liquor to the other inmates, who include an ex-general and a pregnant Hollywood actress, along with the stock gaggle of advertising men, literary agents, and Pulitzer Prize journalists, "maintain[ing] more or less permananent living quarters in El Healtho Sanitarium."

The sharpest scenes tap insider's lore Thompson culled from lost weekends: the techniques for palming Antabuse or hiding bottles, or the symptoms that unlock the clinic drug cabinet. *The Alcoholics,* as noted earlier, traces alcoholism to "a fear of self." Thompson reproduces the detachment of chronic alcoholics who abstractly discuss their craving as though it were happening to someone else. He reprises the "Chinchilla out of a hat" thesis from his *SAGA* article, "An Alcoholic Looks at Himself," in language that mirrors the "two-way pull" of the psychopathic novels:

> The alcoholic's depressed mood pulls him two ways. While it insists that great deeds must be done by way of proving himself, it insidiously resists his doing them. It tells him simultaneously that he must—and can't. That he is certain to fail—but must succeed.
> It was a maddening sensation. . . .

Thompson himself makes an unannounced, italicized entrance to El Healtho on the final page of *The Alcoholics:*

> *"We have a new patient, Doctor. I think you better see him."*
> *"Bad?"*
> *"Pretty well into delirium. Beaten up, rolled, apparently. . . ."*
> *"Better rig up a saline drip. . . . What's his name, anyway? His job?"*
> *"Couldn't quite get his name, Doctor. But he was babbling something about being a writer."*
> *. . . They grabbed him together, the puke-smeared, wild-eyed wreck who staggered suddenly into the corridor. He struggled for a moment, then went limp in their arms sobbing helplessly.*

> *"T-tomcats," he wept. "S-sonsbitches t-thirty-four f-feet tall an'*
> *. . . n' got eighteen tails, n' . . . n'. . . ."*
> *"Yeah?" said Doctor Murphy.*
> *". . . n' oysters for eyeballs."*
> Doctor Murphy chuckled grimly. *"Yes, sir,"* he said, *"we'll knock*
> *him out, wash him out, and get him back to work. I've got a job all*
> *picked out for this character."*
> *"C-cats,"* sobbed the writer. *"N' every damn one a lyric*
> *soprano. . . ."*
> Doctor Murphy regarded him fondly. *"A grade-A nut,"* he said. *"A*
> *double-distilled screwball. Just the man to write a book about this*
> *place."*

The novel bears a noticeable resemblance to Ken Kesey's *One Flew Over the Cuckoo's Nest*—published nearly a decade later, in 1962—from the name of the hero (McMurphy in Kesey) and the character of the sadistic nurse to the comic-strip style and the prescient counterculture theme of the inmates who emerge as saner than their keepers.

But *The Alcoholics* actually is a pale rewrite of a celebrated Oklahoma alcoholic confessional Thompson praised as director of the Writers' Project. *Behind the Door of Delusion* appeared in 1932 under the pseudonym "Inmate Ward 8." The author was widely known to be Marion Marle Woodson, a Tulsa newspaperman, who committed himself for treatment to the Eastern Oklahoma Hospital for the Insane. Nothing in *The Alcoholics* equals the terror—or the black comedy—of Woodson's documentary of his year locked in the asylum. Thompson dropped a mention of *Behind the Door of Delusion* into the automobile tours section of the Oklahoma state guide.

The Autobiographies

The most interesting fact about Thompson's autobiographies *Bad Boy* (Lion Books, July 1953) and *Roughneck* (Lion Books, April 1954) is that they exist at all. No other Lion novelist was permitted to log his life story, and Thompson proposed the two volumes long before there was interest in him as a writer. "Jim wanted to do them, and he assured us that they would be stories," Arnold Hano recalls. "We cheated on the packaging—we didn't scream 'autobiography' or 'nonfiction.' I don't think they sold as well as the novels, but they didn't do badly. It was important to do them, I thought. He wrote two, and there was a third he never got around to."

Bad Boy charts the period between Thompson's birth and his departure for college in 1929, while *Roughneck* advances the calendar to 1941, the year of his father's death and the writing of *Now and on Earth*. Both chronicles are as peculiar for their wooden, sentimental prose as they are for their elisions, caprices, and pulled punches. As Thompson bent his life into a personal mythology of the Prodigal Son and the Victim, this fascinating algebra of need trivialized his experience into blandly charming tall tales. For the McCarthyist 1950s he expunged the Wobblies, Haywire Mac, the Oklahoma Communist Party, the Social Forum School, the Southwest Writers' Congress, Bill Cunningham, Ned DeWitt, Gordon Friesen, and Woody Guthrie—in short, nearly all his public crossroads. Private censorship diluted his romantic, work, and family imbroglios to folksy anecdote. Thompson whitewashes the Hotel Texas, the oil fields, the Writers' Project, and his alcoholism. There is no mention of Lucille Boomer, little about his mother, his sisters, Alberta, or their children, and only a few dispirited pokes at his father.

Despite the consuming inwardness of his fiction, Thompson—strange to say—possessed no gift for introspection. With *Bad Boy* and *Roughneck* he failed to mint a memorable autobiographical language and retreated into abstractions like Fate and Luck to explain why his world turned out the way that it had. At one remove, in his crime novels, Thompson could discharge his anger, fears, failures, and desires, and tell his secret history. Reduced to his own solitary voice, he can seem as much a juggler running out of hands as do any of his characters.

Lion Books also published Thompson's desk drawer novels from a few years previous, *Recoil* (February 1953) and *The Golden Gizmo* (March 1954). "Since he had written them before he came to us," Arnold Hano remembers, "we suggested that we not pay him as much as we would for something fresh. Instead of $2,000, he probably got $1,500. We did skinflint people—that wasn't very nice."

• • •

Jim Thompson suddenly was a novelist with a considerable body of work. Flush on his Lion advances—five for 1953 alone—he moved his family from the Elizabeth and Gregory apartment to a home in Flushing, a rambling, two-floor stucco barn of a house at 149th Street and Elm. The peaceful Victorian neighborhood promised good schools for the younger children, Sharon and Mike, and a safe commute for Pat, who hoped to work in the city as a model and actress. Jim surprised Alberta with a ring, diamonds set in platinum, and a mink stole on the occasion of their twenty-second wedding anniversary, September 16, 1953. He was forty-seven. There were manuscripts in his pipeline to sustain a writer for a lifetime.

His course would be stalled before Lion could catch up with the backlog. The spring of 1954 stunned Thompson with a double whammy. First, Arnold Hano revealed his intention to quit editing for a career in freelance journalism. Then, publisher Martin Goodman announced that Magazine Management was dropping out of the paperback originals field. "I have sold nothing for almost six months," Thompson groaned to Anthony Boucher in August. For the balance of the decade—five and a half fugitive years—he found a publisher for a mere two of his new novels.

The demise of Lion Books seems no less accidental than its creation. Goodman negotiated with the American News Company and gave up Atlas Magazines, his distribution agency, "for a price he just couldn't refuse," according to Noah Sarlot, overseer of the men's adventure stable at Magazine Management. This king's ransom, Sarlot winces, "was a stupid mistake":

> Goodman signed blindly with the American News Company to handle all of his publications, the magazines, Marvel Comics, and Lion. Then American News went out of business, and this nearly put Goodman out too. There was a month, maybe two months, I think, when everything just piled up at the warehouse, nothing was sold. Goodman finally signed with the Independent News Company—but on the condition that he kill Lion. They distributed Signet/New American Library, and it was in their contract that they couldn't take on any other paperback originals line. Lion by this time was a $250,000-a-year business. Goodman had no choice but to make the deal. And that was the end of Lion Books.

Under the Lion Library imprint the firm continued to market books, like *The Kill-Off,* already under development. Title production dipped from seventy-two in 1953 to forty-three in 1956. Lion Library closed shop in the summer of 1957.

Despite troubles at Lion, the mid-1950s saw the maturation of the American paperback industry. During 1955 overall softcover production yielded a record 1,798 titles, some 300 of which were originals. As a prolific popular and critical success, Thompson should have been a coveted trophy. Fawcett Gold Medal was assembling a crime list that spanned the generations from W. R. Burnett, Cornell Woolrich, and Sax Rohmer to Charles Williams, Harry Whittington, John D. MacDonald, David Goodis, Gil Brewer, and Peter Rabe. Beacon nurtured Charles Willeford. Perma Books introduced Ed McBain. Yet everywhere Thompson or his agent knocked, they were turned away. As Ingrid Hallen pleaded in a bewildered letter to Boucher in the fall of 1954:

> You have written so many glowing things about Jim Thompson's work that I am sure you will be interested to know what is happening to his writing career.
>
> Since Lion Books discontinued its line of softcover originals, I've been trying to find a publisher for Jim. And, believe it or not, I'm having a very tough time of it. I've tried Gold Medal,

Popular Library, Avon, Ace Books and NAL's Signet books. No soap anywhere.

I wonder if you can suggest anyone else to me? Jim is beginning to feel very frustrated, and naturally he needs money to support his family. I can't understand why such a good writer would go begging. He has built up a following—thanks partly to you—and that should count for something with a publisher. Many thanks for any help you might give me.

Boucher responded, "I'm just plain baffled." Thompson himself came to believe that the violence in his novels was the crux of the impasse, and spent the next few years, as we shall see, clumsily damping his ferocity. But the wild card in both his astonishing surge of the early 1950s and his subsequent downslide is Arnold Hano. The symbiotic liaison of author and editor cannot be misprized. Prior to meeting Hano, Thompson published only three novels, each in a radically disparate mode. Working alongside Hano during 1952–54, he swiftly realized fourteen books—more than half his life's achievement—nearly all of them composed around a core of thematic and stylistic obsessions.

Hano trusted Thompson like no publisher did before or after him. At Lion he secured the writer a platform and then left him alone. Hano edited *The Nothing Man* for Dell, and placed *After Dark, My Sweet* at Popular Library, where he had connections (Jim Bryans would shortly go there as editor in chief). He left New York for Laguna Beach, California, in 1955. Although Thompson eventually managed other adventurous novels, particularly *The Getaway* (1959), *The Grifters* (1963), and *Pop. 1280* (1964), they were random gems scattered among dreck. He would never write so consistently well again.

As Hano himself summarizes his effect on Thompson in the early 1950s:

This is hard for me to talk about. But I think I became a kind of surrogate father for him, a big brother, or uncle, God knows what. He was a few years older, but that didn't seem to matter. Jim was always needy in terms of other people. He had to have other people, because he really didn't take care of himself.

Jim was dry then. To the best of my knowledge during the time I was working with him he was totally sober. When I told him that I was leaving Lion to freelance, and that there was some question whether Lion Books was going to continue, Jim kind of panicked at the thought of my no longer being his editor, and maybe the whole publishing venture dying on him.

Almost immediately after that Jim started to drink.

Or, finally started to drink in front of Hano. After two fruitful years of counting his glasses and holding back his binges, except with fellow carousers like the Milburns, Thompson no longer masked his alcoholism. He began to act out before his younger editor, mentor, and friend with mounting despair. During the winter of 1954 Hano received a telephone call from Alberta directing him and his wife, Bonnie, to a midtown hotel. They found Thompson "absolutely drunk, crying, and going through this amazing mea culpa." It was then that Hano first heard the writer perform the suicide of James Sherman Thompson. "He told us the excelsior-in-the-mattress story. And also that his father had done this to get back at Jim, so that Jim would be carrying this burden of guilt all his life. It took us a long time to calm Jim down." That Thompson selected Hano as the conduit for this fantasy of parental abandonment and retribution itself shapes a prickly tale, the hotel episode transpiring in the wake of the editor's own inadvertent "abandonment" of his writer and the "death" of Lion Books.

Thompson fell back into his old habit of vanishing. Sometimes he wound up at Maxine's in Florida, or at Freddie's new place in Connecticut. Often, though, the family couldn't predict the origin of his call. "When my Aunt Pauline got sick and mother went back to Nebraska, he started drinking," Sharon recalls. "We were upset because we couldn't find him for maybe two days. Somehow he ended up in New Jersey. . . ."

During one of his absences, Alberta vacated the Flushing house for a cheaper apartment in Jackson Heights. On his return Thompson refused to stay, claiming the rooms were too noisy for him to write. He fled to a hotel until she found a quiet building in Sunnyside. A letter signed by Dr. Max Jacobson about her husband's health allowed Alberta to break the lease.

Part of the redbrick Celtic Park complex, the Thompson apartment at 48-02 43rd Street overlooked a rustic courtyard, and Jim struck up a friendship with three FBI agents who lived down the hall. One morning while he was trying to work, a ball crashed through the bedroom window, strewing glass over his desk and typewriter. The culprit turned out to be Patty McCormack, a young neighbor girl. She perhaps was rehearsing for her upcoming movie role—Patty would star the next year as the demon child in *The Bad Seed.*

•   •   •

Thompson may have appeared to collapse at this meanest twist of "flukish Fate," appeasing his fury at Lion and Hano with sodden self-pity. But even as he guzzled and sobbed, ran away and groused, he fought to reorder his direction as a writer. The ensuing months and years drove him down five incongruous paths concurrently.

Following his rebuff at the New York paperback houses, Thompson moved to soften the savagery of his novels and pursued a contract with

Harper and Brothers, his hardcover publisher for *Nothing More Than Murder.* "It would puzzle Jim that anyone would see his books as ultraviolent," Hano reviews. "He never saw that he was writing a violent story. He was writing a story that was very internalized. And if it manifested in violence, that happened to be how it manifested itself." But faced with the liability of selling no books at all, Thompson blinked and swerved away from his "internalized" fiction.

In the fall of 1954 he signed with Harper for two novels, "Advance $500, payable on signature, against both books, and an advance of $1,500 payable on each of the two completed acceptable manuscripts—minus $250 against each $1,500 (half of $500 signature payment)." The postscript to editor Joan Kahn's memorandum of October 22 underscored his desperation:

> The agent asks that we note that reprint money (if any) due to author will be payable on demand or when received (author needs dough)—and that we've done this sort of thing before.
> And I said we'd get contract through fast.
> Delivery of the first ms. (untitled) in about a month.

The Harper files mention no titles. Yet it's probable his contracted manuscripts involved a pair of reconciliations with the American literary mainstream Thompson tackled mid-decade. Maintaining his customary fever pitch, he soon knocked out an entire new novel, *The Expensive Sky,* and sample chapters of *The Spy.*

The books seem the agency of another writer. *The Expensive Sky* ran down the denouement of a once fashionable Manhattan hotel—"this hostelry of hostelries . . . the magnificent Hotel Van Anstruther"—with arch, stilted whimsy. *The Spy* (subsequently revised as *The Concrete Pasture*) is a maundering highbrow thriller that fuses sex to politics as *Capitol Casebook* reporter and Communist spy Galen "Gay" White essays to leave the Party amid the counterclaims of wife and mistress, friends and functionaries. Each novel dangled follies and howlers, as Thompson labored to stifle his instincts and relax into genre. But *The Expensive Sky* was particularly harebrained—and sad, sinking to fat jokes and comic-strip blue bloods:

> [Whitman's] voice trailed off wearily, helplessly. If the Van Anstruthers had heard a word he was saying, or were impressed by a word of it, they gave no sign of the fact. Miss Hattie, a human dumpling, an overstuffed wad of antique lace and musty black satin: Miss Hattie sat absorbed in her knitting. . . . As for the Commodore, his unwinking gaze still roamed restlessly around the

room, around the walls, moving, leaping rather, from the crossed duelling swords to the shelves of pewter and pottery steins to the gilt-framed pictures of Kaiser Wilhelm, Bismarck *et al.* The Commodore was a great admirer of the Germans. In his opinion, insistently if insidiously perpetrated in the Van Anstruther chain of newspapers, the Germans were the only civilized people in Europe. . . .

"Scum," said the Commodore, with a kind of absent-minded firmness. "Degenerates. Decadent beasts. That's what they are over there, Whitman. The whole kit and caboodle of them."

Harper and Brothers elected to issue neither of these novels.

Thompson, meanwhile, tapped the monthly crime fiction digest market for quick money. During the mid-1950s seven stories appeared in *Mercury Mystery Magazine, Ellery Queen's Mystery Magazine,* and *Alfred Hitchcock's Mystery Magazine.* Some merely recycle prior efforts. "Bellboy" (*MMM,* February 1956) and "Prowlers in the Pear Trees" (*MMM,* March 1956) were chapters from *Bad Boy.* "Murder Came on the Mayflower" (*MMM,* November 1956) glanced back at John Billington—the "Mayflower Murderer" of his 1938 Writers' Project radio play, *First Murder.*

The short fiction continued his flirtation with mainstream culture. For a linked pair of novellas, "The Cellini Chalice" (*AHMM,* December 1956) and "The Frightening Frammis" (*AHMM,* February 1957), Thompson breezily paraded the misadventures of gold buyer and con man Mitch Allison as though he were auditioning for a television pilot ("The Frightening Frammis" would, in fact, be filmed for Showtime under the direction of Tom Cruise in 1993). Digest crime tends to accent craft over vision. But his two wittiest stories proved more than rote. "The Threesome in Four-C" (*AHMM,* December 1956), printed over his *SAGA* pseudonym Dillon Roberts, drew on Thompson's recent experience with the noisy Jackson Heights apartment for an elegant tale of madness. "The Flaw in the System" (*MMM,* July 1956) arranged a sly raid on corporate capitalism in the form of a fable about a mysterious deadbeat who embezzles thousands of dollars in merchandise from an installment sales chain simply by pleasantly telling the truth. "Why, a man like that could wreck us if he took a notion to!" an auditor exlaims. "He could wreck our entire economy!" As Thompson's original title put it, he's "The Most Dangerous Man in the World."

On a third front, Thompson assaulted the men's adventure rags. During 1956–57 he tossed off at least six articles for what editor Jim Bryans calls the "hairy armpit" wing of Magazine Management. These too replayed blasts from his past. "America's First Murderer" in *For Men Only* (September 1956) took another crack at John Billington. "Private Lives of a Hellraiser" in *Men* (November 1956) excerpted more of *Bad Boy.* "They Wouldn't

Stay Dead" in *True Adventures* (September 1957) catalogued three cases of individuals who were thought dead but weren't: a sixteenth-century noblewoman, an eighteenth-century gardener, and, of course, John Stink.

Thompson's fresh outings betrayed kindred lack of imagination. "The Innkeeper's Passionate Daughter" in *Ken* (February 1957) slung a vapidly ribald account of "Bloody Kate" Bender, a Kansas murderess from the 1870s. "Bert Casey, Wild Gun of the Panhandle" in *Man's World* (September 1957) circled his father's finest hour in Oklahoma Territory—yet without ever mentioning him. Perhaps his oddest sortie into men's adventure was the hatchet job on the legend of Charles Arthur "Pretty Boy" Floyd he performed for *Real* (September 1956). Floyd played Robin Hood, Thompson charged, but really he "had run all his life—ran from something, someone, he could not face. A guy called Pretty Boy Floyd." So much, then, for the heroic outlaw celebrated in novel and song by his friends Bill Cunningham and Woody Guthrie.

Thompson also reverted to true crime. After his blowup over the union at *SAGA,* he couldn't appear in most Macfadden publications using his own name. Since 1953 he was occasionally submitting through friendly editors at *Master Detective* lurid chronicles of the Texas and New York underworlds via an avuncular nom de plume, Bob Wicks. Tracking Thompson's contributions is tricky, as Macfadden files suggest that Bob Wicks quickly became one of the in-house monikers assigned to any writer who preferred anonymity. He manifestly was not responsible for all—or most—of the dozens of articles by Bob Wicks that suddenly erupted in the pages of *Master Detective* and *True Detective* after 1954. Some of the Bob Wicks true crime stories can be traced back through the Macfadden archives to a Carlos Lane, a writer who appeared in one issue of *SAGA* while Thompson served as assistant editor, but the nature of his contribution, a woolly Western about Texas gunman Bill Longley titled "Lightning in his Hand" (December 1950), suggests that Carlos Lane too may have been a Thompson or Macfadden pseudonym. Likely Thompson-Wicks *Master Detective* features include "The Slasher and the Showgirl" (November 1953), "Find the Phantom Slugger" (December 1953), "Texas Massacre" (February 1954), "The Woman Who Couldn't Cry" (May 1954), "A Noose for Eleanor" (March 1955), and "Girl in the Dragon's Lair" (June 1955).

"My dad started hanging out with the New York City Police Department," Thompson's daughter Sharon remembers. "He became familiar with their hangouts, the coffee shops and bars where they'd go after work in the morning. They let him ride with them all night, and gave him leads for stories. Daddy got to know the city block by block, the most dangerous places. If you asked him for directions, he would tell you the streets to stay away from."

Thompson finally took a day job. He joined the New York *Daily News,* not as a reporter or rewrite man, but as a copy editor. He "hated checking other writers' spelling and grammar," according to his wife, Alberta, and lasted only a few months—"not long enough to be in the union." Arnold Hano, once more, found himself enmeshed in the numbing resolution:

> Shortly before we moved away, Jim came to the apartment that Bonnie and I had on 105th Street and Broadway after work, and he was slightly sloggered. He said he had been laid off—they may have laid him off because he was drinking; he didn't say that, and I don't know. He spent most of the evening with us, he ate a little and drank a lot.
>
> When it was time for him to go home, I had to take him home. It was a typical New York City scene. We walked through the driving rain to my car, which was parked on Riverside Drive, and I turned the key and nothing happened. I opened the hood and the battery was gone. Someone had left the four screws neatly in the corner where the battery once had been.
>
> It didn't matter to him—it mattered to me—Jim was so out of it that it didn't matter. We walked to the subway, and waited what seemed forever for a train—it was very late at night by then. Just as one came, Jim decided he had to pee. So I carted this big, hulking man off to the men's room. Finally, there was another train, and we took it to Queens.
>
> When we got home, he said to Alberta, who must have been frantic by this time—I think we had called, but she was still frantic—he said to Alberta, "They laid me off today." There was one instant where her face showed what he had said. And then she said, "Jimmie, you should have seen what the wind did before we got the windows closed. It knocked down the lamp. We just had a terrible time here." She just shifted the thing to some little domestic problem. That was the way she handled things.
>
> I've never forgotten that moment.

• • •

For Thompson it was as if the previous two and a half years—and his fourteen new books—never happened. "Nineteen fifty-four, fifty-five was the worst time of all," Sharon reckons. "After the paperback market dried up for him Daddy kept writing, but he didn't know where to turn. The drinking was the worst too. He was desperate and had to get away. He felt he could write better at Maxine's, and he went down to Florida for three or four months. He was away for Thanksgiving. We couldn't afford a turkey, so that year Mother bought some pork chops with all the trimmings. My dad had this little saying that he used all the time: 'What's the use of kicking?' "

Director Stanley Kubrick (Courtesy of Stills
Archive of the Museum of Modern Art)

Stanley Kubrick rescued Thompson from an early retirement into hack-
dom. A few months into 1955 the young Bronx-born filmmaker—then just
twenty-six—approached him to adapt Lionel White's novel *Clean Break* for
the screen. "Are you familiar with a guy named Jim Thompson?" Kubrick
asked his partner, producer James B. Harris. "He's this terrific writer who's
written some stuff I really love."

Thompson also was rescuing Stanley Kubrick. A staff photographer for
Look magazine since high school, Kubrick recently wrote and directed a
low-budget *film noir, Killer's Kiss,* that despite staggering visuals lacked dialogue and a story—in short, a script. "That's the thing that's missing when
you look at *Killer's Kiss,"* suggests Alexander Singer, associate producer of
The Killing, as *Clean Break* came to be retitled by United Artists. "It's a
genius piece of filmmaking in terms of craft, lighting, editing, and sometimes even performances. But you don't get the feeling of a well-crafted narrative." *The Killing*—with each scene tensely plotted in a raw, eloquent
American vernacular—would be Kubrick's breakthrough film, and a cult
masterpiece.

A full generation apart, Thompson and Kubrick nonetheless forged a "real symbiotic relationship," in the words of Robert Goldfarb, the Los Angeles agent who helped sell *The Killing* to Hollywood. Thompson ultimately created three screenplays and a novella for the Harris-Kubrick Pictures Corporation; "these boys," as he branded them in a letter, introduced him to agents, advanced him loans, and furnished the lion's share of his writing income through 1959. "Stanley and Jim"—Goldfarb recounts—"they just kept coming back to each other."

Working out of an office on West 57th Street, Kubrick and Thompson sat down to convert *Clean Break* into a feature film. Thompson retreated to a nearby hotel for the duration, yet Kubrick became a dubious guest at the Sunnyside apartment. "Stanley came out to our place, and just drove us all insane," Sharon comments. "He was a beatnik before beatniks were in. He had the long hair and the weird clothes. They'd go to a nice restaurant, and my dad would be thinking, Oh, God, they're not going to let Stanley in! He would be really worried about this. My dad was very refined in many ways, and if they wanted you to wear a tie in certain restaurants, well, you wore a tie."

Disparities of dress code aside, the pair fell into a comfortable writing routine. "After some preliminary discussions, Jim would go off and work and bring in scenes," according to Jimmy Harris. "Stanley was responsible for outlining what the scenes in the picture were going to be, and Jim was then going to write the dialogue. I guess Stanley structured the thing—but we followed the structure of the book. People begged us to make a straight-line story. But we had enough sense to realize this structure was the most interesting thing about the story."

Published in 1955, Lionel White's *Clean Break* recaps the daring robbery of a New York racetrack by means of crisscrossing narratives. The powerful stylistic signature of the film—constantly returning to a point in time and then bringing each character forward—emerged intact from the novel. This unsettling strategy, which Kubrick and Thompson played for a parody of the classic *noir* flashback as well as for suspense, actually was a formula from White's days as a true crime writer. During the 1940s he edited *Underworld Detective, Detective World,* and *Homicide Detective* before turning to fiction. *Clean Break* preserves the surreal just-the-facts-please formality of vintage true crime:

> It was exactly six forty-five when George Peatty climbed the high stoop of the brownstone front up on West a Hundred and Tenth Street. He took the key from his trouser pocket, inserted it and twisted the doorknob. He climbed two flights of carpeted stairs and opened the door at the right. Entering his apartment, he carefully removed his light felt hat, laid it on the small table in the

hall and then went into the living room. He still carried the half dozen roses wrapped up in the green papered cornucopia.

Thompson filled in White's caper with flourishes reminiscent of his own novels. He focused the homoerotic tension between aging bookkeeper Marvin Unger (played by Jay C. Flippen) and ringleader Johnny Clay (Sterling Hayden). He eliminated the trampy daughter of track bartender Mike O'Reilly (Joe Sawyer) and instead burdened him with an ailing wife. Thompson reprised the criminal-as-artist motif from *The Nothing Man*. "I often thought the gangster and the artist are the same in the eyes of the Master," wrestler Maurice Oboukhoff (Kola Kwarian) philosophizes in broken English. "They are admired and hero-worshipped but there is always present on the land which would see them destroyed at the peak of their glory." He even found a place for his pet phrase that year, as policeman Randy Kennan (Ted de Corsia) sighs to a mobster, "What's the use of kicking?"

In his major modification Thompson fleshed out the faithless marriage of George and Sherry Peatty, expanding a trite plot device from *Clean Break* into a definitive dramatization of a sadomasochistic relationship for the film. Mousy George (Elisha Cook, Jr.) and vampish Sherry (Marie Windsor) spar like the battling Dillons of *A Hell of a Woman:*

> GEORGE
>
> I got to go out tonight. I don't suppose there's anything for dinner.
>
> SHERRY
>
> Of course there is darling—there are all sorts of things. We have cake, asparagus and potatoes.
>
> GEORGE
>
> I don't smell nothing.
>
> SHERRY
>
> That figures—because you're too far away from it.
>
> GEORGE
>
> Too far away from it?
>
> SHERRY
>
> Certainly. You don't think I have it all cooked, do you? It's all down in the shopping center.

At the conclusion of White's novel the dying George shoots Johnny Clay at La Guardia Airport. George's final act in the movie is his point-blank murder of Sherry after she tells him, "I never had anyone but you—not a real husband—not even—just a lot of—bunch of liars." The script ran through different endings before arriving at an absurdist finish out of John Huston's *The Treasure of the Sierra Madre*, where the $2,000,000 stake bursts out of a rickety suitcase, blows pointlessly down the runway, and

Johnny is arrested. In the first draft, for instance, Johnny dies chasing the money when he stumbles into the propeller of a taxiing plane.

The Harris-Kubrick Pictures Corporation mailed the completed screenplay, titled *Day of Violence,* to Robert Goldfarb of the Jaffe Agency in the spring of 1955. "We represented Lionel White, so I guess we were the nearest they had to a Hollywood connection at the time." The crude packaging and format of the script raised more quizzical eyebrows than its idiosyncratic writing:

> I remember that it arrived one day in a cardboard carton big enough to live in, the kind of box which might have contained rolls of toilet paper at the supermarket. The script itself was typed on legal-size pages running sideways and bound at the top. It was humongous—maybe three hundred pages long—not at all in a conventional form physically. The whole thing smacked of amateur night.

Ronnie Lubin, another Jaffe agent, persuaded United Artists to bankroll the off-kilter project with a $330,000 deal that had the studio putting up $200,000 to Jimmy Harris's $130,000. Goldfarb, on the strength of an endorsement from Harris-Kubrick, started to shop around Thompson's new novels, while on the East Coast Ad Schulberg, another Kubrick contact, fell into the same role. With two talent agencies plugging for him, the writer still could not snag a publisher. "The feeling I had from my mother," cautions Ad's son, novelist Budd Schulberg, "was that Jim Thompson was what they call 'a character on board.' I believe it was pretty frustrating for both of them."

Kubrick and Harris shifted operations to Hollywood in the fall of 1955 to film the screenplay, now retitled *Bed of Fear,* at the old Charlie Chaplin studio at the corner of Sunset and La Brea. Alexander Singer shot the racetrack footage at Bay Meadows, near San Francisco.

Prior to departure, Jimmy Harris signed Thompson to write a short novel for possible development into a movie. "There would be these calls from Jim at three or four in the morning, mainly to Stanley. Jim would be 'under the weather,' needing help of some kind, usually financial. I made him some loans, which I decided to let him pay back with work. That seemed more dignified than a handout. Plus the fact we thought he was so terrific that I was sure it was for our mutual benefit."

On June 6 Thompson contracted privately with Harris to submit a "story . . . concerning the adventures and relationships between an American soldier and a psychopathic female with homicidal tendencies" in exchange for forgiveness of a $1,000 debt and additional money upon delivery. He also would be a profit participant in any film.

Evocatively called *Lunatic at Large,* this legendary "lost" Thompson novella was long believed to have disappeared. "He delivered it to us and we misplaced it," Harris regrets. "Stanley and I never copied it, and Jim hadn't made a carbon." The concluding three pages of a seventy-six page typescript, however, came to light from a Southern California storage chamber in 1992.

Thompson telescoped his story in dialogue with rudimentary stage directions. The soldier is named Johnny, the female psychopath Joyce. At the violent climax of *Lunatic at Large,* she stalks him with a hot poker until the intrusion of a pair of policeman, Mike and Joel:

> Johnny attempted to grab it, let out a keen howl as he scorched his fingers.
>
> "You're crazy," he stammered. "You don't know what you're doing, kid. Why do you want to?"
>
> He kept backing away from her. "Listen to me, honey. This is Johnny. Johnny! Don't you remember? I'm the guy that loves you. I wanted to marry you."
>
> "I know, Johnny." Joyce moved toward him steadily, still swinging the poker. "That's why I have to do it. It's the only way I can marry you. The only way I can make sure you never belong to anyone else. You wouldn't want to do that would you, dearest, if you love me. And you'll be so happy, darling. So, so happy. No more pain, no more trouble, no more heartache. Nothing but peace and quiet, darkness and sweet, silent warmth, while you're waiting for me to come to you. You want that, don't you, sweetheart? You want to—"
>
> "Cut it out," Johnny stammered. "Don't! Drop that thing, baby. You hear me? You don't know what you're saying, what you're doing."
>
> He had been backing away while he pleaded with her. Now his ankle struck against the hassock, and his words ended in a frightened yell as he stumbled and went over backwards. His head struck against the bare floor. Dazed and helpless he stared up at Joyce.
>
> With a loving laugh she raised the poker over her head.
>
> "You do understand, don't you, darling" she paused, "that it's only because I love you so much? Because I want us to be together forever and forever."
>
> She paused again. Then, as he looked up unable to speak, she swung the poker down at him. Then there was the crack of a gun shot.
>
> Mike and Joel hoisted Johnny to his feet. He looked at them dazedly, first one, then the other.
>
> Mike gave him a nudge that was half-stern, half-sympathetic.

"Come on," he said. "Snap out of it, Mac. You got some talking to do to get out of this one."

"Get out of it?" Johnny gave him a dull stare. "Get out of it?" He looked across the room, staring at something that lay on the floor. Then curtly shaking off the cop's hand, he slowly walked over to Joyce, knelt quietly at her side.

"Sorry, baby," his voice broke. "I'm so sorry baby."

Joyce's eyelids fluttered open. She smiled the smile of one who is at last entirely at peace with the world. Then one of her hands closed gently over his.

"You," she coughed. "You kept your promise, didn't you, Johnny?"

"Promise?" Johnny brushed at his eyes. "Honey, I don't know what's wrong, how this all happened. But I know you couldn't help it. And if there's anything I can do—"

"You said you wouldn't let them arrest me," Joyce said. "You said you wouldn't . . . and you . . . you. . . ."

She coughed again, and her whole body shook with the effort. Then her eyes closed again, and she lay entirely still.

Johnny stared at her wonderingly. After a time he said brokenly, "Joyce! Joyce! Come back to me, baby. There's something," his voice broke again. "There's so much I got to say to you. We never really got to do no talking, and all the things I wanted to say, how much I loved you, and how happy I was going to make you, and . . . and. . . ."

Mike's hand came down on his shoulder, interrupting him.

"Later, Mac," he said gently. "I don't think you need to do it, but you'll have to tell her later. Some other time. Some other place."

For all the predatory women in Thompson's fiction, Joyce proved his only female psychopathic killer. Harris-Kubrick never moved to mold *Lunatic at Large* for the screen. Sometime during the 1960s Thompson approached Harris for the rights, claiming that he planned to rework the story into a novel. Harris consulted Kubrick, and they agreed to release it; by then no one could locate the manuscript. "Now publishers call me up asking about *Lunatic at Large,*" Harris rues. "Stanley even went down in his cellar to look for it. But we still can't find it!"

• • •

Thompson first viewed *The Killing* in a Manhattan screening room with his family. As the credits rolled—"Screenplay by Stanley Kubrick with Additional Dialogue by Jim Thompson"—he was livid. "My father nearly fell off his chair when he saw that," his daughter Patricia remembers. Neither Kubrick nor Harris was in attendance. "There were fireworks when he next saw Stanley," Sharon adds. "He couldn't believe that Stanley would cheat him out of his credit."

Jimmy Harris supports the "additional dialogue" tag for Thompson. "You have to give Stanley that credit because he laid the movie out. It would be different if we had said to Jim, 'See you in ten weeks.' It's a fair credit, but you wouldn't give it today." Kubrick's lawyer, Louis Blau, reports, "Mr. Kubrick is not going to talk about Thompson and the Thompson controversy. He is not going to dignify the claims being made by the family. [Thompson] received additional dialogue credit, to which he was entitled. [Stanley Kubrick] is not at all pleased by the unfounded claims that are being made. He doesn't want to defend himself. He doesn't have to defend himself."

Others close to *The Killing,* such as associate producer Alexander Singer, disagree. "I think we're talking about the person who wrote the script," he says of Thompson. "Attribution of credit on a screenplay is frequently a central issue. As directors get more recognition for their work, they are more likely to be generous with their attributions." Agent Robert Goldfarb believes similarly:

> Jim was very much indebted to Stanley Kubrick, who gave him work but wasn't generous with the credits. Stanley was an auteur, and his name is certainly deserved. But he didn't offer to share the glory—and it's quite possible that he didn't recognize it. Guys who are as intense and driven and visionary as Stanley Kubrick may receive lots of input from other people, but they so promptly internalize what is of interest to them that they truly don't realize that it isn't their own. So it could be that. On the other hand, Jim Thompson was the inside man in the Kubrick skunkworks. Stanley kept him in the closet, and Jim really did things for him.

All available circumstantial evidence around the screenplay—Kubrick's amateurish writing for *Killer's Kiss,* the embellishments from Thompson's novels, the account of the New York work sessions offered by Harris—indicates that *The Killing* issued from an intensive collaboration. Thompson merited, at least, a solid co-writing line. His "additional dialogue" credit seems a nasty slap in the face—and a perverse trick to anyone who knew Lionel White's book. Since the structure and most of the plot of *The Killing* derived from *Clean Break,* the original elements in the script would fall under the heading of "additional dialogue." Kubrick experienced problems over attributions and permissions on subsequent films. Calder Willingham was still venting his anger about *Paths of Glory* to his death.

Composer György Ligeti charges that Kubrick included his music in *2001: A Space Odyssey* without first obtaining the rights.

Thompson's contribution to *The Killing* ranks with his Lion novels among his crowning accomplishments. *"The Killing* really made a huge impression on me," novelist James Ellroy once told the Los Angeles *Times*. "Thompson not only writes great dialogue, but he's great at capturing the psychology of his characters. You get such a sense of darkness and loss—it's the kind of feeling you don't find in movies anymore."

•   •   •

That Stanley Kubrick "cheated" him out of his credit on *The Killing* became another of Thompson's personal myths in the sense that for the rest of his life he rehearsed his grievance to all who would listen—Arnold Hano, R. V. Cassill, Tony Bill, Pierre Rissient, Jerry Bick, John Ptak, or Mike Medavoy. His "betrayal" by Kubrick is an anecdote that everyone who knew him after 1955 can recite.

His family maintains that Thompson took the matter to the Writers Guild for arbitration. The Guild, Alberta affirms, decided in his favor. "They asked Jimmie if he would accept an assignment of $750 a week to write *Paths of Glory* for Harris-Kubrick if they would change the credit for *The Killing*. He accepted it—he would have been a fool not to. They did this over the phone, with Jimmie in New York and Stanley out in Hollywood."

This next episode in Thompson's life could not have been launched at the Writers Guild. Arbitration was technically impossible for him in 1956. By his own admission, from a 1972 letter to the Guild Arbitration Committee about *The Getaway,* he did not join the Writers Guild until two years later. Thompson admitted, moreover: "I have been subject to many credit arbitrations (though none was instigated by me; and this is the first time I have protested a producer's designation of credits)."

Yet Alberta manifestly was not hearing voices. The telephone conversation she so vividly recollects *sounds* like a personal deal struck between Kubrick and Thompson.

Jim and Alberta left New York for Hollywood in June 1956. His fee for writing *Paths of Glory* would, in truth, be $500 a week. But his screen credit this time was written into his contract with bold capitals: "SCREENPLAY BY STANLEY KUBRICK AND JIM THOMPSON."

"Now, I was in this town twelve years
ago, before I went back east and concentrated on book writing. I'd done
three books at the time, plus a few
dozen stories. I was all full of piss and
high spirits and ideas, ready and rarin'
to go. And I went from one end of
agency row to the other, because you
have to have an agent, you know; you
can't approach a studio direct. . . ."

"I know."

"And I couldn't get one. They weren't
adding to their lists, they said. There
were too many writers in Hollywood
already."

"But you got one now. You're here now."

"And I wish to God I
wasn't," said Blake. "I wish to hell I
was dead."

—Sanderson Blake,
Sunset and Cienega

Satan's Quarter-Section: 1956–1965

Thompson gravitated toward Hollywood from his earliest introduction to the nickelodeon. As a starstruck Oklahoma City schoolboy he mounted a Theda Bara shrine over his bed. He acted a bit part in a Fort Worth two-reeler. With his father he operated the Big Springs Theater. Jim and Alberta, it should be remembered, celebrated their wedding night inside a Lincoln picture palace. Submitting his first story idea to Warner Brothers in 1937—a true crime saga, "The Osage Murders"—Thompson angled to move to Hollywood as far back as 1940. Once he settled there, in 1960, he datelined his letters with a single word, "Hollywood," as though the place were a magic talisman and any street address redundant.

The 1930s generation of American hard-boiled novelists—Hammett,

Chandler, Cain, and McCoy—influenced and wrote for the movies. Their laconic prose, colloquial and racy, came to dominate *film noir* screenwriting. The next generation—including Thompson and Goodis—cut their individual styles on the great 1940s *noir* films, mastering their métier as much in the plush dark of a cinema as at their desks poring over stories and books.

Two *film noir* strains, in particular, bore down on Thompson's fiction: the extreme tradition of the psychotic masculine hero, *Christmas Holiday* (1944), *Scarlet Street* (1945), *Born to Kill* (1947), *Kiss of Death* (1947), *White Heat* (1949); and an opposite tradition, rarer and more interior, perhaps best represented by *Detour* (1945). Following his posthumous revival, Thompson's novels would inspire young directors—such as Joel Coen, *Blood Simple* (1984) and *Barton Fink* (1991); Tim Hunter, *River's Edge* (1986); Joseph Ruben, *The Stepfather* (1987); and Quentin Tarantino, *Reservoir Dogs* (1992) and *Pulp Fiction* (1994)—whose films, paradoxically, thrust deeper into his savage art than new releases actually based on his books.

Jim Thompson loved the *idea* of Hollywood, especially the old Hollywood that endured around such vintage establishments as the Musso & Frank Grill—Hollywood's oldest restaurant, a dark, woody chop house, fortified with two matching bars, on Hollywood Boulevard. But he never understood the workings of the film industry, never would be mistaken for an insider. Story meetings made him jittery, and he couldn't accommodate to writing by committee. Thompson tended, like his father in the Texas oil fields, to seal deals with a drink and a handshake instead of a signature. "Hollywood"—his sister Freddie explained—"Hollywood basically killed him off."

•   •   •

Jim and Alberta rode the train to Chicago, then the *Super Chief* into Los Angeles. Only their young niece Randi made the trip with them. Thompson appeared buoyant and playful. "Uncle Jimmie was like someone I didn't know," Randi marvels. "I had always seen him drinking and morose, and here he was light and laughing and giggling with me over some silly book I was reading." After Stanley Kubrick greeted them at the station, the Thompsons took a furnished apartment on Sunset Boulevard—the same suite, Alberta notes, where Lilly Dillon lives in *The Grifters.*

Harris-Kubrick Pictures was not planning *Paths of Glory* as its next production. MGM already had signed them to develop a Stefan Zweig story, *The Burning Secret,* with novelist Calder Willingham co-writing the screenplay. The "boys" apparently proposed to work Thompson on the sly, and Kubrick began to drop by evenings for script sessions on *Paths of Glory.* "Jimmie and Stanley never wrote together," Alberta recalls. "Every night they would go over what Jimmie had written. They'd scream at each other until it drove me mad."

Sometime around the completion of a first draft, the clandestine arrangement boomeranged. "Hiring Jim Thompson got us fired from MGM," Jimmy Harris discloses. "We had an exclusive contract to make *The Burning Secret,* and they chose to nitpick. MGM found out we were doing *Paths of Glory* and canceled us. *The Burning Secret* went down the drain. We were able then to concentrate fully with Jim on *Paths of Glory.*"

Published in 1935, Humphrey Cobb's First World War novel *Paths of Glory* drew on historical scandals along the Western Front. A vainglorious French general—named Assolant in the book, but Mireau for the film—orders an assault on the "Pimple," an impregnable German fortification. When his regiment is driven back, the general fires on his own troops and spitefully arranges for one soldier from each company to be court-martialed and executed as an example to the others. Cobb's caustic vignettes seared a pitch-black comedy comparable to Joseph Heller's *Catch-22*—and a foreboding violence reminiscent of Thompson's Lion novels.

Stanley Kubrick's *Paths of Glory* has been acclaimed "one of the strongest anti-war statements ever made on celluloid." The genealogy of the screenplay is as tangled in intrigue as the wrangle surrounding *The Killing.* The script rolled through at least five drafts before it was ready for the cameras. Thompson wrapped an initial version with Kubrick late in the summer of 1956. Harris-Kubrick Pictures then recruited Calder Willingham, cashiered along with them by MGM from *The Burning Secret.* "Jim understood," Harris believes, "that sometimes you write yourself out on a project." A "second-draft" screenplay, dated November 26, 1956, bears the credit, Stanley Kubrick, Jim Thompson, and Calder Willingham, as do a subsequent pair of screenplays, both labeled "third draft" and dated February 25, 1957, but differing from each other. Working on location with Kubrick in Germany, Willingham polished the shooting script during the spring and summer of 1957.

Kirk Douglas apparently read the second- and third-draft screenplays (they are among his papers). As he recounts in his autobiography, *The Ragman's Son,* "I saw a small picture called *The Killing. . . .* I was intrigued by the film, and wanted to meet the director, Stanley Kubrick. . . . I asked him if had any other projects. He said he had a script called *Paths of Glory,* by Calder Willingham and Jim Thompson. . . . Stanley told me he'd had no success setting the picture up, but he'd be glad to let me see it. I read the script and fell in love with it." Douglas secured financing for *Paths of Glory* through his own Bryna Productions. He signed on to act the role of Colonel Dax.

When Douglas arrived at the Hotel Vierjahrzeiten in Munich to begin filming *Paths of Glory,* Kubrick rattled him with "a completely rewritten script." *The Ragman's Son* continues:

> He had revised it on his own, with Jim Thompson. It was a ca-
> tastrophe, a cheapened version of what I thought had been a beau-
> tiful script. The dialogue was atrocious. My character said things
> like: "You've got a big head. You're so sure the sun rises and sets
> up there in your noggin you don't even bother to carry matches."
> And "And you've got the only brain in the world. They made yours
> and threw the pattern away? The rest of us have a skullfull of Corn-
> flakes." Speeches like this went on for pages, right up to the happy
> ending, when the general's car arrives screeching to halt the firing
> squad and he changes the men's death sentence to thirty days in
> the guardhouse. Then my character, Colonel Dax, goes off with the
> bad guy he's been fighting all through the movie . . . to have a
> drink, as the general puts his arm around my shoulder.
>
> I called Stanley and Harris to my room. "Stanley, did you write
> this?"
>
> "Yes." Kubrick always had this calm way about him. I never
> heard him raise his voice, never saw him get excited or reveal any-
> thing. He just looked at me through those big, wide eyes.
>
> I said, "Stanley, why would you do that?"
>
> He very calmly said, "To make it commercial. I want to make
> money."
>
> I hit the ceiling. I called him every four-letter word I could
> think of. "You came to me with a script written by other people. It
> was based on a book. I love *that* script. I told you I didn't think this
> would be commercial, but I want to make it. You left it in my hands
> to put the picture together. I got the money based on *that* script.
> Not this shit!" I threw the script across the room. "We're going back
> to the original script, or we're not making the picture."
>
> Stanley never blinked an eye. We shot the original script. I
> think the movie is a classic, one of the most important pictures—
> possibly the *most* important picture Stanley Kubrick has ever
> made.

The offending script, the "catastrophe," and "this shit"—unbeknownst to Douglas—apparently was Jim Thompson's first-draft screenplay, mystify-ingly revived by Kubrick at zero hour. Or maybe not so mystifyingly. Stan-ley Kubrick might have been playing some ego chess with his illustrious star, then ablaze from triumphs in *Lust for Life* and *Gunfight at the O.K. Cor-ral.* Colonel Dax occupied a smaller, less heroic niche in Thompson's script than he would in the eventual film. Many of the late revisions in the story

involve a strengthening of Dax's character. Douglas performs actions originally distributed among other soldiers, and ascends to a higher moral
plane. Neither Humphrey Cobb nor Thompson, for instance, has Colonel
Dax dominate the court martial—a bravura turn for the actor in the movie's
climactic and most eloquent sequence. Cobb's earthy novel shot vertically
through the ranks, indicting doughboys and brass alike, and except for the
slapped-on "commercial" ending, Thompson closely shadowed the mocking realism of his source. Kubrick's film ultimately concentrated on the
French officer class. Perhaps the shrewdest way of summarizing the evolution of the various scripts is that *Paths of Glory* was restyled steadily into a
vehicle for Kirk Douglas.

Calder Willingham alleged his near complete authorship—"99%"—of
the final screenplay for *Paths of Glory*, allocating merely two lines of dialogue to Kubrick and none to Thompson. His contention peppers a spicy
letter about his collaboration with Kubrick, whom he deemed "a curious
study of the artist as psychopath in our time":

> I am sorry to have to inform you that Jim Thompson, what-
> ever his merits otherwise and I have heard from varying
> sources they were considerable, had extremely little to do with
> the final script of *Paths of Glory*, as it was written and shot at
> Geiselgasteig in Munich now some many years ago. I myself was
> there and I know.
>
> In those days machinery did not exist for arbitration of
> screen credits by the Writers Guild and I myself was a screen-
> writing novice, indeed a novelist little concerned with questions
> of screenwriting credit. A constant underlying acrimonious
> envy-need element existed in Stanley Kubrick's attitude toward
> me at that time, I believe. Jim Thompson had been a close asso-
> ciate of Stanley's, a buddy. It is for these reasons Stanley in his
> control of the film bestowed screenwriting credits as he did:
> "Screenplay by Stanley Kubrick, James Thompson, and Calder
> Willingham." I didn't care at the time to any degree worth not-
> ing; when I heard of it I smiled and shrugged ruefully, only
> mildly annoyed at Stanley's sheer gall. What he did, however,
> was outrageous.
>
> The screenplay of *Paths of Glory*, as the film was shot in Mu-
> nich line by line, was 99% my own work, a lot of it done right
> there on a typewriter at the studio. Stanley had in the script lit-
> erally two lines, and they were not important lines. Jim Thomp-
> son wrote not a single line of dialogue that appeared in the film.
> I must add the narrative structure, the conceptual approach,
> the characterizations were similarly my own, to a lesser degree

but very dominatingly. The interpretation, of course, on film was that of Kubrick, and this I often found antagonistic or contradictory to the intent of my script, but about that I could do little beyond angrily pointing out to Stanley his deficiencies, which in the main were a result of his near psychopathic indifference to and coldness toward the human beings in the story—a failing, I might add, which has sadly limited the work of Kubrick throughout his career; he doesn't like people much, they interest him mainly when they do unspeakably hideous things or when their idiocy is so malignant as to be horrifyingly amusing. Stanley Kubrick, with whom I have had a friendly but remote personal relationship now for many years, is a curious study of the artist as psychopath in our time. I am not, please, calling Stanley himself a psychopath or anything like that; it is his aesthetic, his artistic preoccupations and concerns which are psychopathic. Or, as the intolerable and insufferable Pauline Kael accurately observed, his "arctic spirit." It is a severe limitation, as I discovered by personal experience.

In a recent letter to my agent a question of my "fluency and persuasiveness" came up, in an altogether different context than that of motion pictures. I wrote to her:

"Years ago Stanley Kubrick almost refused to read my memo on the final scene of *Paths of Glory,* wherein I argued that the stark brutality of ending the film with the execution of the soldiers would be intolerable to an audience and philosophically an empty statement as well (this is what he was determined to do), that the scene I had invented (wherein the German girl sang in an amateurish and pathetic way *Der Truer Husar* [*The Faithful Soldier*] and caused the French soldiers to be moved and then to sing with her and share her tears in a common humanity) was essential if the story was to be bearable at all, or the truth about human life. Stanley said: 'I can't resist your arguments when you put them in writing, my circuits are overloaded and I blow a fuse and start agreeing with everything you say, like I am hypnotized.' The German girl he later married sang the song and German extras in World War I French uniforms sang with her and wept for pittance pay, tears of recognition of the tragedy of this life which in that moment lifted the film above any other Kubrick has made."

This is the whole and complete truth about *Paths of Glory* direct and straight from the horse's mouth and known to very few people, since I have never bothered to reveal the emptiness of Kubrick's claims in regard to that picture, although such an emptiness might be inferred by the canny filmgoer in the light of Kubrick's failure ever to make another film like it. Insofar as *Paths of Glory* was a great film, leaving aside clever photography, it was a great film on account of the inspiration and struggle of

Yours truly,
Calder Willingham

Willingham's *j'accuse* echoes—even as it aims to contradict—Thompson's. Persistent, unrelenting ire from the only other novelist to write for Kubrick early in the director's professional film career reinforces the litany of betrayal Thompson imparted to friends and family. Yet Willingham's memories of *Paths of Glory*—his aspiration to sole credit for the script, and his remarks on the Writers Guild—square with neither the screenplays themselves nor the internal correspondence around the production. Willingham may have contrived the tearful denouement, as he notes (it first appears in one of the February 25 manuscripts). But a scrupulous inventory of the extant drafts establishes that Thompson was as vital to the success of *Paths of Glory* as Willingham.

Thompson's contributions, in fact, accounted for roughly half of the film's eighty-nine-minute running time. Seven major episodes from his screenplay survived into the shooting script of *Paths of Glory* after only condensing or editing by Willingham, with hundreds of essential lines of dialogue emerging verbatim on the screen. Segments principally crafted by Thompson include:

- The opening meeting between the French generals, which establishes the assault on Ant Hill (as the "Pimple" was renamed for the film).
- The reconnaissance patrol led by the alcoholic Lieutenant Roget, who panics, murders his own man, and then covers it up.
- Colonel Dax's confrontation in his dugout with General Mireau over taking Ant Hill.
- Private Arnaud and Private Duval's pre-assault conversation about dying.
- General Mireau's firing on his own forces.
- Colonel Dax's heated discussion with General Mireau after the attack on Ant Hill fizzles.
- The scenes with the court-martialed soldiers in the guardhouse on the eve of their execution.

Throughout his screenplay, Thompson found his cues in the novel. Following Cobb, he devoted many pages to the selection of the infantrymen who will stand trial, individuating each scapegoat as vividly as he did their French officers. Regarding the speeches that so flustered Kirk Douglas, Jimmy Harris reports, "What Stanley liked about Jim's work was his dialogue." Harris can still recite Thompson's snarling epithet—retained for the film—about Lieutenant Roget: "A sneaky, booze-guzzling, yellow-bellied rat with a bottle for a brain and a streak of spit where his spine ought to be."

Other omitted scenes, unfortunately, tip this taut prole wit into tired, Beetle Bailey clowning:

PVT. MYER

Barber, who is this man? I thought you were running a high-class shop.

PVT. FEROL

(whining apologetically) I do my best, sir. But the neighborhood— you should excuse the expression—is lousy. Always the bums and the loafers are drifting in from the street.

SOLDIER

(grinning) Boy, you sure got a dirty skull, Myer. I'll bet there ain't that much rust on the Eiffel Tower.

PVT. MYER

(sternly) Don't criticize our national monuments! It's still a good tower, even if it is relatively rust-free.

SOLDIER

I'd get my hair cut if it wasn't for the dirt showing. I figure if a guy can't get rid of the rust he'd better keep it covered up.

PVT. MYER

Brilliant! Oh, but you *are* brilliant, aren't you. Will you let me polish your medals when you get to be a general?

SOLDIER

Not until you clean your bean. I don't want none of that rust on my medals.

Thompson's first-draft screenplay suggests that Kubrick planned a radically different film: rougher-edged, plainer-spoken, tilted more toward the common soldier and, like the absurd storming of Ant Hill, void of heroes or stars.

The script's Hollywood "happy ending," however, is as vulgar and witless as Douglas intimates. Shouting "I knew it, by God . . . I knew I wouldn't die!" the prisoners are delivered from the firing squad, and Dax and Mireau stroll arm in arm, if not into the sunset, back to the general's château for a brandy. Oddly, though, the soldiers continued to

Jim Thompson with Joe Kouba—the night of
the Writers Guild award dinner, after Paths of
Glory *was nominated as "the best written*
American drama of 1957" (Courtesy of the
Thompson family)

be pardoned in the second-draft screenplays—and as late as one of the
third draft—which would seem to indicate the nod was Kubrick's rather
than Thompson's.

Despite Calder Willingham's caveat about the Writers Guild, *Paths of
Glory*—unlike *The Killing*—was submitted for arbitration of the screen
credit. Since none of the principals, Harris, Kubrick, Willingham, and the
Thompson family, can or will say who sought a ruling, and the Guild refuses
to comment, the agent for the action remains anonymous. But in a memorandum dated September 24, 1957, Stan Margulies, then a publicist for the
film, wrote, "Stanley Kubrick has just informed me that as a result of a recent Screen Writers Guild decision, it will be necessary to change the
screenplay credits on *Paths of Glory*. It should now read: Screenplay by
Stanley Kubrick, Calder Willingham and Jim Thompson." This recast the
prior alphabetical listing of the authors, and would appear to reward Willingham for his time in Germany.

Thompson resented the alteration from his contract, grumbling to Arnold Hano that "the finished version was so close to his that it was practically impossible to tell the difference."

Indignation did not prevent him from renting a tuxedo and attending an awards banquet at the Moulin Rouge after *Paths of Glory* was nominated by the Writers Guild as "the best written American Drama of 1957." The prize went to Reginald Rose for *12 Angry Men.*

• • •

When Harris-Kubrick Pictures decamped for Munich, Jim and Alberta slipped back to New York. On the home front, their three children all were grown up by the spring of 1957. Thompson was proving as a middle-aged father something of a twinkly curmudgeon. Until Sharon turned eighteen he wouldn't let her serve beer at parties; a few years later when she wished to go camping with some male and female friends, he put his foot down. Michael, more troublingly, "hung around with the boys on the street," as he says, "drinking wine," after he dropped out of high school. "I can't remember exactly what Dad said, but I can remember his look. He was very distressed." Patricia, his eldest daughter, was married and living on her own.

Thompson plunged into the rhythms of the city he was about to depart. Wet nights with the Milburns chasing the legend of Joe Gould down at the Minetta Tavern in the Village. Meals with Jim Bryans near Magazine Management's digs at the old Hotel Marguery. He was amused to see that Noah Sarlot's office occupied a former toilet, white tiles still adorning the walls: the "hairy armpit" brigade—in Bryans's phrase—of men's adventure magazines, consigned to a men's room.

Yet there were fresh places to travel, and new friends. His sister Freddie, married since 1950 to Irving Townsend, a writer and Columbia Records executive, resided in Wilton, Connecticut, and Jim rode the train there for country weekends. Through Irving, he met John Hammond, courtly "discoverer" of Billie Holiday, Count Basie, Teddy Wilson, Bob Dylan, and Aretha Franklin. Hammond and Thompson found common ground in 1930s radical politics. "Jim Thompson was a very good friend of mine," Hammond wrote shortly before his death. "I happen to be crazy about Jim's novels."

Thompson returned to Celtic Park to pack up his apartment for the inevitable move to Hollywood. But before leaving the East Coast for good he hoped to salvage his career as a fiction writer. The past January Lion Library had published *The Kill-Off,* the last novel from his astounding streak of the early 1950s. Thompson had not sold a book for three years.

When Signet/New American Library rejected *The Spy* in July 1954, a young editor named Marc Jaffe wrote Ingrid Hallen that, "we would probably want a book more along the lines of his earlier things for Lion." Now back in New York, Thompson delivered to NAL a recent manuscript that fulfilled Jaffe's words with the literalness of a fundamentalist reading the Gospel: *Wild Town* revisited Lou Ford, his first and most fabled Lion creation.

"Jim Thompson was absolutely *sui generis,*" remembers Jaffe. "He wasn't like anybody else. He did not attempt to develop an image as a writer. Jim was a big bear of a man, but very easygoing. Considering the kind of books he wrote, his personality was 180 degrees opposite. He seemed to hold everything down."

Jaffe accepted *Wild Town* for the fall list. Founded in 1947 by Kurt Enoch and Victor Weybright, New American Library of World Literature vied with Bantam Books as the most illustrious paperback house. Editor in chief Weybright owned a discerning ear for Southern vernacular— Faulkner's *Wild Palms* became his first NAL title, and he reaped record sales with Erskine Caldwell. Soon NAL's Signet and Mentor imprints mounted a stellar roster of American and European authors, from contemporary to classic. Early Signet books have become prized among collectors as much for their sharp covers as for their contents, displaying the art of Robert Jonas, James Avati, Stanley Metzoff, and Robert McGuire, the illustrator for *Wild Town.*

Wild Town (Signet, September 1957) is neither a sequel to *The Killer Inside Me* nor properly a prequel, although the action likely occurs decades previous, just after the oil boom of the 1920s. The novel transpires, rather, in a parallel universe to *The Killer Inside Me,* an inverted mirror world called "Ragtown," where everything a reader of the original *knows* about Lou Ford turns out to be wrong. The West Texas setting may be similar—Ragtown resembles an earlier incarnation of Central City—along with some of the characters, such as Ford's girlfriend Amy; the deputy sheriff may still be a posturing "country clown" belching cornpone and dread. Yet as Thompson told his cousin about the plot of all stories, "things are not as they seem." Ford goes to bed with the devil, but this time he rises with the angels.

Ford initially hovers on the perimeter of the main action—a sop for Thompson's old fans. David "Bugs" McKenna, an awkward, insecure ex-con, signs on as the house dick at the Hanlon Hotel, the fourteen-story prairie monstrosity erected by Ragtown's invalid oil millionaire, Mike Hanlon. Aroused by "a growing impression in his mind that he had been given his job for a sinister purpose," McKenna finds that his every inquiry appears to expose the secret, invidious hand of Ford. "Ford's clownish mannerisms were too exaggerated, no more than a mask for a coldly calculating and super-sharp mind . . . he gave the impression of raging, barely controllable fury." Bugs eventually comes to believe that he has been hired to knock off his sickly boss in an adulterous cabal engineered by Hanlon's young wife, Joyce, and the dubious sheriff. He also falls for Ford's schoolteacher fiancée, Amy.

Thompson infused McKenna with many of the hard-luck traits he discovered for "An Alcoholic Looks at Himself" and his autobiographies, *Bad
Boy* and *Roughneck*. A "frightened child" and a "self-doubting, insecure
youth," Bugs grew into an "introverted, defensively offensive man" who
"seemed to have a positive knack for doing the right thing at the wrong
time." The doctor's son Ford tenders a more acute diagnosis:

> He *made* trouble for himself, Ford had said. He deliberately
> plunged himself into one scrape after another. In so doing, he
> bulwarked his self-pitying conviction that the whole world was
> against him—and it was a hell of a lot more fun, as well as a hell of
> a lot easier, than doing something constructive. . . .
>
> Ford had a lot more to say, but it was all in the same vein. He
> liked being in jams. He'd rather have things go bad than good.

The emergence of a kinder, gentler Lou Ford slings the only bombshell
into an otherwise *poshlust* western potboiler of Texas crude, blackmail, hot
sex, betrayal, and murder. *Wild Town* packs the deputy's cartoon persona
with enough doleful history to fold the charade of *The Killer Inside Me* inside out. His hawbuck routine conceals not *"the sickness"* but thwarted brilliance and family necessity. As Amy explains to Bugs:

> "He graduated from high school when he was fifteen. He went
> through pre-med in three years. Then, in his first year of medical
> college, his father took very ill and Lou came home. Doctor Ford—
> his father, that is—didn't get any worse, but he didn't get any bet-
> ter either. He just lingered on, year after year. And Lou. . . ."
>
> Ford had felt that he had to stay with the old man. But there
> was nothing in the small town for him to do. No suitable work, no
> real challenge for his mind. Still, he had to do something, and be-
> cause he was "old family" he had been given a deputy sheriff's ap-
> pointment. It was no job for a book-learned dude, obviously. For a
> man with ambitions which would be interpreted as pretensions.
> You had to blend with those around you, with the public's concep-
> tion of a cowtown deputy. So Ford had blended. He had fitted him-
> self into the role with a vengeance, exaggerating it until it bordered
> on caricature. And with this outward twisting of the man, there had
> been an inward one. In the brain—the intelligence—which could
> not be used as it had been intended to be.

In *Wild Town*, Ford once again plays God, covertly jerking the strings
on Bugs, Amy, the Hanlons, and everyone else around Ragtown, but his
scheming here is for a good cause. He not only solves the case like "a man

of honor"—as Raymond Chandler apotheosized the detective hero in "The Simple Art of Murder"—he even rises to the Christian sacrifice of his own happiness so that Bugs and Amy might achieve theirs. The final page sounds a note of tragic isolation:

> Ford's face tightened, pain stabbed through his heart, flooded the jeering black eyes. For a moment his world had been penetrated—that private, one-man world—and he knew a sense of loss so great that it was almost overwhelming. . . .
>
> The loneliness swept over Ford again, the loneliness and the bitterness. But only briefly; it was gone almost as soon as it came. He grinned and stood up quietly. He tiptoed out of the room.

"Rag Town" was the original name of Anadarko, Thompson's Oklahoma birthplace. If the Lou Ford of *The Killer Inside Me* sketched, at least in part, an angry and unappeased profile of his sheriff father, "Big Jim" Thompson, then *Wild Town* embodies a move toward healing and reconciliation. Overturning outer treachery to inner rectitude, vindication to understanding, the later Ford novel all but recants the volcanic odium of its darker twin. Thompson's future writing about Pop—the soft, idealized shadings of *King Blood;* the lurid, harsh strokes of *Pop. 1280*—would reel between these implacable extremes.

• • •

Wild Town showed Thompson for the first time winking at his Lion cult, if cult can be the word for so sizable a readership as he collected by the late 1950s. Over the following thirteen months the novel sold a vigorous 238,987 copies. With his $2,500 advance, Jim quit New York City for California, a New American Library author, in May 1957.

Sustaining a familiar Thompson tribal ritual, he squatted with his sister Maxine, now back at Camp Pendleton. Captain Joe Kouba was away touring Japan, and Jim acted the doting if slightly dotty uncle for his nephew Tony. "He bought me a set of classic books, *Treasure Island, Les Misérables,* etc., all uniformly bound, at a time when what I really wanted was a model ship of the *Missouri.* Jimmie was a very astute observer when he was sober—he had good antennae. He saw great humor in the oddities of the common world. He thought it was a roar that he went into a public bathroom one day, and a man walked in and meticulously washed his hands, lathered them up, dried them off, and then walked over to the urinal, pulled out his cock, and pissed. Put it back in his pants and then walked out. He thought it was the funniest thing in the world that someone would do that. And why anyone would pay attention to it is a strange thing, but he was always seeing things of that nature. Jimmie made it a study of a sort. Those powers of perception, I think, could make him perceive things in deranged people, which led him then to express it for his books.

"In the fifth grade I had to write a historical paper about the settlers in America," Tony adds. "Jimmie said, 'Why don't you write about the first murder in America?' So he told me about someone called John Billington, and I did. That was my essay, thanks to Uncle Jimmie."

On the West Coast also, recycling old characters seemed the only trick up the writer's midlife sleeve. From Camp Pendleton Thompson took his own—and now fourth—whack at the "America's first murderer" of his Writers' Project radio play and *Mercury Mystery Magazine* and *For Men Only* stories. The twenty-six "sample" pages from Billington he submitted, along with a synopsis, to New American Library in early June once again conveyed precious little of his obsession with the Pilgrims and violence. The novelist who recently scaled the rarefied formal elevations of *A Hell of a Woman* and *Savage Night* tumbled headlong into a Hollywood approximation of seventeenth-century speech:

> Well, law! We were not well set-up at all, that first time that we sailed from Southhampton. I knew nothing of ships—how could I?—(and 'tis happy I would be if I had never known nothing!)—so when we got downstairs, below decks, I should say I had himself, my John-O, take the first bunks we came to.

Around July 1 Jim and Alberta leased a small, furnished house in Los Angeles, at 848 Winchester Place, to be closer to the movie studios. He sprained a thumb during "the settling down process," but the accident could not prevent him from knocking out seven chapters of a contemporary thriller, *The Glass Whirlpool,* and mailing them to Marc Jaffe in less than a week. "I hope you can give me some fairly fast action on this, Marc," Thompson begged. "It's seldom that I find myself squeezed financially— and it's even rarer for me to mention it. But I feel I know you well enough to say that the move here cost me twice what I thought it would, and for once I'm really feeling the pinch."

The new novel fared no better than *Billington.* A slight, convoluted tale about a college-educated window washer, Johnny Blair, who suspects a Park Avenue doctor is diagnosing false cases of leprosy to blackmail wealthy female patients, *The Glass Whirlpool* struck NAL editor in chief Victor Weybright as "unconvincing" and "far-fetched." Thompson protested the rejection—"And I say this as one who, in more than twenty-five years of writing, has never before protested a rejection"—alleging that an "overloaded inventory" and "expediency" rather than literary merit determined the judgment. "Due to circumstances beyond my control, and yours as well perhaps," he dressed down Marc Jaffe in August, "I've been treated in a very unfair manner; and as a professional writer of longstanding, I felt I had to say so. But I don't mean anything personal by it." Jaffe rushed to field Thompson's salvo: "I feel very strongly that the negative decision was not based on any but editorial considerations." But behind the scenes he lobbied Weybright to reconsider, especially since "the agent said the author would be willing to come down a little on the advance . . . and can be counted on to make any changes we require."

Jaffe, for all his goodwill, was not Arnold Hano, just as New American Library, for all its prestige, was not Lion Books—a publisher that, as Thompson told Anthony Boucher, "took me as I was, allowed me to write the only way I know how." NAL did not so much encourage and challenge Thompson as endeavor to mold his talent according to profitable crime formulas. During the frustration around *The Glass Whirlpool,* Jaffe pressed for a shift from serial killers to serial protagonists. "I've been trying to get [Thompson] to settle down to a series character of some sort— private eye, laywer, police officer, etc.," he informed Weybright by inter-office memo. To the writer, Jaffe embroidered his series notion beyond even the preposterousness of Thompson's own designs for *The Glass Whirlpool:*

> I keep coming back to the series idea, and more specifically to a character similar to Lou Ford . . . Ford, moved into urban surroundings, would have considerable opportunity to flex his sardonic humor and muscle in a variety of criminal situations. Matter-of-fact, he could even be woven into the window-washer plot if Johnny's sister were made a widow and "Ford" a close friend—let's say a member of the D.A.'s Special Squad (which would allow him a good deal of mobility), or even a private investigator with good police contacts, if this seemed better in terms of future stories.

Such confused editorial meddling offered a noose disguised as a lifeline. Thompson did not bother NAL with his strongest fiction from the summer, the novella *This World, Then the Fireworks.* Venting yet another psychopathic killer, he so concentrated his most extreme Lion obsessions and techniques that, as novelist Max Allan Collins once quipped, "reading it will be for some rather like drinking a can of frozen orange juice without adding the water." The merely fifty-seven page manuscript counts down from a hideous Oedipal prologue, entitled "1-Minus." Narrator Martin Lakewood flashes back on the summer night ("our fourth birthday") when he and twin sister Carol followed shotgun blasts to a neighbor's house:

We burst into laughter simultaneously. It was so funny, you see. It was funnier even than Charlie Chaplin in the movies, or Krazy Kat in the funny papers.

The man on the floor didn't have a head, hardly any head at all. And that was funny, wasn't it? And it was funny the way Mom was laughing, spraying out pink stuff and making shiny red bubbles with her mouth. But the funniest thing, what we laughed loudest about was Dad and the woman. The woman who was the wife of the man without any head. The wife of the man Dad had killed to keep from getting killed.

Dad and the woman. Dad who went to the electric chair, and the woman who committed suicide. Standing there naked.

After this primal scene *This World, Then the Fireworks* skyrockets into incest, prostitution, matricide, Carol's fatal Mexican abortion, and still more sex, more murder. For a symmetrical finale, Martin creates his own lethal suburban triangle, involving his policewoman girlfriend, Lois, and her brother—or is the overseas soldier actually her *husband*? The Lakewood twins' amoral precocity harks back to the bad seed shenanigans of Bobbie Ashton in *The Kill-Off,* while Martin's Babel/biblical blasphemies ("Yea, verily, sayeth the Lord Lakewood, better the blind man who pisses through the window than the knowing servant who raises it for him") foretaste the bent religiosity of *Pop. 1280.* Inside the Lakewood calculus people are "no more than . . . symbols in an allegory," and "We are culpable only to the degree that all life, all society, was culpable."

With a stripped-down style reminiscent of the Harris-Kubrick–inspired *Lunatic at Large, This World, Then the Fireworks* hints that Thompson may have intended a film treatment rather than a literary work. Yet no director, even a maverick independent such as his old San Diego journalist buddy Sam Fuller could have leached the purulent subject matter for a 1950s movie screen. Thompson took his novella to *Playboy,* whose fiction editor praised "a strange and fascinating story," but demurred. *This World, Then the Fireworks* could only be published after his death, as part of a 1983 small-press chapbook edited by Max Allan Collins and Ed Gorman, *Jim Thompson: The Killers Inside Him,* which—along with Geoffrey O'Brien's *Hardboiled America*—would spur the Jim Thompson revival.

•   •   •

Thompson's collaboration with Stanley Kubrick on two of the decade's seminal films did not translate into instant cachet with Hollywood. Since his 1937 submission of "The Osage Murders" to Warner Brothers, he had circulated all his novels, hardcover or paperback, and much magazine fiction around studio story departments. His most innocuous writing was returned to him stamped XXX: Box Office Poison. A reader at Warner Brothers scolded the comparatively spineless *Cropper's Cabin,* "Following the formula of sex and sadism, the story is too censurable in every step of the plot to be considered for the screen." Brasher books, such as *A Swell-Looking Babe,* fared no better: ". . . rough people, rough talk, and a liberal sprinkling of sex. The whole thing is downbeat and depressing, with not one sympathetic character in the cast."

Kubrick would not return to the States before fall, and *Paths of Glory* would not have its world premiere until Christmas Day. The spring and summer of 1957, Thompson couldn't even sell a teleplay on his own. In May, Warner Brothers rejected his original story "The Guy in Jake's Shoes," and in July, more humiliatingly, gave a thumbs-down to an untitled outline for an episode of *Maverick.*

Part of the problem involved Thompson's chronic shyness among strangers, a snag for an industry where charm and affability are commodities. A natural storyteller, he never came to terms with "high concept" or the distillation of a complex plot idea to a single, irresistible phrase. "Jimmie just didn't understand the workings of it," his sister Freddie recalled. "He'd go into the studio and some creep would sit there picking his nails while Jimmie tried to lay out a story line. They wouldn't pay any attention to him. Those things did damage; they hurt him deeply." As Thompson himself groused in *Sunset and Cienega,* his abandoned late-1950s novel about a declining Hollywood writer he called Sanderson Blake:

> If you were lucky, you have to do your selling to only one or two people—the producer and/or the story editor—and that could be tough going enough with guys who yawned in your face, talked over the telephone while you were talking and assured visitors that they would be through with you "in just a minute." Sometimes, however, you might have an audience of as many as four—producer, executive producer, story editor and story analyst. All of them poisonously critical, pitching curved-ball questions at you, doing everything they could to rip your story apart.

His *Wild Town* advance all but exhausted, Thompson made plans to move from Los Angeles to more modest San Clemente—into a scenic if tiny waterfront cottage available at winter rates; this, also, would bring him nearer to Maxine at Camp Pendleton. Prior to heading south, he pounded out the opening chapters of a novel that took a subtler approach to New American Library's commercial strictures than either the timid skylarking of *The Glass Whirlpool* or the reckless depravity of *This World, Then the Fireworks.*

The Getaway may be Thompson's most subversive fiction because it so completely masks itself as a routine caper. A couple of likable crooks, a classic bank heist, and a cross-country scram to Mexico pave a descent into—literally—hell. The writer, moreover, incorporated his subversion into his tactics for marketing the book to NAL. His forty-page "sample" contained only the humorous and suspenseful set-up, and not a hint of what Lou Ford would call *"the sickness"* to follow.

Self-confident, good-natured, clever Carter "Doc" McCoy is an affable Thompson psycho:

> Doc McCoy's breakfast had cooled before he could get rid of Charlie, the night clerk. But he ate it with an enjoyment which may or may not have been as real as was apparent. It was hard to tell with Doc; to know whether he actually did like something or someone as well as he seemed to. Nor is it likely that Doc himself knew. Agreeability was his stock in trade. He had soaked up so much of it that everything he touched seemed roseately transformed.

Carol, his partner and wife, used to be a backwater librarian—but "approach with caution," as her police record now warns.

Thompson narrates the spectacular robbery of a Beacon City bank with the same cross-cutting, circular style he borrowed from Lionel White for *The Killing*. After Doc shoots a guard from his hotel window down the street, and diverts the crowd with a fiery haytruck and some dynamite, his accomplices, Rudy and Jackson, make off with the quarter-of-a-million-dollars haul. Rudy then guts Jackson with a knife. On the outskirts of town, Doc meets up with Rudy, and shoots him. The McCoys embark on a joyful flight to wealth and freedom—only to hear, over the radio, that he didn't actually kill Rudy. The "sample" breaks off just as Doc and Carol realize their perfect crime is unraveling.

NAL promptly signed *The Getaway,* and issued Thompson a contract on November 15 for a $2,500 advance, $1,000 on signing, $1,500 on delivery. But seemingly sniffing the rat he couldn't name, editor Marc Jaffe also dispatched a cautionary letter about the absence of "the higher moral values" in the trial chapters:

> I don't know how much [literary agent Ad Schulberg] wrote you about our reaction, but I must say that it was entirely favorable. There was one very basic point made, however, in our editorial discussion about the first section of the manuscript. There does not seem to be any representative of the higher moral values in society—either a cop or a private citizen—to help cope with the criminal situation. One's sympathy seems to be with the master-mind bank robber. It was difficult—in fact im-

possible—to tell just how you were going to work things out, but there should develop some opportunity for the law to enter in a very specific and positive way. Or failing that, the protagonist must ultimately pay for his crime—not simply to meet the standards of an arbitrary Code, but so that his actions are placed in proper perspective.

Thompson received this didactic counsel at his new perch in San Clemente, a steep hike up from the pier and railroad station, at 907 Buena Vista. "I have a wonderful place to write here," he wrote, "high on a cliff overlooking the ocean. It's very isolated." A later section of *The Getaway* would, in fact, memorialize the view from his desk. "He had always thought this was the most beautiful stretch of country in the world, this area of orange and avocado groves, of rolling black-green hills, of tile-roofed houses—all alike yet all different—stretching endlessly along the endless expanse of curving, white-sand beach."

Elated at his success with NAL—"Just got the good news about *The Getaway*, and am very happy that we're going to be working together again," Thompson crowed, "I believe this may well be the book to hit the jackpot"—he engaged Jaffe's scruples mainly by bobbing and weaving around them:

> I'm completely in accord with your view that the criminals must come to a bad end, and I've worked one out that is at once quietly terrifying and completely realistic. The seeds for this have been planted in the sample pages. These begin to sprout as the story proceeds, and the criminals (Doc and Carol, that is) are plunged into one harrowing experience after another in their flight across the country. They know all the angles. They are master crooks: super shrewd, daring, desperate. So they actually do get away, and reach their sanctuary in Mexico. *But!*
>
> But may I lower the curtain at this point? I hate to tip my ending, and a bald statement just wouldn't do justice to it. And the above should demonstrate that I have the book plotted out, and that no one reading it will be tempted to follow a criminal career. We do, of course, feel a certain sympathy (broadly speaking) for the criminals; we have to or we wouldn't care what happened to them. But it is more or less a case of loving the sinner while abhorring his sins.
>
> I hope this scheme of things is satisfactory to you. I'd give you an outline, but, as you know, I'm just not any good at them, and I've never made any on any of my other books.

Thompson's hammy, organ point *But!* was the hinge on a trapdoor leading to all the acid genius of his novel. *The Getaway* shoots past genre into
erosive fantasy, as the breakout for the border culminates in a three-stage
tumble through an inferno of Doc and Carol's own devise. Each sequence
turns on sly, gruesome objectifications of crime fiction commonplaces. In
the first, the cornered McCoys hole up, as it were, inside a pair of coffin-
sized underwater caves provided them by a crime moll named Ma Santis
for forty-eight hours—and for eight pages as claustrophobic as anything in
Samuel Beckett:

> Tucking her chin against her chest, [Carol] raised herself ex-
> perimentally. Six inches, a foot, a foot and a half, a—the stone
> pressed against her head. She shoved against it stubbornly, then
> with a suppressed *"Ouch!"* she dropped back to the floor.
>
> She rested a moment, then tried again. A kind of sideways try
> this time, with her knees pulled upward. That got her up a little far-
> ther, though not nearly far enough. But it did—or seemed to—
> show her how the trick could be done.
>
> She was very lithe and limber, more so now than ever after
> the arduous thinning-down of their cross-country journey. So she
> sucked her stomach in, drew her knees flat against it, and pressed
> her chin down against them. And thus, in a kind of flat ball, she
> flung herself upward and forward.
>
> Her head struck the roof with a stunning bump, then skidded
> along it gratingly, leaving a thin trail of hair and scalp. She would
> have stopped with the first painful impact, but the momentum of
> her body arced her onward. And then at last she was sitting up. Or
> rather, sitting. Bent forward as she was, it would have been far
> from accurate to say she was sitting up.

Next, Doc and Carol are forced to hide inside a room dug from a mound
of dung—everything they've touched having turned to shit. Naked, mop-
ping sweat with soiled clothes, they wait until the "heat," in at least three
senses of the word, is off:

> Head tilted to one side, she gave him an impish look. Then,
> leaning forward suddenly, she took his bristled face in her hands
> and . . .
>
> A soggy mass struck her on the forehead, slid down against
> her face. She sat back abruptly, scrubbing and brushing at herself.
> "Gaah!" she spat disgustedly, nose wrinkled. "Ugh! Of all the filthy,
> messy . . ."

"Now, that was a shame," Doc said. "It's the heat, I suppose. It softens the stuff up and . . ."

"Please!" she grimaced. "Isn't it bad enough without you drawing me a picture?"

That was the end of any lovemaking. . . .

"Which would you say was the funniest?" Doc asks Carol. "Me or the symbolism of the situation?"

Finally, there comes the escape to the sanctuary of El Rey and the "happy, decent life" Thompson's people are always killing for, imagined here as a Swiftean paradise of eternal blankness. "You tell yourself it is a bad dream. You tell yourself you have died—you, not the others—and have waked up in hell. But you know better. . . . There is an end to dreams, and there is no end to this. . . . They call him the devil, and accuse him of thinking he is God. And El Rey will nod to either charge. 'But is there a difference, Señor? Where the difference between reward and punishment when one gets only what he asks for?'"

El Rey's kingdom, which "appears on no maps and, for very practical reasons . . . has no official existence," reshuffles the itches and appetites of life beyond the law into a winsome social code. El Rey, for instance, "provides only the best for his guests. Isn't that what they have always wanted elsewhere . . . regardless of cost?" But his "guests," of course, must subsist on the fixed sum of their booty. El Rey's bank, furthermore, charges rather than pays interest. For criminal couples strained by diminishing joint accounts, "the outcome depends on which of the two is the shrewder, the more cold-blooded or requires the least sleep." As Thompson summarizes:

> El Rey does only what he has to. His criminal sanctuary is a big improvement over most. He does not kill you for your loot. He gives you value for your money. He runs a first-class place, and he could not do so if you were allowed to be miserly. Nor can he permit you to linger on when your money is gone. There would be no room for newcomers if he did; and allowed to accumulate, you and your kind would soon take over. You would be in his place, and he would be in yours up on that cobblestoned street with its sparkling whitewashed buildings. And he knows this. He and his native subjects know it. It explains their delight in irony, in symbolism; in constantly holding a mirror up to you so that you must see yourself as you are, and as they see you.

An ironic Savanarola in his republic of crime, El Rey squeezes his fugitives to a crisis of self-perception. The hungry preying on society by parasites like the McCoys will shade ultimately into, well, cannibalism. *"That smell that filled the air. The odor of peppery roasting flesh* . . . 'Quite fitting, eh Señor? And such an easy transition. One need only live literally as he has done figuratively.'"

After the total horror of El Rey dawns, Doc and Carol scheme to murder each other. Terrified, then amused by their mutual betrayal, they conclude the novel with a toast to their "getaway."

The closing chapters of *The Getaway* exploded a theme park of crime fiction motifs. But New American Library was not overwhelmed by Thompson's highjinks; it had contracted a caper, not a symbolic demolition of one. When Marc Jaffe reviewed the completed manuscript on March 20, 1958, he once more saluted the opening—"in many respects it's the best thing of yours I've read in a long long time"—before he wrestled with his uneasiness about the finish:

> The only important thing that I question is the final sequence, when our two criminals wind up in the land of El Rey. I think I know what you're getting at in this kind of development, but I wonder whether the element of fantasy and symbolism isn't a bit too strong? After all the book is pitched very realistically at the outset, and most of the way through—at least until we reach the meeting with Ma Santis. Without running this thing into the ground, could the old lady be a sort of Charon guiding two sinners first underground then across the water into a private hell?
>
> I don't question the irony of your conclusion, I simply feel that it would be just as effective if the setting were clearly identified as a small town south of the border with a local crime boss in charge. The town could be described realistically . . . and the plot twist would still work. What is the significance (or perhaps better necessity) of the suggestion of cannibalism as it appears in the present version? Why the necessity of the strange financial manipulations?

Thompson, for once, drew a line in the sand and volunteered to change nothing. Yet his artful reply did not challenge Jaffe on grounds of ethics or literature, disentangle confusions, or even dispute specific questions. The novelist's letter of March 22 was all mirrors and smoke—movie options, magazine serials, greenbacks, back slapping, and his own criminal contacts:

> Received your good letter this morning. . . .
> Ad [Schulberg] called me, after our talk yesterday, and she

was really raving about the book. Must have talked all of twenty minutes at person-to-person rates, and you know Ad just doesn't do things like that ordinarily. She thought it was one of the very best manuscripts she had ever handled. She has already submitted it to the *Saturday Evening Post,* and has high hopes for a serial sale. Then, last night, my Hollywood agents phoned me again. Gary Cooper had already read their copy of the ms. and, to use their expression, had "flipped" over it. But he was afraid his public would not accept him as a bank robber, so the book is now being read by Tyrone Power—and this is unusual—at his own urgent request. The final words of the agents were: "Jim, we don't just think we can sell this for a big picture production. We know it."

I am telling you all this because I know you will be as happy about it as I am. It should make for a far larger book sale than we had originally planned. Briefly, however, what I am trying to say is this:

The book as it stands is seemingly a very good one. It should make all parties concerned a lot of money. Should we then run the undeniable risk of making it less good by attempting to make it better?

As you know, I spent more than twice as much time on this book as I have on any other—although it is relatively short. For every page of finished copy, I must have discarded three or four others. I broke completely away from all the tired old situations; everything that went into it was solidly authentic. Perhaps the ending does achieve a certain symbolism—but is that bad? At any rate, it is completely factual.

I have been on a first-name basis with a number of criminals. Following his release from prison, I was the room-mate one summer of the notorious bank-robber, "Airplane Red" Brown and I served as best-man at his wedding. . . . This background does allow me to write with authority. And such characters and situations as Ma Santis and her underwater hideouts, do have real life parallels.

As for El Rey's sanctuary, how could it serve as one—a place from which no one could be extradited—if the Mexican government admitted its existence? Obviously, it couldn't. Not as the next-door neighbor to such a powerful and friendly government as the United States.

Now, I won't take up the things you questioned item by item. Suffice it to say, I believe them to be as they should be, and—as I say in the book—as they just about have to be. And if I changed them, it would be with the conviction that I was making a mistake. . . .

Best regards to you, Marc. And thanks very, very much for the prompt action on the check. This page a day stuff—which was about what *The Getaway* worked out to—is undoubtedly best in the long run; but as an immediate thing, it's sure hard on the pocketbook.

Jaffe, to his credit, arranged for New American Library to print *The Getaway* (Signet, January 1959) exactly as it issued from Thompson's typewriter. More than thirty years after publication, he admits that "Jim knew exactly what he was doing. We had more lengthy discussions, and I must say I still had some reservations—but he won." Still, NAL remained so nervous about the possible immorality of *The Getaway* that its publicity department addressed the ending with an in-house editorial dopesheet: "The forces of the Law do not emerge triumphant over crime, it is true, but the fate of the criminals is sure, they will pay for their crimes in a private Hell of their own making."

While New American Library may have been the most literary house to release a Thompson paperback original, the correspondence around *The Getaway* spotlights the problem of whether they ever understood him. Missing the sympathetic editorial guidance he enjoyed at Lion, Thompson saw his future NAL projects retreat from *The Getaway*. His next proposals would backtrack to the upbeat serial character recipes of the previous summer. In July 1958, he launched a private eye series with *The Red Kitten,* and then in November a con man series featuring Mitch Allison, from his *Alfred Hitchcock Mystery Magazine* stories "The Cellini Chalice" and "The Frightening Frammis," under the improbable titles *Find 'em, Fool 'em, Forget 'em* or *The Barbed-Wire Bikini.* Both ventures failed to outlive their insipid "samples."

Thompson's desperation for cash only tossed stones in his passway. "Anything I could find for him, he needed," Robert Goldfarb, his Hollywood agent, insists. "Jim would grab these deals, grab the advances, then suffer an agony of paralysis and say, 'I just can't write that stuff.' " Goldfarb introduced Thompson to Ted Loeff, a Beverly Hills book packager who hatched ideas for novels and then found writers to nurture them. Loeff and his partner, Charles Bloch, at the Literary Projects Company originated *The Dirty Dozen,* an international best seller. In May 1959, Thompson took a $4,000 advance from NAL to create a book, tentatively called *Lydia Karmer,* about a female murderer with a "compulsion to confess." Ted Loeff—Goldfarb's agency notes reveal—"is going to supply a certain amount of documentary material to Jim and pay him an additional $1,500 for which he will receive 25% of the net in the event of a motion picture sale." Thompson never carried through on the novel. In November he contracted privately with Loeff for a supplemental $1,250 "to write a book on the Dora Jones peonage case," the sensational 1947 San Diego "slave" trial he had covered for the *Journal*. That novel, also, he never finished.

Internal NAL memoranda chimed with louder and haughtier peals of condescension. One note actually chided Thompson for "the overtones of psychological torment with which he has belabored his characters in the past." An anonymous NAL editorial hand would eventually sneer in pencil at the bottom of an interoffice message, "I'm getting dubious about poor old Jim!"

• • •

Doomed brainstorms like *The Barbed-Wire Bikini* and *Lydia Karmer,* or haggling over irony and fantasy with New American Library could not squander his entire attention. During the fourteen-month lag from signing to publication for *The Getaway,* Thompson jockeyed his collaboration with Kubrick into—if not a feature film—steady script work for television. Early in the summer of 1958, agent Bob Goldfarb found him a single-shot rewrite job for an episode of *Tales of Wells Fargo* broadcast as "The Last Stand"; series producer, legendary pulpmeister Frank Gruber, admired Thompson's crime fiction. "Frank recognized a fraternity brother," Goldfarb suggests, "and threw him a bone." Whether or not *Wells Fargo* was an audition, Thompson passed. By August, he joined Ziv Television Programs to write a Western, *Mackenzie's Raiders,* for syndication in the fall.

Jim Thompson "hated writing for TV," according to Alberta, "there were too many people to please along the line," and he ridiculed the Ziv setup amid a Christmas letter for his sister Freddie and brother-in-law Irving Townsend:

> At long last, I've got my foot firmly in the door of television—I'd like to put it up the industry's collective butt. . . . Everything I've done so far has been for Ziv Productions, which is polluting the air waves with a dozen-odd idiots' delights, and is a very low-pay, slave-driving outfit, but by no means the worst. (Give me time, give me time.) . . . Meanwhile, I've received encouragement from Warner Brothers TV and Revue, who pay quite a bit better and do not bracket writers so severely as to production costs. (My spies tell me that all Ziv productions are shot in the producer's garage with a Brownie camera.) Believe me, it's a hell of a job to stage an Indian war with only one Indian. . . .

Ziv may have been cheap; it wasn't insignificant. Frederick W. Ziv presided as the nation's ranking packager of radio programs until 1948, when he expanded into television. A decade later, Ziv and CBS accounted for one-third of all TV syndication revenues.

Thompson's writing for television, with the freak anomaly of a 1965 *Dr. Kildare* episode he irritated into a *noir* pearl, would never transcend schlock. Yet like his true crime reporting, his oral histories, or his *SAGA* articles, he somehow managed to personalize the most formulaic and generic teleplays. *Mackenzie's Raiders* resembled his outlaw tales, such as "Bert Casey: Wild Gun of the Panhandle," for *Man's World* and other men's adventure magazines. As Ziv announcer Art Gilmore intoned over the musical theme at the top of each weekly installment, "From the archives of the U.S. Cavalry, the true story of Colonel Randal Mackenzie and the Cavalry men he led." The Southwestern Indian plots recalled stories Thompson's sheriff father had sifted from territorial Oklahoma.

Mackenzie's Raiders was a Texas horse opera set at Fort Clark during the 1870s. President Grant gave Colonel Mackenzie secret orders to rid the Southwest of Mexican marauders and renegade Indians, pursuing them across the Rio Grande if necessary. The show's gimmick—soon to become a TV cold war staple—is that should Mackenzie be caught on foreign soil, the United States would have to disown his mission to prevent a dreaded "international incident." *Mackenzie's Raiders* starred Richard Carlson, fresh from a stint exposing Communists as Herbert Philbrick on the long-running *I Led Three Lives,* another Ziv production.

Preserved on sixteen-millimeter film and viewed from an archive screening room, *Mackenzie's Raiders* can seem the unwieldy artifact of a distant country: too hokey and dated to warrant revival, yet too solid and competent to be dismissed as camp. Thompson earned about $1,300 for a half-hour teleplay, and an additional $297.50 whenever an installment was repeated. "Jimmie would watch the programs when they aired," says Alberta, "and complain that they changed things on him, that's all." He received author's credit for four episodes of *Mackenzie's Raiders,* "Death Patrol," "Indian Agent," "Blood on the Rio," and "Joe Ironhat." At the head of his scripts he inset brief summaries, among them:

> "Death Patrol": After mopping up on an outlaw gang, Mackenzie must get hi patrol back to Fort Clark—150-mile journey through drought-stricken wasteland. He has three prisoners. Two of his own men are unable to walk, and he is critically short of food, water and ammunition. Pete Lemond, the gang's leader, snipes at the patrol. Two of Mackenzie's men are killed. He and the one-remaining able-bodied man are wounded. Mackenzie ultimately en-

lists the aid of one of the prisoners, Chief Redwing, and is thus able to kill Lemond and reach the fort.

"Joe Ironhat": Despite the sympathetic help of Mackenzie, Joseph Topanga, the first educated Indian in the Fort Clark area, is thwarted and insulted at every turn as he attempts to find suitable employment. Criminal Indians—taking advantage of his discouragement—dupe him into taking part in a robbery. Believing that he has killed the victim, he flees into Mexico with the criminals. Mackenzie's task: To bring the true culprits to justice without harm to the innocent man, Topanga.

Thompson indicated in his December letter to Freddie and Irving that he "dropped in to see [Ziv Television Programs] just before Christmas, and was informed that they were counting on me for five or six programs during the coming year." There would be no further adventures of *Mackenzie's Raiders* with his name on them after "Joe Ironhat" aired in January. His only other contribution to television during 1959 involved a story idea he first pitched to Warner Brothers TV as "Satan's Quarter-Section." The plot reversed a neat jest from his second novel, *Heed the Thunder*. Whereas Ma Fargo had deeded her Nebraska farm to God, Mr. Ames in "Satan's Quarter-Section" wills his ranch to the devil:

Two HEAVIES have stumbled upon gold deposits in Mr. AMES' worthless ranch. When Ames refuses to sell the ranch to the heavies, they kill him, figuring they can force Ames' daughter to sell. HERO finds body, suspects treachery. When Ames' will is read, it reveals that he jokingly willed his "worthless" acres to the Devil. The heavies try to take over the ranch, claiming they have as much right as the girl. Wise to heavies' scheme, Hero files suit against the Devil to recover property for the girl, wins back property through legal means.

Warner Brothers declined. Thompson, however, sold the idea to *Man Without a Gun,* a Ziv western about a crusading Dakota Territory newspaperman. He fashioned a teleplay, but was cut off after the first draft. "Satan's Quarter-Section" would be broadcast in August as "Devil's Acres."

Thompson assaulted Hollywood from the awkward distance of San Clemente, a diabolical drive for an early-morning meeting or shoot. The erratic, often insecure fate of the scriptwriter blighted what was left of his novelist's discipline, and alcoholic stimulation once again paced his days and nights. His family had lived with Jim's binges for decades now, but his electric mood swings under the influence could shock even the battle-scarred. If Alberta and Sharon wearied of coaxing him to bed, they sent him on to Maxine at Camp Pendleton. "Jimmie would call and say, 'Maxine, this is your bad penny, can I come and stay?' "

When Maxine moved back east, after Captain Kouba was reassigned to Arlington, Virginia, Sharon spent a terrible March alone with Thompson at the San Clemente house: "My Aunt Pauline was being operated on for cancer, and my mother went back to Nebraska. My dad drank while she was gone, which upset me more than usual because mother wasn't there to settle things."

She remembers that Thompson, although a disbeliever to his final breath, "came in one night after he had been drinking and said, 'Sharon, I don't know how we're going to do it, but we're going to get Pauline to Lourdes. She's going to be all right if we can get her to Lourdes.' We both just sat there and cried, we were so upset."

• • •

Stanley Kubrick ransomed Thompson from Ziv Television Programs with a surprise telephone call. After *Paths of Glory* he had wasted six months on preproduction for *One-Eyed Jacks* with Marlon Brando before the actor decided to direct the film himself. Kubrick then took over *Spartacus* from Anthony Mann, at the urging of Kirk Douglas. But from as far back as February 1958, he envisioned another caper, *I Stole $16,000,000,* based on the autobiography of Herbert Emerson Wilson, the self-styled "king of the safecrackers."

Thompson initially hoped that Kubrick could be induced to film *The Getaway.* "Kubrick should see it and certainly the majors and some of the independents," Ad Schulberg prodded him, and Marc Jaffe mailed copies of the manuscript to Columbia Pictures and Twentieth Century-Fox. But Kubrick, who once talked about directing *The Killer Inside Me,* passed on *The Getaway,* as did the Hollywood studios. "The opening is promising, but then it becomes pretty much of a routine yarn in its category," the Fox New York story department informed Jaffe.

After *The Getaway, I Stole $16,000,000* must have spooked Thompson with déjà vu. Herb Wilson, a former Baptist minister and "mastermind of crime . . . who never made mistakes, who . . . had blasted or torched safes throughout America during the Roaring Twenties . . . who always dressed for dinner," suggested a still more calculating and debonair Doc McCoy. Like Doc, Wilson approached his felonious trade as a painstaking mental discipline:

> . . . I studied crime as a science that could be and had to be
> mastered—and I mastered it. I knew where to strike, when to

strike, how to strike. I knew how to make a phantom-like departure, with no clues left behind me and puzzled cops running
around in circles, complaining of aching flat feet. The burglar tools
and techniques I invented set a standard still used in the underworld although criminals today, I am told, do not have the same
skill and nerve I possessed. . . .

His reverie on the self-masking appeal of safe cracking allied him with other
Thompson characters:

> I picked safe-cracking as my criminal specialty for several rea-
> sons, but principally because it is done at night. I would be a
> shadow and shadows have no faces.
> That was how I wanted it, and that was the way I carried it out
> for practically my entire criminal career. Even to the unavoidable
> few who witnessed my raids, I was little more than a shadow,
> a nameless, flitting form, who was here, there, then presto—gone.
> . . . I remember the enjoyment I got out of reading the morning
> papers after a Cincinnati job, where the released watchman of the
> plant we had looted informed reporters that "the leader of the mob
> looked like Lon Chaney in *The Phantom of the Opera.*"

Wilson's episodic confession traced a larcenous spree from Los Angeles to Boston, "with even my identity unknown to the police, while I blasted
sixty-five big safes and vaults and robbed armored cars from coast to coast
for a total take of more than $16,000,000." Only after a confederate turned
stool pigeon would Wilson be arrested as he basked inside his Southern
California El Rey, a Venice mansion where dressed in a silk smoking jacket
he read Gibbon's *Decline and Fall* and anticipated Christmas dinner. A
twelve-year stretch in San Quentin Penitentiary served as his descent into
the underworld. "Don't let anyone kid you that crime doesn't pay," he concluded his memoir. "Crime always pays—with a living hell on earth!"

"We picked up the rights to *I Stole $16,000,000,*" remarks Jimmy Harris,
"and United Artists financed the development. We had to meet with Herb
Wilson in Mexico, I remember, because he couldn't come into the United
States."

Was Thompson interested in writing the sceenplay of *I Stole
$16,000,000*? Kubrick wanted to know. On May 7, 1959, he signed with
Harris-Kubrick Pictures "to deliver a completed screenplay in not more
than 20 weeks for a flat figure of $6,000 payable in weekly increments of
$300 a week." On the "first day of principal photography" he would pull
down an additional $9,000.

Thompson was not the first writer to take a shot at *I Stole $16,000,000.*

The projected film, curiously, reproduced the bloodline from his original Kubrick collaboration. Lionel White, author of *Clean Break,* the novel behind *The Killing,* had sketched a treatment and step outline for Harris-Kubrick Pictures under the tentative title of *The Theft.* Stanley Kubrick then fleshed this out into a structured screenplay. The spring of 1959, Thompson worked toward the shooting script, featuring his trademark hard-boiled dialogue, with typical dispatch. On June 1, scarcely three weeks after he inked his contract, he presented the director with a completed screenplay of 135 pages.

Kubrick no doubt requested cuts and changes. For it was while Thompson was revising *I Stole $16,000,000,* just a few mornings later in his secluded writing room overhanging the Pacific surf, that he suddenly collapsed. He had been warned about his high blood pressure for more than a decade. And recently he had experienced dizzy spells—one so incapacitating that he canceled a rare dinner date with his brother-in-law Irving Townsend in Hollywood. Jim was alone at the house. When Alberta returned from an appointment at her beauty salon, she discovered him conscious yet woozy and disoriented near his desk.

She rushed him by car to the family physician, a Dr. Pine, in nearby Capistrano Beach. Dr. Pine believed that Thompson had suffered a mild stroke. Smoking and heavy drinking are commonly branded as prime risk factors in many types of strokes, and since high school Jim had not curtailed his two-plus-packs-a-day cigarette habit, and only sporadically tempered his alcohol intake. The amphetamine cocktails he had injected under the sway of Max Jacobson could also have contributed to his condition. His speech was not affected, nor either of his legs. But Thompson's right hand was paralyzed.

Remarkably, his physician did not hospitalize him for tests. Alberta and Sharon set up a hospital bed in the front bedroom and nursed him at home, with almost daily visitations from Dr. Pine, who seems to have ruffled the Thompson dog, Sandy. "[The doctor] has been here enough to acquire the status of a dependent, but Sandy attacks him more vigorously with each visit," Jim subsequently regaled Irving Townsend. "Think this is highly significant." Less jocularly, he struggled to restore feeling to his hand by squeezing Sandy's ball.

"The stroke really scared Daddy," Sharon recollects, "because he couldn't type." As the days passed, Thompson, who bashed out his books on a lumbering old Smith Corona manual typewriter, wondered if he would ever write again. The family attempted to reassure him with accommodating gadgets. "We rented an electric typewriter for him because the keys were lighter," Sharon continues, "but he couldn't work that at all. He had a habit of stopping and contemplating and leaning, and the typewriter would jump on him. Then we bought him a tape recorder, so that he could dictate, and I got my girlfriend Betty to transcribe for him. But he had a lot of trouble dictating because that wasn't the way Daddy worked." Betty, then engaged to a minister, lasted long enough to contribute the most succinct pronouncement on the contrast between Thompson's social personality and his writing that has animated virtually every description of him since the University of Nebraska. "I can't believe this sweet old man knows words like that!"

The "old man" was not yet fifty-three. Jim was laid up for almost three months. But Harris-Kubrick never abandoned him, continuing to send $300 weekly checks throughout his illness. With physical therapy his hand would gradually recover full movement, and by July 5 he was able to peck out a cranky letter to Irving Townsend that mocked his physical plight:

> Thanks for your good letter; it was nice to hear from you. Sorry we couldn't get together as planned when you were in Hollywood. I believe the illness I was suffering then was a prelude to my stroke. I left a message at my hotel for you, but having witnessed some marvelous examples of their inefficiency, I suspect it was never delivered.
>
> As you can see, am able to function after a fashion, with the aid of a hospital bed and desk, and an electric typewriter which requires very little effort from me. At least, I have been able to do enough to hang onto my motion picture contract. Stanley Kubrick and Jim Harris have been very tolerant of my affliction, insisting that I take good care of myself and assuring me that my pay would continue whether I could work or not. However—and I should probably be ashamed of my suspicions—I can never quite see these boys as philanthropists, and am always uneasy when they engage in nominally kindly deeds. And, anyway, I would rather work. I tried dictating to a secretary for a time, but gave up in bewilderment after having histrionic translated as "historic," pious as "pieass," and intrinsic as "iroxic" (that last one really threw me). Don't know what the public school system has substituted for spelling and English, but think it could bear looking into.
>
> We are all looking forward to seeing you and Freddie when you come out this month. I hope to be up and about by that time, although the doctor tells me that the status quo will probably obtain for perhaps another six weeks, adding, by way of comfort, that I should be glad it isn't six months. The guy has an amazing ability to bear up under my troubles, and seems to grow more cheerful and patient the longer they continue. . . .
>
> Everyone is about the same here, except for being pretty well pooped out from waiting on me. And they have, bless them, done a

wonderful job of it. I was glad to hear that Randi had found employment. From the experiences of my nonage, I know there is
nothing like a routine job for inspiring one to so-called better
things.

Well, I seem to have used several hundred words in talking
about my indisposition and corollary subjects. But the topic is ad-
mittedly much on my mind. . . .

Thompson, as Alberta wrote George and Mary Milburn in New York,
soon was managing seven new pages of script each day. But if he ever finished a second draft of *I Stole $16,000,000,* the manuscript has vanished.
Harris-Kubrick, in any event, decided not to make the film. "One of the reasons we never bothered with it was that it was too close to *The Killing,*" reports Jimmy Harris. "Stanley, as his subsequent films show, wasn't one to
stay in the pattern of the same kind of story. Once we did *The Killing* and
Paths of Glory, we started to think of different genres. We acquired the
rights to *Lolita,* and we didn't think of Jim Thompson in that vein. After
that, we started to drift apart."

• • •

Jim subsisted on the noblesse oblige of Harris-Kubrick Pictures through
September. Without TV or fiction prospects he toughed out the fall only by
another advance from book packager Ted Loeff. Early in 1960 Loeff
glimpsed an occasion to retrieve his investment. Buck Houghton, producer
of Rod Serling's *The Twilight Zone,* was looking for a writer who could turn
an original screenplay into a novel. "I don't say this proudly, but I advanced
some money to Thompson since he had a rough time recuperating from his
stroke," Loeff wrote Victor Weybright at New American Library. "He appears to be healthy now and I would say he could very well complete the
novel. I have insisted that both background and characters bear certain
unique qualities that will take the novel out of the straight suspense category . . . and I believe Thompson has a good approach to the yarn. . . .
Houghton is willing to hold up the film for at least a year and a half if we
agree to arrange publication—both hard covers and paperback."

On February 1 Thompson signed a $4,000 letter of agreement with NAL
for "a novel entitled *Cloudburst* based on a screenplay owned by Ohio Films
(Buck Houghton)." One-quarter of the payment was canceled by his prior
NAL advance for *Lydia Karmer,* and the publisher fastened more control
than theretofore over the book. Thompson would realize the balance in
three stages, $1,000 on signing, $1,000 "on delivery of one-half of the manuscript satisfactory to NAL," and the final $1,000 on completion. Because the
work was a novelization NAL additionally stipulated, "You warrant that
your grant of rights to us for *Cloudburst* violates no rights of Ohio Films."

Other Thompson novels, such as *The Killer Inside Me* or *Cropper's Cabin,* issued from similarly lowly origins; but none survived a more difficult birth.

As drafted by Houghton from a story by Frank Burt, *Cloudburst* framed
a western melodrama about a woman who goes out after her husband's
murderer and falls in love with him. Sheriff Jeff Ruskin is holding Rex Crayly
at the local jail when the outlaw's brother Dave arrives to bail him out. Ambitious and arrogant, Ruskin draws first, and the news of his death causes
his wife, Charlotte, to suffer a miscarriage. She embarks on a vengeful
quest, encountering en route the assistance of a mysterious stranger who,
unknown to her, is Dave Crayly. After Rex jealously gives him away, Charlotte wounds Dave but relents into a kiss of sexual awakening. They appear
headed for marriage until Rex needs Dave's help against some Swedish
gold miners who earlier swindled $30,000 from the Craylys in a cattle deal.
Charlotte, believing that Dave will revert to his criminal past, angrily re-
moves the bullets from his gun. She has second thoughts—but arrives too
late in the rain and lightning. Dave Crayly dies in Charlotte's arms as over-
head the cloudburst clears.

Cloudburst assembled a rich, ironic story line—"sounds like real Jim
Thompson territory," as Buck Houghton notes—yet lifeless characters and
a stale frontier setting. Houghton could not find financing for his film as a
western. "We hoped," he recalls, "that we could bring this along a little
faster if Thompson were to write a novel." He inititially wished that the novelization be relocated to modern New Mexico, but after consultation with
Rod Serling opted for North Africa.* "The Serling crowd is interested in
translating the script from the West to a North African background," Loeff
told Weybright, "and I believe Thompson could do this one beautifully." Sitting down with Houghton and Loeff in Beverly Hills, Thompson stripped
the plot to a contemporary psychological thriller:

CLOUDBURST

This is the story of a woman who pursues a man through the
political and physical jungle of North Africa with the intent to kill
him.

It could be categorized as an action story, but only in a narrow
sense. Much more than that it is a study in character: a woman
who believes that right is right and wrong wrong, whenever or
wherever they occur, and a man whose basic code is expedience.

The woman lacks a description of the man (he has killed her

---

* For his 1981 adaptation of *Pop. 1280, Coup de Torchon,* director Bertrand Tavernier, fascinatingly yet coincidentally changed the setting of the film from the American Southwest
to French Equatorial Africa.

husband, the shock of which causes her child to be stillborn). She knows that he will have changed his name. Still, when the nominal authorities cannot or will not bring him to justice, she takes on the job herself.

Several times she almost catches up with him. At last she succeeds . . . but without knowing who he is. He offers to help her find the man she is looking for. They fall in love, and then she learns his identity: that he is responsible for the death of her husband and her unborn child. . . .

She shoots him. Then, grief-stricken and very much in love with him, she nurses him back to health. But he's learned nothing from the experience; he hasn't really changed. And she comes to the unwilling realization at last, that he never will. He likes being what he is. He is too selfish, too filled with self-love, to love her.

So, finally, she must face up to an eternal truth—that evil wears many guises, but never changes—and an age-old question: Has she the right to love such a man? Can she really love him?

Her conclusion is that, while she may love him she must kill him. She must, perhaps, because she *does* love him. End of story.

Jim immediately departed San Clemente for Falls Church, Virginia, and his sister Maxine, to carve out the North African *Cloudburst*. But the "first one-half (approximately) of the new book, as per our contract," he mailed NAL two weeks later, on Valentine's Day, jettisoned nearly everything he arranged with Houghton and Loeff. Instead of North Africa, the locale was Big Sands, West Texas. And instead of an avenging widow, the principal protagonist was Deputy Sheriff Lou Ford.

For his third Ford novel Thompson lightly rode the bones of Houghton's story, transposing cattle into oil and Swedish con men into Sicilian mobsters, yet the wily lawman substituted not for Sheriff Ruskin but for Dave Crayly. This latest rehabilitation of Lou Ford embellished the mitigating family background in *Wild Town*. Descended from the conquistadores, the deputy was abandoned by his mother during early childhood, and later forced to quit medical school when his doctor father lapsed into a lingering illness. Ford III also hides behind the "drawling, doltish" mask of the "yokel's masquerade," flashing his verbal needle like a concealed stiletto:

He, the real man, became smaller and smaller as the years went by, and the outer shell became thicker. But he was there, all right. A little of him was constantly poking through to the surface, showing up in exaggerated Westernisms and savagely sly gibes— blindly, bitterly striking back at the world he could not change.

Ford has been waging a public vendetta against Aaron McBride, the field boss for the Highlands Oil & Gas Company, who cheated him out of the mineral rights to his land. A mad confrontation by a drilling rig results in McBride's accidental death. All witnesses, prostitute Joyce Lakewood (not quite Joyce Lakeland from *The Killer Inside Me*) and two roughnecks, Curly Shaw and Red Norton, vouch for Ford's innocence. But McBride's young wife, Donna, losing her husband and baby the same week, intends to hunt down the killer. When she reaches Big Sands exhausted and sick, Ford wraps Donna in his mother's old nightgown and soothes her with his father's medicine. The Fort Worth syndicate behind Highlands Oil & Gas, meanwhile, has fingered the deputy for a hit. The ninety-seven page opening concludes as Fat August Pellino incites Donna McBride to shoot Ford.

New American Library gave its blessing to Thompson's *Cloudburst* without a sniffle of trepidation. The author traveled to New York on March 3, and editor Walter Freeman didn't even mention North Africa. NAL mainly appeared relieved that the novel was not *The Getaway.* "Jim came in town today and said that he will finish the book ahead of schedule and then take up any major editorial changes," Freeman apprised Victor Weybright. "I think that this is quite good. The neurotic-bum sort of air that has been a hardship in some of Jim's work is not a problem here. Only some dialogue may be re-worked." But on the West Coast, Ted Loeff and Buck Houghton began to intuit a double cross. Thompson owed him money, Loeff notified Weybright on April 9, and he hadn't shown them a word of *Cloudburst:*

> Please note developments on this Project:
>
> This is a proprietary work owned by producer Buck Houghton—who currently supervises the production of *The Twilight Zone,* the Rod Serling TV show.
>
> There is a problem here, in that Thompson owes LPC [Loeff's Literary Projects Company] $1,350—has sent a large number of pages to NAL directly—has left the proprietor, Mr. Houghton, in the dark completely—while LPC has no idea what kind of copy has emerged. We would appreciate, henceforth, NAL's relaying information concerning "on-the-spot" deals, since our lack of information has caused a redrafting of contracts for the entire set-up. A personal contract is being drawn between Houghton and Thompson (based on the type of proprietary contract we have been using); and a new NAL contract will be required, with Houghton as proprietor.

By then Jim not only had cashed his NAL advance; he was back in New York with the completed novel.

Departing still further from Houghton's screenplay or the Beverly Hills treatment, Thompson canted *Cloudburst* toward a romantic final act. *This* Lou Ford may be sarcastic, but aside from some dreamy moments when he burbles to Donna McBride as though she were his mother ("You remember, don't you? Even when I was a toddler, and you used to . . .") he lacks *"the sickness."* Foreseeing that she will try to shoot him, he replaces the bullets in Donna's gun with blanks. This gives her time to recognize that Ford didn't plan to kill her husband. And when Joyce Lakewood winds up dead and he is without an alibi, Donna lies and says she was in bed with him. Together they vanquish whatever threatens them—the Fort Worth Mafia or the roustabouts Curly and Red, who return to blackmail Ford. Lou and Donna make love "in the far-west Texas night, in the incredible, heartbreaking beauty of the night," and the book simmers to a close. When Houghton hired Thompson he wanted the soft edges of *Cloudburst* roughed up into what Loeff called "a 'hard' quality yarn." The novelization simply creamed the Hollywood corn.

From Los Angeles, Loeff threatened New American Library via telegram and letter. Once the smog of Thompson's deception receded, NAL learned that the writer had never signed his proprietary contract with Houghton. Walter Freeman finally sent the manuscript of *Cloudburst* to Loeff air mail special delivery on June 7. "I am very unhappy about this situation," Loeff riposted. "The result is almost disastrous for Houghton in that he has six months and considerable cash in the screenplay—which he was not able to finance because of a semi-western background." Loeff cursed Freeman and Victor Weybright: "Thompson said that one of the editors at NAL approved a switch-over of background to Texas. . . . It goes back to NAL closing a deal, without my knowledge, when the property belongs to someone else." But he conceded that all parties were operating under the genial spell of Thompson's con. "No doubt, Jim Thompson did not reveal the facts behind the situation but it is so screwed up from every standpoint that I am at a loss how to move. . . . Someday, I'd like to find out how this all happened. . . ."

The novel disposed an irritating quandry for NAL. Editor in chief Weybright esteemed *Cloudburst* more than any fiction Thompson had offered him. "We think Jim Thompson's 'West Texas Cloudburst'—the title could be changed—is a very good book of its kind," he enthused. But NAL was forbidden to publish without a written release from Buck Houghton. A palpably frustrated Weybright tendered Thompson a set of stern ultimatums in July:

> Under the . . . circumstances, it seems clear to us that the resolution of this situation is in your hands. We suggest the following three alternative solutions:

1. You get clearance from Ohio Films to let us publish the book as an independent work, completely disassociated from the original film property, with such changes in title and content as to satisfy Ohio Films in this regard, provided they are satisfactory to us. We would have to insist, however, that all clearances be obtained, and all modifications in the book completed and approved by Ohio Films no later than September 1, 1960. We are now already over a month past our June 1 deadline. (Since we like the book as it is, what we fear here is the likelihood of departing too far from the present version.)
2. You submit to us not later than January 2, 1961 an entirely new book in substitution for *Cloudburst,* the advance already paid to be applied against it if acceptable to us, and the terms otherwise to remain the same as agreed.
3. You return to us all royalty advances paid to date, and the whole agreement will be cancelled.

Weybright remained pessimistic as he looked to agent Bob Goldfarb, who represented both Thompson and Houghton in Hollywood, for a resolution. "Goldfarb told us he can straighten this out," he briefed Loeff. "Do you think that he will persuade Houghton to accept the manuscript with the present setting? If nothing can be done about the change to Texas something else may be worked out to everyone's satisfaction, but I cannot see just what it would be."

Cloudburst would still drag at this impasse come Christmas.

• • •

Down in Falls Church, Virginia, Thompson revolved another dilemma. When Marc Jaffe had called on him at San Clemente the previous August, "Jim was still not well yet, from his stroke. We took a walk along the Pacific and talked. I think he was having some marital problems—what they were exactly, I can't remember now. But that was the impression he gave me." On his extended writing visit with Maxine the winter and spring of 1960, Thompson unburdened his discontent to his older sister as they rode out his nocturnal jags. "We'd sit up some nights to four in the morning because I couldn't get him to go to bed, but he would talk freely. The stories were always the same when he'd be drinking, and I was always kind of worried and upset. I would listen all night if I had to. I never tried to stop him—I knew I couldn't."

According to Maxine, "In his opinion Jimmie wasn't understood at home at all. He was so sensitive, and he just couldn't take the cracks, and everything else that went on. Jimmie was crazy about his family, but he wasn't the kind of person who could stand to be called names, referred to as a drunkard, or put down. He wanted to be admired more at home—admired more and recognized more. I think he felt removed in some way as a man."

Maxine, of course, originally opposed her brother's marriage to Alberta, and she stayed a critical witness:

> I always tiptoed through those years because I did not want to do anything that Jimmie would get blamed for or criticized for or be accused of saying. Alberta never knew what he said to me because I never told her.
>
> The man when sober cooked all the meals, and worked under very difficult conditions. The home atmosphere was never geared to him. He was not catered to in any way at all. They did not try to keep things clean for him; he had to write in rooms that were filled with papers and magazines, and that was not my idea of what you do with the man of the house, the head of the family.
>
> He adored his children, but Jimmie didn't mince words, and didn't always approve of what they were doing. Now they are all so proud of him, and maybe they always were, I don't know. It was always poor Mother—all I ever heard was poor Mother. I felt that somebody should have said poor Daddy, and it might have done an awful lot of good.
>
> Jimmie was a different kind of man—probably very hard to live with over a long period of time because he was so different. The drinking was just not Alberta's way of life, and she couldn't adjust to it. He wasn't my husband, and maybe I would have acted the same way in the same circumstances. I saw beyond the drinking into what his mind was, and his desires and his hopes. She didn't want to see him drink at all, but didn't seem to understand that berating him and belittling him was not going to keep him from drinking. A little more understanding would have helped. The lack of seeing through to what he really was might have been the thing that got him to drink in the first place.

Maxine fretted about her role as what would eventually be tagged in A.A. circles an alcoholic enabler: "People might think that if I hadn't been around, Jimmie might have gotten on his feet on his own. I don't know. I still believe everybody needs somebody, and I tried so hard not to blame him. He was a man who needed help, and he came to me for help, because he had no place else to go. I was fortunate that Joe would put up with it. And even Tony, I don't think he holds it against me at all. I almost neglected him because I couldn't do everything. I was trying to save Jimmie, but looking back it seems ridiculous. I don't think you can."

One afternoon as they drove around the Virginia countryside and Thompson downshifted into his clutch of family complaints, Maxine cut him off. Since his domestic life sparked so much anger, unhappiness, and pain, why didn't he just terminate the marriage and begin a new life? The question, she recalled, genuinely seemed to stun him—as his answer did her:

> He was saying that it was a mistreatment of his mind, that he was not appreciated, and I had the sense, again, that he felt put down, that his ego had been hurt. So I said, Jimmie, maybe this isn't going to work, maybe things aren't ever going to be right for you, why don't you get a divorce? So after all these years he said, "Maxine I care very much for Alberta and for the family. I would never do anything like that." He just came right out and said it. So I thought, I guess so.

He drifted back to California by late spring. That summer and fall were emotional, with lots of drinking and overwrought telephone calls to Victor Weybright, Ted Loeff, or Bob Goldfarb. Buck Houghton would not budge on *Cloudburst,* and Thompson could dig up no other work. His double dealing with NAL, Ohio Films, and the Literary Projects Company may have netted a snap $3,000, but he had firebombed his bridges with anyone in a position to assist him.

Jim moved to Hollywood with Alberta and Sharon in October, suspecting that his best luck reposed in television. A few days after Christmas he was wheeled into a hospital emergency room with bleeding ulcers. At breakfast he couldn't keep down his coffee—the hot, black brew that every morning he boiled hobo-style and sipped as he wrote. When he started heaving blood, Alberta phoned Freddie, who reached her doctor. She also summoned Sharon away from her job at the Ross-Loos Medical Center in downtown Los Angeles.

Everyone convened at the Cedars of Lebanon Hospital on Beverly Boulevard. The Thompsons carried no health insurance, Jim had no money, and at first it appeared as if he wouldn't be admitted. He struggled to a telephone and tried to call Victor Weybright at NAL in New York, but with the holidays the editorial staff was on vacation. Jim then passed out in the lobby. "I was able to get into a hospital here without the usual financial arrangements," he later deadpanned during a letter to Weybright. Tests revealed massive internal hemorrhaging. His hemoglobin level had dropped to four (sixteen might be normal for a man his size; he had lost more than three-quarters of his blood). A tube was placed down his throat, and an in-

Christmas at Maxine and Joe Kouba's—
Alberta, Michael, Sharon, and Jim, 1962
(Courtesy of the Thompson family)

travenous line into his arm. "The doctors told us," Sharon remembers, "that if Daddy hadn't been in a hospital when he collapsed, he would have died."

Joe Kouba, Sharon, even some of Sharon's friends from Ross-Loos, all donated blood—Thompson topped off at a sobering seven pints. He languished at Cedars of Lebanon for more than three weeks. "When he was really sick with the tubes up his nose," Sharon suggests, "he realized how bad he was." Once out of intensive care, Jim refused to play the virtuous patient. "Daddy really hated that hospital because he was hungry all the time. God forbid if Mother didn't show up with a sack of food. He asked us to sneak in things he liked, such as hard-boiled eggs. He'd say, 'They're starving me!' "

Jim was released from the Cedars of Lebanon Hospital on Friday, January 20, 1961, the morning of John F. Kennedy's inauguration as president—with a mortal caution never to drink or smoke again, and Alberta drove him to their new residence in the Hollywood Continental Apartments at 7741 Hollywood Boulevard. The following Monday he heard from Bob Goldfarb that Buck Houghton agreed to drop all objections to the publication of *Cloudburst.* Inertia, if not illness, had prevailed. "No one wanted to make a film of it," says Houghton. Thompson subdued his euphoria. "Dostoevsky didn't know what he was talking about when he equated eternity with a fly buzzing around a privy," he wrote NAL. "An apter simile is me, trying to get this book in the clear."

Yet *Cloudburst* continued to draw snags, like flies. Ohio Films, for one, still owned the title. "The title of the new book *must* be changed," Thompson notified Walter Freeman. "This is not a matter of preference, as I at first thought: We are simply forbidden to use the title *Cloudburst* (and small loss it is, if you ask me)." For a replacement, in March he proposed *This World, Then the Fireworks*—a phrase out of the novel that also was the name of his unpublished 1957 novella. "It's intriguing; it conjures up a picture; it's colloquial, suitable to the locale. And titles equally as long are used every day." Freeman resisted: *"This World, Then the Fireworks* just won't go at all, according to everyone I checked around here."

NAL championed *The Evil That Men Do*—over Thompson's sour protest. "I'm pained to say that *The Evil That Men Do* is, in my opinion, pretty wretched. Possibly it's a hangover from high school days, when I had to listen to one bored kid after another monotonously recite, 'Friends, Romans, countrymen . . .' but I just can't see what this would do for a book except kill it completely." On September 5, fighting a winter publication date, Freeman offered the novelist a last week to "come up with something better." By telegram Thompson rolled the dice . . . *The Transgressors?*

Freeman inquired too, as he put it, "Why make all the gangsters Wops?" Thompson's ethnic representation of the Fort Worth Mob "hurts not only the sensibilities of Italo-Americans, but also the book's verisimilitude. . . . Particularly in the context of this far-west Texas story, the introduction of a kind of slur against this group seems out of place. Now, if the story were in New York, where it is a fact that most of the gambling is controlled by Italians, who are mobsters, Pellino, Onate, & Co. would be right at home. . . . Conclusion: let's dump Pellino et al, and substitute some home-grown Texans with suitably indistinguishable names."

Thompson countered with insider tips from his beat at *Daring Detective* and *Police Gazette:*

> I am a little confused here as to why there should be any
> confusion. Pellino is the Texas representative of a nation-wide

Mafia-like syndicate. All this has been spelled out in detail, or so I thought. All bigtime "action" is syndicate, and the taking over of the Highlands Oil Company would be very bigtime. Needless to say, syndicate money is constantly being poured into legitimate or nominally legitimate enterprises. Although, naturally, it is very careful to keep the fact hidden. . . .

All bigtime crime is traceable to the Unione Siciliano and its offshoots (the syndicate). Not all such criminals have Italian names—I don't regard Onate as one—although inevitably the majority do. In any case, they are always the key men wherever they operate; i.e., Capone in Chicago, Costello in New Orleans, Siegel in Los Angeles (until his death and takeover by Cohen). Mob money is behind Columbia Pictures; the mob is a big investor in Howard Johnson Restaurants. But you doubtless know all this anyway, so I won't elaborate unnecessarily. Under the circumstances, however, I'm sure you will agree that we cannot swap our present group of gangsters for home-grown Texans.

Finally, it hit Thompson that Deputy Sheriff Lou Ford's presence in the novel imperiled a future sale of *The Killer Inside Me* or *Wild Town* to Hollywood. "The book's principal protagonist, Lou Ford, must be given a name other than Lou Ford," he alerted Freeman, *"any* other name, such as Ben Cord, Tom Lord or whatever. This is imperative, although I've just been informed to that effect, since Mr. Houghton controls the motion picture rights to this book, and thus might encumber such rights in my other books in which Lou Ford is a character." Someone at New American Library combed his galleys and mechanically altered every "Lou Ford" to "Tom Lord."

The Transgressors (Signet, December 1961) warranted neither such editorial involutions nor Thompson's monkeyshines with Loeff, Houghton, and NAL. The Lou Ford of *The Killer Inside Me,* and even of *Wild Town,* focused a supple instrument for the novelist to probe the root conflicts of his life. Lazy, cynical, dishonest, *The Transgressors* dramatized his immediate fiscal crisis, yet little else.

The novel also revealed a bookish self-consciousness new to his fiction. By the early 1960s Thompson started to read the French existentialist writers that critics, such as Anthony Boucher and R. V. Cassill, were invoking for reviews of his novels. His recent short story, "The Tomcat That Was Treetop Tall," set inside a Greenwich Village dive, flaunted some barstool jokes about Sartre:

The little guy was smiling at me now, a smile that was about as deceptive as the dash you see in a book in place of a four-letter word. "You look like an intelligent man," he said. "I trust you've heard of George Saul Partre, the inventor of Essentialism?"

"Well," I said, "the name sounds familiar. Would he be any relation to Jean Paul Sartre, the father of Existentialism?"

"Don't be a wise guy," he snapped. "You call him Sartre, and I call him Partre, so what's in a name? Anyway, his theory is that you aren't really here, and if you aren't here you must be someplace else. So you go on to wherever else you are before you get lonesome."

I started to tell him that he was just a little mixed up. The theory of Existentialism, as I understood it, was that the past is dead and the present was non-existent, which left nothing but the future. He cut in on me before I could finish. . . .

Tom Lord in *The Transgressors* similarly tends to theorize about his split rather than play it out. "Absently, he lighted a cigar, stood outside of himself as he puffed it, curiously considering the man at the desk," Thompson expounds. "Looked about like anyone else out here. Talked like them. Acted like them. *Was* like them except for what went on inside him. . . . It was easy to believe that the irking contradictions of his life justified almost anything he did."

His self-consciousness within the work was matched by a sudden grandiosity about it. From now on Thompson would steadily exaggerate the bulk of his achievement. *The Transgressors* is "a sort of milestone," he ventured on his NAL author questionnaire, "my twenty-fifth book." (It was his twentieth.) Ultimately he would all but double his official output, claiming to be "the author of more than fifty novels."

• • •

Nineteen sixty-one and sixty-two were misplaced years for Jim Thompson. New American Library had turned against him; and stranded without a market for new novels, he wasn't producing any. His hulking correspondence over *The Transgressors* moved into the vacancy. Jim convalesced from his deathbed bout with bleeding ulcers—after a fashion. "One day I came home," Sharon relates, "and he was sitting in the chair with a cigar in his hand and a drink by the chair. The doctor told him he couldn't ever smoke or drink again, and I had an absolute conniption fit. Daddy calmed me down and said, 'It's a cigar not a cigarette. . . .' "

Although living in Hollywood, Thompson boarded the coastal train back to San Clemente for his weekly errands, his banking, or his haircuts. "He found it very hard to tear up his roots, whatever they might be," Arnold Hano posits. From San Clemente, Jim would usually try to hook up with Hano, now a freelance journalist working out of nearby Laguna Beach. He extolled his favorite editor in a letter he sent Walter Freeman about *The Transgressors.* "Had a nice talk with Arnold Hano, who asked me to say hello to you. He's really a helluva swell guy—just how swell I didn't realize until my recent, prolonged and damned near fatal hospitalization." Hano, for his part, could not sound so jaunty about the deterioration of his friend:

> We would see Jim and Alberta every so often, but it wasn't any-where as frequent as before. It became difficult when he was drink-ing, and he was drinking nearly all the time. An evening with the Thompsons was no longer fun. He never passed out, or anything like that. He would just become less coherent, and start rambling. The amount he drank in the beginning was just phenomenal, and after a while he didn't need a lot to get drunk. Then he'd sober up enough to write a book. I never knew how he did that.

Sober up enough to write a book. . . . Over the thirty months following his delivery of the *Cloudburst* manuscript to NAL in April 1960, Thompson's fit-ful sobriety yielded a seven-page story and a one-hour teleplay.

Both pieces emulated his Lion novels. The short story, "Forever After," helped kick off the inaugural issue of *Shock* in May 1960. For this "magazine of terrifying tales" slanted toward science fiction and horror, Thompson married his fascination for torture by cliché to his obsession with the hell of one's own making as (shades of *The Twilight Zone!*) a wife is condemned to an eternity of listening to the platitudinous husband her lover murdered with a meat cleaver. " 'Stop it! STOP IT!' Her screams filled the room . . . silent screams ripping through silence. 'He's—you're dead! I know you are! You're dead, and I don't have to put up with you for another minute. And—and—!' "

One AWOL year later, Thompson patched together a script with Nor-man Katkov for the NBC television series *Cain's Hundred.* A police proce-dural allegedly culled from case histories and filmed in quasi-documentary style, the program starred Mark Richman as Nick Cain, a onetime gangland lawyer turned federal undercover agent who is determined to bust the hun-dred most dangerous denizens of the criminal underworld. Cain, like his Old Testament original, fared a shrill, dreary avenger, and the show would be pulled before he could collar more than thirty mobsters.

Thompson's episode, "Five for One: James Condon," recycled a plot from *The Golden Gizmo* and a name from *Savage Night.* Businessman Karl Bigger smuggles gold disguised as cheap costume jewelry into Mexico for James Condon, a San Francisco crime boss. His oddball factory includes Goethe-quoting accountant and kleptomaniac Adolph Hans Saltzman ("I left Heidelberg with the Dean's watch . . .") and a murdered partner.

Through the droll connivance of Saltzman, Cain snags Condon, crossing off another villain from his personal hit list—a stick-figure scorecard concluded each show. But Cain's earnest sermons interred the script's comedy inside a lead box:

> CAIN
> *(rising)*
>
> I'll tell you why. Because all over
> this country there are little men, as
> you put it. And they feed a few big men.
> Without you . . . and thousands like you,
> there couldn't be a Public Enemy Number
> One. . . . There couldn't be any Public
> Enemies.

"Five for One: James Condon" aired in August 1961.

During these lost days and weeks Thompson lived off the sale of the foreign rights to his old novels. The advances might oscillate—Gallimard in France, for instance, paid $770, minus commissions, for *The Getaway,* Kadokawa Shoten in Japan $1,500, and Gyldendall in Norway just $200—yet he had rolled up so many books, and the allure of American hard-boiled fiction abroad flamed so intensely that Thompson was cashing monthly checks for subsidiary rights.

He entered the ragged pantheon of American artists—descending from Poe to David Goodis, Horace McCoy, Chester Himes, Sidney Bechet, Samuel Fuller, Memphis Slim, Joseph Losey, and Nicholas Ray—revered as prophets in France while annexed to obscurity at home. Not every imported Gallic fancy is a Jerry Lewis or Mickey Rourke joke. Starting in 1950 with a translation of *Nothing More Than Murder,* Gallimard released nine novels for *Série Noire* during the author's lifetime and, unlike his stateside houses, kept them in print. Gallimard honored Thompson in 1966 by selecting *Pop. 1280* as the thousandth title to carry the *Série Noire* imprint. Scarcely two years after his death the Parisian journal *Polar* would commit an entire issue to a discussion of his life and work. And, as noted earlier, a French critic proclaimed Thompson "one of the great American writers of the twentieth century" and "the greatest author of *série noire.*" French directors have styled the most sympathetic and resonant adaptations of Thompson's novels for film—Alain Corneau in 1979 with *Série Noire* (from *A Hell of a Woman*) and Bertrand Tavernier in 1981 with *Coup de Torchon* (from *Pop. 1280*); Claude Chabrol and Jean-Luc Godard also expressed interest in shooting a Thompson film.

Jim attempted to return to teaching. In the fall of 1962 he approached

R. V. Cassill, the novelist who had published a panegyrical essay on *The Killer Inside Me,* about joining the faculty of the famed University of Iowa's Writer's Workshop. Thompson posted a letter, then telephoned with his beadroll of woe:

> Thompson was making doleful noises about the need to get out of Hollywood. He said that he had come out to Hollywood with Stanley Kubrick. He was raging and storming because Kubrick had double-crossed him and dumped him on his ass. He was destitute, trying anything, and wondered whether I could steer him to some kind of academic job, so that he could make a living.

"I tried at Iowa, where I was teaching," Cassill wraps up, "and a few other programs—that was the extent of my clout. At Iowa I talked about him with Paul Engle and Vance Bourjaily, and they said we don't need anybody. . . . I never spoke to Thompson again, or heard from him after that."

• • •

Jim crawled back with a new literary agent. He had met Robert Mills in New York during the mid-1950s when the tall, bespectacled, fair-haired Montanan officiated as the managing editor of *Ellery Queen's Mystery Magazine* and *Mercury Mystery Magazine* and Thompson was shopping his short fiction. Mills counted James Baldwin, Edgar Snow, Walter Tevis, Richard Farina, and Harlan Ellison among his clients. "Bob Mills was a very great gentleman, mild, soft-spoken, and urbane," Ellison comments. "He drank— not a drunken tosspot, a very elegant drinker—but I believe he was an alcoholic. He loved the book business, loved the lunches, loved talking to writers. He treated each of his writers as if he was important, and always had money to advance to his writers. Bob always spoke very highly of Jim."

Jim retained Robert Mills as the principal salesman of his novels for the remainder of his life—his longest professional liaison, and one of his most intimate friendships. Mills, who died in 1986, once evoked Thompson as "a quiet man, very gentle, but he warmed up a little when he got a few drinks in him. . . . I think he saw himself as someone who told stories about the way the world is. He didn't particularly think in terms of literature, or art, or in terms of commerciality. He wanted to show the way things were, the way human beings were, whether in a Texas oil field or on the Bowery."

Borrowing train fare from his daughter Sharon, Thompson coasted into Mills's Central Park West office late in 1962 with a novel about a young con man. The agent stood him to a private advance, and forwarded the manuscript to Harlan Ellison, then moonlighting as an editor in Chicago. "I started a line of paperbacks for Bill Hamlin, Regency Books," Ellison recalls.

"Of course, I had met Jim at Lion. I contacted Bob Mills, and he sent me *The Grifters.*" The short-lived Regency Books flexed the same radical ambitions as Lion Books, crooking an arc of paperback originals that stretched from B. Traven and Philip José Farmer to Robert Bloch, Hal Ellson, W. T. Brannon, Donald Honig, and Matthew Gant. Ellison "made the contract for *The Grifters,* but it was published after I left Regency. [Editor and novelist] Algis Budrys picked up the reins, and went ahead and did it."

The Grifters (Regency Books, May 1963) would stimulate the strongest American-produced film of a Thompson novel: British director Stephen Frears's deep-colored essay on sexual corruption from an elegant script by Donald E. Westlake. The book, by contrast, laid down a flat patchwork of greys and blacks—an overcast and opaque Southern California backdrop, a triad of unredeemable hustlers. Roy Dillon is the last character to bear Thompson's Party alias, and *The Grifters* shines most darkly when most personal. The twenty-five-year-old Dillon aims to become a modern master of the short con Jim learned from "Airplane Red" Brown at the Hotel Texas during the 1920s. "Thus, for the tenth time that day, he had worked the *twenties,* one of the standard gimmicks of the short con grift. The other two are the *smack* and the *tat. . . .* It took practice, sure. Everything did." After Dillon is whomped in the stomach by an unappreciative mark wielding a sawed-off bat, Thompson transports him to a Los Angeles hospital with internal injuries that eerily re-create his own recent bleeding ulcers:

> Suspended from a metal stand on the left side of his bed was a jar of syrupy-looking blood. A tube extended from the upended top of it to a quill-like needle in his arm. On the right side of the bed, a similar device dripped saline into the artery of his other arm. The blood and water had been fed into him thus since his arrival in the hospital. . . .
>
> He'd had a long look at death, and he hadn't liked the look of it at all. . . .
>
> The doctors themselves had practically said as much, hadn't they? It was scientifically impossible, they'd said, for a man to live when his blood pressure and hemoglobin fell below a certain level. Yet his had been well below that level *when* he arrived at the hospital. Unassisted, he had been clinging to life on his own *before* anything had been done for him.

Lilly Dillon and Moira Langtry—Roy's look-alike mother and girlfriend—constitute the other "grifters" of the title in a claustrophobic triangle. Moira is a slice of vintage cheesecake with a dry irony about her status as a sexual commodity. Trading carnal favors for rent, she amuses herself by reciting commercial advertisements as her landlord pants over her.

"'The automatic clutch, Charles,'" she murmured. "'It comes with the deluxe upholstery and the high-speed wiry zone.'" A fading racket broad, Moira wants Roy to move off the grift into "the long end," "the big-con."

Lilly Dillon, who works the racetracks for a Baltimore syndicate, runs on "a fatalistic do-or-be-damned philosophy which could accommodate itself to anything but oblivion"—a stoicism put to a sickening test when she crosses her boss, the pungent Bobo Justus. (He threatens to beat her with some oranges wrapped in a towel, then burns her with a cigarette as she fouls her clothes with urine.) Lilly was only thirteen when she gave birth to Roy, and their erotic fever hurls the novel to the final murderous pages:

> Roy sighed. . . . And yet, talking to [Lilly], watching her distress, there was in his mind, unadmitted, an almost sadistic exulting. *Harking back to childhood, perhaps, rooted back there, back in the time when he had known need or desire, and been denied because the denial was good for him.* Now it was his turn. Now he could do the right thing—and yes, it was right—simply by doing nothing. *Now now now the pimp disciplining his whore listening to her pleas and striking yet another blow Now now now he was the wise and strong husband taking his frivolous wife in hand Now now now his subconscious was taking note of the bond between them, the lewd, forbidden and until now unadmitted bond.* . . .

Frears and Westlake domesticated the bloody climax for the 1990 film, insinuating that Lilly kills her son haphazardly, by mistake. Thompson accents her calculation—her exquisite sensual taunting, her thoughtful offer of a drink of water, her cool thrust of the glass shards into Roy's neck.

The Grifters was Thompson's fourth novel in a row with a third-person narration, and only one, *The Getaway,* touched the inwardness and the intensity of his first-person psychopathic ventriloquism. Roy Dillon, like Tom Lord in *The Transgressors,* archly philosophizes about his fate—an existential Tintin in Tinseltown. "He was his own victim, his own slave," Thompson tutors. "He had made personality a profession, created a career out of selling himself. And he could not stray far, or for long, from his self-made self."

A startling sequence—omitted from the film—strips down to the moral ooze of *A Hell of a Woman* or *The Nothing Man.* Carol Roberg is the childlike nurse Lilly throws at Roy to keep him away from Moira. After they make love, Carol reveals she is a survivor of the concentration camps, that she was sterilized in Dachau. Unable to censure himself, Roy releases a foul belch from deep inside his culture. "Roy wanted to vomit. He wanted to shake her, to beat her. . . . It was *her* own fault."

Less offensive, and more poignant, is a digression that Thompson, stumbling toward fifty-seven, permitted himself on aging: ". . . fear was the worst part of being old. . . . A fella knew he wasn't much good any more—oh, yes, he knew it. . . . And thus he made mistakes, one after the other. Until, finally, he could no more bear himself than other people could bear him. And he died."

• • •

With the publication of *The Grifters,* Jim relocated with Alberta and Sharon to a larger apartment in Hollywood, occupying the second floor of a two-story white stucco building at 1922 Whitley Avenue, four short blocks from the Musso & Frank Grill. A family crisis dictated the move, as much as did his Regency advance, his faith in Bob Mills, or proximity to his favorite bar, a hideaway for writers since the 1930s when the offices of the Screen Writers Guild were across the way on Cherokee Street and Stanley Rose's famous Hollywood Boulevard Book Shop was next door.

Thompson's only son, Michael, twenty-five years old that spring, attempted to kill himself. He had joined the Army in 1960, after he was laid off from his job at a San Clemente chemical plant. Discharged in March 1962, he fled back to his parents' home, awash with alcohol trouble. "I was drinking very heavy every day in the Army," Michael relates. "I used to keep a bottle in my locker. Then I got out, and I started hanging around with some wrong people, started taking speed. Bad stuff—one time I was arrested in Hollywood for fighting the cops. I had a breakdown in 1963, and I tried to commit suicide. At the hospital they asked me if I wanted to volunteer for Camarillo [State Hospital], and I said I would. I stayed there for three days . . . I became worse at Camarillo; I don't know whether it was the medication they gave me, or a relapse, but I became very paranoid. I was ill for quite a number of years."

Maxine, living now with Joe and Tony in neighboring Brentwood, drove the Thompsons to the Camarillo State Hospital, near Thousand Oaks. "Jimmie was very upset about Mike's emotional problems after he left the Army," she noted. "I remember seeing Jimmie on the grass talking to Mike, trying to help him."

Once Michael settled into the Whitley apartment, Alberta chauffeured him to his psychiatrist for counseling and to a clinic for electroshock treatments. "I was receiving shock therapy for years, twice a week, sometimes three. My dad used to try and keep me awake—I always wanted to sleep, but he'd give me books to read, or say there was something on the TV. He looked after me, which I was very grateful for. He'd cook me special dinners. My dad tried in his own way, but I guess some of his problems got in the way. He was the last person to lecture you about not drinking. I always tried to absent myself from him when I was drinking. I wouldn't be there, so he *couldn't* lecture me."

He would linger at home with Jim and Alberta for the balance of the decade—and then some. "I moved to San Diego in 1969, and stayed there with another guy. We were drinking then, too. I moved back up to Long Beach. I was there for maybe eight, nine months, and the drinking got heavier again. I moved back home until 1972, when I got my own place." He subsequently became a professional gambler in Las Vegas.

Michael was, perhaps, a casualty of the California 1960s. Yet Maxine cited a sad face-off between father and son that mimicked Jim Thompson's early friction with *his* father:

> After Mike got out of the Army it was a particularly harrowing period. Jimmie was crazy about him, loved him dearly, he was his only son and he wanted to help him. But Jimmie was very outspoken and very straightforward about these things, so maybe he seemed a little harsh.
>
> I think that he wished that Mike had done more with his life. He wished that Mike would go to school or work, instead of what he was doing. He was proud when Mike got into the Army—he thought that would be a lifesaver—but Mike got out of it as fast as he could. Mike was just not Jimmie's idea of what a young man should do. He thought he should work, try to make something out of himself. But whenever Mike got a job something would happen, always the other fellow was wrong, and he would quit.
>
> I guess Mike got to resent him a lot. . . .

"I read quite a bit when I was ill, and I got to know my father more than I had," Michael says. "I needed somebody to take care of me; I was in really bad shape. He seemed to hover over me more then. But I remember one time there was this gasoline station where I was helping this guy out working nights in Hollywood, and he said that I can't go there anymore. I had a big argument with him about—What the hell harm is there, you know? But really, at the time, I don't think he trusted me, like maybe I might do something in the station. Brings back bad memories, a lot of it. I wasn't as close as I wanted to be to my father."

• • •

Thompson poured his own filial distress into *Pop. 1280,* the nightmarish monologue of lawman Nick Corey—obese, obscene, manipulative, murderous and, probably, psychotic—who, à la Sheriff James Sherman Thompson, administers justice in a small Southwestern town around the turn of the century. Harlan Ellison was in Los Angeles, Regency was folding, but for this return to Lion form, Thompson's last major novel, Bob Mills tapped another old friend, Walter Fultz, executive editor at Fawcett Gold Medal and a

former Lion editor. Fultz pronounced *Pop. 1280* "a lot of fun," and congratulated Jim: "It's good to be in touch with you again after all these years—and
a pleasure to discover you're still writing such fine stuff."

Founded by Wilford H. "Captain Billy" Fawcett and overseen by his
sons Roscoe, Roger, Gordon, and Wilford, Jr., the Fawcett Publications
Group, arose, like Thompson, from the sensational pulp magazines of the
1920s and 1930s: *True Confessions, True, Daring Detective, Startling Detective,* and *Front Page Detective.* Gold Medal contracts were coveted among
crime writers for their generous terms. The contract Thompson signed for
Pop. 1280 on October 9, 1963, guaranteed him a royalty of $4,000 for a first
run of 250,000 copies; he preserved, moreover, subsidiary and film rights.
With a paperback original list that by the early 1960s featured David
Goodis, Harry Whittington, John D. MacDonald, Peter Rabe, Richard S.
Prather, Dan J. Marlowe, and Charles Williams, Fawcett Gold Medal was the
house that should have absorbed Jim Thompson after the passing of Lion.

At Gold Medal he worked most closely not with Fultz, who would
shortly commit suicide over unhappiness in his sexual life, but with Knox
Burger. "You could see that Jim was something of a broken tourist—
hunched over, overweight, a chronic drinking problem, just a depressed
fellow with a load of personal problems," Burger observes. "Still, Jim had a
lot of arcane and oddball knowledge, so he could be very entertaining that
way." To Burger, Thompson reiterated many of the domestic gripes he had
assayed for NAL's Marc Jaffe: "Jim was a whiner. I went out to dinner with
him in Beverly Hills, and he complained a lot about his family. His children
were not a joy, but an anchor, and he had a wife who was somewhat disap-
proving, who ran him on a very tight rein. I had the impression that his family was a burden." In California, as at later meetings in New York, Thompson
impressed Burger as "very mild, gentle, almost obsequious. All the violence
that came out in the writing was quite Freudian."

Pop. 1280 (Gold Medal, August 1964) unloaded Thompson's bitterest
slam against his father, pumping Pop's extravagant appetite to loutish gar-
gantuanism, his politician's bonhomie to addled servility, and his bully's
bluster to apocalyptic vengeance. Duplicating locale, silhouetting similar
characters, even conjuring up the same dubious plot devices, such as a
staged double slaying, the novel can seem a rewrite of *The Killer Inside
Me*—one more clownish sheriff mutates into a homicidal schizo:

> Well, sir, I should have been sitting pretty, just about as pretty
> as a man could sit. Here I was, the high sheriff of Potts County, and
> I was drawing almost two thousand dollars a year—not to mention
> what I could pick up on the side. On top of that, I had free living
> quarters on the second floor of the courthouse, just as nice a place

as a man could ask for; and it even had a bathroom so that I didn't have to bathe in a washtub or tramp outside to a privy, like most folks in town did. I guess you could say that Kingdom Come was really here as far as I was concerned. I had it made, and it looked like I could go on having it made—being high sheriff of Potts County— as long as I minded my own business and didn't arrest no one unless I couldn't get out of it and they didn't amount to nothin'.

And yet I was worried. I had so many troubles that I was worried plumb sick.

I'd sit down to a meal of maybe half a dozen pork chops and a few fried eggs and a pan of hot biscuits with grits and gravy, and I couldn't eat it. Not all of it. I'd start worrying about those problems of mine, and the next thing you knew I was getting up from the table with food still left on my plate. . . .

Nick Corey might introduce himself in a comic dialect out of Mark Twain or Bret Harte, tickling the ironies of a jocular tall tale. But *Pop. 1280* travels a still darker trajectory than *The Killer Inside Me,* just as Corey's malice and intelligence are more cloaked—and sharper—than Lou Ford's. As his tired, self-loathing babble, creased by seemingly random religious wrinkles ("Kingdom Come was really here. . . ."), tightens after a few giddy turns of the screw into the conviction that he is the scourge of God, Corey emerges as, perhaps, the scariest, and most unnerving of Thompson's creations.

Corey shoulders a standard mutant pedigree, with a mother who died giving birth to him, and a father who beat him every day for it. Yet as he excoriates "people looking for easy answers to big problems," Corey moves *Pop. 1280* beyond any convenient psychological or social explanations. Behind his buffoonish stance, "just grinning and joking and looking the other way," he comes on like a rip in the fabric of the universe. Sheriff Corey is a demonic trickster. His most innocent prank involves loosening the boards to a public privy so that Potts County bank president, J. S. Dinwiddie, tumbles into a thirty-year accumulation of night soil. And Corey's usual solution to his "many troubles" is a whimsical murder, starting with his slaughter of two disrespectful pimps—a crime he dupes his friend, the condescending Ken Lacey, into all but boasting that he committed.

The gorbellied Corey is another puzzling Thompson ladies' man. "That's *one* thing I never had no shortage of," he drools. "I was hardly out of my shift . . . when the gals started flinging it at me." Besides his wife, Myra, who thinks him "the poorest excuse for nothing I ever laid eyes on," he dangles two lovers, Rose Hauck, Myra's best friend, and Amy Mason, his intended before Myra railroaded him into wedlock under threat of a rape charge. Marriage, Corey has learned, winds up "bawling and accusations and mean talk: the woman taking it out on the man because he was too stupid to get away from her." And women flash their incisors, like a drawerful of knives. "I'd been chasing females all my life, not paying no mind to the fact that whatever's got tail at one end has teeth at the other." Corey's resolution of these "troubles" also demands murder—crude and brutal, as he blasts Rose's husband, Tom, with a shotgun; or slick and crafty, as he snookers Rose into killing Myra.

Corey answers nearly every question, taunt, or charge with a shuffling, "I wouldn't say you was wrong, but I sure wouldn't say you was right, neither." Unlike Lou Ford, however, he rarely drops his dopey cover for his Potts County gulls or his nervous readers. He remains, pretty much, a perfect foil, a sealed envelope. Yet one time the veiled Nick Corey pokes through an episode straight out of the biography of Jim Thompson's father. Just as Sheriff Thompson, according to his niece, enjoyed shocking people who pegged him "just an ignorant country fool" by "suddenly . . . talking in a learned way about anatomy, or the Roman emperors, something they didn't expect him to know about," so Corey slides a sly piece of arcanum past Ken Lacey:

> I picked myself up, trying to rub my ass and my arm at the same time. . . .
> "Hurt your arm?" Ken said. "Whereabouts?"
> "I'm not positive," I said. "It could either be the radius or the ulna."
> . . . But of course Ken didn't notice anything. Ken had so much on his mind, I reckon, helping poor stupid fellas like me, that he maybe didn't notice a lot of things.

Another time, his relaxed gaze freezes Myra's blood:

> I looked at Myra, and her smile stiffened and faded. . . .
> "N-Nick—" She broke the long silence with a trembly laugh. "W-What's the matter?"
> "Matter?" I said.
> "The way you're looking. Like you were about to kill Lennie and me both. I-I never saw you look that way before."
> I forced a laugh, making it sound easy and stupid. "Me? Me kill someone? Aw, now!"

For all Corey's malignant mayhem, *Pop. 1280* is Thompson's fiercest political novel since *Always to Be Blest* back in the 1930s. Some of this rampageous jester's most spirited capers strike against the legacy of slavery. Early on, Corey happens upon Tom Hauck—the name a tart pun on Twain's Tom and Huck—beating an old black man, Uncle John, who knocked into him on the street. "You tellin' me a white man can't whip a nigger if he feels like it?" Hauck challenges. "You sayin' there's some law against it?" Rather than contradict him, Corey defuses the angry white mob by pointing out that Hauck is hitting Uncle John with a sidewalk plank—civic property. "All I had to do was change the issue a little, make it between me and him instead of between a white man and a black." As County Attorney Robert Lee Jefferson upbraids him—and then backs down:

> "Why, you should have arrested Hauck, of course! Thrown him in jail! I'd have been delighted to prosecute him."
> "But what could I arrest him for? I sure couldn't do it for whippin' a colored fella."
> "Why not?"
> "Aw, now," I said. "Aw, now, Robert Lee. You don't really mean that, do you?"
> He looked down at his desk, hesitating a moment. "Well, maybe not. . . ."

Later, although Corey is the only white man who helps extinguish a fire in "colored town," the Potts County business community again implicates him—and themselves: "Do you know what can come of a thing like this tonight, Nick. . . . Scarin' them god-dam poor niggers could cost us all a pisspot full of money!"

From local racist corruption, Corey spreads out to the violence of American institutions. When an operative from the Talkington Detective Agency—Pinkerton, of course, and a dig at the hard-boiled detective hero—arrives in Potts County to investigate the deaths of those two pimps, the sheriff slips him the needle:

> "Why, god-dang if I ain't heard a lot about you people! Let's see now, you broke up that big railroad strike, didn't you?"
> "That's right. . . . The railroad strike was one of our jobs."
> "Now, by golly, that really took nerve," I said. "Them railroad workers throwin' chunks of coal at you an' splashin' you with water, and you fellas without nothin' to defend yourself with except shotguns an' automatic rifles!"

Yet joke by joke Corey absorbs the slime he dredges up, like a scavenger fish crunching filth at the bottom of a polluted stream, and eventually embodies the most toxic strains within Potts County and America. His sympathy for Uncle John does not prevent him, after a piquant speech about racial inequality, from drilling the former slave with his shotgun. The sheriff steadily transforms his pity into his terror. As he admits, "I start feeling sorry for people, like Rose, for example, or even Myra or Uncle John or, well, lots of folks, and the way it eventually works out is it'd be a lot better if I hadn't felt sorry for them. Better for them, I mean."

Beginning with some casual invocations of his "plans" and his "labors," Corey lurches to the belief that he must be the Potts County messiah, "Christ on the Cross come right here to Potts County, because God knows I was needed here, an' I'm goin' around doing kindly deeds—so that people will know they got nothing to fear, and if they're worried about hell they don't have to dig for it." Persuaded that he has been elected by God "to exercise His wrath," Corey is chillingly detached from the consequences of his mission. He bandies with Rose:

> "Just because I put temptation in front of people, it don't mean they got to pick it up."
>
> "I asked you a question, damn you! Who planned those murders? Who tells a lie every time he draws a breath? Who the hell is it that's been fornicating with me, and God knows how many others?"
>
> "Oh, well," I said. "It don't count when I do those things."
>
> "It don't count! What the hell do you mean?"
>
> I said I meant I was just doing my job, following the holy precepts laid down in the Bible. "It's what I'm supposed to do, you know, to punish the heck out of people for bein' people. To coax them into revealin' theirselves, an' then kick the crap out of 'em. And it's a god-danged hard job, Rose. . . ."

He even manages a religious justification for murder:

> I shuddered, thinking how wonderful was our Creator to create such downright hideous things in the world, so that something like murder didn't seem at all bad by comparison. Yea, verily, it was indeed merciful and wonderful of Him. And it was up to me to stop brooding, and to pay attention to what was going on right here and now.

In his disgust and anguish Corey ultimately straddles the inspired notion that he is not only the Anointed, the Expected One, the Lord of Our Righteousness, but also something like His opposite: "The fella that gets betrayed and the one that does the betrayin' all in one man!" That betrayer might be Judas, but more likely, given Corey's Christian name, he is Old Nick, the Prince of Liars, the Devil.*

Like *The Killer Inside Me,* Thompson's first paperback masterpiece, *Pop. 1280,* his final triumph, grinds an allegory about the situation of the pulp novel and its author. Both books, as much as their anarchic narrators Ford and Corey, loose their menace from behind masks of idiocy, crying havoc on the world, and the world of fiction. Yet while *The Killer Inside Me* exulted in the sinister disclosures, grown slow and secret as fungus, await-ing a reader under its sensational, two-bit exterior, the parable *Pop. 1280* hones is bleaker and more devastating. Here, a trashy façade disguises—more trash. "I raised up on one cheek of my butt, and eased out one of those long rattly farts," Corey confides, close to the end. "I scratched my balls, tryin' to decide at what point a fella stopped scratchin' and started playin'." His vision wriggles past private madness, or American rot, to uni-versal horror:

> There were the helpless little girls, cryin' when their own dad-dies crawled into bed with 'em. There were the men beating their wives, the women screamin' for mercy. There were the kids wettin' in the beds from fear and nervousness, and their mothers dosin' 'em with red pepper for punishment. There were the haggard faces, drained white from hookworm and blotched with scurvy. There was the near-starvation, the never-bein'-full, the debts that always outrun the credits. There was the how-we-gonna-eat, how-we-gonna-sleep, how-we-gonna-cover-our-poor-bare-asses thinkin'. The kind of thinkin' that when you ain't doing nothing else but that, why you're better off dead. Because that's the emptiness thinkin' and you're already dead inside, and all you'll do is spread the stink and the terror, the weepin' and wailin', the torture, the starvation, the shame of your deadness. Your emptiness.

The Killer Inside Me allowed Thompson—and the reader—a way out. The limits and liabilities of Lou Ford's perspective, like the holes in his ali-bis, are unmistakable, if you listen closely enough, a last straw of solace. But nowhere in *Pop. 1280* does Thompson hint that there could be anything

---

* American fiction begins with Charles Brockden Brown's *Wieland* (1798), a sort of early-American *Pop. 1280.* Theodore Wieland hears a voice—he is convinced it is the voice of God—commanding him to "render" his family "in proof of thy faith." He kills his wife and children, and then advances on his sister Clara. "This minister is evil, but he from whom his commission was received is God. Submit then with all thy wonted resignation to a de-cree that cannot be reversed or resisted. . . ." Did the voice come from Carwin, the diabol-ical "biloquist" (ventriloquist), or did it arise from Wieland's own troubled imagination? The same questions of madness or calculation, God or the Devil, agitate *Wieland.*

Sharon Thompson's wedding—from left to right: Alberta, Jim, Phylis Wiseley, Patricia Thompson, Helene Miller, Sharon and Jim Reed, Ralph Maunel, and Jim McDonald, November 23, 1963 (Courtesy of the Thompson family)

better, or even different from what Nick Corey sees, or says. "And what else is there to do but laugh an' joke," Corey asks, "how else can you bear up under the unbearable?"

• • •

The week after he delivered *Pop. 1280* to Gold Medal, Jim Thompson guided his youngest daughter, Sharon, down the aisle for her marriage to Jim Reed, a young photographer who shared an Oklahoma background. The Catholic ceremony took place at the Church of the American Martyrs in Manhattan Beach on November 23, the mournful Saturday between the Kennedy assassination and the Oswald slaying. "Daddy was shattered," Sharon recollects.

"We all were such staunch Democrats, and big Kennedy fans." Merriment during the reception evinced a dash of desperation, a forced few hours revelry amid the tragic weekend. "Everyone who came to the wedding did not seem to want to talk about the fact that President Kennedy had been shot."

Editor Knox Burger marveled that Thompson was "a kind of American Louis Céline," and the writer would stay with Fawcett Gold Medal for two more original novels and a reprint of *The Killer Inside Me.* Yet the resurgance signaled by *Pop. 1280* vanished on the nail. Nick Corey's sulfurous musings did not so much log a creative fresh start with an appreciative publisher as dispose an ultimate dead reckoning, the conflagration of a lifetime's obsessions and tics. On March 9, 1964, Thompson signed with Gold Medal to write a novel, tentatively titled *How Fast Money Goes in Texas.* *Texas by the Tail*—as he finally restyled it, with a blue pun—abandoned the artistic and personal extremes of *Pop. 1280,* and Thompson retrenched once again into genre and, new for him, nostalgia.

Texas by the Tail (Gold Medal, February 1965) charges through the story of Mitch Corley, a high-stakes gambler and con man, and his shapely accomplice, Harriet, a.k.a. "Red." During the course of a brisk week's criminal misadventures, Corley runs afoul of a sadistic Fort Worth mobster, Frank Downing; a powerful Texas oil millionaire, Jake Zearsdale; and the state's oldest and most corrupt family, the Lords. Love, for Corley, knits a matching tangle. Red does not know about his estranged wife, Teddy, now a pathetic streetwalker; nor does she know that payoffs for Teddy's silence have all but fried their ill-gotten nest egg. Private and public crises dovetail as Zearsdale accuses Corley of cheating at dice, Downing sends thugs out after his errant spouse, and the luckless hustler is tossed down an oil well on the Lord estate—while back home Teddy confronts Red.

Thompson subseqently declared to director Tony Bill that *Texas by the Tail* was his "most autobiographical novel," and he entrusted Mitch Corley with sizable chunks of his past: his itinerant boyhood—"Mitch changed schools every two months on the average"—trailing a father on "the perilous periphery of the big time," his night doorman's job at the Worth Hotel, and his starter's position at the Parrent Garage. Yet nearly every character in *Texas by the Tail* shouldered a seasoned Thompson souvenir. Jake Zearsdale and his mother ran a cookshack for the oil field drilling crews, just as Jim did with Birdie in West Texas. To roughneck Art Savage, Thompson delivered up a wildcatting venture outside Big Spring with his father in 1926, and his adolescent little black book. "Airplane Red" Brown entered in the guise of a grifter named Turkelson. Otto Lucy also etched a cameo as Dr. Fritz Steinhopf, the psychiatrist who diagnoses Teddy—like Corley, or Jim—as the product of a "dominant mother" and a "defeated" father.

For the rare reader steeped in Thompson's life story, *Texas by the Tail* scatters a covert, connect-the-dots memoir. But his shuffled memory cards accommodate no intimacy of *tone*. This remote third-person novel aims for the light, high notes of the professional thriller, and frequently hits them. Allusions to "lint-like threads of cigarette smoke" and "faint fumes of very good whiskey" abound—as does a brittle machismo cloned from Mickey Spillane: "the well-stocked commissary of her flesh was closed until further notice." Thompson translates his darkest themes into wry set pieces. He soft-pedals the tormented emasculation of *The Nothing Man* and *A Hell of a Woman* to a comic aside on the American husband:

> It is an unquestioned tradition in the lore of the American fam-
> ily, that the adult male would go the way of the buffalo except for
> the protection and guidance of his wife and children. He may be
> trusted to perform brain surgery, but never to sharpen a pencil. He
> may be a chef, but in his own home he cannot boil water. He may
> be a writer, but his help on a freshman theme is a virtual guarantee
> of a failing grade.

Or he muffles the anxious opacity besetting human motives at the conclusion of *Pop. 1280* into a silky digression on the elusive mathematical symbol *pi* ("the answer to such imponderables as true *pi* and man's meanness were not his to provide. . . .").

Texas by the Tail harmonizes all Mitch Corley's vexations, felonious or romantic, in a snappy epilogue—uplifting and incredible. As Red undergoes an instant epiphany, "a new and mature insight," Mitch convinces Zearsdale that he's "the straightest player you'll ever come up against," simply by saying so.

Thompson—despite the previous November's events in Dallas—even arises as a born-again Texan, elevating his adopted state above what he brands the "shameful spectacles" and "this scum" of American violence. "No Texan would have stood idly by while a dozen brutes stomped a decent man to death," he bristles. "No Texan, you could be sure, would look on unconcerned while a woman was being raped. . . ."

It's almost as if he hadn't read his own books.

• • •

By the mid-1960s Thompson "displayed an alcoholic's nervousness," according to Jerry Bick, his new Hollywood agent for film and television. "His hands shook, and he was a sad guy—financial problems, family problems, drinking problems always, and he had a real problem with his self-esteem. Jim was less than proud of what he was doing. And he was very needy, like a baby who's lost all his toys."

For his fiction, Thompson was staring down a cul-de-sac. As he circled sixty, but looked and acted a decade older, there seemed small prospect that he would ever top the incandescent ambitions of *Pop. 1280,* a career-capping novel. The bronze age of the paperback original, moreover, was passing, a victim of—New York editors ruefully informed him—television.

With Bick's encouragement, Thompson tried to resume his screen work. His first assignment appeared a long shot: a one-hour teleplay for *Dr. Kildare,* the long-running NBC medical drama starring Richard Chamberlain. Thompson's prior writing for television stood in the same relationship to his screenplays for Stanley Kubrick as his *SAGA* articles did to his Lion novels. But on an improbable Thursday evening at 8:30 in 1965, he infused *Dr. Kildare* with the saturnine intensity of *film noir.*

The surviving manuscripts chart a ten-month course from page to tube. On April 1, 1964, Thompson submitted a treatment to *Dr. Kildare* producer David Victor at MGM under the title "A Penny in the Dust." Only the opening "teaser" was set up as a script with dialogue and directions; the four acts of the story followed as prose. Over the summer and fall he collaborated with James F. Griffith, and they completed a teleplay, now called "Pardon Me for Living," on October 20. The episode was broadcast as "My Name Is Lisa and I'm Lost" early the next year.

"Lisa" follows the progress of Lisa Dowling, a nurse at Blair General with a mousy manner Jim Kildare diagnoses as "pardon-me-for-living-itis," as she struggles to escape the clutches of two older women. At home Lisa is dominated by her Aunt Martha, a savagery shrouded in kindness. "How many people in this world would have taken in the bastard child of a sinful sister," Aunt Martha taunts her. "She defiled the God-given temple of her body, and God punished her by taking her life. Now, in spite of everything I've done, I see you becoming more and more like her." Aunt Martha's religious mania—a nod, perhaps, to the dour prairie fundamentalism of Thompson's Grandmother Myers—irradiates the small screen:

> O God, grant me the strength and wisdom to guide the footsteps of this child of sin away from the paths of darkness and evil that would corrupt her mind and body and doom her soul to eternal hell. . . .

Dr. Kildare draws out Lisa over coffee, gently impelling small cracks in her shell with the patience of a twelve-step program. "The prescribed treatment is to stand in front of the mirror every morning and repeat to yourself ten times: I'm Lisa Dowling—I'm intelligent, attractive, and a very nice person to know."

At Blair General a new patient in for tests, a Mrs. Pettigrew, also terrorizes Lisa, provoking her with sarcasm, insults, and flying plates. The problem is that Mrs. Pettigrew comes on like a pussycat to the established male staff, such as Dr. Gillespie (played by Raymond Massey). When Mrs. Pettigrew is found screaming in her room, bruised and apparently badly beaten, she points the incriminating finger at Lisa Dowling. The nurse is dismissed, Aunt Martha's fears corroborated, and the hospital faces a lawsuit.

A tense settlement hearing eventually exposes Mrs. Pettigrew as a "dummy chucker," a professional accident faker. She has been running the same frammis Thompson called "the oranges" in *The Grifters,* during a sordid confrontation between Lilly Dillon and crime boss Bobo Justus. As the hard-boiled Blair General attorney explains:

> You've heard of people being beaten with a rubber hose—it breaks them all up inside. Well Mrs. Pettigrew's little trick has just the opposite effect. She places an orange in a stocking, or a cloth of some kind, then proceeds to hit herself all over her body—bruising herself outside, without doing any real damage inside. Bingo! She ends up looking like she'd been hit by a truck.

The episode concludes with Dr. Kildare helping Lisa move out of Aunt Martha's house into her own apartment.

An idiosyncratic television script enhanced by edgy performances, particularly Lois Nettleton as Lisa Dowling and Nina Foch as Mrs. Pettigrew, "My Name Is Lisa and I'm Lost" merits revival as a minor "lost" Thompson smash. His next NBC commission, "The Duel," a half-hour teleplay for the short-lived Second World War series *Convoy,* never surmounted its humdrum occasion. *Convoy* searched the dangerous transport of troops and supplies across the North Atlantic to Europe for high adventure, but mainly found the monotony of a single, recurrent plot: Nazi cruisers attempt to smash the convoy. "The Duel" (co-written with John and Ward Hawkins from an original story by Thompson) draws a bead on a pill-popping German captain who recklessly attacks against the Fuhrer's orders, yet the drama is all frantic motion:

GUN CONTROL VOICE
Bridge—gun control. Target in right turn.
TALBOT
One eleven, this is Fox Command. Immediate execute, turn nine. Execute. Over.
O'CONNELL
Right standard rudder.
HELMSMAN
Right standard rudder.
DD 111 BRIDGE. THERE IS AN EXPLOSION AFT.

"The Duel" aired on October 22, 1965. *Convoy* would be canceled before the conclusion of a first season.

Other, more substantive and alluring screen projects mediated by Jerry Bick teased and then fizzled. In 1965 Thompson became one of a number of Hollywood writers to assist Sam Peckinpah on a screenplay, *Ready for the Tiger,* from the suspense novel by Sam Ross, a former Lion author. His emissary to Peckinpah appears to have been Sam Fuller, who recalls introducing them soon after the publication of *The Getaway.* "Dave Goodis was there too, I think," Fuller relates. "Peckinpah really loved old Jim, and he loved his books about the dispersed, the depraved, and the recalcitrant. I can still see Jim telling his stories to Sam in that hoarse voice of his." *Ready for the Tiger* languished at MGM for years. Thompson and Peckinpah would not work together again until 1972, on *The Getaway.*

In July actor Sal Mineo engaged Thompson to write a screenplay about the Hells Angels. His conduit to Mineo was Harlan Ellison, who says "Sal was going do a movie about the Hells Angels. He had just discovered Thompson as a great lost writer. Sal loved Jim's work and wanted him to do the script. We went over to see Jim one day where he was living in Hollywood, off Sunset." Over the summer Thompson and Mineo researched their Hells Angels film all around Southern California. As Sharon remembers:

> They were allowed to go to several of the Hells Angels meetings and rallies. I was scared something horrible would happen to Daddy, because you don't fool around with the Hells Angels! It was both a book and a film project, a book that was going to be made into a film.
>
> Daddy told some wild stories. Different members would get up and speak at the meetings. He said that if anyone fell asleep when someone was talking, then everybody else would go over and urinate on him.
>
> Sal came over to the house many times; he was very fond of Daddy.

Thompson completed a treatment and a first-draft screenplay, but the movie was never made. The following year he would have to haul Mineo in front of the Writers Guild before he could obtain his entire $5,255.25 payment, Guild minimum.

Bick himself aspired to float *The Grifters* as a film late in 1965: "Robert Wagner was interested in playing it, I was going to produce, and Jim would do the screenplay. I thought it could be a nice, low-budget picture. But we had no success with it."

●　●　●

When Fawcett Gold Medal reissued *The Killer Inside Me,* touting the novel with a full-page advertisement in *Variety* as a "great crime classic" and "the book that censorship couldn't kill," Jerry Bick recollects that he "was struck by the relationship between the man and his books." Bick, who would stay a close friend until the novelist's death, came to believe,

> Jim Thompson was very much like the people in his books. On a conscious, acting-out level, he was ingratiating, always apologizing, a big shambling teddy bear. But nobody can be as obliging and meek as Jim was and not have a lot of pent-up rage inside. He was a saintly character in many ways—kind, pure, innocent in a sense, a really good person, too good for this world. He was the kind of guy whose feelings are easily bruised, who felt pain very easily and to a greater degree than most people. Jim felt everything—he couldn't even pass a panhandler on the street. When you meet someone like that in the real world, it's painful. You know he's not going to survive.
>
> But Jim lived in a fantasy—this innocent, well-meaning person who was drawn to lawlessness. He was capable of lashing out at those who had hurt him, or did him wrong, and Jim would lash out in violence. But there was only one place this came out, and that was at the typewriter.

Yet not always the only place, and not just against those who hurt him. . . . That fall a ferociously intoxicated Thompson frightened Laurence Janifer, a young New York science fiction writer, over the long-distance telephone. Janifer had recently mailed Thompson a fan letter about *The Getaway:*

> One night at two in the morning, the phone rang. It was Jim Thompson. He sounded about one stage past passing-out drunk. I've been a writer, I've been an agent, I have known a lot of people who drink past the point of no return. But Thompson not only sounded drunk but, in a weird sort of way, *dangerous.*
>
> Here I was in the middle of the night listening to someone I never met. We carried on a circular conversation for a little while, then he hung up.

• • •

Shortly before Christmas, 1965, Thompson entered the Daniel Freeman Hospital in Inglewood, complaining of abdominal pain. His doctor, E. H. Bisharat, recommended exploratory surgery. The following afternoon the surgeon, coincidentally Dr. Bisharat's brother, removed his gallbladder and also nearly one-half of his ulcerated stomach. From his hospital bed prior to surgery Jim dictated his last will and testament.

Thompson, to his own wonderment, survived the monstrous operation, and was released from Daniel Freeman three weeks later, but some several thousand dollars in debt. From New York, agent Bob Mills endeavored to rush a collection of his short stories through Gold Medal. "The money Jim might get for that contract," Mills wrote Anthony Boucher, "is not quite, but almost, a life-and-death matter."

We just got this world,
then the fireworks, boy.
Just this world, then the
fireworks, and we ain't
long for this world.

> —Old Man Billy
> Boy Bentley,
> *The Transgressors*

Exit Screaming: 1966– 1977

When Patricia, Sharon, and Michael were younger and given to complaining about a sad or violent movie Daddy ushered them into on a Saturday ramble, Thompson would shush his children with a smile and a wave of his hand. "Life doesn't have a Hollywood ending," he'd say.

But during the early 1970s a downcast and often disabled Thompson undertook to ghost a Hollywood coda for his own biography. Over lunch one afternoon in Laguna Beach he asked Arnold Hano if, as a favor, his old friend and Lion Books editor would compose an article about him. "There was bitterness that he was not famous," Hano recalls. "Jim thought it would help if he was presented to Hollywood in a magazine like *Los Angeles* or

New West. I didn't know what I could write that would be of use to him. So I said it would be really hard, but let me think about it."

A few days later a manuscript arrived in Hano's mailbox—about Jim Thompson, and also *by* Jim Thompson. "He sent me the article he wanted me to sign off on. It was a portrait of a courtly, greying gentleman, a distinguished Hollywood screenwriter who would go to his favorite booth at Musso & Frank's, order a drink and have the pot roast special, and people knew him and respected him. It went on to tell us who this distinguished gentleman was, what he had written, and so forth, but the main thing was the respectability. It was Jim all cleaned up, and totally unlike my version of him. I sent the story back, and said, Gee, Jim, I can't do this."

The decorous article, perhaps the last of his private myths, "represented a picture of Jim Thompson as he would have liked to have been," Hano proposes, "his life as he would have liked it to turn out."

·   ·   ·

Thompson's stomach problems, his bleeding ulcers—the overloaded fuses of nearly four decades' bad habits and complications—had landed him for a second time in the tube-tangled hollow of a hospital recovery room. The climb back from his killing surgery of December 1965 was oppressive and painful, his physical trauma exacerbated by distress over medical bills and family finances. More than a year of dull recuperation would have to pass before he could brook any extended writing. Yet there were a few lucky runs of the cards. In January 1966, NBC spliced "The Duel" onto another *Convoy* episode for a Friday Night Movie, *Adventure in the North Atlantic,* providing Thompson with a double paycheck for his teleplay. In February, Sal Mineo heeded the remonstration from the Writers Guild and settled his balance on the Hells Angels script, an indispensable $3,500. And Dr. E. H. Bisharat, Thompson's physician, gallantly bartered his services for writing lessons from his novelist patient.

Once Thompson proved capable of working again, Jerry Bick discovered that Hollywood was impervious. Even his sharpest stories, such as "My Name Is Lisa and I'm Lost" for *Dr. Kildare,* demanded the intervention of a studio professional before his ideas could be adapted to television, and the networks apparently caught on. "Jim could write a novel in ten days," Bick surmises, "but he couldn't write a screenplay on his own in ten years." The short story collection Bob Mills negotiated with Gold Medal also miscarried, when Anthony Boucher failed to promise an introduction. Mills, and then Knox Burger, begged for "a paragraph—even a sentence—about Jim Thompson as a writer," yet Boucher kept his silence. "I am afraid that your not sending in those words about Jim Thompson has probably killed the deal with Gold Medal," Mills tweaked the *Times* critic in March. Yet disappointment did not prevent Thompson from enjoying a meal with

Boucher two months later in Berkeley, during a restful Northern California vacation with Alberta.

Jim borrowed money from his older sister. "We helped out quite a bit, no question about that," Maxine reported. "We never asked him to, but he always wanted to pay us back. Jimmie always strove, even in the later years. He was determined all his life to be a writer, and nothing in the world was going to stop that, no matter what happened or what he did. That came first."

· · ·

When Thompson returned to his fiction early in 1967, he revived a mellow book he had contracted with Gold Medal as an "untitled pipeline novel" prior to his operation. *South of Heaven* (Gold Medal, May 1967) tapped deeper into his nostalgic vein, but exchanged the shuffled reminiscences of *Texas by the Tail* for a synoptic self-portrait of a roughneck coming of age in the West Texas oil fields. His only first-person novel since *Now and on Earth* not to manifest a criminal protagonist, *South of Heaven* re-created Thompson's experiences as a "powder monkey," blazing a path with dynamite for the Texas Company pipeline to Port Arthur in 1927; absorbed the college poems, such as "A Road and a Memory," he sent Lucille Boomer and published in the *Prairie Schooner;* and included his senior hobo sidekicks, Whitey Ford and Harry McClintock, and the name of the small Nebraska town where he was raised.

Tommy Burwell is a would-be poet and novelist turned derrick tramp, a prodigal twenty-one going on forty:

> . . . a hard crack with a gun can have a sobering effect even on a twenty-one-year-old, and mine had taken a little of the perkiness out of me. . . . I was a drifter, a day laborer, a tin-horn gambler—a man wasting his life in a wasteland. That's what I was now. That's what I'd be in another twenty-one years if I lived that long. . . .

An orphan whose caretaker grandparents—"my only living kin"—also were killed, by a dynamite blast, Burwell finds a mentor in a salty bindle stiff and crapshooter he calls Four Trey Whitey. The grizzled Whitey strikes a composite of Ford and McClintock, fusing one's facility with bones and cards to the other's Wobbly politics. "So it's you and me alone from here to the Gulf," he cajoles Burwell. "You on blackjack and me with the dice. Now, about your cut. . . ." But just as Haywire Mac spurred young "Slim" Thompson into quitting the oil fields and becoming a writer, Whitey eventually promises to "kick the crap out of" Burwell if he doesn't wise up:

Four Trey said not to say anything; just to get the hell away from the kind of life I was leading and go to college like I'd always talked about doing.

"I'm going to count on you doing that, Tommy. For your sake, I hope I'm not mistaken."

"Well," I said, kind of looking away from him. . . . "I sure can't claim I don't have the money for college."

"And?"

"And I'm sure obliged to you," I said, still not looking at him. . . .

"You have no job on the line. I'm through with you. . . . There's nothing for you out here any more."

The piquant memories of *South of Heaven* do not so much structure a novel as loop episodic western yarns in the spirit of *Bad Boy* and *Roughneck*. Most trade on oil field lore. The hoboes strain canned heat, and disport in giddy riot when the pipeline company advances them booze instead of checks on payday. Burwell joins the "dope gang," and the asphalt fumes burn his face "so badly that the skin hung in strips." His spotter is crushed by a heavy mortarboard, and then interred beside the pipe. He recites his vagrant poems, songs, and some bawdy limericks for Whitey. But a loose plot slowly coils through the skein of anecdote. A hobo known only as Bones winds up dead on a flatbed truck, perhaps murdered. Bud Lassen, a Lou Ford–like deputy sheriff, shoots Burwell's friend Fruit Jar; when Lassen's body is discovered near camp, Burwell is accused of the killing. Burwell falls for a mysterious woman named Carol, who may or may not be a prostitute in league with the notorious Long brothers. The Long brothers stand up as witnesses for Burwell, strangely intent on ensuring his release from jail. Whitey, too, appears to have thrown in with the Longs. Or is he avenging the slaying of his wife?

Tommy Burwell hovers, much as Thompson did over his own autobiographies, at an eerie and finally incredible remove from all the violence and deceit, untouched and unsullied. He is not a martyr—by the end he is forced to cut a man's throat to save Carol; but he stays a tall tale hero, simple, pure, and true. As he assembles the stray pieces of the Long brothers jigsaw, he recalls no literary detective so much as the Hardy Boys. Whitey mocks his spectral innocence:

"Do any writing in jail, Tommy? You know. . . ." He went on before I could answer him. "I think you ought to try a novel some time. Maybe a crime story. Take this pipeline, for example. Wouldn't it make a hell of a background for a payroll robbery?"

The oil field epiphanies in Burwell's *Bildungsroman* toll rote and hollow. "I met maturity and accepted it," he resolves early on. Then, fifty pages later, "I'd suddenly had enough of myself as I was. . . . Nothing would help but a completely new life."

The autumnal personal recollections and the insistent happy endings of *Texas by the Tail* and *South of Heaven* suggest that by the mid-1960s Thompson was rooting through his remote West Texas past for other paths he could have taken, the other lives he might have led. Tommy Burwell lets us know that he grew up to write novels, but his companionable, aw-shucks persona before a "prospective publisher" provides a parallel fantasy to the genteel eccentric in the article Thompson sent Arnold Hano:

> Years later, I told a prospective publisher about that county at-torney and some of the other people I'd bumped into in the Texas of those days. And long before I'd finished talking, he was shaking his head. People didn't act like that, he flatly assured me. There were no such people. That's what the man said, and I didn't try to talk him out of his ignorance. But he couldn't have been wronger.

His old nemesis, Louis L'Amour, could not have sounded more picturesque.

• • •

Hanging out with Jim during the late 1960s, Harlan Ellison remembers, "It always felt like twilight." After he introduced Thompson to Sal Mineo, and renewed the friendship that began in New York over a pack of Dentyne gum at Lion Books, Ellison became one of the few regular visitors to the Whitley Avenue apartment: "Jim would sit there through a long after-noon, and I could pretend it was the 1940s—here was this link back to my childhood. I have nothing but really good memories of Jim. He was always a gentleman, always mild in the way people who have spent a lot of years on the road and who have done a lot of hard-knock jobs get mild, become phlegmatic."

Because Ellison didn't drink, he preferred—when they ventured out—to hit All-American Burger rather than the Musso & Frank Grill, where Thompson would sit at the bar and nervously pick at his zucchini Floren-tine. "We talked writing, and learning to write," Ellison says. Thompson be-moaned the demise of the pulps. "One of his laments was that there were so many bad novels because people didn't have any magazines to write short stories for. They were immediately writing novels instead of starting with short stories and novellas and learning their craft."

Thompson kept a scorecard on other writers, Ellison discovered:

There wasn't a whine in his voice, but Jim had a very clear sense that it should have worked out better for him. He'd look at Dick Prather and Evan Hunter [Ed McBain] and say, they were in the same bag I was and they hit it big, while he kept plugging along at $2,000 a book, and his turn never came around. Jim thought that he had worked hard enough and originally enough, but that the books were going down the tubes and no one would ever know about them. He had the sense that his life should have been a little bit better at that point.

Besides writing, the pulps, and old New York, Thompson shared with Ellison a fascination for magic, a legacy from his days on the grift. "There was this private club started by magicians, The Magic Castle, on Franklin Avenue in Los Angeles, a dining and magic performance place. Jim liked sleight of hand—and so did Bob Mills. One night we went. He did a lot of drinking that night."

• • •

The month before Gold Medal released *South of Heaven,* Thompson printed his last short story, "Exactly What Happened," in *Ellery Queen's Mystery Magazine.* Submitted as "The Guy in Jake's Shoes," the story recast his teleplay of the same title that Warner Brothers rejected a decade earlier.

Neil Keller is a janitor at the Wexler Building. By disguising himself as night watchman Jake Goss, "One-Eyed Jake with the missing teeth, the mushy voice, the mole on his right cheek—a guy with a face you could never forget," he plans to knock over Old Man Wexler, a loan shark, for a hundred grand. Only Jake has beaten him to the same scheme, with one crucial twist. When Neil-as-Jake tumbles before Jake-as-Neil, Thompson stitches a metaphysical purl into a familiar motif:

> In his last brief moment all he saw was himself. The one man he had not guarded against. The one man every man faces sooner or later. All he saw was that he was about to be murdered by himself—which, in a sense, was exactly the case.

The story attained its *EQMM* title when Fredrick Dannay edited the concluding phrase to "exactly what happened."

"Exactly What Happened," following on *Texas by the Tail* and *South of Heaven,* demonstrates that Thompson might have played out his career as a proficient merchant of professional crime fiction, another honorable if bland entry in the murder marketplace. But over the summer of 1967 he abruptly shifted tack again. Thompson did not attempt to reclaim the experimental aspirations of *Pop. 1280, The Getaway,* or his Lion novels. Far from it. He angled off, instead, scurrilous and coarse, confronting Gold Medal with a smutty, witless western, *King Blood,* and then, a few months later, with *White Mother, Black Son,* his scatological account of a young mulatto monster. Gold Medal blanched, and gave up on him. "They were so badly crafted and so self-indulgent," editor Knox Burger comments, "so mordant and so sour, that commercially they would have been tough to publish."

Still, Bob Mills soon managed to locate a berth for *King Blood* at Avon Books, yet with an indifferent advance of only $1,750. Thompson signed his contract on August 23 and delivered the novel, as promised, in March 1968. The vulgarity of *King Blood* did not distress Avon—on the internal contract memo it was already oiling the publicity machine: "Raw, powerful, tremendously colorful yarn of an amoral young man's pursuit of an inheritance in Oklahoma: sex and murders galore."

King Blood was Thompson's third successive novel to rifle his remote personal history. Set around territorial Oklahoma at the turn of the century, it provided extended cameos for his father, Deputy Marshal James Sherman Thompson, and his great-uncle, U.S. Marshal Harry Thompson, who now entered his fiction under their own names.

Twenty-three-year-old Critchfield King is returning to the house of his elderly father, Ike King, after he was abducted as a child by his mother when she ran away with a handsome con man. On his way to King's Junction, Critch lifts a money belt containing $72,000 from the Anderson sisters (modeled on, Thompson informs the reader in a footnote, "the Bender family, operators of a murder-for-money roadhouse in southern Kansas"). Once Critch is home, his older brother Arlie—who has already murdered the third King brother, Boz, over a land dispute—steals the money from Critch. His efforts to recover the haul; elude the homicidal Arlie, the vengeful Andersons, and the suspicious U.S. marshals; and gain the trust of his failing patriarch suffuse the rambling—and forgettable—action.

Thompson may have envisioned *King Blood* as a Lone Star *King Lear,* but his style more closely approximated a *Playboy* "Ribald Classic." A leering, locker room swagger—"Ray was pounding his mother's meat. Ray was diddling his mother's pussy"—furnished the dominant texture. And Thompson occasionally lurched beyond that. Here Arlie King plans to "scalp" Big Sis Anderson's "puss":

> "Wish I had me a nickel for every puss I cut off," he went on, carefully reinscribing the circle with his knife. "An ol' Indian trick, y'know, an' us Kings are prob'ly more Indian than white. Funny thing is the woman don't hardly feel it—you don't feel nothin' do you?—till a long time afterward. That's maybe because it's mostly muscle, you know, an' stretchy; got more give to it than a mile o'

cat gut. Why I seen a fella stretch a gal's puss clean over her head, an' then let it snap shut around her neck. Man, oh, man, what a sight to see!" His body shook with laughter. "That gal was flingin' herself around like a chicken with its head off; strangled to death by her own tokus. Now—*lay still!* You keep up that kickin' and squirmin', you'll *really* get hurt. . . ."

Everyone in *King Blood* is either a ruttish hillbilly or a saintly marshal. Thompson rendered his father and all the other territorial lawmen—Uncle Harry, Bill Tilghman, Heck Thomas, and Chris Madsen—with reverence and awe, apparently expanding his revisionary nostalgia to embrace the period before he was born. Another footnote proudly acknowleged that he is "the son of James Sherman Thompson," but his Oklahoma heritage ran as addled as the sex. Thompson situated Tulsa inside Oklahoma Territory rather than Indian Territory, and he reproduced the family canards exactly as his father handed them down to him—the race for Congress against Thomas P. Gore, and the "smashing defeat" due to his too liberal racial principles. . . . "Several towns in the state bore some form of the family name; for example, *Jimtomson.*"

Avon paid the final installment on Thompson's advance in November 1968, but never issued *King Blood.* His author's card was stamped "Cancelled," yet offered no reason for the late disenchantment. Sphere Books, a small English house that reprinted *The Killer Inside Me* and *The Getaway,* eventually would publish the novel in 1973—but with an erroneous 1954 copyright date, as though it were vintage Thompson. "Wrong by twenty years," Thompson complained to Bob Mills. *King Blood* did not appear in America during his lifetime.

Perhaps the most gracious view of *King Blood* marks it as Thompson's stiff try to catch up with the freewheeling 1960s—the summer of 1967 was, after all, the Summer of Love. But Arnold Hano, still his informal editor, poses a sorrier slant: "Jim showed me *King Blood, White Mother, Black Son,* and two or three others in his 'sample' format. They were getting grosser, there was more dirty language, less humor, and less of an ameliorating edge to the rough side of it. I think that this was the result of Hollywood, drink, age, and the general diminution of creativity. I was kinder than I probably felt about them."

• • •

Harlan Ellison, like so many among the writer's writer friends over the decades, possessed "no sense of his family life. It was always Jim, all alone."

Thompson's thirst survived the loss of half his stomach, and he proceeded to drink, whether at Musso & Frank's or at home, with his customary recklessness. He preferred Jack Daniels with Heineken chasers, but settled for Ten-High when money was low. His alcoholism insinuated a time bomb into his household, and Alberta and Jim enacted a ruinous ritual for containing it. After a calm period of abstinence or control, something would trigger a binge that might last for days. "I never knew what set him off," Alberta admits. "But the fact that he got no recognition for his work ate away at him in the later years. Sometimes he'd start laughing and say, 'I don't know why I'm doing this,' and just stop." But if he couldn't stop, or when he turned too sarcastic, Alberta would kick him out; and Jim would phone one of his sisters, usually Maxine. He would slowly, shakily sober up, and return home sick with self-loathing and regret.

"This went on all through the 1960s, right up to two years or so before he died," Maxine remarked. "When Jimmie was having a big drinking bout, he very often got shipped out. He just couldn't shut it off because Alberta said, 'Don't drink in front of me.' " Maxine would drive over to Hollywood, pick him up, and pilot him to Brentwood. "I used to be alarmed when some project Jimmie was working on didn't pan out. Because, I thought, oh, dear, I'm going to have to take over."

His alcohol jag often persisted for two or three days after he arrived at Maxine's: "He'd wait for Joe to go to bed, which was early, and then he'd start drinking and talking." Maxine noted that she "always knew what would happen. It was always the same few stories over and over when he was drinking, sometimes in the same words." The sun might almost be coming up when she finally got him to bed.

Just as in his recent novels, his late-night stories backtracked to his father—but with a darker timbre than the heroic airs of *King Blood:*

> It was the same horrible things about the way it was way back with Papa. About Papa not understanding him, how he felt inadequate to what Papa wanted, that Papa was disappointed in him. It was nothing Papa ever said, but a feeling within Jimmie, something that Jimmie would have stewed over and thought over, and the drinking opened him up so he could talk. I think he felt Papa was to blame for a lot of his troubles.

Alberta sent her husband off bearing tranquilizers on these episodes, according to Maxine. "She told me if Jimmie was to continue drinking that I should give him the Valium, and then he'd be all right. Well, he never wanted to take it—he was pretty smart about a lot of things. But he would finally take one. Now I think that was wrong, but I was told what to do."

His benders wound down with Jim asking Maxine to telephone Alberta. "He would be afraid to call home, so he'd have me call. I would find out how the land lay, and eventually he would go back, looking awfully sad and sorry."

• • •

As Thompson waited on Avon and *King Blood,* another Lion associate flagged his concern with some light, makeshift assignments. Although Jim Bryans, since 1958 editor in chief at Popular Library, declined *White Mother, Black Son* as "a little too raunchy," he commissioned the writer to create a "sort of novel" from *Ironside,* the hit NBC television show starring Raymond Burr as former Chief of Detectives Robert T. Ironside, a San Francisco crime fighter confined to a wheelchair after an assassin's bullet left him paralyzed from the waist down. "My intention was to throw Jim any work I could," Bryans recalls. "The poor guy in his later years had trouble getting two bucks for a drink and dinner." *Ironside* aired for the first time on September 14, 1967. By November 21, Popular Library stocked paperback racks across the nation with Thompson's book. His fare for this fleet feat of meta-fiction was $2,000, more than he could now pull down for a new novel.

Since his "novelization" does not adapt the series pilot or any other teleplay, Jim Thompson's *Ironside* is a centaur fusion of the TV characters and an original plot. On the trail of a blackmailer-murderer known until the final pages only as The Killer, Ironside and his associates, Mark Sanger, Eve Whitfield, and Detective Sergeant Ed Brown, ricochet through a carnival ride of Thompson thrills. The Killer is another avenging Almighty, "No other than God, self-appointed. For it follows, as night the day, that one who elects to kill assumes the role of Deity." The San Francisco waterfront bar for heroin addicts The Killer operates from—where the piano player mixes *Deutschland Über Alles* and "The Internationale" into his medley of pop standards—is once more evoked as "a madman's concept of Hell." Thompson endowed Ironside with his own financially turbulent adolescence ("For a time, during Robert Ironside's boyhood, his father had been a very wealthy man. The wealth hadn't lasted long. . . ."), and a peculiar dash of his West Texas oil fields Marxism ("So pastoral man, as represented by Chief Robert Ironside, was once again in the clutches of an industrialized society. . . ."). He even lifted the opening from his unpublished short story "The Tomcat That Was Treetop Tall."

Ironside, after a fashion, is Thompson's only detective novel, and he displayed scant tolerance for the diligent elucidation of a mystery. Just as in his true crime articles from the 1930s and 1940s, solutions can occur to the crippled gumshoe with the clank of psychic clairvoyance—"All Ironside knew is that he had a hunch"—and fresh evidence is introduced when convenient. Thompson evinced significantly more empathy for The Killer, particularly the seedy, apocalyptic atmosphere he diffuses like stale cologne. The Killer's most memorable rumination rides the "preposterous music" of Hell's piano player to a vision of nuclear annihilation:

There was beauty in the music, or, more accurately, the memory of beauty, now as lost as a lost love; something that lay buried in an unknown dimension like the final decimal of *pi*. Now, as though avenging itself upon an evil and uncaring world, it had sprouted into hideousness—a seed gone mad. And its terrible blossoms of sound hinted at a greater terror to come. Here, said the music, was a taste of Armageddon. Here, the Ultima Thule. Here the inevitable destination of a planet whose mass of six sextillion, four hundred and fifty quintillion short tons was turned into a slaughterhouse instead of a garden. Here, the fruit of neglect, that socially approved form of murder. Here, the basic lie in its final extension.

A whole *was* greater than its parts . . . or was there no Bomb, no minute amalgam of neutrons and protons? Add three billion to the planet's mass, and subtract kindness and caring, and you were left not with an unkindly, uncaring three billion, but death. So said the seed, the music, now sunk in a morass of wilderness from which it had vainly cried out. There would be no refuge from the coming terror. No place to hide. No familiar thing to cling to. Something would become nothing, robbed of its intrinsic beauty and safety, and all else. There would be only a smoking, steaming blown-apart, crushed-together mishmash where brother was himself eaten by brother while eating brother, ad nauseam, ad infinitum.

From Lou Ford to Nick Corey, Thompson's creatures rose on drunken heights to destroy the world. Astonishing, then, that he should finally enact their supreme holocaust inside a stopgap curiosity like *Ironside*.

If Hollywood no longer looked to Thompson for movie or television scripts, studios and producers increasingly scanned his old novels for possible films. He signed on with the Brand Agency on Sunset Boulevard. In November 1968, Warner Brothers paid $1,000 for one-year option on *The Killer Inside Me*. The following July, Alan Factor of Bedford Productions expended the same amount for a one-year option on *Pop. 1280*, with the screenplay to be written by Milt Rosen.

Neither option would be renewed. Come October, Popular Library released another Thompson novelization, this time for *The Undefeated*, Andrew V. McLaglen's post–Civil War western featuring John Wayne, Rock Hudson, and a pair of football stars, Roman Gabriel and Merlin Olsen. Although carved from a film rather than a television program, *The Undefeated* descended still another rung from *Ironside*. Editor Jim Bryans cautioned against the personalizing signatures Thompson imported into the earlier book. "This is not, incidentally, to be written in any depth. . . . The vio-

lence and the sex ought not to be built up at all. . . . You use only dialogue that's in the script, and you don't try to do more, really, than tell the
story that's already there." For the sake of the easy $2,000, Thompson
obliged—and almost comically, going so far as to telegraph the dramatic
shifts at the head of his short chapters with single-word paragraphs—"Midnight . . . ," "Louisiana . . . ," "Dawn . . . ," "Dusk . . ."—his prose flat
as roadkill.

• • •

By the fall of 1969 Thompson, with just his recent few Gold Medal novels
and reprints in circulation, did not always own copies of his books. As producers and agents came calling, he often had to satisfy them with third- or
fourth-generation photocopies, two spotted pages to a sheet. So Jim
arranged with the owner of the Cherokee Book Shop, a used bookstore on
Hollywood Boulevard, for his old novels to be sold back to him whenever
any turned up.

Tony Bill also approached the Cherokee for Thompson titles. Then a
young actor, Bill first read *The Killer Inside Me* when he was drifting around
the writing program at Stanford, and heard Jim Harrison, Gus Blaisdell,
Tom McGuane, and Wallace Stegner recommend Thompson. In partnership
with director Vernon Zimmerman at Bi-Plane Cinematograph, Inc., he envisioned a film about the American hobo. "I thought that maybe Jim Thompson would be a good guy to write it," Bill recollects. "I wanted to read some
more of his books, so I phoned the Cherokee Book Shop and asked if they
had any. They said no, but we sure wish we did. He lives right up the street,
and he doesn't have any of his own books." Bill located Thompson through
the Cherokee, and invited him to lunch. "I found out he did indeed know an
awful lot about the American hobo."

Jim was sixty-three, Tony Bill not quite thirty. Sometimes accompanied
by Vern Zimmerman, they started to meet at one of the red plush leather
booths in the Musso & Frank Grill, long storytelling sessions that might
spill over into supper at Bill's Hollywood Hills house. "I really liked Jim, and
I think he liked me," Bill recalls. "He told me about the legendary back room
at Musso & Frank's where the Hammetts and the Faulkners and the McCoys
used to hang out. Jim was part of that world. I liked his hard-boiledness, his
sense of adventure, his toughness. But in many ways he was a very youthful, unsoiled kind of guy, despite the fact he had this road map of a face,
was a very serious drinker, and I'd usually have to roll him home."

Thompson apparently regaled Bill and Zimmerman with grisly—and
embroidered—sagas from his family life, a bibulous custom he indulged
among younger admirers. "Jim told me that his son would get so disturbed
that he would have to sit on him all night to control him. That's the image
of Jim Thompson that sticks so strongly in my mind." Bill claims that the

Jim Thompson, Robert Redford, and Tony Bill
at Redford's Utah ranch, 1970 (Courtesy of
the Thompson family)

writer once "was so desperate for money that he offered to sell me the rights to all his work for basically whatever I wanted to pay—$500, $1,000, anything."

Through the spring, and into the summer of 1970, the American hobo film progressed at Musso & Frank's until Columbia Pictures agreed to back the development of a screenplay. Bill would produce, and Zimmerman would direct from Thompson's script. Bill planned the film as a vehicle for his friend, Robert Redford. Jim went to work in an office on the Columbia lot.

Whereas Tony Bill stresses that Thompson was preparing "an original screenplay" from the outset, *South of Heaven* somehow became ensnared in the arrangement. The producer suggests that it was Thompson who broached his 1967 West Texas novel. "Jim said, 'You ought to read this book that I wrote called *South of Heaven,* because it's about hoboes, men on the road, and oil wildcats.' I read it and said, 'Yes, it's got some interesting stuff in there, but that's not the script I want to do.' " Yet Bi-Plane Cinematograph nonetheless managed to capture the motion picture rights to *South of Heaven.* Bill maintains that the impetus to sell the novel also came from Thompson. "The rights to the book were tied up because either Jim wanted to use stuff from the book, or he had used stuff from the book. Since Columbia was financing the script, they wanted to be protected if there was anything from the book we used as well."

Bill's chronology isn't entirely on target. *South of Heaven* was the substance of the two initial—and the only—agreements Thompson signed with Bi-Plane Cinematograph. His contract letter of May 15, in fact, specified "your employment by us as a scenario writer in connection with our proposed motion picture based upon that certain published work presently entitled *South of Heaven.*" He would collect $1,500 for signing, $4,500 upon completion of a first draft, $2,000 more for any revisions, and a final $2,000 for the shooting script. Also on May 15, but with a separate document, Bi-Plane Cinematograph took possession of all film and television rights to *South of Heaven* for a token $10.

The first-draft screenplay Thompson delivered to Tony Bill by early June, for all that, carried the title *Hard Times,* not *South of Heaven,* and intersected his novel solely at the point of its 1920s oil field setting. He forsook the autobiographical rambles of Tommy Burwell and Four Trey Whitey for a radical salute to his Wobbly mentor, Harry Kirby McClintock.

Different traits of Haywire Mac inspired two lead characters in *Hard Times.* His musical aspect Thompson poured into the Minstrel, who guides and comments on the action, while his political stance agitated Joe Rock, an IWW organizer and "trouble-makin' red," who sustains his quest for a "fair share of the profits" with his fists. *Hard Times* opens as Joe Rock knocks a railroad dick off a speeding train because he clubbed a defenseless hobo. Rock soon clashes with an oil field foreman over a boiler mishap, and runs afoul of a caustic, small-town lawman, Burt Tate. When he rushes to stop Tate from raping a black woman ("What's the matter, Joe Rock? Got something against black meat?"), the sheriff accidentally kills himself with his own gun. Rock is sentenced to twenty-five years on a county prison farm, and punished on a "wooden lady," a crosslike device that racks his body with electricity. The warden of the prison farm colludes with local landowners to provide inmates as forced labor. The surviving manuscript breaks off after Nancy Courtland, Tate's wealthy former girlfriend, chooses Rock to work for her.

By late July, Robert Redford climbed aboard as both co-producer and star of what the announcement in *Variety* designated an "untitled screenplay by Jim Thompson." Tony Bill escorted Thompson up to Redford's ranch in Utah: the novelist's virgin airplane flight. "I think Bob was very taken with him, because Jim was the genuine article," Bill remarks. "Jim was a very entertaining yarn spinner to sit around and listen to for hours."

Following his caucus with Redford, and a later story conference in New York, Thompson returned to his Columbia Pictures office and completed a second screenplay. This draft he titled *Bo,* Wobbly slang for hobo. His plot retained the essential trajectory of *Hard Times,* yet with Robert Redford confirmed for the role of "the archtypal American hobo," Joe Rock accrued a gentler nobility to match his blond hair and blue eyes. Thompson toned down Rock's violence—Sheriff Tate dies not in a brawl but when a dragline bucket crashes down on him, as the bo shouts, "Look out!" And Thompson enhanced Rock's high-mindedness, as the bo coaxes a farmer to stop beating his deaf daughter and send her to school.

The balance of the *Bo* script shadows Nancy Courtland's courtship of the Wobbly activist, and his eventual flight from her to the Texas pipeline. Even after Nancy chases Rock into the hobo jungle, and offers to purchase his pardon, he resists, pleading his revolutionary principles. Money divides them, Rock says: "That's a fence down the middle there, and you're on one side of it and I'm on the other." Only when the workers' struggle has been won, can they come together:

> Maybe someday, what's simply fair and decent will become law. Safe working conditions and a decent wage. A five or six day week instead of seven. Maybe even a forty-hour week. Disability pay when you're hurt, and unemployment when you're out of work. I know it sounds pretty far-fetched, but—

Nancy finally tells him to "shut up." But through *Hard Times* and *Bo,* Joe Rock never amounts to more than a heroic cipher, or a jackstraw messiah. "Everyone ended up thinking Jim's script was pretty thin," Bill remembers, "and like millions of other scripts, it didn't go any farther. I guess he was pretty burned out as a writer."

Bi-Plane Cinematograph paid Thompson his full $10,000 for his work. Tony Bill went on to co-produce *The Sting* for Robert Redford. Vernon Zimmerman would eventually direct *Deadhead Miles* and the cult splatter sensation *Fade to Black.* On August 6, 1970, Bi-Plane Cinematograph and Robert Redford's Wildwood Enterprises reassigned the motion picture rights for *South of Heaven* to Columbia Pictures.

• • •

Thompson notched the last of his three novelizations for Popular Library while researching the American hobo screenplay with Bill and Zimmerman. The celluloid source was his richest—*Nothing but a Man,* Michael Roemer's heartbreaking 1964 black-and-white African-American film, transcribed to the page some five years after release. But Thompson appears to have snoozed through everything but the cashing of his advance. "Poor Jim was doing all these damn adaptations," Harlan Ellison rues. "He felt that he had been screwed by the universe." *Nothing but a Man* sold 31,000 copies, and Jim Bryans never hired him again.

No sooner had the Tony Bill whirlwind wound down than Jim was swept away by another youthful enthusiast. The Parisian film distributor Pierre Rissient contacted the American writer around 1966, after reading all his novels in French or English. Thompson shared his latest fiction "samples" over subsequent visits, and Rissient nurtured a fascination for *White Mother, Black Son,* the first-person study of a raging, biracial prodigy. "I found the concept of *White Mother, Black Son* fantastic, among the most shocking things that he had written, the synthesis of all Thompson. . . ."

A fresh round of story meetings soon usurped the bar at Musso & Frank's. Rissient descried on these excursions into Hollywood numerous *"problèmes très thompsoniens . . .* Our rendezvous were a pretext for him to escape from the control of his wife, to go out and drink. He was very moved when anyone expressed an interest in his writing, and these encounters often turned into a kind of soliloquy and confession, where he spoke of his life." Much as with Tony Bill, Jim enacted the hard-bitten raconteur, recounting visits to Southern California massage parlors in the company of Musso & Frank's bartender Albert Niego. He blamed his vexations in Hollywood on the blacklist. He apparently also convinced Rissient that he had fled New York for California in 1956 because of "a very serious affair with a woman. . . . There was a huge family drama. . . . His hopes for movie contracts were undoubtedly only pretexts. . . . He spoke very badly about his wife, his family, and his sons [*sic*]." Jim pitched so many stories about Mike that he left Rissient with the impression that he was the father of two boys.

By the summer of 1970, Rissient persuaded Les Films la Boetie to procure the motion picture rights for *White Mother, Black Son* for $5,000, so that Thompson could finish his novel. In early August Jim flew alone to Paris, where Rissient installed him at the Hotel des Belles Feuilles. Any fantasies the *cinéaste* may have cherished about introducing the next Chester Himes to France atomized amid transatlantic Thompson family histrionics:

> When he came to Paris . . . he arrived dead drunk. The next day, while he was starting to recover, he received a telegram from his wife telling him of a suicide attempt by his son. He was not duped, and knew that it was most certainly a ploy to to make him return. While he would have been delighted to remain in France for four or five months, he left immediately. In spite of everything he was very submissive, although he understood the situation perfectly.

Alberta Thompson intimates that Rissient, not her husband, was the intended gull of her telegram:

Jimmie wanted to get out of Paris right away, he just couldn't handle it. We discussed what to do over the phone. He knew that if I said that there was an emergency with Mike everyone would understand. But Mike was acting very strange at that time too, so in some ways it was the truth. He threatened suicide, and I phoned Jimmie. He wanted to come back, and used Mike as an excuse.

Drunk and frightened, Thompson also was flustered by impediments of advancing age. Rereading his own writing proved difficult because of cataracts in his eyes, and the arthritis that swelled his fingers stymied efforts to manipulate Rissient's typewriter. Still, Thompson actually lasted some ten days in Paris—long enough for him to transfer hotels, or peck out a touristy note to Alberta: "As you can see I am having considerabl e trouble with this strange thpewriters. . . . Pierre has been extremelh nice to me; has already shown me a great deal of Paris, and I find it a beautiful and interesting city. All in all, though, there is no place like home."

●   ●   ●

Back in Los Angeles, Thompson slowly expanded *White Mother, Black Son.* Allen Smith is the "kinky-haired nigger kid" of a "swell-looking white broad," a self-proclaimed "unadulterated, .999-fine, 24-karat, 180-proof, 100-percent pure son-of-a-bitch. The *only* one in the fiction-history from which life is copied." A proudly offensive, if cartoonish parable of racial and sexual anxiety, *White Mother, Black Son* attested once again to Thompson's propensity to insinuate the personal into his most vile or outrageous creations. Titled after a childhood charade young Jimmie used to perform with his mother, Birdie, back in Burwell, the novel is set around Astoria, Queens, by the East River's Hell Gate site of the Elizabeth and Gregory apartment complex, where the middle-aged *SAGA* editor and Lion novelist resided during the early 1950s. Thompson had been stewing this bad seed story at least since the Bobbie Ashton chapter of *The Kill-Off,* and he skimmed off rank episodes for another 1960s "sample," *The Horse in the Baby's Bathtub.*

For Allen Smith, Thompson added the spice of race to his psychopathic prankster recipe of domineering mother, absent father, incest, abuse, impotence, and a holy fool who believes that he's God and the devil. Like an adolescent African-American Lou Ford or Nick Corey, Allen locks up his prodigious IQ behind a shuffling dumb show. On his first day at his new high school, his math teacher, Mrs. Carter, asks if he has already studied plane geometry:

"Plain, ma'am?" I scratched my head, letting out a big happy-nigger heehaw. "Sho' didn't seem plain t'me, deed it didn't, ma'am! Seem awful dagnab com-ple-cated!"

That Allen immediately goes on to torture poor Mrs. Carter with the virtuoso demonstration of a problem lifted from "a doctoral-candidate's thesis on mathematics," which he discovered while "browsing in the public library," releases the other needle in his arsenal. His stunts tend to combine intellectual superiority with physical crassness, a high art of low humor discharged in a flash of hate.

Allen, for instance, manages to slip a hypnotic drug to his psychiatrist, and then dyes the shrink's penis with green, indelible ink. Or he gulls the radical Black Students Club into claiming that they saw the principal, Mr. Velie, make a pass at him in the men's room. "Don't you ever read anything?" he taunts, "Mao or Marx or Che. . . . The president of a college or the principal of a high school is always the first to be discredited"; then, of course, he denies everything. Or Allen lures two classmates, Lizbeth and Steve Hadley, the offspring of a black doctor, to his mother's deluxe apartment, by stroking their bourgeois aspiration to "our class of people." There, he plies the Hadley siblings with vodka, persuades Lizbeth to let him shave her vulva ("Only niggers go around with hair all over their dingus"), and orchestrates the ludicrous coupling:

> Lizbeth came dancing out, naked as a baby jaybird.
>
> She wasn't exactly drunk now, just insensitized enough to have lost the edge of her inhibitions. While Steve gaped, she whirled and skipped around the room, pointing to her crotch and voicing a little chant: "Whee, whee, look at me, got no hair on my pee-pee. . . ."
>
> Steve's booze hit him abruptly. He let out a guffaw, and pulled her down on his lap. "Hey, that's really something, Liz! Guess I better have some of that."
>
> "Uh-uh!" She giggled and wriggled, trying to squirm away from him. "Gonna give it to Allen."
>
> He said, hell, there was plenty for everyone, and he was going to take a great big share of it right now.
>
> He grabbed it and squeezed so hard that she groaned with pain. But when he stood up and started toward the bedroom with her, she threw herself out of his arms and stubbornly pushed him away from her.
>
> "I said *no.* Gonna give it to Allen. You already had plenty. . . ."
>
> "Go on, Liz," I said. "We'll make it a triple-header."
>
> "Mmm?" She looked at me interestedly. "Triple-header?"
>
> "Sure," Steve broke in eagerly, "we'll have it at the same time. You just get on your knees on the bed, and turn your little butt up for us, and Al or I will—"
>
> "I know. Unnerstand perfeckly," she mumbled impatiently. "Don' need to draw me a picture."

She marched into the bedroom, with Steve right behind her and me behind him. By the time she had arranged herself on the bed, her head in the pillows and her tail up and her knees spread, Steve was out his clothes and on her and in her.

They groaned simultaneously in an agony of sheer delight. Steve gave me an over-the-shoulder glance and mumbled, what the hell? Why was I still in my clothes?

Allen flaunts a sniggering, motiveless malignancy. "All the other so-called sons-of-bitches of other races and mine are merely semis," he crows. "Their son-of-a-bitchery is motivated, which is another way saying there is a reason, and excuse, for it." But Thompson actually belabors two obvious sources for Allen's rage. One is the heritage of slavery, which Allen has internalized as racial self-loathing; his cruelest frolics humiliate fellow blacks. The other is his prostitute mother, who since Allen was a baby has drawn him into her bed, where she masturbates against him, achieving the satisfaction for herself that she denies him. Both strains converge during the ugly confession Mrs. Smith spills to a concealed Allen, mistakenly believing that he is one of her old black johns:

> ". . . You can understand what a lousy thing it would be for a white woman to have a black child. Me, getting stuck with a wooly-headed little nigger! Sorry . . . no offense. I hated that black bastard from the first time I laid eyes on him. And believe me, I made him pay for what he'd done! Of course, I fed him; saw that he had his bottle whenever he wanted it. But I made him nurse between my legs. Peeled it back where could get it at the clitoris. And why the hell not, anyway? It felt good, and it didn't hurt him any. The little black brat was too young ever to remember. . . ."
> *Too young? TOO YOUNG?*
> The subconscious never forgets. I would be bound to her . . . impotent with any other, without ever knowing why.

Allen piles up his incisive gibes. Is he, for all his obscenity, any more corrupt or racist than the official voices of authority here? His mother? The school principal who seduces a black student aide? The psychiatrist who rejects his claims of child abuse and urges him to turn homosexual? Doesn't he only release Lizbeth and Steve's hidden desires? Allen boasts of his standing among Satan's "legions," and also that he is "God . . . I'm running the store for him while he's out of his head." But sorrow alloys the rationalization behind his wrathful theology. "Right and wrong were so intertwined in my mind as to be unidentifiable," Allen calculates near the end, "and I had had to create my own concepts of them."

White Mother, Black Son, even more than *King Blood,* shows Thompson struggling to roll over his obsessions into a new, more permissive era. His twisted riffs on motherhood, Black Power, Indians, sex, student demonstrations, education, Freudian psychology, marriage, the police, or Norman Mailer's *Why Are We in Vietnam?** suggest an epic Lenny Bruce routine but without the comedian's wit and timing. The hip patter, topical satire, and ricocheting profanity sound affected and desperate, a psychedelic rinse over his tired palette.

From *The Killer Inside Me* through *Pop. 1280,* Thompson cooked his boldest novels from inside an atmosphere of cultural and private censorship. As William Carlos Williams—a poet whose work he assigned to his USC fiction students—once remarked of Poe, he "could not have written a word without the violence of expulsive emotion combined with the indriving force of a crudely repressive environment." Thompson at his best operated by indirection, stealth, and subversion. As he framed the explicitness issue as far back as *Heed the Thunder,* observing of his young stand-in, Robert Dillon: "Generally, he did not swear much. He did not object to others cursing—he even enjoyed it. But for himself he preferred using, searching for, words and phrases which expressed the same vehemence and decadence, but yet were acceptable in any company."

Much as crime fiction, popularly thought of as confining, stretched Thompson as a novelist, so sexual license, popularly thought of as liberating, curbed his savage art. Finally granted the latitude to write whatever he wished, all he could muster was a flippant comic book, didactic and shrill:

> "Well, it's this way," I said. "The intelligent man can only function behind a mask of stupidity, or conformity, if you will excuse the redundancy . . . he should pinch girls on the butt and pee in alleys, instead of going to the john. Always, whatever the circumstances, he must reveal his intelligence in an aw-shucks, turd-kicking manner; as much as to say, well, gosh-durn! Look what I went down! Is I learnin' you anything, gal? You want me to tell you de courses leadin' to the [Applied Owl Crap] degree?"
>
> "Y-yassuh, b-b-boss. P-please tell me about dem dere courses!"
>
> "Very well," I said. "Electives should consist of such subjects as Bad Music Appreciation, How to Join a Hate Group, The Art of Unzipped Trousers and Acceptable Sloppiness, and Raping, Lynching, and Other Indigenous Pastimes. Major courses would be comprised of What D'Ya Think about Them Dodgers, Let's Drop A

---

*As the author of an essay called "The White Negro," Mailer would be a sore spot for Allen Smith.

Bomb On Mos-kow, Sending the Kikes to Jerusalem, Sending the Niggers to Afrikur, and Why Don't They Unleash Chang Kai-shek."

Pierre Rissient lamented that Thompson could not seize the promise of his original "sample," and Les Films La Boetie never pursued a film: "That moment was the hinge, let us say, for his creative vitality. After that he was not able to write any more." Lancer Books, a New York house that marketed everything from *Conan the Conqueror* to *The Nude Who Never,* issued *White Mother, Black Son* in 1972 under the title *Child of Rage.*

Dedicated to Pierre Rissient, *Child of Rage* was Jim Thompson's last novel.

• • •

Young Hollywood continued to court Thompson in his decline. During the abortive American hobo affair, Tony Bill introduced him to Mike Medavoy, already at thirty the head of the Creative Management Associates, a precursor of ICM. Medavoy remembers that, "Jim came in with a number of old small pocket books. He said that every one of these would make a good movie story. The pages were all yellow—that's what he wanted me to sell." His curiosity kindled by more charming tales from the old back room at Musso & Frank's, the agent agreed to take Thompson on. "Here I was representing Steven Spielberg, George Lucas, Terrence Malick, Michael Ritchie, Tony Bill, John Milius—the cutting edge of the up-and-coming generation— *and* Jim Thompson," muses Medavoy, who later would preside over United Artists, Orion, and TriStar. "Jim was my only novelist client, but his real bent then was on becoming a screenwriter." The machinery for repackaging Thompson as This Year's Model appeared shaky, even for high-octane CMA. And the initial test run rattled: an agency newsletter intended to "highlight some of CMA's new young writers" twice mangled *The Grifters* as *The Drifter.*

But early in the summer of 1970, Bill showed Medavoy a crumpled photocopy of *The Getaway:*

> Since Jim didn't often have copies of his own books, he gave me a Xerox of *The Getaway.* I thought it would make a great movie. But as a young, struggling producer, with only a Xerox of an unknown book in hand, I didn't think I had much of a chance of getting it made. I mentioned it to my agent, a young, energetic, aggressive agent named Mike Medavoy, and before I knew it, Mike turned around and sold the rights to David Foster.
>
> That's how *The Getaway* got made. Mike always felt guilty about it, but I've never held it against him. It taught me a lesson. Don't go around talking about great unknown books!

David Foster was a publicist who had worked with Steve McQueen since the actor starred as bounty hunter Josh Randall in the CBS series *Wanted: Dead or Alive* during the late 1950s. For several years Foster had been looking to produce a movie for McQueen. "Steve was interested in playing a Bogart character," Foster explains. "He had never played an out-and-out gangster." On August 5, Foster sent the photocopy of *The Getaway* to France, where McQueen was filming *Le Mans.* "A week later a cable came back from Steve saying, 'Lock it up.' "

Thompson's local saloon served, as before, as an impromptu office. "I made the reservations at Musso & Frank's, got there, and told the guy that when a Jim Thompson came in he should send him over," Foster recalls. "But Jim was already drinking at the bar. He introduced himself, talking very fast and slurry. Jim would always drink his lunch while I sat beside him eating a salad or a hamburger. He struck me as this gentle, scared, dear man. Jim was like a sparrow on a branch afraid to fly off. Yet his books were so tough. I came to see that the writing was a way for Jim to vent a bit."

Perhaps because Foster was older than his other Hollywood suitors, Thompson exposed more of his life. Jim and Alberta socialized with the Fosters at restaurants around Los Angeles, such as The Bistro. Foster dubs the Thompsons "an unlikely couple":

> Alberta is very sophisticated. Jim could have a soup stain on his tie and a smudge on his shirt—he didn't care, his appearance was secondary to him. She, on the other hand, wore pearls, was coiffed perfectly, nice designer dresses, really turned out well, and she took pride in that.
>
> Jim said that his education was in the hotels and gambling parlors of the Southwest. He would always tell me these stories about how, when he was a bellboy, he had to deal with all these shady characters—how he would send them booze, broads, drugs—and all the wild card games and gambling that went on.

Once Steve McQueen returned from France, and then shot *Junior Bonner* in Arizona with Sam Peckinpah, *The Getaway* moved toward a deal. Backed by Paramount Pictures, Foster would produce. McQueen would act the role of Doc McCoy. After viewing *Targets* and the as-yet-to-be-released *The Last Picture Show,* Foster and McQueen selected Peter Bogdanovich as their director. Thompson signed his agreement letter on Feruary 1, 1971, and his contract on April 13. He received $1,500 for an eighteen-month option, and $20,000 for the motion picture rights. He would be paid $15,000 for the screenplay, and a "bonus" of an additional $25,000 if he merited a screen credit. The potential $61,500 package roughly matched Thompson's total income over the previous decade.

Director Sam Fuller once acclaimed *The Getaway* as "the most original gangster story ever written. I could film it without a script." But for Thompson the path from novel to movie snaked past another Hollywood gauntlet. He sketched a prose treatment during the first week of February. On April 23 he submitted a ninety-five-page first-draft screenplay that covered the plot down to the final chapter, promising that "the concluding section on El Rey follows shortly." David Foster sent back almost as many pages of reactions and recommendations. Toiling over *The Getaway* for some sixteen weeks, Thompson dispatched his first draft, portions of a second draft and, as he later reviewed, "about eight ten-by-thirteen envelopes filled with material I had written, 'try-it-on-for-size' scenes, 'well, do it this way, and see how it works,' etc." By June 1 he was fired and replaced with Walter Hill, a novice screenwriter who would go on to direct such prosperous action-thrillers as *The Warriors, The Long Riders, Southern Comfort, 48 Hours,* and *Red Heat.* Hill gleaned sole screen credit for the script when *The Getaway* was released.

Foster claims that he found Thompson's screenplay "too talky" and "not very exciting. Jim simply took the book and tried to literally turn it word for word into a screenplay format. He didn't add the invention of movies." Mike Medavoy demurs, however, at this recollection of the firing. "Jim's draft actually wasn't too bad, but they [Foster and McQueen] didn't like it, though. It was too dark for them. I was disappointed that they didn't like the script. But there was nothing I could do about it."

Thompson believed that Foster and McQueen had consigned him a mandate to re-create his novel. As he subsequently protested to the Screen Writers Guild Arbitration Committee:

> The producers forbade me to depart from the story in my novel. "We bought the book because we liked the story. So stick to it." I was, on a few occasions, able to invent a bit of business which they found so appealing that I was allowed to use it. But the general rule was, Stick to the book. Don't invent anything else. Mr. Hill, apparently, was under no such restriction.

His screenplay inhabited the spirit of his novel from the Beacon City bank heist to El Rey, accommodating discreet cuts while preserving the bleak, downward spiral (trimming the shit house at Ma Santis's hideout, for instance, but not her underwater caves). Thompson localized the symbolic geography of the book with concrete backdrops (KANSAS CITY STATION), a specific date (1955), and topical references to President Eisenhower, Vice President Nixon, and Adlai Stevenson. He winked humorously at McQueen ("Probably best described as the BULLITT of footchases—Doc in pursuit of the thief"), and reluctantly incorporated a few of the star's earnest script proposals, such as having Doc and Carol escape via bus, against his own criminal instincts. "I still don't believe that desperate, highly publicized fugitives take flight on Greyhound buses," he told the Guild Arbitration Committee. "It was suggested to me by Steve McQueen, and I begged off doing it."

Thompson's prose treatment for *The Getaway* was, as Foster complains, gassy and prolix, but his screenplay advanced an estimable, often mordant concision. Here Ma Santis guides Doc and Carol to her underworld:

MA

Let me have a good look at you. *(looks him up and down, beaming)* It's been a long time.
Doc nods, swallowing a mouthful of sandwich.

DOC

Too long. Not since I pulled that bank job in Montana with Earl and Johnny. *(shakes head, regretfully)* Sorry I couldn't make it to their funerals, Ma, God rest 'em.

MA

Didn't make it myself. They wasn't no nicer about funerals at Chino than they was at Huntsville.

DOC

The way it goes. . . . What's the route to El Rey's from here, Ma?

MA

Have to do some arrangin' about that. Meantime, whilst the heat's dyin' down, I better bury you folks.
She gestures to them. They draw close and she squats on the brink of the gravel pit, beaming a flashlight down on the dark water.

MA

See them two clumps of bushes? *(Doc nods)* Now, look right below 'em, there at them kind of shady places just under the water line.

DOC

Caves?
Ma shrugs, straightens and stands, as do Carol and Doc.

MA

More like homes than caves. Just about big enough to crawl into an' get out of sight. But that's all you need, ain't it?

DOC

(glancing at Carol's taut face) How long do you figure, Ma?

MA

Depends. A day or two, say—three at the outside. . . . It ain't so bad, Doc. No smoking an' no grub, o' course. But the air an' water's

sweet enough an' they's plenty of sleepin' pills. (*to Carol*) I'll get a
rope to let you down with. (*goes offscreen*)

The final descent into Hell appears to have put the chill on Thompson
with Foster and McQueen, much as that infernal sequence almost deep-
freezed *The Getaway* with New American Library thirteen years earlier. "We
felt the second half of the book was a whole other movie," Foster reports.
Although he suggests that "Jim was completely amenable to changing the
ending," all the paper evidence indicates otherwise. The ironic El Rey survives in both the treatment and the first-draft screenplay. "The darkness
was one of the many things they changed," Mike Medavoy remarks. "They
didn't exactly shoot the book. They shot the film that they wanted to make."

Coincident with the firing of Thompson from *The Getaway*, Peter Bogdanovich departed to make *What's Up, Doc?* with Barbra Streisand and
Ryan O'Neal for Warner Brothers, and Paramount Pictures withdrew over
budget complications. McQueen transferred the project to his own company, First Artists, and proposed Sam Peckinpah as director. "When I took
Sam to lunch to discuss *The Getaway,*" Foster relates, "I discovered that he
had read the book years ago, and had already met Jim. Sam said that he
had wanted to make the movie back then, but no one would let him." Foster
describes Thompson as "tremendously excited that Sam was going to do
the film." Yet Peckinpah opted to shoot Walter Hill's script.

Filming commenced in February 1972 at the Huntsville State Penitentiary, near San Marcos, Texas. Peckinpah would start belting tequila at
eight in the morning with selected crew. But the set probably wrested its
chief notoriety for the scandal that rippled across American tabloids when
Ali MacGraw, hired fresh from *Love Story* for the part of Carol McCoy, left
her husband, Paramount Pictures executive Robert Evans, for McQueen.

Opening with a long, incongruous prologue about Doc's release from a
Texas prison, and closing with the McCoys' deliverance inside the choked
maw of a garbage truck over the Mexican border to safety and freedom,
Hill's screenplay pumped *The Getaway* into a scuttle of car chases, triple
crosses, and shoot-outs. The rote Hollywood resolution particularly rankled Thompson. "Except for its irony, perhaps, there is absolutely no resemblance between my wrap-up of the script and Mr. Hill's," he clamored to
the Guild Arbitration Committee. "In fact, I would refuse any credit for it if it
was offered." Stripped of El Rey, *The Getaway* lost any objective beyond its
own frantic action and bloody spectacle.

If *The Getaway* no longer belonged to Jim Thompson, the film ultimately also slipped away from Hill and Peckinpah. Steve McQueen's contract allotted him final cut. The actor chose takes that cast him and
MacGraw in a glamorous luster, emphasized some cute physical business

he improvised on location—such as the scene where Doc cooks breakfast for Carol—and accented his skill with guns. He even replaced Jerry Fielding's sound track with a score by Quincy Jones. According to McQueen biographer Marshall Terrill, "When Peckinpah saw McQueen's final cut at his home in Mexico, he stood up in his living room, moved forward, and pissed on the screen, loudly announcing, 'This is not my film!' "

Jim and Alberta attended an advance screening of *The Getaway* on the Warner Brothers lot. "Before everything started, David Foster leaned over and joked with me, 'Hold onto Jim, because he's not going to like it,' " she remembers. When the lights came up Thompson slapped Foster on the back, assuring the producer that he was "pleased as hell." Afterward, he condemned and disowned the film among family and friends. "He really hated what they did to *The Getaway*, especially the ending," Alberta discloses. "Jimmie didn't make a fuss. Steve and Ali were always very nice to Jimmie, and he really liked David Foster. He was happy that it made him a lot of money, and brought the book back in print."

Thompson lodged his grievance with the Guild Arbitration Committee on July 11, anxious to salvage his $25,000 bonus. He supported his appeal with a bound pamphlet of some thirty-three pages "representing his contribution remaining in the final script," and concluded:

> I have now been a member of the guild for some fourteen years. During that time, naturally, I have been subject to many credit arbitrations (though none was ever instigated by me; and this is the first time I have protested a producer's designation of credits).
>
> In so doing now, I am not denying that Mr. Hill's work is substantial and excellent—even, perhaps, to a far greater degree than mine.
>
> However, I worked sixteen weeks on this script, and I have probably made very substantial contributions to the work. Also, despite the introduction of new material—characters and scenes— the basic story and numerous scenes are my own creations.
>
> In my other arbitrations, some of which dealt with far less work than I did on *The Getaway*, I have always received some credit; the very least was screen story credit. To be excluded from any credit at all is, to me, an unprecedented experience. And I find it very hard to account for.
>
> Under the terms of my contract with the producers, I was to be paid a bonus of $25,000 if I got screen credit. Or, to put it another way, the producers would save themselves $25,000 if I could be excluded from credit. I would not say this is the reason for their otherwise baffling attitude. I am merely stating a fact.

The confidential Guild Arbitration Committee ruling rejected Thompson's petition for a screen credit, thus restricting his payment to $36,500. "The arbitration was a tense time," his daughter Patricia observes. "Everybody was very upset and devastated when it didn't go our way."

The Getaway opened at Christmas to largely derisive press. Vincent Canby in *The New York Times:* "From where any critic sits, it's impossible to tell whether this confusion is the result of the writing, the direction or the editing. . . . The movie just unravels." Pauline Kael in the *New Yorker:* "There's no reason for this picture—*another* bank heist—to have been made, and there's no energy in the tossed-together script. . . ." While many critics praised the solid supporting performances—especially Al Lettieri's as Rudy, and Sally Struthers's as Fran Clinton, the veterinarian's wife—Ali MacGraw's Carol McCoy heaped the harshest scorn. Jay Cocks in *Time:* "As a screen personality, MacGraw is abrasive. As a talent, she is embarrassing. Supposedly a scruffy Texas tart, MacGraw appears with a designer wardrobe and a set of Seven Sisters mannerisms." And Kael concluded: "As for McQueen and MacGraw, they strike no sparks on the screen. . . . The audience, which had a good time hooting at her, loved it when he smacked her face—her haughty nostrils and schoolgirl smirk seemed to ask for it. . . . Last time I saw Candice Bergen, I thought she was a worse actress than MacGraw; now I think that I slandered Bergen."

Director Peckinpah retreated into reappraising his work as a "satire." Despite scelerate reviews, *The Getaway* realized $18 million domestically, $35 million worldwide, making it the fifth highest-grossing film (after *The Godfather, The Poseidon Adventure, Jeremiah Johnson,* and *Deliverance*) of 1972.

• • •

With his earnings from *The Getaway,* Thompson leased an upscale, twelfth-floor penthouse down the hill, at 1850 Whitley Avenue. Jim and Alberta refurbished the sunny two-bedroom apartment with Hollywood touches, arranging a grand piano in their spacious parlor. A veranda jutted over a vast kidney-shaped swimming pool, and Thompson posed before the scintillating water for the Los Angeles magazine *Westways,* discordantly caparisoned in a black suit and shirt as tanned swimmers cavorted behind him.

Mike Medavoy witnessed no correspondent elevation of his client's industry status. "The hope was that Jim would write a good-enough screenplay for *The Getaway* that it could become a credential for him to go on to write other films, whether they were based on his own work or not," Medavoy recapitulates. "But he didn't last long enough to get the credit." The agent negotiated small options on *A Hell of a Woman* and *Pop. 1280* with a forgotten French producer. "I didn't see great big movies coming out of these things; I saw interesting films, and got Jim whatever I could." For all his clout, Medavoy couldn't sell Thompson as a commercial scriptwriter. "Jim never adapted to the Hollywood mold. He really wasn't a screenwriter per se, he was a novelist who wrote a certain kind of book very well. Jim was too dark for Hollywood. And everybody was going with the new, young talent. The irony is that today, all the young guys love his stuff."

Thompson fired Medavoy in June 1973. His portfolio traveled to John Ptak at the International Famous Agency, the other talent stream that, after merging with CMA, created ICM, who remembers:

> Most of the time Jim talked about the old days. He seemed less concerned with what was going on than what had gone on. He talked about the early years writing for true crime magazines, and told a lot of those stories. He was like an old fisherman with his stories.
>
> In a short period of time he would have three or four shots of bourbon out of a shot glass. That's painted in my mind. It's not something you see—more out of a cowboy movie. I think Jim had a particular image of himself: a guy who's a crusty old man, who's bitter, and who drinks out of a shot glass. He knew that's who he was, but he didn't like it. But he *played* it, played the role. That was the irony. People get very good at what they play, whether they like it or not.
>
> I think Jim got very caught up in his own persona. That's the way people would come on to him. We had this image of who he was, and he played to that image, he was very good at it. And he could write that way. But at the end of the day, that writing is just paperback original stuff—there's no remuneration for it. Jim looks around, sees other kinds of things happening, and the time's passing by. The very thing he was so good at really did make him somewhat bitter. He lost some time—like, what happened to the sixties, or something? And here you've got all these Hollywood types hanging around him, and kind of exploiting him. Because what does he get out of hanging around and telling people stories?

"Neither Mike Medavoy nor I were his agents in the classic sense of knowing the guy well," Ptak summarizes. "There was no commerce there, so it often really wasn't clear who was representing Jim."

• • •

Sphere Books finally issued *King Blood* in 1973, the last of Thompson's twenty-three original books to see publication. For his author's note on this mongrel western that raised a hymn to his father over the bray of territorial bawdry, he glanced back at his stunted Fort Worth adolescence, silently encoding a less romantic view of Marshal Thompson: "Jim Thompson over-worked his way through high school as a part-time journalist, hotel-worker, burlesque actor-writer, and as a jack-of-all-trades." The retrospective au-thor also overworked his lifetime accomplishment here, inflating his pro-duction to "over fifty novels . . . and innumerable novelettes."

Thompson continued to ply his New York agent, Bob Mills, with "sam-ples." By the early 1970s he seemed long past righting his internal gyro-scope, and the new projects doddered, betraying his personal fatigue and disorientation over the paperback market. In *Kingdom Come* he essayed a stiff historical novel about a fictional 1930s Oklahoma governor, Francis "Crazy Frank" Barrow (loosely modeled on William H. Murray), that resur-rected his old prop, Osage Indian John Stink, comically invoked as Jacob Skunk. For *The Dog* he reprised *Pop. 1280* as a *Beverly Hillbillies* farce of rus-tic spoonerisms and more "funny" names: Jug Slurble, Patience Virtue, Chastity May, George Surprise, and Plinkplank Plunk. Thompson embarked on another hotel novel, *The Jesus Machine,* in the mock-racist cant of *Child of Rage,* and he conjured up another Southern Californian psychotic news-paperman for *Sunrise at Midnight.*

Only one of these late "samples," *The Rip-Off,* he bothered to carry through, apparently convinced that Sphere Books would print it. But the radical chic title couldn't resuscitate the creaky double-indemnity insur-ance scam story, or the spent Thompson shtik. Nearly everyone seems out to kill narrator Britton Rainstar: his crippled (or is she?) estranged wife, his mercurial girlfriend, his baffling nurse (if that's what she is), and the sinister PXA Corporation. A few quirky, promising strokes around the margins—Rainstar's employment as a writer of ecological reports for the Rockefeller-like Hemisphere Foundation, his crumbling mansion on the city dump, the information that his ancestors number among them an In-dian chief whose portrait, by Remington, hangs in the Metropolitan, or that his professor father was destroyed by the House Un-American Activities Committee—dissipate in the mash of feeble motives and Thompson's least plausible women. The reader runs whole chapters ahead of the plodding Rainstar, who floats through *The Rip-Off* on a raft of self-pity:

> I don't know how you are in such situations, but I always feel guilty. The mere need to explain, that such and such is a mistake, et cetera, stiffens my smile exaggeratedly and sets me to sweating profusely, and causes my voice to go tremulous and shaky. So that I not only feel guilty as hell, but also look it.

Thompson also interjected what would be his final word on alcohol: "Drink-ing was probably all that made life-become-existence tolerable . . . as it probably is for all who drink."

Sphere Books passed. *The Rip-Off* would appear posthumously and heavily edited as a serial in *The New Black Mask Quarterly* (1985). When Thompson mailed his manuscript to Mills on June 18, 1974, he appended a sad, pointed crack about his cataracts, and the novel. "I think it might have been better if I could have seen what I was doing."

• • •

Over the Labor Day weekend, the Thompsons moved from their scenic penthouse into a narrow, second-floor apartment at 1817 Hillcrest Road, not far from the Hollywood Bowl. Although the white Moroccan-style building bordered a sloping park with a banyan tree, "the place was a real dump," according to their daughter Sharon, who along with her husband, Jim, and the two young grandchildren, Terri Ann and Jami Michelle, provided assistance. "My daughter Jami remembers my father teasing and playing with her the day they moved to the last apartment," Sharon recalls. "My dad was drinking very heavily that day. Jami remembers him going *putt-putt-putt* like a gun or a car, and she thought this was hilarious. My dad could be very charming that way. But he also wasn't helping them move. He didn't do things like that." Sending his new address to Bob Mills in New York, Thompson enclosed another prickly joke as his postscript: "Hope you can notify any interested parties, if such there be, of the above change."

His friend and former agent, Jerry Bick, took over Thompson's Hollywood business after the departure of Medavoy and Ptak. "There were a lot of late-night phone calls from Jim," he complains. "Jim was always frustrated, because he was not really in demand." While Bick proved no more resourceful for dredging up script work, he steered Thompson to his first acting role since his 1922 walk-on in a lost Texas silent comedy. That summer Bick optioned *Farewell, My Lovely,* intending to produce a third film version of Raymond Chandler's novel, this time with Robert Mitchum as Philip Marlowe. Believing that Thompson might be perfect for the part of the ailing Judge Baxter Wilson Grayle, "the most powerful political figure in Los Angeles," he proposed the writer to director Dick Richards.

Alberta drove Jim to the Goldwyn Studios for his audition shortly before Christmas. As Richards narrates:

> I had been reading his stuff for years and years. I was a fan. I didn't test Jim actually, I just talked with him for a long time. We looked at many people for Judge Grayle, but right away I knew he was my guy. I liked the fact that Jim was forthright, just like Mitchum; he was completely in the spirit of the movie. He wasn't going to tell you a lie about anything. Plus, Jim had a Southern aristocratic quality about him, an elegance. He looked like he could

A publicity still from Farewell, My Lovely—
Jim Thompson with Robert Mitchum as Philip
Marlowe (Courtesy of the Thompson family)

own half of L.A., or he could collect jade, the way Judge Grayle
does . . . a connoisseur's look.

We sat for a long while talking about Chandler, and what I was
attempting to do with the movie, with Mitchum, and the period. We
talked about who Judge Grayle is—I wanted him to really understand that. But you don't have to say very much to a guy who's
written so many good books. When someone has lived as full a life
as Jim, you don't tell him how to act.

Thompson was paid scale for his performance, yet "getting into
Farewell, My Lovely was a big boost for Jim," Bick counters. "It got him medical coverage through the Screen Actors Guild, and Jim needed that badly.
And he just felt good because he was doing *something,* as his writing wasn't
exactly coming along at that point."

In February, Thompson joined the *Farewell, My Lovely* troupe of Mitchum, Charlotte Rampling, Sylvia Miles, Anthony Zerbe, Jack O'Halloran, Harry Dean Stanton, John Ireland, and Sylvester Stallone at the old Harold Lloyd estate in Beverly Hills for his shoot. "While Jim Thompson wasn't what he is today, of course, there was this underground knowledge of his work," Dick Richards remarks, "and Mitchum certainly knew who he was." (Jim told Alberta that he had interviewed Mitchum inside the Los Angeles County Jail for the *Mirror* after the actor's 1948 conviction for marijuana possession.) Thompson's four days on the set upended the Hollywood caste system: Mitchum solicitously fetched him sandwiches and coffee, as the writer dispensed supper invitations to a young stunt double, Jim Sparkman. "It was the first time I had ever been around a movie," reviews Sparkman, who would later stand in for Bruce Dern on *After Dark, My Sweet.* "And he was a little bit uncomfortable being an actor, because that was something new for him. He introduced me to his wife, and they used to invite me over to his house all the time, and to Musso & Frank's. I remember him as a lovely, sweet old man, and I quite enjoyed Alberta."

Anchored by Mitchum's iconic Marlowe, and the moody, neon-lit 1940s ambience, *Farewell, My Lovely* imparted an elegiac homage to classic *film noir.* Thompson's scenes were brief, but resonant. One framed an electric pop-culture frisson, as Judge Grayle greets Philip Marlowe and two generations of American crime fiction—Jim Thompson's and Raymond Chandler's—shake hands. The judge later opens a door on Marlowe entwined in his young wife's arms. Arnold Hano gilded this moment for the conclusion of his Los Angeles *Times* obituary of Thompson. "When his wife in the film, played by Charlotte Rampling, carried on with Robert Mitchum in front of Jim, there is a look on his face that is part bewilderment, part despair, and all forgiveness."

Richards previewed *Farewell, My Lovely* for Thompson at his house on Mandeville Canyon Road. "Jim said, 'That's right!' the minute Mitchum walked on as Marlowe," the director reports. "Afterwards, I congratulated him on his own great performance. He didn't say anything, but this big smile came over his face."

His other brush with Hollywood that year was not so merry. Four years earlier, on May 20, 1971, Warner Brothers finally purchased the movie rights to *The Killer Inside Me,* evidently compensating Thompson only a few desperate thousand dollars. Directed by Burt Kennedy, with Stacy Keach as Lou Ford, Tisha Sterling as Amy Stanton, and cult actress Susan Tyrrell as Joyce Lakeland, *The Killer Inside Me* almost merits enshrinement at midnight theaters devoted to camp cinema. The setting substitutes rural Montana for small-town Texas, and Ford studies *The Games People Play* instead of Krafft-Ebing. His every manifestation of *"the sickness"* is accompanied by queasy gothic lighting, tortured *Psycho* music, and, most bizarrely, a crescendo of dripping faucets.

Warner Brothers released *The Killer Inside Me* late in 1975, mainly to Southwestern drive-ins. When Thompson witnessed this car wreck of a film, Sharon describes him as "stunned" and "speechless." He regretted to his deathbed the cheap sale of his most celebrated novel. "Daddy could barely speak, but he kept saying over and over, 'Sharon, it was a bad deal. I never should have made it. It was a bad deal, Sharon. . . .' "

• • •

Alberta Thompson suffered a heart attack at home during the spring of 1975, and was transported unconscious by ambulance to Hollywood Presbyterian Hospital. Jim waited for the assurance that she would live before he phoned his daughters, Sharon in nearby Huntington Beach, and Patricia in Scottsdale, Arizona. Throughout Alberta's hospital stay, he visited every day for as long as the doctors would allow. "I've never seen a man so upset, and so determined to see his wife, if only for ten minutes," his sister Maxine conceded. "When everything was said and done, he really cared."

Jim assumed all nursing responsibilities upon Alberta's release. Although he was hobbled himself now by poor circulation, he transacted the shopping and cleaning, along with his customary stint in the kitchen. "Seeing Mother sick must have just terrified him," Sharon suggests. "He did everything he could for her until she was out of danger."

While he attended Alberta, Thompson was approached by Alain Corneau, who invited him to adapt *Pop. 1280* for "an American film with a French production." At thirty-two, Corneau, a former jazz musician, had recently scored a critical success as the director of *France Société Anonyme.* "*Pop. 1280* was a mythic book," he explains. "It was number 1,000 in the *Série Noire.* "

Corneau drafted a scenario in London, and then flew into Los Angeles with the financial backing of Jacques Perrin to work with Thompson on an English screenplay. "I remember that our adaptation was close enough to the novel, but more violent. The script opened with some people eating dirt. Jim said that he had seen people do this." Corneau hoped to reassemble the cast of *The Wild Bunch* for *Pop. 1280,* with Warren Oates as Sheriff Nick Corey, Ernest Borgnine as Ken Lacey, and smaller roles for L. Q. Jones and Strother Martin.

Much like Dick Richards, Corneau was moved by the aging American novelist's courtliness; yet he also came to observe Thompson's fury:

> I found him a very funny man, very dapper, with considerable class, even though he was handicapped a bit physically, and

Jim in the Hollywood Hills, 1975 (Courtesy of
the Thompson family)

walked with difficulty. There was also in him a kind of dark rage. I
saw him get angry; it was very impressive. He was angry at everyone around him. At Americans. At his family. He thought that the
entire world was crazy. He also thought that the entire world
wanted him to be crazy too. His books clearly were a life raft for
him.

Jim spoke to me many times about his Indian origins. He had a
very noble physique, why not? He was of mixed blood, Cherokee
he told me. He also told me that his Indian origins disturbed him
enormously, and there are often racial problems in his books, characters caught between two worlds.

Thompson executed a passable 108-page screenplay for *Pop. 1280,* but
he never resolved the puzzle of translating Nick Corey's inward menace
into filmic images, and the dialogue slumped under the freight of his
speeches. Corneau eventually pronounced the project "infeasible."

Two years after Thompson's death, the director would adapt *A Hell of
a Woman* as *Série Noire* from a cunning script by the experimental novelist
Georges Perec, each conversation a sinuous shroud of French clichés.

"Perec found Thompson's novel formidable," Corneau notes. "He saw in *A Hell of a Woman* the myth of Orpheus."

• • •

Emboldened by Alain Corneau's reverence for *Pop. 1280*, Jim flew to New York in August 1975 with an idea for a new novel. He tested his "white bell-boy, Negro porter" story on Jim Bryans, who "expressed an interest," as Thompson notified Bob Mills. He also met Knox Burger for a drink at the Lion's Head on Christopher Street, where they ran into novelist David Markson, once an associate editor at Lion Books. "Jim looked like a man whose feet hurt him," Burger remarks, adding, "I said I'd buy him lunch sometime, and he just sort of shuffled off. This was the last time I saw him."

Back in Hollywood, Thompson buckled down to *A Penny in the Dust*, a title he recycled from his *Dr. Kildare* treatment. Posting his "sample" to Bob Mills on September 23, he confessed that "*Penny* is, in many respects, a true story, and a portrait of the author as a young man. It has not been an easy one to write, but I felt impelled to write it." Set around "Fort Value," Texas, during the early 1920s, *Penny in the Dust* tracks the circumstances leading to the crack-up of young Robert Hightower, promising high school student, night bellhop for a dissolute downtown hotel, and the improbable mainstay of his unraveling family. Thompson exposed his ambivalence about the wisdom of such a manifestly autobiographical book, only tangentially connected to the crime genre. "I am sure it has many things wrong with it," he wrote Mills. "I am similarly convinced that much about it is right, and as it has to be." He sealed the letter with a wry biblical allusion to Alberta's hospital bills: "Needless to say, my financial situation is what it almost always has been, though I am still unaccustomed to it. Which is another way of saying that time is of the essence: *Heb. 13–8.*"

Never published, never finished, *A Penny in the Dust* is the major loss among Jim Thompson's lost novels. Shunning the tall tales of *Bad Boy* and *Roughneck,* or the drunkard's pathos of "An Alcoholic Looks at Himself," he chased the ghost of his estrangement back to the Hotel Texas, Polytechnic High School, and his own disintegrating Fort Worth clan. His spare, barbed phrases snag period attitudes toward race (Robert Hightower is carrying on with a black maid at the hotel), homosexuality (Robert's beloved English teacher, Edgar Allan Linker), and unemployment (Robert inadvertently causes the firing of his predecessor on the night bells), but his portraits cut the deepest. The ineffectual mother—"a tall, graying, severe-looking woman in an old gingham dress and a floppy picture-hat"—who can relax her anger only by "banging things around on the stove" or while weeding, "swinging the hoe in quick short chops, lips moving with what could only be a stream of doggones and goshdarns." The defeated father—"he looked shabby and rumpled and beaten (and like he expected to be beaten some more)"—who waits for Robert to come home from school so that he can borrow money, and "found sanctuary in dreams of the glorious past, or wandered gloomily, broodingly through a hell without exit." The bewildered son, who admits, "I could only talk by being what I was not."

Coming near the end of his life, *A Penny in the Dust* transmitted the urgency of a secret disclosure, as though Thompson yearned to peel back the lurid husk from his crime fiction. When Robert Hightower musters his verbal masks, or performs his "role" as the "Typical Teenage Son," or needles his school principal with praise, it's impossible for a reader not to hear in this "portrait of the author as a young man" the distant original of Lou Ford's voice, Nick Corey's, Dolly Dillon's, Clinton Brown's, Charlie Bigger's, and Allen Smith's. . . . The lines and angles rebound from novel to novel like mirrors on mirrors down a long hallway.

Bob Mills immediately forwarded *A Penny in the Dust* to Jim Bryans. The old Lion editor, now an associate editor at Bernard Geis Associates, silently shelved it.

Six weeks later, on November 3, Thompson impatiently mailed Mills another manuscript that, unfortunately, shaped not so much self-revelation as self-parody. A slapstick television serial profiling a clumsy, Mr. Magooish detective, and more redolent of the mid-1950s than the mid-1970s, Thompson's teleplay for *Peter Parker (Private Peeper)* was unremarkable. Not so his miserable letter that accompanied it:

> I wrote this several years ago, and presented it to a team of agent-packagers. They were wildly enthusiastic, amd made a pitch on it. (I mean they just didn't submit the manuscript; they went in personally, and pitched.)
>
> But—and here comes the sad part, the kind of terrible bad break which has pursued me all my life—*but* at this point in my career, a relative by marriage [Irving Townsend, Freddie's husband, and a CBS executive], who was highly placed in the industry, stepped in. Unbeknownst to me, he had picked up a copy of the script and passed it on to the executive in charge of such projects. And he advised said executive that I was his brother-in-law, and that he would like to see him "do something for me." He meant well, of course. But when my agents-packagers appeared, they were curtly dismissed (a scandal was building at the time about nepotism in the business). They, needless to say, were furious with me. And the script was thrown back at me with some rather nasty comments. So I never showed it anywhere else.
>
> Incidently, it should never be shown at CBS—repeat, never at CBS, as I am identified there as a brother-in-law seeking help. . . .

"Flukish Fate," again. Thompson's late letters to Bob Mills often grind with resentments and self-pity, melancholy asides tossed into the gears of his business:

- *Everything looks a little dim to me these days, so I am never sure whether something actually is or isn't.*

- *This is my last copy of* The Killer Inside Me.

- *Whoever the person is, in your office, who addresses me as James I wish she would stop. The name infuriates me. (Which is why I don't use it.)*

Shortly after Thanksgiving, 1975, Jim entered Hollywood Presbyterian Hospital for cataract surgery on his right eye. The procedure transpired smoothly but failed to improve his vision. Depressed, he canceled an operation scheduled for his other eye.

His poor eyes, if only by tactful retrospection, haunted his own account of the next downturn. Universal City Studios approached his latest Hollywood agent, Peter Thomas of Bart-Levy Associates, regarding the purchase of movie rights to *South of Heaven.* Robert Mulligan, director of *Fear Strikes Out; To Kill a Mockingbird; Baby, the Rain Must Fall; Up the Down Staircase;* and *Summer of '42,* was eager to adapt the novel. The sale Thomas negotiated with Universal apparently promised Thompson more money than his step-deal for *The Getaway.*

Alberta drove Jim to the Bart-Levy offices on Wilshire Boulevard for the formal contract signing. But instead of the anticipated celebration and the grandest check of his life, he found a grim, annoyed Peter Thomas. Columbia Pictures was pressing a chain-of-title claim to *South of Heaven* based on the reassignment of motion pictures rights from Bi-Plane Cinematograph, Thomas informed Thompson. He showed the writer his signature on the May 15, 1970, purchase agreement; the $10 contract licensed Bi-Plane Cinematograph as "the Purchaser [to] assign all or any portion of the rights granted to him hereunder to any person, firm or corporation." The novel did not belong to him. For slightly more than the price of a bottle of Jack Daniels, Thompson had lost his rights to *South of Heaven* "forever."

"Jimmie came down to the car looking like someone had kicked him in the face," Alberta recalls. "He didn't remember signing away the rights. And he knew nothing at all about Columbia getting them. He kept saying, 'I cannot believe what's happened. I can't believe Tony [Bill] and Vern [Zimmerman] would do this to me.' He said his signature on the contract looked like he had been drunk."

With the aid of his nephew, Tony Kouba, Maxine's son and a lawyer in

the firm of Arrigo & Kouba, Thompson prepared to sue. The complaint
Kouba filed with the Superior Court for the County of Los Angeles against
Tony Bill, Vernon Zimmerman, and Columbia Pictures the following summer alleged "mistake" as the secondary cause of action, and "fraud" as the
first cause—Thompson's anguished memoir of bad faith and duplicity
cloaked in stilted legalese:

> 7. . . . Defendants TONY BILL and VERNON ZIMMERMAN de-
> veloped a close and confidential relationship with the Plaintiff.
> During this period of time, TONY BILL, who was 29 years of age in
> 1970, and VERNON ZIMMERMAN, who was 32 years of age in 1970,
> on numerous occasions praised and flattered Plaintiff, who was 64
> years of age in 1970, for the quality of his literary works. Further,
> they were invited to Plaintiff's home, invited Plaintiff to their
> homes, traveled with Plaintiff to various locations throughout the
> United States in apparent mutual efforts to promote the produc-
> tion of various literary works of Plaintiff, frequently dined with
> Plaintiff, were frequently asking for, and were loaned, rare copies of
> Plaintiff's novels which previously had gone out of print, and gen-
> erally developed and sustained a relationship with Plaintiff as
> friends, confidants, and trusted business relations. . . .
>
> 10. . . . in or about June or July of 1970, Plaintiff and Defen-
> dants entered into an oral agreement pursuant to which Plaintiff
> was to prepare such an original screenplay in return for provision
> to him of office space at the offices of Defendant COLUMBIA PIC-
> TURES INDUSTRIES, INC., plus the payment of money.
>
> 11. . . . Plaintiff began the preparation of such a screenplay
> at an office provided to him within the COLUMBIA PICTURES IN-
> DUSTRIES, INC. facility. During this period of preparation of the
> screenplay, no written agreement was entered into between Plain-
> tiff or Defendants, although Plaintiff was paid by Defendants in ac-
> cordance with their promises.
>
> 12. In or about August of 1970, Defendants informed Plaintiff
> that it would be necessary to sign a written contract with reference
> to the screenplay.
>
> 13. Defendants, TONY BILL and VERNON ZIMMERMAN orally
> stated to Plaintiff that said contract in no way affected Plaintiff's
> rights to SOUTH OF HEAVEN, which Defendants were aware ex-
> isted, but only memorialized the agreement with reference to the
> preparation and use of the unnamed original screenplay. . . .
>
> 14. In reliance upon these representations, and without the as-
> sistance and advice of legal counsel or a literary agent, Plaintiff
> executed documents apparently comprising that agreement pre-

sented to him by Defendants without reading their terms. Said agreement was lengthy and detailed and was presented to Plaintiff at a time when his eyesight and physical condition were poor, and when Plaintiff and Defendants were in an informal setting.

15. The representations referred to in paragraph 12 hereinabove were false and were known by Defendants to be false, and were made by Defendants to Plaintiff with malice and the intent to deceive and defraud Plaintiff into signing an agreement which purportedly disposed of all his screen rights to SOUTH OF HEAVEN in favor of Defendants in return for $10.00 consideration.

16. Plaintiff's apparent agreement to said agreement was obtained through said fraud and deceit and breach of fiduciary relationship between him and Defendants, and Plaintiff would not have given his consent to said agreement without said fraud, deceit, and breach of fiduciary relationship, in that Plaintiff relied solely upon Defendants' advice and judgement and representations in signing said agreement. . . .

For each of his two causes of action, Thompson sought $100,000 in compensatory damages, and $5,000,000 in exemplary damages.

The Thompson family contends that the court complaint's references to "poor eyesight" and "an informal setting" were euphemisms for a still darker deception. "Tony Bill and Vernon Zimmerman met Jimmie at Musso & Frank's, got him drunk, and had him sign papers," Alberta claims. "*Hard Times* was supposed to be an original screenplay that had nothing to do with *South of Heaven.* These were people he knew and trusted, and they stole it." Tony Kouba's rough notes on the complaint specify that Thompson asserted that it was Zimmerman (and not himself, as Bill reported) who first introduced *South of Heaven* into the *Hard Times* discussions: "At one pt. Vernon said 'you wrote novel about Hobos in *South of Heaven*'—didn't want competition—Jim agreed to hold book off market *before* contract was signed—Zimmerman said we'll pay—Jim refused—later got $10 check 'to make oral agreement legal'—Zimmerman said that's O.K."

Tony Bill has occasionally denied remembering that Bi-Plane Cinematograph ever acquired *South of Heaven.* "I think Jim may have made a side deal with Columbia when we were making a deal for his hobo script," he explained to the Los Angeles *Times* in 1990. "But in tracing down the rights . . . [producer] Mark Lipson determined that I originally owned the rights to it. But I have no recollection of that." Bill's denial sounds, at best, disingenuous, particularly given the legal action against him. But Thompson's court complaint also dodged a few awkward items. On May 15, 1970, the Plaintiff, of course, signed another agreement with Bi-Plane Cinematograph "as a scenario writer in connection with our proposed motion picture based upon that certain published work presently entitled *South of Heaven.*" Did Thompson forget—or misunderstand—this contract, as well?

Still, the sawbuck deal appears suspect. The $10,000 Thompson received from Bill and Zimmerman for *Hard Times* disposed a fair wage for a screenplay in 1970, yet a shameful sum for a screenplay *and* the motion picture rights to a novel. If Bi-Plane Cinematograph and Columbia Pictures merely intended to protect *Hard Times,* why did they find it necessary to bind the rights "forever"? *South of Heaven* could have been tied up through a limited option. Ten-dollar options occur in Hollywood, usually to float a project. But a $10 sale smacks of flimflam.

The intrusion of *South of Heaven* onto an American hobo script that all parties agree was an original screenplay probably will stay a riddle. Because of recent changes in the copyright laws, film rights to the novel reverted to the Thompson estate twenty-eight years after publication, that is, in 1995.

Thompson's court complaint portrayed him much as he had shaded his oilman father for his 1930s oral history, "The Drilling Contractor": naive, unsuspecting, each Jim Thompson ready to close a negotiation over a congenial meal instead of at a lawyer's office, their trust and generosity betrayed by men they deemed friends. For both father and son the vexation of bad bargains exacted its toll. "To this day I think that what happened with *South of Heaven* was partially to blame for his death," Thompson's daughter Sharon insists. "That really was the beginning of the end for my father."

• • •

Scarcely two weeks after his cataract operation, Thompson dispatched a new "sample" to Bob Mills in New York. His pages were typed so erratically that his agent could not decipher them. Over Christmas, Thompson sifted the opening chapters of the novel back through his Smith Corona "with some extra-powerful glasses, and I hope I've been able to catch any boners." Early in the new year he posted the manuscript again. "This is an offbeat, scarily humorous crime story which builds to a hair-raising climax," Thompson chimed for Mills, in lieu of an outline. "Having been a newspaper man here, with first-hand police and criminal contacts, and having worked extensively in motion pictures and television, I think I am uniquely qualified to tell a story which is itself unique." His hero was a hoot: a crusty Hollywood police captain, gourmet cook, Tom Lehrer fan, and, apparently, still a virgin, whose furtive erections keep bursting the fly on his trousers despite a rig of safety pins and staples. The ominous set-up, involving a hazy organization known only as "The Holders," blew a whiff of paranoia into the sketchy plot. This was the last book Thompson would ever work on. His title, aptly enough: *Exit Screaming.*

On the Saturday morning of January 24, 1976, as he read a newspaper at the kitchen table of his Hillcrest apartment, Thompson suffered a severe stroke. "We were going to the grocery store, the way we did every Saturday, and Jimmie was looking at the ads in the paper," Alberta remembers. "I said something to him, and he didn't answer. I looked over and his glasses were cocked funny. So I got hold of Dr. Bisharat, and we got him to the hospital right away."

Hollywood Presbyterian Hospital held him just a week, although at first Thompson couldn't speak at all. Gradually he recovered sufficient language to formulate words and phrases, but for the rest of his life his mind raced ahead of his mouth, while his sentences, agonizingly, misfired. "It took him a long time to say anything, and the family often had to guess what he was saying, help him get it out," Alberta relates. Then, three Saturdays after his stroke, seizures started, much like aftershocks from a quake. "Jimmie started shaking, like epilepsy, and I called the paramedics, and he was back in the hospital."

For the next ten months, Thompson shuttled in and out of Hollywood Presbyterian Hospital, with seizures, small strokes, and for an operation on his carotid arteries. Sharon and Michael huddled close by, on call. Patricia flew in from Scottsdale with her husband, Max Miller, and the four grandchildren, Helene, Marla, Lisa, and Bryan. A smattering of old friends visited—Arnold Hano, Jerry Bick, Bob Goldfarb. And, of course, his sisters, Maxine and Freddie. To Maxine, Thompson haltingly confided his distress: "You know, I'm a man of words. . . ."

From his bed in Room 373 at the Hollywood Presbyterian Hospital, Thompson dictated his final changes for the complaint against Tony Bill, Vernon Zimmerman, and Columbia Pictures. Tony Kouba filed the papers with California Superior Court on August 10. "Jimmie was too ill to give his deposition," Kouba regrets, "so the complaint was dropped." Kouba discloses that Thompson contemplated a second lawsuit, this against Bill and Robert Redford for *The Sting*. "Jimmie believed that they got the idea for *The Sting* from *The Grifters.*"

Over the summer, a young Hollywood cameraman reached Thompson at the Hillcrest apartment about a movie he wished to co-write with Orson Welles. "I stumbled across *The Killer Inside Me*, looking for a good story," Gary Graver relates, "but when I contacted the publisher, I found out that the picture had already been made. I got Thompson's address—he was living in a building a friend of mine owned back of Grauman's Chinese Theatre, an old Raymond Chandler kind of place."

Graver phoned Alberta, and she invited him over. "Jim was very weak from his stroke, but they gave me a whole bunch of books, which I Xeroxed." says Graver. He conveyed the photocopies back to Welles:

> Orson and I split up the books—he read half, and I read half, then we switched. First, I wanted to do *Pop. 1280,* but Orson figured

it would be way too expensive, with the black shanty-town burning. So we both agreed that *A Hell of a Woman* would be the one.

I optioned it for $2,000 a year, and Orson and I set out to write the screenplay. Orson had me go down to the butcher shop and get a roll of paper. I was at his house, and we rolled it out and hung it up on all four walls. From there we wrote down what happened in each chapter—some things we were going to leave out, some things we were going to keep in, and some things we mixed around. Then we wrote the screenplay together.

I changed the title to *The Dead Giveaway,* which I thought was more commercial and simpler, and because it was about a guy going door to door giving gifts away, and there were so many murders. I announced in *Variety* that I was going to direct the picture with my friend Bud Cort as Dolly Dillon. Orson was going to play Staples, the manager of the store. And I talked to Jocelyn Brando, Marlon's sister, about playing the aunt.

The Dead Giveaway joined the scrapheap of lost Welles, and lost Thompson films.

Early in November, while at home, Thompson suffered another massive stroke. An ambulance delivered him to Hollywood Presbyterian Hospital, where he hovered in a coma for four days. "The doctors never thought that Jimmie would come out of it," Alberta remarks. "But when he did, they started to call him Superman." The CAT scan revealed "a stroke on top of the stroke," registering further damage to his speech center. Thompson remained under intensive care for nearly a month, before he was transferred to a skilled nursing facility across the street, known as The Chalet.

Alberta and the children attended him in shifts, since The Chalet would only permit Thompson to smoke if a family member was present. As his son Michael recounts:

> He would signal me with his fingers, like he was smoking, or I would take out a cigarette and show it to him, and he'd nod and get a big smile on his face.
>
> When you walked into the place, it was like a funeral parlor. It was dark, and he was in the middle of a three-bed room with nobody else in there.
>
> After he was lying there for about a week, he said to me, "You got to get me out of here." So I went right up to the front office, and we got him out that night.

When he arrived home, Jim made Alberta promise that she would never put him in the hospital again.

• • •

The decorous article about "a courtly, greying gentleman, a distinguished Hollywood screenwriter who would go to his favorite booth at Musso & Frank's, order a drink and have the pot roast special" that Arnold Hano sent back to Thompson could not be located among the writer's papers.

Something like him, though not the elegant Hollywood Squire Jim exactly, but his stranger, more slippery down-home twin, turned up from the October 1973 issue of *Westways:*

> This is my country. Raised on a horse ranch in Northwestern Nebraska. Father a criminal lawyer. Brilliant man, but couldn't handle money. Relatives raised me; half English, half Iroquois. My job was to clean out the stalls. One day, when I was six, I forgot to pat a horse on his flank as I was fixing to pass behind him. He kicked me into the next stall. Cried for days. Couldn't stop. Relatives finally sent me to my grandfather. He stopped me with a shot of whiskey.
>
> Grandfather taught me to drink regular, smoke cigars and play cards. He kept a lot of pulp magazines out in the privy. Told me some men made a good living just writing stories for those magazines. "How do you write a story?" I asked him. "Well, you have a good guy and a bad guy," he told me. So I wrote my first story and sent it off and sold it for eight dollars. Lost the eight dollars to grandfather, who cheated at poker.
>
> Been writin' ever since. Work twenty hours a day, seven days a week. Worked on newspapers. Then put out a magazine. Wrote the whole thing myself, letters to the editor included. Became executive editor of the Police Gazette. That's about as low down as you can get. Then I moved into paperbacks. That's where the money was. Few years ago met a fellow named Stanley Kubrick. Had some trouble with him, but worked it out. Followed him out to Hollywood to write films. Last week my wife told me we needed $25,000 right away to make ourselves whole. Can't raise that kind of money in Los Angeles. New York is my town. Always did well in New York. . . .

Shuffling and drawling through a journalist named Leonard Gross, Thompson went on to rearrange and derange his private myths. His *Bad Boy* saga of his solitary transcontinental bus trip to New York for *Now and on Earth* he transposed from 1941 to 1958. The book that he pounded out, "massively hung over . . . in eleven days . . . in a fleabag hotel," now was *The Getaway.*

. . . The Thompson revival would start to simmer. Alain Corneau released *Série Noire* in 1979. Bertrand Tavernier beat Jean-Luc Godard to *Pop. 1280,* and directed *Coup de Torchon* in 1981. Geoffrey O'Brien published *Hardboiled America.* William Morrow & Company reprinted *The Killer Inside Me* as a Quill Mysterious Classic in 1983. Max Allan Collins and Ed Gorman edited *Jim Thompon: The Killers Inside Him,* including the text of a novella, *This World, Then the Fireworks,* and interviews with Arnold Hano and Alberta Thompson. Barry Gifford reissued *A Hell of a Woman, The Getaway,* and *Pop. 1280* at Creative Arts/Black Lizard in 1984 and, over the next three years, continued with ten more novels. Film options followed on *The Grifters, After Dark, My Sweet,* and *The Kill-Off.* . . . "Just you wait," Thompson told his wife, "I'll become famous after I'm dead about ten years."

• • •

Thompson passed his last Christmas at Sharon's house in Huntington Beach. After dinner on Christmas Day, he asked to be driven down to the ocean. He sat inside the car for a long time, quietly looking out at the Pacific.

Back in his Hillcrest apartment, Thompson struggled to tell stories as Sharon, Michael, or Patricia sat by him on the bed, spooning him food. "Daddy enjoyed telling stories," Sharon says. "Even though he couldn't really speak, he still told stories." They were stories his father told him as a child—"criminals his dad caught, the hanging judge, men who had been misjudged and hung no matter what. I wish that we put all this down someplace."

Then, he stopped eating. "He made up his mind that he wasn't going to eat anymore, and he wouldn't," Alberta concludes. "He would say, 'I don't know whether I'll ever be able to write again, and I couldn't stand that.' And I don't think Jimmie could have, because writing was his life." He wasted away, by the end, to seventy-five pounds.

Jim Thompson died beside Alberta early on April 7, 1977, Holy Thursday. His ashes were scattered from a plane over the Pacific Ocean.

The previous Saturday, Sharon had brought him a malt and two packs of Pall Malls. The malt, he hardly touched. But when she searched for the cigarettes the morning of his death, he had smoked every one.

Notes and Sources

These notes constitute a prose record of the interviews, reading, viewing, and archival research performed in the course of this book. Jim Thompson's life could not have been written without the cooperation I have enjoyed from his family, his friends, his colleagues, and his editors—and my apologies to those individuals whose assistance with letters, manuscripts, photographs, newspaper articles, and information may have been inadvertently overlooked. I also wish to acknowledge background sources not explicitly indicated in the text. For the story of Thompson's life could not have been completed without the aid of many books, essays, articles, and pamphlets, few of which contain his name.

I wish to express, at the outset, my gratitude to the libraries and other organizations that furnished me with materials for this biography, or responded to my inquiries with prompt skill and kindness. In Oklahoma: the Anadarko Public Library; the Anadarko Philomathic Museum; the Anadarko *Daily News;* the Caddo County Election Board; the Oklahoma Historical Society; the Western History Collection of the University of Oklahoma, Norman; the University of Oklahoma Archives, Norman; the Oklahoma City Public Library; the *Daily Oklahoman;* the Oklahoma Attorney General's Office; and the Oklahoma Secretary of State's Office. In Nebraska: the Carnegie Public Library, Burwell; the Burwell School Board; the Nebraska State Historical Society; the Lincoln Public Library; the Library and University Archives of the University of Nebraska, Lincoln; and the Big Springs Public Library. In Texas: the Fort Worth Public Library; the Eugene Barker Texas History Center, University of Texas, Austin; the Texas Secretary of State's Office; and the Harry Ransom Humanities Research Center, the University of Texas at Austin. In Washington: the Library of Congress and the National Archives and Records Service. In California: the San Diego Public Library; the Los Angeles Public Library; the Bancroft Library, University of California, Berkeley; the Margaret Herrick Library, the Academy of Motion Pictures; the Doheny Library, University of Southern California, Los Angeles; and the University Research Library of UCLA, Los Angeles. In New York: the New York Public Library; the New York Public Library for the Performing Arts, Lincoln Center; the Fales Library, New York University; the Elmer Bobst Library, New York University; the Raymond Fogelman Library, the New School for Social Research; the Rare Book and Manuscript Library, Columbia University; Butler Library, Columbia University; the Journalism Library, Columbia University; the Law School Library, Columbia University; and the Rockefeller Foundation Archives, Pocantico Hills, North Tarrytown, New York. Also: Widener Library of Harvard University, Cambridge; the Southern Historical Collection, University of North Carolina Library, Chapel Hill; the Country Music Foundation, Nashville; the Library of the Grand Ole Opry, Nashville; the State Library of Ohio, Columbus; and the State Historical Library of Wisconsin, Madison.

No manuscripts survive for Thompson's hardcover fiction and his Lion books, or even for all of his later novels. While I have attempted to quote only from first editions, on the assumption that these contain the smallest number of typographical and other errors, I have also made use of recent reprints issued by Black Lizard/Creative Arts, Donald I. Fine, Inc., Mysterious Press, and Vintage Crime.

The epigraphs at the head of each chapter come from Thompson's published and unpublished writings. Where the lines were originally spoken by a character or a first-person narrator I have included that name along with the title of the book or manuscript.

All interviews were conducted by the author except for those rare few whose circumstances are indicated in the chapter notes.

These notes, as much as possible, follow the order of appearance of topics within a chapter.

Prologue: Art Savage and His Savage Art

The account of Jim Thompson's death and his memorial service reflects interviews with Alberta Thompson, Sharon Thompson Reed, Patricia Thompson Miller, Freddie Thompson Townsend, Maxine Thompson Kouba, Jerry Bick, Arnold Hano, and the Reverend Ray S. Harris, who presided; and correspondence with K. C. Huse, office manager at the Pierce Brothers Westwood Village Memorial Park & Mortuary.

The quotation by Donald E. Westlake on the Thompson revival originally appeared in an article by Patrick Goldstein, "Hard-boiled Hollywood," for the Los Angeles *Times,* March 11, 1990. Luc Sante's essay-review on Thompson, David Goodis, and Richard Stark, "Gentrification of Crime," was published by *The New York Review of Books,* March 28, 1985. The quotation by William Burroughs is from *Naked Lunch* (New York: Grove, 1962).

For "The Drilling Contractor," my appreciation to the Southern Historical Collection, University of North Carolina Library, Chapel Hill.

A small portion of the prologue originally appeared in a somewhat different form, first in my article "Savage Nights" (Boston *Phoenix,* December 10, 1985) and later in the introduction to *Fireworks: The Lost Writings of Jim Thompson* (New York: Donald I. Fine, 1988; Mysterious Press, 1989).

Hell's Fringe: 1906

The opening sequence on Jim Thompson's first meeting with his wife draws on interviews with Alberta Thompson, and with his Alpha Gamma Rho fraternity brothers Boyd Von Seggern, Eugene Dowell, and William Ralston.

For the descriptions of territorial Oklahoma, the natural setting, the peace officers, outlaws, and territorial politics both at the beginning and later in this chapter, I am indebted to the following books: John Thompson's *Closing the Frontier: Radical Response in Oklahoma, 1889–1923* (Norman: University of Oklahoma Press, 1986), Glen Shirley's *West of Hell's Fringe* (Norman: University of Oklahoma Press, 1978) and *Temple Houston: Lawyer with a Gun* (Norman: University of Oklahoma Press, 1968), Frank Richard Prassell's *The Western Peace Officers* (Norman: University of Oklahoma Press, 1993), Frank M. Canton's *Frontier Trails* (Boston: Houghton Mifflin Company, 1930), Floyd Miller's *Bill Tilghman: Marshal of the Last Frontier* (Garden City: Doubleday, 1968), Elmer LeRoy Baker's *Gunman's Territory* (San Antonio: Naylor, 1969), Danney Goble's *Progressive Oklahoma* (Norman: University of Oklahoma Press, 1980), Moman Pruiett's *Criminal Lawyer* (Oklahoma: Harlow Publishing Corporation, 1944), and *Oklahoma: A Guide to the Sooner State* (Norman: University of Oklahoma Press, 1941); also to interviews with John Thompson, Danney Goble, and Frosty Troy.

Mrs. Jimmy Dark and Jim Thompson's cousins Harriet Cowan Keller, Esther Cowan Winchester, and Pauline Ohmart, wove the Dark/Thompson genealogy from their family documents, birth and death certificates, obituaries, and Bibles. Another cousin, Edna Myers Borden, related the Myers family history for this and the following chapter.

For knowledge of turn-of-the-century Anadarko, I am grateful to Paula McBride, who sent me "The Anadarko *Daily News* Visitors Guide 1988–1989," containing reminiscences by original settlers and other vital texture. Also consulted: Phillip T. Dickerson's *1901 History of Anadarko, O.T. August 6, December 25, Its Past Present and Bright Future;* the Reverend J. J. Methvin's *In the Limelight: History of Anadarko and Vicinity from the Earliest Days;* articles in the Anadarko *Daily Democrat,* the *Daily Oklahoman,* and *Sturm's Oklahoma Magazine;* and an early anonymous *Anadarko Business Directory.*

The record of James Sherman Thompson's tenure as sheriff of Caddo County relies primarily on the frequent reports about him in local newspapers, the Anadarko *Daily Democrat,* the Caddo County *Times,* the Anadarko *County Democrat,* and the Anadarko *Tribune,* as well as on stories in the *Daily Oklahoman,* the *Indian Citizen,* and the *Kingfisher Weekly Star & Free Press.* John H. N. Tindall's *Makers of Oklahoma* (1905) and Homer Croy's *Trigger Marshal: The Story of Chris Madsen* (New York: Duell, Sloan and Pearce, 1958) proved valuable, as did interviews with Edna Myers Borden, Harriet Cowan Keller, Esther Cowan Winchester, and Pauline Ohmart.

The history of Sheriff Thompson's stand for Congress at the August 1906 Oklahoma Republican convention follows accounts in the Guthrie *Daily Leader,* the *Oklahoma State Capital,* the Blackwell *News,* and the *Daily Oklahoman.*

Also interviewed: Maxine Thompson Kouba, Freddie Thompson Townsend, Paula McBride of the Anadarko *Daily News,* and Anadarko county clerk Jack Van Deventer.

White Mother, Black Son: 1907–1919

Edna Myers Borden guided me through Jim Thompson's Burwell childhood, sitting for repeated interviews and supplementing them with her letters, family documents, and a scrapbook of newspaper articles. Pauline Ohmart, Harriet Cowan Keller, Neddie Pinnell, Ted Cowan, and Jocelyn Wicks Rock also were indispensable sources. His Nebraska cousins collectively compiled the inventory of Thompson's boyhood reading in his uncle Bob's library. His friends Elva McWharter and Rex Wagner related their memories of his Burwell school days. General background for Burwell and Nebraska included: H. W. Fought's *Trail of the Loup* (Ord: 1906), *The Garfield County Roundup* 1867–1967, Mari Sandoz's *Old Jules* (Boston: Little, Brown, 1935), *Nebraska: A Guide to the Cornhusker State* (New York: Hastings House, 1939), Sharon O'Brien's *Willa Cather: The Emerging Voice* (New York: Oxford, 1987), and articles in the *Nebraska Farmer.*

For Thompson's childhood residence in Oklahoma City, interviews with Maxine Thompson Kouba, Freddie Thompson Townsend, and Harriet Cowan Keller were crucial. More generally, I benefited from William Cunningham's *The Green Corn Rebellion* (New York: Vanguard Press, 1935), Albert McRill's *And Satan Came Also* (Oklahoma City: Semco Color Press, 1955), the R. L. Polk Oklahoma City street directories for the years 1910 through 1919, a 1923 pamphlet "Where to Go in Oklahoma City and How to Get There" issued by the Oklahoma City Chamber of Commerce, as well as the Oklahoma State Guide, and the books by John Thompson and Danney Goble cited above.

James Sherman Thompson's letters to his family here and in subsequent chapters were preserved among the papers of his daughter Maxine. For the depiction of his business ventures, particularly his partnership with Jake Hamon, I followed "The Drilling Contractor," Francis Russell's *The Shadow of Blooming Grove* (New York: McGraw-Hill, 1968), Samuel Hopkins Adams's *Incredible Era: The Life and Times of Warren Gamaliel Harding* (New York: Capricorn Books, 1964), Ione Quimby's "The Strange Death of Jake Hamon" (in *Master Detective,* August 1930), along with Elmer LeRoy Baker's *Gunman's Territory,* articles in the Tulsa *Daily World,* the *Daily Oklahoman,* and the Oklahoma *News,* and the newspaper clipping file on Hamon at the Oklahoma Historical Society. Kevin Brownlow discusses *Fate,* the film starring Clara Barton Smith Hamon, in *Behind the Mask of Innocence* (New York: Knopf, 1990).

The interview with Jim Thompson about his 1914 summer, traveling Oklahoma with his family, was printed in the Oklahoma *Daily News,* October 21, 1937. He discussed his plans for "a boy's adventure book" in a January 17, 1941, letter to William T. Couch of the University of North Carolina Press, preserved in the Southern Historical Collection, University of North Carolina Library, Chapel Hill.

Also interviewed: J. Anthony Kouba, Patricia Thompson Miller, and Don Vogeler.

My Little Black Book: 1919–1929

Geoffrey O'Brien first addressed the implications of Oklahoma, Nebraska, and Texas geography for Jim Thompson's novels in his essay "Les Thompson Inedits" (*Polar,* Spring 1983). Larry McMurtry's article "How the West Was Won or Lost" was published by *The New Republic,* October 22, 1990.

The sketches of Fort Worth during the 1920s reflect the following books: Robert H. Talbert's *Cowtown—Metropolis* (Fort Worth: Texas Christian University Press, 1956), *Texas: A Guide to the Lone Star State* (New York: Hastings

House, 1969), Robert Norval Richardson's *Texas: The Lone Star State* (New York: Prentice-Hall, 1943), Oliver Knight's *Fort Worth: Outpost on the Trinity* (Norman: University of Oklahoma Press, 1953), the R. L. Polk Fort Worth street directories for the years 1919–29; also: articles and advertisements in the Fort Worth *Press.*

The Texas secretary of state's office furnished incorporation and dissolution papers for James Sherman Thompson's company, Planters Petroleum. The descriptions of the Harding whistle-stop campaign through Oklahoma and Texas follow "The Drilling Contractor," articles in the *Daily Oklahoman* and the Oklahoma *News,* as well as the Russell biography of Harding, *The Shadow of Blooming Grove.*

For valuable background on the West Texas oil fields, relating to the activities of both Jim Thompson and J. S. Thompson: C. A. Warner's *Texas Oil and Gas Since 1543* (Houston: Gulf Publishing, 1939), Kenny A. Franks and Paul F. Lambert's *Voices from the Oil Fields* (Norman: University of Oklahoma Press, 1964), Roger M. Olien's *Oil Boom: Social Change in Five Texas Towns* (Lincoln: University of Nebraska Press, 1982) and *Easy Money* (Chapel Hill: University of North Carolina Press, 1990), Bryce Finley Rynan's University of Texas Master of Arts thesis, *A Sociological Study of the Mail-Order Oil Promoter and His Methods* (1933), Mody C. Boatright's *Folklore of the Oil Industry* (Dallas: Southern Methodist University Press, 1963), and articles in *Western World* and the Fort Worth *Press.*

"The Drilling Contractor" underpins the narrative of Jim Thompson's high school years, his employment as a bellboy at the Hotel Texas, and his 1925 illness, as do interviews with Maxine Thompson Kouba, Freddie Thompson Townsend, Edna Myers Borden, and Harriet Cowan Keller, and correspondence with Ralph Waller of the Fort Worth school system. Thompson's student file in the archives of the University of Nebraska, Lincoln, supports the conclusion that he did not graduate from Polytechnic High School. Weldon I. Hudson assisted me in tracking down the 1924 and 1926 Polytechnic yearbooks at the Fort Worth Public Library. Thompson wrote about his friendship with "Airplane Red" Brown in a March 22, 1958, letter to Marc Jaffe, preserved in the New American Library Papers at the Fales Library, New York University. Freddie Thompson Townsend furnished the detail that her brother was nicknamed "Dolly" by his co-workers at the Hotel Texas.

Thompson outlined his early writing for a 1961 author questionnaire for NAL (Fales Library, NYU). Freddie Thompson Townsend identified his jokes from the humor magazines *Judge* and *Life,* and confirmed his authorship of the two James Thompson poems in *The Will-o'-the-Wisp:* "The Darker Drink" (May–June 1926) and "Winter Trees" (March–April 1929). Edith Deen expanded the *Bad Boy* version of his brief apprenticeship at the Fort Worth *Press.* Thompson's reference to his true crime work as "just pap" appeared in a January 17, 1941, letter to William T. Couch of the University of North Carolina Press (the Southern Historical Collection, University of North Carolina Library, Chapel Hill). Also consulted: *Western World.*

Mel Shestack, Jim Thompson's creative writing student at USC, directed me to Harry Kirby McClintock and Whitey Ford; Mel related the stories Thompson told him about his hobo days in the West Texas oil fields with McClintock and Ford, his writing for *Texas Monthly,* and his experiences of country music. Gordon Friesen, a colleague at the Oklahoma Federal Writers' Project, recounted conversations with Thompson about the Wobblies and the novelist's early reading of Karl Marx. The interview with Pierre Rissient relating to Thompson's

Marxism appeared in *Polar,* May 1979 (translation by the author). Henry Young sent me his biography of Harry Kirby McClintock, *Haywire Mac and the Big Rock Candy Mountain* (Temple: Stillhouse Hollow Publishers, 1981), along with a photograph of Mac, and answered my questions. John W. Rumble graciously permitted me to quote from his interview with Whitey Ford for the Country Music Foundation Oral History Project. For the IWW generally I am indebted to: Joyce Cornbluh's *Rebel Voices: An IWW Anthology* (Ann Arbor: University of Michigan Press, 1964), John Greenway's *American Folksongs of Protest* (New York: Octagon Books, 1970), and Nels Anderson's *The Hobo: Sociology of the Homeless Man* (Chicago: University of Chicago Press, reprinted 1961).

Thompson's *Texas Monthly* writing consists of two pieces of oil field folklore, "Oil Field Vignettes" (February 1929) and "Thieves of the Field" (June 1929). His University of Nebraska friend Art Kozelka generously furnished me with his copies of the *Cornhusker Countryman,* the University of Nebraska undergraduate agriculture magazine that included "Incident in God's Country" (May 1931), Thompson's homage to Haywire Mac, along with another oil field short story, "Bo'ger" (April 1931).

In *Bad Boy* Thompson identified the Texas town where he encountered the model for his *The Killer Inside Me* character Lou Ford as "Big Springs." Most likely, he intended Big Spring, not far (following *Bad Boy*) from Midland and Odessa; and perhaps he conflated the name with that of Big Springs, Nebraska, the town where he ran a movie theater with his father during the early 1930s.

Also interviewed: Alberta Thompson, J. Anthony Kouba, Jeremy Townsend, Randi Roberts, Jocelyn Wicks Rock, Rex Wagner, Elva McWharter, Chet Hagen, and George Carnie.

An American Tragedy: 1929–1935

Art Kozelka, Boyd Von Seggern, Eugene Dowell, Emory Fahrney, Claude Rowley, William Ralston, and Joe McGuiness from the University of Nebraska, Lincoln, chapter of Alpha Gamma Rho, are the sources for many of the details relating to Jim Thompson's college education, his fraternity activities, and the circumstances of his campus and off-campus employment. Kozelka additionally sent me the three unpublished Thompson college short stories, "Oswald the Duck," "The Picture," and "Sympathy": unanticipated prizes. Kenneth Keller and Rudolph Umland recalled the Sunday-evening writing workshops at Professor Wimberley's home. Robert Knoll, Jim McKie, and Elvin F. Frolik added essential college or Lincoln background. For Thompson's student registration card and his college transcript I am obliged to the Office of Registration and Records and to Joseph G. Svoboda, university archivist. Thompson's 1940 application to the Rosenwald Foundation containing the explanation of his poor grades is preserved by the Southern Historical Collection, University of North Carolina, Chapel Hill. Also consulted: Robert Platt Crawford's *These Fifty Years* (Lincoln: The University of Nebraska College of Agriculture, 1925) and *The Magazine Article* (New York: McGraw-Hill, 1931), *University of Nebraska College 1929–1931* (college bulletin), James C. Olson's *History of Nebraska* (Lincoln: University of Nebraska Press, 1966), the Nebraska State Guide, the R. L. Polk Lincoln street directories and the Lincoln Classified Business directories for the years 1928–33, and articles in the Lincoln *Sunday Star* and the *Daily Nebraskan.*

For Jim Thompson's early 1930s writing in the *Prairie Schooner,* the *Cornhusker Countryman,* and the *Nebraska Farmer,* I am additionally indebted to the New American Library Papers (Fales Library, NYU), the newspaper collection at the Nebraska State Historical Society, Paul R. Stewart's *The Prairie Schooner Story* (Lincoln: University of Nebraska Press, 1955), R. L. Paget's *Cap and Gown: Some College Verse* (Boston: L. C. Paget Company, 1931), Edward J. O'Brien's *The Best Short Stories of 1932* (New York: Dodd, Mead and Company, 1932), and the Ben Botkin papers preserved at the University of Nebraska, Lincoln.

His *Prairie Schooner* writing consists of "A Road and a Memory" (Winter 1930), "Character at Iraan" (Spring 1930), and "Gentlemen of the Jungle" (Fall 1931). His *Cornhusker Countryman* stories, in addition to the two items listed for the previous chapter, are "Chink" (February 1931) and "Close Shave" (March 1931).

Lucille Boomer Larson Parsley discussed her relationship with Jim Thompson. I am grateful to Lucille, to Maxine Thompson Kouba and Freddie Thompson Townsend, and especially to Alberta Thompson for their candor. Alberta's niece, Marion Danke, also was helpful.

For "A Night With Sally" (Oklahoma *Labor,* September 17, 1936) my appreciation to Mary Moran, Scott Dowell, and Betty Mathis of the Oklahoma Historical Society. "Arnold's Revenge" was published in *Bandwagon,* February, 1935.

Marc Gerald, former managing editor of *True Detective,* writer for the TV series *America's Most Wanted,* and editor of the captivating anthology *Murder Plus: True Crime Stories from the Masters of Detective Fiction* (New York: Pharos Books, 1992), shared his deep knowledge of true crime, along with historical records about the Macfadden house rules, writers' fees, and editorial practices. Jack Heise and Art Crockett spoke to me from their long experience in the true crime field. Also of great value: Harold Hersey's *Pulpwood Editor* (New York: Frederick A. Stokes Company, 1937), Richard D. Altick's *Victorian Studies in Scarlet* (New York: Norton, 1970), Thomas Boyle's *Black Swine in the Sewers of Hampstead: Beneath the Surface of Victorian Sensationalism* (New York: Viking Penguin, 1989), and Bob Kniseley's article "Uncle Billy and the Mystery of the Stolen Gold" (*Daily Oklahoman,* February 3, 1935). Thompson's April 21, 1948, letter to Joan Kahn at Harper and Brothers Publishers about his true crime writing is preserved at the Harry Ransom Humanities Research Center, the University of Texas at Austin.

Thompson's thirteen known true crime articles consist of "The Strange Death of Eugene Kling" (*True Detective,* November 1935), "Ditch of Doom—The Crimson Horror of the Keechi Hills" (*Master Detective,* April 1936), "The Riddle of the Bride in Scarlet" (*Daring Detective,* October 1936), "Solving Oklahoma's Twin Slayings" (*Master Detective,* March 1938), "Secret in the Clay" (*Master Detective,* March 1939), "Frozen Footprints—Solving the Riddle of Cache Creek" (*True Detective,* May 1939), "Oklahoma's Conspiring Lovers and the Clue of the Kicking Horse" (*True Detective,* August 1939), "The Illicit Lovers and the Walking Corpse" (*Daring Detective,* January 1940), "Case of the Giant Footprints (*Startling Detective,* May 1940), "Catch the Keeper of the Calendar" (*Intimate Detective,* May 1940), "The Dark Stair" (*Master Detective,* June 1946), "Case of the Catalog Clue" (*Master Detective,* July 1948), "4 Murders in 4 Minutes" (*Master Detective,* April 1949).

Jim Thompson's letters to his mother survived among Maxine Thompson Kouba's papers; all of his other personal letters in this chapter courtesy of Alberta Thompson.

Also interviewed: Edna Myers Borden, David Foster, Robert Goldfarb, and Mrs. Martin Heflin. Also consulted: the Big Springs *News,* for the Big Springs Theater.

The Concrete Pasture: 1936–1940

Most of the letters and other documents relating to the Oklahoma Writers' Project derive from two manuscript collections: Records of the Works Progress Administration, Federal Writers' Project, National Archives and Records Service; and Records of the Works Progress Administration, Oklahoma Writers' Project, Oklahoma Historical Society. Some materials, mainly involving the Oklahoma state guide, the *Labor History of Oklahoma,* and Zoe Tilghman, are from the Western History Collection, University of Oklahoma, Norman. Although ultimately I disagreed with many of her conclusions, I am most grateful to Mary Ann Slater, who sent me her unpublished Oklahoma State University M.A. thesis, "The Oklahoma Writers' Project: 1935–1942."

This chapter, about 1930s Oklahoma City, the Oklahoma Writers' Project, and the Oklahoma Communist Party, would have been impossible without the courageous and selfless personal recollections of Gordon Friesen and Sis Cunningham (who retrieved Jim Thompson's party alias, Robert Dillon, among so many other vital aspects, large and small), Eli Jaffe, Ina Wood, and Alta Churchill DeWitt. Interviews with Margaret DeWitt, Pete Seeger, and Savoie Lottinville, if less central, were also valuable.

For the 1930s, Depression America, the Federal Writers' Project, and the American Communist Party, I consulted the following books and articles: Jerre Mangione's *The Dream and the Deal* (Boston: Little, Brown, 1972), Monty Noam Penkower's *The Federal Writers' Project, A Study in Government Patronage of the Arts* (Urbana: University of Illinois Press, 1977) and his 1970 Columbia University Ph.D. dissertation, "The Federal Writers' Project: A Study in Government Patronage of the Arts," William F. McDonald's *Federal Relief Administration and the Arts* (Columbus: Ohio State University Press, 1969), Robert S. McElvaine's *The Great Depression, America 1929–1941* (New York: Times Books, 1984), Richard Pells's *Radical Visions and American Dreams: Culture and Social Thought in the Depression Years* (New York: Harper and Row, 1973), Harvey Klehr's *The Heyday of American Communism* (New York: Basic Books, 1984), Warren I. Susman's *Culture as History: The Transition of American Society in the Twentieth Century* (New York: Pantheon, 1984), Oscar Ameringer's *If You Don't Weaken* (Norman: University of Oklahoma Press, 1983) and his newspaper the *American Guardian,* Daniel Aaron's *Writers on the Left* (New York: Harcourt, Brace & World, Inc., 1961), James R. Green's *Grassroots Socialism: Radical Movements in the Southwest* (Baton Rouge: Louisiana State University Press, 1978), Walter Goodman's *The Committee* (New York: Farrar, Straus and Giroux, 1968), George Lynn Cross's *Professors, Presidents, and Politicians: Civil Rights and the University of Oklahoma* (Norman: University of Oklahoma Press, 1981), Kenneth E. Hendrickson's *Hard Times in Oklahoma* (Oklahoma City: Oklahoma Historical Society, 1983), Mary Hays Marable and Elaine Boylan's *Handbook of Oklahoma Writers* (Norman: University of Oklahoma Press, 1939), Harvey Swados's *The American Writer and the Great Depression* (Indianapolis: Bobbs-Merrill, 1966), Daniel Bell's *Marxian Socialism in the United States* (Princeton: Princeton University Press, 1967), John Patrick Diggins's *The American Left in the Twentieth Century* (New York: Harcourt, Brace, Jovanovich, 1967), Joe Klein's *Woody Guthrie, A Life* (New York: Knopf, 1980), and Suzanne H. Schrems's "Radicalism and Song," in *Chronicles of Oklahoma* (Summer 1984), Bob Wood's "Oklahoma Tells Us How," in *Party Organizer* (August 1937), and Bill Richeson's "Be Bold: Don't Hide Your Face" in *Party Organizer* (April 1938).

For Commonwealth College: Raymond and Charlotte Koch's *Educational*

Commune (New York: Schocken Books, 1972); articles and advertisements in the *Windsor Quarterly* and *Oklahoma Labor;* and an interview with former Commonwealth College student Sis Cunningham.

For the Social Forum School: the Oklahoma secretary of state's office provided a copy of the articles of incorporation, filed September 3, 1936. While the school was attacked—though not by name—by the *Daily Oklahoman,* the only direct references to this Popular Front organization appear in *Oklahoma Labor* (May 7 through July 6, 1939; later *State Democrat*), and it apparently has never been written about since. Louis L'Amour fails to mention the Social Forum School during the account of his Oklahoma years in *Education of a Wandering Man* (New York: Bantam Books, 1989).

For the Writers' Project union: articles in the *Daily Oklahoman,* the Oklahoma *News,* Oklahoma *Labor;* Papers of William and Zoe Tilghman, Western History Collection, University of Oklahoma, Norman; and interviews with Alta Churchill DeWitt, Sis Cunningham, and Gordon Friesen.

For the Southwest Writers' Congress: articles in the Tulsa *World,* the Norman *Transcript,* the *Black Dispatch,* the *Daily Oklahoman,* the Oklahoma *News;* the League of American Writers Papers, The Bancroft Library, University of California, Berkeley; the Benjamin Botkin papers, University of Nebraska, Lincoln; interview with Alta Churchill DeWitt.

For Otto Lucy: narrative follows accounts of his arrest, trial, and conviction in the Oklahoma *News* and the *Daily Oklahoman.* Interviews with Alberta Thompson, Maxine Thompson Kouba, and Freddie Thompson Townsend. Particular appreciation to the librarians at the *Daily Oklahoman* for their diligent retrieval of articles and photographs.

For folklore: additional materials from The Manuscript Division, Library of Congress; articles in the Tulsa *World;* and the Benjamin Botkin papers, University of Nebraska, Lincoln.

For the arrests and trials of Bob Wood, Ina Wood, Fred Maxim, Eli Jaffe, etc.: Gordon Friesen's pamphlet, *Oklahoma Witch Hunt* (Oklahoma City: Oklahoma Committee to Defend Political Prisoners, October 1941); the Reverend Owen A. Knox's pamphlet, *Oklahoma Story—1940* (Washington, D.C.: National Federation for Constitutional Liberties, 1940); articles in the *New Masses* and the *New Republic;* and interviews with Ina Wood, Eli Jaffe, Gordon Friesen, and Sis Cunningham.

Jim Thompson's FBI file was obtained from the U.S. Department of Justice, Freedom of Information–Privacy Acts Section, Records Management Division.

Also interviewed: William Terry Couch, Frank Parman, William Savage, Ted Cowan, Mary Ann Slater, Lucille Boomer Larson Parsley, Suzanne H. Schrems, J. Anthony Kouba, Ann Banks, William Stott, and Sam Fuller.

For the 1930s writing by Jim Thompson discussed in this chapter:

"The End of the Book" appeared in *American Stuff: An Anthology of Prose & Verse by Members of the Federal Writers' Project* (New York: Viking Press, 1937).

Always to Be Blest: Jim Thompson's interview about his novel appeared in the Oklahoma *Daily News,* October 21, 1937; letters about the novel from the Viking Press, Inc., Simon and Schuster, Inc., and Vanguard Press courtesy of Alberta Thompson; interviews with Alberta, Alta Churchill DeWitt, and Gordon Friesen (source for the manuscript-out-the-bus-window story, which concludes the chapter).

"Oklahoma Guide" appeared in the *Sooner Magazine,* February 1938.

"Time Without End" appeared in *Economy of Scarcity: Some Human Foot-*

notes, a "pamphlet-of-the-month" issued by Cooperative Books, Norman, Oklahoma, 1939; reprinted in *The Damned* (New York: Lion Library, 1954).

"Snake Magee's Rotary Boiler" appeared in the magazine *Direction,* October 1939.

Oklahoma: A Guide to the Sooner State (Norman: University of Oklahoma Press, 1941).

Labor History of Oklahoma (Oklahoma City: A. M. Horn, 1939).

We Talked About Labor: Materials relating to this project derive from two manuscript collections, The Rockefeller Foundation Archives, Pocantico Hills, North Tarrytown, New York, and the Southern Historical Collection, University of North Carolina Library, Chapel Hill. Daniel Joseph Singal's chapter on William Terry Couch in his *The War Within: From Victorian to Modernist Thought in the South, 1919–1945* (Chapel Hill: University of North Carolina Press, 1982) was a thoughtful guide, as were Couch's *These Are Our Lives* (Chapel Hill: University of North Carolina Press, 1939) and the interview Couch contributed to the Oral History Project, Columbia. Also consulted: William Stott's *Documentary Expression and Thirties America* (New York: Oxford University Press, 1973).

If Tears Were Bombs: 1941–1951

For 1940s San Diego generally I consulted the following: *California: A Guide to the Golden State* (New York: Hastings House, 1939), the R. L. Polk San Diego street directories for the years 1941–49, some 1940s and 1950s pamphlets from the San Diego Chamber of Commerce, and articles in the *Journal,* the *Tribune-Sun,* and the *Union.* For the Thompsons particularly I drew on interviews with Alberta Thompson, Patricia Thompson Miller, Sharon Thompson Reed, Michael Thompson, Maxine Thompson Kouba, Freddie Thompson Townsend, Randi Roberts, Ted Cowan, Harriet Cowan Keller, Neddie Pinnell, Jean and Larry Perrine; also Jim Thompson's letters to William T. Couch preserved in the Southern Historical Collection, University of North Carolina Library, Chapel Hill; and "An Alcoholic Looks at Himself," *SAGA,* December 1950.

For Thompson's employment at Ryan Aeronautical, and at Solar Aircraft I am indebted to the personnel departments of both companies, and to the August 1941 issue of the *Solar Blast,* an employee newsletter; his military records courtesy of Alberta Thompson.

For their accounts of Jim Thompson's visits to New York in 1941, 1945, and 1950, I am most indebted to his friends Sis Cunningham, Gordon Friesen, and Lois McDowell. Also consulted: the New York City street directories and Manhattan telephone books for 1941 to 1950, the personnel department at TASS, "An Alcoholic Looks at Himself," and Joe Klein's biography of Woody Guthrie. Also interviewed: Pete Seeger, Mrs. Joe Jones, William T. Couch, Dorothy Childs, Dorothy Greenberg, Alberta Thompson, Sharon Thompson Reed, and, for the circumstances of James Sherman Thompson's death, Mrs. Ralph A. Smith. John Hammond sent me a letter about Thompson's 1940s politics, dated December 10, 1985. Jim Thompson's interview with the San Diego *Tribune-Sun* appeared on June 6, 1942.

For information about Franz Horch I am grateful to Roslyn Targ; also to his *New York Times* obituary, December 16, 1951. Ruth Jacobson, Dr. Max Jacobson's widow, discussed her husband's treatment of Thompson during the 1940s and 1950s; also consulted: articles in *The New York Times, Newsweek,* and *New York.*

Many of Jim Thompson's colleagues at the San Diego *Journal* and the Los

Angeles *Mirror* shared reminisences and materials: Fred Kinne, Lionel Van Deerlin, Logan Jenkins, Esther Gwynne, Delmar Watson, Jerry Cohen, Jack Goulding, George Getze, J. E. Murray, Casey Shawhan, Howard Chernoff, Kendis Moss, Neil Morgan, Art Goldberg, John Cornell, Roger Beck, and Elaine St. Johns. For Thompson's articles in the San Diego *Journal,* I want to thank the staff of the San Diego Public Library; for his articles in the Los Angeles *Mirror* the staff of the Los Angeles Public Library. His *Mirror* employee card courtesy of the Los Angeles *Times.*

Information and materials relating to Mary MacLaren provided by Patricia Thompson Miller, Alberta Thompson, and the staff at the Margaret Herrick Library, the Academy of Motion Pictures; also consulted: articles in the Los Angeles *Herald Examiner,* the Los Angeles *Times,* and the Chicago *Tribune,* and McLaren's novel, *The Twisted Heart* (New York: Exposition Press, 1952).

Mel Shestack reconstructed his USC writing class with Thompson and their visit to Haywire Mac; also interviewed: Bob Wade.

All of Jim Thompson's letters to his family in this chapter courtesy of Alberta Thompson.

For additional background on Jim Thompson's writing discussed in this chapter:

Now and on Earth (New York: Modern Age, 1942): for information about how this novel came to be written and published I am most appreciative of Gordon Friesen, Lois McDowell, and Dorothy Childs. The New York Public Library preserved some early Modern Age catalogues and promotional materials. The short story by Robert Heinlein, "They," which Thompson paraphrases in chapter twenty of *Now and on Earth,* appeared in *Unknown,* April 1941. For reviews of this novel: the San Diego *Union* (April 19, 1942), the New York *Herald Tribune* (April 12, 1942), the Springfield *Union-Republican* (April 12, 1942), the *New Republic* (May 25, 1942), and the *New Yorker* (March 28, 1942).

"The Dark Stair" appeared in *Master Detective,* June 1946.

Heed the Thunder (New York: Greenberg, 1946): the Greenberg: Publisher archives are housed in the Rare Book and Manuscript Library, Columbia University. Interviews with Lois McDowell, Dorothy Greenberg, and Edna Myers Borden were most helpful. Maxine Thompson Kouba's letter to her Nebraska cousins about the novel was preserved among her papers. For reviews: the New York *Herald Tribune* (February 24, 1946), and *The New York Times* (March 3, 1946).

Jim Thompson and his mother, Birdie, concocted at least four (and probably more) true crime stories under the name Bird E. Thompson for various digests issued by Superior Publishers/Duchess Printing & Publishing Company of Toronto, Canada, during the 1940s. A Bird E. Thompson letter of October 1, 1945, refers to three already published stories, "The Corpse in the Clearing," "Murder in the City of God, and "Mountain Massacre." "The Corpse in the Clearing" appeared in both *The Weeping Widow* (1946) and *Marijuana Murder* (n.d.). A fourth Bird E. Thompson true crime story, "The Innocent Double," was found among Thompson's papers, along with a western, "The Fort Smith Trail."

Nothing More Than Murder (New York: Harper and Brothers, 1949): Alberta Thompson sketched the history of this novel from *The Unholy Grail* to eventual publication. Correspondence between Thompson and editor Joan Kahn preserved with the Harper and Brothers papers at the Harry Ransom Humanities Research Center, University of Texas at Austin. Sales figures for *Nothing More Than Murder* are from the New American Library Papers (Fales Library, NYU).

For reviews: *The New York Times* (March 6, 1949), the *New Republic* (March 21, 1949), *Saturday Review of Literature* (February 26, 1949).

"When I Go Home and You're Not There" (song), lyrics by Jim Thompson, music by Maurice Devin: unpublished, submitted for copyright January 13, 1950.

SAGA: for vital background I am grateful to Margaret Joyce, a former assistant editor; also advertisements in *Master Detective*. Thompson's main *SAGA* articles consist of the following: "This Could Be Gold, Lady" (anonymous; November 1950), "Those Amazing Gridiron Indians" (November 1950), "A G.I. Returns from Korea" (December 1950), "He Supplies Santa Claus" (by "Dillon Roberts"; December 1950), "An Alcoholic Looks at Himself" (anonymous; December 1950), "Prowlers in the Pear Trees" (February 1951), "Oil Sleuths" (anonymous; February 1951), "Two Lives of John Stink" (March 1951), "Who Is This Man Eisenhower?" (April 1951), "Death Missed a Bet" (by "Dillon Roberts"; April 1951), and "Some Hair for Saucy Chief" (July 1951).

Police Gazette: Harold Roswell, Oscar Fraley, and especially Betty Widmayer contributed valuable color and context; Thompson's short profile of Ted Mack appeared in November 1951.

"Blood from a Turnip" appeared in *Collier's* (December 20, 1952).

Also interviewed: Arnold Hano, Jim Bryans, and Joan Kahn.

How Now, Brown Cow: 1952–1956

Arnold Hano enthusiastically endured numerous interviews about Lion Books and his long friendship with Jim Thompson; Jim Bryans, Harlan Ellison, David Markson, Sidney Offit, and Noah Sarlot added their vivid recollections of Lion or Magazine Management. For 1950s paperbacks generally I consulted Thomas L. Bonn's *Undercover: An Illustrated History of American Mass Market Paperbacks* (New York: Penguin, 1982) and Geoffrey O'Brien's *Hardboiled America* (New York: Van Nostrand Reinhold Company, 1981), as well as articles in *Publishers Weekly*. The quotation from Norman Mailer is from his *Advertisements for Myself* (New York: G. P. Putnam's Sons, 1959).

Mary Milburn met with me in the same Greenwich Village walk-up where she and her husband, George, entertained the Thompsons during the 1950s, and she loaned me letters and manuscripts.

Jim Thompson's correspondence with Anthony Boucher (William Anthony Parker White) and Boucher's reviews of his novels are preserved in the Manuscripts Department, Lilly Library, Indiana University, Bloomington.

Thompson's books for Lion Books and Lion Library: *The Killer Inside Me* (New York: Lion Books, 1952), *Cropper's Cabin* (New York: Lion Books, 1952), *Recoil* (New York: Lion Books, 1953), *The Alcoholics* (New York: Lion Books, 1953), *Bad Boy* (New York: Lion Books, 1953), *Savage Night* (New York: Lion Books, 1953), *The Criminal* (New York: Lion Books, 1953), *The Golden Gizmo* (New York: Lion Books, 1954), *Roughneck* (New York: Lion Books, 1954), *A Swell-Looking Babe* (New York: Lion Books, 1954), *A Hell of a Woman* (New York: Lion Books, 1954), and *The Kill-Off* (New York: Lion Library, 1957).

Also: *The Nothing Man* (New York: Dell First Editions, 1954) and *After Dark, My Sweet* (New York: Popular Library, 1955).

For other critical materials cited or utilized during the discussion of Thompson's novels in this chapter: Hervey Cleckley explored the "psychopathic personality" in *The Mask of Sanity* (New York: Plume, revised 1982); David Lehman first invoked Samson in the Temple of the Philistines for a discussion of Lou Ford's destruction of his house at the conclusion of *The Killer Inside Me* in his elegant and exemplary study, *The Perfect Murder* (New York: The Free Press, 1989); the essay by Roger Caillois quoted in connection with Ford's adaptation of protective coloring is called "Mimicry and Legendary Psychasthenia" (*October* No. 31, 1984); Geoffrey O'Brien dubbed Thompson the "Dimestore Dostoevsky" in his afterword to *Savage Night* (Berkeley: Creative Arts/Black Lizard, 1985); Tony Hilfer skillfully treats *A Hell of a Woman* in *The Crime Novel* (Austin: University of Texas Press, 1990); and Daniel Bellis recounts Alain Corneau's film *Série Noir*, in *Georges Perec: A Life in Words* (Boston: Godine, 1993); George Milburn contributed a two-page prologue, "George Milburn Says," to the first edition of *A Hell of a Woman* (New York: Lion Books, 1954); the Oklahoma "Ex-Slaves" narrative quoted for *The Criminal* is preserved in the Collections of the Manuscript Division, Library of Congress; additional information relating to "John Stink" (for *Cropper's Cabin*) from an article "John Stink: The Osage Who 'Returned from the Grave' " by Joe D. Haines ("Chronicles of Oklahoma," Spring 1992); the alcoholic memoir that probably lies behind *The Alcoholics*, 1932's *Behind the Door of Delusion* by "Inmate Ward 8" (Marion Marle Woodson), recently was reprinted with an introduction and afterward by William Savage (Niwot: University of Colorado Press, 1994).

Jim Thompson published seven works of short crime fiction, some of them actually excerpts from his Lion autobiographies, during the mid-1950s: "Bellboy" (excerpt from *Bad Boy*) in Mercury Mystery Magazine (February 1956); "Prowlers in the Pear Trees" (excerpt from *Bad Boy*) in *Mercury Mystery Magazine* (March 1956); "The Flaw in the System" in *Mercury Mystery Magazine* (July 1956); "Murder Came on the Mayflower" in *Mercury Mystery Magazine* (November 1956); "The Cellini Chalice" in *Alfred Hitchcock's Mystery Magazine* (December 1956); "The Threesome in Four-C" (by "Dillon Roberts") in *Alfred Hitchcock's Mystery Magazine* (December 1956); and "The Frightening Frammis" in *Alfred Hitchcock's Mystery Magazine* (February 1957). The manuscript for "The Flaw in the System" is preserved in the Rare Book and Manuscript Library, Columbia University.

Thompson published at least six (and likely many more) pieces in mid-1950s men's adventure magazines: "Pretty Boy: Case History of a Public Enemy" in *Real* (July 1956); "America's First Murderer" in *For Men Only* (September 1956); "Private Lives of a Hellraiser" (excerpt from *Bad Boy*) in *Men* (November 1956); "The Innkeeper's Passionate Daughter" in *Ken* (February 1957); "Bert Casey, Wild Gun of the Panhandle" in *Man's World* (September 1957); and "They Wouldn't Stay Dead" in *True Adventures* (September 1957).

For leads relating to Thompson's mid-1950s articles for *Master Detective* and *True Detective* under the avuncular pseudonym "Bob Wicks," I am grateful to Marc Gerald, who aided my examination of the Macfadden files. Also helpful were interviews with Alberta Thompson and Sharon Thompson Reed.

James B. Harris graciously focused Thompson's various work for Harris-Kubrick Pictures for this and the next chapter in a long interview at his Los Angeles apartment, and later responded to my follow-up inquiries with dispatch and sensitivity. Alexander Singer, Robert Goldfarb, Ronnie Lubin, and Marvin Olshan also assisted with information or materials. Lionel White's *Clean Break* has been reprinted as *The Killing* (Berkeley: Black Lizard/Creative Arts, 1988). James Ellroy's comments on *The Killing* originally appeared in an article by Patrick Goldstein, "Hard-boiled Hollywood," for the Los Angeles *Times,* March 11, 1990. Paragraphing and punctuation (although not the actual words) from what at present appear to be the only surviving pages from *Lunatic at Large* are approximate, since I was not permitted to examine the manuscript but only to hear it read over the telephone. Louis Blau related his remarks on Stanley Kubrick and the credits for *The Killing* when I attempted to reach the reclusive director through him. Additional background or materials for *The Killing* from: the Margaret Herrick Library, the Academy of Motion Pictures, and the University Research Library of UCLA. Calder Willingham's remarks about Kubrick appear in his letter of March 8, 1988, and are quoted in the following chapter. György Ligeti discussed Kubrick's use of his music in *2001: A Space Odyssey* in Lloyd Schwartz's "By György" (Boston *Phoenix,* March 26, 1993).

Also consulted: the New American Library Papers (Fales Library, NYU), the Harper and Brothers Papers (the Harry Ransom Humanities Research Center, University of Texas at Austin), and the Benjamin Botkin papers (University of Nebraska, Lincoln). Also interviewed: Budd Schulberg, Sonia O'Sullivan, Alice Doreef, Maxine Thompson Kouba, Freddie Thompson Townsend, Patricia Thompson Miller, J. Anthony Kouba, and Gordon Friesen.

Satan's Quarter-Section: 1956–1965

Randi Roberts and Alberta Thompson recalled their 1956 train trip with Jim to Los Angeles. For screenplays, correspondence, or other production materials relating to *Paths of Glory* I am grateful to the State Historical Library of Wisconsin, the University Research Library of UCLA, and Alberta Thompson. Kirk Douglas recounted his memories of *Paths of Glory* and of Stanley Kubrick in *The Ragman's Son* (New York: Simon and Schuster, 1988). Calder Willingham sent me his letter about *Paths of Glory,* dated March 8, 1988. *I Stole $16,000,000* (New York: Signet, 1956) was written by Herbert Emerson Wilson with the collaboration of Thomas P. Kelley. Thanks again to James B. Harris and Robert Goldfarb.

Jim Thompson's novels discussed in this chapter: *Wild Town* (New York: Signet, 1957), *The Getaway* (New York: Signet, 1959), *The Transgressors* (New York: Signet, 1961), *The Grifters* (New York: Regency Books, 1963), *Pop. 1280* (Greenwich: Gold Medal, 1964), and *Texas by the Tail* (Greenwich: Gold Medal, 1965).

For guiding me to the New American Library papers at the Fales Library, New York University, I am deeply appreciative to Frank Walker. All of Thompson's letters quoted in this chapter derive from this collection, except for his personal letters to Freddie and Irving Townsend, which were preserved among the papers of Maxine Thompson Kouba, and his correspondence with Robert Mills, which is courtesy of Alberta Thompson. Buck Houghton recalled his experiences with *Cloudburst,* and kindly sent me a copy of his screenplay. Also interviewed about Thompson's NAL novels and abandoned manuscripts: Marc Jaffe and Robert Goldfarb, who also sent me copies of his agency notes.

Arnold Hano, Jim Bryans, Harlan Ellison, Algis Budrys, and Knox Burger contributed vital background about Thompson's novels in the late 1950s and early 1960s. Geoffrey O'Brien kindly shared an interview he conducted with Robert Mills in 1983.

Thompson's teleplays for *Mackenzie's Raiders, Cain's Hundred,* and *Dr. Kildare* are courtesy of Alberta Thompson. MCA Publishing provided a copy of his teleplay for *Convoy.* Also consulted for his television writing: Robert Goldfarb's agency notes; the Warner Brothers papers at the University of Southern California Library; the film and television collection of the Library of Congress; and

The Complete Directory to Prime Time Network TV Shows by Tim Brooks and Earle Marsh (New York: Ballantine Books, 1979).

Material relating to Thompson's writing for *Ready for the Tiger* is from the Sam Peckinpah papers at the Margaret Herrick Library, the Academy of Motion Pictures.

For additional information about Thompson's fiction discussed in this chapter:

This World, Then the Fireworks was first published by Max Allan Collins and Ed Gorman in *Jim Thompson: The Killers Inside Him* (Cedar Rapids: Fedora Press, 1983).

"Forever After" appeared in *Shock*, May 1960.

R. V. Cassill's essay *"The Killer Inside Me:* Fear, Purgation, and the Sopho-clean Light" appeared in David Madden's anthology, *Tough Guy Writers of the Thirties* (Carbondale: Southern Illinois University Press, 1968).

I wish to thank Mark von Schlegell for permitting me to read his Yale senior thesis on *Pop. 1280*, " 'Just Another Lousy Human Being': Jim Thompson's Con-frontation with American Culture" (1989).

Also interviewed: Noah Sarlot, Mary Milburn, R. V. Cassill, Alberta Thomp-son, Freddie Thompson Townsend, Maxine Thompson Kouba, Patricia Thomp-son Miller, Michael Thompson, Sharon Thompson Reed, Tony Bill, Jerry Bick, and Laurence Janifer.

Exit Screaming: 1966–1977

Arnold Hano related his account of the article Jim Thompson asked him to write.

Thompson's novels discussed in this chapter: *South of Heaven* (Greenwich: Gold Medal, 1967), *Child of Rage* (New York: Lancer Books, 1972), *King Blood* (Sphere Books, 1972), and *The Rip-Off* in *More Hardcore* (New York: Donald I. Fine, 1987).

Also his novelizations: *Ironside* (New York: Popular Library, 1967), *The Un-defeated* (New York: Popular Library, 1969), and *Nothing But a Man* (New York: Popular Library, 1970).

Most of the contracts and correspondence relating to Thompson's late fic-tion are courtesy of Alberta Thompson. Jim Bryans recalled the circumstances surrounding *Ironside, The Undefeated,* and *Nothing but a Man.* Kate Fox Reynolds helped me track down material about *King Blood* at Avon Books. Pierre Rissient's comments on *Child of Rage* derive from an interview published in *Polar,* May 1979 (translation by the author), and a telephone interview (in English). Also of significant assistance: Arnold Hano, Jerry Bick, Knox Burger, Harlan Ellison, and David Markson.

"Exactly What Happened" appeared in *Ellery Queen's Mystery Magazine,* April 1967. The manuscript is preserved in the Rare Book and Manuscript Li-brary, Columbia University.

Tony Bill provided an account of the events surrounding the American hobo film, *Hard Times,* or *Bo,* and the *South of Heaven* controversy, as did Al-berta Thompson, Sharon Thompson Reed, Patricia Thompson Miller, and J. An-thony Kouba. Thompson's complaint against Tony Bill, Vernon Zimmerman, and Columbia Pictures was filed with Superior Court of the State of California for the County of Los Angeles on August 10, 1976. Mark Lipson also contributed details from his own research into *South of Heaven.*

Mike Medavoy, Sam Fuller, John Ptak, and Bill Kirby furnished valuable information about Thompson's film work in the 1970s. For information about *The Getaway* (film) I especially wish to thank David Foster. Jim Thompson wrote his grievance letter to the Guild Arbitration Committee, dated July 11, 1972. Also consulted: Marshall Terrill's *Steve McQueen: Portrait of an American Rebel* (New York: Donald I. Fine, 1993) and Marshall Fine's *Bloody Sam: The Life and Films of Sam Peckinpah* (New York: Donald I. Fine, 1991).

Dick Richards, Sylvia Miles, and Jim Sparkman contributed their warm reminiscences of Thompson on the set of *Farewell, My Lovely*.

Samuel Blumenfeld graciously interviewed Alain Corneau for me in Paris (translation by the author).

Gary Graver reviewed his collaboration with Orson Welles on their screenplay for *A Hell of a Woman*.

The drawling recollection attributed to Thompson by Leonard Gross for his article, "From Paperbacks to Greenbacks," appeared in *Westways,* October 1973.

Also interviewed: Michael Thompson, Maxine Thompson Kouba, and Freddie Thompson Townsend.

• • •

Although Jim Thompson died on Thursday, April 7, 1977, his memorial service was delayed, due to the Easter weekend, until the following Monday afternoon at 2:00 p.m., April 11.

The Los Angeles *Times* "lost our announcement," Alberta Thompson recalls. "The paper messed up—there was no announcement until after the service." Only twenty-two mourners signed the register at the Westwood Village Mortuary, most of these immediate family. Among Thompson's friends who attended were Arnold Hano, Robert Goldfarb, Jerry Bick, and Ned and Alta De-Witt from the Oklahoma Writers' Project.

The Reverend Ray S. Harris, the UCLA chaplain who presided at the memorial service, never met Thompson, and misunderstandings inevitably entered his eulogy. "Jimmy [sic] published his first book at the age of sixteen, and over two hundred of his books followed after that first publication," the Reverend Harris ventured. But, prompted by the Thompson family, he also remarked that "Jimmy's courage, during his late period of severe illness, was something special." He pronounced Thompson "an intellectual, but always gentle, very kind, a good cook and a dedicated family man." The Reverend Harris concluded, "Jimmy's mind had remarkable recall. The family was constantly picking his mind about the family history. . . . With the passing of Jimmy, the family feels they have also lost the past."

David Foster sent Alberta a note: "Your call the other day saddened me because Jim was truly one of the nicest and most considerate men I have met in or out of this business." Steve McQueen and Ali MacGraw arranged for a bouquet to be delivered to the Hillcrest Road apartment. And Sam Peckinpah wrote on the card that accompanied his flowers, "I learned it could happen to me but never that it could happen to Jim—I miss him—"

Index

A Note on the Type

The text of this book was set in Cheltenham
Old Style, designed by the architect Bertram
Grosvenor Goodhue in collaboration with
Ingalls Kimball of the Cheltenham Press of
New York. Cheltenham was introduced in the
early twentieth century, a period of remarkable
achievement in type design. The idea of
creating a "family" of types by making variations
on the basic type design was originated by
Goodhue and Kimball in the design of the
Cheltenham series.

Composed by Dix,
Syracuse, New York

Printed and bound by
Quebecor Martinsburg
Martinsburg, West Virginia

Designed by Iris Weinstein